CHINESE

AMERICANS

CHINESE

AMERICANS

THE HISTORY AND CULTURE OF A PEOPLE

Jonathan H. X. Lee, Editor

BLOOMSBURY ACADEMIC
NEW YORK • LONDON • OXFORD • NEW DELHI • SYDNEY

BLOOMSBURY ACADEMIC
Bloomsbury Publishing Inc
1385 Broadway, New York, NY 10018, USA
50 Bedford Square, London, WC1B 3DP, UK
29 Earlsfort Terrace, Dublin 2, Ireland

BLOOMSBURY, BLOOMSBURY ACADEMIC and the Diana logo
are trademarks of Bloomsbury Publishing Plc

First published in the United States of America by ABC-CLIO 2016
Paperback edition published by Bloomsbury Academic 2024

Cover design by Silverander Communications
Cover photos: A wooden bus takes passengers beneath a Chinese-style bridge in Chinatown in
San Francisco. (Uncredited/Corbis); Young family holding moon cakes. (Imagemore Co., Ltd./Corbis);
Chinese and Filipino workers lay track for the Burlington Railroad (formerly the Great Northern Railway)
at Stevens Pass, Washington, ca. 1959. (Josef Scaylea/Corbis)

Library of Congress Cataloging-in-Publication Data
Chinese Americans : the history and culture of a people / Jonathan H. X. Lee, editor.
pages cm
Includes bibliographical references and index.
ISBN 978-1-61069-549-7 (print) — ISBN 978-1-61069-550-3
(e-book)
1. Chinese Americans—History. 2. Chinese Americans—Social
conditions. 3. Chinese Americans—Biography. I. Lee, Jonathan H. X., editor.
E184.C5C4793 2016
973'.04951—dc23 2015035598

ISBN: HB: 978-1-6106-9549-7
PB: 979-8-7651-1604-3
ePDF: 978-1-6106-9550-3
eBook: 979-8-2160-6032-1

To find out more about our authors and books visit www.bloomsbury.com
and sign up for our newsletters.

I wish to dedicate this volume to my sisters:
Lora Lee, Josephine Mu, and Sang Ngo;
to the memories of my big brother, Jason Lee;
and to my son, Owen Edward Jinfa Quady-Lee.

Contents

Part II

**Political Activity and Economic Life: Business Endeavors and
Involvement in American Politics**

Part III

Cultural and Religious Life: People, Institutions, and Organizations

Part IV

Literature, the Arts, Popular Culture, and Sports: People, Movements, and Expressions of Identity

Preface

Virtually every aspect of American culture has been influenced by Chinese immigrants and their descendants. *Chinese Americans: The History and Culture of a People* tells the story of the Chinese American experience—from immigration to exclusion, through complicated and contradictory iterations of assimilation, acculturation, and expressions of hybrid identities, to success and achievement in American life and society and the continued work toward equity and social justice, not just for Chinese Americans but for Asian Americans and other immigrant populations that compose the American mosaic.

Chinese Americans: The History and Culture of a People provides historical analysis and highlights the enormous contributions of Chinese Americans to the professions, politics, and popular culture of America, from the 19th century through the present day.

While the number of Chinese Americans has grown very rapidly in the last decade, this group has long thrived in the United States in spite of racism, discrimination, and segregationist policies. This comprehensive volume takes a global view of the Chinese experience in the Americas. While the focus is on Chinese Americans in the United States, *Chinese Americans: The History and Culture of a People* also explores the experiences of Chinese immigrants in Canada, Cuba, Mexico, and South America. This volume considers why the Chinese chose to leave their home country, where they resettled, and how the distinctive Chinese American identity—or, rather, identities—formed.

Chinese Americans: The History and Culture of a People is organized into four sections: Part I: Context of Chinese American Emigration: Coming to America; Part II: Political Activity and Economic Life: Business Endeavors and Involvement in American Politics; Part III: Cultural and Religious Life: People, Institutions, and Organizations; and Part IV: Literature, the Arts, Popular Culture, and Sports: People, Movements, and Expressions of Identity. Each section contains alphabetically arranged essays that capture a snapshot of everyday life for this immigrant group as they negotiated the mainstream demands for assimilation and acculturation to produce and express variations of hybrid subjectivity that reflect varying ratios of being Chinese and being American (including Hong Kongese and Taiwanese) that is temporally situated. The tussle with being and becoming both Chinese and American is a central theme in the artistic, literary, political, social, economic, civic and educational expressions of being Chinese

American or Chinese in America. This volume includes a chronology of events from the 18th century to the present that highlights the impact of the Chinese Americans across many generations. The primary documents section contains useful primary sources that illustrates the themes of the articles in the volume, and will be useful to students from a variety of academic disciplines. There is a useful bibliography on the subjects covered in the volume as well as a general subject index.

Chinese Americans: The History and Culture of a People can easily be a multi-volume project. Therefore, determining what to include and what to exclude in this one volume project was daunting as Chinese American contributions to American history, politics, civic life, economy, art, literature, film, pop-culture, and so on is deep, extensive, and endearing. I thus focused on unexplored and unexamined topics and personalities in Chinese American studies, such as "Chinese Americans and LGBTQQI," and "Chinese American and Hip-hop," and lesser known contemporary notable Chinese Americans, for example "Huang, Eddie (1982–)," whose memoir *Fresh Off the Boat* (2013) was adapted into an ABC comedy sitcom of the same name, the first since Margaret Cho's *All-American Girl* (1994); "Low, Evan (1983–)," the first openly gay Chinese American politician in California; and "Yee, James J. (ca. 1968–)," a Chinese American Muslim who served in the U.S. military and was investigated by the FBI as a Chinese spy.

I wish to express sincere gratitude to Senior Editor, Michael Millman at ABC-Clio/Greenwood/Praeger who supported this volume and my ability to see it to fruition. I also wish to thank Sidney C. Li, my research assistant; my students and colleagues in the Asian American Studies Department at San Francisco State University; and funding from the College of Ethnic Studies that provided resources and time to dedicate to this volume.

I hope *Chinese Americans: The History and Culture of a People* will be a resource for students who wish to learn about themselves and about the contributions of Chinese Americans, not just at home but around the world.

Jonathan H. X. Lee
Berkeley, California

Chronology of Chinese American History

January 18, 1778   Chinese sailors come to Hawai'i with English explorer Captain James Cook.

February 22, 1784   The *Empress of China* (a.k.a. *Chinese Queen*) leaves New York with cargo of ginseng. On May 11, 1785, it returns to New York. The success of this voyage encourages others to invest in additional trade with China.

August 9, 1785   The first recorded instance of the Chinese in the continental United States are three Chinese seamen named Ashing, Achun, and Aceun, who are left stranded, along with 32 "East Indians" lascars, by Captain John O'Donnell, who left on the *Pallas* after unloading his cargo at Baltimore.

1790   The first U.S. Naturalization Act allows only "free White persons" to become U.S. citizens.

April 1796   Andreas Everardus Van Braam Houckgeest, a Dutchman who was formerly Canton Agent for the Dutch East India Company, comes to the United States from China with a cargo of Chinese arts and five Chinese servants. He settles in Philadelphia, organizes the first exhibit on Chinese art in the United States, and in 1797–1798 authors the first book on China published in the United States.

1818   Wong Arce, Ah Lan, Ah Lum, Chop Ah See, and Lieaou Ah-See are the first Chinese students to receive an education in the United States, when they enroll at the Foreign Mission School in Cornwall, Connecticut. The school was established in 1817 with the expressed goal to teach "heathen" youths from around the world to become Christian missionaries in their own cultures. Lieaou Ah-See becomes the first Chinese Protestant convert in the United States.

1829	The Siamese twins Chang and Eng are the first Thais to arrive in the United States. For four decades they tour the United States and the world. They were born in 1811 of Chinese parents. Before going to the United States, the twins were successful entrepreneurs in Siam (now Thailand). Captain Abel Coffin contracted to manage the twins' touring schedule. They are granted U.S. citizenship in 1839.
1830	The first U.S. Census records three Chinese in the United States.
1840	The second U.S. Census records eight Chinese in the United States. By 1850, the U.S. Census records 758 Chinese.
August 29, 1842	China is defeated by the British Empire in the first Opium War, resulting in the Treaty of Nanjing, the first "unequal treaty," whereby China is forced to cede the island of Hong Kong and to open five ports to foreign commerce.
July 3, 1844	Following Britain's lead, the United States imposes the Treaty of Wangxia (Wang-hsia) on China, which gave the United States most favored nation treatment in trade and extraterritoriality (exemption from Chinese laws) for American nationals in China and the right to be tried by the U.S. consular court.
1846–1850	Southern China is hit with social and political chaos due to a combination of natural disasters that results in crop failures, which leads to famine and poverty, causing an increase in banditry and peasant uprisings.
January 1848	Gen. John A. Sutter discovers gold at Coloma. At the beginning of 1849 there are only 54 "Chinamen" in California. They arrive wanting to be miners but many will become a source of cheap labor for railroads, mines, fisheries, farms, orchards, canneries, garment and cigar factories, and so on along the Pacific Coast. By 1876 there are 151,000 in the United States and 116,000 in California.
April 13, 1850	The California state legislature passes a law that imposes a $20-per-month tax on foreign miners. The

tax is enforced mainly against Chinese miners, who are often forced to pay more than once.

1850	The Taiping Rebellion (1850–1864), a large-scale revolt under the leadership of Hong Xiuquan. In 1847 Hong failed the imperial civil service examination for the third time and reportedly became delirious for 30 days. When he recovered, he believed that he had been selected by heaven to conquer China, destroy the Manchu rulers, and establish the Heavenly Kingdom of Great Harmony, or Taiping Tianguo.
1852	Hawaiian plantation owners import 195 Chinese contract laborers, over 20,000 Chinese migrants enter California, and a Buddhist-Daoist temple to the Empress of Heaven Tien Hau is founded in San Francisco.
November 6, 1853	Missionary William Speer opens the Presbyterian mission for Chinese in San Francisco, the oldest Asian American Christian congregation in North America.
October 1, 1854	California Supreme Court rules in *People v. Hall* that no Chinese person can testify against a white person in court. This ruling stands until 1873. During this period, California has the highest concentration of Chinese migrants in the United States. The ruling overturns the conviction and death sentence of Hall, a white man, for killing Ling Sing, a Chinese man. During the first trail, three Chinese witnesses had testified to the murder. In Hawai'i, the Chinese establish a funeral society, their first community association in the islands.
1856	The *Chinese New Daily News* is launched in Sacramento, California, becoming the first Chinese-language daily newspaper in the world. It is published by Ze Too Yune (a.k.a. Hung Tai. Publ.) It lasts nearly two years, at first daily, then triweekly, then irregularly—sometimes once per week, sometimes once per month.
1858	The California State Legislature passes an exclusion law that prohibits Chinese or Mongolians to enter the state except when driven ashore by weather or unavoidable accident. The penalty for violation of this act is a fine of

	$400–$600 or imprisonment from six months to a year, or both.
1859	San Francisco opens the Chinese School, America's first public school for Asian immigrants. As a result, Chinese students are excluded from San Francisco public schools.
January 10, 1862	In his inaugural address as the eighth governor of California, Leland Stanford promises to protect the state from "the dregs of Asia."
April 26, 1862	The California State Legislature passes an "anti-coolie tax" or "police tax" of $2.50 a month on every Chinese and Mongolian. The goal of the act is to protect white labor from Chinese labor and to discourage the immigration of Chinese labor into the state.
1862	Six Chinese district associations in San Francisco form a loose federation, which will become the Chinese Consolidated Benevolent Association (CCBA).
1863	The first Chinese railroad workers are hired by the Central Pacific Railroad Company to build the western section of the Transcontinental Railroad. They are paid around $28 per month to do the hazardous work of blasting and laying ties over the treacherous terrain of the high Sierras.
1865	Presbyterian Missionary Augustus Ward Loomis and his wife Mary Ann arrive to serve the Chinese in San Francisco from 1865 to 1867.
June 1867	Roughly 2,000 Chinese railroad workers strike for a week demanding more pay and work hours similar to their white counterparts.
July 28, 1868	The United States and China sign the Burlingame-Seward Treaty to facilitate trading and emigration between the two countries. It also guarantees a suitable supply of Chinese labor for the railroad. Although the Treaty establishes friendly relations between the United States and China that encourages Chinese labor migration to the United States, naturalization was prohibited.

1868	Chinese Christian evangelist Samuel P. Aheong (a.k.a. Siu Pheoung, S. P. Ahiona) (1835–1871) starts preaching in Hawai'i and becomes one of the most influential Christian missionaries on the island, encouraging the local Christian community to embrace newly arriving Chinese immigrants.
May 10, 1869	The first transcontinental railroad is completed after Chinese laborers dig over a dozen tunnels through solid granite in the Sierras during cold winter and hot summer months under hazardous working conditions. Ninety percent of the laborers who build the Central Pacific section from California to Utah are Chinese.
July 14, 1870	The Naturalization Act of 1870 is signed into law by President Ulysses S. Grant. The Act limits immigration and naturalization to "aliens of African nativity and to persons of African descent" and "whites," thus excluding all Chinese from receiving citizenship. The Act also bans the entry laborers' wives. Economically, a nationwide recession fuels anti-Chinese sentiments on the West Coast as white labor scapegoat "Cheap Chinese labor" as their problem. Mobs of white labor attack and destroy Chinese communities in many areas of California and other states.
1870	California passes a law against the importation of Chinese, Japanese, and "Mongolian" women for the purposes of prostitution. In Texas, Chinese railroad workers sue the railroad company for not paying them.
October 24, 1871	Chinese residents at Los Angeles's Chinatown are attacked, robbed, and killed by a mob of white men, over 500 strong. The riots happened on Calle de los Negros (now part of Los Angeles Street). A total of 17 Chinese men and boys, including a popular doctor, are hung.
1872	California's Civil Procedure Code drops a law barring Chinese court testimony.
May 1873	San Francisco Board of Supervisors passes the "Queue" and "Laundry" ordinances. The Queue

Ordinance requires that all Chinese prisoners in jail have their hair cut or clipped to a uniform length of an inch from the scalp. The Laundry Ordinance stipulates that laundries using one vehicle with a horse pay a license of $1 per quarter; those that use two vehicles pay $4 per quarter; and those that use more than two vehicles or that use no vehicle, $15 per quarter.

January 30, 1875   The United States and Hawai'i sign a Reciprocity Treaty. The treaty is a free-trade agreement between the United States and the Kingdom of Hawai'i starting in September 1876. In return, the United States gains lands in the area known as Pu'u Loa, which will later house the Pearl Harbor naval base. The treaty encourages increased investment by Americans in the Hawai'i's sugar plantations. The treaty was ratified by the Kingdom of Hawai'i on April 17, 1875, and ratified by the United States on May 31, 1875. The treaty foreshadows the annexation of Hawai'i.

March 3, 1875   The Page Law is enacted, which bars Asian women suspected of prostitution and attempts to regulate contract labor from China. It also bars entry of Chinese, Japanese, "Mongolian" felons, and contract laborers.

1875   The Union Pacific sends 125 Chinese workers to mine in Rock Springs, Wyoming.

March 24, 1877   Five Chinese workers are massacred in a wood chopper's camp two miles from Chico, California.

October 1877   Denis Kearney organizes anti-Chinese meetings in San Francisco and establishes the Workingmen's Party of California, charging that Chinese workers willing to work for lower wages, poorer conditions, and longer hours displace white workers. The slogan, "The Chinese Must Go," was being widely repeated and popular.

April 29, 1878   The California Circuit Court ruling, *In Re: Ah Yup*, declares that Chinese are not white and therefore ineligible to apply for naturalization.

March 6, 1879	California's second constitution prevents municipalities, corporations, and county and state governments from employing Chinese.
October 31, 1880	Hop Alley Chinese Riot, Denver, Colorado. Anti-Chinese hysteria turns into a riot after two Chinese men and three or four white drunks at John Asmussen's saloon at 16th Street and Wazee get into a fight. Most of Chinatown is destroyed. During the rioting, a Chinese man named Sing Lee is beaten and kicked to death; those indicted for his murder are later acquitted. The rioting continues from noon until midnight before the violence is finally suppressed by the militia.
November 17, 1880	The United States and China sign a treaty giving the United States the right to limit but "not absolutely prohibit" Chinese immigration.
1880	Section 69 of California's Civil Code prohibits issuing licenses for marriages between whites and "Mongolians, Negroes, mulattoes and persons of mixed blood."
1881	Hawaiian King Kalakaua takes a trip around the world. He met with rulers and perhaps wants to find more laborers for Hawai'i's plantations. He also wants to learn the ways of other rulers to better protect his own people. He travels first to San Francisco, then to Japan, China, Siam (now Thailand), Burma, India, Egypt, Italy, Belgium, Germany, Austria, France, Spain, Portugal, and England.
May 6, 1882	President Chester A. Arthur signs the Chinese Exclusion Act, which bans immigration of laborers and their wives from China for 10 years. It also bans Chinese immigrants from becoming naturalized citizens. As a result, there is an increase in Japanese immigration to replace Chinese laborers.
1882	The Chinese Consolidated Benevolent Association in San Francisco (CCBA-SF) is established. One of the objectives is to provide leadership in the Chinese community to fight anti-Chinese legislation.

1883	Chinese in New York establish the Chinese Consolidated Benevolent Association.
1884	Joseph and Mary Tape successfully sue the San Francisco school board to enroll their Chinese daughter Mamie in a public school. On January 9, 1885, Superior Court Justice McGuire announces the decision in favor of Joseph and Mary Tape. On appeal, the California Supreme Court upholds the lower court decision on March 3, 1885. Shortly after the decision, the San Francisco school board lobbies for a separate school system for Chinese and other "Mongolian" children. A bill passes through the California State Legislature giving the school board the authority to create an Oriental Public School in San Francisco.
September 1885	Led by the Knights of Labor, local government officials order the expulsion of Chinese from the Puget Sound region of Washington Territory. The episode lasts until March 1886. It results in several Chinese deaths and injuries, and hundreds are driven out by violence or threat of violence.
September 2, 1885	Rock Springs Wyoming, one of the worst instances of anti-Chinese violence. White miners attack Chinese miners: 28 Chinese miners are murdered and 15 wounded, 75 Chinese homes are burned, and hundreds of Chinese are chased out of town.
October 1885	White protesters in Tacoma announce that all Chinese residing in the city must leave by November. In early November, a mob of white residents, led by Tacoma Mayor Jacob Robert Weisbach and backed by the Tacoma police, enter Chinatown and demand that the Chinese residents leave the city immediately. The mob marches the Chinese to a railroad station and forces them to board a train headed toward Portland, Oregon. This becomes known as "The Tacoma Method" and is an example of how to remove the Chinese from cities and towns throughout the United States.
1885	San Francisco builds a new segregated "Oriental School" in response to the *Tape* case.

May 10, 1886	Chinese laundrymen win in *Yick Wo v. Hopkins*, which declares that a law with unequal impact on different groups is discriminatory. In *Yick Wo v. Hopkins*, the U.S. Supreme Court, in a unanimous opinion, invoke the Equal Protection Clause of the Fourteenth Amendment to protect Chinese laundry owners against an ordinance that on its face is race neutral but is applied in a prejudicial manner.
May 27, 1887	A gang of white horse thieves appears on a steep hillside in Hells Canyon, Oregon. They open fire with high-powered rifles, killing 10 unsuspecting Chinese miners. Then they rob the camp and brutally mutilate the bodies and throw them into the river. Their killing spree continues the next day as 8 additional Chinese miners who happen along the river are killed, then another 13 at a second Chinese camp. In total, 34 Chinese miners are slain over the course of two days. This becomes known as the Snake River Massacre.
October 1, 1888	The Scott Act is passed by the U.S. Congress and signed into law by President Grover Cleveland, prohibiting the return of Chinese laborers who temporarily travel to China. It is introduced by Representative William Lawrence Scott of Pennsylvania. At the time of its effective date, 20,000 Chinese laborers possess reentry certificates and 600 of them are in transit back to the United States. None are allowed reentry.
May 13, 1889	The U.S. Supreme Court decides, in *Chae Chan Ping v. United States*, that despite the Burlingame Treaty of 1868, the United States can freely prevent Chinese from immigrating to the United States, thus upholding the constitutionality of Chinese exclusion law.
July 4, 1889	The U.S. Congress passes The Newlands Resolution, which annexes Hawai'i. President William McKinley signs it on July 7, 1889. Under this Act further immigration of Chinese into the Hawaiian Islands is prohibited.
January 1, 1892	Ellis Island is opened. It will be the gateway to the United States for European immigrants.

May 5, 1892   Geary Act renews exclusion of Chinese laborers for another 10 years. Under this Act, all Chinese in the United States are required to carry their registration certificates at all times. Any Chinese without a certificate is subject to immediate deportation.

January 17, 1893   Queen Lili'uokalani, the last native ruler of an independent Hawai'i, is deposed in a bloodless *coup d'état* by five American nationals, one English national, and one German national. All are living and doing business in Hawai'i and oppose her efforts to establish a new constitution. President Grover Cleveland refuses to annex Hawai'i because he feels the Americans in the sugar industry engineered the overthrow and that the Hawaiian people do not want revolution.

May 15, 1893   *Fong Yue Ting v. United States* upholds the constitutionality of the Geary Act. In this ruling the U.S. Supreme Court declares that Congress has the right to legislate expulsion through executive orders. Congress will amend the Geary Act to make it more difficult for Chinese businessmen to enter the country.

November 24, 1894   Sun Yat-sen founds his first revolutionary organization, the Xingzhonghui, in Honolulu to "promote the interest and uphold the dignity of China."

May 27, 1895   In *Lem Moon Sing v. United States,* the U.S. Supreme Court rules that district courts can no longer review Chinese *habeas corpus* petitions for landing in the United States.

1895   The Planters' Labor and Supply Company reorganizes under the name Hawaiian Sugar Planters' Association (HSPA). Its goal is the "advancement, improvement and protection of the sugar industry of Hawai'i, the support of an Experiment Station, the maintenance of a sufficient supply of labor for the sugar plantations of Hawai'i and the development of agriculture in general."

May 6, 1896   The U.S. Supreme Court upholds the "separate but equal" concept in its decision on *Plessy v. Ferguson*. The decision legalizes "Jim Crow" laws for nearly 60 years.

March 28, 1898	The U.S. Supreme Court, in *Wong Kim Ark v. United States*, rules that Chinese born in the United States cannot be stripped of their citizenship under the Fourteenth Amendment.
July 7, 1898	With support of President William McKinley, a joint resolution in Congress to annex the Hawaiian Islands is passed. As a result, thousands of Asian laborers migrate to the continental United States.
Summer 1899	A ship sailing from Hong Kong to San Francisco has two cases of plague on board.
December 31, 1899	The Board of Health begins a controlled burn of a few targeted buildings in Honolulu's Chinatown after the bubonic plague is discovered on the island. More buildings are burned during the first week of January 1900. On January 20, while the wooden buildings between Smith Street and Nuuanu Avenue on Beretania Street are being burned, the fire gets out of control and spreads to several unintended buildings. The fire spreads from the steeple of Kaumakapili Church to the nearby structures, and in the end, the majority of the buildings in Honolulu's Chinatown are destroyed and an estimated 4,000–4,500 people are left homeless.
March 6, 1900	A San Francisco City health officer autopsies a Chinese man and finds organisms in the body that resemble the plague. In April 1901, a clean-up operation of Chinatown is undertaken, scouring approximately 1,200 houses and 14,000 rooms.
April 30, 1900	The Hawaiian Organic Act makes all U.S. laws applicable to Hawai'i, thus ending contract labor in the islands. Under this Act, the Chinese in Hawai'i are required to apply for certificates of residence, and they are prohibited from entering any other U.S. territory or the mainland.
May 7, 1900	The first large-scale anti-Japanese protest takes place in San Francisco. It is organized by various labor groups.
May 19, 1900	San Francisco orders the quarantine and compulsory inoculation to all Japanese and Chinese upon discovery of a bubonic plague victim in Chinatown.

June 14, 1900	The Hawaiian Islands officially become a U.S. territory, and all islanders become American citizens. President William McKinley appoints Sanford B. Dole the first governor.
August 2, 1900	In response to growing anti-Japanese sentiments, the Japanese Foreign Ministry stops issuing passports to laborers headed for the United States and Canada.
1902	The Hawaiian Sugar Planters' Association hires David W. Deshler in Korea to recruit Korean laborers.
1902	Congress extended the Chinese Exclusion Act, but without a termination date.
October 11, 1903	Federal immigration officials and the police raid Boston's Chinatown without search warrants and arrest 234 Chinese, including American-born citizens who allegedly had no registration certificates on their persons. Only 50 are found to be in the country without proper documentation.
November 18, 1904	Hawai'i Sugar Planters' Association's trustees adopt a resolution stating that all skilled positions on the plantations will be filled by "American citizens, or those eligible for citizenship."
December 1904	Two thousand plantation laborers go on strike at Waialua.
1904	The Chinese Exclusion Extension Act makes Chinese exclusion permanent.
February 23, 1905	The *San Francisco Chronicle* front-page headline reads, "The Japanese Invasion: The Problem of the Hour."
May 10, 1905	China begins a nationwide boycott against U.S. products to protest anti-Chinese discrimination in the United States.
May 14, 1905	The Asiatic Exclusion League is established in San Francisco by 67 labor unions. Eventually over 200 labor unions join the league to restrict Asian immigration to the United States.
November 17, 1905	With the Japan-Korea Treaty, Japan declares Korea its virtual protectorate.

1905	Section 60 of California's Civil Code is amended to make marriage between "whites" and "Mongolians" "illegal and void."
April 18, 1906	The San Francisco earthquake and fire destroy government documents, which opens the way for Chinese immigrants to come as "paper sons" claiming birthrights.
October 11, 1906	The San Francisco board of education passes a resolution ordering Japanese and Korean children to be placed in a segregated school with already segregated Chinese.
1906	The Hawaiian Sugar Planters' Association (HSPA) begins recruiting workers from the Philippines after its access to Chinese, Japanese, and Korean labor was limited by immigration legislation. Fifteen laborers are sent to Olaʻa Plantation on the Big Island. In 1909, 554 Filipino laborers arrive in Hawaiʻi, followed by 2,653 in 1910; 1,363 in 1911; 4,319 in 1912; and 3,258 in 1913. By 1930, about 100,000 Filipino workers have migrated to Hawaiʻi.
February 1907	President Theodore Roosevelt's administration persuades the San Francisco board of education and mayor to rescind the segregation order.
February 24, 1907	The Gentlemen's Agreement between the United States and Japan is concluded in the form of a Japanese note agreeing to deny passports to laborers who want to migrate to the United States.
March 13, 1907	The San Francisco board of education formally withdraws segregation order.
September 1907	Shortly after the Bellingham riot, the Japanese and Korean Exclusion League is renamed the Asiatic Exclusion League to include the growing South Asian immigrant community.
September 4, 1907	A mob of 400–500 white working men in Bellingham, Washington gather to drive a community of South Asians out of the city. Many of the South Asians are Sikhs but are mistaken as Hindu. By the end of the day, hundreds of South Asians are driven out of town, 6 are hospitalized, and roughly 400 are held in jail for "protective custody."

September 7, 1907	A riot against Asians in the Chinese and Japanese section of Vancouver, British Columbia erupts.
November 2, 1907	"Demonstration" intended to scare the "Hindus" drive out South Asians from Everett, Washington.
January 27, 1908	Seventy South Asians are driven out of Live Oak, California by a white mob.
January 21, 1910	The U.S. government opens Angel Island Immigration Station on Angel Island in the San Francisco Bay.
August 22, 1910	Korea is formally annexed by Japan through the Japan-Korea Annexation Treaty.
January 1, 1912	The Republic of China (Taiwan) is established, and Sun Yat-sen of the Kuomintang (the KMT, or Nationalist Party) is proclaimed provisional president.
February 12, 1912	China's last emperor Pu Yi is forced to abdicate, or give up, his throne.
May 19, 1913	The California State legislature passes the Webb Act, or Alien Land Act. This Act prohibits "aliens ineligible to citizenship" from buying land or leasing it for longer than three years.
July 28, 1914	World War I begins. It lasted until November 11, 1918. In spite of racial discrimination against Asian Americans, many serve in the war and are awarded naturalization for their military service.
February 5, 1917	The U.S. Congress passes the Immigration Act of 1917, overriding President Woodrow Wilson's December 14, 1916, veto, restricting immigration of anyone born in a geographically defined "Asiatic Barred Zone," excluding Japanese and Filipinos. The Gentleman's Agreement (1907) already restricts immigration of Japanese laborers, and because the Philippines is an American colony, Filipinos are considered American nationals and have unrestricted entry. The Act prohibits all immigration from Asia and India by drawing an imaginary line from the Red Sea in the Middle East through the Ural Mountains: people living east of the line are not allowed entry to the United States. This Act also includes a literacy test requirement.

April 2, 1917	President Woodrow Wilson asks Congress to declare war on Germany. The United States soon formally enters World War I.
November 11, 1918	The armistice treaty formally ends World War I.
December 19, 1918	Judge Horace W. Vaughn of the U.S. District Court for Hawai'i rules that Japanese, Chinese, and Korean veterans of World War I are eligible for naturalization under the Act of May 8, 1918. As a result, 398 Japanese, 99 Koreans, and 4 Chinese are granted citizenship by November 14, 1919. Unfortunately, their citizenship is revoked by the *Toyota v. United States* decision on May 25, 1925.
January 19, 1920	The 1913 California Alien Land Law is amended to close a loophole that permits Asian immigrants to own or lease land under the names of their native-born children.
February 26, 1921	Arizona passes an Alien Land Law.
March 8, 1921	Washington State legislature passes an Alien Land Law.
April 1921	Texas passes an Alien Land Law.
May 19, 1921	President Warren G. Harding, pressured by the Immigration Restriction League, signs into law the Johnson Act, also known as the Emergency Quota Act of 1921 or the Immigration Act of 1921. It is the first quota immigration act that limits the annual number of immigrants to 3 percent of the number of foreign-born persons of most nationalities living in the United States in 1910.
July 19, 1921	White vigilantes deport 58 Japanese laborers from Turlock, California, driving them out by truck at gunpoint.
September 22, 1922	The U.S. Congress passed the Cable Act, which strips any woman of European or African ancestry of her citizenship if she marries an "alien ineligible to citizenship." She can regain her citizenship through the naturalization process if she divorces her alien husband or if he dies. The Act is repealed in 1936.
November 13, 1922	The U.S. Supreme Court, in *Takao Ozawa v. United States*, upholds the 1790 Naturalization Act and rules

	that Japanese (and other Asians) are ineligible for naturalized citizenship: naturalization is limited to "free white persons and aliens of African nativity."
1922	New Mexico passes an alien land law.
February 19, 1923	The U.S. Supreme Court, in *United States v. Bhagat Singh Thind*, upholds the 1790 Naturalization Act and declares South Asians ineligible for naturalized citizenship.
November 12, 1923	The U.S. Supreme Court, in *Terrace v. Thompson*, upholds the constitutionality of Washington's Alien Land Law.
November 12, 1923	The U.S. Supreme Court, in *Porterfield v. Webb*, upholds the constitutionality of California's Alien Land Law.
November 19, 1923	The U.S. Supreme Court, in *Webb v. O'Brien*, rules that cropping contracts between a citizen with legal rights and a noncitizen with no legal rights are illegal, because it is a ploy that allows Japanese to possess and use land in California.
November 19, 1923	The U.S. Supreme Court, in *Frick v. Webb*, forbids aliens "ineligible to citizenship" in California from owning stocks in corporations formed for farming.
1923	Idaho, Montana, and Oregon pass an Alien Land Law.
May 16, 1924	President Calvin Coolidge signs the Immigration Act of 1924 into law, which establishes a national origins quota, limiting the number of immigrants by country and excluding all immigrants from Asia, except for Filipinos, who are "nationals" because the Philippines is a U.S. protectorate.
November 4, 1924	Nevada passes an Alien Land Law.
April 18, 1925	The Chinese Hospital, the first in the United States devoted to the health needs of Chinese immigrants and residents, opens its door in San Francisco.
May 25, 1925	The U.S. Supreme Court, in *Chang Chan et al. v. John D. Nagle*, rules that Chinese wives of American

citizens are not entitled to residence and therefore are not allowed to enter the United States, in accordance with the Immigration Act of 1924.

1925	Kansas passes an Alien Land Law.
June 6, 1927	The U.S. Supreme Court, in *Weedin v. Chin Bow*, rules that a person born aboard of an American parent or parents and who has never lived in the United States cannot be a U.S. citizen.
November 21, 1927	The U.S. Supreme Court, in *Gong Lum v. Rice*, rules for separate but equal facilities for Mongolian children in Mississippi.
February 20, 1928	The U.S. Court of Appeals, Ninth Circuit, in *Lam Mow v. Nagle, Commissioner of Immigration*, rules that children born of Chinese parents on American vessels on the high seas are not born in the United States and are thus not citizens.
October 29, 1929	The U.S. stock market crash, known as "Black Thursday," triggers the Great Depression.
March 3, 1931	An amendment to Cable Act declares that no American-born woman who was stripped of her citizenship (by marrying an alien ineligible to citizenship) can be denied the right of naturalization at a later date.
July 7, 1937	Japan invades China.
November 6, 1937	Japan and Nazi Germany signs the Anti-Comintern Pact, directed at the Soviet Union.
September 22, 1940	Japan is granted rights to station troops in Indochina from the Vichy French government. By 1941 Japan extends its control over the whole of French Indochina.
September 27, 1940	Germany, Italy, and Japan signed the Tripartite Pact, which is known as the Axis alliance.
May 19, 1941	The Viet Minh, the League for the Independence of Vietnam, is founded.
December 7, 1941	Japan attacks U.S. military bases at Pearl Harbor, Hawai'i. Over 3,500 U.S. service men are wounded or killed.

December 8, 1941	President Franklin D. Roosevelt brings a declaration of war on Japan to Congress: Congress passes it.
February 19, 1942	President Franklin D. Roosevelt signs Executive Order 9066, authorizing the secretary of war to delegate a military commander to designate military areas "from which any and all persons may be excluded." Executive Order 9066 is chiefly enforced against Japanese Americans.
March 18, 1942	President Franklin D. Roosevelt signs Executive Order 9102, ordering the creation of the War Relocation Authority, the agency responsible for forcefully relocating Japanese Americans from their homes to internment camps.
March 21, 1942	Congress passes Public Law 503 to punish anyone defying orders to carry out Executive Order 9066.
March 27, 1942	Second War Powers Act repeals the confidentiality of census data, allowing the FBI to use this information to round up Japanese Americans, and changes naturalization restrictions to allow persons serving the U.S. military during World War II to become naturalized.
October 30, 1942	The U.S. Army completes its transfer of all Japanese American detainees from 15 temporary centers to 10 permanent War Relocation Authority detention camps: Manzanar, Poston, Gila River, Topaz, Granada, Heart Mountain, Minidoka, Tule Lake, Jerome, and Rohwer.
December 17, 1943	The Magnuson Act is signed into law. This Act repeals the Chinese Exclusion Act, allows Chinese to become naturalized citizens, and gives China a quota of 105 immigrants per year.
May 7, 1945	Nazi Germany surrenders unconditionally to the Allies. Japan fights on alone.
August 6, 1945	The United States drops the atomic bomb on Hiroshima.
August 9, 1945	The United States drops the atomic bomb on Nagasaki.

August 19, 1945	The Viet Minh successfully seize power in Hanoi, which they later declare the capital of the Democratic Republic of Vietnam.
August 25, 1945	Emperor Bao Dai is forced to abdicate to Ho Chi Minh and the Viet Minh.
September 2, 1945	Japan formally surrenders to the Allies on board the battleship USS *Missouri*. After the capitulation of Japan to Allied forces, Ho Chi Minh and his People's Congress establish the National Liberation Committee of Vietnam to create a provisional government. Japan transfers all power to Ho Chi Minh and the Vietminh. Korea is divided at the 38th parallel: the Soviet Union with military presence in the North, while U.S. military forces are in the South.
October 15 to December 15, 1945	All War Relocation Authority internment camps are closed except for Tule Lake Center.
December 28, 1945	Congress enacts the War Brides Act that was signed into law by President Harry S. Truman. This Act allows 722 Chinese and 2,042 Japanese women (European women also) who married American servicemen to come to the United States between 1946 and 1953.
February 16, 1946	Ho Chi Minh writes letter to President Harry S. Truman asking for support of the United States in Vietnam's independence. The United States does not respond to his letter.
March 20, 1946	Tule Lake "Segregation Center" closes.
June 29, 1946	Congress enacts the Alien Fiancées Act (also known as the G.I. Fiancées Act) that grants fiancées of American servicemen during World War I a special exemption from immigration quotas to enter the United States.
June 30, 1946	The War Relocation Authority program officially ends.
July 2, 1946	President Harry S. Truman signs the Luce-Celler Act into law, which grants naturalization rights to Filipinos and South Asians.

December 19, 1946	First Indochina War starts when Viet Minh forces attack French forces at Hanoi.
December 23, 1947	President Harry S. Truman grants full pardons to 267 Japanese American draft resisters who had violated the Selective Training and Service Act of 1940.
June 5, 1948	With the Halong Bay Agreements, a unified State of Vietnam is created, replacing Tonkin (North Vietnam), Annam (Middle Vietnam), and the Republic of Cochinchina (South Vietnam) under the auspices of the French Union. Former Emperor Bao Dao is installed by the French as Head of State. Shortly after, President Harry S. Truman recognizes the Associated States of Vietnam and agrees to send aid ($15 million of more than $2.6 billion sent over the next five years).
June 25, 1948	President Harry S. Truman signs the Displaced Persons Act into law. This Act helps individuals who were deemed to be victims of persecution by the Nazi government; who were fleeing persecution; or who could not return to their country because of fear of persecution based on race, religion, or political opinions. This Act focuses on individuals from Germany, Austria, Italy, and Czechoslovakia who, on January 1, 1948, were in Italy or the American sector, the British sector, or the French sector of either Berlin or Vienna or the American zone, the British zone, or the French zone of either Germany or Austria. This Act will influence subsequent policies on refugees, especially those fleeing communist countries, including refugees from Hungary, Cuba, China, Vietnam, Laos, and Cambodia.
March 8, 1949	Bao Dai signs the Elysée Agreement, which confirms the independence of Vietnam as an Associated State of the French Union. As part of the agreement the French pledge to assist in the building of a national anti-Communist army.
October 1, 1949	Chinese Communist leader Mao Zedong declares the creation of the People's Republic of China.

January 18, 1950	The People's Republic of China recognizes Ho Chi Minh's government, the Democratic Republic of Vietnam.
January 30, 1950	The Soviet Union recognizes Ho Chi Minh's government, the Democratic Republic of Vietnam.
June 25, 1950	North Korea invades South Korea, initiating the Korean War.
June 27, 1950	President Harry S. Truman deploys the 7th Fleet to the waters off Taiwan to prevent the spread of the conflict in Korea to neighboring countries.
June 29, 1950	First U.S. ground troops are deployed in Korea.
August 3, 1950	A U.S. Military Assistance Advisory Group (MAAG) of 35 men arrives in Saigon to evaluate French requests for military assistance, support in training South Vietnamese troops, and advice on strategy. By the end of the year, the United States is bearing half the cost of France's war efforts in Vietnam.
April 17, 1952	The California Supreme Court finds California's Alien Land Law of 1913 unconstitutional.
June 27, 1952	The Immigration and Nationality Act of 1952, also known as the McCarran-Walter Act, revises and consolidates all previous laws regarding immigration and naturalization. The Act upholds the national origins quota system, which limits the number of immigrants allowed to enter the United States annually by country. It eliminates the Asiatic Barred Zone, allots each Asian country a minimum of 100 visas annually, and creates a preference system that determines eligibility based on skills and family ties in the United States.
July 27, 1953	The United States, North Korea, and China sign an armistice, which ends the Korean War but fails to bring about peace. To date, the Republic of Korea (South) and Democratic Peoples' Republic of Korea (North) have not signed a peace treaty.

October 22, 1953	Laos gains independence from French rule.
November 9, 1953	Cambodia gains independence from French rule.
April 7, 1954	President Dwight D. Eisenhower coins one of the most well-known Cold War phrases when he suggests the fall of French Indochina to the Communists could generate a "domino" effect in Southeast Asia. The "domino theory" will dominate U.S. thinking and foreign policy about Vietnam and Southeast Asia for the next decade.
May 7, 1954	Ho Chi Minh's Viet Minh forces defeat the French at Dien Bien Phun after a battle of 55 days. Three thousand French troops are killed, 8,000 are wounded. The Viet Minh suffer much worse, with 8,000 dead and 12,000 wounded. This battle shatters France's resolve to carry on the war.
July 20, 1954	The Geneva Conference on Indochina declares a demilitarized zone at the 17th parallel, with South Korea under the leadership of Prime Minister Ngo Dinh Die and North Korea under Communist rule.
September 1954	An exodus from North Vietnam to South Vietnam of some 850,000 North Vietnamese—mostly Catholics. Conversely, 80,000 residents in South Vietnam move to the North.
October 24, 1954	President Dwight D. Eisenhower pledges support to Prime Minister Ngo Dinh Diem and military forces.
March 21, 1956	James Wong Howe wins the Academy Awards for Best Cinematography, Black-and-White for *The Rose Tattoo* (1955).
November 6, 1956	California Proposition 13 repeals California's 1913 Alien Land Law by popular vote.
1957	The Nobel Prize in Physics is awarded jointly to Chen Ning Yang and Tsung-Dao Lee "for their penetrating investigation of the so-called parity laws which has led to important discoveries regarding the elementary particles."
July 28, 1959	Hiram Leong Fong is elected to the U.S. Senate from Hawai'i. He is sworn into office on August 24, 1959.

Fong is reelected on November 3, 1964, and on November 3, 1970. He retires on January 2, 1977.

November 8, 1960 John F. Kennedy barely defeats Richard M. Nixon in the presidential election.

December 20, 1960 The Viet Cong, or National Liberation Front, is formed.

May 12, 1961 During his tour of Asian countries, Vice President Lyndon B. Johnson meets with South Vietnamese President Ngo Dinh Diem in Saigon. Johnson refers to Diem as "the Churchill of Asia," while assuring Diem that he is crucial to U.S. objectives in Vietnam.

1962–1971 The U.S. military sprays 77 million liters of chemical defoliants (Agent Orange or Herbicide Orange) on South Vietnam. The goals are to reduce the Communist forces' cover; to deny the Communist forces the use of crops for food; and to clear sensitive areas, such as military-base perimeters.

April 13, 1964 James Wong Howe wins the Academy Award for Best Cinematography, Black-and-White for *Hud* (1963).

August 2, 1964 The USS *Maddox*, a destroyer located some 30 miles off the coast of North Vietnam in the Tonkin Gulf, is allegedly torpedoed by three North Vietnamese gunboats. No causalities and little damage are reported as a result of the attack.

August 4, 1964 The USS *Maddox* is allegedly attacked again by North Vietnamese gunboats.

August 5, 1964 In response to the two attacks on the USS *Maddox*, President Lyndon B. Johnson requests Congress for a resolution against North Vietnam.

August 7, 1964 The Gulf of Tonkin Resolution is debated by Congress and approved. It authorizes President Lyndon B. Johnson to "take all necessary measures to repel any armed attack against forces of the United States and to prevent further aggression." The resolution passes unanimously in the U.S. House of Representatives and by a margin of 82-2 in the U.S. Senate. The resolution allows President Johnson to wage all-out war against North Vietnam without ever securing a formal Declaration of War from Congress.

November 3, 1964   Lyndon B. Johnson wins the presidential election in a landslide victory over Republican Barry Goldwater of Arizona.

February 7, 1965   The Viet Cong attacked the U.S. Air Force base at Pleiku, South Vietnam, killing 8 Americans and wounding more than 100.

February 13, 1965   In response to the attack at Pleiku, President Lyndon B. Johnson authorizes Operation Rolling Thunder, a sustained American bombing offensive in North Vietnam.

March 8, 1965   The first American combat troops arrive in Vietnam.

April 7, 1965   The United States offers North Vietnam economic aid in exchange for peace but the offer is summarily rejected.

October 3, 1965   The U.S. Congress passes the Immigration and Nationality Act, which eliminates national origins quotas. Twenty-thousand people per country are allowed entry annually. Priority was given to those with skills and/or family residing in the United States.

December 31, 1965   The number of U.S. troops in Vietnam exceeds 200,000.

December 31, 1966   The number of U.S. troops in Vietnam reaches 385,000 men, plus an additional 60,000 sailors stationed offshore. By the end of the year, more than 6,000 Americans have been killed and 30,000 have been wounded.

December 31, 1967   The number of U.S. troops in Vietnam increases to 485,000.

January 30–31, 1968   During the Tet (Lunar New Year) holiday, the Viet Cong launch an attack on Hue and more than 100 other South Vietnamese cities and towns. American forces are able to recapture most areas but is a disastrous blow of public support for the war.

March 16, 1968   In the hamlet of My Lai, U.S. Charlie Company kills some 200 Vietnamese civilians. Only one member of the division is found guilty of war crimes. The massacre fuels increased anti-Vietnam War public sentiments.

March 31, 1968   President Lyndon B. Johnson declines to run for reelection.

April 4, 1968   Dr. Martin Luther King, Jr. is assassinated at the Lorraine Motel in Memphis, Tennessee.

November 1, 1968   After three-and-a-half years, Operation Rolling Thunder ends.

November 6, 1968   The Black Student Union and the coalition of other student groups known as the Third World Liberation Front lead a strike at San Francisco State University to demand establishment of ethnic studies programs and classes.

November 6, 1968   Republican Richard M. Nixon is elected president of the United States and promises to achieve "Peace with Honor" in Vietnam.

March 18, 1969   President Richard M. Nixon approves "Operation Breakfast," a covert bombing of Cambodia, to destroy Communist supply routes and base camps in Cambodia. It is conducted without the knowledge of Congress or the American public and lasts 14 months.

March 20, 1969   The student-led protest at San Francisco State College (now University) ends with a settlement to establish the country's first and still only School (now College) of Ethnic Studies. Asian American Studies is one of the programs, along with American Indian Studies, Black Studies (now Africana Studies), and La Raza Studies (now Latina/o Studies).

November 3, 1969   President Richard M. Nixon gives a public speech on the policy of "Vietnamization." The goal of the policy is to transfer the burden of defeating the Communists onto the South Vietnamese army and away from the United States.

1969   Him Mark Lai and Philip Choy teach the first Chinese American studies class at San Francisco State College (now University).

March 8, 1970   Prince Norodom Sihanouk is ousted as Cambodia's Chief of State in a bloodless coup backed by the

	United States, by pro-Western Lt. Gen. Lon Nol, premier and defense minister, and First Deputy Premier Prince Sisowath Sirik Matak.
June 13, 1971	The *New York Times* publishes a series of daily articles based on the information contained in the Pentagon Papers, which was given to them by Daniel Ellsberg, a military analyst who had worked on the study. Ellsberg came to oppose the war and decided that the American public should be made aware of the information contained in the Pentagon Papers, because it revealed a legacy of deception concerning U.S. policy in Vietnam on the part of the military and the executive branch.
January 1, 1972	Only 133,000 U.S. troops remain in South Vietnam.
February 21, 1972	President Richard M. Nixon visits China.
December 13, 1972	Peace negotiations between North Vietnam and the United States break down in Paris.
January 8, 1973	Peace negotiations between North Vietnam and the United States resume in Paris.
January 27, 1973	All warring parties in the Vietnam War sign a cease-fire agreement. It is signed in Paris by Henry Kissinger and Le Duc Tho.
January 21, 1974	The U.S. Supreme Court, in *Lau v. Nichols*, rules that school districts with children who speak little English must provide them with bilingual education. The Court says, "The failure of the San Francisco school system to provide English language instruction to approximately 1,800 students of Chinese ancestry who do not speak English, or to provide them with other adequate instructional procedures, denies them a meaningful opportunity to participate in the public educational program and thus violates 601 of the Civil Rights Act of 1964."
November 5, 1974	March Kong Fong Eu is elected California's Secretary of State.
April 17, 1975	The Communist Party of Kampuchea (CPK), otherwise known as the Khmer Rouge, takes control of Cambodia. The CPK creates the state of Democratic Kampuchea in 1976 and rules the country until

	January 1979. While in power the Khmer Rouge commits a genocide of its own people: the numbers of Cambodians who die under the Khmer Rouge remains a topic of debate. Vietnamese sources say three million, while others estimate one to two million deaths. Many who die are Chinese Cambodians.
April 23, 1975	President Gerald Ford announces, in a speech at Tulane University, that the Vietnam War is "finished."
April 29, 1975	U.S. Marine and Air Force helicopters begin massive airlift of American civilians out of Saigon. In total, over 1,000 Americans and 7,000 South Vietnamese refugees are airlifted out of Saigon.
April 30, 1975	Fall of Saigon.
May 12, 1975	*Time* magazine declares Ho Chi Minh "The Victor."
May 24, 1975	The Indochina Migration and Refugee Assistance Act is passed. The Act reimburses state governments for the expenses of state resettlement programs for Vietnamese refugees. Under this Act, more than 130,000 refugees from Vietnam, 4,600 from Cambodia, and 800 from Laos enter the United States.
December 2, 1975	The Pathet Lao establish the Lao People's Democratic Republic after forcing King Savang Vatthana to abdicate, and capturing Vientiane.
February 19, 1976	President Gerald Ford rescinds Executive Order 9066, 34 years after World War II.
1976	The United States receives 10,200 refugees from Laos who had fled to Thailand.
January 21, 1977	President Jimmy Carter extends a full and unconditional pardon to nearly 10,000 men who evaded the Vietnam War draft.
1978	Tens of thousands of "Boat People"—mostly Chinese—Vietnamese refugees flee Vietnam, mostly by boat and end up in neighboring Southeast Asian countries.
January 7, 1979	Vietnamese troops capture Phnom Penh.

June 1979	Over 54,000 Chinese Vietnamese refugees arrive by boat in neighboring Southeast Asian countries and Hong Kong.
July 1979	At an international conference in Geneva, Switzerland, the Orderly Departure Program (ODP) is established under the auspices of the United Nations High Commissioner for Refugees (UNHCR). The goal is to encourage refugees to leave their country safely, instead of undertaking the dangerous voyage by boat. On September 14, 1994, registration for the ODP is closed. Under the ODP, from 1980 until 1997, 623,509 Vietnamese were resettled abroad, of whom more than 450,000 went to the United States. Refugee camps opened in Thailand to house some 160,000 Cambodian and 105,000 Laotian refugees. UNHCR assisted another 350,000 Cambodian refugees who lived in Thailand outside of the camps and some 100,000 Cambodians who fled to Vietnam.
March 17, 1980	President Jimmy Carter signs the Refugee Act into law. Under this Act, the Office of Refugee Resettlement is established. It also adopts the definition of "refugee" used in the United Nations Protocol and provides regular and emergency admissions of refugees.
March 30, 1981	Architect and sculptor Maya Lin submits winning design for the Vietnam Veterans Memorial in Washington, D.C. There were more than 1,400 submissions and a prize of $50,000.
June 19, 1982	Twenty-seven-year-old Chinese American Vincent Chin is brutally murdered in Detroit by two white men, Ronald Ebens and Michael Nitz, who mistake him for a "Japanese." Ebens and Nitz blame Chin for losing their jobs in the auto industry. Chin is struck repeatedly with a bat, including blows to the head. Chin is taken to the Henry Ford Hospital, where he was unconscious, and died June 23 after four days in a coma.
June 23, 1983	The Commission on Wartime Relocation and Internment of Civilians reports that Japanese American internment was not justified by military

necessity and that internment was based on "race prejudice, war hysteria, and a failure of political leadership." The Commission recommends an official government apology, redress payments of $20,000 to each of the survivors, and a public education fund to help ensure that this would not happen again.

October 4, 1983	The Federal District Court of San Francisco reverses Fred Korematsu's original conviction and rules that the U.S. government had no justification for issuing the internment orders.
November 28, 1983	Lily Lee Chen is inaugurated as the nation's first Chinese American woman elected as mayor in Monterey Park, California.
1983	Andrew and Peggy Cherng open first Panda Express in the Glendale Galleria's food court.
March 25, 1985	Chinese Cambodian Dr. Haing S. Ngor wins the Oscar for best supporting actor for his role in *The Killing Fields*.
November 6, 1986	The U.S. Congress enacts the Immigration Reform and Control Act, which includes civil and criminal penalties on employers who knowingly hire undocumented "aliens."
1986	The Nobel Prize in Chemistry is jointly awarded to Yuan T. Lee, Dudley R. Herschbach, and John C. Polanyi "for their contributions concerning the dynamics of chemical elementary processes."
May 4, 1987	President Ronald Reagan issues proclamation of Asian/Pacific American Heritage Week.
December 22, 1987	The U.S. Congress enacts the Amerasian Homecoming Act, which eases immigration of Amerasian children born (war babies) during the Vietnam War—mostly the offspring of American fathers and Vietnamese mothers. By 2009, about 25,000 Vietnamese Amerasians and 60,000–70,000 of their relatives enter the United States under this law.
September 1989	Vietnam completes troop withdrawal from Cambodia.

November 29, 1990	The Immigration Act is enacted and increases the annual visa cap to 700,000. The Act also creates the Diversity Immigrant Visa program.
December 1991	The United States lifts a ban on travel to Vietnam.
April 29, 1992	The United States eases trade embargo on Vietnam.
December 14, 1992	President George H. W. Bush allows U.S. companies to open offices, sign contracts, and do feasibility studies in Vietnam.
June 1, 1993	Connie Chung becomes permanent coanchor with Dan Rather on The *CBS Evening News*.
February 3, 1994	President William Clinton announces the lifting of the trade embargo in Vietnam.
March 1995	Jerry Yang and David Filo launch Yahoo.
1996	David Ho is named *Time* magazine's "Man of the Year" for his role in developing the "drug cocktail" therapy for HIV-positive patients.
July 1, 1997	At midnight on this day, Hong Kong is returned to China and becomes a Special Administrative Region.
1997	The Nobel Prize in Physics is jointed awarded to Steven Chu, Claude Cohen-Tannoudji, and William D. Phillips "for developments of methods to cool and trap atoms with laser light."
November 3, 1998	David Wu is elected to the U.S. House of Representatives for Oregon's 1st Congressional District. Wu is a member of the Democratic Party. He is reelected in 2000, 2004, 2006, and 2008.
1998	Michelle Kwan wins silver medal in figure skating at Nagano Olympics. She wins the bronze medal at the 2002 Salt Lake City Olympics.
January 20, 2001	Elaine Lan Chao is sworn in as the 24th U.S. Secretary of Labor in the George W. Bush administration for two terms.
2002	Jacqueline Mates-Muchin is ordained by Hebrew Union College, Jewish Institute of Religion as rabbi. She is the first Chinese American rabbi.

2005	Steven Shih "Steve" Chen launches Youtube with Chad Hurley and Jawed Karim.
March 5, 2006	Director Ang Lee wins the Academy Award for Best Director for *Brokeback Mountain* (2005).
January 21, 2009	Steven Chu is sworn in as the 12th U.S. Secretary of Energy in the Barack Obama administration.
2009	The Nobel Prize in Physics is jointly awarded to Charles Kuen Kao, Willard S. Boyle, and George E. Smith. Kao is noted "for groundbreaking achievements concerning the transmission of light in fibers for optical communication."
January 3, 2011	Jean Quan is sworn in as the first female mayor of Oakland, California.
January 11, 2011	Edwin Mah Lee is appointed by the Board of Supervisors as the 43rd Mayor of San Francisco, California. He serves as Interim Mayor until he wins the election on November 8, 2011. He was sworn in on January 8, 2012. Lee is the first Chinese American mayor in San Francisco's history, and the first Asian American elected to the office.
July 27, 2011	Gary Locke is confirmed unanimously by the U.S. Senate as President Barack Obama's U.S. Ambassador to China.
January 3, 2012	Yiaway Yeh is elected by city council to serve as mayor of Palo Alto, California. He is the first Chinese American to hold this office.
June 19, 2012	The U.S. House of Representatives unanimously passes a bipartisan resolution introduced by Congresswoman Judy Chu of California, who represents the 27th Congressional District (which includes Pasadena and the west San Gabriel Valley of southern California), which formally expresses the regret of the House of Representatives for the Chinese Exclusion Act of 1882 and other anti-Chinese legislations that discriminated against people of Chinese heritage in the United States.

2012	Asians surpass Hispanics as the largest group of new immigrants in the United States. An estimated 18.2 million Asians are recorded as residing in the United States, making them the fastest growing racial-ethnic group in the country.
February 24, 2013	Director Ang Lee wins Academy Award for Best Director for *Life of Pi* (2012).
2013	A comprehensive immigration reform is introduced to the U.S. Congress. If enacted, the bill will create a DREAM Act that provides a path toward naturalization for undocumented persons living in the United States.
February 20, 2014	Julie Chu wins silver medal with the U.S. women's national ice hockey team at the Winter Olympics in Sochi, Russia.
January 2015	Jacqueline Mates-Muchin is elected "senior rabbi" at Temple Sinai, located in Oakland, California (officially the First Hebrew Congregation of Oakland). She is the first woman in that position.
February 10, 2015	*Fresh Off the Boat*, a television series about a Chinese American family, based on Eddie Huang's best-selling memoir of the same title, airs in its prime-time slot.
February 11, 2015	American Chef Mei Lin wins *Top Chef: Boston* (Season 12).

PART I

CONTEXT OF CHINESE AMERICAN EMIGRATION: COMING TO AMERICA

HISTORICAL OVERVIEW

In Mandarin Chinese, America is *meiguo* (in Cantonese: *meigok*), meaning "beautiful country," and California is *jinshan* (in Cantonese: *gamsan*), meaning "gold mountain." This reveals an interesting irony in the perception of America versus the lived experience of America by Chinese Americans. The Chinese were the first Asian immigrants to come to the United States. To date, the Chinese have lived in America for over 150 years. Today, about 35 million Chinese live outside of China in over 130 countries. Today the total population in China is over 1.35 billion. Chinese Americans are a complex and highly diverse ethnic and culture group. Their statistical data shows that they straddle both ends of the sociological spectrum, from rich to poor, from college graduates to illiterate dropouts, from doctors and lawyers to sweat shop workers, and from high-tech professionals to unskilled workers.

By 1800 China faced a bleak future. Its military was weak and unable to protect its people from Western colonial powers. In addition, population growth and pressure exacerbated China's inability to protect its people from internal and external pressures. By 1800 the population of China totaled 300 million, representing a twofold increase since the 1660s. Agricultural land did not develop with this population growth, because so much of China consisted of arid and mountainous land. Between 1661 and 1812, the population increased by more than 100 percent, while arable land had only increased by less than 50 percent. Population growth became a significant social, economic, and political problem for China because the economic system did not develop, and the impact of the global industrial revolution was not significantly felt. The displaced Chinese, the poor, and unemployed had to result to social vices, such as banditry, or rebellion, or move to survive.

The British Opium Wars of 1839–1842 and 1856–1860 forced China to pay large indemnities to the Western imperialist colonial powers and drained the Chinese spirit as opium was imported into China to advance British economic interest. This resulted in the Qing government's high taxation on the peasant farmers, who were unable to pay their taxes, which resulted in them losing their land. Once displaced from their land, they were unable to find employment elsewhere because China's industrial sector was underdeveloped, a result of foreign competition imposed on China after the Opium Wars undermining domestic industries such as silk production. In fact, according to Tong, Guangdong produced many mass-produced goods, but foreign goods flooded the local markets, limiting the demand for Chinese-made goods, such as premodern Chinese handicrafts. The rapid growth of the colonized islands of Macao and Hong Kong, by as early as the mid-1850s, captured much trade from Guangdong. By 1870, free trade and competition from other coastal ports in China exacerbated the unemployment rate for the urban proletariat in Guangdong. Unemployment, high taxation, growing population pressure, and natural disasters such as flooding deepened the problems of hunger and poverty in the Guangdong province. The hardest hit population was subsistence-based peasantry who also bore the heaviest taxation. These immigrants defied Chinese law, since the Ming and Qing dynasties forbid overseas travel on pain of death.

The greatest outflow of Chinese immigrants occurred between the 1840 and 1900. An estimated two-and-a-half million people left China and went to Hawai'i, the United States, Canada, Australia, New Zealand, Southeast Asia, the West Indies, South America, and Africa. During this early period, the majority traveled to the Kingdom of Hawai'i and the mainland United States. Civil unrest, political, and military chaos pushed Chinese immigrants out of their country to seek sanctuary elsewhere. Virtually all the Chinese who emigrated came from only five small regions in the two provinces of Fujian and Guangdong and the island of Hainan. Three of the groups settled mainly in Southeast Asia, while the other two traveled across the Pacific to Hawai'i and mainland United States. A vast majority of the first wave of Chinese immigrants who landed in California during the 19th century came from the Guangdong Province. The Guangdong natives in the United States can, in turn, be divided into three subgroups, each speaking its own Chinese dialect. *Samyup (sanyi)* people came from three districts immediately south and west of the city of Guangzhou, in the Pearl River Delta; *Szeyup (siyi)* inhabitants hailed from four districts to the southeast of San yup; while Xiangshan natives originated from a district between Guangzhou and the Portuguese colony of Macau, some 40 miles west of Xianggang (Hong Kong). To Cantonese immigrants, emigration represented a means for a better life in the face of population pressure, economic hardship, political upheaval, religious persecution, and natural disasters. Although aspiring immigrants had many places to choose from, places where gold had been reportedly discovered—most notably California, Australia, and the Fraser River Valley of British Columbia—were the most alluring.

The discovery of gold at Sutter's Mill in 1848 provoked a distant gaze toward the West Coast. This includes the Pacific Northwest and British Columbia. Australia was also a central object of the gold gaze. San Francisco was known as "Old Gold Mountain" (*Jiujinshan*) while Australia was known as "New Gold Mountain" (*Xinjinshan*). Between 1848 and 1882, waves of Chinese immigrants, predominantly from the southern provinces of Guangdong (also known as Canton) and Fujian, came to California, Oregon, Washington, and Idaho in search of gold. Although their search was for gold, many ended up in coal mines, railroad construction, and service work (e.g., cooks, laundry workers, and shopkeepers). Chinese pioneers began to establish Chinatowns, either by necessity or by choice, and started to re-create and reproduce a perception of community. A high percentage of these immigrants were young men in their working prime, chosen by their families to journey to Gold Mountain (Mandarin: *Jinshan*; Cantonese: *Gam San*), overblown with hopes of making it rich and returning home after several years aboard. San Francisco was a major port of entry for Chinese immigrants during the early period of the Gold Rush.

In 1876 the Pacific Mail Steamship Company began regularly scheduled runs between Hong Kong and San Francisco and, as a result, between 1870 and 1883, an average of 12,000 Chinese immigrants were arriving through the port of San Francisco each year. Before the steamship, the voyage took from 55 to 100 days. With the advent of the steamship, and the famous China route that began in 1867 and lasted until the turn of the century, the time taken to reach San Francisco shortened to weeks. The steamships could hold more passengers than the traditional sailing ships. Immigration was further encouraged when the price of the tickets for the steamship dropped threefold. By 1870 there were 63,000 Chinese immigrants living on U.S. soil—between 75 and 80 percent living in California, with sizable communities in Idaho, Montana, and other areas in the Southwest and New England. For this reason, along the West Coast, but primarily in California, there were many Chinese communities of various sizes, as far south as Baja California and San Diego and northward to Vancouver, Canada.

A major pull factor in their decision to leave their villages for distant lands since the late 18th century was the exaggerated tales of the riches of America, on Gold Mountain. The people of Guangdong had been exposed to American influences by way of Yankee traders and missionaries. Prejudice, disfranchisement, and social exclusion marked their daily existence and Gold Mountain dreams.

The travelers were mainly poverty-stricken young men. Some of them were married, generally illiterate or had very little schooling, but all were inspired by the tales of Gold Mountain. There was more than just gold to be mined but employment opportunities as well. The poor peasants entered into contract, a form of forced slave labor, to afford their passage to the Kingdom of Hawai'i and the mainland United States. For example, arrangements for their Pacific passage were made by an emigration broker representing the sugar plantation owners in Hawai'i. They were offered "free passage" to the island in exchange for their labor. The terms of the contracts usually lasted five years and included shelter, food, and medical care. The other way to finance their passage was through the "credit-ticket system." Here, a broker would loan money to the migrant, who would later pay off the loan with interest out of his earnings. Unlike the "coolie trade" of Africans to Cuba and Peru, the Chinese were not coolies. Coolies are kidnapped and forced into labor through coercion. On the other hand, the Chinese laborers voluntarily left their villages in hopes of making money and riches to support their families back in China. Many also simply borrowed money from their relatives for their trans-Pacific journey. The coolie trade was finally banned in 1862 with the passage of An Act to Prohibit Coolie Trade.

Chinese immigration also included merchants. They were venture capitalists seeking new opportunities in a foreign land. Like the peasant laborers, this class of people were also mostly, if not all men. Single women did not travel alone to distant foreign lands. The married ones often stayed home to care for their families and elders. They also stayed behind because the family simply could not afford their passage. Because husbands and sons where separated from wives and families, the Chinese immigrants are described as *sojourners*. Sojourners are people on the move, involved in temporary migration who plan to eventually return to those they left behind. However, two-thirds remained—for legal, financial, or personal reasons—in America, to live, work, and settle.

Before 1900 Hawai'i was an independent monarchy. Hawai'i's lucrative sugar industry entered the world market in the 1940s, replacing small local farms with plantation fields, improved refinement of sugar processing, and increased output. Hawai'i's sugar industry was fueled by the growing population of California and Oregon. The U.S. Civil War also fueled the development of Hawai'i's sugar industry as the North was cut off from the South's raw material. The North thus became a steady market for higher-priced imported sugar and cotton. The need for cheap labor surely influenced the sugar plantation owners to recruit contract workers from China, the Pacific Islands, Japan, Korea, the Philippines, Puerto Rico, Europe, and California. Starting around 1852, the plantation owners imported Chinese laborers in large numbers.

By 1882, the Chinese population in the United States was about 110,000, or one-fifth of 1 percent, of the total U.S. population. When Chinese laborers were no longer needed, political agitation against the Chinese intensified, and the U.S. Congress enacted a series of very harsh anti-Chinese laws, beginning in 1882, designed to exclude Chinese immigrants and deny their naturalization rights and basic civil liberties. In the spring of 1882, the Chinese Exclusion Act was passed by Congress and signed by President Chester A. Arthur.

Section 14 of the Act declares, "hereafter no State court of the United States shall admit Chinese to citizenship; and all laws in conflict with this act are hereby repealed." Section 15 states that "the words 'Chinese laborers,' wherever used in this act, shall be construed to mean both skilled and unskilled laborers and Chinese employed in mining." By 1888, the Act was extended to include all Chinese, not just laborers. It was renewed by the Geary Act of 1892 and extended indefinitely in 1902. The Chinese Exclusion Act was the first U.S. law ever passed to prevent immigration and naturalization on the basis of race, which later was extended and expanded to include other Asian immigrants, such as the Japanese, Korean, and Indian. The exclusionist policies led to an immediate and sharp decline in the Chinese population: from 105,465 in 1880 to 89,863 in 1900 to 61,639 in 1920.

This demographic decline resulted in the steady disappearance of China-towns throughout America. For example, the Chinese communities in California towns such as Cambria, Riverside, Yosemite, Hanford, Mendocino, Santa Barbara, Ventura, and San Luis Obispo slowly disappeared as the remaining Chinese moved northward to San Francisco or southward to Los Angeles, two cities with major Chinese centers and more possibilities for employment. China-town communities in Evanston, Wyoming; Silver City, Idaho; and Walla Walla, Washington, gradually disappeared as well. It is estimated that by 1900, nearly 45 percent of Chinese immigrants resided in the San Francisco Bay area. At the same time, those years witnessed an increasing number of Chinese American families, which resulted in a new generation of acculturated English-speaking Chinese Americans who grew up between the 1930s and 1940s. In the 1880s cities and towns with a Chinatown were scattered throughout the West, though the Chinatown might consist of only a street or a few stores and its inhabitants might number only a few hundred. Eventually, these enclaves disappeared alto-gether. By 1940 only 28 cities with Chinatowns could be identified; by 1955, only 16. Enforcement of the exclusion laws by immigration officials resulted in additional exclusionary measures that doubly hindered Chinese immigration but also reinforced the popular conceptions and construction of the Chinese as "Orientals," "perpetual foreigners" who threatened the American landscape.

Living in America was difficult. Attempts to settle and create families was not easy, especially with the passage of alien land laws that made it illegal for immigrants ineligible to become naturalized citizens from buying and owning real estate. In 1913, California passed its first alien land law, the Webb-Haney Bill. This law also stipulated that aliens ineligible for citizenship may not lease land for agriculture for terms longer than three years. This, along with vio-lence and attacks fueled by anti-Chinese sentiments, pushed Chinese laborers out of the agricultural industries and into the urban ghettos of San Francisco's Chinatown. Throughout the 1920s, 1930s, and into the 1940s, Chinatowns in urban communities grew and became tourist economies. Their survival in

Chinatowns was forced as they were not allowed to make homes elsewhere in the United States. The majority were also employed in the self-service industries: restaurants, laundries, and so on. U.S.-born Chinese children were also forced to attend segregated schools.

World War II and the postwar period witnessed great social changes for Chinese living in America. The United States and China became allies during World War II, which brought about changes in restrictive immigration policies that resulted in the repeal of the Chinese Exclusion Act in 1943 with the passage of the Magnuson Act. The Magnuson Act repealed 61 years of official racial discrimination against the Chinese. This allowed for a modest increase in Chinese immigration, especially after the Chinese Communist revolution of 1949 sent many Chinese in search of refuge abroad. The postwar period was also the time when Chinese gained naturalization rights and eventually the end of anti-miscegenation laws prohibiting the marriage of a Chinese to a white person. The culmination of progressive social change was realized with the passage of the 1965 Immigration and Nationality Act that lifted national origin quotas, and allowed for large-scale Chinese immigration to the United States resumed.

The first wave of Chinese migrants was fairly homogenous in that they came from the Pearl River Delta region of Canton China and consisted of mostly men. In addition, most were sojourners with peasant backgrounds and low levels of education. There was a small merchant class in the mix. The Hart-Celler Act of 1965 transformed the homogenous Chinese American society into a heterogeneous one reflecting diversity in religious, social, economic, educational, linguistic, and ethnic backgrounds. The majority before 1965 spoke Taishan and Cantonese dialects. Today, there is an increase in Mandarin, Chaozhou, Fujianese, Hakka, and Shanghai dialects among the Chinese American populations, whose countries of origins include mainland China, Hong Kong, Taiwan, Singapore, and Malaysia. There is also a sizable sector of the population who are ethnic Chinese from Southeast Asia (e.g., Cambodia and Vietnam) who entered the United States as refugees after the fall of Saigon in 1975. Chinese immigrants from Taiwan, Hong Kong, and Singapore come from higher sociocultural backgrounds with higher educational levels. As such, they tend to enter into professional white-collar or high-tech employment. Since the 1980s, Chinese migration has continued and reflects the heterogeneity of the Chinese American mosaic.

ALIEN LAND LAW (1913)

In 1913, California passed the Alien Land Law, which denied aliens who were not eligible for U.S. citizenship the right to own agricultural land in California. This law was cowritten by California Attorney General Ulysses S. Webb and attorney Francis J. Haney, so it was also known as Webb-Haney Alien Land Law. After the passage of the Alien Land Law in California, other western states, such as Idaho, Montana, Oregon, and Washington, passed similar land laws.

After the passage of the 1882 Chinese Exclusion Act, the supply of cheap Chinese laborers was down. However, the coming of Japanese laborers was not affected by this Act. Japanese agricultural laborers helped the Californian agriculturalists since they needed cheap agricultural laborers. When Japanese began to own more agricultural lands in California, California agriculturalists worried about the competition from Japanese agriculturalists. Anti-Japanese tensions soon rose in California as Japanese immigrant numbers rose, and as it had done with Chinese immigrants, California used legislation to solve the matter, in spite of the federal government's fear that such action would hurt foreign policy. In 1913, California passed the Alien Land Law that targeted Asian immigrants, especially Japanese, because they were banned from naturalization and illegible for U.S. citizenship. Since more Japanese immigrants owned lands in California, the new law affected Japanese more than Chinese. The 1913 California Land Law permitted only aliens eligible for citizenship to acquire, possess, enjoy, transmit, and inherit real property. These aliens illegible for citizenship were also barred from taking the lands on lease for longer than three years. The significance of this law lay in the high percentage of Japanese immigrants working on the land and in agriculturally based jobs. Prior to the law's passage, nearly 50 percent of Japanese immigrants worked in jobs related to the agricultural industries. Considering this high involvement with agriculture and land, it was clear how the new law directly restricted Japanese development in California.

Although the 1913 Alien Land Law was passed, it did not stop Japanese from holding more land in California. Some Japanese agriculturalists used their U.S-born children and relatives to own the land. Some opened companies and used these companies to own land. In 1920, anti-Japanese activists in California succeeded to push for an amendment of the 1913 Alien Land Law. The 1920 Alien Land Law closed the loopholes of the 1913 Alien Land Law. Under the new law, the majority shareholders of these land-holding companies could not be aliens illegible for citizenship. The new law also barred leases of agricultural land, trusteeships, and guardianships in the name of aliens illegible for citizenship. In 1923 and 1927, the California legislature passed more amendments that required these aliens to sell inherited land, and they could not own stock in a corporation that also owned agricultural land. In 1923, the Alien Land Laws were challenged but upheld in the U.S. Supreme Court. In 1952, the Supreme Court of California made the laws invalid.

See also: Chinese Exclusion Act (1882)

Further Reading

Gaines, Brian J., and Wendy K. Tam Cho. 2004. "On California's 1920 Alien Land Law: The Psychology and Economics of Racial Discrimination." *State Politics and Policy Quarterly* (Fall): 271–93.

Ichihashi, Yamato. 1915. *Japanese Immigration: Its Status in California.* San Francisco: The Marshall Press.

Edy Parsons

AMERICAN FEDERATION OF LABOR

The American Federation of Labor (AFL) was a national coalition of labor unions that played a significant role in American labor relations for nearly 70 years. The AFL was officially founded in 1886 during a convention in Columbus, Ohio. The first president of the AFL was Samuel Gompers (1850–1924), a member of a cigar-making union. In contrast to the idealism of the Knights of Labor and the revolutionary and violent behavior of the Industrial Workers of the World (IWW), the AFL focused its attention on practical matters, such as wages, working conditions, and establishing the eight-hour workday. In addition to its pragmatism, the AFL recognized the autonomy of its member unions while simultaneously maintaining control over major structures and vital programs. This recognition of autonomy proved controversial, considering that several unions within the AFL retained discriminatory practices against various racial and ethnic groups. There were several affiliated unions that either practiced segregation or excluded African Americans from their ranks. In reference to immigrants, the AFL and other unions seemed to focus on Chinese immigrant workers. In 1882, the U.S. Congress passed the Chinese Exclusion Act, officially prohibiting the immigration of Chinese laborers into the United States for a period of 10 years. This prohibition was reviewed and renewed in 1892 and another 10-year ban was confirmed. At the turn of the 20th century, Chinese immigrant workers were permanently banned from entering the United States until the exclusion law was formally repealed in 1943. However, by this time, the AFL had suffered losses following the establishment of the Congress for Industrial Organizations (CIO). The division between the AFL and CIO remained in place until the unification as the AFL-CIO in 1955. This unified AFL-CIO continues to remain active in labor issues across the United States.

See also: Anti-Chinese Violence

Further Reading

Dray, Philip. 2011. *There Is Power in a Union: The Epic Story of Labor in America.* New York: Anchor Books.

Lorwin, Lewis L. 1972. *The American Federation of Labor: History, Policies, and Prospects.* Clifton, NJ: Augustus M. Kelley.

Robertson, David Brian. 2000. *Capital, Labor, and State: The Battle for American Labor Markets from the Civil War to the New Deal.* Lanham, MD: Rowman & Littlefield.

John Cappucci

ANGEL ISLAND IMMIGRATION STATION

History books depict the waves of immigration during the late 19th and early 20th centuries as being primarily Western European in their composition. While there were scores of immigrants that were both legal and illegal from Germany, Italy, Ireland, and a wealth of other nations, there were also waves of immigrants flocking to the western United States. Angel Island was opened in 1910 and was touted as the "Ellis Island of the West." The purpose of its creation was to control the flow of Japanese and Chinese immigrants (particularly laborers) to the country. Even after the flow of laborers from Japan was

A group of Chinese and Japanese women and children wait to be processed as they are held in a wire mesh enclosure at the Angel Island Internment barracks in San Francisco Bay in the late 1920s. The Angel Island Immigration Station processed one million immigrants from 1910 to 1940, mostly from China and Japan. (AP Photo)

curtailed in 1907, it is estimated that upwards of 19,000 "Picture Brides" were still allowed to immigrate through Angel Island and more than 17,000 Chinese were thought to be illegally residing in the United States by 1920. Controversy surrounded the facility from the beginning due to its role in limiting access to the United States by Chinese immigrants. Though Angel Island was the official access point for immigrants from more than 80 countries, many stayed for months as detainees in the barracks. Until 1915, Chinese immigrants were the largest single population to pass through the station, when Japanese immigrants outnumbered Chinese immigrants for the first time.

During this time of extreme limitation on the ability of Chinese immigrants to successfully immigrate to the United States, many people began to look for alternate routes to guarantee entry. One such route was to become a "paper son" or "paper daughter" of a citizen. At the time, women's citizenship was tied to their parents or husband, and children who could satisfy immigration officers that they were the legitimate offspring of a citizen could not be denied entry. This led many immigrants to study new identities and family trees in order to successfully satisfy immigration officers during extensive interview sessions.

With the fear of deportation to their homelands constantly looming over them, the detainees sought an outlet for their emotions. Many turned to writing poetry on the walls of the dormitories in which they lived. Some were written in paint, though many were carved into the wooden planks of the buildings themselves, still bearing witness to the exclusion and detention of countless immigrants who passed through the halls of Angel Island.

Angel Island stood as the "Guardian of the Western Gate" until a fire decimated the facility in 1940, when immigration services were moved to the mainland to better facilitate the processes. Though officially repealed in 1943 when China became an ally in World War I, the Chinese Exclusion Act was simply incorporated into an earlier Immigration Act of 1924, which limited the number of Chinese eligible to enter the United States each year to 105. By 1965 this too was repealed and Chinese immigration was on par with immigration of all other nationalities.

With the advent of World War II, the North Garrison of Angel Island became a processing center for Japanese and German prisoners of war. A brief period of expansion due to the housing of prisoners commenced in 1942, with the addition of a mess hall, many barracks, and a recreation facility. Congress enacted the Angel Island Immigration Station Restoration and Preservation Act in 2005 to restore the immigration center, hospital, and barracks. The California State Park Service, largely funded by the Angel Island Immigration Station Foundation as well as funding from the federal government, now operates a museum dedicated to both education related to and preservation of the site. Records are housed at the National Archives and Records Administration.

See also: Chinese American Literature; Paper Sons and Daughters

Further Reading

Angel Island Association. 2013. "Immigration Station." Accessed August 29, 2014. http://www.angelisland.org.

Lee, Erica. 2003. *At America's Gates: Chinese Immigration During the Exclusion Era, 1882–1943.* Chapel Hill: University of North Carolina Press.

Carlise Womack Wynne

ANGELL TREATY (CHINESE EXCLUSION TREATY) (1880)

The Angell Treaty was signed between China and the United States on November 17, 1880. The new treaty targeted only Chinese labor immigration, but left immigration of nonlaborers, such as teachers, students, and merchants, intact.

In the 1870s, the anti-Chinese sentiment was growing in the United States due to the increasing number of Chinese laborers coming to the United States. This led to push for the further limitation of Chinese immigration. In 1880, the U.S. government sent a commission led by James B. Angell to China. The negotiation between China and the United States led to the revision of the Burlingame Treaty of 1868, allowing the Chinese to have the right to immigrate to the United States freely. China and the United States then signed the Angell Treaty, which contained two articles. This new treaty did not exclude all Chinese immigrants but regulated and limited the coming of Chinese immigrants. Within the jurisdiction of the treaty, the U.S. government now had the right to regulate or suspend Chinese labor immigration when the Chinese laborers coming to the United States would affect the interests of the United States. The treaty restricted the coming of Chinese laborers who had never been to the United States when the treaty was signed. However, the treaty allowed Chinese laborers already in the United States to have the freedom of movement between China and the United States. This treaty also gave most-favored-nation status to the Chinese already in the United States, and those nonlaborers could still enter the United States. The interests and opportunities of Chinese immigrants in the United States were surrendered into the hands of the U.S. government. The treaty was ratified in October 1881. In 1882, U.S. Congress passed the Chinese Exclusion Act that was consonant with this treaty.

See also: Burlingame Treaty (1868); Chinese Exclusion Act (1882); Scott Act (1888)

Further Reading

Daniels, Roger. 1988. *Asian America: Chinese and Japanese in the United States Since 1850.* Seattle: University of Washington Press.

Edy Parsons

ANTI-CHINESE VIOLENCE

In the late 1860s, anti-Chinese sentiment began to boil over, and the anti-Chinese violence spread from California to other western states. Most of the anti-Chinese riots happened between the 1870s and 1880s. Anti-Chinese violence in these states emerged for numerous reasons. White workers perceived the Chinese competition as a direct threat to their livelihood in the mines and other industries. Cultural differences made white Americans see Chinese live in an un-American way in the Chinese quarters that had opium dens and prostitution. Furthermore, racial antagonism also caused the tension between white Americans and Chinese. White constituents pressured politicians for action. In some worst cases, violence was used. As a result, Chinese immigrants became targets of anti-Chinese violence.

In spite of an initial positive acceptance when the Chinese first arrived in the United States, Americans, especially in the West, increased their anti-Chinese sentiment. The fear of the Chinese immigrants' negative influence on Americans created a negative image for Chinese. There were several elements, such as the increase of Chinese population in the United States, economic competition, cultural difference and lifestyle, contributing to the shift of American attitudes toward Chinese immigrants. The negative image of Chinese soon became a stereotype for all Chinese immigrants. The anti-Chinese movements of the 1870s and the 1880s received fuel when fears spread that the Chinese would take jobs away from American workers. It was job competition that significantly changed the image of Chinese immigrants from positive to negative in the American West. Growing negative opinion soon changed into active opposition. White American workers felt threatened when

A scene from the Hop Alley Chinese Riot in Denver, Colorado. The riot was born out of anti-Chinese hysteria that turned violent after two Chinese men and three or four white men at a saloon got into a fight. Most of Denver's Chinatown was destroyed. (Library of Congress)

they competed with the cheaper Chinese laborers. By the mid-1860s, over 10,000 Chinese workers had arrived in the United States to build the Central Pacific Railroad, thus creating a large, cheap labor force. Then in May 1869, with the Transcontinental Railroad completed, those Chinese laborers were dumped back into the competitive California labor market. The supply of Chinese laborers increased in the job market. In California, anti-Chinese violence happened in at least 30 urban communities. One worst case happened in October 1871. Nineteen Chinese were killed in Los Angeles Chinatown during a riot that was caused by the death of two policemen trying to intervene in a *tong* battle. The mob also looted stores, burned houses, and beat up Chinese.

Besides California, anti-Chinese violence emerged in several other western states. A large anti-Chinese riot happened in Denver, Colorado in 1880. Denver had about 40,000 people, including 450 Chinese at that time. In 1870, a territorial joint resolution encouraged Chinese laborers to go to Colorado because they would help the development of the territory. Since Chinese laborers were willing to work for low wages and had different customs, fear of these aliens intensified anti-Chinese sentiment. On October 31, 1880, a mob of about 3,000 people gathered at Denver's Chinatown. The mob destroyed buildings and killed one Chinese laundryman before the local police put down the riot.

After the passage of the Chinese Exclusion Act in 1882, the number of Chinese immigrants diminished. However, anti-Chinese violence still occurred after 1882. In 1885, many anti-Chinese riots and attacks happened in various western states. The economic depression of 1885–1886 made the economic condition worse. The fear of job competition from Chinese laborers fueled anti-Chinese agitation. The worst anti-Chinese violence happened in Rock Springs, Wyoming. The Coal Department of the Union Pacific hired about 300 Chinese miners and 150 white miners. Many of these white miners were members of the Knights of Labor, which was a national labor organization pushing for the exclusion of Chinese laborers. On September 2, 1885, white miners beat a Chinese miner to death due to a dispute over work between Chinese miners and white miners. Later, 150 men went to the Chinese quarter, half of them armed with rifles. Twenty-eight Chinese were killed and 15 were wounded. Besides loss of life, property damage in the Chinese quarter was also extensive. Several hundred Chinese were driven out of town. Although 16 whites were arrested for participating in the riot, none of them was indicted. On September 9, 1885, the Chinese who escaped from the massacre were escorted back to Rock Springs by U.S. troops. The Rock Springs Massacre received a lot of press coverage and fueled anti-American sentiment in China. The U.S. Congress agreed to pay compensation. This was seen as a minor victory for China diplomatically.

However, the anti-Chinese violence in Rock Springs also intensified the tension in Washington Territory's coal mines. Regional economic depression in the decade and race prejudice still caused anti-Chinese violence in the region. On September 11, 1885, a group of masked men attacked the Chinese miners at Coal Creek. The Chinese quarters were burned. On September 19, white miners forced Chinese to leave Black Diamond. On November 3, 1885, about 300 Tacoma citizens went to the Chinese quarters and forced them to leave Tacoma. Many of these citizens were armed with clubs. The Chinese did as they were told and left. Some Chinese stores and buildings were burned. On February 7, 1886, white radicals forced the Chinese in Seattle to leave on a streamer. About 350 Chinese were marched off to the dock before the sheriff's forces could stop the radicals. Almost 200 Chinese left. The remaining Chinese were escorted back to their homes by the Home Guards, the University Cadets, and the Seattle Riffles. The white mob refused to give way to the guards. Shots were fired. Governor Squire declared martial law on February 8 and called in the U.S. troops.

Riots in Washington territory were not the last ones. The Snake River Massacre became the last major anti-Chinese violence of the 1880s in the western region. On May 27, 1887, seven white horse thieves robbed and slaughtered 34 Chinese gold miners in Hells Canyon, Oregon. The gold dust was stolen. Three of the horse thieves were arrested and tried, but they were eventually discharged.

In conclusion, a combination of factors triggered anti-Chinese violence. Job competition threatened white workers, especially during economic depression. However, race prejudice also played a big part in anti-Chinese riots and expulsion.

See also: Chinese Exclusion Act (1882); Queue Ordinance (1876)

Further Reading

Daniels, Roger. 1978. *Anti-Chinese Violence in North America*. New York: Arno Press.
Daniels, Roger. 1988. *Asian America: Chinese and Japanese in the United States Since 1850*. Seattle: University of Washington Press.
Saxton, Alexander. 1971. *The Indispensable Enemy: Labor and the Anti-Chinese Movement in California*. Berkeley: University of California Press.

Edy Parsons

ANTI-MISCEGENATION LAWS

Anti-miscegenation laws became the beacon for refusal of any direct assimilation between whites and Chinese. The passage of these laws that prohibited race mixture deeply impacted the two races and societal standards for decades. Behind the rush to pass anti-miscegenation laws lay white America's fear of contaminating its bloodline. This fear spiraled the issue far beyond mere prohibition of marriage between two persons, which was viewed in the United States as an individual, personal right inherent in the U.S. Constitution. The fear had spun interracial marriage into a divisive social and political issue. As the dominant race, white Americans did not once consider assimilation of Chinese as possible. White Americans feared that interracial marriage would create a large population of unwanted mixed race. State authorities stepped in to calm public fear. They protected white superiority and proceeded to restrict, by law, all interracial marriage between whites and Chinese races.

Between the 1860s and the 1910s, 13 separate states passed anti-miscegenation laws specifically prohibiting marriage between whites and the Mongolian race, including Chinese and Japanese. Eight of these 13 states (Arizona, Idaho, Nevada, Oregon, Utah, Wyoming, California, and Montana) were in the American West. Four states prohibited interracial marriage only between whites and Chinese, but only Montana specifically prohibited interracial marriage between white and Japanese. The remaining western states were less specific, choosing to prohibit interracial marriage between whites and the Mongolian race, including Chinese and Japanese.

In 1861, Nevada had the distinction of being the first western territory passing an anti-miscegenation law prohibiting whites from marrying Indians, Negroes, and Mongolians, including Chinese who were labeled as Mongolians. Passed by Nevada's Territorial Legislature, this law remained on Nevada's book for 98 years and was not struck down until 1959. Nevadans, like many other whites, feared the idea of interracial marriage.

In 1864, Idaho became the second western territory to pass an anti-miscegenation law, prohibiting white persons from marrying Mongolians, Negroes, or mulattoes. Between 1887 and 1920, Idaho's anti-miscegenation statues dropped prohibition of marriage between whites and Chinese, and these two races were free to marry during that time. However, in 1921, the prohibition reappeared in Idaho anti-miscegenation law.

In 1865, Arizona enacted anti-miscegenation laws prohibiting white marriage to Negroes, mulattoes, Indians, or Mongolians, and further declared all such existing marriages were illegal and voided. And even though lawmakers had not specifically targeted Chinese, they still feared them. In 1913 a revised and extended anti-miscegenation statute made it difficult for any person with mixed blood to marry at all. The statute prohibited a person with any Caucasian blood from marrying a nonwhite person; the result was that an individual having both Caucasian and Chinese blood could marry neither a white nor a Chinese.

In 1866, Oregon passed its anti-miscegenation law, prohibiting whites from marrying either full-blooded Chinese or any person having at least one-fourth Chinese ancestry. Oregon fear of Chinese males seeking white brides first found fertile soil in the early 1860s when Chinese laborers arrived, mostly in the mining camps. Between 1870 and 1880, the Chinese were not daunted by the anti-miscegenation laws and continued to move to Oregon.

Utah jumped on the anti-miscegenation bandwagon in 1888 when it prohibited whites from marrying Negroes and Mongolians. Passage of the bill grew from fears starting in the 1860s with the arrival of Chinese who came to help build the Central Pacific Railroad from Sacramento to Promontory, Utah. Fears of interracial marriage caused the passage of the 1888 anti-miscegenation law.

Wyoming's anti-miscegenation laws played out like a legal yo-yo. First it passed a law in 1869 prohibiting marriage between whites and Chinese, only to abolish that same law in 1882. Then it swung the other way in 1913 and passed a second anti-miscegenation law that said white persons could not marry Negroes, Mulattoes, Mongolians, or Malayans. As members of the Mongolian race, Chinese were prohibited from marrying whites. The resurgence of anti-miscegenation sentiment by 1913 was based more on fear than any real statistics showing huge rises in Chinese population.

California and Montana were two other states that prohibited intermarriage between whites and the Mongolian race. When the California government passed its anti-miscegenation law in 1872, it prohibited only marriage between white and Negroes. In 1905, the California government amended the anti-miscegenation statute to prohibit marriage between white persons and Mongolians. Prohibiting whites from marrying nonwhites would maintain the purity of the dominating whites.

In 1909, Montana came on board with an anti-miscegenation law, and sections of its law literally specified Chinese and Japanese by word. Montana people viewed Chinese as economic competitors and members of an inferior race. Montana was the only state that specifically stated the prohibition of interracial marriage between whites and Japanese in its statute. The tremendous increase in Japanese population between 1890 and 1900 might be the reason for causing the law to include Japanese specifically.

The passage of anti-miscegenation statutes in the above states showed the construction of a hierarchical race relation between whites and other races. All these western states shared similar motives. The anti-Chinese sentiment was the key for passing the law. The Mongolian race, especially Chinese, were not welcome and especially not on an equal footing with white persons. Whenever the Mongolian race was in these states, the fear of race mixture followed. When supporters of anti-miscegenation statutes gained enough support in the legislature, anti-miscegenation statutes would pass. Chinese became a segregated group under the white race in the United States. The prohibition of intermarriage between whites and Chinese could keep white blood pure. Between the 1870s and 1940s, no Chinese challenged the anti-miscegenation statutes in these states.

See also: Bachelor Society; Chinese Women and the Chinese Exclusion Act

Further Reading

Hardaway, Roger D. 1980. "Prohibiting Interracial Marriage: Miscegenation Laws in Wyoming." *Annals of Wyoming* 52 (Spring): 57.
Wagoner, Jay. J. 1970. *Arizona Territory, 1863–1912.* Tucson: The University of Arizona Press.

Edy Parsons

BACHELOR SOCIETY

An influx of Chinese workers into the United States occurred from the 1840s until 1882, when declining economic opportunities and rising political instability in China forced many Chinese abroad to support their families at home. The majority of immigrants were men who left their wives and children in China or remained unmarried. While most sojourning laborers planned to remain in America only briefly, economic problems in China, rising demand for labor in the United States, and exclusionary laws limiting the movement of foreigners led to increasingly permanent settlement. As a result of these conditions and legislation such as the Chinese Exclusion Act (1882) and Scott Act (1888), which limited any significant Chinese population growth in America by restricting the entry of women, a gender gap developed.

Given the masculine domination of early Asian immigration in the United States, Chinese enclaves became known as "bachelor societies," a phrase that denoted the gender imbalance in these communities. This situation was exacerbated by the fact that many Chinese immigrant women worked as prostitutes, that Chinese communities experienced a massive depopulation following the passage of the Chinese Exclusion Act, and that fraternization of Chinese men with local women often led to regional disputes. The lack of women limited the birth of second-generation Chinese Americans, restricted community development, transformed cultural norms and gender roles from those in China, and hindered the transition from a bachelor- to a family-centered society.

This gender gap also fostered the impression that immigrants were unable to establish traditional families or to assimilate to American social norms. These perceptions in turn led to the increasing segregation of Chinese communities in America, promoted the development of immigrant family associations and community organizations, and led to the growth of illegal immigration networks. The implications of the social composition of bachelor societies shaped Chinese American culture and communities until the 1960s.

See also: International Context of Chinese Immigration to America, to 1870

Further Reading

McClain, Charles. 1994. *In Search of Equality: The Chinese Struggle Against Discrimination in Nineteenth-Century America.* Berkeley: University of California Press.
Siu, Paul. 1987. *The Chinese Laundryman: A Study of Social Isolation.* New York: New York University Press.

Sean Morton

BEMIS, POLLY (1853–1933)

Known also as Lalu Nathoy and Polly Nathoy (according to her marriage certificate from 1894), Polly Bemis is the Pacific Northwest's most famous female Chinese resident. She was born on September 11, 1853, in China, arrived in Idaho when it was still a territory in 1872, and passed away in Grangeville, Idaho on November 6, 1933. The first years of her life in the United States and the exact nature of her arrival present conflicting facts found in chronicles and interviews with people who met her; a film based on a biographical novel of the same name, *Thousand Pieces of Gold*, helped to popularize and perpetuate the legend of "The Poker Bride."

According to Cissy Patterson's interview in 1921, Polly was sold as a slave girl by her parents, smuggled into Portland via San Francisco, and eventually taken by train to Warren, Idaho. Some accounts contend she was a prostitute and that her husband, Charles Bemis, a saloon proprietor, won her in a poker game. The couple settled on a ranch on the banks of the Salmon River, where Polly fished, cooked, gardened, and tended a boardinghouse for miners. Although illiterate, she knew how to count money and play cards and had an extraordinary memory. Her renowned generosity and hospitality made her known as "The Angel of the Salmon River." She provided vegetables to the miners and served as the official nurse for anyone in need. In 1922, her cabin was destroyed by fire and soon after, Charles passed away. Her 30-year neighbors across the river, Charles Shepp and Peter Klinkh, built her a new cabin and helped her with domestic chores. In 1933, Polly Bemis died and was buried in Grangeville, Idaho, but in 1987 her remains were transferred back to the ranch she shared with Charles, which is now the Polly Bemis House museum. A creek near the ranch was renamed Polly Creek in her memory.

See also: Bachelor Society; Chinese Immigration During the Gold Rush; Page Law (1875)

Further Reading

Corbett, Christopher. 2010. *The Poker Bride: The First Chinese in the West*. New York: Atlantic Grove.

McCunn, Ruthanne Lum. 2004. *Thousand Pieces of Gold: A Biographical Novel*. Boston: Beacon Press.

Alejandro Lee

BING KUNG TONG

If the Hongmen is considered the first generation of Chinese secret society, directly transplanted from China to North America in the early 1850s, then tongs like the Chee Kung, Hip Sing, and Hop Sing represent a second generation that became active in the early 1880s. The Bing Kung Tong or BKT (Binggong Tang) also belongs to the second generation. It came into existence by splitting from the Chee Kung Tong, in 1874 according to its own oral history or somewhat later according to early English-language sources. Together the Chee Kung Tong (CKT) and BKT are the only secret societies to call themselves Chinese Masons and to display publicly the square-and-compass emblem of the European-American Masonic Order. Although the two Masonic tongs are not formally recognized by American Freemasons, they often interact with them.

At its peak in about 1940, the BKT had 50 branches in the western United States. It never seems to have spread to Canada or to the United States east of the Rockies, however. In the Pacific Northwest, its early grassroots members included a number of wealthy businessmen. These included no fewer than two honorary Chinese consuls, first of the Qing and then the Republic of China—Moy Back Him (Mei Bo Xian) of Portland and Goon Dip (Ruan Qia) of Seattle. In Moy's and Goon's day, the BKT competed with the CKT for leadership and recognition. Both claimed to have supported the 1911 Chinese Revolution. In 1915, Bing Kung branches in Washington and Oregon absorbed an earlier secret society, the Bow Leong (Bao Liang) to become the Bing Kung Bow Leong Tong. At about the same time, many branches of the formerly powerful CKT disappeared from most western states. The BKT became in many ways its heir.

Like the CKT in previous years, the BKT began to assert a neutral stance in secret society quarrels and even to act as a peacemaker. It did not always succeed in this, becoming embroiled in "tong wars" in Montana and California in 1921–1922 and again in California in 1926. However, it continued to gain status and respectability. In smaller cities it took over many of the CKT's former social service functions, providing temporary housing to travelers, food for the poor and sick, and a gathering place for local Chinese communities. Whether it also helped to protect those communities against physical and legal oppression by non-Chinese is not known. The Society currently claims it did, and that may be so.

Today the Bing Kung Tong Benevolent Association has 12 branches, sometimes called chapters or lodges, with headquarters in San Francisco. While often property rich, all branches struggle to redefine their missions so as not to become outdated. The emergence of young dynamic leaders in several branches suggests that new directions are being found. One sign of the search for redefinition is the history of itself that the BKT published in 2012, marking the first serious attempt by any Chinese American secret society to understand and publicly explain its past.

See also: Chee Kung Tong; Hip Sing Tong (Xiesheng Tang); Hongmen; Hop Sing Tong (Hesheng Tang); Secret Societies

Further Reading

Bronson, Bennet, and Chuimei Ho. 2015. *Coming Home in Brocade: Chinese in the Early American Northwest.* Seattle, WA: Chinese in Northwest America Research Committee.

Gong, Eng Ying, and Bruce Grant. 1930. *Tong War! The First Complete History of the Tongs in America.* New York: Nicholas L. Brown.

Bennet Bronson and Chuimei Ho

BOWL OF RICE MOVEMENT

Chinese Americans and family associations such as the Chinese Six Companies provided humanitarian aid to China and Chinese refugees following the onset of the Second Sino-Japanese War (1937–1945). Raising funds and providing aid were essential aspects of China's resistance against Japan, and a collective effort on the part of Chinese Americans to raise funds, collect supplies, and hinder Japanese efforts was undertaken. Donors were asked to give enough money to assist victims of the conflict or fill the rice bowls of China. To raise funds, Rice Bowl Parties and cultural programs were organized in hundreds of U.S. cities by the United Council for Civilian Relief in China and the Chinese War Relief Association, where entrance fees and donations were collected. These groups also held anti-Japanese parades, encouraged boycotts against Japanese goods, and picketed shipyards accepting Japanese silk products or shipping materials to Japan. In this manner, Chinese Americans supported their homeland, raised awareness of the growing Japanese threat, and improved public understandings of Chinese American culture. Such movements also unified Chinese American communities, decreased the isolation of immigrant enclaves in the United States, exposed U.S. citizens to Chinese American culture, and emphasized the substantial role of Chinese women in community culture and politics.

See also: Rape of Nanjing; World War II

Further Reading

Chen, Young. 2002. *Chinese San Francisco, 1850–1943: A Trans-Pacific Community*. Stanford, CA: Stanford University Press.

Wong, Kevin. 2005. *Americans First: Chinese Americans and the Second World War*. Cambridge, MA: Harvard University Press.

Sean Morton

BOXER INDEMNITY FELLOWSHIP (BOXER REBELLION) (1900)

In 1908, the U.S. government agreed to return the excess Boxer indemnity of over $10,000,000 to China. The indemnity fund was used to establish the Boxer Indemnity Fellowship.

During the Boxer Rebellion of 1900, the Boxers attacked Western missionaries and their converts in China. The Western powers suppressed the Boxers. After the Boxer Rebellion, China was forced to pay indemnity to Western powers. In January 1909, the U.S. government returned the first remission from the Boxer indemnity to China. The Chinese government could only use the indemnity fund for education. According to the plan, the Chinese government sent out 100 students to the United States annually for the first

Tsinghua Xueteng, the study hall of Tsinghua University, in March, 2014. The university was founded in 1911, and had students supported by the Boxer Indemnity Fellowship. (Shaowen1994/Dreamstime.com)

four years. After that, the Chinese sent at least 50 students to the United States each year until 1940.

The Chinese government held competitive examinations in order to select students who would be granted Boxer Indemnity Fellowships. The examinations tested the student's knowledge of mathematics, science, geography, history, and English. However, in 1909, the first year of sending students to the United States, only 47 students passed the competitive examinations and received Boxer Indemnity Fellowships. In 1909, Tsing Hua College, using the American Boxer indemnity fund, was established in Beijing. Graduation from this college qualified a student for the fellowship to the United States. After 1910, the government no longer held competitive examinations. This fellowship allowed more Chinese students to be educated in the United States.

See also: Sino-U.S. Relations

Further Reading

Kwei, Chungshu. 1924. "Tsing Hua College." *The Chinese Students' Monthly* 19 (April): 13–14.

Malone, Carroll B. 1926. "The First Remission of the Boxer Indemnity." *The American Historical Review* 32 (October): 68.

Merrill, H. F. 1910. "The Chinese Student in America." In *China and the Far East*, edited by George H. Blakeslee. 200–201. New York: Thomas Y. Crowell.

Edy Parsons

BURLINGAME TREATY (1868)

The Burlingame Treaty was signed between China and the United States on July 28, 1868. The treaty contained eight articles. This treaty was important because it was the first treaty signed as an equal treaty since the Treaty of Nanjing of 1842.

Anson Burlingame (1820–1870) formerly served as the U.S. minister to China. In 1867, Burlingame was appointed as China's first envoy to the Western nations by the Chinese government. Burlingame's first stop of his mission was the United States, where he arrived on March 31, 1868. Burlingame managed to negotiate with the U.S. government for a treaty that was based on an equal status. The treaty reaffirmed the sovereignty of China. The purpose of this treaty was also about changing the injustices that Chinese were facing in the United States. The treaty benefited Chinese in the United States or those who wanted to go there. Chinese were guaranteed the right to immigrate to the United States and allowed to naturalize as U.S. citizens. The treaty also allowed the Chinese to enter American public institutions to study. Legislations in California that discriminated against Chinese became illegal. However, this treaty was revised in 1880.

See also: Angell Treaty (Chinese Exclusion Treaty) (1880)

Further Reading

Schrecker, John. 2010. "'For the Equality of Men—for the Equality of Nations': Anson Burlingame and China's First Embassy to the United States, 1868." *Journal of American-East Asian Relations* 17 (1): 9–34.

Edy Parsons

CANTONESE

Cantonese belongs to the *Yue* language family (in Cantonese: *Jyutjyu*) and comes from what are now the southern provinces of Guangdong and Guangxi in China. Cantonese is also spoken in Hong Kong and Macau, where it is known as *Gwongdungwaa/Guangdonghua*. The Cantonese that is spoken in Guangzhou (Canton) is sometimes used as a point of reference to that of Hong Kong Cantonese; Guangzhou Cantonese is oftentimes referred to as *Guangzauwaa/Guangzhouhua* in the linguistic literature. It is estimated that there are over 55 million first-language speakers of Cantonese in the world. These numbers, however, do not include the large number of people who speak it as a second or additional language. More crucially, Cantonese is spoken in many diasporic Chinese communities in Malaysia, Vietnam, Singapore, Australia, New Zealand, as well as in the United States and Canada. Cantonese is arguably the most influential and historically significant Chinese language besides Mandarin, due to the influence of Hong Kong popular culture, media, and films. Because of the long history of the Cantonese-speaking diaspora, Cantonese, by extension, play an integral sociolinguistic role in understanding Chinese migration history.

While present trends of U.S. immigration show a vast spread of ethnic Chinese immigrants of various language backgrounds, nearly all Chinese immigrants from the 1800s to 1970s spoke some variety of "Cantonese" originating in the Lliyip/Szeyap/Seiyap or Samyap regions. While there are obvious regional differences to the varieties spoken in these four districts, with much variation even among speakers within a district, these varieties are largely lumped together as "Cantonese," together with regional Standard Cantonese(s) of Hong Kong and mainland China. Yet the exponential rise in the status of Mandarin today has resulted in the heightened demand for and consumption of Mandarin-language classes and bilingual enrichment programs. For all Chinese Americans of these various "Cantonese" backgrounds, then, this shift in the political economy of language requires the negotiation of language backgrounds "new" and "old."

Several issues further complicate the course of "Cantonese" language (any variety) maintenance in the United States. In cities with traditionally high populations of Cantonese-speaking immigrants, like San Francisco, as Cantonese heritage language schools and Cantonese-English bilingual programs are abandoned for Mandarin programs, there are fewer and fewer opportunities for the younger generation to maintain Cantonese institutionally. However, put under a different light, this also means that even without institutional support, despite ongoing repositioning and changes in context of use and esteem, "Cantonese" has still managed to remain visible and operative for over 150 years, through all the phases of ethnic Chinese immigration to the United States. Yet there is a dearth of research when it comes to contemporary Cantonese-language maintenance and teaching, which seems to stem multidirectionally from the lumping effect of "Chinese" and what constitutes a "language" and "dialect" as well as the tendency in China to level language varieties as being part of a single standard due to imagined linguistic and national boundaries.

See also: Chinese Language Schools; Samyap and Szeyap

Further Reading

Lee, Jonathan H. X. 2015. *History of Asian Americans: Exploring Diverse Roots.* Santa Barbara, CA: ABC-CLIO/Greenwood.

Genevieve Leung

CHEE KUNG TONG

The Hongmen seems to have adopted the name "Chinese Masons" in the early 1870s. Yet another name was taken by at least some branches of the Hongmen/Chinese Masons in about 1880: Chee Kung Tong or CKT (Zhigong Tang "Hall of Universal Justice"). By 1886, according to *Harper's Weekly*, the CKT had no fewer than 390 branches in North and South America. Although these kept the Mason name as an alternate and did not forget their other, earlier names, all or almost seem eventually to have settled on "Chee Kung Tong" as name by which they would be called officially in both the United States and Canada. Did some Hongmen branches hesitate to become CKT branches? Perhaps. It took almost two decades for some, including New York's Hongmen, which at first called itself the Loon Yee Tong, to make the switch.

In the 19th century the main CKT headquarters were in San Francisco. Most of its rivals were there as well. Like its Hongmen avatar, the CKT continued to dominate most Chinatowns and may have sought to impose ethical and ritual standards on the spinoffs. Even in San Francisco, with more and more potential rivals coming into existence, the CKT continued to play a controlling role. In 1895, the *San Francisco Chronicle* could state that, contrary to what most Americans believed, the Chinese Six Companies (Zhonghua Huiguan or Chinese Consolidated Benevolent Association) had "little or no authority compared with the Chee Kung Tong." In 1903 the CKT founded its own daily newspaper, *Chinese Free Press* (*Tai Tung Yat Po*, or *Datong ribao*) in San Francisco. This survived until 1927 and had a nationwide circulation. In 1909 its members included at least one-eighth of the Chinese population of San Francisco.

Dr. Sun Yat-sen without doubt was the most celebrated member of the Tong, initiated by his uncle in the Hawai'i lodge in 1904 to assume a high-executive role, Double-ornate Cane (Shuang hua hong gun). The position ensured Sun much help in fund-raising for his revolutionary movement while it assisted him and his allies in modernizing the CKT's governance structure. He succeeded in persuading lodges in the United States and Canada to lend large sums to the anti-Manchu Revolution of 1911–1912. The Canadian branches went so far as to mortgage their land and buildings to raise money. But the financial sacrifices made at Dr. Sun's behest did not work out and

Chinatown residents read the Tong proclamation in Chinatown, San Francisco, ca. 1896. The Tiandi Hui, a secret society that many Tong are connected with, came into existence in China in the late 17th century. It had two main goals: (1) mutual aid among members and (2) resistance to the Manchus, whose alien Qing Dynasty ruled China from 1644 to 1911. Because the Qing emperors saw the Tiandi Hui as dangerously subversive and thus persecuted it mercilessly, the Society stayed deep underground. Outside China, in Hong Kong, Southeast Asia, Australia, and Americas, the danger was not so acute, and the Society and allied organizations not only dared to show themselves but often became, in slightly altered form, the social foci of overseas Chinese communities. According to Bennet Bronson and Chuimei Ho, "No Chinese organization in 19th century BC is likely to have publicly called itself 'Tiandi Hui,' but several spinoff/daughter organizations in the region used Tiandi Hui rituals and regarded themselves as its heir. Among the oldest was the Hung Mun/Hongmen or Chih Kung Tong/Zhigong Tang." (Library of Congress)

may have doomed some CKT chapters. None of those branches were repaid the funds they had loaned to the revolution. Now impoverished and receiving no recognition for their sacrifice, they disappeared from many western U.S. cities shortly after Sun became China's president.

Elsewhere in the United States, the postrevolutionary CKT attempted for several decades to recast itself as a legitimate political party (Zhi gong dang) and later Minzhi dang, representing overseas Chinese in China politics. The question of who in the CKT should represent it in Chinese politics may have been the cause of a major split within the organization between the East and West Coasts of the United States. The eastern CKT pulled back into the local Chinatowns, with a headquarters in New York, which in the 1940s became known as the "Chinese Freemasons Grand Lodge of USA" (Meiguo hong men zhi gong zong tang). Today it is recognized by eight other branches in the East and Midwest: Baltimore, Detroit, Cleveland, Atlanta, Chicago, Boston, Washington D.C., and Philadelphia. The western CKT lost most or all of its local U.S. chapters but became the leader of the CKT chapters mushrooming around the Pacific Rim. Its old San Francisco lodge on Spofford Alley was named the international headquarters of the Five Continents Chee Kung Tong (Wuzhou hong men zhi gong zong tang) in the 1920s. Chee Kung Tong is the only Chinese secret society rooted in the United States that enjoys worldwide membership.

The San Francisco's Five Continents CKT has recently suffered a series of blows with its presidents murdered or arrested. Meanwhile, it is also building close connections with its branches in mainland China, an overture that seems to have never stopped since the political Chee Kung Party was formerly established.

See also: Bing Kung Tong; Hip Sing Tong (Xiesheng Tang); Hongmen; Hop Sing Tong (Hesheng Tang); Secret Societies

Further Reading

Bronson, Bennet, and Chuimei Ho. 2015. *Coming Home in Brocade: Chinese in the Early American Northwest.* Seattle, WA: Chinese in Northwest America Research Committee.

Gong, Eng Ying, and Bruce Grant. 1930. *Tong War! The First Complete History of the Tongs in America.* New York: Nicholas L. Brown.

Bennet Bronson and Chuimei Ho

CHIN, VINCENT JEN (1955–1982)

Vincent Jen Chin was born on May 18, 1955 in Guangdong, China. Chin was the only child of Bing Hing Chin and Lily Chin. Bing Hing Chin brought his bride from China through his service in World War II. After Lily suffered a miscarriage in 1949, they adopted Vincent from a Chinese orphanage in 1961. Chin grew up in Highland Park and, later, Oak Park, Michigan.

On June 19, 1982, Vincent Jen Chin, 27 years old, went to the Fancy Pants strip club in Highland Park with friends for his bachelor's party. There, Chin encountered two autoworkers, Ronald Ebens—a Chrysler plant supervisor— and his stepson, Michael Nitz, who racialized Chin for "Japanese." As many during this period did, they blamed the Japanese for the woes of the American auto industry. Ebens and Nitz harassed Chin with racial epithets and a fight broke out. Although Chin was not Japanese, and worked in the auto industry himself as a draftsman, Ebens was heard saying, "It's because of you little mother-fuckers that we're out of work," as well as other anti-Chinese racial epithets. They were all thrown out of the strip club, but the fight continued in the parking lot, until Chin ran off. Ebens and Nitz pursued him and found Chin at a nearby McDonald's restaurant. There, Ebens and Nitz bludgeoned Chin with a baseball bat until his head cracked open. On June 23, 1982, Chin died.

On March 18, 1983, Ebens and Nitz pleaded guilty to killing Chin. In an agreement with prosecutors, they pleaded to manslaughter (down from second-degree murder). Judge Charles Kaufman sentenced them to three years' probation and fined them $3,780 each. Explaining the light sentence, Judge Kaufman stated, "These aren't the kind of men you send to jail. You fit the punishment to the criminal, not the crime." To the dismay of the Asian American community, neither man spent a single day in jail for murdering Chin.

The brutal murder and light sentence outraged the Asian American community. In Detroit on March 31, 1983, Asian Americans founded the American Citizens for Justice to lobby for a federal trial for Chin's murderers. The campaign was spearheaded by journalist Helen Zia, lawyer Liza Chan, and Lily Chin—Chin's mother. Rallies in Detroit, San Francisco, and Los Angeles galvanized the Asian American communities and attracted national media attention. On June 5, 1984, federal prosecutors charged Ebens and Nitz with violating Chin's civil rights. After 23 days of deliberation, a Detroit federal jury acquitted Nitz but found Ebens guilty of violating Chin's civil rights: Ebens, was convicted and sentenced to 25 years in prison. Although it seemed a measure of justice has prevailed for Chin, but the conviction was overturned on appeal.

In 1987, Lily Chin left the United States and returned to her hometown of Guangzhou, China. She returned to the United States in 2001 for medical treatment and died on June 9, 2002. The violent killing of Vincent Chin in 1982, again, fueled many Chinese Americans to become politically active, especially with regard to civil rights struggles.

See also: Anti-Chinese Violence; Chinese American Activism; Chinese Americans and Civil Rights

Further Reading

Vincent Who? Directed by Tony Lam. Produced by Curtis Chin. Asian Pacific Americans for Progress. 2009. DVD.

Who Killed Vincent Chin? Directed by Renee Tajima and Christine Choy. New York: Film News Now Foundation and WTVS-Detroit Public Television. 1988. DVD.

Zia, Helen. 2000. *Asian American Dreams: The Emergence of an American People.* New York: Farrar, Straus and Giroux.

Jonathan H. X. Lee

CHINA WAR RELIEF ASSOCIATION

The China War Relief Association of America (CWRAA, or Lümei Huaqiao Tongyi Yijuan Jiuguo Zonghui) was an organization founded in August 1937 in response to the Japanese invasion of China during the Second Sino-Japanese War (which later became part of the larger World War II). The CWRAA consolidated the work of the many charities that had been founded to support Chinese war efforts and care for civilians. Headquartered in San Francisco, California, where it was founded by the Six Companies, 47 local CWRAA chapters were established.

Under the leadership of its president B. S. Fong, the association solicited donations and used fund-raisers such as the Bowl of Rice Movement to raise over $19 million. This formed a substantial portion of the estimated $56 million in financial donations and other contributions given by Chinese Americans during World War II. These funds provided assistance for the war effort, training for air force pilots, help for refugees, and care for wounded soldiers.

The CWRAA also organized a boycott of Japanese products and various protests, including picket lines at shipyards in 1939. The organization disbanded at the end of the war, and available funds were used to support Chinese American charities and organizations.

See also: Bowl of Rice Movement; Chinese Consolidated Benevolent Association; Huiguan (The Chinese Six Companies); World War II

Further Reading

Ling, Huping. 1998. *Surviving on the Gold Mountain: A History of Chinese American Women and Their Lives.* Albany: State University of New York.

Oyen, Meredith Leigh. 2007. "Allies, Enemies and Aliens: Migration and U.S.-Chinese Relations, 1940–1965." PhD diss., Georgetown University.

Kevin Hogg

CHINESE AMERICAN BIRTH RATES

Birth rates among Chinese Americans in the early years of settlement are difficult to determine, but historians and demographers can conclude they were very low. Initially, Chinese immigrants were primarily male and they established what was termed a "bachelor society" in California during the last decades of the 19th century. Approximately 90 percent of those who made the journey were men, and they largely remained segregated and did not marry or have families. Numbers declined following the Exclusion Act of 1882, and Chinese men introduced the practice of claiming "paper sons." Constitutional and naturalization laws deemed Chinese born in the United States and their offspring citizens, a status that came with American privileges. As a result, it became common to produce false birth documentation. Chinese men who became U.S. citizens could travel to China and return with boys they claimed to be their sons by presenting papers. This became more widespread when the 1906 earthquake and fire destroyed a majority of vital statistics records in San Francisco. The custom made it more difficult to calculate accurate birth rates and true family size in ways that paralleled measures in the 20th century.

Census records show that in 1930 four times as many Chinese men as women declared themselves married, indicating the majority of men were married to women in China. This practice resulted in a slow birth rate in the United States at least until the mid-1940s. It was then that the War Brides Act (1945) permitted some 6,000 Chinese American men to marry women in China and bring them to the United States. In addition, more Chinese entered under the Alien Fiancées or Fiancés Act (1946). With an increase in women and greater potential for marital relationships, the Chinese American birthrate began to grow. The Immigration and Nationality Act Amendments of 1965 eliminated previously legislated racial barriers, allowed for more young people to migrate from China, and encouraged family reunification. Very importantly, this era helped to create a greater gender balance among Chinese Americans and facilitate population growth through childbearing.

No comprehensive studies on Chinese American fertility or family size have been conducted thus far, but the piecing together of monographic research indicates acculturation in the early post–World War II era influenced the number of children women bore. For example, surveys showed families in New York's Chinatown had an average of 4.4 children, in contrast to an average of 2.9 children among New York's white families. If both parents were born in China, however, the median number of children was 6.2, and if both parents were born in the United States, the median number of children was 3.2. As Chinese became acculturated and Americanized, the average birth rate decreased.

Until the 1960s, couples in China were encouraged to have many children; population growth was viewed as a sign of progress and power. During the 1970s, the Chinese government began to address annual birthrates and total fertility rates, set fertility targets, collect data on contraceptive use, and encourage delayed marriage. The fertility rate in China began to decline due to socioeconomic development, but the government worked to lower it further—below the desired birthrate—in order to stabilize the nation and protect resources. China implemented the first required family planning program in 1979, including a "one child" policy. In migrating to the United States after 1980, Chinese couples were afforded an opportunity to bear as many children as they wanted. Still, birthrates among Chinese Americans did not differ dramatically from those living in China. Many Chinese women sought education and professional opportunities in the United States, which resulted in smaller family size. Chinese women relocated primarily to American urban areas, where birthrates were historically lower. In addition, infant mortality rates were low, resulting in higher survival rates and less tendency among parents to increase their chances of healthy offspring through additional births. Since 2010, fertility rates in China have risen slightly to an expected 1.7 births per woman, while the fertility rates in the United States have declined to 1.9 births per woman.

Though the population rate of Chinese in the United States has grown rapidly in the United States (104.1 percent from 1980 to 1990, 47.5 percent from 1990 to 2000, and 37.9 percent from 2000 to 2010), family size has remained comparatively low. Some statistics show higher rates of intergenerational households—many including grandparents—among Chinese families in the United States (3.8 per Chinese household compared with 3.2 for average American household), but birth rates are low in comparison to other ethnic groups. U.S. births have acted as a driving force in increasing the Hispanic population since 2000, and that trend continued between 2012 and 2013. The U.S. Census Bureau estimated that natural increase (births minus deaths) accounted for 78 percent of the total change in the U.S. Hispanic population from 2012 to 2013. That was not the case with Asian Americans. Increases in the Asian American population are due primarily to immigration. Nearly three-quarters of Asian adults in the United States in 2012 were foreign born,

Comparative Fertility Rates in 2013

	U.S. Total	Chinese American	Mexican American
Women 15–50	76,129,362	1,095,558	3,862,108
Number Who Gave Birth in Last 12 Months	3,930,417	47,363	265,978
Percentage Who Gave Birth in Last 12 Months	5.15	4.32	6.89

Source: U.S. Census, 2014.

and international migration accounted for about 61 percent of the total change in the Asian American population from 2012 to 2013.

Fertility research based on nationality became more complicated in the last decades of the 20th century due to increased intermarriage. Still, the interethnic marriage rates of Chinese remained lower than those of Japanese, Filipinos, and Koreans in the United States, and Chinese continue to be the largest group of Asians. Statistics for those who identified themselves as Chinese remained comparatively stable. In all, birthrates among Chinese after 2000 remained lower than those of the general U.S. population.

See also: Bachelor Society; Paper Sons and Daughters; Wartime Brides Act (1945)

Further Reading

Daniels, Roger. 1988. *Asian America: Chinese and Japanese in the United States Since 1850.* Seattle: University of Washington Press.
Pew Research Center Reports, 2010–2014. Accessed July 16, 2015. http://www.pewresearch.org.
United States Census, 1950–2010. Accessed July 16, 2015. https://www.census.gov.
Zhou, Min. 2009. *Contemporary Chinese America: Immigration, Ethnicity, and Community Transformation.* Philadelphia: Temple University Press.

Kathleen A. Tobin

CHINESE AMERICAN POPULATION TRENDS

Following China's First Opium War (1839–1842), migration to the United States began. Conditions in China for much of its population in the mid-19th century were difficult, with widespread flooding and famine between 1846 and 1848 increasing poverty and hunger. Disease and declining markets for Chinese-made products increased tension and people rebelled against the Qing Dynasty. Suppression of the rebellion resulted in an estimated 100 million lives lost between 1850 and 1875. Prosperity of the 18th century had clearly waned and many in China looked abroad to improve their chances at a better life. The California Gold Rush spurred large-scale emigration of Chinese to the United States beginning in 1850, and in 1870 a category for Chinese was added to the U.S. Census.

More than 90 percent of Chinese immigrants in the early wave were men, as the social roles of both unmarried and married women made it impossible for most to travel. This fact is worth noting for a number of reasons when studying Chinese Americans, but with regard to population it had a direct impact. The presence of women in episodes of migration and settlement influences the potential for population growth of that demographic because of their ability to bear children. Where other immigrant men established marital relationships and families, the Chinese generally did not. Chinese women who did arrive in the United States in the late 19th century were often identified as prostitutes, having made the journey unwillingly and forced into the sex trade. Their numbers are difficult to calculate, but in the larger context of migrant population, there were few. Chinese men journeying to the United States generally intended to return to China after earning enough money to support their families. Considering the scarcity of women and the intentions of men to stay only a short time, the Chinese population of the United States might have gone unnoticed in the course of American history. However, men did stay because their earnings did not amount to what they anticipated and could not afford transportation back to China. Until the Chinese Exclusion Act of 1882, more continued to arrive.

The U.S. Chinese population grew from 63,200 in 1870 to 107,500 in 1890, with the majority residing in western states. Of the 1870 population nearly 50,000 lived in California alone, with 99.5 percent in the West; in 1890, 67.5 percent lived in California with just over 90 percent living in the West. The Chinese population declined following the Exclusion Act to 90,000 in 1900 and 61,500 in 1920. By that time, just more than 62 percent were living in the West. In 1890, nearly 26,000 Chinese lived in San Francisco, or 24 percent of the entire U.S. Chinese population. Not only was the population limited to western states and urban areas within those states, people were segregated into specific neighborhoods. It was a male-dominated culture that differed very much from the majority of Americans and experienced brutal discrimination. These factors contributed to relatively slow acculturation into the general population and American society.

Population trends shifted in the second wave of Chinese immigration, beginning after World War II. Between 1945 and 1953, an estimated 12,000 Chinese came to the United States and an estimated 89 percent were women. Years of economic depression and war had disrupted families, leaving widows and other women with no means of support. The War Brides Act of 1945 permitted some 6,000 Chinese American men to marry women in China and bring them to the United States. In addition, more Chinese entered under the Alien Fiancées or Fiancés Act of 1946 and the Refugee Relief Act of 1953. Immigration restriction had slowed population growth for decades, but China's alliance with the United States during the war had fostered good relations between the U.S. and Chinese populations. This legislation allowed for more young people to enter and encouraged family reunification. This era helped to create a gender balance among Chinese Americans and facilitated population growth through childbearing.

Racial barriers against immigrants began to diminish with the 1952 McCarran-Walter Immigration Act. While the legislation continued to work

Immigration of Chinese by Sex, 1945–1952

Year	Male	Female	Female Percentage	Total
1945	45	64	59	109
1946	71	162	69	233
1947	142	986	87	1,128
1948	257	3,317	93	3,574
1949	242	2,248	90	2,490
1950	110	1,179	91	1,289
1951	126	957	88	1,083
1952	118	1,034	90	1,152

Source: U.S. Department of Justice, Immigration and Naturalization Service, *Annual Reports*, 1945–1953.

Chinese Percentage of U.S. Population, 1860–2010

Year	U.S. Population	Chinese Population in U.S.	Percentage of Total
1860	31,443,321	34,933	0.11
1870	38,558,371	63,199	0.16
1880	50,189,209	105,465	0.21
1890	62,979,766	107,488	0.17
1900	76,212,168	89,863	0.11
1910	92,228,496	71,531	0.07
1920	106,021,537	61,639	0.05
1930	123,202,624	74,954	0.06
1940	132,164,569	77,504	0.06
1950	151,325,798	117,629	0.08
1960	179,323,175	237,292	0.13
1970	203,302,031	435,062	0.21
1980	226,542,199	806,040	0.35
1990	248,709,873	1,645,472	0.66
2000	281,421,906	2,432,046	0.86
2010	308,745,538	3,535,382	1.14

Source: U.S. Census.

on a quota system, favoritism toward European immigration shifted and the United States opened its doors to people from Asia as legal immigrants. Except for minor resistance because China had become a communist country, Chinese were welcomed. As a result, the Chinese American population began to rise and continues to do so. The Immigration and Nationality Act Amendments

Percentage Distribution of Chinese Population by State, 2010

California	New York	Hawai'i	Texas	New Jersey	All Other States
36.2	15.4	5.0	4.6	3.7	35.2

Source: U.S. Census.

of 1965 had the biggest impact on increasing the number of Chinese in the United States. This was a time of optimism and civil rights movements, and race-based restrictions were eliminated. The emphasis lay on family reunification and Chinese took this opportunity to bring in parents, spouses, and minor children. As a result, the Chinese population in the United States grew nearly 85 percent from 1960 to 1970 and more than 85 percent from 1970 to 1980. It more than doubled between 1980 and 1990, from 812,000 to 1,645,000, growing 103 percent compared with a growth of 9.8 percent in the general U.S. population. In 2000 and 2010, the U.S. Census Bureau reported significant growth among Asians originating from other countries, but the Chinese population continued to rank highest.

See also: Chinese Exclusion Act (1882); Chinese Immigration During the Gold Rush; Opium Wars (1840 and 1856); Refugee Relief Act (1953); War Brides Act (1945)

Further Reading

Daniels, Roger. 1988. *Asian America: Chinese and Japanese in the United States Since 1850.* Seattle: University of Washington Press.

Segal, Uma A. 2002. *A Framework for Immigration: Asians in the United States.* New York: Columbia University Press.

United States Census, 1860–2010. Accessed July 16, 2015. https://www.census.gov.

Zhou, Min. 2009. *Contemporary Chinese America: Immigration, Ethnicity, and Community Transformation.* Philadelphia, PA: Temple University Press.

Kathleen A. Tobin

CHINESE AND CUBA'S TEN YEARS' WAR (1868–1878)

Chinese contributions to Cuban history have taken multiple forms, including participation in the Ten Years' War (1868–1878), the first of the Caribbean island's three wars for independence. The war's rebel leaders, in a move to increase support for their cause, declared all inhabitants of the island free, including the tens of thousands of Chinese who labored under abusive conditions on the Spanish colony's plantations. Subsequently, approximately 5,000

Chinese indentured laborers joined them. Some of them fought alongside formerly enslaved Afro-Cubans.

All Chinese who were victims of semi-enslavement desired to be legally emancipated, but not all of those who were promised freedom by the rebels participated in the war. One of the basic factors involved in determining participation was geography. Cuba's Chinese were distributed throughout the island, but most of the battles associated with this movement were restricted to the east. Thus, the uprising directly affected only a portion of the Chinese. Among the latter were men living in Camagüey and Oriente who escaped their plantations and joined the insurrection. In some cases they participated with those who had been their masters.

Chinese participation has been linked to specific military offenses as well as individual acts of leadership and heroism. An assault on Manzanillo, today part of the province of Granma, was led almost entirely by Asians. Chinese also participated in military actions in the province of Santa Clara. A free man by the name of Wong Seng became known for his heroism and military skill after abandoning his herbal medicine practice in order to contribute to the rebel cause. Another hero was Lam Fun Kin, also known as Juan Sánchez. A skilled fighter, he was a veteran of military conflicts in China, including the Taiping Rebellion.

In 1871 Spain issued a royal decree calling for Chinese immigration to be temporarily halted. Building on negative racial stereotypes that date back to its colonization of the Philippines, the decree represented all Chinese as subversives who brought about disorder and impeded attempts to pacify the island. After the decree was issued, many Chinese were incarcerated, and others were forced to work without wages. Among them were men who sought refuge in the capital after fleeing conflicts in the east. Some runaways were captured by colonial authorities and forced to labor on military projects.

Participation in this war was a concern of the Chen Commission, the international delegation that visited Cuba in 1874 to collect firsthand testimony from its Chinese immigrants. Its report mentions 13 men who fled westward after their masters joined the insurgency. Their testimonies indicate that they desired to separate themselves from the war. The Spanish Crown had announced that it would grant those Chinese who remained loyal certificates of freedom. Yet, some were jailed and others forced to work as public laborers.

The Pact of Zanjón, the treaty that officially ended the conflict in 1878, granted unconditional freedom to those Chinese who were registered in the Liberation Army. Today a monument in Havana honors the Chinese who participated in the Ten Years' War. Part of its inscription reads, "There was not one Cuban Chinese deserter, not one Cuban Chinese traitor."

See also: Chinese in Cuba; *Cuba Commission Report, The*

Further Reading

Helly, Denise. 1993. *The Cuba Commission Report: A Hidden History of the Chinese in Cuba. The Original English-Language Text of 1876*. Baltimore, MD: The Johns Hopkins University Press.

López, Kathleen. 2013. *Chinese Cubans: A Transnational History*. Chapel Hill: University of North Carolina Press.

Yun, Lisa. 2008. *The Coolie Speaks: Chinese Indentured Laborers and African Slaves in Cuba*. Philadelphia, PA: Temple University Press.

Don E. Walicek

CHINESE CAMBODIANS

In the 1960s and 1970s Chinese Cambodians were one of the largest minority populations in Cambodia, but by the mid-1980s the population was reduced by more than half. The start of Year Zero under the Khmer Rouge leadership in 1975 and resulting genocide gave some indication of what the new Cambodia, known as Democratic Kampuchea, would look like. The Khmer Rouge transformed the country by relocating people to Khmer Rouge territory and reclassifying urban dwellers into classes of "Old" (or base) people and "New" people. Cambodians were classified by markers of class and ethnicity; those who were deemed to be intellectuals, upper class, and professionals were killed in successive waves. A majority of Chinese in Cambodia were a part of the upper and educated class subject to discrimination. Ethnic Khmer as well as ethnic minorities such as Cham, Chinese, and Vietnamese were classified and killed in different waves of Khmer purges.

Ethnic Chinese Cambodians who were able to escape from Cambodia between 1975 and 1979 made their way to refugee camps on Thailand's border. In some instances, Chinese Cambodians were able to flee through Vietnam by way of masking their Cambodian identity and passing as Vietnamese or as ethnic Chinese from Vietnam. However, from refugee camps and through sponsorship programs, many Chinese Cambodians found their way into Australia, Canada, France, and the United States. About 145,149 Cambodian refugees entered the United States seeking political asylum. From 1975 and onward, larger numbers of Cambodian and Chinese Cambodian refugees began to arrive in the United States but their status as Southeast Asian refugees, similar to Hmong, Laotians, and Vietnamese, set them apart from East Asian immigrants. Southeast Asian refugees migrating to the United States came with limited education, little to no income, and/or had to live with their original sponsors. Refugees were dispersed throughout the United States in clusters to "minimize the negative impact of a refugee population." This was known as Cluster Projects, whereby the United States resettled refugee populations and allocated funds so that no one state had the obligation and responsibility of too many refugees at one time. The project was intended to disperse groups of refugees while also funding the mutual assistance associations, which served as mediators between the larger community and the community they serve. Within the context of the United States and the issues of the first migration for refugees and their families, a secondary migration occurred, whereby refugees no longer stayed with original sponsors. The need for community, finding whereabouts of close family and friends, and other opportunities account for the development of larger Cambodian and Chinese communities found in California, Washington, and Massachusetts. Secondary migration was spurred by the need for community and familial support as Cambodian refugees had difficulties in navigating official government- and state-sanctioned systems. Thus it is important to note the agency of refugees in migration and the significance of family as a source of economic and emotional support. Through the secondary migration and family networks, small businesses became a step toward strengthening community.

Building an ethnic niche and community was important for Cambodians and Chinese Cambodians. Since the 1980s, donut shops have been an ethnic niche for Cambodian and Chinese Cambodian Americans. Family businesses relied on a rotating credit system and unpaid family labor. The rotating credit system among family and friends provided financial support for the startup of a family-operated business and the possibility of expanding into a franchise. The reliance on family as unpaid labor allows for expenditure to be allotted to other necessities. Additionally, the reliance on family labor emphasizes the valuable role of the younger generation who often serve as cultural brokers to assist their parents at the front of the store. Where the mother and father may be limited in English, the children deal with customer transactions by utilizing their English-language skills in the family workplace. First-generation parents increasingly rely on their children as unpaid labor in owning and operating a small business. Concomitantly, second-generation children often struggle in an attempt to balance family life with their own social lives when managing these multiple roles. Though this ethnic niche may incorporate family labor, survival, and attempts to participate in U.S. business models, it is unclear how successful these small businesses are in its present state since its inception in the late 1970s and early 1980s.

Not only did Cambodians and Chinese Cambodians have to navigate displacement and create an ethnic economy for survival, the impact of post-9/11 policies on deportation exposes the continued purveyance of racialization and subject formation in our present and among the newer generation. With the signing of President Bill Clinton's Personal Responsibility and Work Opportunity Act of 1996, Cambodians who have spent a majority of their life in the United States but did not obtain citizenship have been deported on the basis of criminal record, including petty crimes, only to be expatriated. Refugees, who escaped genocide from home countries and were forced to make a new living abroad, are once more exiled to their "home" country. Cambodian refugees in the United States who fled from the Khmer Rouge as already displaced victims are once more displaced through repatriation under the 1996 Immigrant Responsibility Act. This second displacement is ironic because refugees who largely grew up in host countries such as the United States are unfamiliar with Cambodia and, once deported, are castigated as outsiders. The policies on deportation demonstrate the significant role of race and its effect upon future generations and different communities. First- and 1.5-generation Cambodian and Chinese Cambodians now living in the United States as survivors of genocide and those who were impelled to commit to a secondary migration must still continue to face these present issues and realities while still sustaining their lives and their families. This cyclical theme of displacement further prompts second-generation Cambodian Americans and Chinese Cambodian Americans to draw from their personal and family histories, reconceptualize and question how they fit in a white hegemonic America, and attempt to balance their first-generation parents' identities and narratives.

See also: Chinese Vietnamese

Further Reading

Chan, Sucheng. 2004. *Survivors: Cambodian Refugees in the United States*. Champaign: University of Illinois Press.

Ong, Aihwa. 2003. *Buddha Is Hiding: Refugees, Citizenship, the New America*. Berkeley: University of California Press.

Schlund-Vials, Cathy. 2012. *War, Genocide, and Justice: Cambodian American Memory Work*. Minneapolis: University of Minnesota Press.

Angela Tea

CHINESE CANADIAN HISTORY

Chinese Canadians are the largest ethnic minority group in Canada today. Chinese language (including Mandarin and Cantonese) has become the third-most-spoken mother tongue in Canada, next to Canada's official languages, English and French. The history of Chinese Canadians has been one of struggle, survival, and development.

Early Migration in the 19th Century

In 1858, some Chinese laborers began arriving in the west coast of Canada from San Francisco, in response to the gold rush in the Fraser Valley, British Columbia, where gold was discovered in 1857. By 1860, the Chinese population of

British Columbia was estimated to be 7,000. By 1865, the prosperous period of the gold rush was basically over and British Columbia faced severe economic conditions. More and more unemployed white native workers began to blame the Chinese for taking away their jobs because of their willingness to work for much lower wages. Hostility against Chinese laborers emerged in the late 1860s and continued in the forthcoming years. On July 20, 1871, British Columbia entered the Confederation as Canada's sixth province, and the first general election in British Columbia for Legislative Assembly was held. In 1874, the Legislative Assembly passed an act to disenfranchise native Indians and Chinese, which intensified the discrimination against Chinese people.

Ever since the Canadian Confederation was formed in 1867, the federal government had seriously considered creating a national railway from coast to coast. When British Columbia joined the Confederation in 1871, it had to promise to build the Canadian Pacific Railway. In 1879, the Workingmen's Protective Association organized a petition requesting the federal government to not use Chinese immigrants for the construction of the Canadian Pacific Railway. However, there was a shortage of white workers for the construction, and the government had to grant permission for the employment of the Chinese laborers.

The construction of the railway started in 1881. Between 1881 and 1884, about 17,000 Chinese laborers came to British Columbia to build the Canadian Pacific Railway. Some of the workers came from the States; some came directly from China. The Chinese had to do the hardest and most dangerous work, such as blasting tunnels through the rock, but were paid half as much as the white workers. Many Chinese railway workers died due to accidents, cold weather, and illness.

When the Canadian Pacific Railway was completed in 1885, many Chinese workers became unemployed. Some of them returned to China, some stayed in British Columbia or moved east to Toronto, Montreal, and other cities in search of new job opportunities. They were willing to work at any wages for any jobs, such as coal miners, farm laborers, woodcutters, cooks, and servants. Some of them opened small businesses including groceries, laundries, barber shops, and restaurants.

Head Tax

In 1885, the Canadian federal government passed the Chinese Immigration Act, which requested Chinese immigrants, except for diplomats, students, tourists, and scientists, to pay an entry fee (also known as head tax) of $50. At the same time, the government started to keep detailed records of all immigrants from China, and about 95,000 Chinese who arrived in Canada between 1885 and 1949 were recorded by the government. The intention of the head tax was to discourage Chinese people from coming to Canada. The tax was increased to $100 in 1900 and finally to $500 in 1903, the equivalency of a worker's wages for two years. The Chinese were the only ethnic group ever to be explicitly subjected to the head tax in Canadian immigration history. Enduring the heavy tax, Chinese laborers continued to arrive, because they were in extreme poverty and could not make a living in China.

Immigration in the 20th Century

In 1901, according to the census, the Chinese population was 17,312. In the next 10 years, the number reached 27,831. Like their predecessors, the Chinese who came in the early 20th century left home to escape starvation and poverty, looking for better opportunities in Canada. During this period, many Chinese laborers were restricted from bringing their wives and children with them and had to stay alone without family members in Canada. This phenomenon was also knows as the Chinese "married bachelor" society.

In 1923, the Chinese Immigration Act, also known as the Chinese Exclusion Act, was passed by the Parliament of Canada. Between 1923 and 1947, Chinese immigrants were excluded by law, except for those with special permits, from entering Canada. Chinese immigration to Canada almost ceased until 1947, and some Chinese men gave up their immigrant status and returned to China because there was no hope to bring their families to Canada. As a result, the Chinese population declined during this period. Also as a result of this law, the Chinese already in Canada experienced restriction of citizenship rights. They also lost their right to obtain decent works, and for those who could work in the labor market, their wages were much lower than white workers.

During the World War II, the governments of British Columbia and Saskatchewan opposed enlisting Chinese in the army, fearing that they had to enfranchise the Chinese after the war. However, some native-born Chinese volunteered to join the military service to fight for Canada. They were first denied, but finally hundreds of them were able to serve in the war. In May 1947, the federal government repealed the Chinese Exclusion Act. Later, other discriminatory laws against the Chinese were also abolished, in recognition of the contribution made by Chinese Canadians. The repeal of the 1923 Act also allowed wives and other dependents of Chinese immigrants to enter Canada.

Beginning from 1951, the number of Chinese immigrants increased steadily. According to the census, there were 32,528 Chinese in Canada in 1951, and by 1961, the number rose to 58,197. In 1962, Canada abandoned its white racist immigration policy, and admission to the country was to be based on such factors as education and other skills instead of a candidate's ethnic origin.

In 1967, a universal point system was introduced. This system was applied to all applicants, irrespective of country of origin or racial background. People around the world now had an equal opportunity for admission to Canada according to their education and occupational skills. The changes of immigration policies in 1962 and 1967 opened the door to more Chinese immigration and encouraged more professional and skilled Chinese coming to Canada.

In the late 1970s, Canada admitted over 50,000 Vietnamese refugees, also known as the "Boat People," on humanitarian grounds. Many of the refugees were of Chinese origin. Also in the late 1970s, some citizens of mainland China were able to come to Canada to reunite with their long-separated families or relatives in Canada.

The 1981 Census of Canada reported 285,800 Canadians of Chinese origin, about 1 percent of the total population. By 1984, a total of 212,374 Chinese had immigrated since the Chinese Immigration Act was repealed in 1947, and since then, the Chinese have been able to enjoy their civil right as other Canadians.

The implementation of the Investment Canada Act in mid-1980s attracted many Hong Kong investors and entrepreneurs to bring their capital to Canada, in addition to the people from Hong Kong since 1960s. During the early 1990s, a large number of Hong Kong immigrants came to Canada, motivated by the possible political uncertainty after the handover of Hong Kong from the UK to China in 1997. However, Hong Kong's stocks and housing prices soared after 1997, attracting many people return to Hong Kong. On the other hand, some immigrants from Hong Kong had difficulty finding employment in Canada and decided to return to Hong Kong.

Some immigrants from Taiwan also arrived in Canada in the 1970s, and more Taiwanese arrived in 1980s, attracted by the business immigration program. Many Taiwanese immigrants were young students who had completed junior high school education in Taiwan prior to immigrating to Canada, in order to avoid compulsory enrollment of the Taiwan armed forces or to prepare for better university education.

In the 1980s, a growing number of mainland Chinese students came to Western countries to pursue higher education. After the Chinese students' movement in June 1989, the Canadian government enacted a humanitarian program, and thousands of people from China, mainly students, obtained landed immigrant status. In the 1990s, the Chinese government further loosened its restrictions on the exit of its citizens. As a result, a steady flow of mainland Chinese, mainly professionals and skilled workers, arrived in Canada.

Immigration in the 21st Century

By the 21st century, the Chinese had become 3.5 percent of Canada's population, the nation's largest minority group. According to the 2002 statistics from the Citizenship and Immigration Canada, the biggest number of immigrants came from the People's Republic of China since 2000, averaging about 30,000 immigrants per year, which equals to 15 percent of all immigrants to Canada. According to the 2006 Census of Canada, there were 1,346,510 people with Chinese origin in Canada. The census also reported that nearly 86 percent of the Chinese lived in five metropolitan cities: Toronto, Vancouver, Montreal, Calgary, and Edmonton.

As of 2011, according the census, there were 1,487,580 people of Chinese ethnic origin, which was 4 percent of the Canadian population. In addition to professional, investment, and family reunion categories, some Chinese also obtained refugee status in Canada during the past several decades.

In 2014, Canada closed the federal immigrant investor program, ending the process for many Chinese millionaires who are on the waiting list. This program has been in operation for 28 years and helped wealthy Chinese gain Canadian citizenship. Between December 2012 and October 2013, around 16,000 people from mainland China applied for investor visas to Canada.

With more Chinese in professional and technical occupations entering Canada, many are choosing the suburbs, not the Chinatowns, as locations for residence. The Chinatown has ceased to be the center of the Chinese community, as there has been less pressure of segregation in recent decades, compared with the prewar years. With more and more Chinese immigrants coming to Canada with higher education degrees, more Chinese immigrants are working as professionals now than before. In addition, due to the requirement for English or French proficiency as one of the criteria for immigration, Chinese immigrants are in a better position to communicate with native Canadians, compared to immigrants a century ago.

Apology and Recognition

On June 16, 1980, Parliament passed a motion recognizing "the contribution made to the Canadian mosaic and culture by the people of Chinese background." This was the first official recognition of the contribution of Chinese immigrants. In September 1982, the Historic Sites and Monuments Board of Canada installed a bronze plaque at Yale Museum, British Columbia, in honor of Chinese railway workers. In 1987, all three major political parties supported the introduction of an all-party parliamentary resolution to recognize the injustice and discrimination of the head tax and the Chinese Exclusion Act.

On June 22, 2006, Prime Minister Stephen Harper delivered a message of redress in the House of Commons, offering an apology and compensation for the head tax once paid by Chinese immigrants. The government promised to pay survivors or their spouses approximately $20,000 CAD in compensation. There were about 20 people who paid the tax still alive in 2006.

On May 15, 2014, British Columbia's premier Christy Clark formally apologized for racist policies that started more than 140 years ago against Chinese immigrants, calling the regulations a stain on the province's history. She said that, while the governments that passed these laws and polices acted in a manner that was lawful at the time, today this racist discrimination was seen by British Columbians as unacceptable and intolerable.

Chinese Canadians' Participation in Politics

Having obtained the franchise, the Chinese have been able to participate in politics since the 1950s. Douglas Jung was the first Member of Parliament (MP) of Chinese and Asian descent in the Canadian House of Commons representing Vancouver Centre from 1957 to 1962. George Ho won the election as a City of Calgary alderman in 1959 and was elected to the Legislative Assembly of Alberta in 1971. He became the first person of Chinese descent elected to the Alberta Legislature.

In recent years, more Chinese Canadians have been involved in politics at federal, provincial, and municipal levels. Raymond Chan became the first ethnic Chinese to be appointed into the Cabinet of Canada in 1993. Adrienne Clarkson served as Governor General of Canada from 1999 to 2005. David Lam served as Lieutenant Governor of British Columbia from 1988 to 1995. Norman Kwong served as Lieutenant Governor of Alberta from 2005 from 2010. Philip Lee has been the 24th Lieutenant Governor of Manitoba since 2009. There have also been several MPs of Chinese origin: Michael Chong has been MP since 2004, and Alice Wong was MP since 2008, and was later appointed as the Minister of State for Seniors in 2011. Olivia Chow served as another MP from 2006 to 2014. She resigned her seat in the Parliament in 2014 to run for the 2014 Toronto mayoral election. Vivienne Poy and Lillian E. Dyck are currently two Chinese Canadian senators in the Senate of Canada.

Cultural, Social, and Religious Life

Culturally, a great number of Chinese Canadian families maintain their traditional Chinese lifestyle, emphasizing filial piety, education, and other Confucian values. Many Chinese parents send their children to study the Chinese language, music, sports, painting, and other arts during weekends. While the first generation of Chinese immigrants enjoys Chinese food more than Western food, their Canadian-born children are more adapted to Western food and lifestyle. Like people in China, most Chinese Canadians celebrate the Lunar New Year (Chinese New Year). Other Chinese festivals, such as Mid-Autumn Festival, Lantern Festival (Yuanxiao Festival), Qingming Festival, and Dragon Boat Festival (Duanwu Festival) are also celebrated among some Chinese immigrants.

Cultural groups and traditional cultural activities such as Chinese music, folk dance, and martial arts, still flourish among some Chinese immigrants. Chinese-language newspapers and television programs have widespread readers and audience, especially in larger cities such as Toronto, Vancouver, Montreal, and Calgary.

Chinese Canadians have organized into various associations. Some associations are characterized by professional or cultural interests, others are divided by geographical regions where they are originally from. In recent years, Chinese literature in Canada has become a genre of Canadian literature. Novels, poems, and essays written by Chinese Canadians have been published in Chinese, English, or French, and some Chinese writers have become well known for their writings in both Canada and China or even internationally.

According to the 2001 census, 58 percent of Chinese Canadians had no religious affiliation. The largest religious group is Buddhism among religious Chinese Canadians. The others include Catholic, Christian, Islam, and Daoism. Some Buddhist temples and Christian churches were built especially for Chinese Canadians.

The Chinese population in Canada, started with the arrival of 19th-century Chinese laborers, continues to grow, characterized by more highly educated professionals of the postmodern time. The Chinese community has become an integral part of Canada's multicultural society.

See also: Chinese Immigration to Canada

Further Reading

"A Brief Chronology of Chinese Canadian History." 2015. Accessed July 16, 2015. http://www.sfu.ca/chinese-canadian-history.

"Address by the Prime Minister on the Chinese Head Tax Redress." 2006. Accessed July 23, 2014. http://www.pm.gc.ca/eng/news/2006/06/22/address-prime-minister -chinese-head-tax-redress.

Hardwick, F. C., and Moir, P. 1975. *East Meets West: A Source Book for the Study of Chinese Immigrants and Their Descendants in Canada.* Vancouver, BC: Tantalus Research.

Li, Peter S. 1998. *The Chinese in Canada.* Toronto, ON: Oxford University Press.

Mar, L. R. 2010. *Brokering Belonging: Chinese in Canada's Exclusion Era, 1885–1945.* New York: Oxford University Press.

Meissner, Dirk. 2014. "Christy Clark Apologizes for 'Dark Period' When B. C. Had More than 100 Racist Policies Against Chinese." *National Post,* May 15.

Wang, Jiwu. 2006. *"His Dominion" and the "Yellow Peril": Protestant Missions to the Chinese Immigrants in Canada, 1859–1967.* Waterloo, ON: Wilfrid Laurier University Press.

Macy Zheng

CHINESE EXCLUSION ACT (1882)

The Chinese Exclusion Act of 1882 was passed on May 6, 1882. It suspended Chinese skilled and unskilled laborers from coming to the United States for the next 10 years. The 1882 Chinese Exclusion Act affected Chinese immigration until its repeal in 1943.

The Act had shattering effects on Chinese immigrants in many areas. Immediately, Chinese labor immigration was suspended for the next 10 years. However, it did not apply to Chinese laborers who were already in the United States when the Angell Treaty passed on November 17, 1880. This new law did not affect those who might come to the United States within 90 days after the passage of the Act. New restrictions on Chinese laborers already living in the United States allowed Chinese laborers to freely leave and visit China. However, the Act prohibited Chinese laborers from reentry without first obtaining certificates for returning to the United States. The passage of the Scott Act of 1888 canceled all outstanding return certificates. Furthermore, in order to ensure that new Chinese laborers could not enter the United States, this Act also required that Chinese government issue certificates for those who were merchants, diplomats, and other nonlaborers. These certificate holders could then prove their nonlaborer status when they entered the United States. Even nonlaborers could still enter the United States but the quota was small. This Act also prohibited all Chinese immigrants from obtaining citizenship through naturalization. No citizenship meant no vote. Lacking political influence, Chinese immigrants found themselves in an even lower status than before. In 1943, the repeal of the Chinese Exclusion Act of 1882 allowed Chinese to naturalize as U.S. citizens. This repeal put Chinese immigrants in a better status in the United States.

See also: Angell Treaty (Chinese Exclusion Treaty) (1880); Chinese Women and the Chinese Exclusion Act; Scott Act (1888)

Further Reading

Daniels, Roger. 1988. *Asian America: Chinese and Japanese in the United States Since 1850.* Seattle: University of Washington Press.

Lee, Erika. 2005. *At America's Gates: Chinese Immigration During the Exclusion Era, 1882–1943.* Chapel Hill: University of North Carolina Press.

Edy Parsons

CHINESE IMMIGRATION DURING THE GOLD RUSH

On January 24, 1848, discovery of gold in the Sacramento Valley, California triggered the "rush" and an ensuing prosperity. By the beginning of 1849, news of the Gold Rush spread around the world. Gold seekers went to California from every continent. The Gold Rush also attracted Chinese immigrants going to California.

The Chinese immigration movement started in San Francisco when three Chinese, two men and one woman, journeyed from Hong Kong to work for their American boss. Chinese living around Hong Kong and the port of Canton quickly heard the foreign news and word soon spread across China. Thus half a world away, the California Gold Rush ignited Chinese dreams, especially among the poor. At that time, China faced a lot of internal and external challenges. China lost wars to Britain and France. In order to pay the costs of war and indemnity, the Chinese government increased taxes. Furthermore, natural disasters like floods and drought emerged in southeastern part of China. In addition, the Taipei Rebellion (1850–1865) in China also destroyed livelihood in some provinces because of the constant fighting between the Taipei forces and the government forces. Plundering and occupying paralyzed the economy in rebellious areas. People lost their jobs and income. Lands were abandoned. It was a difficult time for the poor. Immigration to the United States became an attractive option. Thus, the Gold Rush in California triggered Chinese immigration.

The great majority of Chinese immigrants coming to the United States were laborers. Some of these laborers were recruited in China as coolie laborers. They were young, and most of them were single. They did not expect to stay in the United States for the rest of their lives. They just wanted to earn more money so they could go back to China with money. They took the voyage to the United States on credit. When they arrived in the United States, they worked for lower wages in order to pay back their creditors. Gold mine owners needed cheap labor so they could maximize their profits. Chinese laborers became their targets. Besides laborers, Chinese merchants also came to the United States. The number of merchants was a lot smaller. These merchants mainly handled and sold merchandise used by Chinese immigrants. Some opened laundry businesses in California. Out of 310 laundry shops, 240 were owned by Chinese.

Of the first wave, around 90 percent were poor Chinese farmers and laborers who worked in and around Hong Kong and Canton, coming mostly from counties located in the Pearl River Delta of China. For example, by 1876, 45 percent of Chinese immigration was from Taishan county of China. While they arrived at a relatively slow pace over the century, California census statistics show that the Chinese population grew by leaps and bounds in one 30-year span, going from 789 Chinese in 1850 to 75,000 in 1880.

In the early 1850s, American western newspapers reported positive news about Chinese immigrants because they, like Californians, saw the new arrivals as an asset to development. Chinese immigrants were welcomed. The press reported news about Chinese immigrants in a positive light. Everything looked good and bright immediately following the 1848 discovery of gold.

White Californians needed labor, and in addition to Chinese immigrants, a huge influx of people came from many different regions of the United States and the world. Right then, things were rosy, and Chinese immigrants were well received by public and politician and press alike. On October 29, 1850, California was admitted into the Union. Fifty Chinese immigrants marched in the parade. During the celebration, California Justice Nathaniel Bennett gave a speech and welcomed both Chinese immigrants and other foreigners.

On April 23, 1852, Governor Bigler's special message to the Legislature of California pointed out that the number of Chinese laborers working contractually in the mines of California was increasing. Bigler suggested that it was necessary to keep track of this tide of Asiatic immigration in order to protect the state's prosperity. When gold was discovered in 1848, it was easily accessible. By 1850, gold was extracted from locations that were not accessible as easy as before. Furthermore, California also faced a depression in 1853. Job competition made the white workers drive the Chinese immigrants away from mines. In 1852, the Californian state government began to push for specific measures restricting Chinese immigration.

Among western states, California had the largest Chinese immigrant population; its white citizens had no intention of accepting this population. They actively sought Asian exclusion. From the mid-1850s, Californian politicians passed exclusion laws on local and state levels. They specifically targeted Chinese with severe restrictions on immigration into the state. California politicians eventually brought their ideas of Chinese exclusion to the federal level. Although the courts found some California state laws to be unconstitutional, this did not prevent the state from amending its laws or passing new ones. In 1852, the Foreign Miner's Tax set the stage for discrimination against the Chinese because Chinese immigrants were not allowed to become naturalized. Under Foreign Miner's Tax law, California charged alien miners a monthly $3 fee, which increased to $4 monthly in 1853. In 1854, the California amended the law to exempt naturalized citizens from paying the Foreign Miner's Tax. This clearly discriminated against Chinese, since they were prohibited from naturalization and had no option but to pay the Foreign Miner's Tax.

Continued arrival of Chinese immigrants in California exacerbated white Americans' fears. Americans felt the threat when the number of Chinese immigrants increased from less than 20,000 in 1852 in California to over 34,000 in 1860 and to nearly 50,000 by 1870. In 20 years, white Americans saw more and more Chinese in their everyday lives. San Francisco's Chinatown, where most Chinese immigrants lived, no longer seemed so far away. Certainly, many Chinese were now seen as part of everyday life, working side by side with whites. Most Chinese worked as laborers, such as miners, domestic servants, and other menial jobs. These roles became the expected norm in the minds of white Americans.

In spite of an initial positive acceptance when the Chinese first arrived in the United States, anti-Chinese sentiment was increasing. In the late 1860s, anti-Chinese sentiment began to boil over, and the anti-Chinese violence spread from California to other western states. Although California tried its best to discourage Chinese immigration, the Burlingame Treaty of 1868 signed between China and the United States overrode that state's law in favor of the Chinese. The Burlingame Treaty restricted the California government from stopping voluntary Chinese immigration and furthermore, guaranteed Chinese immigrants the right to most-favored-nation treatment. However, this treaty did not stop politicians from trying to restrict the coming of Chinese immigrants. It was California Republican Congressman Horace F. Page who successfully began agitating against the Chinese in 1875 and convinced Congress to pass the 1875 Page Act restricting the immigration of Chinese women to the United States.

The Gold Rush brought Chinese immigrants to the United States. They helped build California, but fear of Chinese immigrants triggered the passage of exclusion laws and anti-Chinese agitation.

See also: Anti-Chinese Violence; Chinese Exclusion Act (1882); Scott Act (1888)

Further Reading

Daniels, Roger. 1988. *Asian America: Chinese and Japanese in the United States Since 1850.* Seattle: University of Washington Press.
Sandmeyer, Elmer. 1991. *The Anti-Chinese Movement in California.* Chicago: University of Illinois Press.

Edy Parsons

CHINESE IMMIGRATION TO CANADA

When thinking about Chinese immigration to North America, most people would determine California as the focus of research interest, but Canada also has its own history of Chinese immigration. Until the 20th century many Canadians had not even seen a Chinese person and knew little about China itself; however, people had listened to or read stories from others who had traveled in China or diplomats who had lived there. News about the Opium Wars, the Taiping Rebellion, the Sino-Japanese War, and other events had created a stereotype that was based on war, barbarism, corruption, and intellectual backwardness. Consequently, the first immigrants were confronted by preexisting prejudices.

The white population of Canada disrespected the Chinese, who were depicted as addicted opium smokers who were incapable of assimilating into a modern Western society. When Chinese immigration was discussed by members of the Canadian government, Prime Minister John A. Macdonald requested a thorough evaluation before each Chinese person would be allowed to immigrate. In 1886 the government finally decided on a suitable strategy, which consisted of a $50 head tax for every Chinese immigrant who wanted to enter Canada. However, many of the immigrants considered this to be an investment in a better future, away from wars and corruption, both of which had occurred in Manchu China. For this reason, British Columbia, where most of the new immigrants arrived, tried to secure a higher tax from the incoming Chinese in the early 1890s.

Especially during the Boxer Rebellion in 1900, the local governments tried to further restrict the numbers of immigrants from China by raising the tax as well as demanding language tests for the newcomers. As the Chinese government seemed to be totally unstable in negotiations, the tax was again raised to $500 per head, thereby decreasing the number

Ralph Lee, a 106-year-old former head tax payer, carries the last spike used in the completion of the Canadian Pacific Railway as he arrives at the Ottawa train station in Canada on June 21, 2006. The Canadian government offered a formal apology to Chinese Canadians for a discriminatory head tax charged on Chinese immigrants from the 1880s to the 1920s. (Reuters/Dave Chan/Corbis)

of new immigrants between 1905 and 1907 to little more than 100. However, there was also strong feeling against the existing Asian communities in Canada, so much so that the Asiatic Exclusion Leagues organized a rally against Japanese immigrants in Vancouver, which also destroyed Chinese property in the Chinatown there. Opium factories there especially aroused Canadian criticism, and Mackenzie King, who was the Deputy Minister of Labor and attended the World Anti-Opium Congress that took place in Shanghai in 1909, demanded a ban on opium imports and its nonmedical use in Canada.

At the same time, Canada was trying to negotiate a "Gentlemen's Agreement" that would replace the head tax. King hoped to persuade China to limit its emigration numbers to Canada—between 500 and 1,000 people per year. When

Robert Botden's Conservative government took power in Canada in 1911, the chances of such an agreement seemed to have passed, but the economic growth of China, and especially the creation of a stronger middle class, led to emigration using the head tax as an entrance pass. Between 1911 and 1912 more than 6,000 Chinese immigrants arrived in Canada. However, while the Canadian government welcomed the high revenue, the Canadian population did not welcome the Chinese immigrants. But despite the xenophobia of a "yellow peril" in Canada, more and more immigrants arrived from China, especially after the end of World War I.

To counter this growing number, the Canadian government decided to tighten immigration controls, demanding passports, while the Chinese documents issued in Guangzhou were no longer sufficient to warrant an entrance to Canada. Consequently, the number of arrivals tremendously dropped; in August 1922 just 12 Chinese entered British Columbia. During the 1920s Canadian politicians could win votes by promising to keep the country white. They were financially backed by the Retail Merchants' Association of Canada, because it feared a growing Chinese competition. As the head tax did not seem to limit the problem, Prime Minister Mackenzie King in the 1920s tried to replace it with an official treaty. A bill, signed in 1923, limited entry to Canada to specific groups of people (e.g., university students and Canadian-born Chinese). The Chinese who live in the country declared the day that the bill came into effect to be a Humiliation Day, but could not change the actual situation. It was during the 1930s and the depression changed the Canadian image of China, which was seen as a potential customer of goods produced in Canada. The image of the country was also changed by the Chinese fight against Japan, news about the Rape of Nanjing and the outbreak of the Pacific War in 1941, all of which finally established a permanent sympathy for the Asian country.

In the same year Canada finally sent its first diplomats to China, and Victor Odium became the first ambassador. Both King and the Department of External Affairs were eager to form the best possible relations with China and offered a treaty of reciprocity, allowing Chinese clergy, doctors, and merchants to acquire a status of temporary residence. At the same time, the Chinese already living in Canada demanded a repeal of the anti-Chinese Immigration Act and better conditions for Chinese immigration to Canada in general. In 1946 it was finally repealed, but the Chinese Civil War created new problems. How could it be determined whether the potential immigrants were actually communists, trying to spread the revolution to Canada? The fact that the two countries no longer had official diplomatic relations made it even worse, as the Chinese were still trying to immigrate. The restrictive policies of the Canadian government finally led to an increase of illegal attempts at immigration, and an estimated number of 11,000 Chinese entered the country between 1950 and 1960.

In the late 1960s Canada finally ended its racial discrimination with regard to the immigration policy, and the number of Chinese immigrants legally rose.

The Chinese community of Canada today is an important part of Canadian society, but it suffered from prejudices and racially motivated policies in the first seven decades of the 20th century. Fear of economic competition, racial prejudices, and the political instability of China led to a large antagonism toward Chinese immigration in the North American country. The events of the Pacific War and the Chinese Civil War, as well as the "multicultural turn" of society, finally paved the way for a more equal immigration of Chinese people to Canada, where they form an integral part of the nation-state today.

See also: Chinese Canadian History

Further Reading

Li, Peter S. 1998. *The Chinese in Canada.* New York: Oxford University Press.

Mar, Lisa Rose. 2010. *Brokering Belonging: Chinese in Canada's Exclusion Era, 1885–1945.* New York: Oxford University Press.

Roy, Patricia E. 2013. "Images and Immigration: China and Canada." *Journal of American-East Asian Relations* 20: 117–38.

Frank Jacob

CHINESE IMMIGRATION TO MEXICO

The earliest migration of Chinese immigrants into Mexico begins during the Colonial period when small numbers of Chinese arrived as servants of Spanish merchants. A sizable wave of 60,000 Chinese migrants settled in Mexico between 1880 and 1940. The early Chinese migrants journeyed to Mexico for employment and to escape poverty and harsh living conditions in China: similar to the migrants who set sail for California's gold mountains or to Canada and Australia, the migrants headed for Mexico originated from China's southern region of Canton. They called Mexico "Big Lusong," in contrast to "Little Lusong," referring to the Philippines, which was a Spanish colony at the time.

Many Chinese migrants entered Mexico (and Canada) after the passage of the 1882 Chinese Exclusion Act: their time in Mexico was to be temporary as they made their way to the United States, but the majority stayed, despite hard living and working conditions. Many of the Chinese pioneers settled in Baja California, particularly the city of Mexicali, which became colloquially known as "Little Canton."

In the late 19th to early 20th century, similar to the United States, Mexico needed cheap labor to industrialize and modernize, so between 1880 and 1910, the Mexican government recruited Chinese laborers to build its railroads. In 1899, the Mexican government also signed a treaty with China to recruit Chinese laborers to work in agriculture in the northern border areas. By the 1920s, Chinese immigrants who had settled in Mexico were the second largest immigrant group in the nation—after Spanish immigrants—with a population of 26,000. Besides Baja California, Coahuila, Sonora, and Chihuahua states were also magnets for the Chinese. The Chinese had resided in every Mexican state except for Tlaxcala.

Similar to the anti-Chinese sentiments that developed in the United States and Canada, it occurred in Mexico as well. The rise of anti-Chinese sentiment developed in Mexico during the Mexican Revolution (1910–1920). Economic scapegoating started in Torreon, the Coahuila city where 600 Chinese lived and established their own hotel and bank. At the time of the revolution, nativist-Mexicans blamed the Chinese for economic inequality, just as nativist Americans and Canadians blamed the Chinese laborers who competed with them for work. On May 15, 1911, the forces of revolutionary leader Francisco I. Madero (1873–1913), leading a division of Pancho Villa's (1878–1923) army, attacked the Chinese community in Torreon, killing some 300 of them.

Anti-Chinese sentiment amplified in Sonora, Sinaloa, and Chihuahua, where Chinese migrants had come to dominate the merchant class, largely because they were single men without families and could charge lower prices. By the mid-1930s, some 70 percent of the Chinese in Mexico were deported or expelled from the country, repatriated to China, or pushed across the border into Arizona. This occurred well into the 1950s.

Today, Chinese Mexicans are exploring their heritage and largely embraced in Mexican society. Indeed, one of President Enrique Pena Nieto's cabinet secretaries, Miguel Angel Osorio Chong, is of Chinese descent. The smallest Chinatown in the world is Mexico City's Chinatown, known as "Barrio Chino." The two-block Barrio Chino maintains Chinese-style designs and decorations. Barrio Chino is also the site of a large Chinese Lunar New Year festival that attracts not just locals, but also tourists and visitors throughout Mexico.

See also: Anti-Chinese Violence; Chinese Immigration to South America; Chinese in Cuba; Chinese in Peru

Further Reading

Delgado, Grace. 2013. *Making the Chinese Mexican: Global Migration, Localism, and Exclusion in the U.S.-Mexico Borderlands.* Stanford, CA: Stanford University Press.

Hu-DeHart, Evelyn. 1982. "Racism and Anti-Chinese Persecution in Mexico." *Amerasia Journal* 9:2.

Romero, Robert Chao. 2010. *The Chinese in Mexico, 1882–1940.* Tucson: University of Arizona Press.

Jonathan H. X. Lee

CHINESE IMMIGRATION TO SOUTH AMERICA

Although the Chinese presence in Latin America dates back to at least the 16th century in the Viceroyalty of New Spain thanks to the Manila galleons (*las naos de China*) that connected Manila and Acapulco, the main waves of immigration to the rest of Latin America began in the mid-19th century. By and large, we can highlight three types of immigrants: the first are the indentured laborers that were part of the "coolie" trade or "*la trata amarilla*" ("yellow trade") from 1847 to 1874; the second include independent laborers and businessmen, beginning in the 19th century and continuing to the present; and the third comprise investors predominantly from Taiwan. Among the first immigrants in the region, the British brought 192 Chinese from Penang, Calcutta, and Macao to Trinidad in 1806, while in Brazil, 400 immigrants were placed on tea plantations in 1812.

Between 1847 and 1874, about 150,000 Chinese workers were brought to the Caribbean region: 125,000 to Cuba; 18,000 to the West Indies (Guyana, Trinidad, and Jamaica); 2,640 to Surinam; and 1,000 to the French territories, Guadeloupe, and Martinique. Between 1849 and 1874, about 100,000 were

Members of the Colombian police guard a group of ten Chinese whom were transported illegally inside a truck in Cali, Colombia on September 27, 2008. According to authorities, sixty-nine Chinese citizens haven been deported from the Latin American country. (Carlos Ortega/epa/Corbis)

sent to Peru to work on the coastal economy, primarily on sugar plantations and in guano fields or else on the Andean railroad construction. The large majority of these Chinese were recruited from Siyi, Sanyi, Zhongshan, and outlying districts from southern Guandong via deceptive means, promised gold and other riches, only to be kidnapped and shipped off against their will. At the port of Amoy, they were stripped naked and painted or stamped with the letters C, P or S, the destination codes for California, Peru, or the Sandwich Islands (Hawai'i), respectively. Ravaged by illness and malnutrition, many did not survive the sea journey from China. Many others turned to suicide. Historian Juan Pérez de la Riva contends that a few thousand Chinese immigrants living in California were smuggled into Cuba via New Orleans and Mexico. The end of the slave trade in 1807 and the abolition of slavery in the British colonies (1834–1838), Cuba (1886), and Brazil (1888) triggered the need to find affordable manual laborers to either replace or supplement the workforce in the sugar industry and other fields, giving birth to *la trata amarilla*.

The forced immigration to Cuba and Peru was targeted for investigation because of reported atrocities in the recruitment and transportation of laborers as well as their poor working conditions. The report by the Chinese Commission to Cuba (1874), based on oral interviews with the coolies, reveals that most were kidnapped or deceived into signing eight-year indentured-labor contracts and that the harsh conditions forced many to run away from the plantations. Harvesting guano on the Peruvian coast and the Chincha Islands became an unbearable task for many workers, who opted to end their lives rather than continue in misery. At the end of their contract, surviving laborers returned to China, signed another contract, or became small retail traders. Very few returned to China, choosing instead to make their way in their new surroundings. Given the imbalanced ratio of men to women, Chinese men partnered with local women. Some of these were marriages of convenience to avoid being deported or losing property during the anti-Chinese campaigns of the early 20th century in Mexico and Panama.

Public opinion in Brazil was divided concerning Chinese immigration in the late 19th century. While the Chinese, deemed backward and an impediment to progress, could help with work in the cotton and coffee fields, they also signaled the deterioration of the incipient national identity. Chinese immigration to the state of Sao Paulo, mostly from China via Hong Kong, increased after World War II and the Chinese Revolution of 1949. In the 1970s and 1980s, some Chinese entered Brazil from Paraguay. In 2004, out of an estimated 100,000 Chinese in Brazil, 80,000 resided in the state of Sao Paulo.

While the Chinese were generally considered outsiders in their new lands, many Chinese men proved themselves on the battlefield. In Cuba, they participated in the first War of Independence (1868–1878) alongside Cuban nationals in their fight for independence from Spain. Similarly, indentured Chinese men in Peruvian *haciendas* supported the Chilean army during the War of the

Pacific (1879–1883), choosing to fight willingly in exchange for their freedom. Moreover, the Chinese established colonies in the Peruvian Amazon region as early as 1873, a fact deliberately concealed in 19th-century Peruvian historiography, which bolstered the belief that only Europeans could tame the jungle and create conditions for a thriving civilization.

The Gold Rush in California attracted miners from all over the world, which necessitated a more direct route to the west coast of the United States. The Chinese were employed in the interoceanic railroad construction in Panama (1850–1855) and, later, on the Panama Canal (1904–1913). Soon after Panama became an independent nation, a newly enacted law from 1904 prohibited the immigration of Chinese, Turks, and Syrians. This did not deter John Stevens, the Canal's chief engineer, from hiring 2,800 Chinese workers from Fujian province.

As early as 1855, many Chinese migrated from Panama to Puntarenas, Costa Rica, primarily to work on the construction of a railroad connecting with the Caribbean coast, but also in mining and agriculture and as domestics. Chinese migrants mainly settled in coastal and capital cities in Central America, then tended to migrate within the region (from Costa Rica to Nicaragua, from Panama to Costa Rica, etc.).

In the 20th and 21st centuries, a steady immigration, legal or not, from China, Hong Kong, and Taiwan continues to strengthen the presence of the Chinese and their descendants in countries that have traditionally welcomed them. It has also changed the landscape of other countries, such as Argentina, Chile, and Paraguay, which have seen an increase of Asian immigrants in recent years. While the Chinese population, both new immigrants and established generations, is growing in some countries, the Caribbean region has experienced a decline since the 1960s. The Caribbean Chinese tend to migrate to North America and Europe as the natural result of increasing economic affluence and an attraction to metropolitan urban settings. By and large, professional and educational opportunities and the promise of economic prosperity in the United States and Canada are strong incentives for younger generations to migrate north.

See also: Chinese Canadian History; Chinese Immigration to Mexico; Chinese in Cuba; Chinese in Peru

Further Reading

Banco Interamericano de Desarrollo. 2005. *Cuando Oriente llegó a América: Contribuciones de inmigrantes chinos, japoneses y coreanos.* Washington, DC: Banco Interamericano de Desarrollo.

Lai, Walton Look, and Tan Chee-Beng, eds. 2010. *The Chinese in Latin America and the Caribbean.* Leiden, NL: Brill.

Meagher, Arnold. 2008. *The Coolie Trade: The Traffic in Chinese Laborers to Latin America, 1847–1874.* Philadelphia, PA: Xlibris.

Alejandro Lee

CHINESE IN CUBA

The first large-scale migration of Chinese to the Caribbean island of Cuba took place between 1847 and 1874. This migration is part of the infamous "coolie trade," a series of events that took hundreds of thousands of migrants from China's five treaty ports to Latin America and the Caribbean. The overwhelming the majority of the migrants were men who were coerced or tricked into leaving southern China to work under contracts of indenture. Official records indicate that slightly more than half of the sojourners migrated to the Spanish colony of Cuba. Most of the men who reached the island's capital, Havana, departed from Macao.

When the possibility of importing large numbers of Asian plantation workers to Cuba emerged in 1846, Spanish authorities in Madrid voiced their support for the proposal, asserting that their migration would be modeled after its successful experience with Chinese workers in the Philippines. The Chinese were described as industrious, frugal, docile, and hardened to rural labor. But in contrast to the Spanish Crown's reference to its amiable experience with Chinese laborers in Asia, the interactions in question were actually characterized by situations of tension and conflict in which violence was easily triggered. This past foreshadows the nature of daily life in the first chapter of Chinese migration to Cuba.

The Chinese were transported to work as "free" plantation laborers, but they were subject to serious abuses, violence, and semi-enslavement. They arrived in the Caribbean during a period in which the Cuba's sociocultural order was changing rapidly. While the abolition of African slavery and the push for independence were two of the main factors responsible for shifting dynamics, the influx of approximately 125,000 Chinese indentured laborers itself added a new dimension to dynamics of language, culture, race, and religion on the island.

Testimonies collected in Cuba years after the Trade began indicate that offers of employment at high wages lured would-be migrants from their inland homes to the coastal regions of southern China. Many of them sought economic opportunity and hoped to secure employment in Formosa (contemporary Taiwan), Singapore, or the Philippines. Multiple generations of Chinese had gone to work in these places across the centuries. Only a small percentage, however, intended to migrate to the West. Nevertheless, many were kidnapped and sold as de facto slaves. More yet were forced to sign contracts of service, even those who were illiterate and in disagreement with the provisions of indenture. Middlemen involved in the trade, Chinese, Spanish, and Portuguese, said that such signatures were binding and held that they meant consent had been obtained.

The conditions on the ships that took the men to Cuba were deplorable. Poor sanitation and bad food often resulted in sickness and epidemics among passengers. During the first 12 years of the Trade alone, approximately 15 percent of the migrants destined for Cuba perished at sea. Survivors of the journey reported that many of their fellow countrymen had committed suicide by jumping overboard.

Chinese forced to work in Cuba frequently compared the treatment they received upon arrival to that of animals subject to auction. They reported men on horseback threatening them with whips and herding them into the barracoon, a large structure that had been used to detain runaway slaves. Others testified that their queues, at the time of symbol of dignity and male honor in their home country, were cut off and their clothes forcibly removed so that purchasers could examine them, judge their strength, and determine their value before selling them for a profit.

The idea of transporting large numbers of Chinese to the island was the result of attempts to address a shortage of labor by securing "white" laborers. The immigration of Europeans was preferred not just because of international pressure to end the system of African slavery, but also because of racial ideologies that situated persons of African and Afro-Cuban ancestry as a threat to physical security and economic stability of the elite. While some Europeans did immigrate to Cuba, they tended to reject manual labor, especially labor in the fields of large plantations. Within this context, three conditions framed the possibilities of Asian immigration and caused planters to see Chinese laborers, at least initially, as an ideal solution to the problem of securing exploitable labor. First, distinct from Africans, they were legally unprotected by a Western power; second, they were available in large numbers; and third, important in allaying the planters' afrophobia, they were not considered black.

Contracts of indenture, which usually lasted eight years, detailed the obligations of the laborer and employer alike. The laborer was ensured a monthly wage as well as food, housing, clothing, and medical attention, and he or she was free from obligations upon expiration of the contract. While the contract clearly distinguished the conditions of indenture from slavery, these agreements were frequently ignored. The laborers were rarely paid and reported a lack of meals and clothing as well as routine whippings, beatings, shackling, and other abuses. Some were even forced to continue working after their period of indenture had expired. Nevertheless, the details of the contract were very important to the migrants. For them it was a constant reminder of three things: they were not slaves, their period of service was limited, and they had rights under the law.

Chinese immigrants contributed to the Cuban economy and played a key role in the transition from slave to wage labor. Tens of thousands of male workers labored on sugar plantations under harsh conditions. Others worked on tobacco and coffee estates. The small number of women that immigrated tended to serve as domestic laborers in Havana.

Resistance and demands that owners respect the law and a common sense of humanity were frequently articulated. It was common for Chinese to go to great pains to file petitions and complaints with the proper colonial authorities, either for themselves or for their friends and coworkers. This strengthened bonds among the men and extended networks of support. While this solidarity positively impacted many, a substantial number of men could not deal with the misery and ran away or committed suicide in order to escape their plight. At times Chinese assertions of their own humanity reinforced Spanish ideas about their racial inferiority. Negative views of protest, suicide, and cultural difference on the part of politicians and others contributed to the formation of derogatory racial stereotypes and the further dehumanization of indentured laborers.

Unfortunately, those who completed their contracts and began working as wage earners were not always equitably incorporated into Cuban society. They were also frequently subject to verbal and physical abuse from both the general public and the police. In addition, a series of unjust laws that were enacted to benefit plantation owners or the colonial government by robbing the Chinese of equal pay for their labor. Archives of the period suggest that Spanish beliefs about natural order, progress, and national identity led state officials to see racism against the Chinese population as necessary and legitimate.

The Chinese obviously faced many obstacles in 19th-century Cuba. Nonetheless, as a group they proved resilient, determined, and resourceful. By the 1870s, a substantial number had learned Spanish and some served as interpreters for those who did not. Some, especially the upwardly mobile, converted to Catholicism and were baptized, at times in conjunction with unions with Afro-Cuban women. By 1866 the towns of Pinar del Río, Guanajay, and Güines all had Chinese shops, and by 1870 most large cities had at least one Chinese-owned fruit and vegetable stand. As was also the case in Peru, Chinese cooking practices influenced the local cuisine. As these examples suggest, the Chinese contributed to reshaping Cuba's culture and social landscape.

Chinese laborers also participated in events related to the birth of the Cuban nation. They fought alongside whites and blacks against Spanish rule in two of the most important struggles of a protracted movement: the Ten Years' War (1868–1878) and the War of Cuban Independence (1898). Their participation in these wars against colonial rule was clearly a concern of Spain. In fact, colonial authorities accused thousands of Chinese who were not confined to plantations of supporting rebels. These men were arrested, charged with disturbing the peace, and jailed.

Less than 1 percent of the total number of indentured servants that survived the passage to Cuba returned to their homeland. Many more wished to do so but they lacked the resources necessary for their passage. Some who wanted to go back but could not afford to do so made arrangements for their bones to be repatriated to their home provinces after death.

After the end of Spanish rule in 1898, Chinese Cubans were not immediately incorporated as citizens. Exclusion Acts reinforced anti-Chinese attitudes, and exported U.S. fears of the "yellow peril" were instituted in the first decade of the 20th century and the 1930s.

The second chapter of the Chinese presence in Cuba, which began early in the 20th century, took shape with the influx of agricultural workers that began in 1917. Free rather than indentured, the conditions in which these laborers lived were far removed from those of the 19th century. Only a very small fraction of them had "coolie" ancestors on the island. The new wave of migrants tended to either operate or work in restaurants, grocery stores, laundries, and watch and shoe repair kiosks. Unlike the victims of the Trade, many were entrepreneurs with access to resources and infrastructure necessary to maintain ties with their families and villages in China. In fact, many sent back remittances, and return trips home were fairly common.

The vibrancy of Havana's Chinatown, one of the most extensive and well known in the Americas by 1920, was enhanced by the international contacts that members of the community maintained. "Barrio Chino" was especially important for new immigrants. In addition to serving as a commercial center, it was a place where they could easily make arrangements for lodging and employment and receive legal and medical assistance. This helps explain why groups organized around Chinese political issues competed for leadership and influence in Chinatown.

In addition, Havana's Chinatown was the main base of the community's fraternal organizations as well as regional and clan associations that extended to other areas. Their activities contributed to the growth of the island's immigrant population. Chinese were estimated to number 124,000 in 1924.

Many Chinese left Cuba in the 1930s, a decade of significant economic hardship. At this time the Cuban government nationalized labor and antiforeign sentiment intensified. In response to Japan's invasion of China, one workers' organization reorganized itself as the Alliance to Protect Chinese Culture in 1938. Evidence that events in Asia continued to have a local impact, in the decade that followed the group supported communism in China.

After 1940, it became easier for Chinese who had family in Cuba to immigrate to the island. This change, which led to an increase in female migration, was due primarily to the approval of a new constitution. Another step forward was the Cuban state's recognition of the civil rights of persons of Chinese descent in 1941. Chinese cultural performances also became more visible during this period, with groups integrating the "corneta china" and lion dances into annual carnival celebrations. Cantonese opera and Chinese bands started to become popular.

Emigration from Cuba to the United States picked up with the repeal of the U.S. Chinese Exclusion Act in 1943. This change dealt a blow to the island's Chinese theatres and musical groups. The island is one of the many places that received refugees after the creation of the People's Republic of China in 1949. The 3,000 who arrived included Catholic priests and officials from the displaced nationalist government. Most had family members on the island. Some refugees later found themselves at odds with Cuban political movements, including leftist groups that were strengthened by the communist victory in China.

In the 20th century many Cuban-born Chinese felt that they belonged on the island. For members of this group, cultivating an appreciation for and under-standing of the heritage of ancestors was not incompatible with assimilating into local culture. Distinct from first-generation migrants, they were bicultural: "overseas Chinese" who could function in both traditional cultural contexts and those of the West. This helps to explain why a substantial number of them became active in politics.

Cubans of Chinese ancestry from diverse socioeconomic backgrounds sup-ported various actions against the notoriously corrupt Batista government and the 1959 Cuban Revolution led by Fidel Castro. Supporters of popular strug-gle, they were critical of U.S. intervention and government corruption. Among them were three young men of Chinese background: Armando Choy, Gustavo Chui, and Moisés Sío Wong. Decades later each became a general in the Revo-lutionary Armed Forces of Cuba.

In the early 1960s thousands of business-minded Chinese left Cuba, a reaction to dramatic socialist-inspired political and economic changes. Their departure was a result of the state taking possession of private property and nationalizing privately owned businesses and multinational corporations. Chi-nese Cubans settled in the same places as other refugees who left at this time: Miami, New York, and Puerto Rico.

After the Cuban Revolution of 1959, several Cuban historians completed research on the island's Chinese populations, often producing studies that focused on their role in the struggle for independence from Spain and the island's political development during the period in which Fidel Castro was Cuba's president. Some early work promoted the view that all Chinese were revolutionaries. Such assertions formed part of an effort to establish a useful and inclusive narrative chronicling the group's past, but sometimes they failed to recognize the diversity of perspectives, opinions, and decisions that have existed across time. More recent scholarship pays attention to variations in patterns of opinion and social experience at the same time that it acknowledges problems that previously received very little attention, including racism and economic exploitation.

The lives of Chinese indentured laborers and their descendants figure prominently in numerous literary works by acclaimed Cuban writers. Especially notable among these are *The Messenger* (1998) by Mayra Montero and *Monkey Hunting* (2003) by Cristina García. The works of Regino Pedroso and Zoé Valdés, Cuban writers of Chinese ancestry, also address questions about traditional culture and the negotiation of modern identities.

One of most important international relationships for Cuba in the first 10 years of the 21st century was with the People's Republic of China. The two countries signed trade agreements and China set up manufacturing pharmaceutical drugs and appliances. In addition, arrangements were made allowing thousands of Chinese to learn Spanish in island schools, and by the end of the decade approximately 5,000 Chinese students had graduated from Cuban universities. During this same period Havana's Chinatown was revitalized and promoted by the government as an important tourist attraction.

Demographers estimate that there were only 200 foreign-born Chinese Cubans in 2010 but also pointed out that Cuba's population included thousands of "mixed" Chinese ancestry. Investment ties and cultural exchange appear to have fostered the revitalization of a Chinese Cuban identity among members of this group.

China's substantial economic and political influence has contributed to the reshaping of ideas about Asian migration to the island and also influenced how Cuba is perceived internationally. In Cuba, these shifts are contextualized by annual festivals dedicated to members of the Chinese diaspora, regular conferences on Chinese history, and frequent Chinese tourist delegations from the People's Republic of China, Canada, and the United States. Images of China past loom large in the island's national imagination and its vision for the future.

See also: Chinese and Cuba's Ten Years' War (1868–1878); Chinese in Peru; Coolie Trade; *Cuba Commission Report, The*; Lam, Wifredo

Further Reading

Choy, Armando, Gustavo Chui, and Moisés Sío Wong. 2005. *Our History Is Still Being Written: The Story of the Three Chinese-Cuban Generals in the Cuban Revolution*. Edited by Mary Alice Waters. New York: Pathfinder.

García Triana, Mauro, and Pedro Eng Herrera. 2009. *The Chinese in Cuba, 1847–Now*. Edited and translated by Gregor Benton. New York: Lexington Books.

Look Lai, Walton, and Tan Chee-Beng. 2010. *The Chinese in Latin America and the Caribbean*. Boston: Brill.

López, Kathleen. 2013. *Chinese Cubans: A Transnational History*. Chapel Hill: University of North Carolina Press.

Don E. Walicek

CHINESE IN HAWAI'I

The presence of Chinese in the Hawaiian Islands dates back to 1788, when the Kingdom of Hawai'i was an independent nation. At the time, Hawai'i was governed by a system of common law that had its roots in ancient laws called *kapu*. Two ships of English fur traders arrived at the Island of Hawai'i and spent three months there in the winter of 1788, waiting for the seas to calm so that they could resume their journey. Approximately 50 members of the crew were Chinese. A few months later, American fur trader Captain Simon Metcalfe went to Hawai'i, also with Chinese men in his crew.

Widespread Chinese immigration began in 1852 when indentured servants escaping poverty in the provinces of Kwantung (Guangdong) and Fukein (Fujian) went to Maui to work on sugar plantations. Smallpox had decimated the Native Hawaiian population in 1853, creating a more urgent demand for laborers. Chinese immigrants were recruited to fill the void. Working under five-year contracts, Chinese plantation workers were paid in room, board, credit toward the cost of their passage from China, and an extra $3 a month. By 1882, almost half of the plantations laborers in Hawai'i were Chinese.

Working on the sugar plantations was physically demanding work, and the majority of Chinese laborers did not work beyond their initial five-year contracts. Some returned to China, while others found work on the islands as domestic servants or became entrepreneurs. Others worked as rice or taro farmers. A few of the Chinese men who left later returned to Hawai'i with their wives but many more Chinese men married Native Hawaiian women. The majority of the immigrants who stayed settled along the waterfront in Honolulu. The area, which came to be known as Chinatown, even though it was quite culturally diverse, attracted many Chinese businesses, ranging from produce stands and laundry facilities to the more disreputable opium dens and gambling halls. In the 20th century, the increased military presence in Hawai'i added to Chinatown's unfavorable reputation, as businesses primarily catered to the soldiers and sailors on leave.

Chinese immigration to Hawai'i was severely restricted in 1898 when the United States annexed Hawai'i. This led to Hawai'i becoming subject to the Chinese Exclusion Act, and only select Chinese people, such as students, teachers, or merchants, were permitted to move to the Islands. When China became an ally of the United States in World War II, immigration laws were relaxed. As more whites left Hawai'i for the mainland after the war, Chinese Americans stepped in and took a more prominent role in Hawaiian business and politics. Today about 6 percent of Hawai'i's population is Chinese, although the number of Hawaiians of mixed Chinese and Native Hawaiian descent is much higher, accounting for approximately one-third of the state's residents. There is a strong Chinese presence in Hawai'i, with over 200 Chinese societies, including social and religious clubs as well as professional organizations.

Chinatown has also experienced a renaissance in the 21st century after enduring many years of crime and neglect in the 1980s and 1990s.

See also: Bachelor Society; Chinese Immigration During the Gold Rush; Chinese Immigration to South America; Contract Laborers (Credit-Ticket Laborers); Coolie Trade

Further Reading

"Chinese in Hawai'i." 2011. University of Hawai'i. Accessed July 16, 2015. http://www .hawaii.edu/news/docs/chinese-in-hawaii.pdf.

McKeown, Adam. 2001. *Chinese Migrant Networks and Cultural Change.* Chicago, IL: University of Chicago Press.

Nordyke, Eleanor C., and Richard K. C. Lee. 1989. "The Chinese in Hawai'i: A Historical and Demographic Perspective." *The Hawaiian Journal of History* 23: 196–215.

Amy Lively

CHINESE IN PERU

The first known documentation of Chinese in Peru dates to the early 17th century. Their presence in the Andean region is a result of ongoing exchange and commerce that linked New Spain (present-day Mexico) and the East through the Manila galleon trade. Mexican silver and Chinese luxury goods (including silks, porcelain, and spices) were the center of the trade, but patterns of contact that existed for over three centuries led a very small number of Chinese, including some who migrated from southern China to the Philippines and later took up service on Spanish galleons, to disembark at ports such as Acapulco and then travel to Peru and other parts of Latin America.

Peru's first large-scale wave of Chinese immigration dates to the period 1849–1874 when almost 100,000 indentured servants arrived. Many of the members of this overwhelmingly male population traced their origins to the southern Chinese province of Guangdong; however, the group was culturally and linguistically diverse. Most had been kidnapped or duped into service as part of the "coolie trade" to the Caribbean and Latin America

Chinese laborers pick cotton on irrigated land at the foot of the Andes in Vitarte, Peru, ca. 1907. (Library of Congress)

and then forcibly taken to Macao and the other British-controlled treaty ports from which they began their trans-Pacific voyage. Once in the ports, many of the men, a large portion of whom were poor and illiterate, were forced to sign contracts of indenture. The few who left willingly believed they would be protected by legal contracts and international treaties, but efforts to enforce the provisions of these documents almost always proved to be in vain.

Chinese migrants traveling to Latin America as indentured servants faced brutal physical abuse aboard the ships that transported them. Flogging, chaining, inadequate food and water, as well as prohibitions on movement and speaking were commonplace during the voyage of three to four months. Many Chinese men committed suicide in protest. Others died from the insanitary conditions and mistreatment they faced at sea. Traders responded to these deaths by packing in larger numbers of migrants, an attempt to ensure their economic profits.

Shortly after reaching Lima, Peru's capital, many of the men were auctioned off to the highest bidder after potential purchasers examined them as if they were animals. Most would work under a contract that lasted for eight years, an agreement that many were forced to renew. The majority of the arriving Chinese were taken to coastal enterprises dedicated to the harvesting guano and sugar, lucrative industries of the period, but significant numbers also contributed to the construction of the Andean railroad. Guano pits were often located on the Chincha Islands, and sugar plantations tended to be located in rather remote areas. In both cases men worked in relative isolation, a factor that led many of the abuses against them to go unchecked.

Slavery was abolished in Peru in 1854, but Chinese arriving before as well as after this date faced some of the same abuses that Africans in bondage endured. Daily life was especially difficult for indentured Chinese in rural areas. Many were denied clothing and medical care and some were locked up at night on the farms where they worked. Inhumane living conditions and constant economic exploitation prevented many from forming families and healthy social relationships. In response to abuse, they rebelled, ran away, and did what they could to press for more humane treatment. Runaways who were caught were fined and forced to pay their owners the costs of their capture and return. Very few of these men had anything to show at the end of their service. These circumstances led some laborers to become depressed. Their situation only worsened when the Peruvian government facilitated their access to opium.

While by no means easy or comfortable, life tended to be better for migrants who lived in cities. Many of these men were artisans. They worked as carpenters, tanners, bakers, and mattress makers. Some made and sold cigarettes. Others labored in domestic service, serving as cooks or servants. Men working in kitchens are likely to have been the first to introduce Chinese culinary traditions to the wider population.

Distinct from the situation that faced enslaved Africans, indentured Chinese did have rights under the law. In fact, leaders among them tended to be experts in the details of their contracts and consistently argued that the protections they were afforded by law should be respected. Those laborers who successfully completed the term of their contracts sought economic opportunities to improve their condition. Some joined Chinese work gangs. Others chose to recontract with their masters, usually for a period of between a few months and two years. Those in rural zones often hoped to save enough to relocate to a city and then establish a business or take up a craft. Some dreamed of returning to China as free men, a goal that was difficult to realize.

Just 15 years after indentured laborers arrived, the early signs of a Chinese section of Lima were already visible. Entrepreneurs rented places in the market and chose the area as a base for the associations and guilds. In the late 1860s they were joined by merchants of Chinese ancestry from California. By 1876 the population of Lima's Chinese community had reached 15,000. The Chinese quarter, increasingly associated with Asian heritage and traditions, was a bustling center of commerce and a space of cultural contact.

By 1873 small Chinese colonies had been established in various parts of the Amazon. These communities appear to have consisted of runaways, men who had completed their contracts, and free migrants. While existence in this frontier region was somewhat precarious for outsiders, residents of the colonies relied on networks and personal industry to make a living. They did so as small-scale investors in manufacturing, trade, and agriculture. Within a few decades they made significant economic gains and contributed to the development of the region.

The immigration of indentured laborers from China officially ended in 1874. At this time only the Caribbean island of Cuba had received more of China's "coolies" than Peru. Both international condemnation of the conditions facing forced migrants and actions of the imperial government in Beijing contributed to the abolition of involuntary migration; however, the phenomenon of indenture continued for a few years. Men still under their contracts had to complete them.

The last group of contracts expired in the 1880s. It was about this time that Chile invaded Peru in the War of the Pacific, a conflict that lasted from 1879 to 1883. Some Chinese living in coastal areas cooperated with the invading army in exchange for their freedom and the opportunity to work as wage earners. Among them were men who participated in the siege of Lima. The men who united with the invading troops were shocked when their liberators attacked the stores that their fellow countrymen owned in Lima's central market. In response to what was seen as betrayal, as many as 1,000 Chinese were murdered, and many Chinese-owned shops were destroyed.

The second part of the 19th century was a period of growth for Chinese cultural institutions. Three important groups were established in Lima: the Ku

Kong Chao Association in 1868, the Pun Yui Society in 1887, and the Tung-shin Society in 1898. The members of these benevolent societies were people from Guangdong, Cantonese immigrants, and persons of Hakka ancestry, respectively.

Peru's Chinese population grew significantly through free immigration in the 20th century, with about 30,000 people arriving in the first two decades alone. In this period, more than 30 Chinese brotherhood and fraternal-political associations as well as several Chinese schools, newspapers, and publications operated. In addition, the term *Tusán* began to take root in the local lexicon. The word nuanced what it meant be to Chinese by serving as a label for those considering Peru their homeland.

While some Chinese started to see themselves as belonging to Peruvian society, the population as a whole was far from integrated and was frequently represented as a source of pressing social problems. Peruvian workers accused the more-prominent Chinese of fixing prices, exploiting employees, and monopolizing neighborhood grocery stores and small industries. Politicians and labor leaders echoed these accusations and portrayed Chinese religion and culture as monolithic and incompatible with the customs and values of Peruvian society. They did so in political debates, in the press, and at labor rallies.

The result was a wave of anti-Chinese protests and an increase in everyday racial violence. On two occasions tensions culminated in riots that led to the loss of life and the destruction of private property. The insularity of Chinese family and kinship structure and the closed nature of their business networks contributed to conflict and misunderstanding. Remarkably, prominent members of Lima's small Chinese elite failed to speak out against anti-Chinese riots in 1909 and 1918. Negative cultural stereotypes pitted Peru's racial groups against one another and contributed to solidifying the power of the elite. This undermined the organization of a cohesive movement of workers from all of Peru's main groups: persons of Asian, Spanish, Amerindian, and African ancestry.

By 1920 controversial restrictions on Chinese immigration were in place. In the decades that followed marriages between Chinese men, most of whom were speakers of Cantonese, and indigenous women became more common. Their children, distinct from those of previous generations, tended to acculturate to the norms of dominant society, learning Spanish and converting to Catholicism. Many operated *chifas*, restaurants serving Chinese food, and small neighborhood stores. In the 1940s and 1950s middle- and upper-class Chinese began moving to suburban municipalities.

The establishment of a military government in 1968 led to economic problems and fragmentation of the Chinese community. Wealthy businessmen fled to the United States and Canada. Government officials decreed the Chinese quarter unsanitary and evicted numerous merchants. Even though some remained, the activities of temples, clubs, and institutions waned, and older generations charged that younger ones had strayed from traditional values.

In addition, Lima lost status as node of commerce and international networks with significant Chinese participation. The quarter was not revitalized until 1999, the year of the 150th anniversary of the introduction of Chinese indentured laborers. At that time funds were allocated to stimulate economic activity and install traditional Chinese architectural features.

Economic and social developments demonstrate that China and Chinese cultural traditions are important in 21st-century Peru. Distinct from the period of the coolie trade, which focused on the exportation of human labor, China has become a strategic partner and a major capital investor. Billion-dollar projects, including controversial mining ventures and ongoing robust commercial exchange function as mainstays of the economy. These encourage new patterns of Chinese immigration, both legal and illegal, from various countries in Asia. While estimates of Peru's contemporary Chinese population differ substantially across sources, it is clearly the largest in the region. The community, including Chinese nationals, appears to have numbered 120,000 in 2000.

Persons of Chinese ancestry have shaped Peruvian national culture in politics and the arts. Victor Joy Way was the first prime minister of Chinese-Peruvian ancestry. He served in 1999. José Antonio Chang served in the same office from 2010 to 2011. Julia Wong and Siu Kam Wen are examples of acclaimed writers of Chinese ancestry who have explored the significance of their heritage in fiction. Like *chifa*, which has become so ingrained in Peruvian food culture that dishes with Szechuan and Cantonese roots are considered Peruvian rather than Chinese, their contributions weave a history of immigration into the fabric of everyday life.

See also: Chinese in Cuba; Coolie Trade

Further Reading

Lausent-Herrera, Isabelle. 2011. "The Chinese in Peru and the Changing Peruvian Chinese Community(ies)." *Journal of Chinese Overseas* 7: 69–113.

Look Lai, Walton, and Tan Chee-Beng. 2010. *The Chinese in Latin America and the Caribbean.* Boston: Brill.

López-Calvo, Ignacio. 2014. *Dragons in the Land of the Condor: Writing Tusán in Peru.* Tucson: University of Arizona Press.

Meagher, Arnold J. 2008. *The Coolie Trade: The Traffic in Chinese Laborers to Latin America, 1847–1874.* Philadelphia, PA: Xlibris.

Don E. Walicek

CHINESE IN THE MISSISSIPPI DELTA

The Mississippi Delta is an alluvial plane that is situated between the Mississippi and Yazoo Rivers in northwest Mississippi. It is notable for its fertile soil as well as its distinctly Southern culture, earning the Delta the label of "The Most Southern Place on Earth" by historian James C. Cobb. While the Mississippi Delta has never had a large number of Chinese residents, the Chinese have been a part of the region since the middle of the 19th century.

The first Chinese immigrants in Mississippi arrived following the end of the Civil War in 1865. The abolition of slavery led to fears among white plantation owners that the mass exodus of newly freed African Americans would create a labor shortage. Chinese immigrants, many of them from the *Szeyap* region of southern China, were actively recruited to take the place of slave labor. By 1880, just over 50 Chinese immigrants were living in Mississippi. However, the Chinese quickly learned that there was little money to be made as plantation workers and many turned to owning and operating grocery stores as a means of financial survival.

Mississippi's first Chinese residents cared little for integrating into the state's racially segregated society. Their primary concern was making money to send back to China. They lived in African American neighborhoods and catered to a mainly African American clientele, who were unwelcome throughout the Jim Crow South. African Americans of the Delta found the Chinese grocery stores to be both a safe meeting place and a suitable option for purchasing essentials with little likelihood of harassment. For the Chinese, their respectful treatment of African Americans led to disapproval from the white residents. Interracial dating between the Chinese and African Americans further aggravated the whites and, as a result, the Chinese came to be considered as "nonwhite" and were subjected to the same discriminatory laws as African Americans.

Over time, though, acceptance by the white residents of the Delta became more important to the Chinese. After World War II and into the 1960s, the Chinese adopted the religious customs of the region, becoming very active in the Baptist church. They made a greater effort to separate themselves socially from African Americans and, in an attempt to assimilate into white society, gave their children first names more commonly associated with whites.

Following the end of segregation in 1964, Chinese grocers were no longer the only option for African Americans of the Delta. Restaurants, serving either Chinese food or the traditional barbecue of the South, have become a more viable option for Chinese business owners. While less than 1 percent of the population of Mississippi today is Asian, the Chinese continue to have a presence in the Delta, and Delta State University in Cleveland, Mississippi maintains the Mississippi Delta Chinese Museum to help preserve the unique role of the Chinese in the region's past.

See also: Chinese Fisheries in California; Chinese in the U.S. Civil War

Further Reading

Cobb, James C. 1992. *The Most Southern Place on Earth: The Mississippi Delta and the Roots of Regional Identity*. New York: Oxford University Press.

Wilson, Charles Reagan. 2002. "Chinese in Mississippi: An Ethnic People in a Biracial Society." Accessed July 16, 2015. http://mshistorynow.mdah.state.ms.us/articles/86/mississippi-chinese-an-ethnic-people-in-a-biracial-society.

Amy Lively

CHINESE IN THE U.S. CIVIL WAR

The first study of Chinese in the U.S. Civil War, published in 1996, identified only 10 who served, and although researchers combing through muster rolls have since added dozens of names and will undoubtedly find more, the number of Chinese will always be minuscule in the face of the three million who fought. As their profiles in this volume indicate, however, the range of their participation was broad and the challenges they faced as soldiers and veterans unique.

The challenges for researchers must also be noted: "Chinese-sounding" names often turn out to be nationals of other countries; many of the Chinese who served had completely Western names; microfiche are frequently illegible; census data are flawed. In this brief overview, individuals of mixed race are included in the count of Chinese, and their names and service data are drawn from the 1996 study and Terry Foenander's "Asians in the Civil War"; the 1860 Census data for Chinese are from Him Mark Lai's statistical breakdown by state.

At the start of the fighting in 1861, scarcely 200 Chinese resided east of the Mississippi where the war was primarily waged. So, discounting the five who enlisted in California, the current total of 58 Chinese servicemen means the level of combatants in proportion to the population was substantial—and these figures do not take into account the percentage of the Chinese population that was male and of age for military service.

Because the smallest number of Chinese resided in the South, it stands to reason that far fewer fought for the Confederacy than the Union. Even fewer seemed to have been committed to the Confederate cause. Certainly the Bunker cousins in the Virginia cavalry, coming from slaveholding families, were. But Cao Zishi, underage and in the nebulous position of student, apprentice, and servant, could not have chosen freely when accompanying his master into the cavalry in Tennessee.

Some Chinese had no interest in fighting for either the Confederacy or the Union. John Fouenty, conscripted in Savannah, Georgia, ran away to Union-held St. Augustine but did not join the Union cause. Having been captured from his native Hong Kong for the notorious "coolie trade," he had survived a four-year labor contract in Cuba and been homeward bound when forced to disembark on the American continent and then to don Confederate gray; once within Union lines, Fouenty resumed his broken journey home to China.

A strong case can be made that another runaway, Thomas Sylvanus, was devoted to the Union because he reenlisted twice after a battle-related disability discharge. Hong Neok Woo, in the Pennsylvania militia, is on record as supporting the North because he opposed slavery. Edward Day Cohota, like many peers in the general population, enlisted simply because he did not want to be left behind by friends when they went soldiering.

The range of choices and motivations for service among the Chinese reflects those of other native and foreign-born males. Desertions likewise occurred, but the reasons prompting the handful by Chinese have yet to be uncovered. The small cluster of desertions from the Second Louisiana Infantry points to a problem within the regiment. Possibly James Johnson, who had been a sailor before joining the 18th New York Cavalry, realized in the few months between his enlistment in New York and desertion in New Orleans that he preferred the sea.

American cargo vessels had long included Chinese on crews, and most of the Chinese veterans identified to date served in the Union navy, which was open to all races, and where they held similar positions: cabin boys, stewards, cooks, and landsmen. Because the navy did not maintain personnel files for enlisted men until 1885, constructing profiles of Chinese who served at sea and verifying their claims is virtually impossible. According to newspaper reports, some were involved in combat: John Akomb, steward on a gunboat, was twice wounded, once seriously in the chest; the heel of John Earl—a cabin boy on Admiral Farragut's flagship, the *Hartford*—was smashed by solid shot in Mobile Bay; and William Hang, serving on the same vessel as a landsman, handed out powder during the battle.

Unlike the navy, the Union army initially excluded "colored" volunteers; then African Americans were allowed to fight in segregated "colored" regiments officered by whites; and it is here that the unique position of Chinese in America's racial landscape is most evident. There were only three categories in the 1860 Census—white, black, or mulatto—and how a Chinese was identified seemed to depend on the enumerator, economics, and geography. In North Carolina, the slaveholding Bunker family was—from the two Chinese fathers and two white mothers to their mixed-race children—considered white. Also marked white was Antonio Dardelle, a servant in Connecticut. But in Maryland, a census enumerator expressed his confusion over the appropriate designation for servant Thomas Sylvanus by making something akin to an exclamation mark.

Similarly stumped was a Confederate general over a captured Union soldier, John Tomney, which may account for the Confederate cavalry and infantry's acceptance of Chinese and mixed-race men to fight alongside whites. At least two Chinese served in the Union's Colored Troops, whether from personal preference or after being rejected by white regiments cannot be determined. But Yale graduate Yung Wing *was* rejected when he offered his services in Washington, D.C., in 1864, perhaps because he expected to be commissioned as an officer rather than serving as a private.

Period magazines were rife with negative images of Chinese, and the widely used school text *Peter Parley's Universal History* proclaimed Chinese as rat-and-dog-eating liars addicted to cheating. Chinese displayed in tours sponsored by missionaries or P. T. Barnum projected more positive yet no less stereotypic images. Given the scarcity of Chinese in the east, though, most people did not personally encounter any except in New York City's lower wards, where an estimated concentration of about 70 worked as peddlers and operated boarding houses and small businesses.

That Chinese won acceptance, even admiration and respect in white regiments, with three earning promotion to corporal, can be attributed to the nature of a soldier's small, tight-knit community where men depended on each other for survival, not just on battlefields, but also on long, hard marches, when felled by sickness, or as prisoners of war. Veterans reluctant to surrender this camaraderie sought to preserve it through regimental reunions and formation of a fraternal organization, the Grand Army of the Republic, and Chinese actively participated in both. Invariably, the anomaly of their service was commented upon, sometimes by the Chinese veteran himself for whom it seemed a point of pride.

Among the veterans, only one has been identified as native born: James Earl, the California-born son of a Mexican mother and Chinese father, who ran away to sea as a boy, attended school in Salem, Massachusetts, and served in the navy from 1863 to 1870. But foreign-born Chinese veterans, having fought for the United States of America, sought to become its naturalized citizens. Congress had promised any honorably discharged foreign-born veteran citizenship upon petition. The 1790 Naturalization Law restricted naturalization to whites, however, and the Fourteenth Amendment, by which African Americans gained citizenship, did not apply to Chinese; then Congress passed the Exclusion Act in 1882 explicitly forbidding their naturalization. Yet these laws were applied so inconsistently that Hong Neok Woo was naturalized in Lancaster, Pennsylvania before the war; Thomas Sylvanus shortly after; Antonio Dardelle, despite Exclusion; but Edward Day Cohota denied; and William Hang, a Navy veteran, thoroughly ensnared in the contradictions.

Granted citizenship in New York on October 6, 1892, Hang voted until August 17, 1904, when he was arrested when exercising his franchise. Producing his naturalization papers, Hang was then subjected to a tirade by Joel M. Marx, assistant U.S, attorney, who accused the judge issuing the papers of inexcusable ignorance. Hang fought the ruling to no avail: On October 21,

1908, the New York Supreme Court vacated and set aside his citizenship. Thus Chinese veterans, however acculturated in language, religion, dress, and cultural practices, were relegated to permanent outsider status, whereas European veterans found their service and citizenship accelerated their complete assimilation. For European veterans, then, their ethnicity could be "just one aspect of their character, not the burning core of their very being." Chinese veterans, their ethnicity their sole definition by law, enjoyed no such luxury. And, after passage of the 1892 Geary Act, which extended exclusion and required all Chinese to carry identification proving their legal entry, Joseph Pierce changed his identity to Japanese; his children and those of Antonio Dardelle passed as white.

So powerful is the legacy of exclusion that despite its repeal in 1943, Chinese in the United States continue to be marginalized in the 21st century: Rep. Mike Honda, seeking passage of a resolution honoring Asian American and Pacific Islander soldiers who fought in the U.S. Civil War, found himself in an uphill battle; staying the course for five long years, he finally succeeded on July 30, 2008.

See also: Chinese in the Mississippi Delta; World War I; World War II

Further Reading

Association to Commemorate Chinese Serving in the American Civil War. 2012. Accessed September 11, 2012. http://sites.google.com/site/accsacw/.

Burton, William L. 1998. *Melting Pot Soldiers: The Union's Ethnic Regiments*. New York: Fordham University Press.

Costa, Dora L., and Matthew E. Kahn. 2008. *Heroes & Cowards: The Social Face of War*. Princeton, NJ: Princeton University Press.

Foenander, Terry. 1996. "Asians in the Civil War." Accessed September, 2012. http://www.tfoenander.com/Asians.html.

McCunn, Ruthanne Lum. 1996. "Chinese in the Civil War: Ten Who Served." *Chinese America: History & Perspectives* 10: 149–81.

Tchen, Jack Kuo Wei. 1999. *New York Before Chinatown: Orientalism and the Shaping of American Culture 1776–1882*. Baltimore, MD: The Johns Hopkins University Press.

U.S. Census. 1860. Files of Him Mark Lai.

"Vote Cast Here by Shipmate of Farragut." 1920. *San Francisco Chronicle*, November 5.

Ruthanne Lum McCunn

CHINESE VIETNAMESE

The term *Chinese Vietnamese American* reflects what many consider to be America's strength: diversity. This signifier reflects three complementary yet competing national, ethnic, cultural, linguistic, religious, and social groups and identities. Moreover, it reveals the inherent diversity associated within Chinese or Vietnamese or American and bespeaks the heterogeneous nature of Chinese

America and Vietnamese America. Understanding and accepting their inherent diversities will inevitably impact political representation and enfranchisement and possibly address the social, educational, economic, and health issues directly impacting several Southeast Asian refugee communities in America, in particular, with Chinese Vietnamese Americans. The "model minority" stereotype that suggests that Asian Americans (as a homogenous category) are somehow exemplary "Americans" when compared to other ethnic groups (e.g., blacks, Native Americans, and Latinos) ignores the real needs and concerns of refugee Southeast Asian Americans (e.g., Vietnamese, Hmong, Lao, and Cambodian Americans). Asian American scholars, activists, and community workers are aware of the negative consequences of lumping refugee Southeast Asian Americans into the "model minority," but the

Chinese Vietnamese refugees are rescued by the USS *Blue Ridge* in May 1984, after eight days aboard a tiny craft. Fleeing their homeland on crowded fishing boats and makeshift vessels, Chinese Vietnamese refugees became an ever-visible reminder of the Vietnam War for decades after the fall of Saigon in April 1975. (Defense Visual Information Center)

U.S. Census and major funding institutions (e.g., Ford Foundation) have yet to accept these communities as distinct communities with specific needs, which results in racializing them as "Asian" and perpetuating disparities in access to educational, social, and political resources. A long-standing problem for the Chinese Vietnamese American communities in the United States is their having to claim one or the other as their ethnicity and ancestry. There has been a dearth of studies addressing their needs and concerns.

A considerable segment of Chinese Vietnamese refugees arrived in America via Hong Kong. The duration of their stay in Hong Kong varied, but their displacement from Vietnam connects them all. Changing immigration patterns has drastically transformed what it means to be Asian in America. This chapter provides an experiential account of first-generation refugee resettlement and

the formation of identities for Chinese Vietnamese refugees who arrived in America via Hong Kong. An examination of generational conflicts and historical awareness among those of the first generation and their American-born children will illuminate the complex process of identity formation and community identification. Although the dislocation and displacement was a tremendous reference point for refugees, the powerful forces of American cultural values and ideals have caused intergenerational fractures. The process of settlement and integration into American society has thus been uneven, slippery, and difficult.

Post-1975, immigration reveals the dynamic changes in the Asian American landscape in general, and Chinese American landscape in particular, over the past three-and-a-half decades, which was significantly reconfigured by Indo-Chinese immigrants who arrived in the United States following the fall of Saigon. As the United States pulled out of the disastrous Vietnam War in April 1975, about 130,000 Vietnamese who were generally highly skilled and well educated, and who feared retaliation for their close associations with Americans, were airlifted by the U.S. government to bases in the Philippines, Guam, and Wake Island in the Northern Pacific Ocean. Although the task of resettling the initial wave of refugees from Vietnam (130,000 Vietnamese and 5,000 Cambodians) was complete by the end of 1975, many refuge-seekers continued to leave Cambodia, Laos, and Vietnam after the American evacuation and resettlement efforts ended. In the two years after the Communist victory, relatively few people escaped Vietnam, because the new authorities announced that certain groups of people (e.g., elected officials, employees of various counterinsurgency, religious leaders, intellectuals, military officers, the middle class, and ethnic Chinese Vietnamese) would be taken to "re-education camps" located at "New Economic Zones." There they were forced to till uncultivated land and admit to crimes against the new Communist State.

In light of these punitive measures, middle-class people and merchants, both ethnic Chinese and Vietnamese, began to escape by sea. At first, the American public did not hear much news about them because their numbers were small. The country of first asylum also wanted to keep their arrival as quiet as possible because they feared a larger exodus and influx if people in Vietnam found out that their compatriots managed to successfully seek refuge. By late 1977, as the number of boat refuge seekers increased—reaching an average of 1,500 refuge-seekers a month—Thailand, Singapore, and Malaysia, unable to accommodate refuge-seekers, began to push boats back to sea. Pressured by the international community for its moral and social responsibility, the United States started to respond through legislation. To counter the humanitarian crisis, President Jimmy Carter ordered the Seventh Fleet to seek vessels in distress in the South China Sea. A sizable percentage of refugees coming from Vietnam,

Laos, and Cambodia were of ethnic-Chinese backgrounds, speaking either Cantonese or the Chaozhou dialects.

From 1978 to 1989, ethnic Chinese Vietnamese were persecuted amid international power struggles, increasing ethnic tensions, changing Vietnamese government policies that force Vietnamese citizenship and, by extension, military duty, and changes in economic policies. Fear of being pushed into the jungles resulted in 160,000 ethnic Chinese from all over Vietnam migrating to China's southern provinces. By the end of this exodus, nearly a quarter-million Chinese Vietnamese had returned to China.

In May 1975 Hong Kong encountered its first batch of roughly 4,000 boat people, who were picked up by a Danish ship in the South China Sea. In 1976 only 191 refuge-seekers reached Hong Kong; 1,007 made it in 1997; and by 1978 nearly 9,000 arrived by small boats. Some were ethnic Chinese Vietnamese merchants who were able to utilize their contacts in Hong Kong to arrange for their passage. By spring 1979 Hong Kong housed 17,000 boat people. The trafficking of refugees became a lucrative business in Vietnam and resulted in an international refugee crisis. The massive influx of new refugee-seekers placed greater and greater pressure on the limited resources in Hong Kong, which resulted in changing policies. A conference convened by U.N. Secretary General Kurt Waldheim in Geneva (July 17–19, 1979), with the participation of the United States, Great Britain representing Hong Kong, and ASEAN countries all agreed that something had to be done to assist the country of first asylum (e.g., Hong Kong). The Geneva Conference resulted in immediate change, although the Hong Kong government became increasingly bitter because it was shouldering 35 percent of the boat people but was only allocated 13 percent of the resettlement to countries of second-asylum slots.

Like many refugees before them, the new arrivals had to be processed and resettled in America. Upon arriving in the United States, refugees were first sent to four government reception centers, located at Camp Pendleton, California; Fort Indiantown Gap, Pennsylvania; Fort Chaffee, Arkansas; and Eglin Air Force Base, Florida. There they were interviewed by voluntary agencies and matched with countrywide sponsors. They were initially distributed across all 50 states to minimize the negative impact of a refugee population. Despite the government's attempt to disperse the refugee population, California emerged as a concentrated center as a result of tertiary migration from other states. In southern California, a sizable population of Vietnamese refugees resides in Los Angeles, Orange County, and San Diego. In northern California, they are located in the Silicon Valley City of San Jose.

The United States responded to the international refugee crisis by increasing its intake of refugees to 168,000 per year. Soon the U.S. Congress passed the Refugee Act of 1980 as a way to facilitate the resettlement of refugees. The Act established the Office of Refugee Resettlement within the U.S. Department of Health and Human Services to administer the domestic resettlement program. Under the resettlement program, refugees can receive cash assistance, medical assistance, and supportive services intended to ease their initial adjustment to the United States, with the goal of facilitating for their economic self-sufficiency. Henceforth, a sizable portion of Chinese Vietnamese refugees have arrived in the United States after spending time in Hong Kong.

The immigration of the Vietnamese refugees to America is generally divided into two periods. The first period is divided into three waves. The first Vietnamese came just before the fall of Saigon (in total, about 10,000–15,000 refugees arrived), then another wave during the fall of some 80,000 refugees. Most of them were airlifted by helicopter. These refugees worked with the Americans and many had marketable skills and spoke at least functional English. This wave benefited from the large-scale guilt that Americans were struggling with, which translated into social services and a lot of government resources to assist them in their resettlement. The third wave witnessed 40,000–60,000 refugees who fled Vietnam, but by this time the American guilty conscience was wearing thin.

The refugees who started to flee Vietnam after 1978 were considerably worse off than those who had escaped in the first period. After 1978 most of the refugees who fled escaped in small boats that were not seaworthy. Overall, these refugees were called "boat people," and many were ethnic Chinese Vietnamese refugees who risked their lives to escape Vietnam. Some of them made it to the United States; many more were caught in detention facilities and either stayed there or were shipped back to Vietnam. Many ethnic Chinese Vietnamese who had long ago made Vietnam their home also left during the second period; specifically, the years between 1978 and 1980. Unlike the refugees who fled during the first period, they did not benefit from America's guilty conscience; rather, they entered during a period of economic recessions caused by a bust in the real estate market and high unemployment, which translated into "compassion fatigue." Antirefugee Americans invoked the popular question of the day: "Why are we taking care of the refugees from Indochina, and not our own people?"

There are four distinct stages in the development of Vietnamese and Chinese Vietnamese communities in America. The first stage was the wave of exiles who fled Vietnam immediately after the fall of Saigon in 1975. Most of them were from middle-class backgrounds, were Catholic converts, had English proficiency, and worked with the U.S. government before the fall. They built communities that revolved around manufacturing in California, and fishing in the Gulf Coast (e.g., Texas and Louisiana). The second stage included refugees who arrived between 1979 and 1982. The majority of these refugees were Chinese Vietnamese, popularly called "boat people." They were members of the petite bourgeoisie, were rural poor, had little or no English skills, had lower socioeconomic status, and arrived in large numbers. They were scattered by resettlement, but secondary migration led them to California and Texas, where there were Vietnamese refugee communities already established. The third stage occurred since the 1980s. This stage was community oriented based on the flourishing of ethnic businesses, civic organizations, and other community social structures that were established to serve the immigrant refugee population. The fourth stage reflects the development since the 1990s, when 1.5- and second-generation Americans grow up and become politically active. Their parents, refugees who fled Vietnam since 1975, began to become naturalized citizens and became politically active themselves, since their dream of returning to Vietnam was no longer realizable.

Similar to many immigrants before them, the first- and second-generation Chinese Vietnamese Americans will struggle to balance themselves between the forces of traditions and the new American ways, between being Chinese, Vietnamese, and American. Children who grow up in households with first-generation refugee parents expressed their childhood experiences positively, indicating that their parents have been successful in transmitting traditional values, morals, and customs to them, even though they may rebel against them. Many 1.5- and second-generations expressed that their parents did not talk to them about important topics like sex and birth control, and that they had to rely on their schools and friends to learn about it. They also said that a lot of what they learned about social values and norms, they learned indirectly through the hierarchical nature of their family structure, which emphasized respect for the elders that included their parents and their older siblings. Among the 1.5- and second-generation Chinese Vietnamese Americans, the process of identity formation is complex and complicate and reveals that for them, identity is fluid, flexible, and ever changing.

Chinese Vietnamese refugees and their U.S.-born children are understudied and underrepresented. They are, unfortunately, the invisible demographic group in America's political and academic landscape, even though they are physically visible in Chinatowns and Little Saigons in most of the urban centers. The Asian American movement must shift its focus from pan-Asian American solidarity to ethnic specific social justice to correct the historical imbalance of the last three-and-a-half decades. Southeast Asian refugees and their American children are at a disadvantage educationally, economically, and politically. To continue to ignore their real needs, even if unwillingly, in favor of pan-Asian American identity, benefits the first wave of Asian American immigrants and their descendants at the expanse of Southeast Asian American refugees and the generation who is growing up in America.

Not fully Chinese, Vietnamese, or American, Chinese Vietnamese refugees and their children are located outside of these communities, yet straddle them all simultaneously. For this very reason, future research on Chinese Vietnamese refugees and their children may reveal aspects of community, ethnic, identity, and cultural formations in Asian America that has not been documented and confirm that identity (e.g., Vietnamese, Chinese, and American) are always already shifting and situational.

See also: Chinese Cambodians

Further Reading

Gold, Steve. 1994. "Chinese-Vietnamese Entrepreneurs in California." In *The New Asian Immigration in Los Angeles and Global Restructuring*, edited by Paul Ong, Edna Bonacich, and Lucie Cheng. Philadelphia, PA: Temple University Press.

Trieu, Monica. 2009. *Identity Construction Among Chinese-Vietnamese Americans: Being, Becoming, and Belonging.* El Paso, TX: LFB Scholarly Publishing.

Jonathan H. X. Lee

CHINESE WOMEN AND THE CHINESE EXCLUSION ACT

The Chinese Exclusion Act, one of the most significant restrictions on the immigration of a specific racial group in American history, was signed into federal law by President Chester Arthur on May 6, 1882. It was drafted in response to the widespread anti-Chinese sentiments throughout the American western territories and sought to exclude Chinese immigrants from entering the United States. The Exclusion Act developed the terms of the Angell Treaty (1880) and made revisions to the Burlingame Treaty (1868) by restricting the immigration of Chinese laborers regardless of their conduct for a decade and prevented them from becoming U.S. citizens. In addition, all Chinese traveling in or out of the country were required to obtain an employment status certificate; individuals caught bringing Chinese into the country could be fined or imprisoned. As a result, families were separated; the number of Chinese women allowed into America was restricted, leading to a bachelor society; and illegal immigration surged with travelers claiming to be the children of U.S. citizens, known as paper sons and daughters. The Exclusion Act was amended (1884), expanded by the Scott Act (1888) and Geary Act (1892), revised by the McCreary Amendment (1893), and made permanent in 1902. In addition, the constitutionality of the Chinese Exclusion Act was upheld by the Supreme Court in *Chae Chan Ping v. United States* (1889), *Lem Moon Sing v. United States* (1895), and clarified in *United States v. Wong Kim Ark* (1898). The Exclusion

Act also foreshadowed similar migration restrictions put in place throughout the 1920s, such as the Immigration (1924) and National Origins Acts (1929), which limited Asian immigration. With the American-Chinese alliance during World War II, the Exclusion Act was repealed by the Magnuson Act (1943). However, only a limited number of Chinese were allowed to immigrate until the passage of the Immigration and Nationality Act (1965), which eliminated national and racial policies, permitted Chinese immigration, and allowed naturalized peoples to become citizens. In 2012 the U.S. House of Representatives passed a resolution formally apologizing for the Chinese Exclusion Act.

The Chinese Exclusion Act is seen as a response to the influx of Chinese immigrants during the California Gold Rush (1848–1855), the construction of the Transcontinental Railroad, and western development from the 1840s until the 1870s. By mid-century most Chinese settled into crowded urban regions such as San Francisco and held low-wage employment as servants and laundrymen. As regional prosperity slowed the previous toleration of immigrants declined and anti-Chinese sentiments were expressed by individuals such as California Governor John Bigler (1852–1856) and Denis Kearney as well as groups like the Supreme Order of Caucasians, Knights of Labor, and unions who blamed immigrants or "coolies," for depressing wage levels by working for less. Other detractors of immigrants argued that Chinese were racially inferior, that they refused to assimilate and accept American culture and values, and that they often lived in unsanitary conditions that fostered social diseases.

In response to these sentiments throughout the American west, legislation including immigration taxes and laundry-operation fees were imposed in order to limit the success of the Chinese workers and communities. Further laws during the period, including the Page Act (1875), specifically prohibited the entry of Asian "undesirables," including prostitutes, felons, and contract laborers. In addition, California law was modified, allowing the state to limit the types of employment opportunities open to Chinese immigrants. By 1879 Congress sought to pass national anti-Chinese legislation, which was vetoed first by President Hayes and later by President Arthur, as it violated the Burlingame Treaty (1868) with China. However, in 1880, with the modification of the Burlingame Treaty, the United States was free to restrict Chinese immigration and the Exclusion Act was passed.

With the passage of the Exclusion Act, Chinese women faced a different set of problems, given the law's focus on female immigration, employment, and marital status. In processing immigration applications, wives were classified as laborers, the same as their husband. As a result, immigration officials preferred single men in order to limit the number of workers entering the United States. Married women who sought to come to America often had to provide difficult-to-obtain government documentation guaranteeing their status. Even then, preferential treatment was often given to those women who were thought to be the wife of a merchant to avoid admitting laborers and prostitutes. Adding to this complexity, American-born Chinese women who had left the country and attempted to return often were left to deal with inconsistent admissions criteria. As such, the Chinese Exclusion Act limited the rights of Chinese women in particular with regard to their ability to immigrate with their families and by restricting the type of employment they could undertake in America. As a result of state and federal legislation targeting Asian women, the ratio of females to males in the Chinese community remained extremely low for decades, destabilizing families and restricting cultural development, limiting the range of occupations available to women, and, in many cases, directly leading to a disproportionate number of Chinese prostitutes in cities such as San Francisco.

See also: Chinese Exclusion Act (1882)

Further Reading

Chan, Sucheng, ed. 1991. *Entry Denied: Exclusion and the Chinese Community in America, 1882–1947.* Philadelphia, PA: Temple University Press.

Gyory, Andrew. 1998. *Closing the Gate: Race, Politics, and the Chinese Exclusion Act.* Chapel Hill: University of North Carolina Press.

McClain, Charles. 1994. *In Search of Equality: The Chinese Struggle Against Discrimination in Nineteenth-Century America.* Berkeley: University of California Press.

Sean Morton

CUBA COMMISSION REPORT, THE

This document presents excerpts of petitions and oral testimonies collected in the Caribbean island of Cuba in 1874. That year, the 27th year of the shipment of involuntary laborers from China's British treaty-ports to approximately 15 sites in the Caribbean and Latin America, an international commission traveled to Cuba to investigate claims that migrants were the victims of exploitation, physical violence, and other abuses characteristic of semi-enslavement. Its main findings, presented as *The Cuba Commission Report*, were officially published in Chinese, English, and French in 1876.

The person in charge of the report was Chinese dignitary Ch'en Lan Pin, thus occasional references to it as *The Ch'en Commission Report*. Ch'en was accompanied by numerous Chinese officials appointed by the Ch'ing government in Peking, Mr. A. Macpherson, British Commissioner Customs at Hankow, and Mr. A. Huber, Commissioner of Customs at Tientsin. Interpreters fluent in the languages of southern China, the homeland of most migrants, also worked with the commission.

At the time of the commission's visit, Cuba, still a Spanish colony, had received about 125,000 Chinese laborers, more than any other participant in the region's infamous "coolie trade." The commissioners were charged with meeting with Spanish officials and collecting firsthand information. They visited plantations, barracoons, jails, sugar warehouses, and small shops, conducting interviews and receiving documents in which men answered their questions. Of the more than 2,000 migrants with whom the commissioners came into contact, 90 claimed to have left China freely, and only 2 attested to humane treatment by their employers.

The report consists of two main parts. The first, entitled "Dispatch to Yamên," lists the places the commissioners visited and describes the investigation and general findings. Describing a situation in which cruelty is rampant and abuses often unendurable, they report kidnappings, suicides, whippings, maimings, and extortion. The second and longer part, "Replies to Inquiries," presents 50 questions, each of which is followed by excerpts from laborers' responses. Many migrants are identified by name, using Chinese characters as well as roman letters. The report establishes that the rights and provisions central to the contract of indenture had almost always been totally disregarded by recruiters, government officials (British, Chinese, and Spanish), and those purchasing contracts of indenture. It also documents "owners" withholding certificates of completion and forcing the Chinese to work for multiple years, well beyond the terms stipulated in contracts.

The publication of the report by the Imperial Maritime Customs Press in Shanghai suffered delays. It probably had a minimal impact on ending the illegal transport of migrants to Cuba, given that the last shipment of laborers took place in 1874. Nevertheless, the commission's work succeeded in raising awareness about the many problems faced by overseas Chinese in general, suggesting that laborers' grievances were exacerbated by both racism and the absence of Chinese consulates and missions. The commissioners' use of detailed, first-person accounts to confront widespread abuse and simultaneously influence international policy make *The Cuba Commission Report* a significant publication in the 19th-century history of human rights.

See also: Chinese and Cuba's Ten Years' War (1868–1878); Chinese in Cuba

Further Reading

Helly, Denise. 1993. *The Cuba Commission Report: A Hidden History of the Chinese in Cuba. The Original English-Language Text of 1876*. Baltimore, MD: The Johns Hopkins University Press.

Walicek, Don E. 2007. "Chinese Spanish in 19th-Century Cuba: Documenting Sociohistorical Context." In *Synchronic and Diachronic Perspectives on Contact Languages*, edited by M. Huber and V. Velupillai, 297–324. Amsterdam, NL: John Benjamins.

Yun, Lisa. 2008. *The Coolie Speaks, Chinese Indentured Laborers and African Slaves in Cuba*. Philadelphia, PA: Temple University Press.

Don E. Walicek

DOLLAR DIPLOMACY IN CHINA

Dollar Diplomacy is a term associated with U.S. foreign policy during the presidency of William Howard Taft (1909–1913). It was enacted by Secretary of State Philander Knox (1909–1913) to enhance U.S. international influence, promote American business and financial interests, and improve the stability of foreign nations, while limiting European intervention into zones of strategic importance to the nation. This policy was initially focused on protecting and expanding U.S. interests in Central America by extending Theodore Roosevelt's (1901–1909) Corollary to the Monroe Doctrine, which asserted the right of the United States to intervene when nations became so politically or economically unstable that they were vulnerable to European intervention. The proposed solution promoted the expansion of U.S. investment and business institutions into these regions to foster reform and thereby benefit U.S. interests.

While initially focused on Central America, Taft and Knox also hoped to offset increasing Russian and Japanese influence in Southeast Asia by implementing the policy of Dollar Diplomacy. In particular, the administration lobbied U.S. banks to invest in Asian projects that could be used to simultaneously repay loans to European, Russian, and Japanese creditors, promote regional development, and grant control of Pacific markets to U.S. businesses, the hope being that this would eliminate foreign investment and influence in the region as well as begin to incorporate Asian markets into the U.S. economy. The goal was to control these regions by slowly dominating their financial infrastructure, which by extension would provide America leverage in international political decisions. In creating a stable environment for U.S. investment, these policies would prompt regional development, facilitate further U.S. commercial growth, and increase the international influence of the United States while avoiding the need for direct military intervention. Taft argued that the policy traded "dollars for bullets."

However, U.S. investment into Asian projects, such as the construction of major rail lines in China, ultimately produced only a minimum profit as both Russian and Japanese interests undermined the undertakings. Future investment by U.S. institutions became increasingly limited, and Taft's Dollar Diplomacy in Asia was deemed a failure. Neither the regional stability nor rising U.S. influence ever materialized, and U.S. policies simultaneously became increasingly and evidently exploitive.

The phrase "Dollar Diplomacy" gained negative connotations and is now used to refer to the manipulation of a foreign nation's internal affairs for another country's financial gain. It is critiqued as economic imperialism and criticized as the wasteful use of government resources and interests to promote independent commercial and business goals without evident benefit to the nation. For these reasons, by 1913 Taft had essentially abandoned Dollar Diplomacy and the policy was later rejected by the Woodrow Wilson administration (1913–1921). Despite this, however, the essential strategy of Dollar Diplomacy—using businesses, loans, and economic policies to control foreign nations and achieve international goals through economic means—survived. A prime example is the Bretton Woods system, which utilized financial institutions, humanitarian organizations, corporations, and other private agencies as instruments to advancing U.S. policies without the formal involvement of the U.S. government.

See also: Sino-U.S. Relations

Further Reading

Coletta, Paola. 1973. *The Presidency of William Howard Taft*. Lawrence: University Press of Kansas.

Rosenberg, Emily. 1982. *Spreading the American Dream: American Economic and Cultural Expansion, 1890–1945*. New York: Hill and Wang.

Rosenberg, Emily. 1999. *Financial Missionaries to the World: The Politics and Culture of Dollar Diplomacy, 1900–1930*. Cambridge, MA: Harvard University Press

Sean Morton

HIP SING TONG (XIESHENG TANG)

Another spinoff from the Hongmen, the Hip Sing Tong (Xiesheng Tang) shares similar rituals and regulations with other Chinese secret societies in America. Unlike other secret societies, it claims to have started in Victoria, Canada, rather than in San Francisco, as early as the 1860s. Despite that claim, contemporary newspaper articles make it clear that it came to Victoria from somewhere else—probably San Francisco—in the mid-1880s. Further, it lasted only about two years in Victoria, after which it disappeared and never returned to Canada. Its known early lodges appeared in several western U.S. cities in the 1880s. By the 1890s it had reached smaller cities like Lewiston, Idaho, Astoria, Oregon, and Spokane, Washington. Branches on the East Coast and then the Midwest followed in the late 1890s. Its expansionary policies helped it become the only Chinese secret society besides the Chee Kung Tong to have a truly national presence.

The Hip Sing Tong has a colorful history. After decades of peaceful coexistence, especially in the Northwest, the society became involved in a series of bloody "tong wars" in California and New York. Its quarrels with the On Leong Tong in New York were led by several outstanding but unscrupulous individuals who some regard as Chinese Godfathers: Mock Duck, Eddie Gong, and Bennie Ong. In 1930 Eddie Gong published a personal memoir, *Tong War!*, which provided the first detailed insider's account of any Chinese tong in America. Although he and his collaborator, a reporter named Bruce Grant, treated the history of the Hip Sing as a series of gallant but violent episodes, much like chapters in the classic Chinese gangster novel, *The Water Margin*, Gong makes it clear that even then the Hip Sing had a benevolent, public-spirited side. Later he was one of those who led the Hip Sing into raising significant financial support for China in its war against Japan.

Since World War II, the Hip Sing has changed directions to play a positive role in Chinese communities. In 1951 it officially changed its name to the Hip Sing Association (*gonghui*). It is now involved in many civic programs, providing scholarships for the young as well as senior services. In the 1970s it even started a federally insured credit union for its members. Hip Sing members quite often hold leadership positions in other organizations, several serving as directors of the Chinese Consolidated Benevolent Associations. Far from the old Mock Duck days, recent Hip Sing officers have a reputation as educated and responsible community leaders. Today the Hip Sing occupies a prominent place in many Chinatowns. With national headquarters in San Francisco (*Jinmen xie sheng zong gonghui*), it has semi-independent branches in Boston, New York, Philadelphia, Washington D.C., Atlanta, Cleveland, Pittsburgh, Minneapolis, Chicago, Houston, San Antonio, Denver, Seattle, and Portland.

See also: Bing Kung Tong; Chee Kung Tong; Hongmen; Hop Sing Tong (Hesheng Tang); Secret Societies

Further Reading

Bronson, Bennet, and Chuimei Ho. 2015. *Coming Home in Brocade: Chinese in the Early American Northwest*. Seattle, WA: Chinese in Northwest America Research Committee.

Gong, Eng Ying, and Bruce Grant. 1930. *Tong War! The First Complete History of the Tongs in America*. New York: Nicholas L. Brown.

Bennet Bronson and Chuimei Ho

HONG KONG

Hong Kong, now officially known as the Special Administrative Region of China, shares a land border with mainland China in the north and consists of four main areas: Hong Kong Island, the Kowloon Peninsula, the New Territories, and the outlying islands. Formerly a fishing village with a small population, Hong Kong became a British colony during the First Opium War (1839–1842) on August 29, 1842, under the Treaty of Nanking. The city remained under British administration from 1841 to 1997, excluding the Japanese occupation from 1941 to 1945. While a British colony, Hong Kong became an important trading center regionally as well as an influential international financial hub. As stipulated in the 1984 Sino-British Joint Declaration, Britain returned Hong Kong's sovereignty to China in 1997. During the 1990s, a wave of transnational Hong Kong migrants entered the United States before the return of Hong Kong to China, fearing the loss of civil liberties, investments, and finance. By mid-2000s, as a

Protesters raise placards with Chinese words that read "End the one party dictatorship" and yellow umbrellas, the symbol of their democracy movement, as hundreds of people march on a downtown street in Hong Kong on May 31, 2015. The march marks the 26th anniversary of China's bloody crackdown on Tiananmen Square on June 4th, and was followed by an annual candlelight vigil. (AP Photo/Vincent Yu)

result of relative stability and exponential growth in the Chinese market, many returned to Hong Kong, some investing in real estate in growing Chinese cities, such as Shenzhen, situated immediately north of Hong Kong.

With the "One Country, Two Systems" policy, the People Republic of China promised Hong Kong a high degree of political and economic autonomy for 50 years. After the handover, there have been visible changes in Hong Kong's economic, language, and political systems. Economically, labor-intensive industries in Hong Kong have transferred to mainland China and Hong Kong now focuses more on finance, trade, and shipping. A bilingual/trilingual policy has been introduced to schools to make sure students learn Cantonese, English, and Mandarin. Politically, despite the promise of "One Country, Two Systems," the Hong Kong government has had difficulty balancing independence and the growing influence of Beijing. For example, an electoral process outlined by the Chinese government on August 31, 2014, only notionally allows for full democracy by providing a limited number of preselected candidates. The protests and events that have taken place in the months following Beijing's announcement, and which are still continuing, have become known as the Umbrella Movement.

See also: Cantonese; Opium Wars (1840 and 1856); Taiwan

Further Reading

Courtauld, Caroline, May Holdsworth, and Simon Vickers. 1997. *The Hong Kong Story*. Hong Kong: Hong Kong University Press.

Scott, Ian. 1989. *Political Change and the Crisis of Legitimacy in Hong Kong*. Honolulu: University of Hawai'i Press.

Tammy Ho Lai-Ming

HONGMEN

The father of all North American secret societies was the cluster of closely linked secret societies called Hongmen ("Hong Gate"), said to have been generated from the Hongshun Tang, the second of the original five divisions of the Tiandi Hui ("Heaven and Earth Society"). In its early days in America, the Hongmen seems to have been considered identical with the Hongshun Tang and was also known as Yixing Gongsi ("Company for Promoting Integrity"), or Sanhe Hui ("Triad Society" or "Three Harmonies Society"). The Triad name, now almost a synonym for Chinese crime in East and Southeast Asia, soon went out of use in the Americas. For more than 150 years, the Hongmen has not used the Triad name.

All members were sworn to overthrow the Qing Dynasty that ruled China, which meant they were fiercely persecuted by the imperial government in Beijing. Such societies existed in China from the 18th century onward, had spread to Southeast Asia by the early 19th century, and came to California with the first Chinese gold miners in 1849–1850. As early as 1854, local English-language newspapers reported that the "Hung Society" was active in San Francisco.

The Hongmen Society not only was among the earliest Chinese organizations to appear in North America but was also the first to be open to members who did not have the same birthplace or surname. For most of the 19th century, the Hongmen and its immediate derivatives held sway over Chinese North America, adding new names along the way. By 1871 it had begun calling itself in English "the Chinese Masons" and by 1880, Chee Kung Tong (Zhigong Tang, "Hall of Universal Justice"). Today, the Chee Kung Tong is the only secret society that still carries "Hongmen" as part of its title. It and the Bing Kung Tong are the only ones that retain the ancient Tiandi Hui style of tracking years by using the term "*tianyun*," or "heaven cycle." A few objects with that term can still be seen in Hongmen-CKT and BKT lodges at the present day. These derivative societies often used Tiandi Hui rituals and considered themselves to be, in part at least, its heirs. They protected and provided benefits to members, emphasizing loyalty and comradeship, qualities embodied by Guandi, the patron deity of all secret societies

Because membership was not restricted to birthplace or family names, the Hongmen Society was able to absorb large numbers of members from different walks of life. In derivative societies, even though Chinese men were the majority, women and even non-Chinese men became members. These societies, however, courted notice by the Chinese and non-Chinese public. Historically, their dragon and lion dances in Chinese New Year parade often elicited very positive reports from journalists. Showy funeral services for deceased leaders were other eye-catching events for the press.

It must be said, however, that certain of these derivative societies are remembered as violent and criminal. Like the modern Triad societies of East and Southeast Asia, which those derivatives closely resembled, some lived by extorting protection money from gambling houses, brothels, and legitimate businesses. They also fought fiercely for control of those revenue sources. Later, the white press would call these quasi-criminal organizations, "tongs," and their disputes over turf, "*tong* wars."

Four derivative secret societies are the Chee Kung Tong, which was in many cities identical with the Hongmen, the Bing Kung Tong, the Hip Sing Tong, and the Hop Sing Tong. Although all have had episodes of disagreement and fought occasional tong wars, these four large tongs should also be regarded as important grassroots organizations. They did much for their members and communities, joined in support of such causes as Chinese independence and resisting Japanese aggression in the Pacific, and assisted many sojourner members to survive problems and to return to their families in China. Most rarely engaged in crimes more severe than gambling.

Many other tongs existed. Among those of real historical importance, although not discussed here, are the Suey Sing Tong (Cuisheng Tang) on the West Coast and the On Leong Tong (Anliang Tang) in the eastern United States. Those have survived. Most of the rest have simply disappeared.

See also: Bing Kung Tong; Chee Kung Tong; Hip Sing Tong (Xiesheng Tang); Hop Sing Tong (Hesheng Tang); Secret Societies

Further Reading

Bronson, Bennet, and Chuimei Ho. 2015. *Coming Home in Brocade: Chinese in the Early American Northwest*. Seattle, WA: Chinese in Northwest America Research Committee.

Gong, Eng Ying, and Bruce Grant. 1930. *Tong War! The First Complete History of the Tongs in America*. New York: Nicholas L. Brown.

Bennet Bronson and Chuimei Ho

HOP SING TONG (HESHENG TANG)

Judging by mentions in the English-language press, the Hop Sing Tong (Hesheng Tang) is older than most other American secret societies. Like the Hip Sing, with which its historical relations were touchy, it must be either a spinoff or a quasi-facsimile of the Hongmen. Also like the Hip Sing, it does not use either the Hongmen or Chinese Mason names.

Interestingly, the Hop Sing first appeared not in a coastal city but in a rich silver-mining area in the interior, Virginia City, Nevada. It is mentioned there repeatedly by California newspapers in the mid-1870s but is not said to be in California itself until 1881 and in the Northwest until the late 1880s. The official history of the Hop Sing states that its first branch was founded in 1875 in San Francisco. Because several newspapers place it in Virginia City a year earlier, that 1875 date may have to be modified. A possible relic of its early Nevada career is the existence of a chapter, apparently still active, in Reno.

Almost from the outset, the Hop Sing had a reputation for aggression, at different times fighting for or against most of the other warlike tongs in the western United States: the Suey Sing Tong (Cuisheng Tang), the Hip Sing Tong, the Bing Kung Tong, and many others. Even the Chee Kung Tong, normally sacrosanct, seems to have been targeted by the Hop Sing on at least one occasion, when the Hop Sin succeeded in taking over the CKT's temple, and presumably the rest of its property, in Boise, Idaho, in about 1915. To the society's credit, it seems to have taken good care of the temple after acquiring it. That kind of interconnected relationship with other tongs continues. In 2014, when San Francisco's Chee Kung Tong got into trouble with the law, Hop Sing Tong too was investigated. This is partly because membership of the two tongs can overlap. Today Hop Sing and Hip Sing still jointly sponsor the annual Bomb Festival in Marysville, California.

The Hop Sing Tong stands out among other secret societies in valuing such traditional cultural symbols as good calligraphy and acknowledging a connection with the imperial Manchu regime in Beijing. The tong seems to have made an effort in finding high-level imperial officials to compose and pen its dedicatory signboards. Today we can still admire the splendid calligraphy on an inscription at the front door of Seattle's Hop Sing building, brushworked by Xia Tonghe in 1898, and on another inscription in the San Francisco headquarters of the Society, written by Zhu Ruzhen in 1909; fittingly, the latter was inscribed for the Hop Sing's recreational/economic subbranch, "*yiqiang gongsuo.*"

Both of the calligraphers involved were noted scholars as well as officials of the Manchu regime. Zhu in particular was a confirmed loyalist who remained outspokenly faithful to the Manchus until the very end. The interesting question is, did the Hop Sing know about or mind Zhu's political preferences, at a time when most Chinese in America supported either the Chinese Empire Reform Association or Sun Yat-sen's revolutionaries? Surely, literate observers pointed out to the Hop Sing that posting Zhu's inscription meant that the Tong was taking the side of the Manchus, whom all secret societies in the Tiandi Hui tradition were sworn to overthrow. Why did the Tong commission and keep the inscription? Could they have allowed the love of beautiful calligraphy to override the spirit of the Tiandi Hui?

Today, the Hop Sing joins the Hip Sing and others as a bulwark of the traditional Chinese American community in a number of western Chinatowns: In San Francisco (where its headquarters is located), Portland, Seattle, Denver, Boise, Reno, Marysville, Vallejo, San Jose, Monterey, Santa Barbara, Los Angeles, Calexico, and perhaps Folsom. Some of branches, like that in Marysville, is inactive for lack of members. Others, however, like the one in Seattle, appear to be thriving.

See also: Bing Kung Tong; Chee Kung Tong; Hip Sing Tong (Xiesheng Tang); Hongmen; Secret Societies

Further Reading

Bronson, Bennet, and Chuimei Ho. 2015. *Coming Home in Brocade: Chinese in the Early American Northwest.* Seattle, WA: Chinese in Northwest America Research Committee.

Gong, Eng Ying, and Bruce Grant. 1930. *Tong War! The First Complete History of the Tongs in America.* New York: Nicholas L. Brown.

Bennet Bronson and Chuimei Ho

HUIGUAN (THE CHINESE SIX COMPANIES)

Huiguan are family associations or district groups composed of peoples from the same regions in China. Central to Chinese and later Chinese American communities, Huiguan were mutual aid societies that influenced the lives of most Chinese immigrants in the 19th century by providing social, economic, and legal assistance to those of Chinese descent. Huiguan in America aided laborers with their passage by providing temporary housing, financial assistance, help in finding employment, social support and credit, care for the sick, and death benefits, and maintaining correspondence between American Chinatowns and families in China. They also promoted the development of Chinese immigrant communities and sought to deter rising anti-Chinese sentiments, retained lawyers to defend the rights of Chinese immigrants, and pursued lawsuits against discriminatory legislation such as the Chinese Exclusion Act (1882), Scott Act (1888), and Geary Act (1892), as well as lobbying politicians.

Huiguan were organized by a hierarchy of self-appointed merchants who were successful community leaders in immigrant enclaves and Chinatowns throughout America. They maintained strict social control arbitrating local disputes and enforced the repayment of loans by Chinese immigrants. In the 1850s, in response to discriminatory laws and rising anti-Chinese public sentiments in California, Chinese community associations were established and unified as the Four Houses. When two more organizations in San Francisco joined in 1862, the existing Huiguan became known as the Chinese Six Companies until the passage of the Chinese Exclusion Act, when they formed the Chinese Consolidated Benevolent Association (CCBA).

These organizations were politically active in negotiations for the Burlingame Treaty (1868) and in reminding President Ulysses Grant in 1876 of the contributions of Chinese immigrants to western development in the United States. In response to the Geary Act, which sought the mandatory registration of all Chinese in America and established that any such individuals could be deported without judicial recourse, the CCBA advised Chinese immigrants to refuse to register or carry identity cards. As a result, by the legislated deadline few Chinese had complied with the law, and a new deadline was set by the McCreary Amendment (1893). Despite opposition from the CCBA, the Supreme Court upheld the government's right to register and deport noncitizens in *Fong Yue Ting v. United States* (1893). Regardless, the Chinese Six Companies, concerned that the law would lead to harassment of Chinese merchants and laborers, promoted enforcement of the legislation to pursue criminals and convicts rather than earnest Chinese immigrants. The CCBA's resistance to the Geary Act and the Supreme Court's decision established precedents for legislation and legal debates regarding immigration and Civil Rights in America for the coming century.

The CCBA later lobbied Congress during World War II (1939–1945) for the repeal of the Exclusion Act and advocated immigrant rights. However by the 1960s–1970s the organization was seen as too conservative amid the Pan-Asian and civil rights movements of the period and owing to shifting demographics in Chinese immigration was increasingly critiqued by members of the Chinese American communities as nonrepresentative. Regardless, from the mid-19th century through the late 20th century the Huiguan and later the CCBA were among the most influential organizations in Chinese American communities.

See also: Chinese Consolidated Benevolent Association

Further Reading

Chan, Sucheng, ed. 1991. *Entry Denied: Exclusion and the Chinese Community in America, 1882–1947.* Philadelphia, PA: Temple University Press.
Lai, Mark. 2004. *Becoming Chinese American: A History of Communities and Institutions.* Walnut Creek, CA: AltaMira Press.

Sean Morton

INTERNATIONAL CONTEXT OF CHINESE IMMIGRATION TO AMERICA, TO 1870

Chinese immigration to the United States in the 19th century until 1870 was shaped by a combination of factors, including internal political turmoil and financial instability throughout China, growing Western Imperial and economic influences in Southeast Asia, China's deepening trade deficit with European nations, and industrial and technological innovations. Concurrently, the rising demand for inexpensive labor during the California Gold Rush (1848–1858), development of national railway projects, and the range of economic possibilities in the United States provided many Chinese sojourners with the opportunity to support their families and villages at home. Therefore, an understanding of the international context of Chinese immigration to America is necessary to fully understand the dynamics and complexity of the period.

From 1800 until 1870 there was a period of worldwide political change. This included a political transformation for the French Empire following the rule of Napoleon Bonaparte (1804–1814, 1815), a shift away from slave labor and the reign of Queen Victoria over the British Empire (1837–1901), the rising international influence of Russia, the slow collapse of the Ottoman Empire following the Crimean War (1853–1856), the faltering control over Latin America by Spain, and the growth of European Imperialism and trade in Southeast Asia. In addition, the growth of market capitalism and international trade dominated by corporations such as the East India Company increased Western influence in China and exacerbated its financial problems.

For the British Empire in particular, this period led to further development of trade with China as Westerners sought products such as silk, tea, and ginseng, as well as markets for manufactured products. However, European and American demand for Chinese goods resulted in a trade deficit, which British businesses sought to offset by becoming involved in the illegal opium market. The result was a rise in tensions between Britain and China and the eventual outbreak of the First Opium War (1839–1842). This conflict concluded with passage of the Anglo-Chinese Treaty of Nanjing (1842), which greatly favored Western political and commercial interests, granting them almost complete access to Chinese products and markets. These events subsequently led to the collapse of the Cantonese monopoly of the opium trade and the decline of the Pearl Delta and Guangdong Province's regional economies. In addition, throughout this period, the Chinese junk was no longer used as the primary vessel for transporting cargo in the region, and traditional Chinese trade networks were soon replaced with a limited number of ports, such as Penang (1786), Singapore (1819), and Hong Kong (1842). These new ports facilitated European and American shipping and promoted increasing Chinese involvement in world affairs. It is also important to note that the context of this era and the increased demand for cheap labor in the West is necessarily defined by the British closure of the Atlantic slave trade with the passage of the Abolition of the Slave Trade Act (1808) and the need to inexpensively replace their workforce.

In the United States, the 19th century was characterized by rapid growth into the Midwest and the Pacific Coast of North America. Expansion occurred following purchase of the Louisiana Territory from France (1803), purchase of Florida from Spain (1821), independence of Texas (1821), annexation of New Mexico (1846), and purchase of Arizona (1854). These acquisitions fostered American desire to develop and assert control across the continent. Concurrent to these events were developing racial tensions leading to Civil War (1861–1865), Reconstruction (1863–1877), and a shift away from the use of slave labor. These conditions coupled with expansion of the manufacturing industry to create a demand for cheap labor. Therefore, while Chinese American relations and trade had existed since the late 18th century, it was the onset of the California Gold Rush, construction of the Transcontinental Railway (1863–1869), rapid regional development in the West, and agricultural growth in America that led to the demand for an abundance of cheap labor. America's willingness in the mid-19th century to expand its relations with China is evidenced in the Wangxia Treaty (1844), which opened new ports and increased trade between the nations as well as allowed foreigners to own land in China. In addition, the United States passed the Act to Encourage Immigration (1864) to promote the migration of laborers and the Burlingame Treaty (1868), which guaranteed and protected the rights of Chinese immigrants in America.

In response to the global context of expanding European Imperialism, as well as British and American industrial capitalism, many of the internal problems within China were exacerbated and in turn facilitated the international migration of Chinese labor. Indeed, throughout the 19th century, owing to the economic decline of China, political instability of the Qing Dynasty, rising national taxation, peasant rebellions, and loss of land, people in coastal villages were increasingly willing to explore international opportunities to support their families. This drive was amplified by technological innovations of the period, including the advent of steam-powered shipping (1823), improved transoceanic travel, widespread use of the telegraph, and modernization of postal services that enabled Chinese sojourners to maintain ties with their families and villages. Hence, a combination of regional problems in China, coupled with the economic prosperity available abroad in locations such as Australia, Hawai'i, Brazil, Mexico, and the United States led to the migration of Chinese men, either as coolie laborers or entrepreneurial sojourners. The result was that local economies in coastal regions throughout China soon developed around the international demands for migratory labor and wages that were returned to the region.

The mass migration of Chinese laborers to the United States reached its zenith between 1850 and 1870, but declined throughout the 1870s during a period of deepening economic recession in America, which fostered growing public and legislative demands to limit the success and development of Chinese culture in the United States. As a result, the unrestricted immigration of Chinese persons largely ceased by 1882 with passage of the Chinese Exclusion Act, which effectively halted migration of Chinese into America until World War II.

See also: Burlingame Treaty (1868); Chinese Immigration During the Gold Rush; Opium Wars (1840 and 1856); Sino-U.S. Relations

Further Reading

Chan, Sucheng. 1990. "European and Asian Immigrants into the United States in Comparative Perspective, 1820s to 1920s." In *Immigration Reconsidered: History, Sociology, and Politics*, edited by Virginia Yans-McLaughlin. New York: Oxford University Press.

Yans-McLaughlin, Virginia, ed. 1990. *Immigration Reconsidered: History, Sociology, and Politics*. New York: Oxford University Press.

Sean Morton

LOCKE, CALIFORNIA

This historic town of Locke is a unique example of a rural Chinese American community that was established, built, and inhabited exclusively by Chinese during the early 20th century. Locke is an unincorporated community in California's Sacramento-San Joaquin River Delta. Originally, it was named Lockeport, after George Locke, the owner of the land it was built on. In August 2, 1970, Locke was listed on the National Register of Historic Places, then in December 14, 1990, it was designated a National Historic Landmark District.

Locke was not built until the Chinese had been engaged in the Sacramento-San Joaquin River Delta region's agriculture for half a century. The town began in 1912 and was built overnight, when three Chinese merchants, two from Vorden—they were Chinese immigrants from the Zhongshan district of Guangdong province—and one from Walnut Grove, who was from the *Szeyap* region (a collective name for the four districts of Xinhui, Thaishan, Kaiping, and Enping) contracted tradesmen to construct three buildings. The first building, built by Chan Tin Sin, was a dry goods store and beer saloon. Yuen Lai Sing built a gambling hall, and Owyang Wing Cheong built a hotel and restaurant. Shortly afterward, the Canton Hotel was built, along with several other structures. Chinese Americans went to Locke to escape anti-Chinese violence in places like San Francisco. These early businesses reflected the needs of the Chinese migrant labor force who needed rooms to sleep in, stores to shop in, and gambling houses to relax in.

Locke grew after the Chinatown in Walnut Grove was destroyed by a fire on October 7, 1915, and Zhongshan district Chinese merchants relocated to

Members of the St. Mary's Drum and Bell Corp. from San Francisco march down Main Street during a celebration in Locke, California, on May 11, 2002. The sale of the town's land to Sacramento County will enable building owners to get loans to make improvements to the nation's last remaining free-standing rural Chinese American town. (AP Photo/Steve Yeater)

nearby towns instead of joining the *Szeyap* residents to rebuild. The Zhongshan natives were Yuehai-speaking Chinese from the Zhongshan region of Guangdong province in China. A committee of Chinese merchants, led by Lee Bing, Chan Hing Sai, Tom Wai, Chan Dai Kee, Ng So Hat, Chan Wai Lum, Chow Hou Bun, and Suen Dat Suin was created to approach George Locke with a proposal to build on his land. George Locked reached an agreement with the Chinese merchants, and they leased land from him because the California Alien Land Law of 1913 prohibited ownership of land by immigrants who are ineligible to become naturalized citizens. Locke thus became a town built for and by the Chinese and resided by the Chinese until the early 1990s. By 1920, Locke was completed and the all-wooden hamlet has remained unchanged for over a century. During its prime, Locke, similar to other Chinatowns, had a town hall that later housed the Chinese-language school, general stores, herb shops, fish markets, brothels, clothing stores, restaurants, and theatre. At one point, Locked even housed a Chinese Kuomintang political party local chapter.

The early Chinese migrants went to work on the Sacramento-San Joaquin River Delta building levees. From the late 1850s to the early 1920s, thousands of Chinese migrants found employment in agriculture in California, except in the Imperial Valley. As such, Chinese agricultural laborers played a significant role in the success of many California corps. The population of Locke waxed and waned with the harvesting season that reached as much as 1,500 Chinese residents, with farmhands sharing rooms in boarding houses. Chinese residents who lived in residential homes behind Main Street took in boarders during this season. For nearly five decades Locke was inhabited sole by Zhongshan Chinese. During the 1940s and 1950s a large portion of the Chinese American population moved out of Locke after receiving their education and moved to major urban centers, such as Los Angeles and San Francisco. In 1977 a Hong Kong-based developer purchased the town from the Locke heirs and sold it in 2002 to the Sacramento Housing and Redevelopment Agency. In 2004, the Agency sold the land to the families who have been living there for many years.

See also: Alien Land Law (1913); Anti-Chinese Violence; Samyap and Szeyap

Further Reading

Gillenkirk, Jeff, and James Motlow. 1978. *Bitter Melon: Inside America's Last Rural Chinese Town.* Berkeley, CA: Heyday Books.

"Locke, California." May 18, 2015. Accessed July 16, 2015. http://www.locketown.com/.

"Locke, California: Historic Chinese Town." 1998. Accessed July 16, 2015. http://www.scrapbookpages.com/photoessays/Locke/Locke02.html

Jonathan H. X. Lee

OPIUM WARS (1840 AND 1856)

By the 1830s Chinese products were in high demand in Europe but European products in China were not. This resulted in silver flowing from Britain to China. In an effort to counteract the deficit, Britain introduced opium to the Chinese market. The Qing government quickly banned it, and Britain contested the ban in force. Britain and China fought the First Opium War between 1839 and 1842. Britain won. The war ended with the Treaty of Nanking, which granted Britain gold, five treaty ports, preferential trading rights, and Hong Kong. This defeat, anti-Qing unrest, and subsequent economic difficulties began a long-term trend of Chinese immigration to the United States, spurred on by the discovery of gold in California in 1849. This was not the end, however; the failure of the 1842 treaty to satisfy Britain's ambitions in the region led to the Second Opium War 14 years later.

Britain and China fought the Second Opium War between 1856 and 1860. For China, the result was equally as disastrous as the first. Due to the defeat, Britain was able to further exploit Chinese trade at the expense of local populations, yielding increasing numbers of emigrants to the United States in the process.

See also: International Context of Chinese Immigration to America, to 1870

Further Reading

Lovell, Julia. 2014. *The Opium War: Drugs, Dreams and the Making of Modern China.* New York: Overlook Press.

Waley, Arthur. 1958. *The Opium War Through Chinese Eyes.* Palo Alto, CA: Stanford University Press.

Zachary S. Kopin

PAGE LAW (1875)

Enacted by the U.S. Congress on March 3, 1875, An Act Supplementary to the Acts in Relation to Immigration required that "the immigration of any subject of China, Japan, or any Oriental country" be "free and voluntary." The law was officially repealed in 1974.

Introduced and sponsored by Representative Horace F. Page, Republican of California, the so-called Page Law also required that the "the consul-general or consul of the United States residing at the port from which it was proposed to convey such subjects . . . ascertain whether such immigrant has entered into a contract or agreement for a term of service within the United States, for lewd or immoral purposes." Upon the completion of a satisfactory inspection and inquiry into the labor status and moral character of the immigrants, the consul would then issue a certificate permitting passage to the United States.

The law proscribed a maximum fine of $2,000 and imprisonment for not more than one year for any citizen or legal resident of the United States who knowingly transported immigrants from the Far East as laborers under "all contracts and agreements." Any such contractual arrangements and agreements were deemed "illegal importation" and void. It prohibited "the importation into the United States of women for the purposes of prostitution" and voided any such contracts "made in advance or in pursuance of such illegal importation." The law made it a felony for any person who "knowingly and willingly" engaged in the "importation of women into the United States for the purposes of prostitution," punishable by a maximum fine of $5,000 and imprisonment for not more than five years. The same penalty was applied to any person convicted of "knowingly and willingly" conveying "any woman to such purposes, in pursuance of such illegal importation and contract or agreement."

The Page Law provided penalties for violation of the revised immigration statutes of the United States and "any other section of the law prohibiting the [coolie]-trade." Any person convicted in a U.S. court "in advance or in pursuance of such illegal importation . . . to supply to another the labor of any [coolie] or other person brought into the United States" was subject to a fine "not exceeding five hundred dollars and imprisoned for a term not exceeding five years." The law reinforced section 2158 of An Act to Prohibit Coolie Trade of February 19, 1862, prohibiting any owner or captain of any seagoing vessel "registered, enrolled, or licensed" in the United States from participating in the transportation of contract laborers to foreign ports, and kept in place the 1862 law's provision of a maximum fine of $2,000 and a maximum imprisonment of one year for any such violation.

The law made it "unlawful" for "persons who are undergoing a sentence for conviction in their own country of felonious crimes" to immigrate to the United States, but allowed the immigration of those convicted of crimes deemed "political or growing out of or the result of such political offenses," and those "whose sentence has been remitted on condition of their immigration." Almost as an afterthought, it further prohibited immigration of any "women 'imported for the purposes of prostitution'" from any foreign port worldwide, not just ports of departure in the Far East.

The process by which the lawful or unlawful status of a ship's passengers was determined was vested in the law "under the direction of the collector of the port at which it arrives." Upon arrival, the law required that each vessel undergo an inspection to determine if "any such obnoxious persons are on board." No passenger could disembark until inspection, and if it was determined that any passengers were "of either of the classes whose importation is hereby forbidden," they were denied entrance to the United States "except in obedience to a judicial process issued pursuant to law." If any "aggrieved" person(s) denied entry under the law instituted a judicial review of the collector's decision, "it shall be the duty of the collector at said port of entry to detain said vessel until a hearing and determination of the matter are had."

If a judicial review determined that the inspector's decision to deny entry to "the obnoxious person or persons" was "in accordance" with the law, the immigrant was "returned on board of said vessel, and shall thereafter not be permitted to land." If the immigrant-petitioner sought a subsequent appeal to a higher federal court, the law required that "the master, owner, or consignee of the vessel shall give bond and security, to be approved by the court or judge hearing the case, in the sum of five hundred dollars for each such person permitted to land." Finally, the Act set in place the potential for forfeiture of "the vessel, by the acts, omissions, or connivance of the owners, master or other custodian or consignees . . . as in cases of frauds against the revenue laws, for which forfeiture is prescribed by existing law."

Scholars across all disciplines agree that the Page Law was the first race-based immigration restriction in the United States. Most of what has been written about the impact of the law focuses on the law's prohibition of Chinese

BEFORE THE PAGE LAW OF 1875

1854. A municipal committee visits Chinatown and reports to the Board of Alderman that most of the women were prostitutes. San Francisco passes municipal ordinance 546, To Suppress Houses of Ill-Fame Within the City Limits, directed at Chinese and Mexican brothels.

October 17, 1865. San Francisco municipal ordinance 666 empowers the San Francisco police with "the removal of Chinese prostitution and its concomitants, disease and filth, from the central portions of the city."

March 31, 1866. The California Legislature in An Act for the Suppression of Chinese Houses of Ill Fame declares all Chinese brothels "public nuisances."

July 23, 1866. San Francisco municipal ordinance 5766 empowers municipal health authorities to relocate Chinese brothels "as they shall deem advisable."

March 18, 1870. The California Legislature approves both An Act to Prevent the Importation of Chinese Criminals and to Prevent the Establishment of Coolie Slavery and An Act to Prevent the Kidnapping and Importation of Mongolian, Chinese and Japanese Females, for Criminal or Demoralizing Purposes, stating in the preambles to both acts that the laws were an "exercise of the police powers pertaining to the state."

February 7, 1874. The California Legislature amends the 1866 public nuisance act by striking the word "Chinese." The amendment was driven by concern that the 1866 act would not withstand constitutional scrutiny under the Fourteenth Amendment.

September 21, 1874. The U.S. Circuit Court for the District of California rules the 1870 California kidnapping act unconstitutional in the case *In Re Ah Fong*. Regarding the exclusion of the Chinese from California, U.S. Supreme Court Justice Stephen Field, presiding in circuit, writes that "If their further immigration is to be stopped, recourse must be had to the federal government, where the whole power of this subject lies."

Further Reading

The Codes and Statutes of the State of California. 1876. San Francisco, CA: A. L. Bancroft.

The General Laws of the State of California, from 1864 to 1871 Inclusive. 1871. San Francisco, CA: A. L. Bancroft.

San Francisco Municipal Reports for the Fiscal Year 1865-6, Ending June 30, 1866. 1866. San Francisco, CA: Towne and Bacon.

women. Historians of the Asian American immigrant experience conclude that the law inhibited the growth of Chinese American families in the United States, creating an imbalanced sex ratio that lasted for more than a century.

Other scholars look at the law in the context of the history of sexuality, acknowledging that at the most conservative estimates, 50 percent of the Chinese women who migrated to California in the last quarter of the 19th century were sex workers. The "Chinese Question" was written in California municipal ordinances and state laws that sought first to contain and control and then ultimately prohibit Chinese prostitution. These same scholars also examine the Page Law in the context of the role of concubinage and polygamy in Chinese cultural practice and the American popular belief that like contract labor and prostitution, concubinage and polygamy were forms of slavery. In this context, the Page Law has been viewed as an incidence of moral panic in American cultural identity. All agree that prostitution was a social problem not just limited to Chinese immigrant women at the time. For these scholars, racist assumptions about Chinese women's unredeemable and inherent immorality, as well as the fear that the disease-ridden Chinese prostitute could infect not just the physical body but the American body politic as well, motivated the exclusion of Chinese women.

Labor historians look to the economic origins of the Page Law, concluding that the Chinese laborer became a scapegoat for political demagogues during The Panic of 1873. Pointing to the earlier experience of anti-Chinese labor agitation in post–Gold Rush California, labor historians view the law, for better or worse, through the lens of white working-class labor solidarity and identity, and the popular belief among the California working class that Chinese docility threatened both employment and wages. These scholars also point out that the Page Law, sensitive to the "most-favored-nation" language of the Burlingame Treaty of 1868, privileged the Chinese merchant and scholar class while penalizing the unskilled laborer.

Political historians view the law in the context of reconstruction of the union at the end of the Civil War and how the economic downturn in the 1870s brought the Democratic Party to power in the House of Representatives while also narrowing Republican control of the Senate. That Horace Page was a Republican and a Californian has led some scholars to conclude that his anti-Chinese stance was partially a calculated decision to appeal to the popular sentiments of California's working-class voters. However, Page's congressional career was pronounced for his sponsorship of failed anti-Chinese bills and resolutions to restrict Chinese immigration and to renegotiate the Burlingame Treaty. In 1882, Page successfully sponsored the Chinese Exclusion Act of 1882.

Three months before the enactment of the Page Law, Republican President Ulysses S. Grant wrote in his annual message to Congress of "a generally conceded fact—that the great proportion of the Chinese immigrants who come to our shores do not come voluntarily." Grant's message failed to acknowledge that the Immigration Act of 1864 allowed for wage contracts to pay for an immigrant's cost of transportation and that such contracts were recognized under the 1864 law as neither slavery nor servitude, nor did he acknowledge the most-favored-nation status of the Burlingame Treaty. For Grant, involuntary servitude, "in a worse form does . . . apply to Chinese women," and "If this evil practice can be legislated against, it will be my pleasure as well as duty to enforce any regulation to secure so desirable an end." The Page Law was the solution.

Historians interested in the intersection of political and legal history look at the law in the context of the federal legislative branch embracing the federal judiciary's belief that under the Commerce Clause of the U.S. Constitution, the Page Law was the only constitutionally legitimate way to regulate immigration. They point out that the law was enacted months after the U.S. Circuit Court ruled that the California Legislature's enactment of An Act to Prevent the Kidnapping and Importation of Mongolian, Chinese, and Japanese Females, for Criminal or Demoralizing Purposes (1870) was an unconstitutional infringement on the federal government's regulation of commerce and not a proper application of police powers reserved to the states under the Tenth Amendment. While the states could not regulate immigration, the federal government could and, finally, would. These scholars point to the shared language of the voided California Act of 1870 and the later wording of the Page Law as a new but ultimately surmountable challenge for the Chinese and their allies. The Chinese in America now turned toward a tactical reliance on the Fifth and Fourteenth Amendments to the U.S. Constitution in their battle for civil rights.

For the student or scholar interested in contributing to a greater understanding of the significance of the Page Law, one area in need of exploration is an assessment of the law as a topic of study in the history of capitalism. From the bureaucratic management of the Page Law from ports of embarkation to ports of arrival, to the fines, imprisonment, and seizure of property sanctioned under the Act, no one has yet investigated the reactions and responses of the shipping companies to the law. Depending on the existence and accessibility of business archives and the personal papers of shipping company owners, executives, and lawyers, one might be able to more fully understand the significance of a law that not only demonized Chinese women in late-19th-century America, but also reduced their humanity to a cost/benefit calculation as a "human cargo" now deemed an undesirable import. The needs for further study are abundant.

See also: Chinese Exclusion Act (1882); Chinese Women and the Chinese Exclusion Act

Further Reading

Abrams, Kerry. 2005. "Polygamy, Prostitution, and the Federalization of American Immigration Law." *Columbia Law Review* 105 (April): 641–716.

Luibhéid, Eithne. 2002. *Entry Denied: Controlling Sexuality at the Border*. Minneapolis: University of Minnesota Press.

McClain, Charles J. 1994. *In Search of Equality: The Chinese Struggle Against Discrimination in Nineteenth-Century America*. Berkeley: University of California Press.

Peffer, George Anthony. 1986. "Forbidden Families: Emigration Experiences of Chinese Women Under the Page Law, 1875–1882." *Journal of American Ethnic History* 6 (Fall): 28–46.

U.S. Congress. 1875. *Revised Statutes of the United States, Passed at the First Session of the Forty-third Congress, 1873-'74*. Washington, DC: U.S. Government Printing Office.

U.S. Congress. 1875. *The Statutes at Large of the United States from December, 1873, to March, 1875, and Recent Treaties, Postal Conventions and Executive Proclamations*. Washington, DC: U.S. Government Printing Office.

David Alan Rego

PAPER SONS AND DAUGHTERS

The paper son or daughter system was a means through which Chinese immigrants circumvented exclusionary laws to enter the United States on identity papers claiming U.S. citizenship. This system evolved in response to legislation such as the Chinese Exclusion (1882), Scott Act (1888), and Geary Act (1892), which targeted Chinese immigrants and restricted who was allowed to enter America in an attempt to limit the growth of ethnic communities and their cultural influence within the United States. As a result of these acts, Chinatowns were bachelor societies with few families, prompting Chinese laborers to circumvent the system by using exemption clauses within the immigration codes, which stated that children of U.S.-born citizens could not be denied entry and could claim citizenship. Following the San Francisco earthquake (1906), which destroyed the majority of immigration and citizenship records, the government was unable to challenge claims to citizenship by Chinese immigrants. A system of falsified identities evolved that became popularly known as "paper sons," wherein Chinese immigrants would declare the birth of a child and then either use or sell the documentation, allowing others to claim to be the descendants of U.S. citizens and thereby gain entry into the country.

See also: San Francisco Earthquake (1906)

Further Reading

Lau, Estelle. 2007. *Paper Families: Identity, Immigration Administration, and Chinese Exclusion*. Durham, NC: Duke University Press.

Sean Morton

QUEUE ORDINANCE (1876)

The Queue Ordinance, also known as the Pigtail Ordinance, was one of a series of legislation passed in order to discriminate against the Chinese immigrant population living in California, specifically, the city of San Francisco. Chinese immigrants who helped to build the Transatlantic Railroad now settled in the area. California attracted people because of the mining industry; however, after the Gold Rush, it housed a great number of unemployed residents. The Transatlantic Railroad made travel easier, so despite the lack of opportunities available, people continued to travel west in search of a better life. This socioeconomic situation created tension between white Americans and Chinese immigrants. Many saw the immigrants as a growing problem and found a solution by enacting discriminatory policies.

On July 29, 1870, the Board of Supervisors of the city and county of San Francisco, which held the legislative power of the city and county, passed the Cubic Air Law, an ordinance that required all lodging houses and sleeping apartments to maintain 500 cubic feet of open space for each adult resident. Although the law did not appear discriminatory, the police department enforced it in Chinese areas but not in poor white areas. The ordinance required owners of the lodging houses guilty of breaking the law to pay a fine that ranged from $10 to $500, face imprisonment from 5 days to 3 months, or both. Occupants found guilty had to pay a fine that ranged from $10 to $50, face imprisonment of five days, or both. The majority of the Chinese residents chose imprisonment instead of paying the fine in order to protest the discriminatory practice. They filled the jail cells, so to force them to pay the fine instead of going to jail, on May 25, 1873, the Board introduced order number 1097, the Queue Ordinance.

A portrait of a Chinese prospector wearing the queue hairstyle in the California gold fields, ca. 1853. (Getty Images)

The Queue Ordinance declared that male prisoners upon arrival at the prison had to have their hair cut within an inch of their scalp. During this time, Chinese men wore their hair shaved in the front and the back portion in a long braid called a queue. This hairstyle signified their allegiance to China. Chinese people in America held on to this tradition because although they lived abroad, they planned to return home one day. Cutting off their queue would alienate them not only from their country but also from their community abroad. They also believed it would bring misfortune and one would suffer even after death. The Board of Supervisors passed the ordinance knowing about this belief system; it wanted to force the Chinese to pay the fine. The main goal of the policy was to discourage anymore Chinese from immigrating to California and encourage those already there to leave.

Because of the blatant purpose of the ordinance, the mayor, William Alvord, vetoed it, citing that it was discriminatory in nature, went against the Treaty of Peace, Amity, and Commerce between the United States and China, and violated the Civil Rights Act of 1870. The mayor also noted that the Board of Supervisors did not have the power to impose a punishment other than fines and imprisonment. On June 23, 1873, the Board tried to pass the ordinance despite the mayor's veto and needed 8 out of 12 votes; the Board only received seven votes, so the order did not pass.

Unfortunately, the Queue Ordinance did not end there. On April 3, 1876, the legislature of the state of California passed a lodging act entitled An Act Concerning Lodging Houses and Sleeping Apartments Within the Limits of Incorporated Cities, which was identical to the Cubic Air Law. Tenants could not occupy a space that provided less than 500 cubic feet per adult. The misdemeanor resulted in a $10–$50 fine, imprisonment, or both. The Board of Supervisors saw this state law as an opportunity to reinstate the Queue Ordinance because it believed the law would not be effective without it. The measure passed 10-2, and the then-current mayor Andrew Jackson Bryant signed it on June 14, 1876.

The Chinese community protested once more—men who were forced to cut their queues filed lawsuits. One decisive case was *Ho Ah Kow v. Nunan*. In April 1878, Ho Ah Kow was charged with breaking the lodging act. Because he did not pay the fine, he was imprisoned and his queue was subsequently cut off. As a result, he sued Matthew Nunan, the sheriff who ordered the cutting. Ho Ah Kow won the case; the federal district court of California found the act to be discriminatory and, therefore, unconstitutional. The Queue Ordinance finally ended, and one discriminatory practice against Chinese immigrants was put to rest.

See also: Anti-Chinese Violence; Chinese Americans and Civil Rights; Chinese Immigration During the Gold Rush

Further Reading

Field, Stephen J. 1879. *The Invalidity of the "Queue Ordinance" of the City and County of San Francisco*. San Francisco, CA: J. L. Rice & Co.

Esther Spencer

RAPE OF NANJING

The Rape of Nanjing (also Nanjing Massacre) refers to deliberate atrocities of mass murder, systematic rape, and terrorization committed by the Japanese Army against civilian populations and prisoners of war (POWs) in the capital city (Nanjing) of the Republic of China between 1937 and 1938. Between 40,000 and 30,000 (according to scholarly consensus) civilians were killed. Between 20,000 and 80,000 women were raped. It is one of the most significant cases of war crime in the 20th century. The bloodshed involved instances of burning buildings, stabbings, drownings, strangulations, theft, and destruction of personal property.

During the summer of 1937, the military leaders of the Empire of Japan acted on their expansionistic plans and waged war with China (known as the Second Sino-Japanese War, July 7, 1937–September 9, 1945). Expecting to conquer all of China in three months, the Japanese Army attacked the city of Shanghai, landing forces to the north (Yangtze River) and to the south (Hangzhou Bay) of the city. Firm Chinese resistance spoiled the timetable of the Japanese offensive, extending the summer battle into autumn. The Japanese Army launched a coordinated drive toward Nanjing in November. Poor organization and leadership of Chinese soldiers at Nanjing led to a large and disorderly retreat.

The city was captured in four days by Japanese soldiers who were ordered to "kill all captives." The 90,000 Chinese soldiers who surrendered were viewed as cowardly threats and not deserving of life. They were taken to remote locations beyond the city and subjected to brutality. Japanese soldiers were ordered to inflict as much pain as possible with the aim of preparing them for the hardships of future battles. Their actions were also deliberate attempts to move beyond civilized notions of warfighting and acclimatize Japanese soldiers to ideological dimensions of war against China. Soldiers were photographed smiling while executing civilians and POWs by means of firing squads, bayonets, and beheadings. Severed heads were displayed as trophies. Other killing techniques involved machine gun fire and burning using gasoline.

Special attention was given to women and children in Nanjing. Sexual assaults took place against elderly women and young girls. Following gang rapes, victims were usually killed in order to eliminate eyewitnesses. Pregnant

Visitors mourn the victims of the Nanjing Massacre at Memorial Hall in Nanjing, China, on March 28, 2015, just ahead of Tomb-sweeping Day. The traditional Chinese Tomb-sweeping Day comes on April 5th, according to the Chinese calendar, and marks a time when Chinese will mourn their dead ancestors. (ChinaFotoPress/Getty)

women were included in these atrocities. Many were forced to engage in acts of violence against family members. During wartime occupation, the city's population was given addictive narcotics, including opium and heroin. The establishment of an infamous Comfort Women system for the Japanese Army saw many girls and women enter into sexual slavery.

Stories of atrocities were not easily accepted by North Americans, where skepticism over the possibility of such events was considerable. Political issues in Europe concerning the rise of Adolf Hitler and the militarization of Nazi Germany overshadowed the macabre events in Nanjing. Following World War II, revisionist accounts emerged in Japan despite evidence of the events. In 2013, former Japanese Prime Minister Yukio Hatoyama (2009–2010), during a visit to the Nanjing Massacre Memorial Hall dedicated to the victims, apologized for Japan's war crimes against China. Japanese politicians visiting Yasukini Shrine in Tokyo are criticized for paying tribute to former military leaders complicit in the Rape of Nanjing.

See also: World War II

Further Reading

Chang, Iris. 1997. *The Rape of Nanking: The Forgotten Holocaust of World War II.* New York: Basic Books.

Fogel, Joshua. 2000. *The Nanking Massacre in History and Historiography*. Berkeley: University of California Press.

Yamamato, Masahiro. 2000. *Nanking: Anatomy of an Atrocity*. Santa Barbara, CA: Praeger.

Scott Nicholas Romaniuk

REFUGEE-ESCAPEE ACT (1957)

An emergency refugee bill introduced by Massachusetts Senator John F. Kennedy on June 4, 1957, An Act to Amend the Immigration and Nationality Act, and for Other Purposes, was signed into law on September 11, 1957. The Refugee-Escapee Act was a response to the 1956 failed anticommunist uprising in Hungary as well as an effort to make good on the promise of the Refugee Relief Act of 1953, when over 5,000 nonquota visas for refugees and escapees remained unused at the expiration of the 1953 Act on January 1, 1957.

While much of the language of the Refugee-Escapee Act concerned amendments to the 1952 McCarran-Walter Immigration and Nationality Act's definition of "orphan" eligible for admission into the United States on nonquota basis, there is little evidence that the law had a significant impact on the number of Chinese children who entered the United States as orphans—unlike the experience of Eurasian orphans from Korea, where the law did increase the entry of Korean children as nonquota immigrants.

The Refugee-Escapee Act was intended as a foreign policy statement during the Cold War, but for Chinese Americans, the greatest impact of the law was on the domestic front. Section 7 of the law created a process where an alien who "was admitted to the United States between December 22, 1945, and November 1, 1954, both dates inclusive, and misrepresented his nationality, place of birth, identity, or residence in applying for a visa" could avoid deportation if they could "establish to the satisfaction of the Attorney General that the misrepresentation was predicated upon the alien's fear of persecution because of race, religion, or political opinion if repatriated." Section 7 also provided that "any alien who is the spouse, parent, or child of a United States citizen or an alien lawfully admitted for residence" who committed fraud or perjury in obtaining a visa could reapply for lawful visa status and permanent residency.

Estimates of the number of illegal Chinese immigrants residing in the United States who pursued legal status under section 7 vary from 8,000 to 30,000. Scholars of the mid-20th century Chinese immigrant experience view the Refugee-Escapee Act as an early example of an immigration amnesty provision in U.S. law. The Refugee-Escapee Act provided the "paper" sons and daughters of late 19th- and early 20th-century Chinese exclusion a path to legal residency and citizenship after decades of hiding in the shadows. The journey of these thousands of men and women awaits a monumental social history that will not only tell their story, but will also inform our current understanding of the struggle for legitimacy faced by the estimated 12 million illegal aliens in the United States in the second decade of the 21st century.

See also: Refugee Relief Act (1953); War Brides Act (1946); World War II

Further Reading

Gudykunst, William B. 2001. *Asian American Ethnicity and Communication.* Thousand Oaks, CA: Sage.

Immigration and Nationality Act of 1957. Public Law 85-316. 71 Stat. 639-644. September 11, 1957.

Reimers, David M. 2005. *Other Immigrants: The Global Origins of the American People.* New York: New York University Press.

David Alan Rego

REFUGEE RELIEF ACT (1953)

Enacted on August 7, 1953, An Act for Relief of Certain Refugees, and Orphans, and for other Purposes authorized the issuance of 205,000 "special non-quota" visas above the national origins quota restrictions promulgated in An Act to Revise the Laws Relating to Immigration, Naturalization, and Nationality, and for Other Purposes (The McCarran-Walter Act) of June 27, 1952. The Refugee Relief Act of 1953 provided 205,000 nonquota visas for any "refugee" who met the legal definition of "any person in a country or area which is neither Communist nor Communist-dominated,

Mrs. Wan Ju Pan Chan, widow of a Chinese college professor, her son, Bun Chan, 13, and three adopted boys, Kwai Keung Chan, 12; Yam Tai Chui, 14; and Ying Yeung Yam, 14, are some of the first refugees from China to arrive under the U.S. Refugee Relief Act on September 15, 1955. All five escaped from Communist China and were brought to the U.S. with the help of Church World Service and the Protestant Episcopal Church. (Bettmann/Corbis)

who because of persecution, fear of persecution, natural calamity or military operations is out of his usual place of abode and unable to return thereto, who has not been firmly resettled, and who is in urgent need of assistance for the essentials of life or for transportation."

Under the Act, less than 1 percent of nonquota visas were available "to two thousand refugees of Chinese ethnic origin whose passports for travel are endorsed by the Chinese National Government or its authorized representatives." However, section 6 of the law increased the number of visas open to Chinese refugees by 5,000 through an "Adjustment of Status" provision where "Any alien who establishes that prior to July 1, 1953, he lawfully entered the United States as a bona fide nonimmigrant" and "is unable to return to the country of his birth . . . because of persecution or fear of persecution on account of race, religion, or political opinion," could gain permanent U.S. residency. After the outbreak of the Korean War in 1950, the U.S. government, citing national security reasons, prohibited the exit of any Chinese National who had originally entered the United States under a nonimmigrant student visa. For students wishing to remain in the United States, section 6 changed their status from national security detainees to permanent residents.

See also: Refugee-Escapee Act (1957); War Brides Act (1946); World War II

Further Reading

Han, Yelong. 1993. "An Untold Story: American Policy Toward Chinese Students in the United States, 1949–1955." *The Journal of American-East Asian Relations* 2 (Spring): 77–99.
Refugee Relief Act of 1953, ch. 336, 67 Stat. 400.

David Alan Rego

SAMYAP AND SZEYAP

While present trends of U.S. immigration show a vast spread of ethnic Chinese immigrants of various language backgrounds, nearly all Chinese immigrants from the 1800s to 1970s spoke some variety of "Cantonese" originating in the Lliyip/Szeyap/Seiyap (literally: "Four Districts") or Samyap ("Three Districts") regions. In Modern Standard Mandarin they are called *Sanyi* and *Siyi*, respectively. The Lliyip/Szeyap/Seiyap region is an area in Guangdong province in mainland China, which consists of four districts (in pinyin: Taishan, Kaiping, Enping, and Xinhui). The Samyap district comprises Nanhai, Panyu, and Shunde. Speakers of Samyap speak a variety that is more linguistically similar to Standard Cantonese, while speakers of Lliyip/Szeyap/Seiyap have maintained the voiceless alveolar lateral fricative [ɬ], which is a remnant sound of Old and

Middle Chinese. This sound has been leveled to voiceless alveolar sibilant [s] in Samyap.

Because of the proximity of the Lliyip/Szeyap/Seiyap region to various seaports, it is no surprise that much of the early ethnic Chinese immigration to the United States came from these four districts, with Taishan sending off the largest population of people, mostly as laborers. Speakers from the Taishan region of the Four Districts spoke Hoisan-wa, also known as "Toisanese" or "Toishanese," as it is called in Standard Cantonese, and "Taishanese," as it is called in Modern Standard Mandarin. While there are obvious regional differences to the varieties spoken in these districts, with much variation even among speakers within a district, these varieties are largely lumped together as "Cantonese," along with regional Standard Cantonese(s) of Hong Kong and Guangdong. Linguistically, varieties spoken in these districts are relatively mutually intelligible, especially for cities and towns in close proximity to each other, but this disregards the sociolinguistic stigma and rural-urban divide that exists for speakers of a "less standard" Cantonese. It is not uncommon to hear Lliyip/Szeyap/Seiyap speakers call themselves "Cantonese" speakers, qualified with a phrase to the effect of, "But I speak a rural form of Cantonese."

Chinese Americans who can trace their ancestors' arrival in the United States to the 19th and mid-20th centuries come from a shared Lliyip ancestral heritage language that differs greatly linguistically, culturally, and historically from Mandarin, the current standard language of China and Taiwan. This particular population is not at all small, as it encompasses a sizable proportion of third-generation Chinese Americans and nearly all fourth-generation-plus Chinese Americans. Statistics show that up until 1965, which marks the passing of the Immigration and Nationality Act, nearly two-thirds of the Chinese in the United States came from Lliyip/Szeyap/Seiyap.

The terms *Samyap* and *Szeyap* refer to different varieties of Cantonese, perhaps because of the need to distinguish the various "Cantonese" speakers before 1965; with the arrival of various other Chinese languages (e.g., Shanghainese, Taiwanese, Hakka, Mandarin), Samyap and Szeyap were subsumed into a larger, pan-Cantonese entity. Thus these two terms are more likely to be used by Chinese American elders and less frequently by younger generations of Chinese Americans.

See also: Cantonese; Chinese Family Associations

Further Reading

Lai, Him Mark. 2004. *Becoming Chinese American: A History of Communities and Institutions.* Walnut Creek, CA: AltaMira Press.

Genevieve Leung

SAN FRANCISCO EARTHQUAKE (1906)

Considered one of the worst natural disasters in the history of the United States, the San Francisco earthquake of 1906 virtually destroyed one of the west coast's most vibrant cities, killing at least 3,000 people. It also gave city official the opportunity to promote a plan designed to permanently drive thousands of Chinese American residents from their San Francisco homes.

During the last half of the 19th century a significant Chinese American community developed in San Francisco as a result of the Gold Rush and the increase in railroad building in the American West, and by 1900 around 15,000 residents of the city were of Chinese descent. Many lived along Grant Avenue and Stockton Street in a section of the city that became known as "Chinatown." As the city's population grew, a significant backlash against these citizens developed. Driven by prejudice and a desire to control the valuable real estate on which Chinatown rested, local politicians made plans to relocate the Chinese American population to less valuable property on the outskirts of the city. The process was already under consideration when the earthquake struck just after 5:00 a.m. on April 18, 1906. The earthquake devastated San Francisco as brick and wooden structures crumbled. Fires broke out and city officials watched helplessly as broken water lines made it impossible for firefighters to combat the flames. A major movement along the San Andreas fault caused the disaster and shock waves were felt as far north as Oregon and as far south as Los Angeles. Modern seismologists estimate that the earthquake measure around 7.8 on the Richter Magnitude Scale, which was not developed until the 1930s. In the aftermath, San Francisco's mayor declared a curfew and federal troops

Chinatown was rebuilt after the 1906 San Francisco Earthquake and Fire. This photo captures a partially delapidated Kearney Street in Chinatown, from the vantage point of Telegraph Hill. (Library of Congress)

were sent in to discourage looting. The fires burned for five days, consuming thousands of buildings amounting to 80 percent of the city.

The earthquake completely destroyed Chinatown and the army moved many of the district's residents to segregated refugee camps. Hoping to take advantage of the situation, city officials established the Committee on the Location of Chinatown within two weeks of the disaster, and the group quickly produced a blueprint for permanently relocating San Francisco's Chinese American community. Despite support for the plan, some local businessmen worried that relocating Chinatown would hurt the city's economy, stifling both Asian trade and tax revenues. The Chinese government also weighed in, expressing outrage and generating considerable political pressure against the idea. In the end, the plan failed and Chinatown, like the rest of the city, began to rebuild.

See also: Angel Island Immigration Station; Paper Sons and Daughters

Further Reading

Fradkin, Peter L. 2005. *The Great Earthquake and Firestorms of 1906: How San Francisco Nearly Destroyed Itself.* Berkeley: University of California Press.

Kurzman, Dan. 2002. *Disaster!: The Great San Francisco Earthquake and Fire of 1906.* New York: HarperCollins.

Ben Wynne

SCOTT ACT (1888)

The Scott Act (1888), introduced by Representative William Scott of Pennsylvania, revised the Burlingame Treaty (1868) between China and the United States and extended the Chinese Exclusion Act (1882), which restricted immigration of Chinese laborers by terminating future exit visas and invalidating existing travel visas. The Scott Act was part of numerous legislative attempts to limit Chinese immigration, including the Exclusion Act, Geary Act (1892) and McCreary Amendment (1893). Passage of the Scott Act followed a period of mass immigration during the California Gold Rush and construction of the Transcontinental Railroad, and resulted from rising unemployment in the United States during the 1870s, anti-Chinese riots in the mid-1880s, and rising doubts about the Bayard-Zhang Treaty. While the legitimacy of the bill was not recognized by the Chinese government, it was later upheld by the U.S. Supreme Court in *Chae Chan Ping v. United States* (1889). As a result, thousands of sojourning Chinese laborers who had property and money in the United States and valid travel visas to return to China were prohibited from reentering the country. In addition, Chinese immigration to the United States underwent a massive decline between 1880 and 1890, Chinese American communities became further isolated, the existing gender gap in immigrant enclaves was exacerbated, a need for family associations and community organizations arose, and the illegal "paper sons" immigration process began.

See also: Anti-Chinese Violence; Chinese Exclusion Act (1882); Sino-U.S. Relations

Further Reading

Konvitz, Milton. 1946. *The Alien and the Asiatic in American Law.* Ithaca, NY: Cornell University Press.
McClain, Charles. 1994. *In Search of Equality: The Chinese Struggle Against Discrimination in Nineteenth-Century America.* Berkeley: University of California Press.

Sean Morton

SINO-JAPANESE WAR (1894)

Japan and China fought the First Sino-Japanese War between 1894 and 1895. The nine-month war was a contest for the right to rule Korea as a vassal state, although the war did spill into China itself. Japan's victory signaled its ascendance on the world stage as a colonial power, while China's defeat marked the Qing Dynasty's attempts at modernization as a failure. The war reversed the traditional power dynamic in East Asia and further exacerbated the domestic problems within China created by the increasingly weak Chinese state.

The war was a contributing factor to the mass of Chinese immigrants at the end of the 19th century, both directly and indirectly. Manchuria, especially, suffered from the heavy fighting in the region. The local population experienced heavy casualties during the war and began to look for a peaceful existence

An illustration of a cannon shell exploding against a tree in the midst of four warriors on horseback during the Sino-Japanese War, possbily during the battle at Kaiping. This artwork is one panel from a vertical Oban Nishikie triptych. (Library of Congress)

elsewhere. The war contributed to the contingencies for the Boxer Rebellion and the fall of the Qing Dynasty in 1912, both of which caused an exodus of Chinese. It should not be confused with the Second Sino-Japanese War (1937–1945), which was a contest over mainland China.

See also: International Context of Chinese Immigration to America, to 1870; Rape of Nanjing

Further Reading

Conroy, Phillip. 1960. *The Japanese Seizure of Korea, 1868–1910*. Philadelphia: University of Pennsylvania Press.
Paine, S. C. M. 2005. *The Sino-Japanese War of 1894-1895: Perceptions, Power, and Primacy*. Cambridge, UK: Cambridge University Press.

Zachary S. Kopin

SINO-U.S. RELATIONS

Sino-U.S. relations went through ups and downs since the 18th century. The U.S. government saw China's shift from the rule of Qing Dynasty to the establishment of the People's Republic of China. In the 21st century, China and the United States become the two major economic powers in the world. Sino-U.S. relations became increasingly important. Their economic and strategic relationships play a significant role to stabilize the region and the world.

In 1784, an American vessel, *Empress of China*, was the first to leave New York harbor for China. One important key to Sino-U.S. relations was that, after the mid-1840s, China had grown weak through repeated defeats in wars with Western powers. In 1842, China and Britain signed the Treaty of Nanjing after the First Opium War. Importantly, China opened five treaty ports to Britain. The United States also wanted to negotiate a treaty with China and expand its trade with China. In 1844, the two countries signed the Treaty of Wangxia, opening these five Chinese ports to the United States. However, full consulate services were not established in China until the mid-1850s. China and the United States signed the Treaty of Burlingame in 1868. This treaty guaranteed that Chinese had the right to immigrate to the United States and allowed to naturalize as U.S. citizens. Between the 1870s and 1880s, the U.S. legislature passed more Chinese exclusion laws that made it difficult for Chinese immigrants to come to the United States and to become U.S. citizens.

In 1899, the U.S. government initiated its Open Door Policy, hoping to unlock opportunities for itself and other Western powers, all aggressively seeking a sphere of influence within the vast realm of China. Import and export trade boomed; the number of U.S. companies in China increased tenfold to over 300 firms and $200 million by 1923.

Beginning from 1928, the United States recognized the Nationalist government led by Chiang Kai-shek as the legal government of China. During World War II, the United States supported the Chinese Nationalist government's fight against Japanese invasion. After the end of World War II, the United States also supported the Nationalist government's fight against the Chinese Communist Party during the Chinese Civil War. In 1949, after the Nationalists lost to the Chinese Communists, the Nationalists retreated to Taiwan and established the Republic of China. The United States still recognized the Taiwan government as the sole legal government of China until 1979.

After the Chinese Communist Party declared the formation of the People's Republic in 1949, the U.S. government developed new foreign policies that aimed at containing and isolating China. In 1966, President Lyndon Johnson still followed containment policy, but he did not want to isolate China. In 1969, President Richard Nixon articulated the idea of shifting from confrontation to negotiation. The Vietnam War played a significant role in this shift of policy because the United States wanted to end the war in Vietnam, and China could put pressure on North Vietnam. In 1971, the U.S. government sent out friendly signals to China. On April 12, 1971, the U.S. Table Tennis Team visited China. On July 15, 1971, Nixon announced he would visit China. On February 21, 1972, Nixon arrived in Beijing, China. Nixon's visit brought China back to the international community and ended the isolation of China. On February 28, 1972, the Shanghai Communique was issued. Both China and the United States agreed that there was but one China and that Taiwan was a part of China. Both countries also agreed exchanges in science, technology, culture, journalism, and sports. In August 1972, the United States supported the admission of China to the United Nations. China replaced Taiwan as one of the five permanent members in the UN Security Council. In 1979, Deng Xiaoping, as China's vice-premier, visited the United States. On January 1, 1979, China and the United States established diplomatic relations. On March 1, 1979, China and the United States established embassies in Beijing and Washington, D.C., respectively. In 1979, the United States also signed a trade pact with China and granted it most-favored-nation status. U.S. businessmen could set up offices in China. Chinese businesses could then set up offices in the United States. The incident that made the Sino-American relations tense up was the Tiananmen Square crackdown in 1989. The U.S. Congress called for sanctions on China, but President George H. W. Bush believed that keeping China's door open was more important. China still kept its door open after the crackdown. However, China and the United States had other obstacles, such as China's human rights record, political prisoners, international arms sales, and intellectual copyrights. Trade deficits between China and the United States also grew bigger every year.

On October 10, 2000, the U.S. government granted China permanent trade relation status. China did not need to renew most-favored-nation status anymore. In 2001, President George W. Bush took office. He believed that China was a potential threat and strategic competitor to the United States. Therefore, he used a tougher approach. On April 1, 2001, a U.S. EP-3 surveillance plane collided with a Chinese F-8 fighter. On April 12, 2001, China released the 24 American crew members after the United States apologized for the plane entering China's airspace. This incident created a tension between China and the United States. After terrorist attacks in the United States on September 11, 2001, the United States saw the potential that China could be a partner to fight against terrorism. China cooperated with the United States.

In 2009, the United States and China held the first round of the China-U.S. Strategic and Economic Dialogue. In 2009, President Obama and President Hu Jintao of China met when they both attended the G20 Financial Summit in London. Both presidents agreed that the Sino-American relations should be positive, cooperative, and also comprehensive. In March 2013, China completed its leadership transition. China had a new president, Xi Jinping. In early June 2013, Xi and Obama had meetings in California. Both leaders wanted to build a new model of cooperation.

China has gone through many external and internal challenges and become a rising power in the 21st century. The United States has had to shape and reshape its policies in order to protect its interests. Therefore, the challenges of the Sino-American relations would always be there.

See also: Angell Treaty (Chinese Exclusion Treaty) (1880); International Context of Chinese Immigration to America, to 1870; McCarthyism; World War I; World War II

Further Reading

Garrison, Jean. 2007. "Constructing the 'National Interest' in U.S.-China Policy Making: How Foreign Policy Decision Groups Define and Signal Policy Choices." *Foreign Policy Analysis* 3: 105–26.

Grasso, June. 2009. *Modernization and Revolution in China: From the Opium Wars to the Olympics.* 4th ed. New York: M. E. Sharpe.

Edy Parsons

TAIPING REBELLION

From 1851 until 1864 China was shocked by one of the greatest rebellions in its modern history. The Taiping Rebellion (Great Peace Rebellion) was initially aimed against the rule of the Qing Dynasty and the Western great powers. A lot of the participants were peasants; however, the rebellion was not simply an agrarian one. Hong Xiuquan, who led the rebellion and preached beliefs that were inspired by Christian teachings, and his followers conquered large parts of China for more than 10 years. He was able to attract a large number of followers who were hoping for a better life, but the Taiping uprising was finally suppressed by local provincial armies that had been supported by French and British troops.

The increasing Western influence in Manchu China, symbolized by the occupation of the Chinese harbor by the imperial powers and a wish to reinstall the Ming rulers, who were overthrown by the ruling Manchus in the middle of the 17th century, increased the rebellious potential of the common population. The majority of the population, the Han Chinese, suffered from governmental mismanagement as well as corruption. While the foreign-led bureaucracy became rich, the majority of the population was suffering from high taxes.

The harsh life of the peasantry—whose number had grown due to a population increase from 250 million to 430 million between 1750 and 1850—opened their ears to new messages. But it was not only the peasants who became involved, but also the workers, many of whom had lost their transport privileges in the aftermath of the First Opium War (1839–1842) as a consequence of the Treaty of Nanking.

The Taiping teachings were promising a better life in which everyone would be equal and social classes would no longer divide the society, so Hong Xiuquan, who depicted himself as a messiah and Jesus's brother, was able to attract many followers. The leader preached social, economic, political, and gender equality, causing many people to follow these new religious teachings.

After the outbreak of the Taiping Rebellion in the province of Guangxi in 1851, it grew tremendously in just a couple of weeks, finally even reaching Beijing and Shanghai as well as Tibet. The movement was able to attract followers from different social classes, because it promised the establishment of a new social order, based on equality rather than corruption. The common people hated the Manchu rulers, who had taken over all positions of power and control in the country. After the Taiping rebels managed to occupy large parts of the country, Nanjing was made into the new capital, where the revolutionary leadership resided and founded the Taiping Tianguo (Heavenly Kingdom of Great Peace). Due to the support of the population and the military miscalculations of the Manchu rulers, the rebellion became a successful attempt to overcome the existing society. As a consequence of the Christian motivation, the new movement was praised by Western observers. However, the British and the French in the end supported the Manchu rulers, because they needed a stable trade condition in China. In 1864 the rebels lost Nanjing and had no hope of being victorious against the combined forces of the Manchu rulers and the Western powers, which were better equipped and trained than the Chinese rebels. Additionally, the rebellion was weakened by internal struggles regarding

Hong's role and leadership, especially since he had decided to live the life of an emperor instead of the life of equality that he had propagated for all people who believed in the Taiping teachings. His luxurious lifestyle as well as his numerous concubines created an internal struggle between him and his followers, who believed in the original demands of the rebellion, asking for an equal treatment of all Chinese. Through the communist historiography of the later periods it was constructed as the first semblance of revolutionaries in China. The fact that the rebellion was based on Western ideas that were brought to the country by different missionaries was neglected. It also showed that the Western powers would not support a Chinese independence movement, because the weak Manchu rulers were thought to be better trade partners than a new government that might ask for better trading conditions. Despite the fact that this first rebellion since the lost Opium War failed, it paved the way for the many other uprisings that would demand a change in Chinese society. When in 1911 the revolution was successful, its leaders were able to look back on a very long history of rebellion against the Manchu, starting with this major uprising that had already almost led to the decline of the Chinese Empire.

The Taiping Rebellion was not a simple peasant uprising because the rebels were longing to create a new societal order. It also attracted intellectuals who wanted to abolish the Ching to reinstall the Ming Dynasty. It was a religiously motivated rebellion that shook the bases of China, showing the weakness of the ruling power and its dependency on Western support, and stimulating the growth of further revolutionary activities in China. The Taiping Rebellion thereby was one of the first steps that led to the decline of the Manchu rulers and the Chinese Revolution of 1911.

See also: International Context of Chinese Immigration to America, to 1870

Further Reading

Jen, Y. W. 1993. *The Taiping Revolutionary Movement*. New Haven, CT: Yale University Press.

Moore, Barrington, Jr. 1993. *Social Origins of Dictatorship and Democracy: Lord and Peasant in the Making of the Modern World*. Boston, MA: Beacon Press.

Shih, Vincent. 1972. *The Taiping Ideology: Its Sources, Interpretations, and Influences*. Seattle: University of Washington Press.

Frank Jacob

TAIWAN

Taiwan, an island nation-state, was born in 1949 when two million Nationalists, or Kuomingtang (KMT), affiliates fled to Taiwan and established a government after it lost the civil war to the Chinese Communist Party on mainland

China. Taiwan has historically been Chinese territory but military defeat during the First Sino-Japanese War forced China to cede Taiwan to Japan, which maintained colonial power until 1954, nearly a decade following the end of World War II. Since the war, Taiwan democratized and established local representation in its overall governing structure. In 2000, Taiwan accomplished its first peaceful transfer of power from the Nationalist Kuomingtang Party to the Democratic Progressive Party. Post–World War II Taiwan experienced a great economic transformation and modernization and became one of East Asia's "economic Tigers." The biggest national issue for Taiwan since its establishment is the question of mainland China and its "One China" philosophy, which threatens Taiwan's sovereignty. Although Taiwan is a relatively small island geographically, its population as of 2011 was 23.07 million.

Although the "Taiwanese American" can be subsumed in the category of "Chinese American," there are various Taiwanese ethnic groups (Hakka, Zhangzhou, Quanzhou, and other Fujianese "Taiwanese") that distinguish themselves from the "mainlanders" who fled to Taiwan in the wake of the Communist victory. Hence, the cultural, social, economic, and political background of the Taiwanese makes their experience different from other Chinese immigrants. There are two types of Taiwanese from Taiwan: the Fujianese and Hakka compose the majority of the population on the island and are called *benshengren* or "local people"; mainlanders who immigrated to Taiwan after World War II are called *waishengren*, or "outside people." These so-called outside people are mainly Mandarin-speaking Taiwanese. Since the 1990s both benshengren and waishengren on Taiwan and abroad refer to themselves distinctively and declaratively as "Taiwanese." Therefore, Taiwanese Americans are any subjects who immigrated to Taiwan and are loyal to Taiwan's geopolitical sovereignty.

The million-dollar question for scholars studying Taiwanese Americans is: "Is Taiwan Chinese?" This question is much debated, both in academia and in politics between Taiwan and mainland China, as well as within their respective national borders. The question "Is Taiwan Chinese" must take into consideration the intersection of cultural, political, and national identities between and among the various ethnic groups in China and Taiwan. For the purposes of this essay, in discussing Taiwanese immigrants in America, we will specifically refer to them as "Taiwanese Americans," and therefore emphasize their Taiwanese origins because their experiences are different from other "Chinese American" communities.

Taiwan is a dynamic, relatively new democracy that has experienced two peaceful exchange of power since its establishment under martial law. The term "Taiwanese" and hence "Taiwanese American" has crystallized over time to refer to someone from Taiwan who is interested in Taiwan's geopolitical sovereignty. It is also someone who is culturally connected to Taiwan through religious practices and associations. Taiwanese Americans have relatives from Taiwan and are able to return to Taiwan regularly to reconnect with their kinfolks. A Taiwanese centric consciousness has developed in the United States among second-generation Taiwanese Americans as illustrated by the establishment of student and professional organizations and associations. The new generation of Taiwanese Americans maintain multiple identities that they negotiate situational and politically. Taiwanese Americans are simultaneously Chinese American and Asian American. The geopolitical situation between mainland China and Taiwan is not lost among second-generation Taiwanese Americans as attested to by the establishment of Taiwanese American Student Associations across college campuses in the United States. Instead of joining the already established Chinese American Student Associations, they elected to make a conscious political, cultural, and to certain degree ethnic declaration of being from Taiwan, and Taiwanese. As such, they are concern about Taiwan's geopolitical future and sovereignty. Economic interests and Taiwanese investors in mainland China maintain the current status of cross-strait relations, one of political grandstanding by officials on both sides of the Taiwan Straits. The U.S. geopolitical support of Taiwan's political sovereignty results in a wholesale pro-America and pro-American sentiment on the island nation-state and among Taiwanese Americans residing in the United States. The future of Taiwanese Americans and their communities rests on Taiwan's ability, and China's desire, to maintain the current status quo, which has secured relative peace.

See also: Chiang Kai-shek, Madame (Soong Meiling); Sun Yat-sen; Taiwanese American Heritage Week; Taiwanese Immigration History

Further Reading

Berger, Suzanne, and Richard K. Lester, eds. 2005. *Global Taiwan: Building Competitive Strengths in a New International Economy*. Armonk, NY: M. E. Sharpe.

Harrison, Mark. 2006. *Legitimacy, Meaning, and Knowledge in the Making of Taiwanese Identity*. New York: Palgrave Macmillan.

Ng, Franklin. 1998. *Taiwanese Americans*. Westport, CT: Greenwood Press.

Jonathan H. X. Lee

TAIWANESE IMMIGRATION HISTORY

Taiwanese immigration to the United States unfolded in four distinct periods. The first from the end of World War II to the passage of the 1965 Immigration Reform Act. This period witnessed mostly Taiwanese exchange students seeking advanced degrees. Between 1954 and 1976, the Taiwan government administered exams to students who wished to study aboard, but only after they have fulfilled their mandatory military service. Before this period, students from Taiwan mainly studied aboard in Japan and England. According to

Taipei's Ministry of Education statistics, the number of students going aboard to study gradually increased, such that in 1963 there were 2,125 students aboard, and 2,925 in 1969. On average, the United States received roughly 2000 Taiwanese students annually throughout the 1960s and into the 1970s. However, after receiving master's degrees and doctorates, the majority of these students remained in the United States, which resulted in the phenomena that many scholars call the "brain drain." This period also includes the immigration of Taiwanese spouses of American personnel, mainly U.S. soldiers who were stationed in Taiwan after the Korean War. The Korean War and the enveloping Cold War prompted the United States to pledge support of Taiwan's geopolitical safety with the signing of the Mutual Defense Treaty in 1954. Chinese American military personnel also brought their Taiwanese wives back to America with them.

The second period is from 1965 to 1979. The 1965 Immigration Reform Act raised the ceiling for Chinese immigrants to 20,000, including Hong Kong and Taiwan. China, Hong Kong, and Taiwan were not treated as separate entities until the 1980s. This included a provision for the reunification of families of U.S. citizens that was not restricted by numerical limits. Additionally, there was a clause that allowed preferential admissions of immigrants with vital and exceptional skills, such as technical and scientific skills in critical employment arenas. As a result, engineers, scientists, and skilled professionals from Taiwan, trained in either Taiwan or the United States were able to gain permanent residency status. This too, magnified the "brain drain" that had begun in the first period of Taiwanese immigration.

The third period starts in 1979 and continues to the present time. The overall Chinese population in America increased considerably in 1979, when the United States normalized geopolitical relations with the People's Republic of China. Official relations with Taiwan thus ceased. Therefore, instead of an embassy in Taipei, the United States established an American Institute in Taiwan (AIT) that functions like a quasi-embassy and is staffed by U.S. State Department personnel. In 1982, in light of protests from Beijing, the United States established a separate quota for Taiwan at 20,000. This occurred in the context of rapid modernization and economic growth in Taiwan. Trained professionals were not able to find employment in Taiwan because job creation lagged behind economic growth. Consequently, many sought employment in the United States. This period also increased the impact of the "brain drain" from Taiwan. The Immigration Act of 1990 maintained a preference clause for professionals and those with exceptional skills in key growth areas (i.e., computer and other high technologies). Additionally, the Act's employment provisions include investors who saw economic opportunity in America. The 1990 Act made it easier for such investors to move into the United States, which resulted in what has been labeled "flexible citizenship." Flexible citizens are wealthy Taiwanese (and Chinese) immigrants who move between Taiwan (and Hong Kong and Singapore) and maintain dual citizenships, thereby making use of economic policies and fluid nation-state borders.

The normalization of geopolitical relations between the United Sates and mainland China in 1979 aroused fear of China's conquest of Taiwan. Many Taiwanese residents were apprehensive that China might make a move to unite with Taiwan under its "One China" philosophy. Accordingly, many anxious Taiwanese began moving their capital to other countries, in particular to the United States. A similar phenomenon unfolded in Hong Kong during this period. Together, this period witnessed an increase of Taiwanese immigrants (also Hong Kongese) seeking permanent residency status in the United States.

A fourth distinct migration period can be discerned that was most manifest in the 1990s and throughout the 2000s. This period can be described as the "transnational period" of Taiwanese immigration. Chinese immigration to the United States has always been transnational in nature, meaning that immigrants have come to America and maintained connections to their homeland. Early Chinese immigrants from Canton in the 19th and early 20th centuries were transnational because Chinese males immigrants intended to return to China after securing wealth primarily from the Gold Rush. Families and kinship networks facilitated an early transnational lifestyle whereby husbands have worked in the United States and sent money home to China.

Families in the homeland grew because husbands would return to China and become intimate with their wives. The same husbands might have a family and second wife in America. The encounters and face-to-face meetings were limited and occasional, even though transnational. Taiwan lifted martial law in 1987, which, coupled with economic development in Taiwan, created a new type of transnational flow. The new type of transnational flow during the 1990s and 2000s was facilitated by further advances in travel and telecommunications. As a result, scholars have called these new transnational persons from Taiwan (also from Hong Kong and Singapore) *taikongren* ("astronauts"), meaning Taiwanese subjects who move back and forth between the United States and Taiwan for business and work. The families of these so-called Taiwanese astronauts are described as "split transnational families."

This period also witnessed the growth of transnational Taiwanese student populations in America. This is partly a consequence of the competitive nature of the examination system in Taiwan for advancement in school. As a result, parents with the means to do so send their children to the United States to get an education. The economic boom in Taiwan during the 1980s–1990s facilitated this social phenomena. These students have been sent to live with relatives or close family friends or live in homes their parents purchased. They are called "parachute children" or *xiao liuxuesheng*, literally meaning "little overseas students." The toll that such transnational Taiwanese family structures have on marriages and on family relations has been documented and found to be, overall, negative and stressful.

In addition, today's Taiwanese American transnational subjects fly back to Taiwan to vote, and Taiwanese politicians travel to the United States to campaign in Taiwanese American communities. For instance, during the 2004 and 2008 presidential elections in Taiwan, many Taiwanese Americans traveled back to the island to vote because absentee voting was not allowed. While approximately 2,000 Taiwanese-New Yorkers returned to vote in 2004, nearly 10,000 Taiwanese Americans returned from California to Taiwan in 2008 in order to vote. This phenomenon, labeled "political transnationalism," especially includes Taiwanese Americans who actively participate in the politics of their native countries, especially with regard to U.S. foreign policy.

Even though the 1980s and 1990s witnessed high levels of the new transnationalism by Taiwanese subjects living between the United States and Taiwan, it has subsequently revealed a decrease in emigration from Taiwan for the same reasons that there has been an increase in the number of returning transnational Taiwanese/Taiwanese Americans, namely due to economic development, better work opportunities for highly skilled and highly educated professionals, better living conditions, and the end of martial law in 1987. Although many Taiwanese students are staying in Taiwan for their education and advance degrees, as of 2009, Taiwan still ranked ninth among all countries with students in the United States.

The factors that inform Taiwanese immigration to the United States are complex and multilayered. They range from political factors, such as cross-strait relations with China; national security; and, during the early period, restrictions on freedoms due to martial law. However, one still finds many Taiwanese still pushing to leave Taiwan for educational and economic opportunities as a result of a rigorous examination system for educational opportunities as well as a lack of an adequate number of jobs for highly skilled professionals in relation to the number of Taiwanese obtaining advanced degrees. For example, engineers in Taiwan a dime a dozen. In fact, an American engineer can earn more money teaching English in Taiwan than working as an engineer. On the other hand, the United States lacks the educational structure and resources to train and develop homegrown engineers. As such, many engineers from Taiwan (and other Asian countries) are recruited for employment in America's high-tech and computer industries. Changes in U.S. immigration policy after 1965 made it possible for Taiwanese immigrants to gain permanent residency status and sponsor their kinfolks during the ensuing years. Taiwanese Americans, both first- and second-generation, have made their presence well known within Chinese American communities. Their experiences, economic background, and history set them apart from earlier Chinese immigrants as well as more recent ones from the mainland.

See also: Chiang Kai-shek, Madame (Soong Meiling); Sun Yat-sen; Taiwan; Taiwanese American Heritage Week; Taiwanese Americans

Further Reading

Chang, Shenglin. 2006. *The Global Silicon Valley Home: Lives and Landscapes within Tai-wanese American Trans-Pacific Culture*. Stanford, CA: Stanford University Press.

Chee, Maria W. L. 2012. *Taiwanese American Transnational Families: Women and Kin Work*. New York: Routledge.

Ng, Franklin. 1998. *Taiwanese Americans*. Westport, CT: Greenwood Press.

Jonathan H. X. Lee

TREATY OF NANKING (1842)

See: Hong Kong; Opium Wars (1840 and 1856)

TRIADS

See: Secret Societies

WAR BRIDES ACT (1945)

See: War Brides Act (1946)

WAR BRIDES ACT (1946)

When Public Law 271 ("An act to expedite the admission to the United States of alien spouses and alien minor children of citizen members of the United States armed forces") was enacted on December 28, 1945, many Chinese Americans and their allies viewed it as a positive step in righting the wrongs of 70 years of federal legislative enactments prohibiting Chinese immigration into the United States. However, it was soon evident that dismantling almost 75 years of anti-Chinese immigration law was a complicated process requiring a complete overhaul of decades of reactionary legislation directed at the Chinese.

Like the December 17, 1943 Magnuson Act ("to repeal the Chinese Exclusion Act, to establish quotas, and for other purposes") (Public Law 199), the 1945 "War Brides Act" reflected America's wartime and postwar commitment to eradicate racism and ethnocentrism from U.S. law. By allowing "alien spouses or alien children of United States citizens serving in, or having an honorable discharge certificate from the armed forces of the United States during the Second World War" entry into the United States as nonquota aliens, the 1945 Act supplanted the immigration quota barriers put in place under the Immigration Act of 1924, An Act to Limit the Immigration of Aliens into the United States, and for Other Purposes (Public Law 139).

The 1924 law provided that "The annual quota shall be 2 per centum of the number of foreign-born individuals of such nationality resident in the continental United States as determined by the United States census of 1890, *but* [emphasis added] the minimum quota of any nationality shall be 100." In keeping with a half-century of race-based federal legislative enactments against Chinese immigrants, the Chinese were excluded from quota provisions in the 1924 law. The 1924 law also denied any Chinese woman who married an American citizen prior to May 26, 1924 entry into the United States. On June 13, 1930, the 1924 law was amended to remove this prohibition, allowing Chinese wives entry as nonquota aliens. While the 1924 Act provided no quota for Chinese immigration into the United States, the Act of 1930 set the stage for what would follow in the 1940s.

By December 9, 1941, both the United States and the Republic of China had declared war against the Empire of Japan. For Chinese Americans and their allies on the U.S. home front, the exclusion of Chinese immigrants from the United States was an untenable position for a nation committed to the fight for freedom and democracy against German and Italian fascism in the West and Japanese imperialism in the East. Repeal of Chinese exclusion laws dating back to 1875 were necessary to buttress America's commitment to fight a world war against its enemies, as well as respond to enemy propaganda about America's racist and xenophobic immigration restrictions.

Still, anti-immigrant interests in the United States pressured Congress against the repeal of Chinese exclusion. Bowing to demands from groups opposed to Chinese immigration, the 1943 Magnuson Act's repeal of decades of Chinese exclusion laws created a quota number substantially less than the 2,150 visas possible under the 1924 law. In 1890, 107,488 citizens and residents in the United States traced their ancestry to the China. Under the questionable terms of the Immigration Act of 1924, the Chinese allotment in 1943 was set at 105 visas, of which 35 visas were set aside for Chinese residing outside of mainland China. After decades of exclusion, the Chinese were granted a mere five more visas than were granted immigrants from Iceland and Luxembourg under the provisions of the 1924 law.

Importantly, the 1924, 1930, 1943, and 1945 laws made nonquota admissions conditional under the provisions of section 3 of the February 5, 1917 immigration law entitled An Act to Regulate the Immigration of Aliens to, and the Residence of Aliens in, the United States (Public Law 301). The 1917 law prohibited "certain classes of aliens" from admission to the United States, including a sweeping geographic prohibition of immigrants from what was later called an "Asiatic Barred Zone," including portions of the Middle East, the Indian Subcontinent, the Asian portion of the Russia, Tibet, a portion of Mongolia, Nepal, Bhutan, Siam, French Indo-China, the Malay states, the Dutch East Indies, Portuguese Timor, British and German New Guinea, the Mariana Islands, the Solomon Islands, and the Bismarck Archipelago. Also included in this geographic delimitation were the central and western regions of the Republic of China.

Because the 1945 War Brides Act did not repeal the provisions delineated in section 3 of the 1917 law, Chinese American servicemen with wives and children in China were met with a conflict in law that ostensibly barred the promise of family reunification granted to other U.S. soldiers made in recognition and honor of their wartime service. On August 9, 1946, An Act to Place Chinese Wives of American Citizens on a Non Quota Basis modified the both the 1924 Immigration Act and the 1943 Magnuson Act, allowing Chinese wives and children nonquota entry into the United States. The Chinese War Brides Act had a significant impact on the growth of the Chinese American population. By one estimate, between 1946 and 1950, 12,265 Chinese immigrants arrived in the United States, of which 7,071 were women, with 5,365 of those women entering the United States through the port of San Francisco. The 1946 Act did not repeal immigration prohibition from the entire geographic region delimited under the 1917 law; that change would come about on December 24, 1952, under the provisions of the McCarran-Walter Act.

See also: Chinese American Population Trends; Chinese Exclusion Act, 1882; Refugee-Escapee Act (1957); Refugee Relief Act (1953); World War I; World War II

Further Reading

An Act to Repeal the Chinese Exclusion Acts, to Establish Quotas, and for Other Purposes, December 17, 1943, ch. 344, § 2 (1943).

An Act to Expedite the Admission to the United States of Alien Spouses and Alien Minor Children of Citizen Members of the United States Armed Forces, December 28, 1945, ch. 591 (1945).

An Act to Place Chinese Wives of American Citizens on a Non Quota Basis, August 9, 1946, ch. 945 (1946).

Immigration Act of February 5, 1917, ch. 29, § 3 Stat. 876 (1917).

Immigration Act of May 26, 1924, ch. 190, § 4, 9, 11, 13 Stat. 155, 159, 161–162 (1924).

Ma, Xoaohua. 2000. "The Sino-American Alliance During World War II and the Lifting of the Chinese Exclusion Acts." *American Studies International* 38 (June): 39–61.

David Alan Rego

WORLD WAR I

Also known as "The Great War," World War I was an international conflict that lasted from 1914 to 1918. Largely centered on the breakdown the balance of power system in Europe, the conflict nonetheless affected the course of history in Asia because of the far-flung empires of all the major belligerents.

Imperial Designs on China

Had it not been for the presence of imperialist European powers in Asia, World War I might not have "spilled over" into Asia. Britain, Germany, and France particularly found themselves in competition to carve out interests in China and Asia generally, while modernization and industrialization had facilitated Japan's own potential expansionism. At the turn of the century, Japan had already created a "sphere of influence" through military victories in Manchuria and northern China.

In contrast, the United States found itself somewhat insulated from the reach of European imperialism in Asia. Claiming to be a "friend to China," the United States had advocated its Open Door policy to uphold the territorial sovereignty of China in the wake of both foreign incursions, especially from the Japanese, and internal strife in the wake of the Boxer Rebellion and other domestic forces such as the fall of the Qing Dynasty and the establishment of the Republic of China in 1911. The so-called "special relationship" with China, along with its policy of Chinese exclusion, characterized how Americans (and Chinese Americans) viewed the Asian component of World War I.

The Great War Spills Over

In late 1914, the Great War spilled over into Asia. British and Japanese attacked the German port of Tsingtao, and the defeat of Germany there resulted in Japanese control of the northern coastal province of Shandong. Seeking to capitalize on its successes, in 1915 the Japanese government sent its "Twenty-One Demands" to the Chinese in an attempt to expand its sphere of influence and, controversially, take over some of the domestic power of what was left of China.

The Chinese Nationalist government, beset with internal strife and military weaknesses, was not in a position to defend against Japanese incursions. However, as an attack on America's Open Door Policy, the Twenty-One Demands elicited a fairly strong response from the United States, and Japan was not able to gain much more than recognition of its existing sphere of influence.

Still, Japan's expansive presence on the Asian continent was codified later in the Treaty of Versailles. The great powers' acceptance of the Japanese in Shandong inspired the May Fourth Movement, a widespread protest movement that centered on the twin pillars of Chinese nationalism and Wilsonian self-determination. What started as a student protest in Beijing on May 4, 1919, quickly spread throughout China and to the Chinese diaspora.

For instance, in the United States, Chinese American organizations, such as the Chinese Consolidated Benevolent Association, had been protesting against Japan's expansionist policies throughout this period and supported the nascent Kuomintang (Chinese Nationalist Party) in the new Chinese Republic. This support for the KMT, garnered partly because of its strong stance against Japan, would later characterize much of America's Cold War policy toward China.

Chinese Americans in the Service of Their Country

Chinese Americans had served in the U.S. military as early as the Civil War in very limited numbers. However, because of the politics of Chinese exclusion and its related demographic consequences, Chinese Americans were more likely to be drafted than other populations but were not particularly well-represented in the U.S. military until World War II. Other Asian Americans were more active in the military, particularly Filipinos (some of whom were of Chinese descent) since the Philippines had been at the time a territory of the United States.

Still, some Chinese Americans did indeed serve in World War I, such as Private Henry Chin, who was mobilized to the defense of France but was killed in action. Sing Kee Lau (also known as Sing Kee Low) was born in 1895 in Saratoga, California, and after the war became a prominent businessman in New York City. Lau was awarded the French Croix de Guerre and the Distinguished Service Cross for his heroism in France. He had single-handedly defended a signal station under attack despite being gassed.

Despite these heroic acts, much of the history of Chinese Americans serving during World War I has been lost, and unlike their service later during World War II, their experiences did little to reverse the institutional racism that had characterized the U.S.'s policy of Chinese exclusion.

See also: World War II

Further Reading

Chang, Iris. 2003. *The Chinese in America: A Narrative History*. New York: Viking.

Chen, Shehong. 2002. *Becoming Chinese, Becoming Chinese American*. Champaign: University of Illinois Press.

Lai, H. Mark. 2010. *Chinese American Transnational Politics*. Champaign: University of Illinois Press.

Yvette M. Chin

WORLD WAR II

World War II was a total global war that affected the Chinese American community in unique ways. By the 1930s and 1940s, the Chinese living in the United States included a higher proportion of U.S.-born and English-native Chinese than the previous century's more transient population. The community's demographic imbalances (a result of the Chinese Exclusion Act and related immigration quotas), and the continuing racial discrimination they endured, meant that these individuals experienced the World War II differently from their

Chinese in New York's Chinatown gather around to read newspapers proclaiming Japan's willingness to surrender according to Potsdam terms on August 10, 1945. They joined with the rest of New York in premature V-J Day celebrations touched off by these reports. (Bettmann/Corbis)

white counterparts as well as from the other large Asian immigrant group in the United States—the Japanese.

Before Pearl Harbor

Unlike traditionally Eurocentric views of World War II, the conflict did not start in 1939 with the German invasion of Poland, nor in 1941 with the bombing of Pearl Harbor from the Chinese and Chinese American perspective. Rather, Japanese incursions into China started as early as World War I and Japan's territorial gains from the Versailles Treaty. By 1940, almost all of China's major cities were occupied by the Japanese, making Chinese Americans early advocates of U.S. intervention. Framed as "resistance against Japan" and cast very much into the contexts of Sino-Japanese disputes over territory on the continent as well as China's internal strife, from the turn of the century, Chinese American communities raised funds to assist the Chinese Nationalist government and organized boycotts of Japanese American businesses, while Chinatown community newspapers spread the word, galvanizing Chinese American communities to advocate for American intervention.

Among the most well-known American organizations to respond to Japanese aggression was the Chinese Women's Association, based in New York. On the west coast, Chinese Americans halted U.S. sales of scrap metal to the Japanese and coordinated boycotts of Japanese American businesses. Another organization based in San Francisco, the Chinese War Relief Association (CWRA), formed from the leadership of existing Chinese American groups and successfully raised funds through parades and "Rice Bowl" parties. Funds would be transferred through private means as well as through the purchase of Liberty Bonds, and, when the United States entered the war in response to Pearl Harbor, the Chinese American community welcomed and supported the involvement.

Chinese Americans Go to War

The U.S. war effort afforded Chinese Americans with socioeconomic and political opportunities that they had been denied to them. Barred from travel to and from China because of the Chinese Exclusion Act and suffering from racial discrimination, Chinese Americans (both immigrant and first-generation) often found themselves "stuck" in Chinatown communities, despite having native English skills and/or advanced education.

In addition to being "naturally" supportive of the war, Chinese Americans were disproportionately drafted into the U.S. military: the demographic consequences of Chinese exclusion resulted in a population that was overwhelmingly male, unmarried, and without dependents. Over the course of the war, between 12,000 to 15,000 Chinese men served in the military, approximately 20 percent of the Chinese adult male population, while some figures estimate that, for example, in New York City 40 percent of the Chinese population was drafted. Compared to the general population figures (8.6 percent), it is clear that Chinese Americans were grossly overrepresented in the draft.

Despite their enthusiasm for the war against Japan, Chinese Americans still suffered from discrimination within the military. Unlike the experience of Japanese American or African American soldiers, Chinese Americans soldiers were at least partly integrated into the regular rank and file. Still, the U.S. Navy limited what positions Chinese Americans could hold, restricting them to serving in the mess hall until 1942. Racial segregation in general was the reality in the military until 1948.

While some of the most well-known military actions against the Japanese are ascribed to the famous Flying Tigers, an unofficial group of U.S. pilots flying with the Chinese Air Force to defend the Chinese Nationalist government around Chungking, only a handful of Chinese Americans were among them, primarily mechanics and engineers. It was not until after the Flying Tigers were absorbed into the formal military structure that Chinese Americans were included among the pilot ranks, especially in the Chinese American Composite Wing (CACW), formed in 1943. Trained in the United States, the CACW brought Chinese Americans and white Americans into closer contact, and for some Chinese Americans, military service abroad was also their first personal experience in the motherland.

Formed in 1944, one unit with the largest concentration of Chinese Americans was the 14th Air Service Group (14th ASG), nine units that included about 10 percent of enlisted Chinese Americans and officers. Many Chinese American airmen flew with distinction, such as Henry Wong of Philadelphia, who was stationed with the 3rd Air Cargo Resupply unit, part of the 14th ASG. Later awarded the Distinguished Flying Cross, Wong was a career officer with 22 years under his belt.

Many Chinese Americans served in other branches of the military, such as Captain Francis B. Wai who was born in Hawai'i to a Chinese father and a Native Hawaiian mother. Wai joined the Hawai'i National Guard. Called to active duty in 1940, he was assigned to the 24th Infantry Division of the U.S. Army. His unit landed in the Philippines in October 1944, and Wai was killed in action storming the beach at Leyte. He was posthumously awarded the Medal of Honor.

Reportedly, there is only one known Chinese American prisoner of war. Eddie Fung, born in San Francisco, had run away to Texas to become a cowboy. He then volunteered for the Texas National Guard, which would mobilize soon after Pearl Harbor. Fung was part of the so-called Lost Battalion that was captured in Java by the Japanese on March 8, 1942. He was among the thousands of Allied prisoners of war that were forced to build the Burma-Thailand death railway, perhaps more well-known in the film *The Bridge on the River Kwai*. Fung and other survivors of his battalion were liberated at the end of the war after 42 months of imprisonment.

In addition to direct military service, the need for Chinese translators also furnished new employment prospects within the U.S. military, a need that provided opportunities also for Chinese American women. Meanwhile, war production industries, especially shipyards on the west coast, the overall labor shortage created by war mobilization afforded more opportunities for Chinese Americans to work outside of the Chinatown milieu, for both men and women.

Telling Your Enemy from Your Friend

The attack on Pearl Harbor forced American stereotypes about Asians—and Chinese and Japanese specifically—to be recast for the war effort. Now needing to differentiate among Asians, the Chinese were restereotyped as loyal and peaceful, while the Japanese now became warlike and aggressive. Because U.S.

military involvement was so highly focused on the Pacific Theater, and because multiple kinds of Asian Americans were part of the war effort at home and abroad, magazines and newspapers such as *Time* and *Life* offered "helpful" ways of telling Asians apart, often with pictures to compare facial features between them. Still, despite this attempt at differentiating among Asians, there are reports of Chinese Americans and others still being targets of xenophobia against "Japs."

For the most part, Chinese Americans were hostile to their Japanese American counterparts: Chinese American newspapers organized the community in boycotting Japanese businesses and spread the idea that Japanese Americans were subversive. In areas where the two groups were more integrated, such as Hawai'i, some Chinese American activists like Hung Wai Ching defended Japanese Americans.

Moreover, diplomatic relations between the United States and China during the war also served to elevate the opinion of the Chinese in America. In the early 1940s, Madame Chiang Kai-shek made several visits to the United States. During these visits, and especially with her 1943 address to Congress, Madame Chiang humanized the war effort and galvanized U.S. support for the Chinese Nationalists, a connection that would endure in U.S. policy toward China for decades after the war.

Postwar Paths to Citizenship

Just as military service and wartime production afforded socioeconomic opportunities for Chinese Americans, both civilian and military, so too did service broaden the chances of citizenship and political inclusion. In the context of the Exclusion Act, the very question of Chinese American citizenship ran counter to their record in military service and their shows of loyalty to the United States. The demographic imbalances that made Chinese Americans disproportionately represented in the draft stemmed directly from the discriminatory immigrations quotas established by the National Origins Act.

Deemed "undesirable," the exclusion of Chinese wives from immigrating to America resulted in a high number of eligible draftees (single men without dependents) from among the Chinese American community. Over the course of the war, the formal alliance between the United States and China to fight World War II seemed at odds with the policies of Chinese exclusion. Ultimately, with the war effort, movement to repeal the Chinese Exclusion Act began to gain ground. The 1943 Chinese Exclusion Repeal Act (Magnuson Act) allowed Chinese immigration and permitted some resident Chinese Americans to pursue naturalization. Still, although considered a generally positive development, the Act continued to limit the number of entry visas to 105, thus modestly expanding Chinese immigration, but still very much working within the quota system established by the Immigration Act of 1924.

More positive, however, was the War Brides Act of 1945 that exempted military spouses and dependents from immigrations quotas. Chinese Americans benefited the most from this Act, especially after the end of Chinese exclusion by allowing Chinese American veterans to marry Chinese women and bring them to the United States. Nearly 6,000 Chinese women were brought to the United States under the Act until its expiration in 1949. Because of the somewhat hasty rush to use the War Brides Act before it expired, the Chinese population in the United States grew rapidly went from 77,000 to 117,000 over the course of the 1940s.

Perhaps the most positive development for Chinese American veterans was the Servicemen's Readjustment Act of 1944, or the GI Bill, which provided veterans with low-interest loans mortgages and tuition assistance. With these benefits, many Chinese Americans were able to advance their education or start small businesses, despite the discrimination they continued to face over the decades. Now armed with citizenship, veterans benefits, and positive public opinion, Chinese Americans could expand beyond the Chinatowns that they had been forced into and could become full members of society.

See also: Flying Tigers; World War I

Further Reading

Chun, Gloria Heyung. 2000. *Of Orphans and Warriors: Inventing Chinese American Culture and Identity.* New Brunswick, NJ: Rutgers University Press.

Taylor, Jay. 2009. *The Generalissimo: Chiang Kai Shek and the Struggle for Modern China.* Cambridge, MA: Belknap Press.

Wong, K. Scott. 2005. *Americans First: Chinese Americans and the Second World War.* Cambridge, MA: Harvard University Press.

Yvette M. Chin

WORLD WAR II IN THE PACIFIC

World War II in the Pacific (also the Pacific War or the Asia-Pacific War) included the Pacific Ocean, East Asia, South West Pacific, South East Pacific, China, and parts of North America and Australia. Generally, December 7, 1941, marks the beginning of the war and September 2, 1945, marks the end, although some historians cite the Japanese invasion of Manchuria (1931) and the Second Sino-Japanese War (1937) as competing dates. The main participants were Japan, the United States, the British Empire, the Republic of China, Australia, Canada, the Netherlands, and the Soviet Union.

In September 1931, Japan invaded Manchuria after accusing the local Chinese population of sabotaging the South Manchuria Railway. This event led to the creation of a nominally independent state (Manchukuo). Japan sought to extend its territory, accommodate its growing population, and acquire resources for its military and industrial expansion. After the League of Nations ordered a withdrawal, Japan responded by leaving the League and pursued a policy of armed expansion.

The Russo-Japanese War (1904–1905) and the presence of Japanese forces in Siberia, following the Bolshevik Revolution (1917), formed a tenuous relationship between the two. Consequently, a series of border disputes ensured between Japan and the Soviet Union (known as the Soviet-Japanese Border Wars) from 1932 to 1941. By 1935, several larger confrontations followed (the Battle of Lake Khasan [also the Changkufeng Incident] and the Battles of Khalkhin Gol [also the Battles of Nomonhan]). In April 1941, Japan and the Soviet Union signed the 1941 Neutrality Pact, at which point Japan abandoned its ambitions in Siberia and shifted its focus to South West Asia and the Pacific.

In 1937, clashes between China and Japan led to the Marco-Polo Bridge incident, and erupted into full-scale war. Britain, France, the United States, the Soviet Union, and Nazi Germany (initially) aided China. The Japanese Army seized the major cities of Shanghai and Nanjing and indiscriminately bombed others. As both sides implemented "scorched earth" policies, soldiers and civilians became targets of increasing violence. Between 10 and 20 million Chinese civilians had been killed by the end of the war.

War between Japan and the Western powers was not inevitable. Japan's move from war in China to war with the West involved, among other factors, its entry into an alliance with Nazi Germany and Fascist Italy (the Tripartite Pact) on September 27, 1940, and the view that defeating China meant seizing territory around it in a strategy of isolation. In 1941, Japan invaded Southeast Asia. In response to Japanese aggression, the Unites States froze Japanese assets in the United States and halted supplies of iron, petroleum, and technology to Japan. Pressed for resources, Japan turned to Malaya and the Dutch East Indies. Preemptive attacks were made against U.S. bases in the Pacific in anticipation of a U.S. response.

A popular starting date of the Pacific War is the surprise attack on Pearl Harbor on December 7, 1941. Japan's attack force consisted of hundreds of aircraft launched from six aircraft carriers north of Hawai'i. Airfields, warships, and shipyard facilities were targeted. However, the U.S. aircraft carriers were Japan's primary targets and were absent during the attack. Delays also prevented Japanese diplomats from delivering their declaration of war prior to the attack. The United States and Britain responded by declaring war on Japan, and on December 11, Nazi Germany and Italy declared war on the Unites States. These declarations of war amalgamated the European and Southeast Asian wars into a single global conflict.

In December 1941, Japan attacked Hong Kong, Guam (Mariana Islands), Wake, Thailand, Burma, the Gilbert Islands, Borneo, and the Philippines. Between January and May 1942, the Japanese swept across the South West Pacific, invading the Dutch East Indies, the Bismarck Archipelago, Papua New Guinea, and the Solomon Islands. Several major naval battles took place in the

South West Pacific resulting in Japanese victories. Aircraft from the Pearl Harbor Strike force also bombed Darwin—an attack that shocked Australia.

Japan secured its southern perimeter by March 1942. The Allies also established their defensive perimeter running from Hawai'i to Australia and New Zealand. On April 18, 1942, American bombers, launched from the U.S. aircraft carrier *Hornet*, bombed Tokyo and other Japanese cities. Although the attack resulted in light damage, it heavily impacted Japanese strategy.

The Battle of the Coral Sea (May 7–8, 1942) was the first fleet battle between aircraft carriers. Japan planned to invade and occupy Port Moresby (Papua New Guinea) and Tulagi (Solomon Islands). The battle ended in a tactical Japanese victory but a strategic victory of the Allies, who successfully halted Japanese expansion and damaged two of Japan's fleet carriers. Japan's abandonment of its plans for an amphibious invasion of Port Moresby was the most significant outcome of the battle.

The Battle of Midway (June 4–7, 1942), the second fleet battle between aircraft carriers, was a decisive engagement that marked a turning point in the war. Japan planned to lure the U.S. fleet into battle in order to overwhelm and destroy it. Fully aware, the United States sent aircraft carriers to ambush the Japanese fleet. With the loss of a single aircraft carrier, the United States managed to sink four of Japan's fleet aircraft carriers and destroy nearly 250 aircraft.

By August 1942, the United States invaded and recaptured parts of the Solomon Islands, including Tulagi, Guadalcanal, and the Florida Islands. From August 24 to 25, 1942, the third carrier battle of the Pacific War took place. The attack, part of the Guadalcanal Campaign, resulted in a strategic Allied victory and delayed Japan's plans to reinforce Guadalcanal. The fourth carrier engagement, known as the Battle of the Santa Cruz Islands (also the Battle of the South Pacific), occurred on October 26, 1942. Tactically, victory went to Japan but U.S. industrial power effectively ended Japan's chances of winning the war.

During a two-day sea-battle known as the Battle of the Philippine Sea (June 19–20, 1944), Japan lost three more aircraft carriers and over 300 aircraft. The battle was a decisive Allied victory. It was the last of the five major aircraft carrier battles during the Pacific War. The battle took place during the U.S. invasion of the Mariana Islands (June–August 1944). The islands were important for providing airfields that placed the U.S. Army Air Force's (USAAF) new B-29s in range of Japan.

The USAAF began conducting air raids of Japan in 1944. These attacks, initially yielding little success, intensified as the war continued and inflicted heavy damage on Japanese cities when airbases in the Mariana Islands became available in late 1944. While the United States initially targeted Japan's industrial centers, precision bombing proved difficult and entire cities were bombed. These became known as the infamous "Fire Raids" on Japan, which resulted in the death of between 90,000 and 100,000 civilians in a single attack on Tokyo.

By mid-1944, Allied forces advanced across the pacific to within several hundred miles of the Philippines. The Philippines campaign, from October 1944 to March 1945, saw the return of U.S. forces (and General Douglas Mac-Arthur) to the islands starting with amphibious invasion of the Gulf of Leyte. Japan mobilized its remaining strength to repulse U.S. forces, and was the first battle in which Japanese forces conducted organized kamikaze attacks.

Between February and March 1945, the United States fought for control of Iwo Jima, just 750 miles from Tokyo. The island provided the Allies with a strategically important airbase. To Japan, the attack meant that the larger invasion of the home islands was not far off. The battle lasted only a month but is regarded as one of the bloodiest of the Pacific war, resulting in 7,000 U.S. casualties. As the war in Europe came to an end and Iwo Jima was captured, the Allies invaded Okinawa, only 350 miles from Japan. The 82-day battle claimed the lives of over 10,000 U.S. service personnel and about 70,000 Japanese soldiers. Okinawa was to serve as a staging base for the invasion of Japan.

The human costs of capturing Iwo Jima and Okinawa raised questions about the casualties that could be expected from an invasion of Japan. Both contributed to President Harry S. Truman's decision to use atomic bombs against the Japanese cities of Hiroshima (August 6, 1945) and Nagasaki (August 9, 1945), which brought the war to an end with the unconditional surrender of Japan on September 2, 1945.

See also: Flying Tigers; World War I; World War II

Further Reading

Castello, John. 1982. *The Pacific War: 1941–1945.* New York: Harper Perennial.
Harries, Meirion, and Susie Harries. 1994. *Soldiers of the Sun: The Rise and Fall of the Imperial Japanese Army.* New York: Random House.
Marsten, Daniel. 2011. *The Pacific War: From Pearl Harbor to Hiroshima.* Colchester, UK: Osprey.
Miller, Edward. 2007. *War Plan Orange: The U.S. Strategy to Defeat Japan, 1897–1941.* Annapolis, MD: Naval Institute Press.

Scott Nicholas Romaniuk

YUNG WING (1828–1912)

Yung Wing (1828–1912), a native of Pedro Island, near Macau (now in Guangdong Province), was the first naturalized Chinese American citizen. Yung and two other Chinese students came to the United States in 1842 to study at Monson Academy, Monson, Massachusetts. He became a Christian while studying at the academy. In 1848 he entered Yale University and graduated in 1854. It was at this point that he became eligible for naturalization. China then permitted dual citizenship.

Chinese President Hu Jintao (L) and Yale University President Richard C. Levin (R) stand next to a portrait of Yung Wing, the first Chinese student to enroll in Yale in 1872, which was presented to Hu during his visit to Yale in New Haven, Connecticut, on April 21, 2006. (Mike Segar/Reuters/Corbis)

Yung, a prominent scholar and an educator, was the head of the Chinese Educational Mission to the United States, having shepherded a number of Chinese students to study in the United States. In 1875 when the anti-Chinese sentiment was high in California and other states, the Chinese government appointed Yung, along with Ch'en Lanpin, Imperial Commissioners to the United States, Peru, and Spain. They were responsible for promoting friendly relations and protecting the Chinese nationals.

See also: Ng Poon Chew; Wong Chin Foo; Wu Tingfang

Further Reading

Yung Wing. 2005. *My Life in China and America.* Beijing: Tuanjie chubanshe.

Edmond Yee

PART II

POLITICAL ACTIVITY AND ECONOMIC LIFE: BUSINESS ENDEAVORS AND INVOLVEMENT IN AMERICAN POLITICS

HISTORICAL OVERVIEW

One primary pull factor of Chinese migration to the United States is economic. For the first wave of Chinese pioneers, it was gold. The first wave of Chinese immigrants who landed in the port of San Francisco were viewed favorably, as celestials and strangers who eventually would become good Americans. When California celebrated its admission into the Union in 1850, the Chinese participated in the ceremonies, alongside whites. Justice Nathaniel Bennett declared that even though the Chinese were born and raised under different governments, that day, they stood as brothers, respected as equals, who share one country, one hope, and one destiny. This quickly changed as the nativist cry got louder and louder. White miners demanded that the Chinese, along with the Mexican, Hawaiian, French, and Chilean miners be banned from mining. Competition intensified and the Chinese miners became the targets of hostility and faced rigid racial prejudice from competing white miners as well as from local and state governments. The best example of this can be seen when the California state legislature passed the Foreign Miners Tax of 1852, which was chiefly enforced against Chinese miners, who often had to pay more than once.

As a result of exclusion from mining, and from gold becoming scarcer during the mid-1860s, the Chinese left the mines and ventured into fishing. Eventually Chinese fishing activities stretched from the Oregon boundary down to Baja California and also along the Sacramento River delta. By the 1870s, a number of fishermen concentrated on catching and processing shrimp in the San Francisco Bay, while others collected abalone off the coast of Southern California. A large number of Chinese immigrants established their residences along the California coast and began the business of gathering, drying, and exporting seafood resources, namely seaweed (Ulva), kelp, and abalone, back to China.

Besides the venture into the fishing industries, large numbers of Chinese workers were employed in the railroad industries. In February of 1865, 50 Chinese workers were hired by the Central Pacific Railroad to help lay the tracks for the transcontinental line leading east from Sacramento. The Chinese laborers were praised by Leland Stanford, the company president, and Charles Crocker, the company's superintendent, as hardworking, amiable, and quiet—workers who could learn any skill, quickly and efficiently. They even went as far as to suggest that Chinese workers were more productive and reliable compared to white workers. The Chinese laborers were trained for all aspects of railroad construction: blasting through mountains, driving horses, handling rocks with picks and shovels. Animosity and hostility from white railroad laborers developed, which resulted in their demand that the company stop hiring Chinese laborers. Within a two-year period, the company employed 12,000 Chinese laborers, roughly 90 percent of their workforce. The railroad employed the "dual wage system," paying Asian workers less than white workers as a means to keep wages for both groups low. The dual wage system resulted in "ethnic antagonism," whereby white workers demanded restrictions on Asian workers, which later resulted in immigration exclusion. Not only were the Chinese laborers fast workers, but their employment saved the company a lot of money because the Chinese laborers were paid $31 a month, while their white coworkers were paid $45 a month. White workers also demanded lodging. Because the Central Pacific managers wanted to accelerate construction, they forced Chinese workers to work through the winter of 1866. The Chinese workers lived and worked in tunnels under the snow. Snow slides and landslides occasionally buried the camps and crews. In the spring, the thawing corpses, still with shovels and picks in their hands, were discovered. That spring, Chinese workers went on strike and demanded eight-hour days and $45 a month: 5,000 workers went on strike. The strike was advertised through the Chinese-language print. The Central Pacific managers blamed their rival Union Pacific for masterminding the strike. This allowed them to negate the possibility that the Chinese workers were capable of acting on their own benefit and behalf. As a possible solution to the Chinese strike, the Central Pacific sent a wire to New York, inquiring about the feasibility of sending 10,000 blacks to replace the striking Chinese. Superintendent Crocker responded to the Chinese strikers by cutting off their food supplies, which worked because weeks later, virtually imprisoned in their camps on the mountains of the Sierras, the starving strikers went back to work. In 1869, the Transcontinental Railroad was completed ahead of schedule. The completion of the Transcontinental Railroad is a symbol of America's Manifest Destiny. The construction of the Central Pacific Railroad line was a Chinese achievement, but this fact remains unnoticed and invisible.

Released from railroad construction, the Chinese laborers moved into agriculture. In California's Sacramento-San Joaquin River delta region, they constructed irrigation channels, reclaimed swamplands, and built the levees, dikes, and ditches. As tenant farmers or sharecroppers the Chinese introduced new varieties of fruits and vegetables for the local markets. By 1870, the Chinese constituted 18 percent of all farm laborers in California; by 1880, they represented 86 percent of the agricultural laborers. The dual wage system was also employed in this industry. In 1880, Chinese pickers in Santa Clara County, California went on strike, demanding increased compensation for the fruit they harvested. The 1882 Chinese Exclusion Act reduced the supply of Chinese farm laborers, so they recognized the increased need for their labor and demanded higher wages as a result.

Other ex-miners began working in the salmon canneries on the coastal bays and streams from central California to western Alaska. In Alaska in 1902, the peak year of Chinese employment there, more than 5,300 of the cannery workforce of 13,800 were Chinese. Others traveled to the Pacific Northwest after being recruited to build the North Pacific line or to run lumber mills. Still others worked in small businesses: laundries, restaurants, and dry-goods stores owned by Chinese merchants. During the 1870s, Chinese workers were recruited to replace the emancipated black slaves for plantation work and railroad building in the South: in Louisiana, Mississippi, and Florida. The Chinese did not stay on the plantations long. As early as 1871, the *New Orleans Times* notes that Chinese preferred to work in the small trades and industries in the city rather than toil in the fields. By 1880, there were a recorded 50 Chinese in Mississippi, 133 in Arkansas, 489 in Louisiana, and 95 in New Orleans, working as laundrymen, cigar makers, shoemakers, cooks, and woodcarvers. Chinese workers were also recruited to Massachusetts, New Jersey, and Pennsylvania as scabs to break striking shoemakers, steam launderers, and cutlery makers—most of whom were Irish immigrants. By then, there were 500 Chinese in New York and about 900 in Boston.

San Francisco, also known as *Dai Fow* (Cantonese for "Big City"), became a city with employment opportunities. "Ethnic antagonism," which pitted one ethnic group against another to keep wages low, resulted in anti-Chinese sentiments and violence, driving many Chinese into self-employment. The Chinese laundry was chief among them. The Chinese laundry was an American phenomenon. It did not exist in China; in fact, there were no laundries in China during that period. Back in China, women did the washing, not men. Opening a laundry in America required little capital because the materials were simple: a stove, trough, dry room, sleeping area, a sign, and some English skills. Besides low capital-investment demands, the Chinese were pushed into this line of work because it was one of the few that was open to them, besides restaurants. In 1900, one out of four employed Chinese men worked as a laundryman.

After the railroad and mining, the Chinese population became an urban population because many were "driven out" of rural areas as a result of economic competition and racial discrimination. San Francisco's Chinese population went from 2,719 in 1860 to 12,022 in 1870. Similarly, Los Angeles's Chinese population went from 605 in 1880 to 1,817 in 1890. In the 1870s, the urban Chinese population moved into manufacturing and once again found themselves caught in a racially segregated labor market with low wages. Often Chinese laborers occupied menial positions in tanneries and woolen, paper, and knitting mills, while European Americans took the skilled jobs. In instances where they held the same position as whites, they were paid less for the same work. In the early 1880s, Chinese men earned $1 a day as factory workers, while white men earned $2.

The image of the Chinese American economic status today is drastically different than the historic economic history. Instead of unskilled cheap laborer, the overall image of the Chinese American population is one of success as exemplified by the racialized image of them as the leading "model minority." As a "model minority" Chinese Americans' median household income is equal to or higher than their white counterparts, by extension, they monopolize white-collar professional fields in the sciences, engineering, medicine, technology, and math. However, it does not account for what Chinese American critics call the "bamboo ceiling," which is reflected in the lack of Chinese Americans in top management positions of Fortune 500 corporations and high-ranking offices in American politics. Moreover it hides the thousands of unskilled and undocumented Chinese Americans who share the same aspiration for work and better opportunities as their first-wave ancestors.

Chinese Americans' perceived economic success correlates with their perceived political apathy as well. Historically, Chinese Americans were excluded from participating in American civic life. Legally all ethnic Chinese born in the United States are U.S. citizens as a result of the Fourteenth Amendment and the 1898 *United States v. Wong Kim Ark* Supreme Court decision. Wong Kim Ark was a Chinese American born in San Francisco. His parents moved back to China in 1890. In 1895, when coming back from visiting his parents in China, Wong was detained and denied entry based on the fact that he was of Chinese descent, even though he was born in San Francisco. The U.S. Supreme Court recognized Wong as a U.S. citizen because of the Fourteenth Amendment, because he was born in the United States. It also declared the 1882 Chinese Exclusion Act could not be retroactively used to deny U.S.-born Chinese their rights to citizenship. Things did not change for Chinese immigrants until the passage of the 1943 Magnuson Act, which permitted naturalization of Asian immigrants, repealing the Chinese Exclusion Act of 1882. The Immigration Act of 1965 finally allowed all Asian immigrants, regardless of their country of origin, immigration and naturalization rights. Today, nearly three-quarters

(70.2 percent) of the Chinese American population are U.S. citizens; 58.8 percent of them are naturalized citizens. This means that three out of four Chinese Americans are U.S. citizens and exhibit very high rates of naturalization. However, this is less true among the recent immigrants who have been slower to seek citizenship.

In response to the systemic decimation and exclusion, the Chinese Six Companies, also known as the Chinese Consolidated Benevolent Association (CCBA), which advocated for Chinese rights in the United States, in a letter to President Ulysses Grant in 1876 reminded the President of the Chinese contributions to the development and expansion of America. The Chinese Six Companies also publicly denounced mob violence against the Chinese. The Chinese also employed the U.S. court system in their protest. In 1855, Chan Yong applied for citizenship in San Francisco's federal district court and was denied citizenship on the basis of the 1790 Naturalization Law, which limited naturalization rights to "whites" only. Since the Chinese were not "white" they were therefore unable to become naturalized citizens. In 1862, Ling Sing sued the San Francisco tax collector, challenging a $2.50 capitation tax levied on the Chinese on the basis that it was unconstitutional. The California Supreme Court, in *Ling Sing v. Washburn*, ruled that while the Chinese could be taxed as "other residents," they could not be set apart as "special subjects of taxation." This was a victory for the Chinese, as the California Supreme Court ruled in their favored based on the fact that the state law was unconstitutional.

In 1868, the Chinese Six Companies lobbied for inclusion of a provision to protect the Chinese immigrants in America in the negotiations between the United States and China. They argued that federal protection of the Chinese would not only protect Chinese lives and property in the United States, but also promote Chinese investments in the country and promote trade between America and China. The Burlingame Treaty (1868) recognized the "free migration and emigration" of the Chinese to the United States as visitors, traders, and permanent residents. It also provided the Chinese with rights and privileges of movement and residency as subjects of the "most favored nation." The flow of immigration (encouraged by the Burlingame Treaty) was stopped by the Chinese Exclusion Act. The Chinese population declined until the Act was repealed in 1943 by the Magnuson Act. Official discrimination extended to the highest levels of the U.S. government: in 1888, U.S. President Grover Cleveland, who supported the Chinese Exclusion Act, proclaimed the Chinese "an element ignorant of our constitution and laws, impossible of assimilation with our people and dangerous to our peace and welfare."

The Civil Rights Act of 1870 contained language that included the Chinese in America. This Act nullified the decision in *People v. Hall* (1854), which made it illegal for Chinese to testify against a white person in court. On August 9, 1853, George Hall, a white miner, accompanied by his brother and one other man, assaulted and robbed a Chinese placer miner on the Bear River in Nevada County, California. Ling Sing left his tent after hearing the sound of gunfire and was shot and killed by Hall. The sheriff arrested Hall and his companions. Hall was later tried and found guilty based on the testimony of three Chinese witnesses. The judge sentenced Hall to death by hanging. However, California Supreme Court Chief Justice Hugh Murray overturned the conviction on the basis that "Asiatics" were "Indians" and therefore unable to testify against a white man in court. Murray argued that "Asiatics" long ago traveled over the Bering Strait and "descended" into Indians. Indians were not allowed to testify in court against a white man, so since "Asiatics" (in this case, the Chinese eyewitnesses) were Indians, they too, cannot testify in court against a white man.

Chinese Americans were banned from political participation because they were not allowed to become naturalized citizens. This did not change until the 1943 Chinese Exclusion Act was repealed for military, political, and economic reasons. In the early 20th century, West Coast and East Coast Chinese Americans united to establish the Chinese American Citizens Alliance (CACA) in Los Angeles to organize voter registration among Chinese Americans. In 1943 the CACA was instrumental in getting Congress to repeal the 1882 Chinese Exclusion Act that had banned Chinese immigration. The civil rights movement of the 1950s and 1960s drew more Chinese Americans into American politics, at which time the Chinese for Affirmative Action and the Chinese Progressive Association were both founded in San Francisco. They fought for greater political enfranchisement and better working and living conditions. The violent killing of Vincent Chin in 1982 fueled many Chinese Americans to become politically active, especially with regard to civil rights' struggles.

Chinese American political participation is complex when considering the type of political activity and political affiliation. Chinese Americans may seem to be less inclined to attend political rallies, but they are more inclined, compared to other ethnic groups, to donate money to candidates running for office. Gradually, Chinese American political participation and identity is shifting from the local to the national, especially in cities where there are sizable Chinese American populations. On the national scene, Daniel K. Akaka, part Chinese and part native Hawaiian, was the first to be elected to the U.S. House of Representatives in 1976. Akaka was also elected to the U.S. Senate in 1990. Chinese American Gary Faye Locke was elected the 21st governor of the state of Washington on November 5, 1996. Locke also served as the U.S. Secretary of Commerce and then U.S. Ambassador to China in President Barack Obama's administration. Steven Chu is the 1997 Nobel Prize physicist who was named Secretary of Energy in President Obama's administration.

There are intense transnational activities among Chinese American peoples. Most of it is economic in nature as many Chinese technocrats live and work between Asia and the United States. A large fraction of Chinese immigrants from China, Taiwan, Hong Kong, and Singapore who arrive in the United States are armed with well-developed cultural capital, technologically sophisticated skills, and material wealth, which makes them different from earlier Chinese immigrants. They have been described as high-tech transnationals of today's booming Chinese American "ethnoburbs." They are able to utilize their political, educational, and economic capital to circumvent bureaucratic red tape and benefit from different nation-state regimes by selecting multiple sites for investments, work, and family relocation. This has created transnational Chinese American families, who are "split" between China, Taiwan, Hong Kong, Singapore, and the United States.

It is also happening in the sphere of politics: In the 2004 and 2008 presidential elections in Taiwan, many Taiwanese Americans traveled back to the island to vote because absentee voting is not allowed. Approximately 2,000 Taiwanese New Yorkers returned to Taiwan to vote in 2004 as did nearly 10,000 Taiwanese Americans from California in 2008. Scholars call this phenomenon "political transnationalism," whereby Chinese Americans from China, Hong Kong, and Taiwan actively participate through donations and votes in the politics of their native countries, especially with regard to U.S. foreign policy. For instance, Taiwanese Americans who hold a Taiwan passport may return to Taiwan to vote in elections.

Recently, because China is developing and modernizing at tremendous levels, some Chinese American scientists and engineers are returning to China to take high-status and high-paying positions. It is predicted that more and more Chinese American scientists will return to China to work because their career will not be limited by the racial "bamboo ceiling."

BOGGS, GRACE LEE (1915–2015)

Grace Lee Boggs, a first-generation Chinese American philosopher born in Providence, Rhode Island, was a facilitator of radical freedom movements in the United States for many decades. A close associate of the Caribbean Marxist C. L. R. James during the Age of the CIO labor movement, and a political collaborator with her husband, the African American autoworker James Boggs, before and after the Black Power movement, she maintained a long-term base in Detroit. An advocate of workers' control, women's liberation, black autonomy, and colonial freedom, Grace projected education for popular self-government. She desired to cultivate social individuals who inquire what value they should place on themselves. A forerunner of the Asian American movement and closely associated with the African American community, like the Japanese American Yuri Kochiyama, Grace became an important symbol of Afro-Asian unity, and her early political activism anticipated the mass revolt of Asian Americans against white supremacy and the model minority myth.

Grace's parents, like most Chinese immigrants in that era, were from Toishan, a sector of peasant villages in Guangdong Province. They came to the United States, leaving behind a devastated economy and constant popular rebellion against feudal authorities. Chin Lee, her father, was enterprising, working first in railroads and laundries, and ultimately became a prominent owner of Chinese restaurants. Her mother lived in the shadow of Confucian patriarchy and strove to break out and express her personality through Christianity. Both were burdened by racist immigration policies in the aftermath of the Chinese Exclusion Act and a popular culture degrading Asians as outsiders. Growing up largely in Queens, a borough of New York City, she was raised among mostly European immigrants who disturbed her by asking about her nationality. Her family was middle class and she did not interact with the culture of the Chinatown ghetto (as her father worked among Chinese all week in his restaurants). Comfortable enough to rent a vacation home in Long Island and enjoy the beach, her family faced discrimination and had to have a white friend purchase their home for them. Chin Lee's business was prosperous during and after World War II, and he became friends with politicians and entertainers. But soon after he ran into tax trouble and his businesses were padlocked and confiscated. This foreshadowed the decline of Times Square, which his restaurant once brightened. Chin Lee's energies were reserved for China, following the fortunes of the modern politics of Sun Yat-sen, Chiang Kai-shek, and Mao Tse-tung. His only interest in America was that its economy should do well so his business would prosper.

Grace first attended college at age 16 at Barnard. She initially did not identify with the marginal because her father had a business and owned his own home though he constantly borrowed to pay creditors. But Grace did enjoy asking questions about the meaning of life, and while initially not seeing herself as a teacher, she soon became interested in philosophy. She became captivated by the role the mind played in creating truth and how communities lived by assumptions by which social change led them to rethink, discard, and create new premises for freedom and power.

Grace also revolted against the disposition of philosophers as leisure-class individuals, and in pursuit of meaning she wasn't concerned with grades at Barnard though she graduated on time and did well. She became burdened by racial and gender discrimination in employment—often hearing "we don't hire Orientals"—and became a typist to earn money after realizing there was no work for a woman-of-color philosopher. Her graduate school experience at Bryn Mawr was very satisfying. She studied under Paul Weiss, who made philosophical projections as if life dependent on it. Weiss introduced her to the writings of Kant, Hegel, Alfred North Whitehead, William James, John Dewey, and George Herbert Mead, whom she wrote about in her doctoral dissertation. Through her early studies Grace learned that philosophy should encourage good conduct, respect the dignity of humanity, and not see others as a means to one's own end. Human purpose was constantly in the process of overcoming hindrances, and progress was not automatic but had to transcend contradictions. Necessary was awareness that history had a social motion and we could not live by truths that were already behind us. Through George Herbert Mead, Grace learned aspects of Rousseau's desire to cultivate the popular will, fused it with Hegel's dialectical philosophy, and in her own right Grace became a philosopher of the social individual by constantly asking what values we should place on ourselves and society. This was all before her encounter with Karl Marx.

In the late 1930s and early 1940s Grace lived in Chicago. Aware that Communists affiliated with Moscow were inconsistent in their antiwar stance, she joined Max Shachtman's Workers Party of the Leon Trotsky movement and began writing on politics with the pen name Ria Stone. Soon she met C. L. R. James, who was a member of the Workers Party but quickly formed his own collective among the Trotskyists, called the Johnson-Forest Tendency (JFT). At its height it had about 75 members. C. L. R. was "Johnson" and "Forest" was Raya Dunavskaya, a bold Russian immigrant woman, who would later found the News & Letters group. Grace, though much younger than C. L. R. and Raya, became the third major leader of the collective.

Grace joined the radical movement, inspired by the fight against racism and A. Philip Randolph's First March on Washington Movement. She was soon developing original themes in political philosophy, working closely with C. L. R. She was the first to translate sections of Karl Marx's *Economic-Philosophical Manuscripts* from German into English, and together with C. L. R. and JFT she studied closely Hegel's *Science of Logic* and Karl Marx's *Capital*. She began to articulate a philosophy of popular self-emancipation, which revolted against the one-party state, welfare state, and trade union hierarchy during the Age of the CIO. She picked apart rationalism as an administrative philosophy of the bourgeoisie, where Big Businesses falsely spoke in the national interest when they were only interested in profits. She argued that only by listening to the experiences of the working class at the point of industrial production could the problems of humanity as a whole be understood. This was best expressed in the pamphlet *The American Worker* (1947) she wrote with autoworker Paul Romano. Grace also saw in Marx philosophical fragments that inspired in her an early feminism. Marx reminded that men should not seek in women their "common" needs but their "human" needs. Grace's Marx was always striving for the fully developed individual, looking for a creative impulse to govern society, and saw civilization as an open book of human capacities.

From 1947 to 1951 the JFT increasingly came to rupture with Trotskyism over their lack of appreciation of labor's self-emancipation and African Americans' and women's autonomous struggles. In 1951 they founded the Correspondence group and published a newspaper by the same name. The paper is remembered for an original outlook on popular culture and the notion that ordinary people by instinct understood the way to break out of totalitarian bureaucracy as represented by the Cold War and McCarthyism. After 1955 Grace became editor of *Correspondence*, and her new husband James Boggs became the central personality of the collective. C. L. R. as a result of persecution by immigration authorities had to return to London in 1953. But Grace often visited London to work on book manuscripts and global solidarity projects. There were constant letters of strategy mailed across the Atlantic between Detroit and London.

Grace worked very closely with C. L. R., best known as the author of *The Black Jacobins*, the classic history of the Haitian Revolution. He introduced her to the dynamics of spontaneity and organization in comparative world revolutions (the Puritan, French, Russian, and Haitian revolutions). C. L. R. informed his circle on European, African, and Caribbean historical developments. Through C. L. R., Grace came to work closely with anticolonial politicians such as George Padmore, Eric Williams, Kwame Nkrumah, and Mbiyu Koinange; also libertarian socialist and postmodern thinkers like Cornelius Castoriadis and Jean Francois-Lyotard. Co-writing many pamphlets with C. L. R. and Raya, such as *The Invading Socialist Society* (1947), *State Capitalism & World Revolution* (1950), and *Facing Reality* (1958), Grace was also part of the conversations and helped to edit what became C. L. R.'s studies of Heglian dialectic, Herman Melville, and Ghana's Kwame Nkrumah. Both C. L. R. and Grace always noted with great satisfaction even after their split the years of their political collaboration.

However, beginning in the mid-1950s Grace began to sense that C. L. R.'s perspectives were calcifying. She began to rethink the Age of the CIO as a revolt against the welfare state and trade union hierarchy. She began to see the American working class as burdened by racial and national arrogance and a materialism that obstructed its elemental drive to liberty. Like C. L. R., she always had a deep identification with antiracist and anticolonial movements, and she began to theorize a transition from the Age of the CIO to the centrality of the Third World. Always ambivalent about C. L. R.'s excitement about the Hungarian Revolution of 1956, by 1961 she was rethinking whether spontaneity, workers self-management, and a movement without vanguard leadership was the best way to understand successful revolutionary processes.

In 1961–1962, Grace politically ruptured with C. L. R. around a dispute over an internal organizational manuscript, "State of the Nation," by her husband, which later became James Boggs's *American Revolution: Pages from a Negro Worker's Notebook* (1963). Her husband came from Alabama sharecropper roots and was an insightful, charismatic, and rooted African American autoworker in Detroit. The personification of the organic intellectual, Boggs began to ask difficult questions about the insurgent capacities (or increasing lack thereof) of the working class from close personal observation. The controversy between C. L. R. and James Boggs was about the difference between historical materialist understanding of reality, the relation of popular spontaneity to revolutionary organization, and thus the tactics of radical political education, agitation, and propaganda work. Grace did not take these differences lightly and understood they were of profound significance even if losing close comrades were a personal disappointment.

Black Power

The Black Power movement (1965–1975), generally seen as blossoming after Malcolm X's death and with the Student Non-Violent Coordinating Committee's turn away from nonviolence and multiracialism, has recently been reframed by some historians to account for earlier developments that foreshadowed Malcolm's last full year in 1964. From 1962 to 1964 Grace Lee Boggs, with her husband James Boggs, are seen as facilitating a transition to the Black Power era, for how they recast the tone of the *Correspondence* newspaper, the dialogues they had with Malcolm, how they mentored youth, such as Max Stanford's Revolutionary Action Movement, organized support for Robert F. Williams, the early African American advocate of armed self-defense, and how they anticipated the turn to Third World Marxism. Increasingly Grace saw revolution coming not from the American industrial proletariat but from new nations like Mao Tse-tung's China and Kwame Nkrumah's Ghana and was among the first secular thinkers to recognize the Nation of Islam's contribution to antiracism.

In 1963 Grace facilitated the conference in Detroit where Malcolm X gave his famous "Message to the Grassroots" speech. In 1964 Grace was coordinator of the Michigan Freedom Now Party and began to give lectures on the black freedom movement, which distinguished between reform and revolution and which broke down the conflicting tendencies and social classes within it. By 1966–1967, with James Boggs, Grace co-authored many influential widely circulated articles such as "The City is the Black Man's Land," and "Detroit: Birth of a Nation." The Boggses, early advocates of civil rights, were now trying to help shape the black freedom movement toward seizing power. This meant shaping a consensus that black people would soon govern over whites as mayors and police chiefs. But also black people had to, in light of the potential of the urban uprisings in many cities from 1964 to 1968, consider the revolutionary potential of carrying out their own economic, judicial, and foreign relations independent of capitalism.

James and Grace Lee Boggs were seen by government surveillance records, with Milton and Richard Henry (later founders of the Republic of New Africa), Ed Vaughn (Pan African bookstore owner who later became a congressman), Rev. Albert Cleage of the Shrine of the Black Madonna Church, and H. Rap Brown as responsible for the fiery 1967 Detroit rebellion against police brutality.

The Boggses mentored younger diverse Black Power leaders and organizations from Stokely Carmichael to the League of Revolutionary Black Workers. They would question the trendy call for "black unity" and distinguish between coalition building and the need to develop distinct political programs.

Grace was responsible for editing and pushing forward Cleage's *The Black Messiah*, a pioneering work in black and anticolonial theology. In contrast to her husband, Grace worked to strengthen the church as a social force, was not deterred by corrupt preachers, and always maintained an understated spirituality behind her secular projections.

Grace's 1968 speech, "The Black Revolution in America," was published in an original anthology called *The Black Woman* (1970), edited by Toni Cade Bambara. Including the literary expressions of Alice Walker, Audre Lorde, and Nikki Giovanni, Grace's contribution, the only one by a non–African American woman, was creative in how it delineated what a revolution was, how the black middle class was increasingly seeking coveted positions above society in the name of fighting racism, and how black urban youth instinctively were confronting capitalism and the state. Grace boldly pointed out new contradictions and suggested a way forward.

Beyond Rebellion, Toward a New Concept of Citizenship

By 1970 James and Grace Lee Boggs saw the Black Power movement, as personified by the Black Panthers, as having a crisis of leadership. The Panthers, who initially courageously confronted racist police, despite proclaiming to be a vanguard party, were more of a movement of young people with a lack of perspective, not so much in its anti-imperialism, but in its inability to make projections for what the new society might look like. As the Panthers ruptured between factions that were pursuing electoral strategies and armed liberation, the Boggses were dissatisfied with how "political prisoners" began to increase, and how the very definition was stretched to include all black people in jail. They became disenchanted with their initial alliance with Revolutionary Action Movement and started to pose ideas for a new concept of citizenship.

By the 1970s, as documented in their books *Revolution and Evolution in the Twentieth Century* (1974) and *Conversations in Maine* (1978), the Boggses started to ask new questions about whether the welfare state was liberating, where was women's liberation going, could the end goal of economic liberation be a job in an era of deindustrialization, and how can African American pursue black autonomy without taking up the issue of crime among their communities.

In the wake of the Panthers the Boggses posed a *Manifesto for a Black Revolutionary Party* (1970) in an attempt to give strategic leadership, but by the early 1980s were trying to pose a *Manifesto for an American Revolutionary Party*. Swept up in the era of Third World Marxism, Black Nationalism, and the debate about the role of the vanguard party, by the early 1980s they were returning to the idea of a government of popular councils and assemblies that they developed with C. L. R., but with a new emphasis on popular responsibility in neighborhoods not so much insurgent labor action in workplaces.

They were now for a distinctly American Revolution, where previously American democracy and conceptions of liberty, during the Black Power era, were bankrupt. But now the pacesetter was a people of color–led multiracial organization that led the way from abstract "rights" to a new concept of power reinvigorating national ideals. James and Grace Lee Boggs led the National Organization for an American Revolution from 1982 to 1987. They were not able to overcome the contradictions of electoral and privilege politics, racial insecurity and sexism, the instability of young activists starting families and pursuing jobs where the Boggs were comparatively older and more rooted, even as their ideas were in the best position to challenge a new generation. Reminding their comrades to think "dialectically not biologically" or not narrowly through the prism of race and sex, the Boggses led the way out of the alienation of the collapse of the Black Power and women's movements toward new forms of association.

Grace Lee Boggs also has been a neglected theorist of women's liberation. Publishing individually and collectively written pamphlets in the 1970s and

1980s, "Women and the Movement to Build a New America," "Women and the New World," "What Value Shall We Place On Ourselves?" and "Beyond Socialist Feminism," Grace inquired, what is behind the conflicts between men and women down through the ages? She argued it has been women's deep need to be politically and economically independent from family, while of course respecting the burdens of working-class men and parental responsibility. With the evolution of reproductive technologies, education, and the welfare state, women were finally asking transparently what they desire in conversations with men. Behind loose talk of feelings and emotions women were looking at the world objectively in the face of fears that sex and relations with men are not simply desires but pose questions for how women's lives are permanently shaped and how society is organized. It was not a misunderstanding primarily based on men and women communicating differently but one of power and consequence.

Grace believed women must be challenged to see themselves not as victims or dependents on men. Rather, the intersection of the personal and political is that women must challenge men and themselves to be a whole new human being so a new society can be created. This is especially so among young girls where in urban centers they are preyed on, and encouraged to be sex objects and childbearers (sometimes under the premise of narrow nationalist politics as much as by pimps) as a false basis of empowerment without thinking what value they should place on themselves and how developing their minds could foster a greater autonomy.

In James Boggs's last years, before he died of cancer in 1993, SOSAD (Save Our Sons and Daughters) and *The Awakening* was forged in an attempt to close crack houses, build community gardens, and fight for an ethical redevelopment plan for postindustrial Detroit. As always the Boggses were far ahead of their time. Their vision of a social ecology, while growing to this day, still has not been grasped by the multitudes as Detroit has plummeted into bankruptcy, austerity, and the collapse of its infrastructure.

After James Boggs died, Grace began to reconsider her Asian American identity, finally visiting China for the first time. Since 1970, when she first spoke on "Asian Americans and the U.S. Movement" and helped found the Detroit Asian Political Alliance (APA), Grace was a force of clarifying the contours and conflicts among Asian Americans and linkages between Asians overseas, Asian immigrants, and the desire to learn more about Asian culture navigating racist and Cold War repression. Grace transitioned from critiquing Mao Tse-tung's communism to embracing him as a modern philosophical role model.

Grace's role in the Asian American movement, like all movements, was less to project ethnic leadership than to ask difficult questions about social change. Grace made clear that, while having the courage to disagree with her parents (she would not have married an African American if she did not), the Asian American experience, despite different diaspora origins, is really about the search for self-reliance and reconciliation between modernity and tradition. She implored globally minded Asian Americans that the American experience is not one of peasant villages but coming to terms with the fact that the United States has great technological "know-how" but little historical and philosophical "know-why."

Grace Lee Boggs often projected a vision of an American Revolution distinguished by popular councils and assemblies, while asking difficult questions about welfare, crime, rights, trade unions, social ecology and the limits of cities, automation, and a postindustrial economy that challenged the mainstream of socialist and progressive movements. A chairperson of small revolutionary organizations dedicated to radical education, agitation, and propaganda; an editor of original political newspapers and writer of dynamic pamphlets for more than 50 years; the last two decades of her life were distinguished by greater emphasis on her spirituality, with a new focus on nonviolence (but less disobedience) and a shifting sense of historical materialist evolution, and a more full embrace of her Asian American identity.

Grace's endorsements and silences on President Obama were recognized by those with a long memory as an aberration from the Boggses' stance that the post–civil rights crisis was a product of black people's failure to stay independently organized from capitalist electoral politics. But as she approached the age of 100, Grace despite her heralded innovation, at her best in these later years was really relying on a recycling of her deep archive of ideas developed in the past, which few are old enough to recall. She did not simply live through the rise and fall of many movements for social justice, searching for new identities, discarding one banner for another, in pursuit of fresh perspectives. She is a major figure of the Asian American and black radical traditions not merely because she experimented with Anglo-American and European philosophical ideas ultimately to arrive on her own authority. Boggs as original strategist and theorist was a partisan who reminds of the antagonisms within radical social movements, conflicting tendencies of organizations and ideological dynamics, and the impulse not merely to advise regimes but to overthrow them. The scholarship on her life and work is just beginning and deep probing into her intellectual heritage will reveal that Grace was an original revolutionary.

See also: Chinese American Activism; Chinese Americans and Civil Rights

Further Reading

Boggs, Grace Lee, and Scott Kurashige. 2012. *The Next American Revolution.* Berkeley: University of California Press.

Boggs, Grace Lee. 1998. *Living for Change.* Minneapolis: University of Minnesota Press.

Boggs, Grace Lee. 2005. "The Black Revolution in America." In *The Black Woman: An Anthology*, edited by Toni Cade Bambara. New York: Washington Square Press.

Matthew Quest

CENTRAL PACIFIC RAILROAD
See: Transcontinental Railroad

CHENNAULT, ANNA (1925-)

Born Chen Xiangmei in Beijing, China on June 23, 1925, Anna Chennault gained notoriety through her marriage to a famed American aviator and through her work in the United States for the Republican Party and various Chinese American organizations. After graduating from Lingnan University in Hong Kong, Chennault pursued a career in journalism and in 1944 became a correspondent for the Central News Agency in China. In 1947, she married Claire Chennault, who had commanded to much acclaim the "Flying Tiger" American Volunteer Group in China and later the 14th Air Force during World War II. The union produced two daughters. After the war, Chennault's husband established the Civil Air Transport, a cargo airline and precursor to Air America that flew relief missions into Asia in support of Chiang Kai-shek and the Nationalist Chinese. The Central Intelligence Agency eventually purchased the business and used it as a cover for covert operations in the Far East. Through her husband, Anna Chennault established many international business and political contacts and maintained a high profile, promoting anticommunist causes and making public appearances in the United States. After her husband's death in 1958, Chennault worked occasionally as a correspondent for the Central News Agency and for a short time as a broadcaster for the Voice of America. She relocated with her two daughters to Washington, D.C., where she associated herself with various conservative causes and became part of a social circle that included many leading Republican politicians. She actively support Richard Nixon's presidential campaign in 1960 and founded or worked for a number of organizations that supported Nationalist China and Chinese Americans in the United States. She toured the country and gained notoriety on the speaking circuit as an expert on Asian affairs. She also served as a political go-between for U.S. officials during her frequent trips to visit relatives and friends in Taiwan.

Chennault's relationship with Richard Nixon generated controversy in 1968 as Nixon campaigned for and eventually won the presidency. As the election drew near, the race between Nixon and Democratic standard-bearer Hubert Humphrey tightened after President Lyndon Johnson announced that the United States would halt the bombing of North Vietnam. As part of a political strategy designed to help Humphrey and the Democrats, Johnson hoped that the announcement would encourage the North Vietnamese to come to the negotiating table and discuss a peace settlement. Aware that the strategy would not be effective if South Vietnam refused to take part in negotiations, the Nixon camp used Chennault and her contacts to deliver a message to the South Vietnamese leadership discouraging them from being part of any peace talks until after the U.S. election. Chennault assured the South Vietnamese ambassador that by waiting, South Vietnam would receive better terms from the new Republican administration. Johnson privately called Nixon's attempt to sabotage the peace process "treason," and it was certainly illegal based on laws in place at the time. Nixon won the election, so the affair was never investigated, and he later denied the allegation in interviews. In the years to come, Chennault remained active in Republican politics, serving on numerous boards and for many years as chairman of the General Claire Chennault Foundation.

See also: World War II

Further Reading

Chennault, Anna. 1980. *The Education of Anna.* New York: Times Books.

Forslund, Catherine. 2002. *Anna Chennault: Informal Diplomacy and Asian Relations.* Wilmington, DE: SR Books.

Hughes, Ken. 2014. *Chasing Shadows: The Nixon Tapes, the Chennault Affair, and the Origins of Watergate.* Charlottesville: University of Virginia Press.

Ben Wynne

CHIANG KAI-SHEK, MADAME (SOONG MEILING) (1898–2003)

Soong Meiling (1898–2003), also known as Madame Chiang Kai-shek, was the wife of Generalissimo Chiang Kai-shek and a First Lady of the Republic of China. American educated and fluent in English, Soong played an active role in Chinese politics and was instrumental in garnering U.S. support for China during World War II and the early Cold War. As First Lady, Soong was one of the most influential women in modern China and ranked frequently in Gallup Polls as one of the "10 Most Admired Women in the World."

Soong was born in Shanghai in 1898 but spent most of her childhood and teenage years studying in the United States. She graduated from Wellesley College in 1917 with a major in English but had also taken classes in American

In her official 1942–1943 tour, Madame Chiang also visited and spoke to numerous Chinatown communities across the United States. Her most memorable address came at Carnegie Hall on her third day in New York, where she spoke for over an hour to more than 3,000 Chinese Americans. While in San Francisco she toured up Grant Avenue, which was the main street of the largest Chinese populated quarter in the Western Hemisphere. Many Chinese people also came to see Soong and hear her speak at other major stops on her tour, including Chicago and Los Angeles. When she spoke publicly, Soong told stories from Chinese history and folklore to appeal to the members of the Chinese community living in America.

Madame Chiang Kai-shek, wife of the Generalissimo, rides from the railroad station to the White House in Washington, D.C., with President Roosevelt on February 17, 1943. Madame Chiang was a guest at the White House for two weeks and took part in important war discussions. (Bettmann/Corbis)

literature, English composition, philosophy, and Bible studies. Upon returning to China, Soong met her future husband Chiang Kai-shek in 1922 and the couple married in 1927. After Chiang rose through the ranks to become Generalissimo and leader of the Kuomintang (Chinese Nationalist Party), Soong worked as her husband's English translator, adviser, and spokesperson during the Chinese Civil War and World War II.

During the early 1940s, Soong toured the United States in an effort to gather sympathy, aid, and armaments for her husband's wars against the Japanese and Chinese Communists. She became well-liked by the American public, most evident by appearing on the cover of *Time* magazine three times. On February 18, 1943, she became the first Chinese person and only the second woman to address the U.S. Congress. Her speech, which appealed to American national pride and centered on Sino-American unity in the war against Japan, was received warmly by both U.S. politicians and the American people. She became a popular household name in the United States, prompting strong public demands that the Roosevelt Administration send more aid to the Chinese war effort than it was otherwise sending through the 1941 Lend-Lease Act.

In 1949, Chiang lost the Chinese Civil War to the Communist Party and was forced to flee to Taiwan. In efforts to stabilize the Kuomintang and potentially reclaim the mainland, Soong played a pivotal role in helping Chiang convince the United States to send further financial and military aid to the Nationalists during the early Cold War. With Soong's help, Chiang also succeeded in sign-ing a mutual defense treaty with the United States in December 1954. Soong continued to be an important point of contact in Sino-American relations until her husband's death in 1975. After Chiang's death, Soong retreated from public life and returned to the United States, where she died in 2003 at the age of 105. On top of her many achievements, Soong was one of few people who lived during three different centuries.

See also: Sun Yat-sen

Further Reading

Li, Laura Tyson. 2006. *Madame Chiang Kai-shek: China's Eternal First Lady*. New York: Grove Press.

Pakula, Hannah. 2009. *The Last Empress: Madame Chiang Kai-shek and the Birth of Modern China*. New York: Simon & Schuster.

Andrew Kelly

CHINATOWN GANGS IN THE UNITED STATES

Chinatown gangs in the United States have a varied and sensationalized history within the American discourse. From sinister portrayals as the Chinese "Yellow Peril" to hyperviolent refugees from Southeast Asia, Chinatown gangs have been popularly featured in literature, television, film, and newsprint for more than half a century. Reflective of demographics in Chinatowns across the country, Chinatown gangs appear to continually grow in their diversity beyond southern Chinese immigrants, including those that are U.S.-born, from Taiwan, and from Southeast Asia. Robust understandings of the gangs continue to be elusive and what is known often focuses on long-standing southern Chinese communi-ties in San Francisco and New York. Studies and documentation of Chinatown gangs vary from small youth street "crews" to transnational crime syndicates with origins in the revolutionary Triad organizations during the Qing Dynasty.

Prior to the influx of Chinese immigrants resulting from the 1965 Immigra-tion and Nationality Act, there were very few youth of Chinese descent living in the United States. Thus, there was little recorded on what is usually considered gang activity in Chinatown communities, although there was some criminal group activity that was primarily engaged in by adults. This lack of activity and documentation began to change in the decade after 1965, when thousands of immigrant families and their children began to arrive in the United States, often first settling in Chinatowns.

Located in the urban core, Chinatown residents were often limited in terms of English-language capacity as well as financial, social, and cultural capital. This most likely facilitated "underground" social and economic practices by adults that were both new and established. As the children of many working-class

Chinatown immigrants experienced high marginalization and disenfranchise-ment in schooling, social services, and law enforcement institutions, they were also pulled into practices tied to Chinatown gangs that had been noted by law enforcement to some degree since the 1950s. Here the term "gang" is defined as a cohesive group of people affiliated under certain terms of leadership, geog-raphy, and loyalty. These groups often engage in illicit practices that can some-times be understood as self-defeating forms of resistance, similar to those of working-class Chinatown youth during the 1970s.

Aside from similar class backgrounds, Chinatown gang youth had family ori-gins in southern China, typically from Guangdong (Canton) Province, where many Chinese immigrants to the United States were historically from. Fol-lowing the Vietnam War and the U.S. involvement with Cambodia and Laos, Chinatowns experienced an influx of Southeast Asian refugees and immigrants, many of whom were ethnic Chinese with ancestral roots in Guangdong (i.e., Chaozhou or Chiu Chow). In recent decades, further diversification of Chi-natown gangs has resulted from immigrants from Taiwan and northern China that sometimes settle in Chinatowns but speak different dialects from those in the south, including Mandarin. Other factors that have impacted the gangs are the gentrification of Chinatowns across the country, which has pushed together communities that have historically lived apart, as well as subsequent genera-tions of Asian and Chinese youth born in the United States, many of whom are racially and ethnically "mixed." Another factor in the changing demographics of Chinatown gangs is the emergence of suburban Chinatowns, such as in the San Gabriel Valley in Los Angeles County.

Because of the "underground" nature of Chinatown gangs, it is difficult to accurately account for their practices, development, size, and reach. A signifi-cant factor that has influenced understandings of Chinatown gangs is 20th-century portrayals of Chinatowns in the U.S. news and entertainment media. The discourse has often framed Chinatowns as havens of immorality, rife with gambling, narcotics, and human trafficking tied to prostitution and undocu-mented immigration. Chinatown gangs continue to be viewed as violent and organized perpetrators of such crimes, somewhat like the Italian Mafia in terms of their level of organization and interstate activities. This portrayal has influ-enced academic institutions and the criminal justice system as Chinatowns and Asian gangs have increasingly become the subject of study and policing since the 1970s in cities such as Boston, Philadelphia, Chicago, and San Francisco.

Within the "organized crime portrayal" of Chinatown gangs, they are dis-cussed as organizations with ties to the tongs, which were originally frater-nal support associations first established in the 1800s that eventually became involved in criminal activity. In recent decades, Chinatown gangs are believed to have carried out some of the business activities of the secret tong societ-ies. Teenage and young adult street gang members, mostly males, have been thought to take orders from somewhere along the chain of command within criminal tong hierarchies. If they do not take orders from tongs, the gangs at least have to placate them to conduct their activities with less interference from the existing Chinatown infrastructure. These exchanges and networks have been explicitly documented in the research about New York, particularly with Manhattan Chinatown.

In addition to the ties between Chinatown gangs and the tongs, connections have also been made to the triads that originated as revolutionaries during China's Qing Dynasty. Although many Chinatown street gangs appear to not have been strongly affiliated with the triads when they arose in the 1970s, 1980s, and 1990s, it is thought that these affiliations began to solidify largely because of human trafficking and the lucrative drug trade from Asia with narcotics such as heroin. Ties have been documented between North American gangs and Chinese triads in East and Southeast Asia, but it is unclear to what extent these exist in the United States. Nevertheless, with the tongs, there has been much speculation of transnational criminal conspiracies within the U.S. media and criminal justice system. At times this speculation has been sensationalized to paint portraits of vast and sinister undergrounds in Chinatowns, reminiscent of the historical exoticization and demonization of Chinese and Asians as the evil "Yellow Peril."

Debates continue within the criminal justice system and social science research on what are primary factors of gang development in places like Chinatown. Different theories persist on the role that tongs, triads, and organized crime play. However, there is agreement on how issues of class, language, and schooling are critical factors in youth joining Chinatown gangs, and how there seems to be a reduced public presence of Asian gangs on a national level, due in part to the arrests of some major gang leaders during the 1990s.

Further Reading

Chen, Ko-lin, and Jeffrey Fagan. 1999. "Social Order and Gang Formation in Chinatown." In *The Legacy of Anomie Theory*, edited by F. Adler and W. S. Laufer. Piscataway, NJ: Transaction.

Chin, Ko-lin. 2000. *Chinatown Gangs: Extortion, Enterprise, and Ethnicity*. Oxford, UK: Oxford University Press.

Huang, Hua-Lun. 2006. "Dragon Brothers and Tiger Sisters: A Conceptual Typology of Counter-Cultural Actors and Activities of American Chinatowns, China, Hong Kong, and Taiwan, 1912–2004." *Crime, Law and Social Change* 45: 71–91.

Joe, Karen A. 1994. "The New Criminal Conspiracy? Asian Gangs and Organized Crime in San Francisco." *Journal of Research in Crime and Delinquency* 31: 390–415.

Takagi, Paul, and Tony Platt. 1978. "Behind the Gilded Ghetto: An Analysis of Race, Class, and Crime in Chinatown." *Crime and Social Justice* 9: 2–25.

Toy, Calvin. 1992. "A Short History of Asian Gangs in San Francisco." *Justice Quarterly* 9(4): 647–65.

Benji Chang

CHINESE AMERICAN ACTIVISM

Chinese American activism, and by extension Asian American activism, has become increasingly important in the United States since the 1960s, and it is best conceived of as a variety of different groups, with a shared cultural heritage and experiences that work toward similar goals. Although Asian activism existed to a limited degree as early as the 1850s, small disparate communities and ethnic divisions prevented a unified approach in dealing with common socioeconomic and political issues. It was not until the 1960s when the ideals of the civil rights and women's movements, reactions to the internment of Japanese Americans during World War II, and U.S. intervention into Korea and Vietnam created a unified Asian American identity and clarified a common set of grievances. Asian American organizations were founded upon their members' shared heritage, immigration experiences, and resistance to discrimination. Generally, the goals of these organizations were to promote community improvement, wider awareness of ethnic issues, and equal treatment. In addition to the establishment of ethnic organizations, changing immigration laws in America, rising birthrates in the Asian American community, and greater political awareness transformed the activist role of Asian Americans. Following student strikes at San Francisco State College (now University) and the University of California at Berkeley (1968–1969), where Asian Americans fought against institutional racism for the inclusion of ethnic studies in school curriculums, activists regularly sought to improve communities, overcome national racism and discrimination, and advocate against U.S. imperialism. In the 1980s and 1990s, Asian American activism became increasingly professionalized, focusing on cultural preservation, national electoral politics, Jesse Jackson's 1984 presidential campaign, and reparations for Japanese internment.

While there is a history of political participation by Asians as early as the 1850s, such forms of activism focused primarily on labor disputes and improving living conditions rather than on ethnic grievances. The limited population of the Asian American communities and divisions between national groups meant that these actions were not connected to larger organizations or political goals. It was not until the 1930s and 1940s, following decades of racism and exclusionary laws (Chinese Exclusion Act of 1882, Gentlemen's Agreement of 1907, Johnson-Reed or Immigration Act of 1924) and in the wake of socialist political ideals sweeping Asia (anticolonial, equality) that the roots of the modern Asian American activism began.

In the early 20th century, most Asian migrants were working class, lived in ethnic enclaves, and often held racially segregated jobs. However, following passage of a Laundry Tax in New York City in 1933, which targeted Chinese establishments, business owners formed the Chinese Hand Laundry Alliance to challenge racist laws, present a unified voice to the political establishment, and overcome ethnic isolation. In addition, in 1936 Chinese members of the

National Maritime Union, a labor organization pledged to protect members regardless of race, color, religion, or national origin went on strike to receive equal pay and the right to shore leave. Regardless of the successes of these labor actions, national racism against Asians culminated with the internment of Japanese Americans during World War II, when all Asians (Japanese, Chinese, Koreans, Vietnamese, Filipino) tended to be grouped together. As a result of the activism of the 1930s, the dissemination of new political ideals from Asia, and the national racism presented by the United States in the denial of fundamental rights against most Asian groups during World War II, the development of an increasingly unified Asian American culture began to emerge.

In the 1960s, Asian American activism, building on the women's and civil rights movements and in response to the Korean and Vietnam wars, began in earnest. The developing pan-ethnic Asian American culture was based on shared heritage, experiences, and resistance to discrimination. Asian American activism began in different locations throughout the country, such as San Francisco and New York, with different perspectives and goals but responding to common issues. In general, Asian American organizations during this period sought political and social change rather than promoting a specific cultural identity. The activism of the period is defined by the members of these organizations, who were second-generation Asian Americans, focused more on national issues of race, equality, and the Vietnam War, working with black American organizations to eliminate discrimination.

In San Francisco, community activists in the 1960s began to bring attention to the problems of Chinatown, including poor living conditions, unemployment, and institutional racism. At the same time, students at San Francisco State College and the University of California at Berkeley went on strike to challenge institutional racism and to promote the establishment of ethnic studies. Concurrent with these events was the International Hotel campaign, which focused on the protection of a residential building housing a large number of retired Asian workers and a range of community services and organizations. From these events arose community organizations such as the Third World Liberation Front, Kearny Street Workshop, and Asian American Political Alliance, which garnered national attention and gave way to wider political protests that sought to address institutional racism, protect historical ethnic enclaves, and support cultural as well as artistic movements.

By contrast, in New York Asian American activism is credited as beginning in 1968 when Kazu Iijima and Minn Matsuda sought to start a Japanese American community organization for their children to learn about and maintain their Asian heritage. The result was the creation of the Asian Americans for Action (AAA) group, or Triple A, whose members included students from Columbia University and the City College of New York. AAA, a pan-Asian organization, focused on establishing a political voice in opposition to the

Vietnam War, declaring it to be a military excursion, driven by American racism and imperialist ideals, and arguing that it was a conflict being fought for natural resources and business interests rather than as an effort to protect the rights of people.

Throughout the 1970s, 1980s, and 1990s Asian American activism became increasingly professionalized, focusing on cultural preservation, the continued promotion of civil rights, national electoral politics, and campaigning for reparations for the internment of Japanese Americans. These changes in Asian American activism reflect the growing sophistication of the movement as well as the shifting nature of social and political organizations throughout the nation since the 1980s.

See also: Boggs, Grace Lee; Chinese Americans and Civil Rights

Further Reading

Liu, Michael, and Kim Geron. 2008. *The Snake Dance of Asian American Activism: Community, Vision, and Power*. Lanham, MD: Lexington Books.
Louie, Steve. 2001. *Asian Americans: The Movement and the Moment*. Los Angeles: UCLA Asian American Studies Center Press.
Maeda, Daryl J. 2012. *Rethinking the Asian American Movement*. New York: Routledge.

Sean Morton

CHINESE AMERICAN CITIZENS ALLIANCE

Like other immigrant organizations, the Chinese American Citizens Alliance has its roots in the historical context of the migration of Chinese sojourners in the mid- to late 19th century, as well as in the anti-Chinese sentiments that arose in the American West in response. Chinese immigrants fulfilled the need for inexpensive labor during the Gold Rush (1848–1858) and the construction of the Transcontinental Railroad (1863–1869) in the United States, but negative public perception of Chinese laborers fostered the passage of ethnically targeted restrictive immigration policies such as the Page Act (1875), Chinese Exclusion Act (1882), Scott Act (1888), and Geary Act (1892). This atmosphere of entrenched social segregation and legislative discrimination led immigrants to inhabit increasingly isolated Chinese neighborhoods called Chinatowns, and also gave rise to the organization of family associations and community organizations, which sought to support Chinese interests, provide social support, and present a unified political voice in California and across the nation.

However, in 1895 following the failure of the Chinese Six Companies' challenge to the Geary Act, Chinese American citizens in California organized the Native Sons of the Golden State, which was incorporated by Chun

Dick. The goal of this organization was to change the way Chinese in America were being treated. The Native Sons were later reorganized in 1904 by Ng Gunn, Joseph Lum, and Walter Lum, and by 1912 it had become a statewide organization. By 1915 this association was officially reorganized and chartered as the Chinese American Citizens Alliance (CACA), a national nonprofit organization, which had begun to include a range of out-of-state organizations.

The goals of the CACA were to overcome racial and ethnic discrimination against Chinese Americans, ensure Chinese Americans the rights and privileges of U.S. citizenship, accelerate the process of assimilation into American society, promote the participation of Chinese community leaders in American politics, and provide a unified national voice for Chinese Americans. While laudable, the CACA has been criticized as being more concerned with citizen rights than immigrant rights and thereby negating the needs of a large segment of the early Chinese population in the United States.

From its inception, the CACA provided financial and legal assistance to Chinese immigrants, and between 1920 and 1947 it granted death benefits for the families of its members. During this period, the CACA was instrumental in prompting the amendment of the Immigration Act of 1924 to allow the entry of foreign wives of Chinese immigrants. In addition, members of the organization testified before the U.S. President's Commission on Immigration and Naturalization in 1952 and participated in the pan-Asian coalition promoting the civil rights movement during the 1960–1970s. The CACA in the early 20th century was one of the most prominent National Chinese American political organizations in aiding immigrants, providing a united political voice for the Chinese American community, challenging social and legislative discrimination, and publishing the *Chinese Times* (1924–1988), which was the first Chinese American news publication in the United States.

See also: Chinese Consolidated Benevolent Association

Further Reading

Chan, Sucheng, ed. 1991. *Entry Denied: Exclusion and the Chinese Community in America, 1882–1943*. Philadelphia, PA: Temple University Press.
Okihiro, Gary Y. 2001. *The Columbia Guide to Asian American History*. New York: Columbia University Press.

Sean Morton

CHINESE AMERICANS AND CIVIL RIGHTS

The history of the civil rights of Chinese immigrants and Asian Americans in the United States has gone through four periods. In the first, Chinese

American immigrants used the courts to gain important civil rights while facing hostility. Following, Asian immigrants fought harassing laws stopping them from immigrating, being naturalized, or owning land. Next, political rights were again gained in the 1940s and 1950s and economic rights in the 1960s and 1970s. In the present period, continued Chinese American attempts to gain further rights have produced mixed results in a complex time.

1860s–1880s

Most Chinese immigrants who arrived just after the beginning of the Gold Rush were young male peasants shunted off their land in the rural area near Guangzhou in the large Zhujiang delta in Guangdong Province, China. Approximately 300,000 came to the United States as manual laborers to start again or simply to make some money and so to meet the plentiful demand for cheap labor in the West.

Beginning with the Page Act in 1875—which classified as "undesirable" any Asian coming to the United States to be a forced laborer, any Asian woman in prostitution, and any convicts—and the Chinese Exclusion Act of 1882, the Chinese were the first and only immigrant group to be restricted until 1917. The popular and political mood of the nation at the time was to limit rather than grow the civil rights of the Chinese.

In the face of such opposition, the Chinese immigrants learned quickly that they had to use all aspects of the American judicial system to fight such legal discrimination. This was especially true for Chinese merchants and tradesmen who wanted to do business. The Chinese thus made many court challenges against unfair regulations and legislation.

The initial Chinese immigration wave was stimulated by the Gold Rush, and the Chinese almost immediately ran into related noxious regulations. California's Foreign Miners License Tax of 1852, rendered solely against Chinese miners, was one of the first to be challenged. The Chinese also tried a labor strike. On June 25, 1867, a small group of Chinese working on the Transcontinental Railroad construction for Central Pacific went on strike to protest against both the huge wage differential between them and the whites and the long work hours. They demanded $40 a month, a 10-hour maximum workday, and shorter shifts in the extremely hazardous tunnels. Central's boss Charles Crocker refused their demands. As soon as other camps of Chinese heard about the strike, they joined and raised the strike demand to $45 monthly. In response, the Company stopped all food shipments to the remote building camps and hired armed whites who came to the camps to "be intimidating." After a week of this nonviolent protest, the starving Chinese returned to work.

So the legal route would be pursued. The basis of many of the Chinese's local, state, and federal legal cases fighting discrimination was the 1868 Burlingame Treaty between China and the United States. This Treaty held that Chinese were to "enjoy the same privileges, immunities, and exemptions in respect to travel or residence, as ... enjoyed by the citizens or subjects of the most favored nation." One example was an attempt to get two statutes neutered: a San Francisco municipal ordinance forbidding sleeping in a room with less than 500 cubic feet of air space per person and a municipal ordinance permitting jail wardens to cut short the hair of (Chinese) prisoners. Both were only enforced against Chinese. In a positive step for the Chinese's future legal dealings, the decision in *Ho Ah Kow v. Nunan* (1879) declared that both statutes were unconstitutional. This was the first federal case to state that the "equal protection" clause of the Fourteenth Amendment and section 16 of the 1870 Civil Rights Act were legally applicable to the Chinese as persons under the law.

Despite the draconian Exclusion Law, many of the Chinese avoided expulsion by pressing an individual court case. The critical element was having legal representation. In most of these cases (over 80 percent), the courts acted on the recommendations of government commissioners and reversed the denial of admission.

Chinese civil rights also were expanded by the landmark 1886 U.S. Supreme Court decision in *Yick Wo v. Hopkins*, which held the right of Chinese laundry men to work without being "subjected to the arbitrary power of governments." That is, no longer could Chinese laundry men be put out of business because their placing their laundry clothes on the roof made the wooden houses fire traps. The Court ruled that the rights protected by the Fourteenth Amendment were possessed by "aliens" like the Chinese, and that a law that is "fair on its face" can be illegally discriminatory if it is administered in an unequal way.

In general, state and congressional attempts to restrict the freedoms of the Chinese during this period frequently were defeated on questions of constitutional principles, application of treaty rights, and (occasionally) the President's desire to protect its foreign-policy powers by controlling the treatment of "aliens" and relevant subjects.

1890s–1920s

During this time, people of color in the United States found their civil rights declining sharply as steps forward in the previous era were repudiated and even reversed. After the enactment of the Chinese Exclusion Act in 1882, there followed a number of increasingly stringent laws to restrict Chinese laborers domestically as well as others from entering the United States.

At this time, the U.S. Supreme Court decided several cases that legally linked the concept of national sovereignty to the important question of who could enter the nation as an immigrant. *Chae Chan Ping v. United States* (1889) held that the Scott Act of October 1, 1888, was constitutional. This ended the right of Chinese laborers to reenter the United States when they returned from visits to China.

In *Fong Yue Ting v. United States* (1893), the Court found that the federal government had the power to both exclude and deport aliens. This decision reinforced the power of the Geary Act (1892) that required Chinese registration. In angry response, the powerful Chinese Consolidated Benevolent Association ("Chinese Six Companies") called on the Chinese community to participate in a huge act of civil disobedience by refusing to register. The demonstration then happened, and the Chinese subsequently took their case to the U.S. Supreme Court. They lost. The Court decided that "the right of a nation to expel or deport foreigners . . . is as absolute as the right to prohibit and prevent their entrance into the country."

In another setback for Chinese basic rights as citizens, so-called "aliens" (i.e., Chinese) were prohibited from owning or leasing farmland in 14 states by Court decisions on the 1920 California Alien Land Law in *Porterfield v. Webb* (1923) and on the 1921 Washington Alien Land Law in *Terrace v. Thompson* (1923). In *Webb v. O'Brien* (1923), the Court ruled that even sharecropping contracts were illegal, and *Frick v. Webb* (1923) forbade owning stocks. From a legal perspective, the right of noncitizens to work without harassment thus was not extended to the right to farm.

1940s–1970s

From the low point in Chinese civil rights in the 1920s, the successive years were comparatively a turnaround. In the 1940s, Asian immigrants and Asian Americans won important political rights. When the United States and China became allies during World War II, national restrictions on Chinese immigration, naturalization, and mixed marriage were lessened. Moreover, Americans—and their politicians—were impressed by the great numbers of Chinese men who eagerly joined the armed forces to fight in the war. Hundreds of Chinese women also joined the WAC or the WAVES. The first Chinese woman to join the WAC had to go on a special diet and drink two gallons of water to pass the 100-pound weight minimum. They all were exercising their rights as well as attesting to their citizenship.

Subsequently, legal Chinese immigration to the United States was allowed by the Magnuson Act (1943), ending 61 years of institutional racial discrimination. The Magnuson Act (known as the Chinese Exclusion Repeal Act of 1943) allowed Chinese immigration for the first time since the 1882 Exclusion Act. It also gave a route for Chinese nationals living in the United States to become naturalized, the first time since 1790 that Asians were legally permitted to be naturalized. The Chinese were given a token annual immigration quota of 105 persons plus the right to become naturalized citizens.

An example of this loosening, President Franklin D. Roosevelt signed in 1943 Executive Order 9346 to extend the earlier antidiscrimination order to all business and manufacturing enterprises holding federal contracts. Many Chinese American college graduates now could obtain jobs utilizing their education as scientists, engineers, and technicians. Most Chinese women then obtained either secretarial jobs or helped build "Liberty Ships."

In the Cold War, Chinese Americans were utilized as a virtual political weapon by the U.S. State Department to counteract the influence of Red China in the Asian Pacific region. In effect, the federal government therefore affirmed and legitimated the Chinese's claims to full citizenship without restrictions. However, some analysts later felt that this special portrayal contributed to the "other" label continuing to qualify Chinese Americans' gains in social standing.

Chinese American rights were not central in the civil rights battles of the 1960s, but the community did benefit from the progress that was made. Asian Americans successfully used Title VI of the 1964 Civil Rights Act in *Lau v. Nichols* (1974) to convince a court to rule that a school system that will not consider the needs of limited English-speaking students is denying them equal educational opportunity. That court's decision now is seen as importantly "implicitly mandat(ing) bilingual education." Congress then enacted the Equal Educational Opportunity Act (1974) to have federal agencies monitor how schools were complying with the *Lau* decision.

Asian immigrants with limited proficiency in English benefited from the 1965 Voting Rights Act when the Act's provisions were later held to include language minorities (1975). Therefore, this was a legal basis for the preparation of multilingual ballots and other election information.

Chinese American rights were again strengthened by the 1965 Immigration Act's abolishing of the discriminatory "national origins" quota system and replacing it with a more equal system.

Politically active Asian Americans' prospects were improved when in *United Jewish Organizations v. Carey* (1977), the U.S. Supreme Court refused to overturn redistricting boundaries that had been constructed to further the possibility of minority candidates winning elections.

Since the 1960s and 1970s, Asian Americans have benefited from governmental affirmative action regulations and programs. In turn, their advocates have utilized these as a basis to expand their economic rights.

Post-1990s

In the past few decades, efforts to expand the civil rights of Chinese and other Asian Americans have primarily focused on obtaining social rights. Specifically, activists have worked for increased and/or better defined rights in the areas of education, the general lack of English proficiency, combating anti-Asian violence, and racial profiling. This has included work to make certain that Asian Americans continue to fully achieve their economic rights and to fight attempts to lessen Asian American political rights.

It largely has been a period of retrenchment in general American civil rights. Multiple U.S. Supreme Court decisions have narrowed the reach of affirmative action. Affirmative action became a very controversial issue within the Asian American community because it is so divided by national origin, language, religion, nativity, citizenship status, years of residence in the United States, class, sex, etc. There have arisen questions about who should be promoted, if anyone, and how. There are arguments about whether there are too many Asian Americans at elite colleges, and some colleges have a reverse quota system, which has led to extensive debates. Questions of fairness pervade the discussions and debates.

Minority political power also has been eluded recently by the U.S. Supreme Court. For example, in *Miller v. Johnson* (1995) the Court threw out the recently drawn boundaries of some electoral districts that had been deliberately constructed to enhance the clout of minority voters.

However, the national debate cannot ignore that large numbers of Chinese, primarily those who have recently immigrated, have little education and live in stark poverty. Many paid smugglers to illegally transport them to the United States; many overstayed their visas or permits. Some are held in bondage or other illegal situations as a condition of their immigration. These Chinese represent an extremely vulnerable population that urgently needs legal assistance for the protection—and retention—of their rights and peace.

While it is difficult to predict, it is certain that Chinese Americans will confront similar complex definitions of rights and fairness in the upcoming decades.

See also: Boggs, Grace Lee; Chinese American Activism; Chinese American Citizens Alliance

Further Reading

Chan, Sucheng. 2002. "Asian American Struggles for Civil, Political, Economic, and Social Rights." *Chinese America: History & Perspectives* 16: 56–86.

McClain, Charles J. 1994. *In Search of Equality: The Chinese Struggle Against Discrimination in Nineteenth-Century America*. Berkeley: University of California Press.

Wu, Ellen D. 2008. "'America's Chinese': Anti-Communism, Citizenship, and Cultural Diplomacy During the Cold War." *Pacific Historical Review* 77 (August): 391–422.

William P. Kladky

CHINESE CONSOLIDATED BENEVOLENT ASSOCIATION

The Chinese Consolidated Benevolent Association (CCBA), or Zhonghua Hui-guan, was founded in San Francisco following passage of the Chinese Exclusion Act (1882) to facilitate the need for a more unified and inclusive approach to state and national political discrimination. The CCBA initially differed from other ethnic associations in the immigrant community because it represented a unification of organizations and was dedicated to fighting social segregation, halting anti-Chinese legislation, lobbying politicians, and pursing lawsuits against discriminatory laws. Since its inception, a number of consolidated benevolent associations have been established throughout the United States in locations such as New York, Boston, Philadelphia, New England, and Los Angeles. However, these newer organizations have often deferred to the original in San Francisco. Throughout its existence the CCBA has argued against the Geary Act (1892), sought to repeal the Exclusion Act, lobbied to reform U.S. immigration legislation, defended civil rights, and actively supported Taiwanese nationalism.

Historically the CCBA was rooted in the establishment of *huiguans* in the United States during the 1850s, which occurred in response to rising anti-Chinese sentiments. *Huiguans* are family associations composed of people from the same regions in China, which acted as mutual aid societies influencing the lives of most Chinese immigrants in the 19th century by providing social, economic, and legal assistance to those of Chinese descent. *Huiguans* in America aided laborers with their passage, providing temporary housing, financial assistance, help in finding employment, social support and credit, care for the sick, and death benefits. By 1862, the existing *huiguans* were known as the Chinese Six Companies until the passage of the Chinese Exclusion Act, when they formed the CCBA.

In response to the Geary Act, which sought mandatory registration of all Chinese in the United States and established that any such individuals could be deported without judicial recourse, the CCBA advocated widespread civil disobedience among Chinese immigrants, urging them to refuse to register or carry identity cards. As a result, by the legislated deadline few Chinese had complied with the law, and a new deadline was set by the McCreary Amendment (1893). Despite opposition from the CCBA, the Supreme Court upheld the government's right to register and deport noncitizens in *Fong Yue Ting v. United States* (1893). Regardless, the CCBA, concerned that the law would lead to the harassment of Chinese merchants and laborers, promoted enforcement of the legislation to pursue criminals and convicts rather than earnest Chinese immigrants. The CCBA's resistance to the Geary Act and the Supreme Court's decision established precedents for legislation and legal debates regarding immigration and civil rights in the United States for the coming century.

The CCBA later lobbied Congress during World War II (1939–1945) for the repeal of the Exclusion Act and advocated immigrant rights. However, by the 1960s–1970s the organization was seen as too conservative amid the pan-Asian and civil rights movements of the period and owing to shifting demographics in Chinese immigration was increasingly critiqued by members of the Chinese American communities as nonrepresentative. Regardless, from the mid-19th century through the late 20th century the CCBA was among the most influential organizations in Chinese American communities.

See also: Chinese American Citizens Alliance

Further Reading

Lai, Mark. 2004. *Becoming Chinese American: A History of Communities and Institutions.* Walnut Creek, CA: AltaMira Press.

Lai, Him Mark. 1987. "Historical Development of the Chinese Consolidated Benevolent Association/Huiguan System." *Chinese America: History & Perspectives* 1: 3–51.

Sean Morton

CHINESE FAMILY ASSOCIATIONS

Like many immigration organizations, Chinese family associations have their roots in the historical context of the Chinese migration to the United States beginning in the 1850s as well as in the anti-Chinese sentiments that arose in the American west in response. The influx of Chinese workers into the United States was a result of declining economic opportunities and political instability in China, and many Chinese were forced abroad to support their families at home. Until 1888, these sojourners fulfilled the need for inexpensive labor during the Gold Rush (1848–1858) and construction of the Transcontinental Railroad (1863–1869) in the United States. In the 1870s, declining economic prospects and increasing anti-Chinese sentiments fostered by hostile politicians, business owners, and unemployed white workers prompted the passage of ethnically targeted immigration policies such as the Page Act (1875), Chinese Exclusion Act (1882), Scott Act (1888), and Geary Act (1892). Such legislation not only restricted the movement of Chinese immigrants but also taxed their businesses, divided their families, and led to a gender imbalance their communities, which became known as bachelor societies. These situations led immigrants to inhabit increasingly insular Chinese neighborhoods called Chinatowns and also fostered the continued growth of family associations that sought to support Chinese interests, provide social support, and present a unified Chinese political voice in California as well as in a range of other states. As such, the needs of the expanding Chinese immigrant population, rising anti-Chinese sentiments, and discriminatory laws in the United States led to the establishment of family associations as a means of founding a support system and providing mutual aid throughout the Chinese American community.

Two essential family associations arose in the Chinese community of the period were called *huiguans* and *tongs*. *Huiguans* were traditional family associations or district groups composed of peoples from the same region or family in China. Central to Chinese and later Chinese American communities, *huiguans* were mutual aid societies that influenced the lives of most Chinese immigrants in the 19th century by providing social, economic, and legal assistance to those of Chinese descent. *Huiguans* in America aided laborers with their passage by providing temporary housing, financial assistance, help in finding employment, social support and credit, care for the sick, and death benefits. They also promoted the development of Chinese immigrant communities, maintained traditions and ties with families in China, arbitrated disputes, and exerted a degree of social control over the community. Typically *huiguans* in the United States were organized by a hierarchy of self-appointed merchants who used their success in America to become intermediaries and leaders in Chinatowns. Tongs were also family associations, which represented Chinese immigrants, provided assistance, and offered community protection from the rising anti-Chinese American sentiments of the period. However, unlike *huiguans*, *tongs* lacked hereditary and financial support from established families and soon became associated with organized crime, such as prostitute and the collection of protection money to finance their organization. In the 1880s, owing to increasing anti-immigrant sentiments, many Chinese continued their migration east to cities such as New York, Boston, and Chicago, establishing both *huiguans* and *tongs* across the country.

While initially family associations were exclusively for family members, the growing number and diversity of immigrants, declining economic conditions in the American west, and the rising need for a unified and more inclusive organization to represent Chinese Americans as a group led associations to combine their resources and influence. In this manner, by 1862 the *huiguans* in California had united and become known as the Chinese Six Companies. In 1882, following passage of the Chinese Exclusion Act, this collection of family associations reorganized into a national association and became the Chinese Consolidated Benevolent Association. The CCBA, or Zhonghua Huiguan, initially differed from other family associations because it represented a unification of organizations and was less focused on regional support, and increasingly dedicated to fighting social segregation, halting anti-Chinese legislation, lobbying politicians, and pursing lawsuits against discriminatory laws.

Notably, such family associations and later national organizations were politically active through the late 19th century, aiding in negotiations for the

Burlingame Treaty (1868) and lobbying legislators and presidents against the passage of increasingly restrictive ethnic laws. In response to the Geary Act, which sought the mandatory registration of all Chinese in America, and established that any such individuals could be deported without judicial recourse, *huiguans* advised Chinese immigrants to refuse to register or carry identity cards. As a result, by the legislated deadline few Chinese had complied with the law, and a new date was set by the McCreary Amendment (1893). Despite opposition from the CCBA the Supreme Court upheld the government's right to register and deport noncitizens in *Fong Yue Ting v. United States* (1893). In response, family associations, concerned that the law would lead to the harassment of Chinese merchants and laborers, promoted enforcement of the legislation to pursue criminals and convicts rather than earnest Chinese immigrants. The CCBA's resistance to the Geary Act and the Supreme Court's decision established precedents for legislation and legal debates regarding immigration and civil rights in the United States for the coming century.

In 1895, following failure of the Chinese Six Companies' challenge to the Geary Act, Chinese Americans began to turn toward national organizations such as the Chinese American Citizens Alliance (CACA) and Chinese Equal Rights League (CERL), which represented a transition away from family associations. Regardless, family associations such as the *huiguans* and the CCBA remained influential, lobbying Congress during World War II (1939–1949) to repeal the Exclusion Act, advocating the protection of immigrant and civil rights, as well as supporting Taiwanese Nationalism. By the 1960s–1970s, such associations were often seen as too conservative amid the pan-Asian and civil rights movements of the period and, due to the shifting demographics in Chinese immigration, were increasingly criticized by members of the Chinese American communities as nonrepresentative. Regardless, from the mid-19th century through to the late 20th century the *huiguans* (later, the CCBA) and the tongs were among the most important organizations in Chinese American communities.

See also: Bing Kung Tong; Chinese American Activism; Chinese American Citizens Alliance; Chinese Hand Laundry Alliance; Hip Sing Tong (Xiesheng Tang); Hongmen; Hop Sing Tong (Hesheng Tang); Huiguan (The Chinese Six Companies); Samyap and Szeyap; Secret Societies

Further Reading

Lai, Mark. 2004. *Becoming Chinese American: A History of Communities and Institutions.* Walnut Creek, CA: AltaMira Press.

Lai, Him Mark. 1987. "Historical Development of the Chinese Consolidated Benevolent Association/Huiguan System." *Chinese America: History & Perspectives* 1: 3–51.

Sean Morton

CHINESE FISHERIES IN CALIFORNIA

Chinese fishermen came to California just after the state joined the nation in the 1850s. These men were among the first nonnative fishermen to capitalize on the natural resources found along the Pacific coast. During the next few decades, Chinese fishing camps and villages were established from the Oregon border to Baja California, on offshore islands, and along the Sacramento River Delta. For over 100 years, the California fisheries provided employment for thousands of Chinese fishermen. These pioneers helped establish the commercial fishing industry in California and introduced important and valuable delicacies such as shrimp and abalone to 19th-century tables.

Shrimp camps dominated the San Francisco Bay Area, Monterey specialized in abalone and squid, and San Diego was primarily concerned with abalone. The marine resources from these areas were dried and shipped to China and Chinese communities in the United States and sold fresh locally.

A vast number of the Chinese fishermen who settled in California displayed great skill in their ability to obtain and process marine products. For example, although the fishermen living in the Monterey Bay region were known for harvesting abalone and capturing squid, they also had the knowledge to catch and process rockfish, cod, halibut, flounder, red fish and blue fish, yellow tail, mackerel, sardines, and a variety of shellfish.

The skills of these men were developed in regions of China where fishing was a livelihood. Census data from 1880 provide evidence that fishermen who worked the fisheries at Point San Pedro on San Pablo Bay in Marin County hailed from areas of the Guangdong Province where shrimp fishing was an occupation.

Chinese fishermen in California maintained traditional fishing methods, and their adherence to these practices is best displayed by their use of traditional watercraft such as Chinese junks. In China these vessels have traditionally been used for many purposes, such as fishing, transportation of cargo, and ferrying. In California, Chinese shipwrights built traditional watercraft at several locations, including San Diego, Santa Barbara, San Mateo, San Pablo, Point San Pedro, San Bruno, and Hunters Point.

There are several characteristics, such as a sharp bow and a rounded stern, that positively identify 19th-century Chinese watercraft. The large unbalanced rudder was retractable and displayed perforated, diamond-shaped holes and served as a keel in the lowered position. The distinctive sails featured battens secured near the mast. Most California junks were made from redwood and seem to have been left unpainted; they were simply treated with tung oil.

Fisheries in San Francisco

The shrimp fisheries located in the San Francisco Bay region provided jobs for hundreds of Chinese fishermen from the 1870s to 1930. Point San Pedro was one of the largest Chinese shrimp fishing villages. Today, a part of this settlement still exists and is known as China Camp State Park, located in Marin County, California. The fishing village spanned 10–15 acres and consisted of 32 houses, a boat building, and shipping facilities. The 1880 U.S. Census recorded 347 fishermen along with cooks, boardinghouse keepers, servants, gardeners, a junk dealer, a barber, and a school teacher who worked to support fishing activities and the fishermen. The total population for Point San Pedro that year was 469 residents.

Shrimp was caught with bag nets staked to the bay floor. This equipment represented a major investment and the choice of fishing ground was very important. An experienced fisherman who understood the currents would dictate the exact location where the net stakes would be placed. Chinese fishermen recognized ownership of fishing territories, yet they were not legally sanctioned.

Fisheries in Monterey

The earliest Chinese fishing village in the Monterey Bay region was established at Point Lobos, where a building, known as the Whalers Cabin, was built in the early 1850s. This structure provides physical evidence of Chinese fishing activities in the Monterey Bay region and is believed to be the oldest remaining wooden-frame residence of Chinese origin in California.

There was competition in the Monterey Bay fishery between ethnic groups. Portuguese whalers established a settlement in Monterey in 1855 and additional fishermen from Portugal arrived in the area in 1860. Italian fishermen arrived in Monterey County from San Francisco in 1873. Yet, more than half of the fishermen in the area were Chinese. These men, using methods learned from their respective homelands, frequently came into conflict. In 1880, Chinese fishermen sued Portuguese fishermen for cutting their fishing nets; however, the Portuguese men prevailed in the lawsuit.

Point Alones, located in Pacific Grove, one-and-a-half-miles northwest of Monterey, was established in the 1850s. This village was among the most prosperous of the Chinese fishing settlements in California. It was a self-contained community that provided its residents with traditional goods for sale at the general store, an employment agency, a cemetery, an outdoor shrine, and an association hall. The community was a cultural center where Chinese residents from nearby towns would gather and share traditional customs from the homeland. Many Chinese fishermen raised families at Point Alones, and together they worked in the fishing industry where squid was their primary marine product. This village thrived for 50 years and burned down in May 1906.

Fisheries of San Diego

Chinese fishermen dominated the fishing industry in San Diego from the early 1850s until the 1890s. Two Chinese fishing colonies were established on Point Loma, and another fishing village was located at the waterfront adjacent to the Stingaree district and Chinatown. Chinese merchants and contactors in San Diego's Chinese community worked as marketing agents and handled export operations. In some cases, Chinese merchants owned vessels used in the fishing industry.

By the time Chinese fishermen arrived in San Diego, the abalone population had exploded. Sea otters are native to California, and their fur was highly desired, yet because of overhunting, the animal was driven close to extinction. An element of their diet is abalone; consequently, abalone flourished and multiplied once their natural predators were removed.

Abalone was the perfect resource for Chinese fishermen to pursue. Dried abalone was considered a delicacy in China, and Chinese fishermen in San Diego harvested the mollusk with very little competition. Abalone was pried from the rocks and the meat was dried and exported, whereas the shells were shipped to China to be used for cabinet inlays and jewelry, and to France and Germany to be used for buttons and curios.

Expanding their activities, Chinese fishermen worked the waters and shores of the Channel Islands and Baja California. They maintained San Diego as their base of operations for drying their catch, shipping, and fresh market sales. Abalone was abundant in Baja California and Chinese fishermen would sail their junks up to 400 miles from San Diego in pursuit of their prey. A newspaper account from 1871 described two junks arriving at the San Diego port from lower California with eight tons of abalone meat (*San Diego Daily Union*, October 14, 1871).

Decline of the Chinese Fisheries

During the 1860s, Chinese fishermen began to be attacked from several fronts, culminating in the decline of the Chinese fishing industry in California. Restriction on Chinese fishing began with investigation and regulation. The first restriction placed occurred in 1860, when a license fee of $4 was levied upon fishermen by the state. The license fee was repealed in 1864. During the 1870s the U.S. Commission of Fish and Fisheries began to investigate the Chinese fishing industry. Although the federal government recognized that the regulation of the fisheries should be left up to the states, the Fish Commission's mandate was to gather information and study coastal fisheries in the United States. In 1879 and 1880, David Starr Jordan surveyed the Pacific Coast fisheries in conjunction with the tenth U.S. Census. The conclusion of the survey was that the quantity of fish was being "constantly and rapidly diminished by Chinamen with their fine-meshed nets" (*San Diego Daily Union*, January 14, 1880).

Most members of the federal and state fish commissions were political appointees but not scientists. They did not have the expertise to understand biological processes that affected the fisheries, such as climatic changes, pollution, and a shift in predator/prey populations. Moreover, the diversity of the marine life harvested by Chinese fishermen reduced the danger that fish populations would be decreased.

Hostility toward the Chinese population in the United States reached a fever pitch, and in 1882 Congress passed a bill restricting immigration of Chinese laborers for 10 years. Additional laws that extended exclusion and limited Chinese employment opportunities were passed in 1892 with the Geary Act. This legislation specifically defined "persons engaged in taking, drying, or otherwise preserving shell or other fish for home consumption or exportation," as laborers. In effect, Chinese fishermen were redefined as laborers, an excluded class, and subject to deportation. Laws and regulations placed upon Chinese fishermen were harsh and based on the racism of the time.

See also: Anti-Chinese Violence; Chinese Grocery Stores; Chinese Laundries; Chinese Restaurants in the United States

Further Reading

Jordon, David S. 1887. "The Chinese Fishermen of the Pacific Coast." In *The Fisheries and Fishery Industries of the United States. Section IV: The Fishermen of the United States*, edited by George Brown Goode and Joseph W. Collins, 30, 33. Washington, DC: U.S. Government Printing Office.

Lydon, Sandy. 2008. *Chinese Gold: The Chinese in the Monterey Bay Region.* Capitola, CA: Capitola Book Company.

Nash, Robert A. 1973. "The Chinese Shrimp Fishery in California." PhD diss., University of California, Los Angeles.

Linda Bentz

CHINESE GROCERY STORES

When Chinese immigrants arrived in the United States in the latter stages of the 19th century, they found their employment opportunities limited. While work could initially be had as field laborers or as construction workers on the nation's growing railway system, these jobs paid very little. In the case of railroad construction, the work could also be very dangerous. Discrimination against Chinese immigrants grew in the United States as the Chinese were blamed for high unemployment and declining wages. When the Chinese Exclusion Act was passed in 1882, immigration from China was severely limited. However, merchants were one of the few classes of Chinese immigrants who were granted entry into the country. Opening a grocery store was one of the only methods of economic survival for Chinese immigrants and their descendants.

In most cases, Chinese grocery stores were located in the lower socioeconomic neighborhoods of urban areas, largely because that is where the Chinese were most welcome. For example, in the Jim Crow South, this meant catering to a primarily African American clientele, who found the Chinese grocery stores a safe option for both shopping and meeting friends and colleagues. In the Southwest, Chinese grocers catered to Mexican Americans. Understanding local tastes helped the Chinese integrate into their communities. One of the first examples of fusion cuisine could be found in one of the many Chinese grocery stores in the Tucson, Arizona, barrios, where one merchant offered a very popular house blend of meat and Chinese spices that he called Chinese chorizo.

The goods sold at most Chinese grocery stores were a combination of Chinese imports and the most common and desirable local products. Chinese merchandise, including teas, spices, and a variety of traditional Chinese staples, were typically purchased wholesale from distributors in San Francisco, New York, or Chicago. Merchants sold these items at retail prices alongside

Sam Jue and his wife Susan Jue stand in their shop, the last Chinese grocery store on China Street in Rolling Fork, Mississippi, on June 10, 2005. "I still offer credit to some of my long time customers," says Jue, 86. (AP Photo/Rogelio Solis)

American canned and packaged goods. Locally grown produce was also sold in these stores, many times for lower prices than could be found in non-Chinese markets. In fact, many Chinese grocers were able to sell most of their merchandise more inexpensively than their American competitors because of the reliance on family labor. It was not uncommon for the family of a Chinese grocer to live in the back of the store. Family members, including children, were expected to work in the store but they were paid no wages. This free labor allowed the merchants to sell their products at lower prices.

Following World War II, the presence of independent, community grocery stores began to diminish with the emergence of chain supermarkets. Not only did Chinese grocers struggle to compete with these larger markets, the growth of the suburbs left many urban areas in decline. Younger generations of Chinese Americans were less interested in continuing family grocery businesses and were more likely to join the exodus away from city centers. Chinese grocery stores still exist today, although now they are primarily specialty markets.

See also: Chinese Laundries; Chinese Restaurants in the United States

Further Reading

"Chinese Grocers." 2015. Southern Foodways Alliance. Accessed July 15, 2015. http://www.southernfoodways.org/oral-history/chinese-grocers-in-the-mississippi-and-arkansas-deltas/.

Tong, Benson, ed. 2004. *Asian American Children: A Historical Handbook and Guide.* Westport, CT: Greenwood Press.

Amy Lively

CHINESE HAND LAUNDRY ALLIANCE

Chinese hand laundries began in the mid-19th century. The low-investment, labor-intensive hand laundry industry proliferated in cities across the country, coinciding with the expansion of industrial capitalism, becoming a central "economic lifeline" for the Chinese community. Over time, hand laundries began to threaten the industrial dominance of large white power laundry companies and what followed were attempts by the state to advantage the dominant group.

The Chinese Hand Laundry Alliance (CHLA), an organization of Chinese American laundry owners, formed in 1933 to resist a proposed New York City ordinance that would have instituted an annual license fee of $25, a $1,000 bond on all public laundries, and restricted laundry ownership to U.S. citizens. CHLA was an overtly left-wing and rank-and-file alternative to the more established, top-down, and nationalist-affiliated Chinese advocacy organizations that were seen as ineffective in preventing passage of the law.

The ambulance that the Chinese Hand Laundry Alliance sent to China to care for wounded soldiers, ca. 1900. (Underwood & Underwood/Corbis)

As an economic lifeline, the law would hurt everyone in the Chinese community, and as a result, with the exception of the merchant elite and the Chinese Consolidated Benevolent Association (CCBA), there was a broad grassroots base of support for the formation of the CHLA. The CCBA leadership believed the CHLA to be an existential threat to both the CCBA and the traditional power structure. Both organizations continued to maintain an antagonistic relationship. The creation of the CHLA was brought on by the intensified economic conditions of the Great Depression and its diverse leadership, and democratic decision-making represented a dramatic departure from hierarchical organizations that had traditionally operated within the Chinese community. At an overflow meeting on April 26 in Chinatown, the founding constitution was voted on by the 254 Chinese laundrymen in attendance. The stated mission was to concentrate their strength, internally keep unity and defend the interests of the members, and outwardly resist and try to abolish any discriminatory acts against the Chinese hand laundries.

The CHLA quickly got to work organizing the community to take collective action against the ordinance. Although the law passed, amendments reduced the license fee to $10 and the security bond to $100 and added an exemption for "Orientals" in the U.S. citizenship requirement. The CHLA and Chinese community declared victory, popularized as the "Victory of May," ensuring the longevity of the CHLA. The CHLA went on to organize successfully against other chauvinistic laws, provide legal assistance for its members, and defend itself against attacks by the CCBA.

Like many politicized Chinese Americans, CHLA members were tremendously influenced by political changes within China. The CHLA came out fiercely against the Japanese invasion of Manchuria and Chiang Kai-shek's position of "nonresistance" through its "Resist Japan and Save China" campaign. By the 1940s the CHLA was publishing the "only Chinese-language newspaper in the U.S. that was not pro-Nationalist," which caught the attention of Senator Joseph McCarthy's officials and kept them on constant alert for alleged communist subversives. The CHLA members were targeted for sending remittance back to relatives in China as a violation of the Trading with the Enemy Act. CHLA leaders were arrested, associates were hounded, and CHLA's membership fell precipitously as a result. In the decades that followed, CHLA's membership would continue to wane alongside the decline of the U.S. Chinese hand laundry industry.

See also: Chinese Consolidated Benevolent Association; Chinese Laundries

Further Reading

Song, Jingyi. 2010. *Shaping and Reshaping Chinese American Identity: New York's Chinese During the Depression and World War II.* Lanham, MD: Lexington Books.

Yu, Renqiu. 2011. *To Save China, to Save Ourselves: The Chinese Hand Laundry Alliance of New York.* Philadelphia, PA: Temple University Press.

Ashok Kumar

CHINESE HOSPITAL, SAN FRANCISCO

The Chinese Hospital is the only hospital in the United States that seeks to serve the Chinese American community. It roots date back to 1899 when the Tung Wah Dispensary opened its door in San Francisco's Chinatown. By the early 1920s, the Tung Wah Dispensary was not able to meet the growing health-care demands of the Chinese American community, and other medical providers in San Francisco denied service to the Chinese residents due to anti-Chinese sentiments and racism. To meet the health-care needs of the Chinese residents, the Chinese Hospital Association, a nonprofit public benefit corporation, was created in 1923 comprising 15 community organizations. The Chinese Hospital Association's Board of Trustees raised funds for construction of a new hospital at 835 Jackson Street, and the Chinese Hospital opened its doors with 60 acute beds on April 18, 1925. In the mid-1970s, the Chinese Hospital's Board of Trustees raised funds to construct a new hospital that opened on September 29, 1979, at 845 Jackson Street, next door to the original Chinese Hospital. Today, the Chinese Hospital is undergoing another transformation as it is being rebuilt with 21st-century medical technologies to meet the needs of the community. The new hospital plans were contested as historic preservationists advocated that the old structure or parts of the old structure be saved from demolition. However, the Chinese Hospital and its supporters argued that the historical importance of the Chinese Hospital lies in its missions to serve the immediate immigrant Chinese communities. The new hospital will be better equipped to meet the growing needs of the residents. For decades, the Chinese Hospital has served the health-care needs of the communities whose lives are tied in the fabric of Chinatown.

See also: Chinese Medicine

Further Reading

"Chinese Hospital." 2014–2015. Accessed July 16, 2015. http://www.chinesehospital -sf.org/.

Risse, Guenter. 2012. *Plague, Fear, and Politics in San Francisco's Chinatown*. Baltimore, MD: The Johns Hopkins University Press.

Jonathan H. X. Lee

CHINESE-LANGUAGE NEWSPAPERS IN AMERICA

Chinese-language newspapers in America have played a major role in maintaining the identity of Chinese communities and covering the history, culture, economy, and life of these communities. Their reports are relatively objective and authentic, which is different from their counterparts in China or Taiwan. Chinese-language newspapers appeared in America as early as Chinatown but their influence remained minimal until recently. The reasons include the isolation of Chinese American communities from the mainstream American society due to the Chinese Exclusion Act from 1882 to 1943, the low levels of literacy and Chinese-language proficiency among Chinese immigrants, and the limited scale of ethnic economies.

Chinese-Language Newspapers in the Early Years

The *Golden Hills' News* (*Jiujinshan Xinlu*) was the first Chinese-language newspaper in the United States. The first issue was published on April 22, 1854, in San Francisco and its publisher was William Howard. The authors were non-Chinese and showed empathy as well as criticism to Chinese in terms of personality, knowledge, and religion. It also included news, advertisements, and information on economy and transportation. The newspaper was popular among Chinese immigrants as it met their needs. A subscription to *Golden Hills' News* was 75 cents per month—a considerable sum in those days.

The *Golden Hills' News* only survived a few months. Then Szeto Yun (Huang Tai) founded the *Chinese Daily* in December 1856 in Sacramento. Although it was reduced to a weekly, only on Wednesdays, it was published daily in the beginning and was once the first Chinese-language daily newspaper. However, this newspaper ended in 1858.

In the 1860s, the Qing government lifted the ban on Chinese labor working in foreign countries. The Burlingame Treaty (1868) between the United States and China encouraged Chinese immigration to the United States. As a result, the number of Chinese laborers in America increased dramatically. There were also businessmen and intellectuals coming along. The enlargement of Chinese communities, improvement of Chinese-language education, and the increased Chinese-language literacy rate all became impetus for the development of Chinese-language newspapers. There were more Chinese-language newspapers, including the *San Francisco Chinese News* (*Jiujinshan Tang Ren Bao Zhi*) in 1874 and *Hua Ji Bao* and *Tang Fan Gong Bao* in 1875. *Hua Fan Hui Bao* lasted until 1903 and therefore became one of the longest Chinese-language newspapers in the 19th century in the United States.

The period from the 1850s to 1894 was the beginning stage of Chinese-language newspaper development in America: the number of newspapers was still very small, the length of articles was short, coverage was narrow, and circulation was limited.

The Chinese-Language Newspapers in the Early 20th Century

The defeat in the Sino-Japanese War of 1894–1895 aroused Chinese national awareness and some Chinese elites started to promote constitutional reform. For example, the "Gong Che Shangshu (Public Vehicle Memorial)" led by Kang Youwei (1858–1927) in 1895 not only had great influence in China but also influenced the press and publications undertakings about overseas Chinese.

In 1903, Chinese revolutionary leader Sun Yat-sen (1866–1925) went to Honolulu and reorganized *Tanshan Xin Bao* into the Xing Zhong Hui (China Revival Society). The next year, Sun went to San Francisco and reformed *Da Tong Ri Bao* into a prorevolutionists' newspaper. The revolutionists of overseas Chinese included *Tanshan Xin Bao* and *Zi You Xin Bao* in Honolulu, *Wen Xing Bao* and *Da Tong Ri Bao* in San Francisco, *Zhongguo Wei Xin Bao* in New York, and *Xin Zhongguo Bao* in Honolulu.

In 1924, *Jinshan Shibao* (*Chinese Times*), one of the Chinese-language newspapers with longest history in the United States to date, launched its first issue in San Francisco. In 1927, shortly after the death of Sun, the Nationalist party split into the two groups: the Left and the Right. Each group established their own official newspapers, including *Shao Nian Zhongguo Chen Bao* and *Meizhou Guo Min Ri Bao* in San Francisco, *Min Qi Ri Bao* in New York, and *Zhongshan*

Chen Bao and *Meizhou Ri Bao*. *Xian Feng Bao* (1928–1938) was the first newspaper edited by Chinese Marxists in the United States. Later, the Chinese Communist Party founded *Jiu Guo Shi Bao* (1938–1939). *Meizhou Hua Qiao Ri Bao* (1940–1989) was a newspaper leaning to the left.

During the 1950s and 1960s, due to McCarthyism and America's "containment and isolation" policy against China, Chinese American newspapers developed very slowly. The newly established newspapers only included *Lian He Ri Bao* in 1952, the short-lived *Min Zhi Ri Bao* (1960–1966), *Zhongguo Shi Bao* (1962–1979), and *Zi You Zhongguo Ri Bao* (1955–1957).

Chinese-Language Newspapers Today

The lifting of legal bans to Chinese immigration after World War II and the enactment of the 1965 immigration legislation have brought tremendous changes to the Chinese communities in America. Post-1965 immigrants are more diverse in their places of origin. As a result, not only Cantonese but also Mandarin was used widely among Chinese Americans. The majority of new immigrants are proficient in written Chinese as well. In addition, economic development in the Chinese immigrant communities since the 1970s gave rise to Chinese-language media. The Chinese newspapers and periodicals have increased to 700 types, two-thirds of which were established after 1970. The competition among the newspapers became very keen. The traditional and influential newspapers like *Xin Zhongguo Ri Bao* and *Shao Nian Zhongguo Chen Bao* have been replaced by new newspapers.

Chinese-language newspapers have burst into full bloom since the 1990s. The largest and most influential newspapers include the New York–based *Chinese Daily News* (formerly *The World Journal*), the U.S. edition of the Hong Kong–based *Sing Tao Daily*, and the New York–based *China Press*. The *Chinese Daily News* (based in Taiwan) is the largest and most influential Chinese-language daily in the United States. Since its debut in New York in 1976, the *Chinese Daily News* has been politically pro-Taiwan and "anti-communist." The second largest newspaper is the North American edition of the *Sing Tao Daily*. Most of *Sing Tao Daily*'s readership is Cantonese-speaking Chinese Americans from Hong Kong. The third largest newspaper is the *China Press*, which was established in 1990 in New York as an independent paper. Most of the *China Press*'s readers are recent immigrants from mainland China. It is politically pro-mainland China.

In addition, many local community newspapers and magazines have also appeared in the same cities, especially since the 1990s. Community newsletters, mostly owned by immigrant entrepreneurs, are published weekly or biweekly. Most of these community papers are distributed at no cost through Chinese-owned businesses.

There are several constraints on Chinese-language newspapers, such as the difficulties in seeking advertisement sponsorships, the lack of professionalization of staff reporters, the low pay of staff members, and the political inclination due to donors or sponsors' influence.

However, these newspapers continue playing an important role in maintaining the Chinese community identity and offering information for Chinese in America. At the same time, they are useful firsthand materials for scholarly research.

Further Reading

Ma, Yan. 2003. "Chinese American Newspapers and Periodicals in the United States and Their Web Presence." *Serials Review* 29 (3): 179–98.

Zhou, Min, and Guoxuan Cai. 2002. "Chinese Language Media in the United States: Immigration and Assimilation in American Life." *Qualitative Sociology* 25 (3): 419–40.

Zhou, Nanjing, ed. 1999. *The Encyclopedia of Chinese Overseas. Volume of Media & Publication.* Beijing: Chinese Overseas Publishing House.

Yan He

CHINESE LAUNDRIES

San Francisco, also known as *Dai Fow* (Cantonese for "Big City"), became a city with employment opportunities. "Ethnic antagonism," which pitted one ethnic group against another to keep wages low, resulted in anti-Chinese sentiments and violence, driving many Chinese into self-employment. The Chinese laundry was chief among them. The Chinese laundry was an American phenomenon. It does not exist in China; in fact, there were no laundries in China. Back in China, women did the washing, not men. Opening a laundry in America required little capital because the materials were simple: a stove, trough, dry room, sleeping area, a sign, and a few English skills. Besides low capital investment demands, the Chinese were pushed into this line of work because it was one of the few that was open to them, besides restaurants. In 1900, one out of four employed Chinese men worked as a laundryman. In general, the Chinese laundries were successful means of livelihood. However, in 1880, the city of San Francisco's elected officials passed the laundry ordinances that persons could not operate a laundry in a wooden building without a permit from the Board of Supervisors. The San Francisco Board of Supervisors was thus given the power to grant or withhold permits. At this time, 95 percent of the city's 320 laundries were operated in wooden buildings. Moreover, two-thirds were owned and operated by Chinese laundrymen. Chinese owners were denied a permit, while non-Chinese applicants were granted one. The ordinance was challenged in the U.S. Supreme Court in *Yick Wo v. Hopkins* (1886). In *Yick Wo*, the U.S. Supreme Court, in a unanimous opinion, invoked the Equal Protection Clause of the Fourteenth Amendment to protect Chinese laundry owners

Yick Wo was a Chinese laundry owned by Sang Lee. Lee immigrated to California in 1861. After 20 years of owning and operating his laundry as an undocumented immigrant, the San Francisco Board of Supervisors invoked the laundry ordinance to shut it down on the basis that he could not continue to run it in a wooden building. Lee continued to operate his laundry and was convicted and fined $10 for violating the ordinance. Lee sued for a writ of habeas corpus after he was jailed for refusing to pay the fine.

against an ordinance that on its face was race neutral but was applied in a prejudicial manner.

See also: Chinese Grocery Stores; Chinese Hand Laundry Alliance; Chinese Restaurants in the United States

Further Reading

Siu, Paul. 1987. *The Chinese Laundryman: A Study of Social Isolation.* New York: New York University Press.

Jonathan H. X. Lee

CHINESE RESTAURANTS IN THE UNITED STATES

Restaurant business was one of the earliest economical enterprises pursued by Chinese immigrants in North America. The Canton (Guangzhou) Restaurant, with a 300-seat capacity in San Francisco, was the first Chinese restaurant in the United States and was founded as early as 1849. During the Gold Rush era, large quantities of Chinese food products such as dried oysters, shrimps, cuttlefish, mushrooms, dried green vegetables and bean curd, bamboo shoots, sausages, sweetmeats, duck liver, kidneys, and water chestnut flour arrived in California. There were at least seven Chinese restaurants in San Francisco by 1851 whereas dozens of Chinese food joints in various mining areas served both Chinese and American customers. However, the number of Chinese restaurants in the late 19th century was actually modest. San Francisco had 11 in 1878 and 28 in 1881. The number dropped to 14 in 1882, probably because of the impact of the passage of Chinese exclusion law in that year. The 1882 *Directory of Principal Chinese Business Firms* in San Francisco listed 175 laundries, 77 general merchandise stores, 62 grocery stores, 22 drug stores, 16 butchers, and only 14 Chinese restaurants.

Chinese restaurants began to thrive only after chop suey houses became popular in New York City in the 1900s. The first Chinese who opened a chop suey house outside of Chinatown was a Chinese man named "Charley Boston" (his Chinese name was Lee Quong June or Li Quen Chong), a thoroughly Americanized wealthy merchant and a leader of the famous On Leong Tong in New York's Chinatown. He did so well that soon many other Chinese followed him. When Liang Qichao, a leading Chinese intellectual, visited the United States in 1903, he noted with surprise that there were over 400 chop suey houses in New York City. Chinese restaurant business enjoyed a golden era from 1900 to the 1920s. During that period, chop suey houses were not only a New York phenomenon but spread into Boston, Long Island, New Jersey, and Connecticut. In 1900, Chicago had only one Chinese restaurant. By 1905, there were 40 but only five were in Chinatown. By 1915, there were 118 but only six or seven were in Chinatown. On the West Coast, the number of Chinese restaurants was also growing, and there were not only Chinese but also Japanese and Koreans chop suey proprietors. In 1905, San Francisco had only 46 Chinese restaurants. Twenty years later, the number grew to 78, which was still far behind that of New York. In 1900, there were but two or three Chinese restaurants in Los Angeles, frequented almost exclusively by Chinese. There were at least 15 by 1910. Several of these Chinese restaurants were outside Chinatown and a few were in downtown Los Angeles. In the 1920s, one of the largest Chinese restaurants in the Los Angeles area was Crown Chop Suey Parlor in Pasadena, owned by a Japanese immigrant, Mr. Kawagoye. However, New York had more Chinese restaurants than any other city.

When catering to white and tourist clients became the focus of the restaurant business, Chinese began to run cocktail bars, café shops, and night clubs in and outside of Chinatowns in New York, Chicago, Los Angeles, and San Francisco in the 1920s and 1930s. Live music and dancing rather than food became the major attraction in those restaurants. In the beginning, such bars purely attracted white clients. Then Chinese customers gradually frequented them as well. Some of them did not serve Chinese food. The most famous Chinese night club was the Forbidden City started by Charlie Low in December 1938 on Sutter Street outside in Chinatown of San Francisco. Food at the Forbidden City was Western and cheap, but the restaurant began to offer nude dancing by Asian girls.

When the Chinese restaurant business established a niche in the American food market, it began to provide important hiring opportunities for the Chinese. The 1920 U.S. Census indicates that of the 45,614 Chinese employed in the United States, 26,488 of them worked in restaurants and laundries. In the 1930s, 6 percent of the Chinese adult males in California and 20–25 percent of Chinese adult males in East Coast cities worked in the restaurant business. According to a 1938 report by the Oriental Division of the U.S. Employment Service in San Francisco, 90 percent of Chinese youth were service workers, mainly in the culinary trades. In 1941, 5,000 young Chinese in San Francisco had no future worthy of their education but seemed destined to wash dishes, carry trays, cut meat, and dry fish in Chinatown when the defense industry was in great need of professional employees. In Chinese American experience, food was not only an ethnic label but attached to their racial status. Restaurant jobs were American-made and self-employed occupations for Chinese Americans.

Following the 1965 immigration reform, Chinatowns in San Francisco, Los Angeles, and New York experienced a heavy influx of new immigrants. When Chinatown was not big enough for the new immigrants, they began to move into suburban cities like Monterey Park in Southern California and Flushing, Queens in New York. Following the immigration boom, the number of Chinese restaurants grew rapidly. In the late 1960s, the number of Chinese restaurants in the continental United States grew to more than 10,000; there was actually a shortage of qualified Chinese chefs in the early 1970s. Before 1965, there was only one Chinese restaurant in Monterey Park. By 1987, the city had over 60 Chinese restaurants, representing 75 percent of the dining business in the city. Harbor Village and Ocean Star, located on Atlantic Boulevard, became two of the largest city revenue generators in Monterey Park. Ocean Star, owned by Robert Y. Lee, had 800 seats and was one of the largest Chinese restaurants in San Gabriel Valley. Recipes, ingredients, and cookery in the post-1965 Chinese restaurant businesses in the United States follow closely their counterparts in Asia. A pattern in the Chinese restaurant business in the San Gabriel Valley is that each city with concentrated Chinese residents has a few famous Chinese restaurants as a major attraction. Monterey Park has the Ocean Star and Harbor Village. Arcadia has the celebrated Din Tai Fung dumpling house. San Gabriel has the high-end restaurant Mission 261. Rowland Heights has the Sea Harbor Seafood Restaurant and Sam Woo See Food Restaurant. Famous Chinese restaurants follow wherever the immigrants have congregated. The emergence of numerous Chinese restaurants has changed the social landscape of Southern California and made Chinese America a visible ethnic community. From a bunch of chop suey eateries in the 1960s, the Chinese restaurant business has evolved into a food capital of Chinese cuisine. As authentic Chinese food has replaced Americanized Chinese dishes, the booming restaurant business becomes a concrete example of how a transnational lifestyle is deeply embedded in Chinese American communities. Different regional Chinese cuisines and restaurant types and operations also illustrate the diverse social origins and the diaspora background of the new immigrants. In the Chinese restaurant world, the San Gabriel Valley in Southern California has become a real global village. By 2004, as home to over 240,000 Chinese residents, the San Gabriel Valley had more than 2,000 Chinese restaurants. In comparison, Los Angeles Chinatown, according to a *Los Angeles Times* article, has about 80 restaurants for 15,000 residents.

Today there are more than 40,000 Chinese restaurants across the nation—a number larger than the total number of McDonalds, Wendy's, and Burger Kings in the United States combined. According to a 2000 report by the National Restaurant Association in the United States, Italian, Mexican, and Chinese cuisines have already joined the mainstream. Those three cuisines have become so engrained in American culture that they are no longer foreign to the American palate. More than 9 out of 10 consumers are familiar with and have tried these foods, and about half report eating them frequently. Hunan, Mandarin, and Szechwan variations of Chinese cuisines, like some European cuisines, are known to between 70 and 80 percent of Chinese restaurant consumers.

Panda Express is the largest Chinese fast-food restaurant chain and the fastest growing Asian restaurant company in America. Established in 1983 by Andrew and Peggy Cherng, an immigrant couple from Taiwan and Hong Kong, Panda Express has become the most visible and popular Chinese fast-food chain in the United States. Targeting mainstream American customers, Panda Express stores usually locate in shopping malls, airports, theme parks, sport stadiums, street plazas, university campuses, hospital cafeterias, and even military bases. By 2009, Panda Express had over 1,200 chain stores throughout 37 U.S. states with $1 billion in annual revenues.

The largest sit-down Chinese restaurant business is P.F. Chang's China Bistro, established by Paul Fleming, a white American restaurateur. In 1993, he opened his first P.F. Chang's in Scottsdale, Arizona and invited Philip Chiang to be his partner. When the restaurant was named P.F. Chang's China Bistro, "P.F." stood for Paul Fleming, and "Chang" stood for Chiang—Philip purposely spelled his "Chiang" as "Chang" as a more contemporary and standardized Romanization of the Chinese name. In 1998, when P.F. Chang's had 10 stores, it filed an IPO at $12 a share, which jumped to $32.75 in March 2000. By then, the chain had opened 39 stores with 13 in development. The chain opened 13–15 new restaurants annually. By 2008, P.F. Chang's ran 189 full-service Bistro restaurants and 159 fast-food Pei Wei restaurants across the country. Though owned by a mainstream American food company, the restaurant imports some ingredients, herbs, and spices directly from China and its menu features some regionally flavored Chinese dishes.

P.F. Chang's phenomenon poses a serious question to Chinese Americans: Who owns culture? Although mainstream American customers tend to stay away from small, family-owned Chinese restaurants, more and more of them have learned to accept genuine Chinese food at P.F. Chang's, which has the financial resources to provide a trendy, comfortable dining environment, attract middle-class professionals and families as its clients, and carve out a high-end Chinese cuisine niche in the competitive American restaurant market. The success of P.F. Chang's reveals the complexity of cultural and economic negotiations between Asian and Western culture, between the struggling, family-owned small Asian American business and giant, publicly traded corporate America.

See also: Chinese Foods; Chinese Grocery Stores; Chinese Nightclubs (1920s–1940s)

Further Reading

Chao, Tonia. 1985. "Communicating Through Architecture: San Francisco Chinese Restaurants and Cultural Intersections, 1849–1984." PhD diss., University of California, Berkeley.

Coe, Andrew. 2009. *Chop Suey: A Cultural History of Chinese Food in the United States.* New York: Oxford University Press.

Gabaccia, Donna R. 1998. *We Are What We Eat: Ethnic Food and the Making of Americans.* Cambridge, MA: Harvard University Press.

Lee, Jennifer. 2008. *The Fortune Cookie Chronicles: Adventures in the World of Chinese Food.* New York: Twelve Hachette Book Group.

Liu, Haiming. 2009. "Chop Suey as an Imagined Authentic Chinese Food: Chinese Restaurant Business and Its Culinary Identity in the United States." *The Journal of Transnational American Studies* 1 (1). Accessed July 16, 2015. http://repositories.cdlib.org/acgcc/jtas.

Liu, Haiming. 2009. "Food, Culinary Identity, and Transnational Culture: Chinese Restaurant Business in Southern California." *Journal of Asian American Studies* 12 (June): 135–62.

Mai, Liqian (Lai, Him Mark). 1992. *Cong huaqiao dao huaren: Ershi shiji meiguo huaren shehui fazhan shi* (From Overseas Chinese to Chinese Americans: A History of 20th Century Chinese American Social and Economical Development). Hong Kong: San Lian Press.

Wu, David Y. H., and Sidney C. H. Cheung. 2002. *Globalization of Chinese Food.* Honolulu: University of Hawai'i Press.

Haiming Liu

CHU, JUDY (1953–)

Judy Chu is a Chinese American politician, the first Chinese American woman to be elected to the U.S. Congress, representing the 27th District of California in the U.S. House of Representatives. She was born on July 7, 1953, in the Bay Area of California. Chu earned a bachelor's degree in mathematics and a PhD in psychology from the University of California. Her career has included serving as a politician as well as a psychology professor.

Chu's political career started in 1985. She was elected as a school board member for Garvey School District. She served for three years until her election to the city council of Monterey Park in 1988. She was a city councilor until 2001. During her term, she was both a councilor and the mayor. She left the city

Rep. Judy Chu, D-Calif., center, and other House Democratic advocates for comprehensive immigration reform speak during a a news conference on Capitol Hill in Washington, D.C., on January 13, 2015. The speakers addressed the implementation of President Barack Obama's executive actions to spare millions from immediate deportation. (AP Photo/J. Scott Applewhite)

council in 2001 to become a state assemblywoman. Chu had sought the assembly seat twice prior to being elected. In 2002 and 2004, Chu was reelected to her seat. Due to term limits, she was unable to run for a third full term. In 2006, she was elected to the State Board of Equalization, representing the Greater Los Angeles area. After a three-year term on the board, she sought a congressional seat.

In 2009, a special election was held to fill the 27th District seat after the prior Congresswoman, Hilda Solis, was appointed by President Obama to be the Secretary of Labor. Twelve people vied for the congressional seat. As a result, no one candidate received a majority of the votes. Chu and her cousin received the most votes and competed in a run-off election. Judy Chu defeated her cousin Betty Chu, 62–33.

Chu won reelection in 2010 with 71 percent of the vote, and 6 percent of the vote in 2012. She is still a sitting Congresswoman.

Chu's political positions are highly aligned with the Democratic Party. She is highly pro-choice, opposing plans to defund Planned Parenthood and opposing restricting federal funding of abortions. Chu strongly favors laws that endorse hiring women and minorities, taxes on the wealthy, expansion of the Affordable Care Act, and same sex marriages. She opposes an absolute right to gun ownership and expansion of the military. Chu serves on two congressional committees, the Committee on the Judiciary and the Committee on Small Business.

See also: Locke, Gary Faye; Low, Evan

Further Reading

"Representative Judy Chu (1953–)." 2014. Accessed July 16, 2015. https://www.congress.gov/member/judy-chu/1970.

"Welcome to Congresswoman Judy Chu." 2014. Accessed July 16, 2015. http://chu.house.gov/.

Douglas R. Jordan

CONTRACT LABORERS (CREDIT-TICKET LABORERS)

Credit-ticket labor flows, which originated at least as early as the early 19th century, relied on networks of Chinese families and businesses to finance the intending laborer's voyage overseas. A person (usually a man) desiring to go to a particular location would seek financial backing from a family member, family friend, or perhaps a sponsor already situated in the country to which he wished to go. Unlike a coolie whose entire person was bound to his employer, the credit-ticket laborer owed his benefactor only an agreed-upon sum of money. There was generally an agreement in place with regard to how the laborer would go about earning that money, but the laborer was legally his own master (though an employer may choose, contrarily to the spirit of such employment, to keep a firmer grasp on the laborer in order to protect his own investment). The laborer's social autonomy was often further circumscribed by the local legal and political climate, which could at times become quite unfriendly toward Chinese during this period.

Such movements had a number of destinations, including places throughout Southeast Asia, like Thailand, Singapore, Indonesia, Malaysia, and the Philippines; South and Central America; and the unsettled frontiers of the United States and Australia. In the case of the United States in particular, such credit-ticket laborers may have accounted for as much as 80 percent of Chinese in California in the 19th century. A large number of Chinese entering the United States in the 19th century did so via San Francisco (and in later years, via the prison-like immigration quarantine station on Angel Island in San Francisco Bay). The Chinese Six Companies (*liuda gongsi*) was one of the major sponsors of credit-ticket immigrants hoping to come to the United States. An arriving laborer was usually received by a representative of the sponsoring organization or by a member of his hometown's association, to ensure that he was immediately situated within a support network.

Golden Ambitions, Bitter Realities

Many of the credit-ticket laborers in the United States hoped to make a fortune mining gold during the Gold Rush of the mid-19th century and to return to China with their newfound wealth; others might become engaged in any number of occupations, from assisting in shops and laundries to mining coal or contributing to public works projects (like the Transcontinental Railroad). Indeed, a substantial number of credit-ticket laborers hoped that they would eventually save enough to return to China, and thus were considered to be "sojourners" rather than true (permanent) "immigrants"; however, the harsh reality of economic conditions in frontier society meant that many were unable to do so. Some left wives and children in China to whom they would never return. Others were able to start families of their own in the United States. (This was difficult, however, as not only did a relatively small number of Chinese women accompany men in the early voyages to the United States, but anti-miscegenation laws in states like California prohibited Chinese men from marrying or living with white women.) Only the relatively successful could afford either to bring their families over or return to China themselves. Even those who could not afford to return often sent back remittances to help support the families they had left behind.

Sinophobia

Once the gold ran out, and after the Transcontinental Railroad was completed in 1869, there was a large surplus of labor in the western United States. White European immigrants and settlers from the East Coast began to fear competition from Chinese laborers, who were often willing to work longer hours for less money. Thus, in the late 19th century, the American West experienced a number of explosions of racist violence against Chinese (e.g., the Rock Springs, Wyoming massacre of 1885 and the Snake River massacre in 1887 in Oregon) and xenophobic incidents of white-on-Asian attacks or destruction of Chinese property. White nativist sentiment ran high, and reactionary politicians were able to build successful party platforms by fomenting fear of the "Yellow Peril." They implemented discriminatory anti-Chinese legislation, like taxes that only applied to Chinese or denial of citizenship or the right to buy land. The Chinese Exclusion Act of 1882, perhaps the culmination of such racist machinations, was not only a testament to the strength with which nativist paranoia had begun to grip the country, but it would also mark the official end of this wave of credit-ticket movements as new laborers were prohibited from entering the United States.

See also: Coolie Trade

Further Reading

Hom, Marlon K. 1987. *Songs of Gold Mountain: Cantonese Rhymes from San Francisco Chinatown*. Berkeley: University of California Press.

Kuhn, Phillip. 2008. *Chinese Among Others: Emigration in Modern Times*. Lanham, MD: Rowman & Littlefield.

McKeown, Adam. 2001. *Chinese Migrant Networks and Cultural Change: Peru, Chicago, Hawaii, 1900–1936*. Chicago, IL: University of Chicago Press.

McKeown, Adam. 2008. *Melancholy Order: Asian Migration and the Globalization of Borders*. New York: Columbia University Press.

Elizabeth Evans Weber

COOLIE TRADE

As the transatlantic trade in African slaves gradually came to be outlawed over the course of the 19th century, and as freed slaves in the Caribbean and the Americas began to demand higher pay for their work (or refused to work at all for their former masters), colonial plantation apparatuses found that their survival would depend on the recruitment of more cheap labor. The trade in "indentured" Chinese labor, more commonly referred to as the "coolie trade," was one such type of recruitment.

Although the ruling Qing Dynasty had passed a series of laws prohibiting its subjects from leaving its territories, treaties established between the Qing government and Britain in the wake of the first Opium War (1839–1842) had granted legal immunity to British citizens in international settlements of newly established "treaty ports." The British government had already begun an experiment with transporting contracted Indian labor to its colonies in the Caribbean, and once guaranteed immunity from Qing law, British merchants and trading houses based in the international districts in China would turn their attention to China's large urban population. Able to facilitate the emigration of Chinese without fear of prosecution, British and other foreign nationals began to lay the groundwork for the mass transportation of Chinese laborers. The first organized shiploads of Chinese coolies, destined for Mauritius, departed in 1843, and were followed by shipments to Réunion in 1845 and to Cuba in 1847. Shipments would become more regular and more numerous by the end of that decade.

The coolie trade differed from credit-ticket labor movements in several ways: the first was that labor contracts involved in the coolie trade bound the coolie to his employer for a certain length of time, during which his personal liberties were greatly restricted. Second, the coolie trade was largely organized and championed by the demand side, that is, by traders and end users of coolies; whereas credit-ticket journeys were generally arranged by the intending migrant. However, certain political considerations at times caused recruiters and employers to obfuscate the terms under which Chinese were being transported and/or employed; as a result of inaccurate or misleading (and often incomplete) record-keeping, it is not in all cases possible to distinguish "coolie" laborers from "credit-ticket" laborers.

Contracts

Given growing international outrage over the inhumanity of the transatlantic slave trade, it was determined that the coolie trade would be better received if administered as a system of contractual indenture: laborers would sign contracts prior to embarkation to demonstrate their volition and upon arrival in their destinations would either be led directly to their place of employment or would have their contract resold in a "coolie market" (much akin to the slave markets that preceded them). Proponents of the trade argued that the use of contracts—which stipulated the number of years a coolie was to remain under contract, the number of days per week he was expected to work, the amount he was to be compensated per month, allowances to be made for food, shelter, and so on—would protect the laborers and prevent many of the abuses of the slave trade. In many cases—but by no means all—the reality was that employers ignored the terms of the contracts and treated coolies much as slaves had been treated previously.

Organization/Structure

To maximize recruitment, the foreign companies relied upon local Chinese agents ("crimps") to seek out and enlist potential recruits. Because such crimps were usually compensated on a "per-head" basis, they often turned to deception and coercion to maximize the number of persons they recruited. Though the majority of contracted laborers did indeed enlist themselves voluntarily, a large minority were tricked or physically compelled onto ships or into barracoons—ramshackle storage sheds along the coast—where they were amassed before being sent to the other side of the world. Such coolie labor was sent to a vast number of different locations: Singapore and Penang; the Dutch East Indies; British Caribbean colonies of Guiana, Trinidad, and British Honduras; Spanish colony Cuba and former Spanish colony Peru; former Portuguese colony Brazil; Dutch Caribbean colony Surinam; French colonies Martinique and Tahiti; Hawai'i (not yet a U.S. territory); and, in a very short-lived experiment, coolie labor was also acquired for sugar plantations in Louisiana.

The trade initially flourished in the port city of Xiamen in Fujian Province. However, within a few years, violent and coercive recruitment methods had sparked the outrage of the city's residents. A violent antitrade riot broke out at the end of 1852, frightening foreign coolie dealers and ultimately driving the trade toward Hong Kong (then occupied by Britain) and Macau (then occupied by Portugal). Abuses persisted out of these locations as well. The British government in Hong Kong attempted to regulate the trade by establishing an emigration house system with designated staff to verify that all laborers were recruited voluntarily; however, this had the unintended consequence of merely driving the bulk of the trade to Macau, where it was almost completely unregulated. Those shipments that did continue out of Hong Kong were generally organized by the British government and British colonial representatives; shipments out of Macau, on the contrary, were largely privately organized and thus more susceptible to corrupt and coercive practices.

Shipping and Mortality

The practice of recruitment often ran thus: a crimp would encounter his mark, and whether the potential laborer agreed voluntarily to go, or whether the crimp had to deceive or otherwise coerce him, he was brought to the barracoon where he would be made to sign a contract. At this time, he was also usually advanced a sum of money and an outfit of new clothes. Upon receipt of these items, he was usually forbidden from leaving the barracoon until embarkation. He might wait in the dank, cramped barracoon for months before being loaded onto a ship.

Once on board, coolies were crammed together in the dark hold of the ship, much as African slaves had been. The closeness of quarters, coupled with inadequate hygienic facilities, meant that illness often spread rapidly through the population. Disease was a common cause of death among the trapped coolies; so too were lack of adequate nourishment and water; dangerous conditions at sea; and the occasional violent mutiny (usually violently suppressed). The journey from China to the Americas and Caribbean might take as long as three to four months, and mortality on an average voyage might be about 7 percent. (There were numerous cases in which mortality was significantly higher. In catastrophic cases such as *Flora Temple*, in which the captain left 850 coolies to drown while he and his white crew escaped on rowboats after the ship struck a reef in a storm, mortality could approach 100 percent.)

Life in the Colonies

Upon arrival in the colonies, those coolies who had already been spoken for were brought directly to their new place of employment. Those who had been contracted on speculation were brought to coolie markets where they were subjected to humiliating examinations and prodding by prospective employers. Though employers were technically buying the *contracts*, rather than the coolies themselves, the transactions often resembled the outright purchasing of slaves.

The roles of coolie laborers were different depending on where they were sent. In Cuba, they worked in sugar refineries and on tobacco plantations; in Peru they toiled under the tropical sun, mining and carting away wheelbarrows of toxic guano to be used in fertilizer and munitions production; in Tahiti, they farmed cotton; in Hawai'i, they planted sugar cane and other cash crops. In certain cases, coolies might land the somewhat more comfortable position of serving on household staff; but generally, Chinese laborers had been recruited to continue performing the demanding, degrading tasks that African slaves had been made to perform before them. In fact, it soon became evident that many employers had really wanted slaves all along: they refused to release the coolies from their contracts—essentially converting them into permanent property.

Indeed, the overseers who controlled the day-to-day tasks of the plantation also treated coolies much as they had treated slaves, with long hours and frequent beatings. As such, mortality on plantations or in mines was also extremely high—many died performing dangerous tasks; others were beaten to death by cruel managerial staff; some died as a result of inadequate rest and nutrition; while still others committed suicide rather than continue living under a draconian labor regime. Because coolies were almost exclusively male, those who did survive life on the plantations either died bachelors or else married into the local population.

Abolition of the Trade

As public awareness of the cruelties that often inhered in the coolie trade increased, governments, plantation owners, and coolie dealers found their own position in the coolie trade less tenable. In particular, the Qing court was so distressed over the abominable treatment of coolies overseas that its representatives began to demand improved conditions for Chinese laborers. After a series of diplomatic disagreements between the Qing court and the British government, the British emigration house system would come to an end in 1873. That year, the Portuguese government recognized the damage that its reputation was sustaining by the continuation of the coolie trade out of Macau and decided to terminate it the following year.

See also: Chinese Immigration to South America; Chinese in Hawai'i; Chinese in Peru; Contract Laborers (Credit-Ticket Laborers)

Further Reading

Hu-Dehart, Evelyn. 1994. "Chinese Coolie Labor in Cuba in the Nineteenth Century: Free Labor of Neoslavery?" *Contributions in Black Studies* 12: 38–54.

Jung, Moon-ho. 2006. *Coolies and Cane: Race, Labor, and Sugar in the Age of Emancipation.* Baltimore, MD: The Johns Hopkins University Press.

Look Lai, Walton. 1993. *Indentured Labor, Caribbean Sugar: Chinese and Indian Migrants to the British West Indies, 1838–1918.* Baltimore, MD: The Johns Hopkins University Press.

Meagher, Arnold J. 2008. *The Coolie Trade: The Traffic in Chinese Laborers to Latin America, 1847–1874.* Philadelphia, PA: Xlibris.

Stewart, Watt. 1951. *Chinese Bondage in Peru: A History of the Chinese Coolie in Peru, 1849–1874.* Durham, NC: Duke University Press.

Yen Ching-hwang. 1985. *Coolies and Mandarins: China's Protection of Overseas Chinese During the Late Ch'ing Period, 1851–1911.* Singapore: Singapore University Press.

Yun, Lisa. 2008. *The Coolie Speaks: Chinese Indentured Laborers and African Slaves in Cuba.* Philadelphia, PA: Temple University Press.

Elizabeth Evans Weber

EU, MARCH FONG (1922–)

March Fong Eu was born on March 29, 1922. She is a third-generation Californian, born in the small Central Valley city of Oakdale, the daughter of Chinese immigrants, Yuen Kong and Shiu Shee Kong. In 1943, Eu earned a bachelor of science degree in dentistry from the University of California at Berkeley; in 1951, she earned a master of education degree from Mills College; and in 1954, she earned a doctorate in education from Stanford University. During World War II, Eu worked as a dental hygienist at the Presidio in San Francisco. She also served as chairperson of the Division of Dental Hygiene and professor of health education at the University of California at San Francisco. Eu has been awarded many honors, including honorary doctor of law degrees from Western State University (1975), the University of San Diego (1977), and Lincoln University (1984). In her successful career, she has achieved acclaim as an American politician of the Democratic Party.

Eu was the first Asian American, and first woman, to serve on the Alameda County Board of Education, where she served three terms; in her last term, she served as the first woman president. Eu was elected to represent Oakland and parts of Castro Valley in the California State Assembly, becoming the first Asian American woman to serve in that body. In 1974, Eu was selected by three million votes as California's first woman Secretary of State, and first Asian American in statewide office. Eu's accomplishments and contributions as California Secretary of State includes implementing voter registration by mail; including candidate statements in the state ballot pamphlet; making the mail-ballot available to all who want to use it; and pioneered reporting of election results on the Internet. In addition, Eu expanded voter outreach efforts, forging partnerships between government and the private sector to create programs to encourage citizens to register and to vote.

In 1994, Eu accepted President Clinton's appointment as the U.S. Ambassador to the Federated States of Micronesia, where she worked to promote cultural exchange and understanding. In total, Eu served 19 years as California Secretary of State (1975–1993), 8 years as State Assemblywoman representing District 15 (1967–1974), 10 years as school board member, and a term as U.S. Ambassador (1994–1996).

In 2002, Eu lost the Democratic nomination for California Secretary of State during the primaries; in 2003, she expressed interest in running for governor of California in the recall special election of Governor Gray Davis, but then withdrew her intention. Eu's life and career as a public servant is groundbreaking, making history for not just Chinese Americans, but for Asian Americans and women as well.

See also: Chu, Judy; Fong, Hiram Leong; Locke, Gary Faye; Low, Evan

Further Reading

California Secretary of State. 1976. *Biography, Secretary of State March Fong Eu.* Sacramento: California Secretary of State.

Ma, Eva Armentrout. 2000. *Hometown Chinatown: A History of Oakland's Chinese Community, 1852–1995.* New York: Garland Publishing.

Jonathan H. X. Lee

FLYING TIGERS

Formally known as the 1st American Volunteer Group (AVG), the Flying Tigers consisted of American volunteer pilots and related personnel under the command of retired U.S. Army captain and aviation advisor to the Kuomintang, Claire L. Chennault. In 1937, Chennault had been hired as a private individual by Madame Chiang Kai-shek to assist the burgeoning and embattled Chinese Air Force in what was supposed to be a three-month mission. In addition to building a network for air raid warnings and a working infrastructure of strategic runways, Chennault formed one of the best-known aviation units of the Pacific Theater of World War II.

Flying with Distinction

The Flying Tigers consisted of three fighter squadrons and were known for the distinctive shark-face nose art decorating their approximately 90 Curtiss P40 fighter aircraft. Officially, the group was part of the Chinese Air Force; at the time, the United States was not at war, and President Roosevelt could not publically call up forces to assist the Nationalist Chinese. Thus, pilots were recruited from all branches of the U.S. military (from which they had to formally resign), and equipment was funneled to the Chinese through the cash-and-carry program.

The initial group of almost 200 personnel, including about 10 pilots, first assembled in Burma in the summer of 1941. At its height, the Flying Tigers assisted in the war against Japanese military encroachment in Burma and China by providing air cover over the crucial Burma Road, working closely with the British Royal Air Force. Until the fall of Burma to the Japanese, for several months, the Flying Tigers were able to keep this vital supply line open to China. The AVG was also vital in protecting the Chinese Nationalist capital Chungking from Japanese air attacks.

Known for their unorthodox tactics, the Flying Tigers repelled Japanese forces despite significant numerical disadvantages. The official record of the Flying Tigers registers 296 combat-related wins, including grounded aircraft destroyed, although there has been some debate about the veracity of this number. Soon, however, the United States would officially join the war, and the Flying Tigers were disbanded on July 4, 1942. Some members of the AVG were incorporated into the 10th Air Force, which later became the China Air Task Force (14th Air Force, sometimes also referred to as the "Flying Tigers"), where the pilots continued to fly with distinction until the end of the war.

Some AVG airmen, such as pilots Eddie Rector and Greg "Pappy" Boyington, were highly decorated flying aces, and with colorful pilot David Lee "Tex" Hill, directly inspired the 1942 John Wayne movie, *The Flying Tigers*, along with several other wartime films. Another notable American that served in the Flying Tigers was Joseph Alsop, the well-known journalist who served as Staff Historian of the AVG. Alsop would later be highly influential, through his syndicated column, in shaping U.S. Cold War policy in Asia.

Eight Chinese Americans (a mix of immigrant and first-generation) were members of the Flying Tigers: seven mechanics and one doctor hired as civilians under the Central Aircraft Manufacturing Company (CAMCO), an American company that had been producing and repairing aircraft since the 1930s. Several other Chinese Americans had been recruited stateside but had not completed training before the unit was shipped out or had difficulties getting passports.

One of these Chinese mechanics was Pak On Lee, who had immigrated from Guangdong Province in 1935, settling in Portland, Oregon, for several years before joining the AVG in 1941. Like his other Chinese American compatriots, his language skills as well as his local experience were vital to the training of the local Chinese support crews in Kunming in Yunnan Province. After the attack on Pearl Harbor, the mission of the AVG shifted away from instruction and toward direct support of the Chinese Air Force. Recently, Chinese researchers have uncovered a cemetery allegedly containing the final resting places of Chinese AVG ground crews, translators, and support personnel.

Thus, although the Flying Tigers are most associated with the defense of China against the Japanese, the actual employment of Chinese Americans in the AVG was limited in scope. It was not until after the Flying Tigers were disbanded, and after the United States entered the war against Japan, that Chinese Americans were incorporated into the pilot ranks, especially in the Chinese-American Composite Wing (CACW), formed in 1943.

Citizenship Through Covert Action?

The history of the Flying Tigers has not been without controversy. First, its legal status (as part of the Chinese Air Force) meant that many airmen had to "retire" from regular U.S. military service in order to join. Further, the degree to which President Roosevelt was personally involved in the AVG has been subject to some debate. Some have argued that FDR signed a secret executive order (no

Chinese crewmen prepare Curtiss P-40, Rose Marie of the 16th fighter squadron, 51st Fighter Group for a mission. The Flying Tigers, the 1st American Volunteer Group (AVG), or fighter group, comprising three squadrons (approximately 60 aircraft), were commanded by General Claire L. Chennault and flew with the Chinese Air Force between 1941 and 1942 (part of the Second Sino-Japanese War and the Second World War in the Pacific). The group was composed of pilots of the United States Army Air Corps (USAAC), Navy (USN), and Marine Corps (USMC), and was part of a unique American air operations system. Bearing the "Flying Tiger" insignia designed by the Walt Disney Company, the group was formed in 1938 in Kunming (China), but was only officially recognized as a unit in 1941. (Bettmann/Corbis)

copy of which has been found) authorizing covert action. Still others focus on the President's tacit approval through assigning his aide Lauchlin Currie to manage the AVG even while most of the supplies, personnel, and training were furnished through otherwise private means.

The Flying Tigers, however, were not a heavily guarded secret. In 1942, President Roosevelt praised the Flying Tigers for their "outstanding gallantry and conspicuous daring." In 1992, the U.S. government officially recognized the Flying Tigers among its military ranks, and several AVG veterans would later be awarded the Medal of Honor.

The ambiguous state of the Flying Tigers also required a certain amount of cooperation from the U.S. State Department. To shield AVG members from the potential consequences of working and fighting for a foreign government, some details on passports would be untrue or ambiguous. Calling them "students," for example, served to obscure their true purpose in China.

However, the issue of passports was all the more vital for the Chinese American Flying Tigers, who, because of the Chinese Exclusion Act and related discriminatory immigration acts, lacked U.S. citizenship. Some of the Chinese Americans that applied but then were rejected from service may have been "paper sons." Thus, these volunteers could be denied reentry into the United States after serving in China. However, the opportunity to be involved with U.S. troops, both under the ambiguous AVG and then more formally after Pearl Harbor, constituted a twisting, but heroic, path to citizenship that would help integrate Chinese Americans into the United States after the war.

See also: World War II

Further Reading

Ford, Daniel. 2007. *Flying Tigers: Claire Chennault and His American Volunteers, 1941–1942.* New York: HarperCollins (Smithsonian Books).
Samson, Jack. 2005. *The Flying Tiger: The True Story of General Claire Chennault and the U.S. 14th Air Force in China.* Guilford, CT: Lyons Press.

Yvette M. Chin

FONG, HIRAM LEONG (1906–2004)

Born Yau Leong Fong on October 15, 1906, in the Honolulu neighborhood of Kalihi on the island of Oʻahu, Hiram Fong is perhaps best known as the first Asian American to serve in the U.S. Senate. His political career spanned over 30 years, 14 years in Hawaiʻi's Territorial House of Representatives, before he became the first U.S. senator elected after Hawaiʻi achieved statehood in 1959. In 1964, Fong became the first Asian American to run for his party's nomination for President of the United States. Unsuccessful, he nonetheless remained in the Senate for 17 years, until his retirement in 1977. He founded numerous successful businesses in the islands, and over the years he has received national and international awards in business and philanthropy as well as 11 honorary academic degrees.

Fong was the seventh of 11 children. His father Fong Sau Howe and mother Fong Lum Shee had both immigrated to Hawaiʻi from the Chinese mainland. As a child familiar with hard work, he assisted his family financially with odd jobs, among them delivering *poi*, shining shoes, selling newspapers, and caddying rounds of golf. He attended local public schools and graduated from McKinley High School in 1924. In 1930, he obtained his degree from the University of Hawaiʻi at Mānoa, and after working to save money for his tuition, he enrolled at Harvard Law School. He was awarded his degree in 1935, and returned to Hawaiʻi to worked in the Office of the Prosecuting Attorney of Honolulu. In 1938, he went into private legal practice and founded the firm of Fong, Miho, Choy and Robinson.

That same year, Fong married Ellyn Lo; they had 4 children, Hiram Jr., Rodney, Marvin, and Meri-Ellen; 10 grandchildren; and 2 great-grandchildren. His wife passed in 2006.

In 1938, Fong, who was but 31 years old, won a seat in the Territorial House of Representatives. During World War II he served as a major in the U.S. Army Air Force as a Judge Advocate of the 7th Fighter Command of the 7th Air Force, later retiring as a colonel from the U.S. Air Force Reserve. With the end of World War II, he returned to his legislative seat. His reputation for bipartisan leadership led to his being named the Speaker of the House, a position he held from 1948 to 1954. During this time, he was one of the foremost leaders in the fight to make Hawai'i a state. He was, however, forced into a premature retirement when the Democratic Party of Hawai'i successfully ended a Republican Party stronghold over the territorial legislature by voting most incumbents out of office.

Perhaps because of his many stressful business and governmental duties Fong began gardening as a hobby in 1950. Over time, he imported numerous flowers and fruit trees from around the world, sufficient enough to plant a 725-acre plot. The site, located in Kahulu'u, on the island of O'ahu, became the botanical garden and recreation center now known as Senator Fong's Plantation and Gardens. Fong and his wife opened their gardens to the public in 1988, and he remained a permanent fixture among the crowds, up until a week before his death.

At about the same time, Fong began to branch out from the political arena and, along with five other island families, began to make inroads into the world of business. They started Finance Factors, one of the first industrial and consumer loan companies to service the growing minorities who were seeking to start new businesses and buy homes. He went on to establish and head Finance Realty, Finance Home Builders, Finance Investment, Finance Factors Foundation, and Market City.

Upon achieving statehood through the Admission Act of 1959, Hawai'i returned Fong to elected office as its first U.S. senator. There, he sought civil rights legislation, and in 1964, he became the first Asian American to receive votes for President at a major party convention. He again ran in 1968, and thereafter, he supported both the Vietnam War and President Nixon during the Watergate scandal.

After retiring from the Senate in 1977, Fong faced increasing financial and legal difficulties, including several lawsuits with a son over the family's numerous businesses. He was eventually forced to declare bankruptcy in 2003.

Fong passed away on August 18, 2004, in Honolulu, Hawai'i. Governor Linda Lingle immediately ordered the state flag to be flown at half-staff. He was interred at Nu'uanu Cemetery near downtown Honolulu. A memorial service to honor his service was held at the State Capitol Rotunda on August 26, 2004.

The Papers of Hiram L. Fong, composed of documents, photographs, videos, and memorabilia, the bulk of which cover the period from August 1959, to January 1977, are housed within the Library of the University of Hawai'i and are readily available through the Archives and Manuscripts Department.

See also: Chu, Judy; Eu, March Fong; Locke, Gary Faye; Low, Evan

Further Reading

Arakawa, Linda. 2004. "First Asian in U.S. Senate Broke Barriers." *Honolulu Advertiser*, August 19.

Faust, Daniel. 2005. *Hiram Fong: Hawaii's First Senator*. New York: Houghton Mifflin.

James A. Wren

GOLD RUSH

Chinese immigration to the United States during the Gold Rush era (1848–1858) in the mid-19th century was driven by a combination of circumstances in China and conditions in the United States. In China, loss of the First Opium or Anglo-Chinese War (1839–1842), rising political turmoil, foreign intervention, declining economic opportunities in the Zhujiang region due to increasing British and American imported goods, overpopulation, drought, the rise of the sojourner class, and improved trans-Pacific travel came together to encourage Chinese emigration. Simultaneously, the need for cheap laborers during the Gold Rush, for railway construction, and to facilitate agricultural and manufacturing developments in the American West provided many opportunities for Chinese workers in the United States. As a result, the Californian Gold Rush and construction of the Transcontinental Railroad (1863–1869) led to an era of relatively open Chinese immigration into America from 1849 until 1882.

This influx of Chinese immigrants was followed by a period of social discrimination and legislative exclusion against Chinese in America from 1882 until 1943. Anti-Chinese sentiments were influenced by federal immigration laws, state legislation, and regional tensions, each of which shaped the structure and development of immigrant communities in America for over a century. In particular, Chinese communities remained predominantly male bachelor societies and consisted of a rising merchant class throughout the 19th century. Furthermore, Chinese immigrants had very restricted economic, personal, and political rights, which limited their employment opportunities and prompted the majority of laborers to work in mining, railway construction, clothing manufacturing, laundry services, and restaurants. Consequently, anti-Chinese sentiments rose and segregation of Chinatowns occurred in a more defined manner and for a longer period than for other immigrant groups in the United States.

This isolation led to increasing solidarity and retention of traditional customs within the Chinese American community, which in turn gave way to the rise of family associations, community organizations, and ethnically based benevolence societies that sought to aid immigrants and provide support throughout this period.

While documented Chinese immigration to the United States existed early in the 19th century, it was with the discovery of gold in California that mass migration began. The majority of Chinese immigrants during the mid-19th century came from the Guangdong Province in southeastern China. While some immigrants during this period may have been coolies or indentured workers who labored for the cost of their passage to America, most had likely borrowed the funds to travel to America and later repaid them at an exceedingly high interest rate. It is probable that the majority of Chinese who came to America during this period were temporary sojourners who intended to earn money and then return home to China and not remain in the United States as permanent residents. Regardless, owing to increasing international intervention into China, its declining internal economy, and raising political turmoil, Chinese laborers began to travel abroad to support their families.

Opportunities for Chinese immigrants arising from the need for cheap laborers during the Gold Rush, for construction of the Transcontinental Railroad, and to facilitate agricultural growth in the American West were made more prevalent by the Emancipation (1862) of slaves in the Southern States as well as legislation such as the Contract Labor Act (1864), which promoted foreign immigration. In addition, the influx of inexpensive labor was facilitated by passage of the Burlingame Treaty (1868) between the United States and China, which protected Chinese people from anti-Chinese legislation and legal restrictions on immigration. As such, the opportunities available in the American West and California between 1850 and 1869 attracted an unprecedented number of foreign and Chinese immigrants into the region. During this time San Francisco served as an immigration port and regional refuge and became the primary enclave in America for Chinese immigrants. However, Chinese communities in the city were mostly segregated ghettos, often resembling transient camps rather than established residential settlements, and they mostly consisted of overwhelmingly male populations of laborers who were on route to work in elsewhere in mines, boom towns, or on the railroads. During this period, in addition to general laborers, miners, and railway workers, typical occupations for Chinese immigrants also included being merchants, laundrymen, restaurant owners, and students.

During the 1850s Chinese immigration to the United States would increase fourfold, the vast majority of which would remain in California. For the most part Chinese immigrants were initially attracted to America by the possibility of establishing claims of their own on Gum Shan, or "the Gold Mountain." Despite these intentions, however, the Chinese who were soon viewed as hardworking ultimately became a source of cheap labor for others. Those few Chinese immigrants who sought to mine for gold were soon undermined with the passage of the Foreign Miners Tax (1852), which set a monthly tax on foreign prospectors and largely served to end Chinese mining operations, eventually prompting most to work for others or open their own businesses. In this regard, while the demand for inexpensive labor in California continued to prompt increasing numbers of Chinese immigrants into the region, it also led to an escalation of anti-Chinese sentiments and growing calls for increasingly restrictive legislation as mining claims began to decline. Regardless, however, the rising numbers of migrants moving from the eastern United States into the Midwest and Pacific coastline had by the late 1850s promoted the development of the Transcontinental Railroad (1863–1869) to facilitate the movement of people and supplies west, a project that paved the way for the continued need for Chinese laborers.

By the 1860–1870s, Chinese people constituted almost one-quarter of California's workforce, and by 1880 San Francisco's Chinatown had dramatically increased in population. This situation simultaneously enlivened immigrant culture, exacerbated local housing difficulties, and provoked regional hostility. Therefore, despite protections afforded by the Burlingame Treaty, increasingly discriminatory state laws sought to limit benefits from the Gold Rush for the Chinese with passage of acts such as the Foreign Miners Tax (1852) and later the Page Act (1875). In addition, declining economic prosperity occurred in America during the 1870s following completion of the Transcontinental Railroad. The significant Chinese population of workers was associated with cheap labor and soon was viewed by U.S. citizens as unwanted competition for increasingly rare jobs, which led to rising anti-Chinese sentiments, social unrest, legislative exclusion, and public discrimination. These tensions reached a breaking point after cigar makers went on strike and Chinese laborers walked across the lines to break the strike in 1877. Those events indicated that immigrant laborers could no longer be relied upon to be a docile and inexpensive workforce. As a result, the limited support that Chinese immigrants had received from the business community soon dissipated, giving way to increasingly widespread anti-Chinese hostility.

In response, both the state of California and the federal government began to pass a succession of exclusionary laws, including the Page Act, Exclusion Act (1882), Scott Act (1888), and eventually the Geary Act (1892). The most influential piece of legislation was the Exclusion Act, which for the first time targeted a specific ethnic group in an attempt to limit their right to immigrate to the United States and exclude them from specific civil liberties. Additional legislation developed and expanded these restrictions, eventually segregating schools, targeting Chinese businesses, making it impossible for Chinese immigrants to become naturalized, restricting their ability to become citizens and bring their families to America, and requiring them to register in order to travel abroad. In addition to exclusionary federal legislation, in 1879 the California Constitution was amended to legalize discrimination against the Chinese. These amendments further limited immigration of Chinese into the state as well as restricting the employment of Asian immigrants by corporations and public agencies. As such, throughout the mid-19th century, the legal status of Chinese immigrants as well as their distinct ethnic, linguistic, racial, and cultural differences became the basis of discrimination against most Asians in America. Therefore, despite the establishment and growth of Chinese communities during the Gold Rush, exclusionary laws effectively halted the development of immigrant families, businesses, and Chinatowns. This combination of social isolation and legal discrimination provided the basis for future anti-Chinese legislation, eventually enabling authorities to criminalize and persecute the Chinese American population. As a result, Chinese immigrants often became victims of lynching and violence, which increasingly isolated them into segregated ethnic communities in the American West.

See also: Chinese Immigration During the Gold Rush

Further Reading

McClain, Charles. 1994. *In Search of Equality: The Chinese Struggle Against Discrimination in Nineteenth-Century America.* Berkeley: University of California Press.
Yung, Judy, Gordon Chang, and Him Mark Lai, eds. 2006. *Chinese American Voices: From the Gold Rush to the Present.* Berkeley: University of California Press.

Sean Morton

GONG LUM v. RICE (1927)

Gong Lum was a resident of Rosedale, Mississippi, and father of nine-year-old Martha Lum, an American-born U.S. citizen, in Mississippi. In 1924, Martha Lum attended the Rosedale Consolidated School in the morning, but by noon recess was informed by the superintendent that she would not be allowed to return to school on the grounds that she was of "Chinese descent" and not a member of the "white or Caucasian race." In a state trial, the court entered a writ of mandamus in favor of Gong Lum, which ordered the members of the board of trustees to readmit Martha Lum. However, on appeal, the Mississippi Supreme Court reversed the order in favor of the board of trustees to exclude Martha Lum from attending school with white children. Gong Lum appealed to the U.S. Supreme Court. In a unanimous decision, written by Chief Justice

William Howard Taft, the Court affirmed the Mississippi Supreme Court decision, arguing that the petitioner had not illustrated that there were no segregated schools she could not attend. In addition, the Supreme Court affirmed that Martha Lum was "not White" and therefore was "colored." Gong Lum argued that classifying Martha Lum as a member of the "colored race" (i.e., black race) denied her equal protection under the laws under the Fourteenth Amendment, but in referencing *Cumming v. Richmond County Board of Education* (1899), Chief Justice Taft argued in favor of state rights to manage and provide public education to its youth. As such, the Supreme Court cited a long list of federal and state court decisions that reach back as far as *Roberts v. City of Boston* (1849)—apparently the first case to introduce the doctrine of "separate but equal"—and *Plessy v. Ferguson* (1896)—which brought "separate but equal" to the national level—which all upheld segregation in the public sphere, especially with regard to public education. *Gong Lum v. Rice* was overturned following *Brown v. Board of Education of Topeka I* (1954) and *Brown v. Board of Education of Topeka II* (1955). In 1971, the San Francisco Unified School District attempted to desegregate its schools and reassign Chinese and other Asian American students to other public schools, but Chinese parents objected because at the Asian schools, their children were able to learn about their cultural heritage, which other public schools did not offer. In *Guey Heung Lee v. Johnson* (1971) the U.S. Supreme Court declined to issue a stay of a federal district court's order to desegregate public schools in San Francisco.

See also: Chinese Americans and Civil Rights; *People v. Hall* (1854); *United States v. Wong Kim Ark* (1898)

Further Reading

Gong Lum v. Rice, Justia U.S. Supreme Court. https://supreme.justia.com/cases/federal/us/275/78/case.html.

Jonathan H. X. Lee

GUEY HEUNG LEE v. JOHNSON (1971)
See: Gong Lum v. Rice (1927)

HO AH KOW v. NUNAN (1879)
See: Chinese Americans and Civil Rights

LAU v. NICHOLS (1974)
See: Chinese Americans and Civil Rights

INTERNATIONAL LADIES' GARMENT WORKERS' UNION

The International Ladies' Garment Workers' Union (ILGWU) formed in 1900 by the largely Jewish immigrant workforce in New York City. For first decade of the 20th century the ILGWU led large-scale strikes but was unable to make significant inroads in the sector. After the tragic fire of the Triangle Shirtwaist Factory in 1911, the ensuing public outcry led to significant workplace regulations. By the 1920s the ILGWU began to develop a strategy of applying economic pressure at the point of production and consumption in order to negotiate with both the contracting factory and the jobber. This "jobber-contractor strategy" allowed garment workers to gain power despite being outsourced, and the ILGWU gained in membership, becoming one of the largest unions in the United States. The numbers of the ILGWU began to decrease in the 1960s and 1970s alongside the declining domestic garment sector, a consequence of production relocating to the global south, part of what became known as "globalization." Today the ILGWU continues as the union Workers United.

The garment sector was one of the first large-scale manufacturing industries in the United States. The word "sweatshop" was first coined in the sector because workers "sweated" long hours in cramped conditions. The industry was susceptible to a high degree of exploitation since it was labor intensive; "vertically dis-integrated," which meant it was outsourced by retailers and "jobbers" (the brands of today); and compounded by gender and racial oppression because it was both highly feminized and had a predominantly immigrant workforce.

Chinese American women, mostly in San Francisco's Chinatowns, began to work as seamstresses in small family-run shops or in their homes in the late 19th and early 20th centuries. By the 1930s these shops had become larger garment factories and were often used as a cheaper alternative to undermine the mostly white unionized garment contractors. In 1938, after years of failed attempts to unionize the Chinatown garment shops, workers formed the independent local Chapter 341 of the International Ladies' Garment Workers Union (ILGWU), known as the Chinese Ladies Garments Workers Union. The Chinese garment workers of San Francisco organizing themselves into an autonomous local in recognition that they might be disadvantaged in the largely white ILGWU San Francisco local.

The first target was the retailer National Dollar Stores. After a 108-day strike and picketing of its retail shop, the company capitulated, agreeing to become a "closed shop," 5 percent wage increase (to $14 per week), time-and-half for overtime, 40-hour work week, improved working conditions, and paid holiday for Labor Day. For many workers the terms did not go far enough, but in the end workers narrowly accepted the agreement. Almost all 100 union members lost their jobs within two years of the agreement and the union local shrunk to less than 40 members. Nonetheless, labor historians concur that the adversarial approach, collective class consciousness, and links with workers outside the community that were emblematic of the campaign changed the course of history for Chinese American women. Crucially, the strike and subsequent factory closure led the Chinese American women, with the assistance of ILGWU organizers, to break the racial barrier and be permitted to work in white-owned union shops.

With the outset of World War II, the ILGWU all but dissipated in Chinatown; nonetheless, Chinese American garment workers would become central to San Francisco and New York's labor movement. Forty years later the ILGWU organized its next large strike in Chinatown, now the center of New York's dwindling garment sector. In June of 1982, 15,000 Chinese American garment workers in New York City would walk out. The final agreement increased workers' wages, holidays, and employer health-care contributions, and improved the cost of living adjustment. Through the ILGWU, Chinese American garment workers had organized across the sector to become outspoken union leaders, agitating strikes and work stoppages and directly confronting the stereotype of Asian passivity and subservience.

See also: Chinese American Activism; Chinese Americans and Civil Rights

Further Reading

Kumar, Ashok, and Jack Mahoney. 2014. "Stitching Together." *WorkingUSA* 17 (2): 187–210.

Song, Jingyi. 2010. *Shaping and Reshaping Chinese American Identity: New York's Chinese During the Depression and World War II.* Lanham, MD: Lexington Books.

Yung, Judy. 1995. *Unbound Feet: A Social History of Chinese Women in San Francisco.* Oakland: University of California Press.

Ashok Kumar

LEE, WEN-HO (1939–)

A Taiwanese scientist, Wen-Ho Lee came to the United States in 1965 and received his doctorate in mechanical engineering from Texas A&M University. Lee eventually became a U.S. citizen and in 1978 was employed as a nuclear scientist at Los Alamos National Laboratory in New Mexico. Lee was fired on March 8, 1999, following a publication in the *New York Times* on the sale of U.S. nuclear secrets to China and the release of the U.S. Government's *Cox Report*, which alleged that China had built a nuclear arsenal similar in design to U.S. technology. Lee was accused of stealing U.S. nuclear data for having downloaded classified information and endangering national security. In December

1999, Lee was indicted and spent nine months in jail, where he was prohibited from speaking Chinese, kept in solitary confinement for 278 days, and had limited access to his family and attorneys. Federal investigators failed to provide evidence of espionage or Lee's intent to sell secrets, but they charged him with improper handling of restricted data, to which he pled guilty. The unfair treatment Lee received compared to similar cases involving non-Asians and the lack of evidence presented led to suggestions of racial profiling. In June 2006 Lee received $1.6 million from the federal government and five media organizations as settlement in his civil lawsuit.

See also: Yee, James J.

Further Reading

Gotanda, Neil. 2000. "Comparative Racialization: Racial Profiling and the Case of Wen Ho Lee." *UCLA Law Review* 47 (6): 1689–1703.

Lee, Wen Ho. 2003. *My Country Versus Me: The First-Hand Account by the Los Alamos Scientist Who Was Falsely Accused of Being a Spy.* New York: Hyperion Books.

Sean Morton

LOCKE, GARY FAYE (1950–)

Gary Faye Locke was born on January 21, 1950, in Seattle, Washington. Much of his early years were spent living in the Yesler Terrace public housing project. Locke is a third-generation Chinese American whose paternal lineage is from Taishan, China. Locke is the second oldest of five siblings. His father, James Locke, served as a staff sergeant in the U.S. Fifth Armored Division during World War II, and his mother, Julie Locke, is from Hong Kong. Locke's paternal grandfather left China in the 1890s and emigrated to the United States, working as a "houseboy" in Olympia, Washington, in exchange for English-language lessons. Locke's first language is Chinese and did not start formal English learning until he entered kindergarten. In 1968, Locke graduated from Seattle's Franklin High School and achieved Eagle Scout rank and the Distinguished Eagle Scout Award from the Boy Scouts of America. In 1972, Locke graduated from Yale University with a bachelor's degree in political science. Then, in 1975, he received his juris doctor from Boston University School of Law.

Locke's political career began in 1982 when he was elected to Washington State's South Seattle district in the Washington House of Representatives. Locke became the first Chinese American governor in U.S. history when he won the general election for governor of Washington in 1996. Locke won reelection in 2000 and did not seek a third term. He was the 21st governor of the state of Washington. Locke was chosen by the Democrat Party to give his party's response to President George W. Bush's 2003 State of the Union Address. Locke received racist slurs, threats to him and his family after his rebuttal, which influenced his decision to not seek a third term. After leaving the governor's office, Locke went to work for an international law firm of Davis Wright Tremaine LLP in their China and governmental-relations practice groups. On February 25, 2009, Locke was selected to be President Barack Obama's Secretary of Commerce. His nominated was confirmed on March 24, 2009: Locke is the first Chinese American appointed as Secretary of Commerce. Locke was again nominated by President Barack Obama as U.S. ambassador to China after Jon Huntsman, Jr. resigned. The Senate confirmed his nomination on July 27, 2011. In late November 2013, Locke announced he would step down as U.S. ambassador to China to spend time with his family in Seattle. In his parting speech as ambassador, Locke said, "I'm proud of my Chinese heritage. I'm proud of the great contributions that China has made to world civilization over thousands of years. But I'm thoroughly American. I'm proud of the great values that America has brought to the entire world and all that America stands for."

Gary Faye Locke, former Governor of Washington, during an interview in Shanghai, China, on April 23, 2007. (Imaginechina/Corbis)

Locke is married to Mona Lee, a Taiwanese American who was Miss Asian America in 1994 and a television reporter for NBC affiliate KING 5 television in Seattle.

See also: Chu, Judy; Low, Evan

Further Reading

Locke, Gary. 2003. "The One-hundred Year Journey: From Houseboy to the Governor's Office." In *Asian American Politics: Law, Participation, and Policy*, edited by Don T. Nakanishi and James S. Lai. Lanham, MD: Rowman & Littlefield.

Yung, Judy, Gordon Chang, and Him Mark Lai, eds. 2006. *Chinese American Voices: From the Gold Rush to the Present.* Berkeley: University of California Press.

Jonathan H. X. Lee

LOW, EVAN (1983–)

Evan Low is an openly gay American politician. Low is a Democrat who represents District 28 in the California State Assembly and serves as Assistant Majority Whip. Low was born in 1983 and grew up in San Jose, California. His father, Arthur Low, is a Chinese American optometrist. Low graduated from Leland High School and moved to Campbell in 2003. He graduated from De Anza Community College, went on to study at San Jose State University, and graduated with a bachelor's degree in political science. After, he completed a Senior Executives in State and Local Government program at Harvard University.

Low's political career began with an unsuccessful run for a seat on the Campbell City Council in 2004. He ran again in 2006 and won. Low made national headline news in 2009 when his colleagues selected him to become Campbell mayor in 2009. At this time, he was the youngest openly gay Asian American or Chinese American mayor in the nation. Low was reselected to serve as Campbell mayor in 2013. In 2014, Low was elected to the California State Assembly representing District 28. District 28 is located in the Silicon Valley and includes Campbell, Cupertino, Los Gatos, Monte Sereno, Saratoga, and the areas of West San Jose, Willow Glen, Cambrian, and Almaden Valley.

Low is known for launching a petition on the website Change.org to get the U.S. Food and Drug Administration to lift its ban on gay and bisexual men from donating blood: as of early 2015, there are 63,208 supporters. He has taught American government and political science at De Anza Community College.

See also: Chu, Judy; Locke, Gary Faye

Further Reading

"Assistant Majority Whip, Evan Low, District 28." 2015. Accessed July 16, 2015. http://asmdc.org/members/a28/.

"Evan Low for State Assembly." 2014. Accessed July 16, 2015. http://evanlowforassembly.com/.

Jones, Carolyn. 2009. "Young, Gay Asian Becomes Mayor of Campbell." *San Francisco Chronicle*, December 2.

Jonathan H. X. Lee

MCCARTHYISM

Soon after the establishment of People's Republic of China, the diplomatic relationship between China and the United States broke up. The success of the Chinese Communist Revolution as well as the formation of the Sino-Soviet Alliance raised keen debates among political circles in Washington. Critics of the Truman Administration portrayed the "loss of China" to communism as a catastrophe. In 1950 when the Korea War broke out, the United States soon launched a "containment and isolation" policy against China.

In February 1950, Senator Joseph McCarthy capitalized on the national mood by proclaiming that he had a list of 205 card-carrying Communists in the State Department. Supporters of Chiang Kai-shek, Republicans, and those who were disappointed by the U.S.–China policy accused the Far East experts in the U.S. government of "sabotage," incompetence, treason, and conspiracy. McCarthy and his followers wanted the U.S. Secretary of State to make it absolutely clear that the United States will never recognize the Chinese membership in the United Nations.

Senators McCarthy and Pat McCarran then conducted multiple investigations and assorted loyalty-security boards. Far East experts, especially "China Hands" in government and academia, were soon purged. McCarthy's charge expanded to Owen Lattimore, who had served as personal adviser to Chiang at the beginning of World War II in a series of congressional hearings, including those in the Institute of Pacific Relations. Foreign Service Officers O. Edmund Clubb, John Paton Davies, Jr., John Emmerson, John S. Service, and John Carter Vincent were forced out of the Foreign Service, while journalists such as Edgar Snow and Theodore White could not continue their careers in journalism.

As a result, in the McCarthy era, anticommunist investigations conducted by the CIA and FBI started from the U.S. Congress and spread to Hollywood, the media, academia, and government.

McCarthyism's Influence on Chinese Immigrants in the United States

McCarthyism spread to Chinatown rapidly. The U.S. government started surveillance of left-wing organizations soon after the People's Republic was founded. Federal authorities kept close contact with liberal Chinese American organizations like the China Youth Club and the *China Daily News* and bugged the headquarters of Chinese Hand Laundry Alliance.

The outbreak of the Korean War altered Chinese American's perspectives. The hostility that the American public harbored toward the Chinese drew on Chinatowns, and the economy of Chinese Americans was under serious attack. This silenced procommunist voices in Chinatowns. Throughout the country, FBI agents visited Chinese Americans and warned them to unsubscribe from the *China Daily News*. Besides, Chinese immigrants found their mail opened, their phone lines tapped, and their movements shadowed in the streets. U.S. authorities even probed the lives of U.S. World War II veterans of Chinese heritage and interrogated children in Chinatown playgrounds.

The darkest moment for Chinese immigrants in the United States came in December 1955, when Everett F. Drumwright, the U.S. consul in Hong Kong, released a report that accused the Chinese community of "a fantastic system of passport and visa fraud." He insisted that almost all Chinese in America had entered the United States illegally. After the release of this report, the entire Chinese community fell under federal scrutiny and no one was immune from investigation. "Chinatown was hit like an A-Bomb fell." Business activities dropped rapidly when investigators raided Chinatowns on both coasts. Chinese merchants in New York City lost $100,000 a week in sales.

In 1956, U.S. Attorney Lloyd Burke subpoenaed 40 major Chinese American associations, demanding that they produce all records and photographs of their membership and a full account of their income within 24 hours. Chinatown leaders appealed to politicians for help. In March, a federal judge threw out the subpoena attack, calling it a "mass inquisition." In the same year, the U.S. government initiated a "confession program," encouraging the Chinese without legal immigration status to voluntarily confess. Those confessing implicated dozens of Chinese relatives who in turn cooperated with authorities to protect themselves. In San Francisco, some 10,000 Chinese confessed. Although only few were deported due to their political activities, the psychological impact instilled in the Chinese community a fear of government authority and a legacy of silence.

Chinese intellectuals were another group vulnerable to accusations of espionage. The U.S. authorities suspected that Chinese intellectuals and scientists in the United States passed secrets to the People's Republic with the fear that China was developing into a world power with high technology and science. The Immigration and Nationality Act of 1952 as well as President Harry Truman's proclamation of 1953 stopped the departure of foreigners whose knowledge might jeopardize national security. As a result, 120 Chinese nationals were detained and not permitted to leave for years. One example is Qian Xuesen (1911–2009), a top Chinese aerodynamicist who helped pioneer the U.S. space program. The authorities charged Qian with being a communist and placed him under visual house arrest for five years. This insulation made Qian decide to return to China. As a result, the case against Qian hurt rather than helped U.S. national defense. The United States lost a first-class scientist from the American lunar and missile programs.

The McCarthy era was certainly a troubled period for Chinatowns. The "old-timers" of Chinatown were aging and dying. The decrease of populations coincided with the government surveillance, which reduced business revenue. An antigambling law passed in 1954 also devastated Chinese casinos and nightclubs. Many young families left Chinatowns and moved to the suburbs. Chinatowns shrank in size and some vanished completely. In 1940, a study showed 28 U.S. cities with Chinatowns, but by 1955, the number had fallen to 16.

Of course, the dark era for Chinese immigrants did not last forever. From the late 1970s, new immigrants came to the United States with rapid speed and soon filled the Chinatown neighborhoods and spread widely elsewhere in the United States.

See also: World War II

Further Reading

Peck, James. 2006. *Washington's China: The National Security World, the Cold War, and the Origins of Globalism*. Amherst: University of Massachusetts Press.

Thomson, James C. 1972. "On the Making of U.S. China Policy, 1961–9: A Study in Bureaucratic Politics." *The China Quarterly* 50: 220–43.

Yan He

PEOPLE v. HALL (1854)

We know not from where or exactly when the Chinese emigrant miner Ling Sing journeyed from southern China to seek his fortunes at *Gum San*, the Golden Mountain of Gold Rush California. In all likelihood he was born in Guandong Province. It is almost certain he was among the tens of thousands of his brethren fleeing China at the beginning of the Taiping Rebellion (1850–1864), a bloody civil war leaving upwards of 20 million dead. Lured by the pamphlets, posters, and broadsides that littered the port cities along the South China Sea, Ling Sing was most likely pushed by war and devastation at home, while at the same time pulled by the promise of great riches to be had from the sediment of rivers flowing down from the Sierra Nevada Mountains.

What we do know is that on August 9, 1853, George Hall was arrested for the murder of Ling Sing. By all accounts it was a robbery gone awry. Hall and two men (one of whom was Hall's brother) entered a Chinese mining camp along the banks of the Bear River, intent on robbing Chinese miners of their meager gold dust. Hearing the shouts of a fellow miner, Ling Sing left his tent and ran to the aid of his countryman. In the ensuing scuffle Ling Sing was shot. Later that month, Nevada County District Attorney William Stewart obtained a grand jury indictment against Hall for the murder of Ling Sing.

Stewart, who went on to serve as Attorney General of California and later U.S. Senator for the state of Nevada, was an antislavery Northerner. Among the witnesses testifying before the grand jury were six Chinese miners. Their testimony was interpreted by William Speer, a Presbyterian minister and medical missionary, who spent five years in Canton, China. Fluent in Cantonese, Speer came to San Francisco in 1852 to evangelize the city's growing Chinese immigrant population.

With an appropriation of $5,000 from the Nevada County Board of Supervisors to prosecute the case against Hall, the trial centered on the testimony of three of the original six Chinese witnesses and one Caucasian witness who also testified for the state. Speer once again served as interpreter. The jury returned a verdict of murder in the first degree against Hall, and Judge William Barbour sentenced Hall to death by hanging. Recollecting the facts of the case some

55 years later, Stewart wrote in his *Reminiscences* (1908), "I had not the slightest doubt that Hall killed [Ling Sing], because he was seen [by the white witness] coming from the camp where the dead body was found."

Hall's conviction was appealed to the three Justices of the California Supreme Court. According to Stewart, "friends" of the condemned murderer "employed" John McConnell to mount Hall's plea before California's highest court. McConnell and Stewart were no strangers to each other. Indeed, when Stewart resumed his legal education, he did so under McConnell's tutelage, entering the study of law in McConnell's Nevada City office in the spring of 1852. Stewart was appointed district attorney in November 1852, filling the vacancy left when McConnell resigned as District Attorney for Nevada County.

McConnell, a Southerner by birth and pro–states rights southern Democrat by political temperament, was the Attorney General–elect of the state when he appeared before California's Supreme Court on Hall's behalf. McConnell focused on section 14 of California's Act Concerning Crimes and Punishments (1850), which provided that "No Black, or Mulatto person, or Indian shall be allowed to give evidence in favor of, or against a White man." McConnell contended that because the statute prohibited the testimony of an "Indian" against a white man, the trial testimony of the Chinese witnesses was inadmissible. Stewart later recalled that McConnell "said Chinese were the same as Indians and that the statute applied." Stewart's rebuttal was that since no objection to the Chinese testimony was made during the criminal trial, the Supreme Court was barred by statute from considering the decision of the lower court. Stewart also argued that in his reading of section 14, while the statute prohibited the testimony of "Indians," no language in the statute prohibited testimony from the Chinese race.

In a 2-3 decision, the California Supreme Court "Held, that the words Indian, Negro, Black, and White, are generic terms, designating race" and "therefore, Chinese and all other people not white, are included in the prohibition from being witnesses against Whites." The verdict against Hall was overturned. Delivering the written opinion of the Court was California's Chief Justice, Hugh Murray. A staunch Democrat in the states-rights tradition, Murray was appointed to the Court in 1852 by Governor John McDougall. Murray won election outright as a Democrat in 1852 and was reelected in 1854 as the candidate of the anti-immigrant Know Nothing Party.

Concurring in Murray's decision was Justice Solomon Heydenfeldt. Southerner by birth, secessionist by political inclination, and proponent of cotton cultivation in the rich soil of California, Heydenfeldt arrived in San Francisco in 1850 to practice law. While a judge in Russell County, Alabama, Heydenfeldt wrote an open letter to Alabama's Governor Rueben Chapman, calling for the termination of the domestic slave trade into that state. Heydenfeldt wrote this letter not because he was an abolitionist, but because he feared race war would exterminate the "White" race of Alabama. When Heydenfeldt left his elected Supreme Court post in 1857, he embarked on a successful career as a lawyer. Heydenfeldt was a founding member of the San Francisco Mining Exchange, president of the Exchequer Mining Company, and holder of substantial land and mining interests in his new home state. Heydenfeldt's brother Elcan, a California state senator in 1853, was so vehement in his opposition to the rights of free blacks in the state that he moved that their petition protesting their second-class status as witnesses in civil cases be expunged from the official record of the legislature.

Dissenting in the *Hall* decision was Justice Alexander Wells. Born in New York City, Wells practiced law on Wall Street. In 1845 he was elected to the New York Legislature with the support of the pro-immigrant Tammany Hall political machine. Drawn to California by the Gold Rush, Wells entered the fray of California sectional politics on June 18, 1852, when while serving as an appointed interim justice in Heydenfeldt's absence, he granted a writ of habeas corpus to three men who were ordered returned to Mississippi in a decision handed down by pro-slavery District Court Judge Lewis Aldrich under California's controversial Fugitive Slave Law (1852). Unlike the federal Fugitive Slave Law enacted as part of the compromise that brought California into the union as the 31st state in 1850, California's Fugitive Slave Law focused not on slaves escaped to California but rather on slaves brought to the free state by their Southern masters.

In the matter of *People v. Hall*, it was the opinion of the majority that California was a free white state and George Hall was a free white man entitled to all the protections of the law. Reaching beyond the issue before them on the admissibility of evidence in the law of criminal practice in California, the Justices decided to correct a contradiction in statutory language between the criminal *and* civil practice acts relative to race-based prohibitions on testimony. The language in the Civil Practice Act (1852) stated clearly that "No Indian or Negro shall be allowed to testify as a witness in any action in which a White person is a party" while the language of the Criminal Act, barred "Black, or Mulatto person, or Indian."

Murray addressed the discrepancy on multiple levels. First, he opined that Christopher Columbus, in service to the King and Queen of Spain, mistakenly named the inhabitants of San Salvador "Indian" because he thought he had reached "one of those Islands of the Chinese Sea, lying near the extremity of India, which had been described by navigators." Columbus's error was merely an error of geography. "Indian" as "an appellation was universally adopted, and extended to the aboriginals of the New World, as well as Asia," reasoned Murray.

Next, Murray turned to the authority of science, citing the French naturalist George Cuvier's "three distinct types of human species" and his designation of the superior Caucasian, followed by the inferior Mongolian and Ethiopian races. Even if Columbus was wrong, science was right. "Many ingenious speculations" supported the court's reasoning that the three races "were subdivided into varieties or tribes" and the Chinese were a type of the Mongolian race. There was no doubt in Murray's mind that the Chinese were Mongolian, "a race of people whom nature has marked as inferior." Moreover, recent theories on human migration were "not without plausibility" and "this continent was first peopled by Asiatics who crossed Behring's Straits, and from thence found their way down to the more fruitful climates of Mexico and South America."

Murray acknowledged that the Bering Straits theory might, like Columbus, be wrong, and the indigenous populations of North and of South America might be a distinct race. To that Murray alluded "to the early history of legislation on this subject, our Statute being only a transcript of those of the older States." In effect, it did not matter where "Indians" came from, as long as it was understood that historically they were not accorded the same rights as white citizens in other states. Even if the Chinese were not "Indian," Murray reasoned they were not on equal footing with whites because, as James Kent had noted in his *Commentaries on American Law* (1826), it was unlikely that "any of the tawny races of Asia can be admitted to the privileges of citizenship."

Notwithstanding Murray's foray into history, race science, human migration theory, and American jurisprudence to support his conclusions on the inadmissibility of Chinese testimony, Murray proceeded to achieve what the California State Assembly had failed to accomplish in the two statutes relating to witness testimony against whites in civil and criminal practice. While section 394 of the Civil Practice Act prohibited "Negro" testimony and section 14 of the Criminal Practice Act prohibited the testimony of "Blacks," the real issue before the Court, wrote Murray, was the meaning of the words "Black" and "White." It was clear in history and in science who was "White" and who was not. Anything not "White" was "Black" and therefore the Chinese were prohibited under both statutes because they were "Indian" (as a matter of historical error) and "Black" (as matter of natural history).

According to Murray, "the Legislature, if any intention can be ascribed to it, adopted the most comprehensive terms to embrace every known class or shade of color, as the apparent design was to protect the White person from the influence of testimony other than that of persons of the same cast." Murray declared "that if it had ever been anticipated that this class of people were not embraced in the prohibition, then such specific words would have been employed as would have put the matter beyond any possible controversy." Murray was either unaware of or completely ignored the fact that Virginia-born California Assemblyman Benjamin Myers had introduced a bill in 1853 to exclude Chinese testimony in criminal cases. That bill failed to make it out of the Assembly's Judiciary Committee.

The case was remanded to the lower court for retrial. Without the testimony of the Chinese witnesses, the only admissible testimony was the white witness who saw Hall leaving Ling Sing's camp. Stewart did not prosecute the case and Hall was a free man. On March 18, 1863, the California legislature codified the *Hall* decision by amending the civil and criminal practice acts to prohibit Native American and "Mongolian" testimony—with the added specific exclusion of "Chinese." In keeping with federal law, the statutes were purposely omitted by codification in 1873. On March 30, 1955, both statutes were officially repealed.

See also: Anti-Chinese Violence; Chinese Exclusion Act (1882)

Further Reading

California Supreme Court. 1906. *Reports of Cases Determined in the Supreme Court of the State of California*. San Francisco, CA: Bancroft-Whitney.

McClain, Charles J., Jr. 1984. "The Chinese Struggle for Civil Rights in Nineteenth Century America: The First Phase, 1850–1870." *California Law Review* 72 (4): 529–68.

David Alan Rego

SECRET SOCIETIES

"Secret society" will be used here rather than such synonyms as "*tong*," "fraternal organization," or "sworn brotherhood." The term is nonpejorative and widely accepted, even though the societies themselves are not particularly secret. Yet they were and are important. During the 19th and early 20th centuries they often dominated local Chinese communities in Hong Kong, Macao, Southeast Asia, Australia, the Pacific Islands, and the Americas. They still play a major role in some of those places.

Coming with the very early waves of Chinese immigrants in 1850s, all secret societies that existed in North America prior to the 1980s can trace their roots to the Pearl River Delta in southern China. They sprang from an old, diffuse group of revolutionary/mutual aid/self-defense/sometimes-criminal organizations that originated in southern China and spread around the world with the early Chinese Diaspora. Often those societies called themselves Hongmen ("Hong Gate") or Tiandi Hui (Heaven and Earth Society) and traced their roots to common, partly mythical, origins but were otherwise independent of one another.

Chinese secret societies in America often have multifaceted natures. They have community-building programs that are social service oriented, but in the past they also behaved in ways that sometimes were against the law. They conducted their activities, both benevolent and illegal, through a highly structured hierarchical leadership with severe penalties for violating regulations. Although all secret societies originally shared the political goal of overthrowing the Qing Dynasty that ruled China between 1644 and 1911, some were mainly social groups that focused on mutual aid and recreation for members. Others served administrative and judicial functions within the community, allocating business locations and cemetery sites, settling disputes, and enforcing the payment of debts. Still others engaged in criminal activities: protection rackets, extortion, and strong-arm methods for controlling such tolerated vices as gambling and prostitution. And, confusingly, a few such organizations were involved with all three sorts of activity at once: mutual help, administration, and crime.

Very little of that crime, incidentally, involved smuggling and selling drugs. Although many authorities assert the contrary, claiming that Chinese tongs have always controlled the smuggling and selling of narcotics, this is no more than sensational, usually racist, propaganda. Not a single instance of secret society drug trafficking was recorded anywhere in North America during the entire 19th century. In the 20th and 21st centuries, the North American secret societies, as distinguished from the Triad societies in Southeast Asia, have only been bit players in the narcotics trade.

Whatever one thinks of them, in almost any Chinese community in the Americas, Australia-New Zealand, or Southeast Asia, the secret societies were, and sometimes still are, dominatingly important. In the United States and Canada, they formerly had more real authority among local Chinese than any other immigrant organization, including regional and clan groupings, benevolent associations, chambers of commerce, and even, until recently, the Chinese and U.S. governments.

See also: Bing Kung Tong; Chee Kung Tong; Hip Sing Tong (Xiesheng Tang); Hongmen; Hop Sing Tong (Hesheng Tang)

Further Reading

Morgan, W. P. 1960. *Triad Societies in Hong Kong.* Hong Kong: Government Press.

Bennet Bronson and Chuimei Ho

SUN YAT-SEN (1866–1925)

Sun Yat-sen is one of the most important figures of the Chinese Revolution of 1911, especially from a Western perspective, because he represented the events like no one else. This charismatic man, who received not only a classical Chinese but also a Western Christian education on Hawai'i, would become the international face of the Chinese Revolution, who connected the Chinese population living overseas with that in the home country. He left a lot of

writings, some especially dealing with future developmental
programs for postrevolutionary China, which show his
ambitions for the country that
would grow through the development of infrastructure and
economic power. All in all, Sun
could be described as a sym-
biosis of Chinese values and
Western education, a man who
would therefore also become a
figure who is memorialized in
both worlds.

Sun, who was born in
1866 in the Chinese village of
Cuiheng in Shandong Prov-
ince, immigrated to Macao
when his father wanted to find
work there in 1882. His elder
brother Sun-Mei had decided
to emigrate to Hawai'i, where
he would work on a vegetable
farm in Honolulu. He became
successful there, opening a cat-
tle farm on Maui some years

A portrait of Sun Yat-sen from his obituary in
1925. (Wellcome Library, London)

later, finally demanding that Sun follow him to the Pacific island to work with
him. Sun Yat-sen followed his brother's lead and went to Hawai'i, where he
received his brother's permission to attend Iolani School, one of the earliest
education facilities on Hawai'i, founded by King Kamehameha IV at the beginning of the 1860s. Sun's brother also agreed to Sun's continuing education at
Oahu College in Honolulu, where the young man was influenced by Christian
values and ideas, which would become the basis for his belief in the overthrow
of the Qing Dynasty that ruled China, depicted by Sun as a regime that ruled
without the consent of the population.

After his education on Hawai'i Sun returned to China, where he attended the
Diocesan Home in Hong Kong, eventually becoming a Christian and studying
English. He also came into contact with the revolutionary ideas and ideals of
the French Revolution. He used these as a basis for his demands for change,
which he began to advocate after enrolling at Canton Hospital Medical College
in 1886. He did not stop his political activities, even when he became an intern

at Chinhu Hospital, one of the most renowned hospitals in the city of Macao. After approaching the Governor General of Tianjin, Li Hongzhang, without any results, Sun returned to Hawai'i in October 1894, where he founded the Xing Zhong Hui (Society for Chinese Revival), which would raise funds for a Chinese Revolution.

Sun was able to raise funds there but at the beginning it was hard to achieve a sum that would be sufficient to buy arms that were much needed for the revolution. When Sun visited London in 1896 he was kidnapped by the Chinese government and became the most well-known Chinese revolutionary leader in the world. Rescued by Sir James Cantile, Sun used his fame to further develop the ideas of revolution and to collect money from the Chinese emigrant circles around the globe. He traveled to Japan in 1897 to gain support from the Japanese government; he also issued bonds in his own name just a few years later to assemble sufficient money to support his revolutionary ambitions in Guangzhou Province, after having organized Chinese anti-Qing movements in different parts of Southeast Asia as well as Europe. In 1905 he founded the Tong Meng Hui (Chinese United League), which he chaired as the president. After a failed uprising in Huanggang in Guangdong Province in 1907, Sun had to travel again in Asia for another fund-raising campaign. His ambitions were still high, but due to some failed revolutionary attempts, it became harder to gather money again and again. In 1909, after having traveled to Malaya and Burma, as well as to Thailand the previous year, he visited Europe and the United States again, to meet influential members of the Chinese communities there, who might be willing to fund the revolution or to establish another branch of the Tong Meng Hui.

When the revolution was finally successful in China, Sun was surprised by it, because he was not even in the country at that time. The uprising against the government in Wuchang was successful and China's feudal regime finally collapsed on December 19, 1911, at which time Sun was elected as the provisional president of the new Republic of China and the last emperor, Pu Yi, was forced to abdicate. However, soon after the success of the revolution, Sun resigned and the powerful military warlord Yuan Shikai took over the republic. Sun reorganized the Tong Meng Hui into the Kuomintang (Nationalist Party) and was elected as its chairman. With Yuan taking over more and more power, Sun was finally forced to leave the country for Tokyo as General Yuan declared himself the new emperor. When revolts broke out in 1916, Sun returned from Japan. Yuan finally died in June 1916 and Sun was able to take over the political power again, becoming elected Generalissimo in 1917, when he declared that his main target would be the protection of the Chinese constitution. In 1918 he resigned as a military leader to focus on his writing over the next few years, but in 1921 he became President of the Republic of China until his death in 1925 from cancer.

Sun was definitely one of the most important Chinese figures of the 20th century, a man who also represented the connection between the home country and the emigrant communities around the globe, where he was able to find and attract financial support for the cause of the Chinese national revolution. His Western education, in combination with his respect for Chinese traditions and values, finally made him the charismatic leader that native Chinese as well as emigrant communities were able to believe in.

See also: Chiang Kai-shek, Madame (Soong Meiling); Taiwan

Further Reading

Bergère, Marie-Claire. 2000. *Sun Yat-sen.* Stanford, CA: Stanford University Press.
Schiffrin, Harold Z. 2010. *Sun Yat-sen and the Origins of the Chinese Revolution.* Berkeley: University of California Press.

Frank Jacob

TAIWANESE AMERICANS

According to a Taiwanese government survey, there were approximately 627,000 persons of Taiwanese ancestry—"members of the Taiwanese diaspora"—living in the United States in 2008, among them 342,000 Taiwanese immigrants. Those Taiwanese were the 24th largest immigrant group in America, comparable in size to the Japanese and Iranian American populations. Overall, these immigrants were concentrated in California and possessed high levels of education and lower levels of poverty than did many other immigrant and native-born American groups.

Based on the U.S. Census Bureau's 2008 American Community Survey (ACS), the 2000 Decennial Census, and the Department of Homeland Security's Office of Immigration Statistics (OIS) for 2008 and 2009, the following conclusions can be drawn about the Taiwanese American population. First, of the 342,000 foreign-born Taiwanese living in the United States, half lived in California, and Taiwanese women (54.6 percent) outnumbered Taiwanese men (45.4 percent). One-third of these foreign-born Taiwanese immigrated to the United States in the 1980s, almost 29 percent during the 1990s, and 93,000 more (nearly 30 percent) were admitted between 2000 and 2009. Second, Taiwanese immigrants had a higher rate of naturalization than did many other immigrant populations; as such, between 2000 and 2009, the 86,362 Taiwanese who became U.S. citizens equaled only one-eighth the number of mainland Chinese naturalized. However, the percentage of foreign born who became citizens and the rapidity with which they applied was not surprising, given that 7 out of 10 Taiwanese-born adults possessed a bachelor's degree or higher. More than half of the Taiwanese immigrant men were employed in highly skilled professional careers, such as finance, information technology, engineering, and health sciences. Third, roughly 113,000 Taiwanese American children under

Four Stradivarius violins are played on stage: Taiwanese American Cho-Liang Lin plays the 1715 "Titian," South Korean Chee-Yun plays the 1714 "Leonora Jackson," Russian American Philippe Quint plays the 1708 "Ruby," and Margaret Batjer plays the the 1716 "Milstein" during a rehearsal at the Colburn School in Los Angeles on March 27, 2014. (AP Photo/Damian Dovarganes)

the age of 18 resided in a household where at least one parent was a Taiwanese immigrant. Seventy-six percent of the Taiwanese Americans were homeowners. About one in nine Taiwanese immigrants (11.2 percent) did not have health insurance in 2008—much lower than the one-in-three uninsured rate (32.9 percent) among all immigrants and slightly lower than among the native born (12.9 percent).

Nearly 93,000 Taiwanese immigrants gained lawful permanent residency in the United States between 2000 and 2009. Furthermore, two-thirds of all Taiwanese immigrants receiving lawful permanent residency in 2009 were admitted based on the family reunification clause. Between 2000 and 2009, roughly 86,000 Taiwanese immigrants became naturalized Americans.

See also: Chiang Kai-shek, Madame (Soong Meiling); Sun Yat-sen; Taiwan; Taiwanese American Heritage Week; Taiwanese Food in America

Further Reading

Chang, Shenglin. 2006. *The Global Silicon Valley Home: Lives and Landscapes Within Taiwanese American Trans-Pacific Culture*. Stanford, CA: Stanford University Press.
Ng, Franklin. 1998. *Taiwanese Americans*. Westport, CT: Greenwood Press.

Jonathan H. X. Lee

Population of Taiwanese Americans

Year	Number
1980	16,800
1990	192,746
2000	292,081
2001	258,735
2002	274,415
2003	268,214
2004	230,997
2005	259,984
2006	274,718
2007	273,841
2008	257,876
2009	275,227
2010	315,792
2011	324,382
2012	314,679
2013	321,587

Table by Sidney C. Lee. Data from *Statistical Yearbook of the Immigration and Naturalization Service* 1982–2013, and Integrated Public Use Microdata Series: (Version 5.0).

TRANSCONTINENTAL RAILROAD

Early Chinese pioneers gold seekers were excluded from gold mining due to social, economic, and political exclusionary actions and policies. As a result, they ventured into working as coal miners or as agricultural laborers or into the fishing industries, and a large number of Chinese workers were employed in the railroad industries. In February of 1865, 50 Chinese workers were hired by the Central Pacific Railroad to help lay the tracks for the transcontinental line leading east from Sacramento. The Chinese laborers were praised by Leland Stanford, the company president, and Charles Crocker, the company's superintendent, as hardworking, amiable, and quiet—workers who can learn any skill, quickly and efficiently. They even went as far as to suggest that Chinese workers were more productive and reliable compared to white workers. The Chinese laborers were trained for all aspects of railroad construction: blasting through mountains, driving horses, handling rocks with picks and shovels. Animosity and hostility from white railroad laborers developed, which resulted their demand that the company stop hiring Chinese laborers.

Within a two-year period, the company employed 12,000 Chinese laborers, roughly 90 percent of its workforce. The railroad employed the "dual wage system," paying Asian workers less than white workers as a means to keep wages for both groups low. The dual wage system resulted in "ethnic antagonism" whereby white workers demanded restrictions on Asian workers, which later resulted in immigration exclusion. Not only were the Chinese laborers fast workers, but their employment saved the company a lot of money because the Chinese laborers were paid $31 a month, while their white coworkers were paid $45 a month. White workers also demanded lodging. Because the Central Pacific managers wanted to accelerate construction, they forced Chinese workers to work through the winter of 1866. Time was a big concern for the company because the amount of payment it received in land and subsidy from the federal government was determined on the miles of tracks they were able to build. The Chinese workers lived and worked in tunnels under the snow. Snow slides and landslides occasionally buried the camps and crews. In the spring, the thawing corpses, with shovels and picks still held in their hands, were discovered. That spring, Chinese workers went on strike and demanded eight-hour days and $45 a month: 5,000 workers went on strike. The strike was advertised through the Chinese-language print. The Central Pacific managers blamed their rival Union Pacific for masterminding the strike. This allowed them to negate the possibility that the Chinese workers were capable of acting on their own benefit and behalf. As a possible solution to the Chinese strike, the Central Pacific sent a wire to New York, inquiring about the feasibility of sending 10,000 blacks to replace the striking Chinese. Superintendent Crocker responded to the Chinese strikers by cutting off their food supplies, which worked because weeks later, virtually imprisoned in their camps on the mountains of the Sierras, the starving strikers went back to work. In 1869, the Transcontinental Railroad was completed ahead of schedule. The completion of the Transcontinental Railroad is a symbol of America's Manifest Destiny. The construction of the Central Pacific Railroad line was a Chinese achievement, but this fact remains unnoticed and invisible.

After the Railroad

Released from railroad construction, the Chinese laborers moved into agriculture. In California's Sacramento-San Joaquin River delta region, they constructed irrigation channels, reclaimed swamplands, and built the levees, dikes, and ditches. As tenant farmers or sharecroppers the Chinese introduced new varieties of fruits and vegetables for the local markets. The majority were laborers who toiled in orchards, vineyards, and hop fields. By 1870, the

Chinese constituted 18 percent of all farm laborers in California; by 1880, they represented 86 percent of the agricultural laborers. The dual wage system was also employed in this industry. Employers paid Chinese laborers lower wages than white workers. The Chinese workers were trapped in a racially based dual wage system, where they were paid less than white workers for doing the same job. In 1880, Chinese pickers in Santa Clara County, California went on strike, demanding increased compensation for the fruit they harvested. The 1882 Chinese Exclusion Act reduced the supply of Chinese farm laborers, so they recognized the increased need for their labor and demanded higher wages as a result.

Other ex-miners began working in the salmon canneries on the coastal bays and streams from central California to western Alaska. In Alaska in 1902, the peak year of Chinese employment there, more than 5,300 of the cannery workforce of 13,800 were Chinese. Others traveled to the Pacific Northwest after being recruited to build the North Pacific line or to run lumber mills. Still others worked in small businesses: laundries, restaurants, and dry-goods stores owned by Chinese merchants. During the 1870s, Chinese workers were recruited to replace the emancipated black slaves for plantation work and railroad building in the South: in Louisiana, Mississippi, and Florida. The Chinese did not stay on the plantations long. As early as 1871, the *New Orleans Times* notes that Chinese preferred to work in the small trades and industries in the city rather than toil in the fields. By 1880, there were a recorded 50 Chinese in Mississippi, 133 in Arkansas, 489 in Louisiana, and 95 in New Orleans, working as laundrymen, cigar makers, shoemakers, cooks, and woodcarvers. Chinese workers were also recruited to Massachusetts, New Jersey, and Pennsylvania as scabs to break striking shoemakers, steam launderers, and cutlery makers—most of whom were Irish immigrants. By then, there were 500 Chinese in New York, and about 900 in Boston.

After the railroad and mining, the Chinese population became an urban population because many were "driven out" of rural areas as a result of economic competition and racial discrimination. San Francisco's Chinese population went from 2,719 in 1860 to 12,022 in 1870. Similarly, Los Angeles's Chinese population went from 605 in 1880 to 1,817 in 1890. In the 1870s, the urban Chinese population moved into manufacturing and once again found themselves caught in a racially segregated labor market with low wages. Often Chinese laborers occupied menial positions in tanneries and woolen, paper, and knitting mills, while European Americans took the skilled jobs. In instances where they held the same position as whites, they were paid less for the same work. In the early 1880s, Chinese men earned $1 a day as factory workers, while white men earned $2. Throughout much of this early period, anti-Chinese sentiments informed much of the public policies and popular racism that discriminated against the Chinese living in America.

See also: Chinese Fisheries in California; Chinese Immigration During the Gold Rush; Gold Rush

Further Reading

Ambrose, Stephen, 2000. *Nothing Like It in the World: The Men Who Built the Transcontinental Railroad 1863–1869.* New York: Touchstone.

Houghton, Gillian, 2003. *The Transcontinental Railroad: A Primary Source History of America's First Coast-to-Coast Railroad.* New York: Rosen Publishing.

Jonathan H. X. Lee

UNITED STATES v. WONG KIM ARK (1898)

See: Chinese Americans and Civil Rights

WU TINGFANG (1842–1922)

Wu Tingfang became the Chinese Minister Plenipotentiary (i.e., ambassador) to the United States (and Spain and Peru) twice, first in 1896–1902 and then again in 1907–1909. Exceptionally able in the eyes of the foreign services of both Beijing and Washington, he was not only one of the most respected diplomats in the history of the Qing Dynasty but also one of the most popular, noted for his excellent English, witty interviews and lectures, and able defense of his nation's interests.

Wu was an international figure from the very beginning. Born in Malaysia to a Chinese family from Xinhui County southwest of Canton, Wu was bought up speaking his parents' Taishanese dialect as well as standard Cantonese and excellent British English. His fluency in Taishanese and Cantonese, the languages of almost all Chinese immigrants to the Americas, would stand him in good stead in future years. After a secondary school education in Hong Kong, he went to London and joined the Inns of Court, where he received a law degree and learned the skills of a practicing lawyer. He then returned to Hong Kong and became both a judge and a key advisor to the British colonial government. In the mid-1880s, he made a momentous decision: he would leave an exceptionally promising career in Hong Kong and accept the invitation of the great Chinese Viceroy, Li Hongzhang, to move to Beijing and become Li's personal assistant.

From then on Wu served only China. However, he took a strong interest in the welfare of his countrymen overseas, not only in his native Southeast Asia but in the Americas as well. This may be why he agreed to leave the exciting world of the Imperial court, where with Li's patronage his career might have risen even higher, to become a diplomat in a foreign country.

He became the ambassador to Washington at a critical junction, when anti-Chinese sentiment among U.S. lawmakers and bureaucrats was at a peak and when conflicts within the Chinese community had become acute. He faced these challenges with intelligence, firmness, and grace. Among his continuing tasks as a diplomat were bargaining for more favorable interpretations of the various Chinese Exclusion acts passed by Congress, persuading the U.S. government to adhere to the terms of earlier agreements affecting Chinese American rights, and arguing for Chinese individuals who had been unfairly treated by the United States.

Like earlier Chinese ambassadors, he often met with stonewalling attitudes on the part of U.S. officials. One of his tactics to overcome this was to cultivate the American press. He became popular among journalists, who enjoyed his novel, witty comments on American and Chinese culture. Another tactic was to build connections with the American social elite. He was sought after as a guest and speaker at numerous receptions and banquets and was reputed to have personal access to almost any U.S. businessman or politician. One American newspaper compared him favorably with the current Japanese ambassador, who spoke English badly and lacked Wu's urbane humor and command of social graces.

Wu was also well received by Chinese Americans. He visited most East Coast Chinatowns and traveled to San Francisco in 1897, 1903, and 1909. On the last of these trips he brush-wrote a text to go above the front door of the new headquarters of the Kong Chow (Xinhui) Association. The fine calligraphy of that text, which still exists, shows his mastery of traditional Chinese cultural skills. Chinese in San Francisco clearly respected him for that as well as his fluent Taishanese and Cantonese, and they may have felt they owed him a special debt for his efforts in 1897 to settle once and for all the bloody conflict between the Taishanese-speaking Sze Yup ("Four County") and Cantonese-speaking Sam Yup ("Three County") factions in Chinatown. He showed the same sensitivity to local Chinese feelings in 1908 when he endorsed a proposal by students and merchants in New York to build a Confucius Temple, allowing Kang Tongbi, daughter of Kang Youwei, founder of the Chinese Empire Reform Association (Baohuanghui), to be included even though her father had been proscribed by the Chinese government.

He apparently was genuinely a fan, although also a trenchant critic, of the United States. In 1914 he published a book in English entitled *America, Through the Spectacles of an Oriental Diplomat*. It was a hit with the reading public who enjoyed his novel viewpoint, evident intelligence, and subtle

A portrait of Chinese minister Wu Tingfang in Washington, D.C., c. 1900. (Library of Congress)

humor. At about the same time he received an LLD degree from the University of Chicago after having been that university's commencement speaker twice, in 1901 and 1908.

Wu continued to be involved in public life after leaving the United States. In 1912, Sun Yat-sen, China's newly chosen president, chose Wu as Foreign Minister of the Chinese Republic. He accepted, also served as acting president of the country during Sun's absence. Leaving office after a year or two, he turned to writing. He died, honored by Chinese and foreigners alike, in 1922 at the age of 80. His son, Wu Chaoshu, who had spent much of his youth in Washington, became Chinese Ambassador to the United States from 1928 to 1931.

See also: Ng Poon Chew; Wong Chin Foo; Yung Wing

Further Reading

Bronson, Bennet, and Chuimei Ho. 2015. *Coming Home in Brocade: Chinese in the Early American Northwest.* Seattle, WA: Chinese in Northwest America Research Committee.

Bennet Bronson and Chuimei Ho

PART III

CULTURAL AND RELIGIOUS LIFE: PEOPLE, INSTITUTIONS, AND ORGANIZATIONS

HISTORICAL OVERVIEW

Similar to all other immigrants, the Chinese have imported their cultural and religious traditions to the United States. Because Chinese migration has waxed and waned since the mid-19th century through today, Chinese cultural and religious traditions and expressions reflects multiple iteration of acculturation and various degrees of integration into American society. The liberalization of immigrant policy after 1965 parallels the changing mainstream attitude and belief in American culture. The initial American perception of Chinese people was ambiguously positive: they were seen as diligent, clean, industrious, and endowed with the potential to become good citizens. But once economic competition in agriculture and gold mining increased, the attitude quickly shifted to one of exclusion. The first decade of the 20th century had ushered in the great image of the melting pot, a process of assimilation by which diverse peoples from around the world gathered on U.S. soil, and, over a period of time, acculturated themselves into mainstream American life. Chinese immigrants, however, did not melt into American mainstream society smoothly. In terms of their cultural religious practices, the first generation of Chinese Americans were creative in their attempts to "fit in." This is well illustrated with the use of the term "church" instead of "temple" for their religious institutions. The historic Taoist Temple located in Hanford, California was officially the "Taoist Church" up until the late 1970s. Despite these attempts, Chinese immigrants found it difficult to assimilate. Due to their physical, cultural, and linguistic differences, mainstream American society concluded that the Chinese were resisting assimilation. As a result, they were perceived as potentially dangerous and subversive to the American way of life.

The end of World War II ushered in the countercultural movements that started to question the normative vision of American social life and with it the expectation that immigrants would assimilate into mainstream society. The civil rights movements of the 1960s through 1970s not only expressed dissatisfaction with racist beliefs and public policies, it also revealed a fundamental problem with the concept of assimilation. To the extent that the American way of life was normatively white and middle class, it was impossible for whole segments of the population to ever become fully "American." The imagined consensus promoted by those who favored assimilation could only be sustained by excluding people with dark skin, non-European ancestries, and limited incomes—in particular, Asian immigrants. The civil rights movements not only demanded practical changes in public policy, they also demanded a transformation of American national self-identity; they insisted that Americans recognize themselves to be a pluralistic people, that there were diverse and legitimate alternative ways of being American. This produced the pluralistic attitude of American life, one that resembles a "salad bar," indicating that Americans and American life comes in a variety of styles, cultures, religions, languages, and so on.

Between 1882 and 1965, exclusionist attitudes gave way to the melting pot attitude, which then gave way to the cultural pluralism of the 1980s. Since 1965 there has been a rejuvenation of the Chinatown communities across the United States, especially in San Francisco, Los Angeles, New York, Chicago, and Houston. These regions have also experienced the formation of "new" Chinatowns in rural areas. In all these areas, the formation of the new Chinatowns has occurred and continues to occur due to the continual flow of Chinese immigrants from Taiwan, Hong Kong, and mainland China, and Indo-Chinese from Southeast Asia. In these recent communities, temples and religious businesses have rapidly appeared on the new pluralistic religious landscape. Contemporary Chinatown communities are now multigenerational, multinational, and heterogeneous. Chinese immigrants are creating and living in "culturally Chinese" communities outside of the China, Taiwan, and Hong Kong. It is possible for them to live without speaking English, to have continuity in the way they live their lives in the United States with the way they lived their lives back home. The cultural and religious lives of the new Chinese American communities are therefore as diverse and complex as the communities in which they are located. This stands in direct contrast to the early homogenous bachelor society, which did not reflect the intrinsic diversity in Chinese cultural and religious traditions.

Chinese Americans, both recent immigrants and older generations, are able to maintain some sense of Chinese cultural practices and identity. Some of this might be an effect of vibrant Chinatown communities throughout all metropolitan cities. In some places, such as Chicago and San Francisco, public schools are offering Chinese-language classes, which provide many second- and third-generation Chinese American youths the opportunity to maintain a sense of Chinese cultural identity. Many Chinese Americans take an interest in Chinese American history in high school and college and will identify as Chinese American and take an active interest in Chinese American social issues and politics. Some Chinese American youths are learning about Chinese legends and heroic figures through popular multimedia video games like *Dynasty Warriors*. Moreover, because Chinese festivals and holidays are generally celebrated and observed in communities where there are sizable Chinese American populations, it is easier for Chinese American youths to maintain cultural awareness and identity.

There are many reasons for Chinese Americans to maintain ties to China, Hong Kong, Taiwan, or Singapore. Many of the recent Chinese immigrants are transnational immigrants who live and work in both Asia and the United States. They therefore have the human capital: educational, language, and technological skills to maintain strong transnational ties and connections. In the 1980s and 1990s, second- and third-generation Chinese Americans took an active interest in their Chinese heritage, which resulted from the civil rights movements of the 1960s and 1970s, which gave birth to the Asian American Studies program at San Francisco State University in 1969. With a new consciousness and awareness of themselves as Chinese and American, these youths traveled back to China to research their ancestral villages and family histories.

New immigrant Chinese American parents will send their children back to China, Hong Kong, or Taiwan to learn Chinese. For Taiwanese American youth, the Love Boat (otherwise formally known as the Overseas Compatriot Youth Formosa Study Tour to Taiwan) is an example of this. The Love Boat provides Taiwanese Americans an opportunity to learn Chinese language and culture. At the same time, it is now an infamous way for young Taiwanese Americans to meet other Taiwanese Americans. It is common for participants to meet on the Love Boat and later get married.

Chinese American youths also employ the Internet and social networking sites to stay connected to family and friends in China, Hong Kong, Singapore, and Taiwan. Because of China's recent economic development and potential domination of the global economy, many Chinese American parents are encouraging their children to learn Chinese so as to have career opportunities in China in the future. Culturally, Chinese Americans have maintained strong connections to the old country. For instance, there is an elaborate belief and ritual tradition associated with ancestral veneration. During the Qingming Festival, many Chinese Americans will travel back to China, Hong Kong, Taiwan, or Singapore to visit the gravesites of their ancestors, to sweep their graves, and share a communal meal together. Thus, cultural responsibilities and practices are a strong force that keeps Chinese and Chinese American family members connected.

Chinese American cultural and religious life and community come in various shapes, sizes, and imaginations. Traditional assimilation is no longer seen as viable, necessary, possible, or ideal. Chinese cultural and religious expressions and traditions have influenced Chinese American identity, boundaries, and borders and will continue to do so. Geographical boundaries no longer solely inform citizenship, nationality, and identity. Chinese identities in contemporary transnational and increasingly global communities are less bound by distinct territorial boundaries and are becoming more defined in terms of cultural heritage. The life of Chinese culture and religions in contemporary American society is being maintained and constructed in the Chinese American diaspora both apart from and within the "American mainstream." Contemporary Chinese cultural expressions and religious life in the American diaspora crosses cultural, religious, social, economic, and national boundaries. This requires creative and imaginative investigation.

Chinese Americans, recent immigrants to fourth-generation, continue to maintain some traditional Chinese holidays and festivals while celebrating Western and American holidays as well, such as Thanksgiving and July 4th Independence Day. The most popular Chinese holiday celebrated within the United States is the Chinese Lunar New Year, or Spring Festival, which commences on the first day of the first lunar month (generally corresponding to the end of January or beginning of February in the Gregorian solar calendar). Traditional activities are informed by Chinese myths, folklore, and folk customs, which emphasize luck and prosperity of the New Year. For example, wearing red is popular as it symbolizes blood and life; eating oranges because it symbolizes nuggets of gold and wealth; and setting off firecrackers to scare away evil spirits and bad luck, to make room for fortune and good energy. Homes will be cleaned from top to bottom to start the New Year fresh and clean. Today, the largest Chinese Lunar New Year celebration takes place in San Francisco. This San Francisco Chinese New Year Parade is televised globally and is one of the biggest cultural civil celebrations of its kind in the city.

One celebration that is not as public as the Chinese Lunar New Year celebration is the Lantern Festival, which marks the end of the New Year. The Lantern Festival is celebrated on a smaller scale through families and locally in Chinatowns across America. Other Chinese festivals celebrated on a smaller scale within Chinese American communities across the United States include the Qingming Festival (Clear and Bright Festival), a day devoted to remembering and venerating ancestors. Many recent Chinese American immigrants will return to China, Taiwan, or Hong Kong to celebrate this holiday. The other popular celebration is the Mid-Autumn Festival, a day connected to celebration of the harvest moon, where family members gather to view the beauty and magnificence of the full moon.

One main similarity between Chinese festivals and holidays and U.S. and Western festivals and holidays is the emphasis on family gathering and solidarity. The continuation of Chinese cultural festivals and holidays is a key way to educate younger Chinese Americans about the customs and heritages of cultural China. It reinforces their identity and identification with the Chinese American communities and reinforces the importance of multicultural celebrations as a means of being a people together.

BOK KAI AND BOK KAI TEMPLE

Established in the 1854, the Daoist Bok Kai (variously spelled Taoist Bok Eye or Boe Ky) Temple, a religious and community center, relocated to its present location on First (or the older name, Front) and D Streets in Marysville, California, in 1869 and then was reconstructed after a fire destroyed the second temple structure in 1880. This is the only extant Daoist temple dedicated to Bok Kai, who is known as the God of Water and the Northern God in the Daoist pantheon in the United States. Bok Kai was responsible for protecting the people against floods, and since 1880 Marysville has not experienced the devastating floods like those of nearby Yuba City. Bok Kai became an important deity in the Daoist pantheon in the mid-15th century when a temple was erected in his honor at the Imperial Palace in Beijing. He is included in the Daoist spiritual guardians known as the Four Saints (Sisheng), and paintings of him can be found in Daoist temples in China and Taiwan as well as the major American Chinese art museums, including the Boston Museum of Fine Arts.

According to the principles of *fengshui* (wind and water, or geomancy), an aspect of Daoism, the temple is situated on the north bank of the Yuba River near the confluence of the Yuba and Feather Rivers with the main entrance facing south toward the river. This allows good spirits to enter. Daoist architectural style, in emphasizing the harmonious unity of man and Nature, creates order and equability in the layout of the buildings. The connection with nature is further developed in the attached or nearby garden that allow meditation and contemplation. Due to the 1913 Alien Land Law, the ownership of the property at one point was transferred to the Chinese Benevolent Association of San Francisco but is believed to be the property of the Hop Sing Tong. Trains used to stop at the front of the temple, making it easier for travelers to visit the temple. Today visitors come from all over the country and from abroad by car.

In recent times a levee has been built between the temple and the river so that initially the main approach to the temple was down a flight of steps from the top of the levee (instead of being level with the riverbank) but now the approach is from a park on west side of the temple at the rear of the building. The government of the Republic of China donated the funds to erect the Memorial Gateway.

Marysville's Chinatown and the Temple Architecture

Marysville, Yuba County's county seat, is part of the Gold Country and developed shortly after the 1848 discovery of gold at Sutter's Sawmill in nearby present-day Coloma. Chinese immigrants flocked to the area in search of gold while others took jobs in agriculture, laundry work, restaurant businesses, and early industries, especially woolen mills. A thriving Chinese community with a Chinatown developed and the population, at its height in 1870, was said to be more than 2,000 Chinese. This figure increased as weekend visitors and others visited the shops, restaurants, and theaters in town. At one time there were three Chinese theatrical troops residing there to entertain the Chinese in the region, at least three fraternal organizations (Suey Sing, Hop Sing, and Chee Kong tongs), several Chinese Christian churches, a Chinese school, a Chinese children's playground, and boarding houses. One of the fraternal brotherhoods (probably the Hop Sing Tong), associations typical of mining towns with a large Chinese population, raised money for the original 1854 temple and the 1869 relocated temple that burned down. The community built the present temple on the 1869 site using traditional Daoist Chinese temple plans; Swain and Hudson, a major construction firm, built the temple at the cost of over $5,000, an astronomical sum for individuals earning $1 per day.

The one-story building is divided into three parts: a central section that is the main temple, with two smaller sections to the right and left of the entrance way. The main temple, which features two red entry doors (red is the color of happiness) and two red-and-gold lanterns, contains one intricately carved gilt wooden altar table and a second, plainer one for offerings of incense, tea, alcoholic beverages, fruits, and flowers. The traditional altar decorations of a large, dragon-handled pewter incense burner, flanked by two pewter candle-stick holders, and vases decorate the table. Fortune-telling bamboo sticks in bamboo containers and fortune-telling blocks are also on the table. A bronze engraved plaque dates from the late 1870s. By the entryway is a large bronze bell and ancient drum, both of which are still in use. Located nearby are the names of the donors for the 1880 temple construction. Both sides of the room have traditional Chinese weapons in wooden holders and silk banners, wooden engraved plaques (one pair dating to 1868), and wooden steles. At the rear of the temple is the primary altar table where the deities reside. Bok Kai, the largest figure, is in the center with a jade tablet and is flanked by six other deities: (1) Guandi, also known as Guan Yu or Guangong, the God of War, Justice, and Martial Arts, Literature, and Brotherhood from the Three Kingdoms period in the third century; (2) Yufeng, representing civil and military activities, including the protection of policemen and officials; (3) Guanyin, the Goddess of Mercy, who was incorporated into the Buddhist pantheon as a major bodhisattva and represents women, fertility, and mercy, especially helping people in times of need; (4) Tianhou, the Empress of Heaven, also known as Mazu, who protects fishermen, overseas travelers, and coastal communities and was a historic person of the Lin (Lum) clan; (5) Huado, the God of Medicine or Health; and (6) Tudi, the God of Earth. According to the local press, over 3,000 people participated in the dedication ceremony led by several Daoist priests from San Francisco.

Above the entrance to the temple in the open veranda area, a skilled Chinese artist painted an exquisite mural depicting several different Daoist themes separated by environmental-related poems written in different calligraphic styles and paintings of the four seasons (fall, winter, spring, summer). Laozi, depicted as an old man, and Guandi, dressed as a general, are among those individuals featured in the Daoist narratives, and in one section a young boy in Western dress is depicted to represent Chinese Americans, present and future. The linear renditions of figures and attention to detail, especially in the clothing, demonstrated the high skill of the artist (a point noted by the local press). Birds and flowers also are present. Many of the vibrant colors have remained through the centuries because of the rich mineral paints that were used. One poem describes the wind blowing through pine trees and rivers and mountains, in keeping with an appreciation of nature.

To the right (east) side of the main temple is a wing that consists of six rooms. An interior door leads to a wooden staircase from the main temple and there is an exterior door as well. A fortune-telling board with slips of paper is located near the staircase. Since roasted pigs are a major part of the celebration, there is a unique brick pig oven, which has not been used since the 1920s. There is a stove for burning spirit money and artifacts to the deities or in memory of the deceased. In one of the small rooms on the northern section there are many carved wooden sayings presented by the members of the temple. There is a room that was used to house visitors or travelers when trains originally stopped in front of the temple. Chinese usually were forbidden to stay in non-Chinese hotels in the late 19th century. Another small room, which has an upstairs section, contains a three-wok burner brick stove, chairs, tables, and perhaps more beds. The room also was used for gaming and other recreational activities, such as reading.

To the left (west) side of the main temple is a large room divided into two sections. There is only one exterior door. This room served as the community meeting room and perhaps an office. Beautifully hand-carved teak or rosewood chairs and tables are in the room. Built without any nails, they represent the best of 19th century Chinese furniture in design and execution. Steles dating back to 1880 are stored here as well as other artifacts and numerous books in Chinese and English, including the priest's accounting records. The gilt sedan chair to carry Bok Kai in parades also is kept there.

This tripartite division of a temple building is typical of one of the two main sects of Daoist temple architecture. The upturned eaves and the two red wood columns with cushioned capitals by the entry temple doorway are characteristic of Song Dynasty (960–1279) temple architectural style. The fact that there is a public park at the west side of the building is in keeping with the Daoist love of nature and gardens.

As the economy of Marysville declined, the Chinese population decreased. Job opportunities opened in other locations after World War II, so young

Chinese Americans moved to places like San Francisco and Sacramento and their suburbs. As a result, the temple is only open on certain days, but on Bomb Day, Bok Kai's birthday, the temple is open with great fanfare and parades.

The Early Priest and Activities of the Temple

Yee Chow Chung (born 1842, immigrated to the United States in 1871) served as the trained Daoist priest until his death or departure after 1920. He was married but left his wife and children in China. He kept records about astronomy as well as account books. When he died, there were no local Daoist priests to take his place because the 1892 extension of the Chinese Exclusion Act of 1882 (known as the Geary Act) had redefined priests or ministers of both Western and Eastern religions as "laborers" and therefore were ineligible for immigration to the United States. This left the Chinese American community without a pool of Daoist priests. A lay minister probably succeeded him and eventually the care of the temple rested in the hands of a lay caretaker who often was chosen as the winner of the Bomb Day Celebration that marked the birthday of Bok Kai, usually held on the second day of the second month according to the lunar calendar (late February to March in the Gregorian calendar).

Bomb Day begins with the lighting of incense and the chanting of prayers and is followed by the lighting of firecrackers and the firing of "bombs," papier-mâché bamboo-framed cylinders wrapped with newspapers and stuffed with gunpowder, one of which holds the lucky number that determined who would be the leader of the community who would serve as caretaker of the temple or who could appoint a representative to care for the temple. A dragon dance is part of the celebration, and the original bamboo dragon frame is among the many artifacts in the Bok Kai Museum. This dragon was 150 feet long and required 100 men to carry it. The account books for 1890 indicated that it cost $575 and the costumes worn to support it were $480. The dragon was exhibited at the World's Fair in New York and then retired in 1937 to give way to a more modern, shorter, wire dragon frame. Bok Kai rides in a gilt wooden intricately carved sedan chair carried by human bearers. In 1880 the local newspaper reported that over 1,500 Chinese participated in the festivities. By the turn of the 20th century, the entire Marysville community participated in the celebration, and in 1930 the city adopted it as one of its main tourist attractions and jointly sponsored Bomb Day with the temple administrators. According to anthropologist Dr. Paul Chace, in 2001 there were 7,000–9,000 participants lighting incense, having their fortunes told, partaking of the 100–200 roasted pigs and other delicacies, and watching the two hours of parades and martial arts performances. Today Marysville's Bomb Day celebration attracts visitors from all over North America and countries around the world.

The other major festival is Chinese Lunar New Year and, like Bomb Day, is celebrated with an elaborate dragon dance and parade.

Structural Problems

The levee and high water table have caused structural problems to the temple. In 1947 members of the temple organized and tried to renovate and strengthen the temple building as cracks appeared. The Friends of Bok Kai organized to raise money and bring the attention of the region and nation to this treasure. In 2001 the National Trust for Historic Preservation named the Bok Kai Temple one of the 11 most endangered sites in the United States. Media attention was immediate. In 2002 the temple was listed on the state and national registers, giving it official significance in the American mosaic. The Friends sponsored lunches, lectures, and other activities to help raise funds. Chinese historical societies sponsored bus tours to Marysville. Sacred Places included the temple in its tours and donated funds for its restoration. The major contributors were the Chinese Benevolent Association of San Francisco, Rotary (for general restoration), and the McBean Family Trust (for mural restoration). Getty Museum restorations helped in the project of restoring the murals. Grants from the California State Historic Preservation Office and National Trust for Historic Preservation also helped in the $1 million fund-raising project.

Other Daoist Temples

Every major Chinese American town or city had temples, often referred to as "joss houses" by the local American population. The term derived from Pidgin English from the Javanese word *deyos*, the Portuguese word *deos*, and the Latin word *deus*, all referring to "gods" in the building. Joss sticks refer to the incense sticks that were burned at the altar. The term first appeared in 1659 and by 1711 English and American writers had connected the Chinese gods or god with the term joss. Americans seldom distinguished whether the "joss house" was Daoist, Buddhist, Confucianist, or an organizational meeting hall (*tang* or *miao*). The Chinese are more specific and the Bok Kai Temple is called a *miao*, or temple/place of worship.

In San Francisco, the Daoist Tin How Temple, originally built in 1852 and reconstructed in 1911, is dedicated to Tianhou (Empress of Heaven), also known as Mazu. The Kong Chow temples in San Francisco and Los Angeles as well as the Mo Dai Miu (Kwan Gong) in Mendocino, a small two-room temple, are dedicated to Guandi (God of War, Justice, Literature; and protector of its followers). The Kong Chow temples also serve as a district association and clan community center. Oroville's Chinese temple consists of three different buildings, one each devoted to Buddhism, Daoism, and Confucianism. Weaverville's 1874 Daoist Temple Amongst the Forest Beneath the Clouds (Won Lim) rivals the Bok Kai Temple as a relatively large Daoist temple but it is dedicated to Guan Yu and is a California state historic park and not a functioning historic Daoist temple like Bok Kai. Historically there were other Bok Kai temples; for example, in Lewiston, Idaho. In 1875, 10 years after their arrival in Lewiston, the Chinese built the Beuk Aie Temple at the confluence of the Clearwater and Snake rivers on A and B Streets. Because A Street was eroded away by the Clearwater River, in 1888 the Chinese built a new temple to "Buck Eye" at 513 C Street, where it remained until 1959 when it was destroyed to facilitate the expansion of the local newspaper office. Another Daoist temple existed in Evanston, Wyoming but was known only as a "joss house." Local newspapers covered the Bomb Day celebrations so it might have been dedicated to Bok Kai. In Honolulu the Daoist temple is situated in the Lin (Lum) Family Association building and is dedicated to Mazu or Tianhou, who is a historical person from the Lin clan. In Merced, California, a Daoist temple built in the 1880s and lasting until the 1960s was located on the second floor of a café but only some of the artifacts still remain. Other such small Daoist worship areas existed wherever there was a large Chinese American population.

The Bok Kai Daoist Temple is one of the oldest, continuously active Daoist temple in the United States and reflects not only the Daoist architectural style but also the beliefs of one of the major religions of China.

See also: Chinese Temples in America; Ching Chung Taoist Association of America; Daoism; Religions

Further Reading

Little, Stephen. 2000. *Taoism and the Arts of China.* Chicago, IL: Art Institute of Chicago.

Sue Fawn Chung

CHINATOWN GHOST STORIES

Chinatown ghost stories are a part of Chinese American oral folklore where ghosts are used as central characters in a story. These stories are categorized as "Chinatown" because all stories not only take place in Chinatown but also contain elements of Chinatown's unique and long history. Chinatown ghost stories should not be confused with Chinese ghost stories, as the latter have a history that goes back to ancient China. Chinatown ghost stories are considered Chinese American. These stories reflect people of Chinese descent living in America: their history, culture, personality, experience, and way of life.

Chinatown ghost stories were never formally written down and may be classified as "ghostlore," a combination of the words ghost stories and folklore. The earliest contemporary usage of the term was by Elliot J. Gorn in his essay "Black Spirits: The Ghostlore of Afro American Slaves." Slave owners, who took

"Disappearing Lady"

Robert's mother always warned him and his younger brother to never go to the movie theaters without her. She warns that gangsters often hang out in movie theaters, assaulting people and raping women.

One day, Robert and his friends decide to skip school and watch a movie at the Great Star movie theater. He does not even think about his mother's warning. Robert and his friends pay for their tickets and scatter for seats throughout the theater. With no girls around, the boys do not want to sit too close to each other.

When the movie ends, one of Robert's friends, Steve, is behaving strangely. He is asking everyone where the lady is. Robert and his friends do not know what he is talking about. Steve tells them that halfway into the movie, he stands up to let a woman into his row and she sits down right next to him. He thinks this is strange because attendance in the theater is sparse. He feels her presence next to him the whole time. When the movie ends, he stands up to let her by, but the woman is not there anymore. She could not have walked to the other side of the row because he would have seen her walk down the long row of seats.

Steve is not the type to play jokes on people, and that day he looked sincere and genuinely scared. After that incident, he does not hang around the group anymore.

advantage of African supernatural beliefs, used these ghostly tales to terrorize slaves and keep them submissive.

The Chinese community, much like the slaves, also has very strong supernatural beliefs. There is a strong belief that spirits of one's ancestors control one's fate, and it is crucial that one never anger them. The fact that these stories were never written down plays a crucial role in their development and is a reflection of the Chinatown community. Early Chinatown was made up of immigrants who were illiterate or possessed limited formal education. Ghost stories were, and are, one way that immigrants use stories to communicate their history, traditions, beliefs, and life experiences.

Many of these stories are passed down in two different ways, from the older generation to the younger generation and within the younger generation themselves. The stories also have two different purposes. When told by the older generation to the younger, the stories are primarily used as cautionary tales. These stories instill fear in children and young adults not only about the supernatural but also about the dangers of living human beings. Since parents cannot supervise their children all the time, ghost stories are used as a form of babysitting when their children step out of the house. Usually children in

"Deadly Waters"

One night Mike and Sean sneak into the Chinatown YMCA through an open window to go swimming in the pool. They have snuck into the YMCA after hours on numerous occasions and have never been caught. They fool around in the pool when Mike starts to struggle in the water. Sean tries to help him but being a kid himself, he can't, and by the time help arrives, Mike has already drowned.

Ever since the drowning, people say that when little kids swim in the pool by themselves, they would feel a hand grab their leg and pull them down. This is why parents always warn their kids about swimming in the YMCA pool.

Chinatown ghost stories encounter a ghost. A few stories are also used to share a bit of Chinese American history, touching on the railroads, Chinatown brothels, and popular longtime organizations like the YMCA. Although stories told within the younger generation are the same cautionary tales told by the older generation, their purpose is slightly different: the stories are used mainly for entertainment purposes, but unbeknownst to the younger generation, they are spreading the cautionary tales among their peers.

Chinatown ghost stories are still being circulated within the Chinese American community, whether used for cautionary or entertainment purposes. As members of the Chinatown community start moving outside of Chinatown and into the suburbs, the stories move with them, spreading the tales to an audience who did not grow up in Chinatown. Chinatown ghost stories are folklore unique to the Chinese American experience. An oral tradition that transmits Chinese and Chinese American culture, history, worldviews, and religiosity, it is also entertaining.

See also: Dying and Death Rituals

Further Reading

Davidson, Hilda R. Ellis, and W. M. S. Russell, eds. 1980. *The Folklore of Ghosts.* Cambridge, UK: D. S. Brewer.

Driver, Nick. 2002. "Old Chinatown's Deep, Dark Secrets." *San Francisco Examiner,* April 18.

Emmons, Charles F. 1982. *Chinese Ghosts and ESP: A Study of Paranormal Beliefs and Experiences.* Metuchen, NJ: Scarecrow Press.

Grant, Glen. 1998. *Chicken Skin Tales: 49 Favorite Ghost Stories from Hawaii.* Honolulu, HI: Mutual Publishing.

Shioya, Tara. 1996. "Chinatown Ghost Story." *SF Weekly,* December 11.

Alice Tam

CHINESE CHRISTIANS IN AMERICA

Christianity, with Evangelical Protestants as the predominant majority, is the most practiced religion among the Chinese immigrants in the United States. Christian churches have become the predominant religious institutions in the Chinese American community. Christianity, especially Evangelical Protestantism, has played an increasingly significant role in the lives of Chinese immigrants. One of the important characteristics of Chinese Christians in America is that they are mostly converts in the host country because Christianity is not a traditional Chinese religion. However, the presence of Chinese Christians in America is almost as long as the history of Chinese immigration. The first Chinese Christian church was established by a returned medical missionary from China with the support of the Presbyterian Board of Foreign Missions in San Francisco in 1853. Since then the Christian population among the Chinese immigrants has increased steadily. However, there are no national data on how many Chinese Christians are in the United States. According to a *Los Angeles Times* survey of Chinese Americans in Southern California in 1997, 32 percent claimed to be Christian with 6 percent Catholics, 20 percent Buddhist, and the remainder with no religious affiliation. Nationally, the reasonable estimate of the Chinese Christian population in America is somewhere between 10 and 35 percent.

The life of Chinese Christians in America is centered on the Chinese churches. The Chinese Christian church has roughly experienced a two-stage development corresponding to the two-stage Chinese immigration history. The first stage of Chinese immigration was from the late 1840s to the 1950s. The overwhelming majority of the Chinese immigrants were from the rural area surrounding the Pearl River Delta; hence the earliest Chinese American population was relatively homogeneous. Most of them spoke Cantonese and were male laborers; some of them were merchants. In this first stage the Chinese laborers and merchants lived mainly in Chinatowns and worked in Chinese restaurants, hand-wash laundries, gift shops, and as domestics. Unlike European immigrants who brought their Judeo-Christian religious tradition to America, the Chinese Christians were mainly converts in the host country. After the establishment of the first Chinese Christian church in 1853, other denominations also started their missions for the Chinese immigrants and established the Chinese churches subsequently. For example, Methodists started their mission in 1868, and Baptists, Congregationalists, and Episcopalians in 1870. In this earlier period all the pastors of the Chinese churches were Caucasian and Chinese Christians served only as their assistants. The Sunday services were mainly in English with Chinese translation. The main goal of these mission churches was to Christianize the Chinese in the United States and send them back to China to help missionaries there. These earlier Protestant missions were not successful in their effort of converting the Chinese. The percentage of the Chinese Christians was very small. The Catholic mission in this time period was hampered because of the Catholic Church's active involvement in the anti-Chinese movement in California. However, the Chinese mission churches were helpful to the Chinese immigrants' adaptation to the host society in that the churches gave them the opportunity to learn English, American values, and lifestyle; to meet non-Chinese Americans; and to receive social services. In this earlier period when Chinese immigrants faced racism and social exclusion, some Chinese immigrants intentionally embraced the Chinese church as a parallel white institution to elevate their racial status in American society. The Chinese churches also played an important role in supporting the revolution in China in the earlier part of the 20th century.

Although 1943 saw the repeal of the 1882 Chinese Exclusion Act and the establishment of the annual quota of 105 Chinese immigrants, the Chinese did not come in large numbers until 1965, when the Immigration and Naturalization Amendment Act passed, which also marks the beginning of the second stage of Chinese immigration.

Starting from the earlier part of the 20th century, a new trend began to emerge in the Chinese Churches in the United States. Some Chinese Christian churches gained financial and leadership independence within the denominations, and a few churches even became nondenominational and independent, although the majority of the churches were still supervised by Caucasians. By 1952, there were 66 Chinese Protestant churches in the United States, among which 47 were denominational, 5 were interdenominational supported by several denominations or a council of churches, and 14 were independent. During this period, most Chinese churches were small in size with an average membership of 155.

Since the 1950s, the number of Chinese churches has begun to increase. The Chinese church started evolving into the next stage. Since the late 1950s and early 1960s, Chinese students have established many campus Bible study groups in American universities. As the students adjusted their status to permanent resident under the new immigration law of 1965, many Bible study groups developed into churches. Most of the churches established in this period were founded by the new immigrants themselves. Many churches were nondenominational. The churches were mainly conservative evangelical theologically and independent and congregational organizationally. This form of Protestantism has become the most practiced religion among the Chinese immigrants since then. Because Chinese Christians in the United States are from different parts of the world (mainly Taiwan, Hong Kong, China, and other Southeast Asian countries, such as Singapore and Malaysia), speak different languages, and have different cultural backgrounds, most Chinese Christian churches have at least two Sunday services. One is in the native language of the first-generation immigrants, either Mandarin or Cantonese; the other service is in English for the 1.5- and second-generation immigrants. If a church provides only one Sunday service, the church also provides an English translation. Some churches have three congregations and three Sunday services based on language—Mandarin, Cantonese, and English. In recent years, some second-generation Christians also participate in pan-Asian American churches.

Not all Chinese Christians participate in the Chinese churches of members with mixed backgrounds. Some Taiwanese immigrants participate in Evangelical Formosa Churches in the United States. In 1970, the first Evangelical Formosa Church was formed in Los Angeles, California. Up to the year 2000, there were 51 churches, 26 of them in the United States. The main languages in the Evangelical Formosa Churches have been Taiwanese and English. However, in recent years, some churches also use Mandarin, the most popular language in Taiwan.

Similarly, in New York Chinatown, Fuzhounese immigrants established a Chinese church consisting of predominantly immigrants, legal and illegal, from Fuzhou, the capital city of Fujian Province on China's southeast coast. The language of the church is mainly Fuzhounese. Since the late 1980s tens of thousands of mostly rural, young Fuzhounese have flooded into the United States. The Fuzhounese church located in New York's Chinatown, the main point of entry for the Fuzhounese youth immigrants, has helped these most vulnerable and marginalized members of American society survive, and has served as a location to access social, financial, and emotional support. The mainland Chinese began to convert to Protestantism in unprecedented numbers after the June 4, 1989, Tiananmen Square incident. The church with the majority members of the mainland Chinese also began to emerge. However, the majority of the mainland Chinese Christians participated in the churches with members of mixed backgrounds.

Post-1965 immigrants have more diverse social class backgrounds, from low-skilled workers to highly educated professionals. However, a typical Chinese church may have more middle- or upper-middle-class professionals, with advanced degrees in different fields, such as mechanical engineering, electronic engineering, and chemical engineering.

Chinese Christians in America have been strongly influenced by the larger American evangelical subculture. Chinese Christians read popular evangelical literature both in Chinese and in English, including books, magazines, and videos. The pastors of Chinese Christian churches were educated at evangelical theological seminaries in the United States, such as Trinity Theological Seminary and Fuller Theological Seminary. American evangelical leaders, such as Billy Graham, Rich Warren, and Chuck Swindoll, are among the most frequently mentioned names in the Chinese churches. The Chinese Christian saints, like John Soong, Watchman Nee, and Wang Mingdao, are also respected as role models for the Chinese Christians.

Most Chinese churches have three regular weekly activities: Sunday services, Friday night fellowship meetings, and prayer meetings. Sunday services for the first generation use English-Chinese bilingual hymn books and sing classical hymns translated from English, some hymns adopted from mainland China and Taiwan or Hong Kong, and others from the Chinese music ministries in the United States, such as Melody of My Heart, Stream of Praise Music Ministry. The first-generation worship has a choir. The second-generation worship style is more contemporary, featuring a worship team and a band. The songs are from the mainstream American evangelical community.

As mentioned earlier, most Chinese Christians in America are converts. This is the result of active and institutionalized efforts of proselytization by Chinese churches and parachurch organizations, both Chinese and American. In fact, proselytization becomes the most important function of the Chinese Christian church. In the United States Chinese conversion is communally informed, although individual choice remains important. Personal networks and social activities of Christian churches are important mechanisms to attract non-Christians and through which the social needs of immigrants are met. For example, Carolyn Chen finds that Taiwanese immigrants become more active in proselytizing after coming to the United States. Chinese festivals, such as Lunar New Year, become an important time for evangelism. Chinese Christians actively invite their non-Christian friends to participate in church activities. Many churches also host an annual evangelistic conference, which becomes an important channel for converting non-Christian Chinese. Parachurch organizations, such as China Outreach Ministry (COM), International Students Inc., and OMF International, have played a vital role in converting Chinese immigrants. For example, COM has developed systematic programs for evangelizing Chinese students, scholars, and their family members. When new students and scholars first arrive in the United States, COM picks them up from the airport and subsequently helps them settle down. They also organize year-round activities, such as sightseeing, sports activities, and English-learning programs as attractions. Chinese American friendship dinners have been frequently used to evangelize the Chinese.

Chinese Christian publications have also played a significant role in evangelizing and nurturing the Chinese Christian spirituality. Since the late 1990s, Chinese Christians have started to publish more magazines, books, and video and audio products in the United States. For example, China Soul for Christ Foundation, Christian Life Press, Inc., Overseas Campus Magazine, and

Ambassador for Christ, Inc. are among the most prominent organizations serving the Chinese Christians in the United States. Their publications become increasingly influential in the Chinese Christian community.

Chinese Christians in America have not only actively proselytized Chinese in the host country, but also started their mission to proselytize Chinese around the globe. Chinese Christian Mission was established in October 1961 with the goal of reaching the world with the gospel, through literature, broadcasting, and sending missionaries. Other organizations, such as the Great Commission Center International and Gospel Operation International for Chinese Christians, have the similar goals. These missions mainly focus on Chinese around the globe, although they have also expanded their mission to reach out to non-Chinese.

Many Chinese churches and Chinese parachurch organizations have supported the Christian churches in mainland China in different ways. Many church pastors went to China to train the house church leaders and sometimes also brought with them financial support.

The conversion to Evangelical Protestantism means a change of worldview. Most Chinese immigrants have an atheistic worldview and are hostile to the Christian faith because of traumatic modern Chinese history, which was filled with sad stories of Chinese people's suffering from Western colonialism and imperialism. Historically, Christianity has been stigmatized in the Chinese culture as a relic of Western imperialism. "One more Christian, one less Chinese" was an old saying directed against Chinese converts. However, today at least for the Chinese Christians, Christianity is no longer a foreign religion. Christianity as a world religion is not owned by any specific ethnic group. Most Chinese Christians believe the 21st century is the century for evangelizing the Chinese. In their words, salvation has come to the Chinese. The traditional Chinese culture emphasizes the hierarchal social relations, which constrains the Chinese from expressing love in an explicit way. For example, parents rarely hug their children and vice versa. The basic doctrine of the Christian religion is love—"God is love," and "love your neighbor." This doctrine has great impact on Chinese Christians. It becomes the driving force of serving people. For example, most Chinese churches have a fund for helping people in need. The doctrine of the egalitarian status before God has fundamentally changed the Chinese view of human relations. Although the Chinese still respect older people and people of higher social status, the fundamental belief that people are equal becomes unshakable among Chinese Christians.

Conversion not only means the change of worldview but also means the change of leaving a family-centered social network and entering a religious community. The Chinese Christian community also becomes influential in the construction of Chinese immigrants' identity. The Evangelical Protestant church provides the social space for immigrants to reconstruct a new community; it provides a new family through which immigrants find the meaning in their new life and achieve a sense of self-hood. The religiously empowered communities enable the immigrants to gain a freedom from traditional Chinese expectation, which is centered on Confucian values or traditional family, kinship ties; at the same time, it is to discover their "authentic selves," which transcend familial and societal definitions. For most Chinese Christians, the Christian identity becomes the most important identity. This does not mean that Chinese immigrants think the Chinese identity is no longer important. On the contrary, their Chinese identity remains strong. The Chinese Christian community becomes the most important social space for them to reproduce and celebrate the Chinese culture. For example, in the Chinese church, people talk in Chinese; eat Chinese food; decorate the church with Chinese characters along with other Chinese culture symbols, such as painting; and celebrate Chinese festivals, such as Spring Festival and Mid-Autumn Festival. Some Chinese churches also have Chinese-language schools. Chinese Christians also selectively preserve Chinese cultural values, such as emphasizing filial piety and educating their offspring.

Chinese churches have also played a pivotal role in connecting Chinese immigrants to the larger community through religious activities. Most Chinese Christian churches have Caucasian members. Some of them are retired missionaries, others are spouses of Chinese Americans, and still others are friends of the Chinese church members. The Chinese churches also cooperate with Caucasian churches and support Caucasian parachurch organizations, such as Cru (formerly Campus Crusade for Christ) and Navigators. For example, some Chinese churches and Caucasian churches and parachurch organizations cosponsor evangelistic conferences.

See also: Falun Dafa/Falun Gong; First Chinese Baptist Church, San Francisco; Religions; Taiwanese American Religions; Watchman Nee and Witness Lee; Yee, James J.

Further Reading

Chen, Carolyn. 2008. *Getting Saved in America: Taiwanese Immigration and Religious Experience.* Princeton, NJ: Princeton University Press.

Guest, Kenneth J. 2003. *God in Chinatown: Religion and Survival in New York's Evolving Immigrant Community.* New York: New York University Press.

Jeung, Russell. 2005. *Faithful Generations: Race and New Asian American Churches.* New Brunswick, NJ: Rutgers University Press.

Loewen, James W. 1988. *The Mississippi Chinese Between Black and White.* 2nd ed. Prospect Heights, IL: Waveland Press.

Yang, Fenggang. 1999. *Chinese Christians in America: Conversion, Assimilation, and Adhesive Identities.* University Park: Penn State University Press.

Zhang, Xuefeng. 2006. "The Impact of Institutional Factors on Chinese Conversion to Evangelical Protestantism in the United States." *Sociology of Religion: A Quarterly Review* 67(2): 149–159.

Xuefeng Zhang

CHINESE FOODS

The foodways of China are exceptionally diverse, varying dramatically by region, ethnicity, and class, and so are the foods Chinese immigrants and their descendants eat in the United States. Overseas Chinese hail from many areas in China and bring to their new homes cuisines that have evolved over centuries of interaction with local ecologies. In the United States, these cooking traditions are transformed by cultural exchange among the Chinese, other immigrants, and Americans. Through these interactions, the Chinese assimilate new food-stuffs and cooking techniques into their foodways while preserving traditional culinary concepts and folk values related to the preparation and consumption of food, like the balance of hot and cold food elements.

Wherever the Chinese settled, they found ways to procure foods of their homeland. In the 1850s, the Chinese started coming to the United States in large numbers and over the next half-century built trade networks across the country and Pacific Ocean. Import firms moved Chinese foodstuffs like rice, soy sauce, and preserved vegetables, meats, and fruits from southern China to remote towns on the U.S. frontier. Chinese fishermen supplied fresh fish and shellfish to coastal settlements and sent dried seafood inland. These items were expensive, rare, and, hence, used sparingly by 19th-century Chinese immigrants. Mainly they counted on local Chinese farmers to supply the bulk of their diet. Small-scale, labor-intensive farms grew traditional vegetables and fruits and a variety of New World crops. Settlers in rural areas also foraged and hunted. Early immigrants were compelled by financial and environmental reasons to eat new foods in addition to the traditional foods they could buy or grow.

Chinese restaurants crossed the Pacific with the Chinese. The earliest ones date to the 1850s and were small, informal dining rooms that served simple Cantonese dishes. Clubhouses and boarding houses similarly fed their residents. As Chinese communities grew in size and wealth, restaurants became places to find elaborate and extravagant meals. The best restaurants imported expensive ingredients and furniture from China and were the preferred venues for the celebration of Chinese holidays, births, and weddings. The average restaurant, whose dishes and decorations were more modest, attracted both Chinese and non-Chinese clienteles, and were the forerunners of Chinese

American restaurants. Around World War I, some eateries started offering on their menus American dishes like roast turkey alongside traditional ones. While these businesses did not cater to the Chinese per se, they exposed the Chinese working in them to foods other people ate. Today, Chinese Americans eat cuisines of many nations and patronize both traditional and fusion Chinese restaurants.

Traditional Chinese foodways are far easier to maintain nowadays thanks to technological improvements in food transportation and preservation. Industrialization has made it possible to produce standardized foodstuffs cheaply and in bulk, which are then distributed via modern highways, waterways, and airways. Chinese farms, once powered by manual labor, are now mechanized and employ the methods of corporate farms for the storage and selling of their produce. Large Chinese supermarkets exist in all major cities. Despite these benefits, rare or regionally unique ingredients are difficult to find in much of the United States, which forces Chinese immigrants to find substitutes.

See also: Chinese Restaurants in the United States; Taiwanese Food in America

Further Reading

Anderson, E. N., and Chun-Hua Wang. 1985. "Changing Foodways of Chinese Immigrants in Southern California." *Annals of the Chinese Historical Society of the Pacific Northwest* 3: 63–69.

Diehl, Michael, Jennifer A. Waters, and J. Homer Thiel. 1998. "Acculturation and the Composition of the Diet of Tucson's Overseas Chinese Gardeners at the Turn of the Century." *Historical Archeology* 32 (4): 19–33.

Libby, Gary. 2006. "Historical Notes on Chinese Restaurants in Portland, Maine." *Chinese America: History & Perspectives* 20: 47–56.

Porterfield, W. M. 1951. "The Principal Chinese Vegetables Foods and Plants of Chinatown Markets." *Economic Botany* 5 (1): 3–37.

Heather R. Lee

CHINESE GENEALOGY

Jiapu 家譜, translated as "Chinese Family Register," also known as *pudie, zongpu, zupu, tongpu, zhipu,* or *jiacheng,* have been used for thousands of years to record the genealogical history of a family, including a family's origin, collateral lines, names and ages of the members, records of marriages, births and deaths, merits and deeds, and some biographical information of male descendants.

The connection between names and a country's language and culture is expressed remarkably in Chinese American names. Information such as family tradition, lineage, religion, education, gender, status, as well as the social values and attitudes of the parents or elders given such a name, are entirely encoded in names. Your surname can further demonstrate certain assets about the history, such as the country from which it originated and the migration patterns of the ethnic group to which it belongs.

At the core of Chinese name traditions are the precepts in regarding names as symbols of family connections. That is, one character within a two-character given name is generally referred to as a "generation name." It was assigned by the progenitor of a clan in which each generation in his lineage was given a character taken from a propitious verse with rhymes and can be repeated in the names of family members belonging to the same generation.

Evolution of Chinese Genealogy

The origin of Chinese family names spans many eras and, according to ancient Chinese documents, family names were created and used by the Chinese people about 2,800 years ago during the Xia, Shang, and Zhou dynasties. Tradition says that the evolution of Chinese clan genealogies was developed in the Xia Dynasty (ca. 2200–1700 BCE), which marked the beginning of a slavery society in place and the establishment of a hereditary throne system within the royal families. The earliest evidence of Chinese genealogical record can be traced to over a 1,000 years ago during the Shang Dynasty (ca. 1700–1112 BCE). In the Zhou Dynasty (ca. 1122–221 BCE), *jiapu* only represented a special symbol for the aristocratic Chinese society within the noble class. Genealogical roots were found in the preoccupation era as evidenced in the oracle bones and bronze inscriptions of the Shang and Zhou dynasties. Not until the patriarchal clan system was disintegrated in the Qin Dynasty (221–206 BCE) that the clan genealogies were emerged and became a clan culture advocated by the common citizens in the Han Dynasty (206 BCE–220 CE). Later, as the feudal pedigree system became legitimatized, there was a large increase of genealogies proliferated that were compiled by the government for prominent clans and feudal lords in the Wei, Jin, and Southern and Northern dynasties (420–581 CE).

As the imperial examination system was adopted during the Sui (581–618) and Tang (618–907) dynasties, the once-dominated clans under landlord influences were in rapid decline. Not until the second half of Tang did genealogies start gradually being compiled in private hands by individual household or lineage organizations. These genealogies covered a broader area of subjects than the earlier documents, with focus on the importance of moral and ethical ideologies to promote the core family values. In the Song Dynasty (960–1279), the contents of genealogies were enhanced immensely with the inclusion of family disciplines, Confucius ideology of Ru Thought, Zhuzhi House Code of Success, ancestral portraits, ancestral tomb charts, and land records. Along with the widespread establishment of clansman and family associations, more and more clan genealogies compiled by individual family or lineage organizations became dominant in Chinese households and families in the Ming (1368–1644), Qing (1644–1910), and the contemporary Minguo (1911–present) eras.

Searching for Your Chinese Ancestral Roots

The compilation of a family genealogy starts with the names of your ancestors and anyone who is blood related to the family. Talk to those directly in your family line such as parents, grandparents, great-grandparents, and close relatives to see whether there is a *jiapu* or *zupu* that exists and kept by family members. *The Book of One Hundred Surnames (Bai Jia Xing)*, which covers the history and origin of over 1,000 most popular Chinese surnames, is an excellent source to start the search. Other useful information includes primary and secondary sources. For instance, the private records such as birth and death certificates, marriage and divorce certificates, baptism records, property records and land deeds, cemetery and funeral records, obituaries, eulogies, and personal diaries are primary sources. It is also important to locate secondary sources from the public records found in national archives and repositories, such as census and population data, vital statistics, naturalization records, military services and pension records, Chinese household register, and immigration records. Some community and ethnic newspapers may carry useful information as well.

You may search the electronic database *NARA Genealogy* available from the U.S. National Archives and Records Administration. A keyword search box is provided to search for information related to genealogy and personal history records; wars and international relations; government spending and private sectors such as businesses, foundations, and labor unions; photographs and other textual records; places, such as countries, states, counties, cities, towns, and Zip codes; as well as the 1940 U.S. Census and all available resources organized by time periods from 1800 to the present.

See also: Chinese Family Associations; Confucianism; Dying and Death Rituals

Further Reading

Boey, Danny. 2002. *Basic Guide to Chinese Genealogy*. Singapore: Chineseroots Pte Ltd.

Chao, Sheau-yueh J. 2000. *In Search of Your Asian Roots: Genealogical Research on Chinese Surnames*. Baltimore, MD: Clearfield Company.

Chinn, Thomas W. 1972. "Genealogical Sources of Chinese Immigrants to the United States." In *Studies in Asian Genealogy*, edited by S. J. Palmer, 221–28. Provo, UT: Brigham Young University Press.

Sheau-yueh J. Chao

CHINESE IMMIGRANT CEMETERIES

Chinese cemeteries and grave markers are silent monuments memorializing Chinese contributions to the growth of the western United States. Most Chinese immigrants were from southern China and brought with them many traditional beliefs and rituals. These led to a singular transformation of the western U.S. landscape, in that Chinese cemeteries are often located on the slope of a small hill, surrounded by higher and wider hills that seem to envelop the main site.

By their location on a sloping, encompassing hillside, these Chinese cemeteries follow a pattern common to cemeteries in southern China. This is a distinctive feature of the Chinese concept of geomancy, or *fengshui*, translated as "wind" and "water," a belief system in which balancing the components of spirituality and geography ensures good fortune. Whether or not actual *fengshui* applications can be demonstrated, very specific traditional concepts appear to be at work.

In central Idaho, on the remote Salmon River, the "River of No Return," the burial site of Charlie Bemis is one such example. Although he was Euro-American, his Chinese wife, Polly Bemis, undoubtedly selected his gravesite. She chose a slight rise in front of an enveloping hillside facing a creek flowing into a river, all significant *fengshui* characteristics. This suggests that even common people were familiar with the basic principles of *fengshui*.

Where a distinctly separate Chinese cemetery exists, such as the one in Pierce, Idaho, it is possible to isolate certain common features; chief among these are empty graves. According to Chinese custom, Chinese immigrants, nearly all of whom planned to return to China after making their fortune in the United States, made provision for the possibility of their death in a foreign land by arranging in advance for their remains to be returned to China. Accordingly, they paid a "death insurance" fee to cover the costs of exhuming their bodies, cleaning the bones, and shipping them to China for reburial in the home village. Exhumation pits are clearly visible in many Chinese cemeteries in the western region of the U.S.

Women often appear to have been excluded from the practice of removal. The emphasis on patrilineal descent and the lack of respect accorded women were contributing factors. This may mean that some Chinese cemeteries, considered empty through removal, are actually still holding female burials.

Graves of men and women interred permanently in U.S. cemeteries were marked in a variety of ways. Wooden markers tended to rot, so stones, concrete, and bricks were preferred. A gravestone in the Lewiston, Idaho, cemetery bears the name Jim Yeeott in English, as the Caucasian community knew him; the stone's Chinese characters give his actual surname, Ng.

In the inland Northwest, a "burner" is an unusual feature of many, but not all, Chinese cemeteries and Chinese sections of Euro-American cemeteries.

This tall brick or masonry structure serves as a place for the ritualized burning of paper and cardboard facsimiles of money, clothing, jewelry, and other household objects. Burning passes them to the spirit realm for use by the deceased in the afterlife.

See also: Confucianism; Dying and Death Rituals; *Fengshui*/Geomancy

Further Reading

Chung, Sue Fawn, and Priscilla Wegars, eds. 2005. *Chinese American Death Rituals: Respecting the Ancestors.* Lanham, MD: AltaMira.

Lai, David Chuenyan. 1974. "A Feng Shui Model as a Location Index." *Annals of the Association of American Geographers* 64 (4): 506–13.

Priscilla Wegars

CHINESE-LANGUAGE SCHOOLS

In the United States, Chinese-language schools have long served as an educational institution for cultural and linguistic maintenance. In the research literature on these types of schools, also called heritage language (HL) schools, Chinese language schools are generally cited as having well-developed programs, oftentimes because some teachers previously taught in their home countries. Currently, because of shifts in perception of economic viability and utility of certain Chinese languages in the United States, there has been rapid change in terms of demographics and underexplored tensions in Chinese-language schools. As language is also entwined with identity, there are also unexpected issues that have to do with Asian American teaching, learning, and identity formation.

The early group of Chinese immigrants who came in the 1850s encountered many barriers that precluded their integration into mainstream U.S. culture. As mostly poor men from Hoisan (Toisan/Taishan) county of Guangdong Province in southern China, many came as contract laborers and their mentality included bearing the injustices and ultimately returning home. In 1877, the California Senate barred the Chinese from attending public schools, which created the first segregated Chinese-language schools, established by Chinese scholars. Since Chinese American students could not take part in public education, the original intent of these Chinese-language schools was to provide the children of Chinese immigrants, who only intended on staying in the United States for a short time, tutelage in Chinese language, history, classics, and calligraphy so that their cultural heritage and linguistic abilities would be maintained when they returned to China. The first formal Chinese-language school, the Ching School, was established in San Francisco in 1886 by the Chinese Imperial Government to do just this. Its aim was to encourage its students to

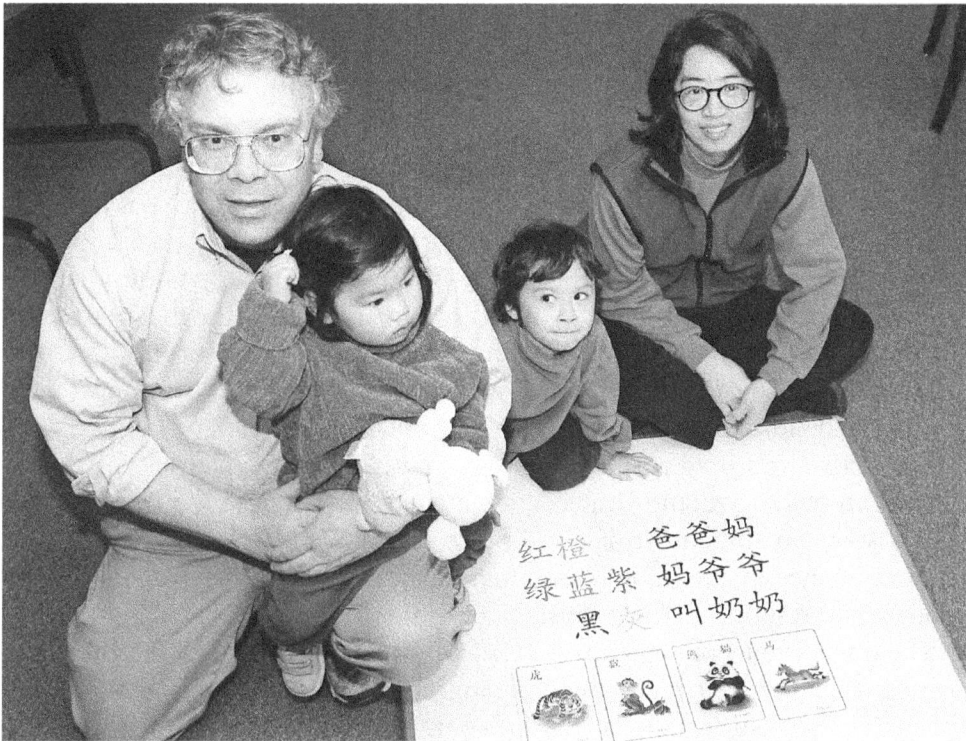

Richard Alcorn and Kathleen Wang, the founders of a Chinese Charter School, with their children, Anna, 2, and Eric, 5, in the community room of the apartment complex where they live in Hadley, Massachusettes, on March 4, 2007. As of 2007, at least 27 states offered Chinese language classes in either elementary, middle, or high schools. (AP Photo/ Nancy Palmieri)

take the civil service examination (which ceased in 1905) through a vigorous schedule: weekday classes were held from 3:00 to 9:00 p.m., and Saturday classes were held from 9:00 a.m. to 9:00 p.m.

Subsequent Chinese-language schools were operated through churches and community centers, with far less rigorous hours. The passing of the Immigration and Nationality Act of 1965 saw a more diverse ethnic Chinese immigrant population from Taiwan, Hong Kong, and various parts of China and other Asian countries. Departing from the sojourner mentality, these more recent immigrants were more likely to settle and raise their children in the United States. Speaking different varieties of Chinese (Cantonese, Mandarin, Taiwanese) and using different scripts (traditional versus simplified characters), Chinese HL programs began to be more and more community based, with tuition used to rent out rooms or community centers where the schooling takes place, usually on Friday evenings or Saturday mornings. Generally which variety of Chinese to be taught was determined by the dominant Chinese population group in a metropolitan area (e.g., long-standing Chinese-language schools in San Francisco Chinatown would be more likely to offer Cantonese, while a small college town with a large population of international students from China would be more likely to offer Mandarin). With no affiliation with the local public school system, the economic viability of these schools relies heavily on the financial sustenance of parents and school administrators; oftentimes the two are one and the same. With limited interaction between the HL schools and public school districts, students oftentimes do not receive foreign-language credits for attending HL programs. Surveying the top issues that face HL schools in research conducted over the last half-century, the following three are most pervasive: teacher training, funding, and student attitudes. Younger children might enjoy spending their Friday nights or Saturday mornings "playing" with friends who speak the same HL, but high school students are often less receptive, rebelling against the program and language, without much academic incentive to attend. Indeed, researchers have long noted the tensions that arise when students in HL schools find it difficult to learn their HL and show resistance in attending these programs, though shifts in pedagogy in HL programs to respond to these tensions remain to be seen.

The tragic events of September 11, 2001, coupled with an increasingly globalized economy, have highlighted the importance of the learning of languages other than English in U.S. K–12 classrooms. Starting from 2004, a series of efforts have been taken on the parts of the Department of Defense and American Council on the Teaching of Foreign Languages (ACTFL) to raise public awareness of the importance for Americans to have language competence in languages other than English to ensure national security and economic prosperity. Both Cantonese and Mandarin are classified by the U.S. Department of State as "Category Three" languages that are considered extremely difficult for native speakers of English to learn. Maintenance of HL competence in communities began to be seen as an important resource that the United States and individuals could draw from to satisfy the national need. This recent initiative seems to represent a promising moment for teaching and learning foreign languages, especially for those languages identified as being strategically important to the United States, like Mandarin.

That being said, many Chinese HL learners need to negotiate the use of different varieties of HLs. In the discussions of Chinese-language programs in the United States, the term "Chinese" nowadays often refers to Mandarin, the official language of the People's Republic of China and Taiwan. However, the very term "Chinese" is highly contested because many Chinese ethnic communities speak other varieties of Chinese (Cantonese, Fujianese, etc.) as their HLs, which are not entirely mutually intelligible with Mandarin. This crucial distinction is often neglected in Chinese HL program design and implementation. For example, in many current Chinese-language programs, speakers of other Chinese varieties are placed with Mandarin speakers in the HL track, but their knowledge in non-Mandarin varieties is discounted by the teachers or programs and their unique needs are often left unaddressed, causing them much frustration in studying a language that is assumed to be their HL. HL speakers and learners are often characterized by their use of "nonstandard" varieties, lack of certain registers in oral production, disproportionate receptive and productive abilities, and limited literacy; such negative attributes are also absorbed by the learners and speakers when talking about themselves. Thus HL learners' existing linguistic knowledge in addition to how they decide to position themselves leads to complex and dynamic pedagogical implications of HL teaching for a heterogeneous body of learners.

Current Mandarin HL programs in the United States have also experienced heightened diversity in enrollment from non-HL learners (e.g., language-majority speakers) as well as ethnic Chinese adoptees. Obviously, with a diverse student population comes different motivation and investment in language learning; as such, the language-as-instrument stance is one that requires a reorientation toward and deeper examination of the needs of the learners and their identities rather than focusing on the perceived instrumentality of languages.

See also: Cantonese; Samyap and Szeyap

Further Reading

Fan, Chen-Yung. 1981. *The Chinese Language School of San Francisco in Relation to Family Integration and Cultural Identity*. Taipei, Taiwan: Institute of American Culture, Academia Sinica.

Lai, Him Mark. 2001. "Retention of the Chinese Heritage, Part II: Chinese Schools in America, World War II to the Present." *Chinese America: History & Perspectives* 15: 1–30.

Genevieve Leung

CHINESE MEDICINE

Chinese medicine can mean several things. "Chinese medicine" can be understood as an indigenous medical system that was developed within the framework of Chinese culture. The medical tradition has roots in Chinese cosmology, Daoist cultivation methods, and Confucian social ethics. "Chinese medicine" is also a dimension of Chinese culture that focuses on practices that heal, maintain, balance, and improve the human body. This broader understanding of Chinese medicine includes not only healing by professional practitioners (e.g., herbalists, acupuncturists, bone setters, and ritualists; see *Beliefs and Practices*, below), but also a wide range of practices that common people use to maintain their health. In today's world, where Western science and biomedicine are considered advanced and authoritative, "Chinese medicine" can also mean an integration of medical systems that tailors to the social, economic, and cultural needs of the Chinese people. Since this entry focuses on Chinese medicine within the Asian American context, we will address mostly the first two understandings of Chinese medicine: Chinese medicine as a traditional medical system and Chinese medicine as a dimension of Chinese culture.

History of Chinese Medicine in the United States

For as long as the earliest Chinese ethnics had been in the United States, the home remedies, herbal formulae, food therapy, acupuncture, bone setting, and other healing techniques had always been part of life in the Chinese American community. Although there were records of Chinese medicine practitioners advertising in English-language newspapers in major cities in America since as early as the 1890s, during the earlier eras when Chinese ethnics were frequently targets of racial discrimination, Chinese American practitioners served patients mostly within the Chinese enclave.

The opening of the People's Republic of China (PRC) in the 1970s and the ensuing diplomatic relationship between China and the United States marked the beginning of a new phase for Chinese medicine in America. Along with the American public's increased interested in Chinese culture, news media coverage on the efficacy of acupuncture also brought Chinese medicine into the mainstream consciousness. The politicking by enthusiastic patients and practitioners led to state certification and licensure of acupuncturists, first in Nevada (1973), then in California (1974), and many other states followed.

Coinciding with the heightened receptivity of the American public toward Chinese medicine, the PRC also actively exported a standardized form of Chinese medicine that highlights the national identity of China's traditional medical theories while eliminating the "contaminations" from China's long history of superstitions and lack of scientific logic. The PRC government called this new system "Traditional Chinese medicine" (TCM; hereafter specified as PRC-TCM) to differentiate from Chinese medicine that could be understood as any practice of medicine (which can include Western biomedicine) provided within the Chinese context. The "Traditional" pays tribute to the power of the antiquity and cultural authenticity of China's indigenous medicine, offering a contrast against the authority of Western biomedicine. Ironically, PRC-TCM and other traditional healing techniques are not the main modes of medical services in the PRC today; they are only supplemental to Western biomedical diagnoses and treatments there.

In response to the rapidly growing popularity of Chinese medicine in mainstream America, the National Center for Complementary and Integrative Health (NCCIH), a division of the National Institutes of Health established in 1991, devotes resources and funding in defining Chinese medicine and verifying the effectiveness of Chinese healing methods. NCCIH defines PRC-TCM as a medical system that "originated in ancient China and has evolved over thousands of years," and within the American context, as a medicine that is complementary to "conventional medicine" (or Western biomedicine). Several major medical schools and medical research centers also have conducted clinical trials and evidence-based research on the efficacy of Chinese medicine, mostly on acupuncture treatments.

In sum, the Chinese medicine in America today is shaped by the Chinese medical tradition, the development of medicine within the Chinese enclave in the United States, the politicized redefinition of Chinese medicine by the government of the PRC, and the defining and regulatory powers of the National Institutes of Health, state medical boards, and licensing agencies.

Education and Knowledge Transmission

Before there were schools for Chinese medicine in the United States, Chinese American practitioners of Chinese medicine were trained as apprentices of already-established practitioners. Some medical families only trained within the bloodlines in order to preserve their heritage formulae and techniques. Other masters sought capable students and transmitted knowledge through long-term master-disciple relationships. When the state medical boards first licensed acupuncturists in the 1970s, many of these home-schooled practitioners were given the first licenses; some of these senior practitioners are still practicing today.

After the opening of the PRC in the 1970, the influx of immigrants from China also brought practitioners who were trained by their state medical schools. Unlike practitioners trained under traditional apprenticeships, state-trained practitioners were trained in a range of programs—some were trained in the new PRC-TCM system, some were trained to integrate Chinese and Western medicines, and others were only trained in Western biomedicine.

Currently, 34 U.S. states regulate their acupuncturists. Many states that certify or license their acupuncturists now require completion of graduate-level programs in TCM or other oriental medicine. The curricula of the TCM programs in the United States typically incorporate PRC-TCM with additional courses on Chinese medical language, counseling, clinic administration, and so on. Based on student demands and faculty interests, some schools also offer courses such as Chinese medical classics and Chinese medical history to enrich the cultural aspect of the medical education.

Furthermore, the National Certification Committee for Acupuncture and Oriental Medicine (NCCAOM) administers standard examinations in acupuncture and Chinese herbology, which are required by most states. California and Nevada administer their own licensing exams. Although acupuncture is also used in other medical systems—it has been used in traditional Japanese, Korean, and Vietnamese healing, and also utilized by some European and American healers who do not use Chinese medical theories—exams offered by NCCAOM and the states of California and Nevada focus exclusively on PRC-TCM theories and applications.

Basic Understanding of the Human Body

In the traditional Chinese conception of the cosmos, a shared life energy, or *qi*, makes and fills all living entities within it. Humans, as part of the cosmos, are made with and sustained by this *qi*. *Qi* inside the human body circulate through 14 invisible pathways (or meridians), each meridian correlating with the functions of an organ in the body. When there is a blockage in one of these pathways, the functions of the correlating organ is compromised. Along these meridians are points that correlate with specific aspects or functions of the organ—these are the acupuncture points. Stimulating the acupuncture points bring about healing because they help regulate specific organ functions.

The "organs" in Chinese medicine are not just the physiological organs. Each organ represents a set of bodily functions, which may or may not directly correspond with how Western physiology understands as the functions of the physiological organ. For example, in Chinese medicine, the function of the liver is to produce blood; in Western physiology, blood is produced in the spine. The discrepancy is rooted in the fact that the liver in Chinese medicine is first understood in terms of a set of functions, and the physiological liver does function to store glycogen, synthesize plasma protein, and decompose red blood cells, all very important aspects of blood production. Some of the organs in Chinese medicine do not have physiological form. The Triple Burner (*sanjiao*), which has no physical form, is an organ responsible for the digestive aspects of metabolism.

Chinese medicine conceptualizes health differently from Western biomedicine. Biomedicine considers one healthy if there are no symptoms of illness and the vital measurements fall within the average range of the population in general. In Chinese medicine, health is defined by the state of balance within the individual, where the dynamics between organ functions are equalized and harmonious. This inner state of health is reflected in the patterns in one's pulse, the smell of one's breath, the tone of one's voice, the manner of one's actions, and the colors and textures of one's tongue, face, ears, palms, and fingernails. A practitioner of Chinese medicine pays close attention to subtle signs and patterns in the patient in order to identify where the imbalances are and what treatments to use to recalibrate to the state of balance.

See also: Chinese Hospital, San Francisco

Further Reading

Barnes, Linda L. 2005. *Needles, Herbs, Gods, and Ghosts: China, Healing, and the West to 1848.* Cambridge, MA: Harvard University Press.

Kaptchuk, Ted J. 1983. *The Web That Has No Weaver: Understanding Chinese Medicine.* New York: Congdon & Weed.

Emily S. Wu

CHINESE OPERAS

Chinese opera is the earliest Chinese musical genres established by Chinese immigrants in the United States. The term "Chinese opera" was rarely used in early writings and Chinese opera was more often referred as "Chinese theatre," "Oriental performance," or "Celestial drama" before the 1920s. Although a problematic term, "Chinese opera" encompasses the qualities of antiquity and foreignness.

The history of Chinese opera in America began in 1850s, when a substantial wave of contracted Chinese railroad workers and gold miners arrived in California from the southern coastal region of Guangdong. In a result, Cantonese opera (*Yueju/Yuht kehk*), along with other Cantonese musical genres, which were popular in the Guangdong region, were imported from China to serve these predominantly male immigrants. They formed a bachelor society and listened to Cantonese opera as their main pastime. On October 18, 1852, the all-male Tong Hook Tong (or Hong Fook Tong) Chinese Dramatic Company from Guangdong staged the U.S. premiere of Cantonese opera in San Francisco. Then from the late 1870s to the 1880s, a period called the golden era of Chinese theater in America, saw the establishment of several Cantonese opera theaters in San Francisco, each giving frequent performances. Some of these theaters were even located within the same block (e.g., Jackson Street, a street that was known as the "theatre street"). According to numerous English-language reports from the 1880s, these Chinese opera troupes performed for the celebration of Chinese New Year, community functions, festivals, and at funerals.

On February 12, 1891, a Cantonese opera performance in the cellar of a Harrison Avenue hotel in Boston was well received by members of the American Folklore Society's Boston branch. Then the first Chinese opera theater in New York City—the Chinese Theatre on Doyer Street—was opened in the heart of Chinatown on March 25, 1893. The Chinese Theatre was a landmark of New York's cosmopolitan culture and one of the city's major attractions. Guided by a Chinese interpreter, non-Chinese tourists typically stayed and enjoyed the hour-long fight scenes in the performance.

Chinese opera theaters suffered declines with the enactment of the 1882 Chinese Exclusion Act. The Act banned immigration of Chinese laborers and their wives as well as prohibited the naturalization of Chinese immigrants. Furthermore, the passing of several ordinances against the use of Chinese ceremonial gongs in San Francisco, an important instrument for Chinese opera; and the arrest of Chun Fong, the manager of a Chinese opera theater in New York, who was accused for producing "an immoral performance" on Sunday, July 14, 1895; contributed to the intense racism against Chinese immigrants during this period. Moreover, most newspaper reports about the performances in this period contained racist and derogatory phrases. Many Cantonese opera musicians were forced to change their occupations in order to avoid harassment. They worked in restaurants or laundry facilities, spoke very little or no English, and isolated themselves from the mainstream American life.

The period between1924 until the early 1930s was the golden age of Cantonese opera theater in New York's Chinatown. Two Cantonese opera theaters were operating concurrently, presenting nightly performances. This period also saw the rise of female opera actors. However, this thriving opera scene soon ended with the arrival of the Great Depression. Due to the disappearance of the touring opera troupes from Guangdong (Canton) and Hong Kong and the increased numbers of stranded Chinese opera artists during the 1930s, Cantonese opera clubs were established within the Chinatown Chinese communities' boundaries. The Cantonese opera clubs functioned as community centers where the members took care of each other by providing housing and financial help to those in need. The recreational singing activities helped the members of the Chinese communities socialize and relate ancient legends and history from the homeland with one other. The heroes and heroines served as role models for Chinatown dwellers during the dark years of exclusion. By the 1950s, Cantonese opera enthusiasts had established a number of Cantonese opera clubs in San Francisco, Portland (Oregon), Boston, and New York. Some of the oldest clubs are the Nam Chung Musical Association in San Francisco and the Chinese Musical and Theatrical Association (CMTA) in New York.

In the early 1950s and 1960s, the increase in the Chinese student and intellectual populations contributed to the emergences of Peking (or Beijing) opera (Jinju) clubs and Chinese instrumental music ensembles (minyue tuan). In 1951, the first North America amateur Peking opera club, Guoju Ya Ji (The Chinese Opera Club in America) was founded in New York by stranded Chinese students in the United States. These Beijing opera clubs, organized mainly by Chinese immigrants from northern China, became more common in the 1980s in major cities such as New York; Washington, D.C.; Seattle; Los Angeles; Chicago; and San Francisco. Although they were mainly clubs for amateurs, they gave annual performances by combining their existing members with invited professional performers, who performed the leading roles and gave instructions to the amateur members. Unlike the early wave of immigrants, the members of these newer groups spoke English as well as Mandarin in addition to their ethnic dialects, and many of them had college or graduate degrees. They generally resided outside Chinatowns and worked in various professional positions in universities, hospitals, and companies outside Chinatowns. These new groups actively reached out to mainstream Americans for their acceptance of Chinese music culture by giving public lectures, demonstrations, and performances in universities, museums, and other institutions.

A new wave of immigrants was made possible after the U.S. Congress enacted the 1965 Immigration Act. Chinese immigrants from China, Taiwan, and Hong Kong soon contributed to the rapid increase of Chinese American population. Unlike the labor immigrants from 19th century, these new immigrants were skilled workers, technicians, and professionals with college or higher degrees.

Cantonese opera: Cantonese opera rose to popularity at the Guangdong and Guangxi regions of China in the 18th century. Unlike Beijing opera that enjoyed the status of being the "national opera" in China, Cantonese opera was regarded as a local "lowly" regional opera genre. However, it was the first type of Chinese opera to be heard in the United States and to represent the Chinese on the international frontier in the 19th century. It is performed through singing and speaking in the Cantonese dialect, acting, and dancing. Since a full or complete opera is rarely produced in America, the most common practice of Chinese Americans is to sing excerpts from Cantonese operas. One or two singers, accompanied by an instrumental ensemble, usually sing these lyrical excerpts. The instrumental ensemble of Cantonese opera is usually consists of *bangu* (drum), *ban* (hollow wood block), *wenchang luo* (large civil gong), *wuchang luo* (small military gong), *bo* (cymbals), *gaohu* (high-pitched two-stringed fiddle), *erhu* (lower-pitched two-string fiddle), and *yangqin* (hammered dulcimer). Since Cantonese opera in China has incorporated several Western instruments such as saxophone, electric keyboard, violin, and electric guitar into its music since the 1920s, some of the instrumental ensembles of Cantonese opera in the United States have also followed such practice.

Despite suffering from a long decline due to events such as the exclusion laws, the 1906 San Francisco earthquake, competition from new forms of entertainment, and the disappearance of regular performances by professional companies, Cantonese opera is still alive in amateur clubs. With the arrival of new immigrants from Hong Kong and Cantonese-speaking regions of China after 1965, Cantonese opera experienced some revitalizations starting the 1980s.

Peking opera: Peking opera is considered the national opera genre in both China and Taiwan, and is historically patronized by the imperial families in China. It was first brought to the United States by the sensational performance of Mei Lan-fang, the most distinguished Peking opera female-role actor, in 1930. Since the presentation of a complete opera is rare, the most popular performance practice for Chinese Americans is to perform a sequence of two to four independent acts drawn from various Peking operas. The musical accompaniment in Peking opera contains fewer instruments than used in Cantonese opera; they include *bangu*, *daluo* (large gong), *xiao luo* (small gong), *cha* (cymbals), *jinhu* (the leading high-pitched two-stringed fiddle), *erhu*, *yueqin*, *sanxian*, sometimes *suona* (double-reed wind instrument), and *dizi* (flute).

Kunqu: Kunqu is one of the oldest opera genres in China, dating back to the mid-14h century. Composed by famous literati, it was a leading opera form during the Ming Dynasty (1368–1644) and enjoyed an elite status before its decline in the 18th century. The texts and music are the most literate and archaic. Singing is accompanied by mimetic dancing. *Dizi* (flute) is the most important accompanying instrument. Since some early Peking opera performers in the United States were also trained in *kunqu*, there were records of *kunqu* excerpts' performance in earlier Chinese immigration periods. The arrivals of some important *kunqu* artists from China in the late 1980s facilitated the founding of Kunqu Society, the first *Kunqu* group in North America, in 1988. A common performance practice of *kunqu* in the United States is to perform four to five acts of various *kunqu* repertoires.

Shaoxing opera: Shaoxing opera is a newer Chinese opera genre that originated in the Shaoxing region in Zhejiang Province near Shanghai in early 20th century. The Zhejiang-Shanghai dialect-speaking immigrants in America favor this genre. In 1991, the Shao-Xing Opera Association was founded in New York and has presented several performances since then.

Among these post-1965 new immigrants were professional musicians who had won international or national recognition and prizes. They include Hua Wenyi (*Kunqu* actress), Pin Chao Luo (Cantonese opera actor), Qi Shu-fang (Peking opera actress), and Tang Lianxing (*pipa* "four-stringed plucked lute" player). These musicians contributed to the further development and growth of Chinese opera in the United States.

Starting in the 1980s, New York City, with its status of being a global city, gradually replaced San Francisco as the most important place in Chinese American musical life as it drew an immense transnational influx of capital, artists, cultural productions, agencies, and political power. Although San Francisco was the center for Chinese opera and music during the first 100 years of the Chinese presence in America, New York City currently appears to host more musical clubs, Chinese cultural organizations, and musical performances.

Currently, four different types of Chinese operas are being cultivated actively in the United States. They are Cantonese opera, Peking (or Beijing) opera, *Kunqu*, and Shaoxing opera. The repertoires of these operas consist of historical stories, legends, myths, and folktales.

Chinese opera in the United States is learned primarily through oral tradition and some written notations such as the cipher and *gung ceik* (gong chi) notations. Besides learning from the veteran Chinese opera performers and professional teachers, members also learn their parts by listening to audio and video recordings of professional performances or previous productions.

An opera club usually consists of three groups of people. The first group is the retired professionals and veterans of Chinese opera who may have achieved the status of being the "national-level" (*gua jia ji*) performers. They are either invited or immigrated to the United States to coach the amateur performers and to pass on the art of Chinese opera. They serve as "artistic directors," and their professional training, lineage, and ties with the professional opera organizations in China help legitimize the amateur performance. The second group consists of middle-aged, middle-class immigrants (mostly working professionals and wealthy homemakers in their thirties to fifties) who have both time and financial ability to afford the expensive hobby of Chinese opera singing. They are the building blocks of the amateur clubs as they raise funds and organize Chinese opera performances in order to keep Chinese opera alive in the United States. The last group of people is a small group of young American-born Chinese in their teens and twenties. They rarely perform the operatic singing (due to their illiteracy in reading Chinese and understanding the archaic meaning of the opera texts) but instead contribute to the dance and physical action parts of the shows.

The cost of a Chinese opera production is usually high because of the rental of the rehearsal and performance spaces, salary for live musicians, and import of exquisite costumes, props, and elaborate backdrops from Asia. Moreover, Chinese opera has no financial viability or marketability; the cost to keep the art alive is shared and funds are raised by the members of the amateur clubs. To raise funds, the production crew may sell "congratulatory notes" and advertisement space/pages in the program book of their performance. One page could be a few hundred dollars; some purchase a full page and some may purchase a half- or-quarter page. A performance is very often presented as a charity event, and part of the funds raised benefit certain Chinatown or non-Chinatown nonprofit organizations or are for the relief for natural disasters worldwide. A typical performance last about four to five hours, featuring 7–10 skits of opera singing, with short speeches, award presentation, and photo opportunities with VIPs in between. The opera arias could be solos or duets from famous Chinese operas, and a children's group dance maybe included in the repertoire. The event is usually extended with a banquet afterwards to celebrate the success of the performance.

The staging and production of Chinese opera in the United States have undergone some changes due to the Western influence and the demographics of the performers. For example, the first wave of Cantonese opera performance used simple props and background, whereas the present productions use microphones, elaborated backdrops, and dry ice. Depending on the nature of the performance, the live band may be placed at the orchestra pit instead of being on stage. The music ensemble is also simplified and has added more Western instruments. Some opera clubs include more physical-action scenes in order to encourage the younger generations (who are more interested in martial arts and modern dance) to perform as well as to reach out to non-Chinese audiences, who do not understand the singing. In contrast to the current development of Chinese opera in Asia, where new compositions and innovations have been introduced to attract younger generations to Chinese opera, Chinese American amateur performers focus only on relearning and perfecting the old pieces and performing Chinese opera in the traditional way. Ultimately, performing Chinese opera in an old-fashioned way reaffirms the cultural Chinese identity of Chinese Americans.

Chinese opera in the United States maintains a transnational tie with Chinese opera in China, Hong Kong, and Taiwan. For example, members of the opera clubs usually bring back some of the latest innovations and trends of Chinese opera after they visited these countries. Chinese opera clubs in the United States depend on the Chinese opera industries in China, Hong Kong, and Taiwan, from which they order and import the costumes, backdrops, and musical instruments for their performance activities in the United States. They also frequently invite professional performers from abroad to teach and perform with the amateur members in the United States. Furthermore, Chinese opera club members celebrate and put on performances during national and traditional holidays of their countries of origin, including the national day of the Republic of China, Chinese New Year, and Mid-Autumn Festival. Therefore, Chinese opera helps Chinese Americans retain their ties with their countries of ancestry.

Currently, there is only one Chinese opera theater operating in the United States—the Great Star Theater (*Damingxing*) on Jackson Street in San Francisco's Chinatown. It was almost demolished by developers but was saved by the efforts of Cantonese opera lovers, preservationists, scholars, and politicians with the launch of the "Saving the Great Star Theater" campaign in 2001. Despite the involvement of the younger U.S.-born Chinese generation in Chinese opera clubs, most of them have expressed that they would not continue to be involved in Chinese opera when they start professional careers. It is very difficult for the U.S.-born Chinese generation to devote themselves to Chinese opera because they lack the literacy in Chinese and disagree with some of the dated themes and archaic values in the repertoire. Therefore, the future of Chinese opera in the United States is at risk if there is a rapid decrease in the population of enthusiastic amateur performers and new immigrants from China, Hong Kong, and Taiwan.

See also: Hong Fook Tong

Further Reading

Duchesne, Isabelle, ed. 2000. *Red Boat on the Canal: Cantonese Opera in New York Chinatown*. New York: Museum of Chinese in the Americas.

Lei, Daphne. 2006. *Operatic China: Staging Chinese Identity Across the Pacific*. London: Palgrave Macmillan.

Zheng, Su. 2010. *Claiming Diaspora: Music, Transnationalism, and Cultural Politics in Asian/Chinese America*. New York: Oxford University Press.

May May Chiang

CHINESE TEMPLES IN AMERICA

Like immigrants the world over, Chinese immigrants to America during the early 19th century brought with them their religions and religious institutions. Chinese temples reflect the religious diversity and unity of Chinese religiosity, which blend Confucian, Buddhist, Daoist, and folk religious beliefs and rituals into a temple. There are Chinese Buddhist temples, Chinese Daoist temples, Chinese Confucian temples, and Chinese popular religious temples. Chinese and Chinese Americans will visit all these varieties of temples based on the ritual calendar, personal needs, and community holidays and festivals.

In China, a temple—be it Buddhist (*si*) or Daoist or popular (*miao*)—is a community center where people meet to discuss politics, seek medical advice, celebrate major festivals, hold meetings, and more important, serves as a Chinese school. These multiple functions of the temple can also be seen in immigrant Chinese communities in the United States, both historically and today. Material evidence found in the temples today speaks to these multiple functions, and they remain centers for community solidarity. As a community temple, it is managed by a local committee, which might or might not have a resident priest. The priest might be an ordained Daoist specialist or a local religious specialist, such as medium or shaman.

A family's prayers are sent to heaven with the scent of burning incense at Kong Chow Buddhist Temple in San Fancisco's Chinatown, 1989. (Phil Schermeister/Corbis)

By the early 21st century, however, most of the historic Chinese temples in California are seeing their role in the Chinese community decline, as new generations of U.S.-born Chinese have moved away. Today, temples are either fully operated by the city and maintained as historic landmarks and museums (e.g., Oroville's Chinese Temple, originally built in 1863), maintained by the State of California (e.g., Weaverville's Joss House, founded in 1874), or are established as nonprofits under local community and board supervision (e.g., Hanford's Taoist Temple of 1893, Auburn's Joss House of 1909, and Mendocino's Temple of Kwan Tai of 1852). Still other temples remain under full Chinese ownership and are still actively used as places of worship (e.g., the Kong Chow Temple of 1857 and Tien Hau Temple from 1852 in San Francisco's Chinatown). A final type, represented by the Bok Kai Temple in Marysville, originally built in 1854, is a temple owned and operated by the Chinese community, which may donate the temple to the city or state as a means to finance its restoration but without fully relinquishing it entirely. These temples are all registered as city, state, or national landmarks except for the two fully functioning temples in San Francisco's Chinatown—the Kong Chow Temple and the Tien Hau Temple.

The Mendocino Temple of Kwan Tai, the Kong Chow Temple, Auburn Joss House, and Hanford's Taoist Temple are all dedicated primarily to the red-faced God of War, Literature, and Social Harmony: Guandi. The Tien Hau Temple in San Francisco's Chinatown is dedicated to the Goddess of the Sea, also known as the Empress of Heaven. The Bok Kai Temple is dedicated to the Dark Emperor of the North, also known as the True Warrior Zhenwu. Each year in early spring the Marysville community celebrates the Bok Kai festival, which includes the oldest continuously held parade in California. These historic temples are vibrant reminders of the bittersweet historical circumstances and conditions of life in America for Chinese immigrants, as they were generally built in Chinatowns—ghettos on the periphery of "white societies." The Mendocino Temple of Kwan Tai was renovated by the descendants of the Hee family. One of the descendants commented that as a little girl she was embarrassed by the little red temple because it reminded her of how different she was from her peers. The majority of the religious artifacts on display at these temples date back to the late Qing period (1644–1911). However, there are Chinese American elements in them as well. For instance, at the Hanford Taoist Temple, there is a display of an "unhewn log," which is a symbol used in the *Dao dejing* (*The Classic Book of Integrity and the Way*) to illustrate the ideal state of being. This is unique to Hanford and is not replicated in Daoist temples in China, Taiwan, Hong Kong, or Singapore.

Interestingly, there is continuity in the role that these historic temples play in their respective local communities—they remain sites of community unity even as they have lost their daily worshipers. Moreover, recent changes in immigration policies, which have allowed large new contingents of Chinese immigrants to come into the United States since the 1960s, have provided fertile ground for new Daoist and Buddho-Daoist temples to be established, such as the Ma-tsu Temple U.S.A. in San Francisco and a Sino-Southeast Asian temple association dedicated to Guandi, the Teo Chow Association, located in major cities throughout California, Texas, and New York.

As a result of modernization and the forces of globalization, Chinese religious temple organizations have become transnational, reflecting Chinese/Chinese American transnational lifeways and subjectivities. Recent developments of Taiwanese Buddhist temples offer the best example of new forms of transnational Chinese temples. The Hsi Lai Temple, the largest Buddhist monastery in North America, completed in 1988 at a cost of $26 million, is situated on 15 acres of a hillside at Hacienda Heights in Los Angeles, near "Little Taipei," a rapidly growing community populated by mostly Taiwanese Americans. Hsi Lai is a satellite community of the mother temple, Foguangshan "Buddha Light Mountain," located at Kaohsiung (Gaoxiong) in southern Taiwan. Foguangshan was founded by Master Xingyun, who is the 48th patriarch of the Linzhi School of Chan (Zen) Buddhism. Foguangshan has branches across the United States, in Denver, New York, San Francisco, and San Diego, as well as in major cities worldwide. Hsi Lai Temple has also established the Hsi Lai University (University of the West), offering undergraduate and graduate degrees in education, business administration, and most importantly, Buddhist studies.

Another global Buddhist organization has left an influential footprint in the American religious landscape, the Tzu Chi Compassion Relief Society (Ciji Gongdehui), a worldwide network with centers throughout Europe, Latin America, Southeast Asia, and North America. The headquarters of Tzu Chi Compassion Relief Society in the United States is located within Los Angeles proper. Tzu Chi Compassion Relief Society has established itself in the new

American religious landscape through the promotion of social services, primarily through its free clinic program. Dharma Master Zhengyan, along with a group of 30 followers, founded Tzu Chi Compassion Relief Society in Hualian, Taiwan in 1966. Currently, Tzu Chi Compassion Relief Society is the largest civil organization in Taiwan. In 1993, the Tzu Chi Compassion Relief Society Foundation established its Free Clinic in Alhambra, California. The clinic is a general health-care facility providing medical assistance to financially disadvantaged residents in Los Angeles. It incorporates traditional Chinese healing with Western medicine and Buddhist philosophies of compassion to serve clients without regard to age, sex, race, class, or religious affiliation. In addition to these two major global Taiwanese Buddhist communities, there is Zhuangyen Monastery located at Carmel, New York, and serving New York, New Jersey, and Connecticut. Another major center is the Jade Buddha Temple associated with the Texas Buddhist Association in Houston, Texas.

A politicized and transnational Chinese Buddhist community that originates from mainland China is also making a great impact in the United States: Falun Gong, or Falun Dafa. Falun Gong is a new Chinese Buddhist movement founded by Li Hongzhi in 1992. In the late 1990s, the Communist Party of China banned Falun Gong, which drove its participations into exile. They have resettled in Taiwan, the United States, and Europe and have successfully established a global network of chapters and temples and grown in membership despite its suppression. They have also established themselves as a global human rights case against China's suppression of religious freedom. Falun Gong participants hold regular demonstrations in front of Chinese embassies worldwide.

The life and vitality of Chinese temples in America depends on whether or not Chinese Americans continue to practice their heritage traditions. As evident from historic Chinese temples, descendants of the immigrant population who established Chinese temples do not continue to venerate or perform rituals there. Instead, temples become historic landmarks and symbols of a once-lively yet vanished Chinese cultural influence. In this way, Chinese historic temples become more akin to a Confucian temple, known as *wen miao* ("temples of culture)." However, in places where new immigrant Chinese resettle, such as Chinatown communities, historic Chinese temples remain relevant and maintain religious and ritual traditions, as is the case with the Tien Hau Temple and Kong Chow Temple. Moreover, changes in immigration policies during the 20th century and the impact of war has diversified the Chinese population in the United States, which reflects the new diversity of Chinese temples established since the 1980s, as is the case with Taiwanese temples and Sino-Southeast temples.

See also: Bok Kai and Bok Kai Temple; Ching Chung Taoist Association of America

Further Reading

Lee, Jonathan H. X. 2004. *Auburn's Joss House: Preserving the Past for the Future (The Auburn Chinese Ling Ying Association House)*. Auburn, CA: Auburn Joss House Museum and Chinese History Center.

Lee, Jonathan H. X. 2004. *Hanford's Taoist Temple and Museum (#12 China Alley): The Preservation of a Chinese-American Treasure*. Hanford, CA: Hanford Taoist Temple Preservation Society.

Lee, Jonathan H. X. 2004. *The Temple of Kwan Tai: California Historic Landmark No. 927—Celebrating Community and Diversity*. Mendocino, CA: Temple of Kwan Tai Inc.

Jonathan H. X. Lee

CHING CHUNG TAOIST ASSOCIATION OF AMERICA

Daoism is one of the oldest religious and philosophical traditions in China, dating back to as early as the 5th millennium BCE. The Ching Chung Taoist Association of America (CCTAA) is an orthodox, lineage Daoist temple located in San Francisco's Chinatown. Established in 1978, the temple community has approximately 1,000 members on its registry and about 60 disciples who actively participate in the daily operations of the Association and perform regular religious ceremonies. The Association traces its lineage to Ching Chung Koon (Azure Pine Monastery) in Hong Kong—now officially registered as Ching Chung Taoist Association of Hong Kong (CCTAHK)—which in turn traces its lineage to the True Dragon Sect of the Quanzhen (Complete Perfection) school from Northern China. Although connected by a shared lineage, the CCTAA and CCTAHK are completely separate in their organizational operations.

Ching Chung Koon in Hong Kong was established in 1949 by Master Hau Po-woon (1912–1999). A Daoist Master from the famed Zhibao Tai community in Guangzhou, Guangdong Province, China, Hau eventually established two temples in Hong Kong—one in Kowloon and another in New Territory. Besides providing worship and ritual services, Ching Chung Koon also offered charitable social services, which over the years expanded to several free medical clinics, senior homes, and schools (preschool through high school).

In 1978, through a sand divination—a Daoist practice where deities possess the body of gifted disciples to write on a tray of sand, and the celestial scripts are interpreted and recorded, usually with other community members as witnesses—Ching Chung Koon's guiding deity, Lü Dongbin, instructed the Ching Chung Koon community to establish a temple in the United States. The Reverends Wilson C. Lee (Daoist name: Li Dazhi, 1931–2005) and Lily L. Wong (Daoist name: Wang Feiqiong, 1933–2002), who were husband and wife and both senior disciples of Hau, were entrusted with the mission. The Lee family immigrated to San Francisco the same year and started with a home shrine. The San Francisco temple at 532 Grant Street was established in 1979 and was officially open to the public in 1981. The home community in Hong Kong shipped a full cargo container of shrine furniture, statues of deities, and other important ritual accessories made by in-house craftsmen. In 1996, the temple relocated to its present location, a larger space, at 615 Grant Street. The husband-and-wife team was dedicated to replicate, as much as possible, all the religious services that were available in the home community in Hong Kong.

The Lee Family

Lily Wong and her family lived close to the Kowloon temple and worshiped deities in the temple regularly. She started regular temple worshipping when she was about 10 years old, but did not become an official disciple until she was 28 years old. She was a 16th-generation disciple, and the only one in the Wong family to become a disciple. Her husband, Wilson Lee, followed her lead into the religious community and eventually became a 20th-generation disciple.

Counting from the establishment of Ching Chung Koon in Hong Kong in 1949, every passing year marked a new generation of disciples. Unlike lay parishioners who only pay respect to the deities and make occasional donations to the temple, disciples are required to study texts from the Daoist canon, make bodily and spiritual cultivation part of their daily lives, and learn to perform official ritual services.

Both Wong and Lee were trained to independently officiate rituals, but Lee was recognized as the leader of the San Francisco Ching Chung community until his death in 2005. With the assistance of his wife and son, Lee also assisted in the establishment of Hong Kong CCTA's Canada branch in Vancouver, British Columbia in 1989 (registered as Ching Chung Taoist Church of Canada).

Their son, Jefferson H. Lee (Daoist name: Lee Dancheng, 1963–) was a godchild of Hau. The younger Lee spent much of his childhood in the Hong Kong temple with his godfather and was later also officially ordained as a disciple (31st generation). He was in his teens when the Lee family immigrated to the United States, and he participated in the founding of the San Francisco community. After the death of his parents, he became in charge of the San Francisco temple. While he assisted in the performance of rituals when his father was alive, he pointed out that it was the spirit of his deceased mother who stayed behind to assist in temple rituals when he became the head of the community. It is a customary duty in this lineage that when an ordained master passes on, his/her spirit stays with the community for seven additional years to guide and assist the next community leader. He expects that when it comes to his time to pass on, his spirit too will stay in the temple shrine for seven years to assist the next community leader.

Fluent in English, Cantonese, and Mandarin, the younger Lee devotes his weekends to serve the CCTAA community and educating the general public about Quanzhen Daoism. During the week, he works full time as a funeral director. He attributes his entry into the funerary business, again, to family tradition—that his uncle established the first funerary parlor in Hong Kong. When he attended a relative's funeral in San Francisco in the early 1990s, the lack of understanding for proper Daoist death rituals motivated him to enter a mortuary school and attain a state license for funeral direction. His funerary career has been a success. At one point, he worked for a large funerary corporation and managed 25 mortuaries and several cemeteries. Currently, he works with a smaller, noncorporate mortuary that has close connections with the Chinese and Japanese communities in San Francisco.

The younger Lee is married and has two sons. Neither of his sons is planning to carry the family torch by becoming an ordained Daoist priest or a funeral director.

Beliefs and Practices

CCTAA's root in Quanzhen Daoism can be easily identified by its worship of three prominent masters in the Quanzhen lineage—Lü Dongbin (one of the Eight Immortals and central guiding deity of the Quanzhen lineage), Wang Chongyang (founder of the lineage, 1113–1170), and Qiu Chuji (Wang Chongyang's disciple who started the Dragon Gate Sect and brought the Quanzhen school to its prominence in the Yuan court, 1271–1368). From this historical lineage, CCTAA inherited a rich literature on philosophy, alchemy, talismans, rituals, and bodily cultivation. After the People's Republic of China opened its door to the outside world, and before his death in 1999, Hau traveled extensively throughout China to visit Daoist masters and continued to reaffirm and expand the content of the religious repertoire of his association.

After the death of Hau, CCTAHK maintained its legitimacy by closely connecting to the Chinese Daoist Association, a government-sanctioned organization that regulated Daoist communities in People's Republic of China, including Baiyun Guan in Beijing. Many of its beliefs and practices of CCTAHK have been adjusted to become more consistent to the Baiyun Guan interpretations. The Lee family remains orthodox in its teachings and ritual practices—the CCTAA maintained the teachings, ritual procedures, and religious wardrobe that were originally transmitted by Hau.

The younger Lee explains that the religious vocation of an ordained priest is only part of a long series of administrative training. As Daoist disciples who are on the path to eventually join the celestial bureaucracy, he, his parents, and other disciples consider that serving as administrators of the religious institution in the human world is a prerequisite of becoming a member of the community of deities who govern all aspects of human affairs. When the disciples leave the human world (not only after their physical deaths but also after the seven years of service in the temple as spirit mentors), they go to a destination called Langhan Gong (Temple or Palace of Esteemed Favor), where they continue their administrative training and mobilize further upward on the chain of celestial commands.

The Lees have been invited to perform public Daoist rituals in Chinese ethnic communities in the United States and Canada. Besides performing Daoist death and funerary rituals upon request, both father and son have officiated public rituals at dragon boat festivals in both Toronto and San Francisco. Like most other Chinese Daoist and Buddhist communities, CCTAA also performs community rituals for Lunar New Year, birthdays of guiding deities and past masters, ancestral memorials on Qingming Festival—a festival that takes place in the spring—and offerings to ancestors and hungry ghosts in lunar July. Introductory rituals are also performed for new disciples who officially join the lineage to study rituals and commit to become core members of the community. Other problem-solving rituals for individuals and households can also be performed for members and nonmembers upon request, where CCTAA charges fees to cover for the cost of offerings and other materials necessary for the rituals.

Official ritual performances only happen a few times in the year. Members of the CCTAA community, whether or not they are disciples, visit the temple shrine to pay respect to the deities. There is no requirement for community members to worship at any regular interval. The temple shrine is also open for public visits and worship. Worshipers, especially CCTAA members, usually bring fruits, sweets, or flowers as their offerings to the deities. All worshippers are expected to pay respect to the deities with lighted incense sticks. Worshippers who request blessings or guidance are expected to burn paper money to show additional appreciation toward the deities.

In the early years of its establishment, there were a few CCTAA members who were able to perform sand divination as a way to channel messages from the deities to the community members. In the recent years, occasions for sand writing have diminished. Instead, the younger Lee receives messages from the deities in his dreams and sometimes also during waking hours. He claims that sometimes he would have a sudden urge to write things down, or observe his own fingers becoming restless and wanting to hold a pen, and as he holds a pen in his hand, deities would channel their messages through automatic writing. Other times a message would appear in his mind, and he would have a knowing that it is a message from the deities; the messages are often fleeting and he would have to write them down as soon as possible. These messages are the deities' direct guidance to the community, as directives for community-level decisions, as forecasting important happenings for individual members, or as orders for specific tasks to be done.

Although generally not a charitable organization, CCTAA tries to support its members and sometimes the larger Chinese ethnic community in times of need. Donations made by members and shrine visitors not only fund the daily operations of the organization but also supplies an emergency fund in case a funeral or other rite needs to be performed and the family of the deceased, ill, or troubled is unable to pay for the ritual offerings and materials. Outside of ritual needs, the emergency aid is generally available only for the organization's members, and the assistance is available not only in terms of monetary funding but also in terms of access to personal connections and resources through the social networks of CCTAA's registered members.

See also: Bok Kai and Bok Kai Temple; Chinese Temples in America; Daoism

Further Reading

Komjathy, Louis. n.d. "Ching Chung Taoist Association of America." *Daoist Organizations in North America.* Accessed July 16, 2015. http://www.daoistcenter.org/organizations.pdf.

Kwok, Man Ho, and Joanne O'Brien, trans. 1991. *The Eight Immortals of Taoism.* New York: Penguin.

Emily S. Wu

CONFUCIANISM

Confucianism, a misnomer created by the Jesuit missionaries in the 16th century, has no counterpart in its native China or East Asia, where the term *Rujia* (school or family of scholars) is the common designation for this tradition. *Rujia*, at once signifying a genealogy, is also a scholarly tradition, political system, code of ethics, worldview, way of life, and spiritual tradition with a strong emphasis on human's capacity for self-transcendence. But unlike Greek humanism, which places human above all things, Confucian humanism is not devoid of the Transcendent. Likewise, the term Confucianism may lead people into thinking that the tradition was founded by a man known in the West as Confucius (551–479 BCE), which actually is a Latinization of the Chinese phrase Kong Fuzi or Master Kong, an honorific form of address to the man named Kong Qiu. He was not the founder of the tradition nor was he given that honor. However, for the sake of the readers who are familiar with the terms "Confucius" and "Confucianism," they shall be so used here.

Confucius: The Master

Confucius was born in Qufu, Shandong Province. By the time he was born his family fortune had fallen from aristocracy to that of commoners. There are many stories surrounding his birth, one of which states that he was born in a cave, which is well preserved today, at the foot of Mt. Ni. His father died when he was young. His mother brought him up and served as his first teacher. He may not have been a diligent student when he was young, for he did not get serious to learn until age 15. From that point on he became a lifelong learner and teacher as well as an occasional holder of minor posts in government. But he was not a very successful official.

At the age of 56 he gathered some of his disciples and began traveling from state to state seeking a prince to employ his political philosophy in government. At the age of 67, after finding no one to accept his ideas and ideals, he returned with the disciples to his native land and began a career as the first private teacher in China until he died at the age of 72. After his death his disciples split and formed schools of their own based on different aspects of the teaching of the Master.

The *Lun Yu* (The Analects of Confucius), the embodiment of the person of Confucius and his ideas, was most likely written by the second generation of his disciples. In this book we not only see Confucius in action and sense his aspirations, fears, joys, and so forth, but also experience his creative transformation of some feudal concepts of the past. He revolutionized, for example, the concepts of the *junzi* (profound person) and *ren* (love, humaneness, or benevolence) by infusing a moral dimension into them.

Confucianism in North America

In *Confucius, the Man and the Myth* (1949), H. G. Creel argued that the American Revolution was indirectly influenced by Confucianism. Whether or not Creel was right is a matter of debate. What we do know is that Confucianism was washed onto the North American shores by the waves of immigration from China as early as 1848. These immigrants brought the tradition with them and built temples in honor of Confucius, as attested to by the now-defunct temple in Stockton, California. By the end of the 19th century, some major universities in the United States began offering Confucian studies through their language, philosophy, or history departments. Today the number of such institutions is on the increase. And as previous mentioned, the Chinese government itself has decided to establish 100 Kongzi Shuyuan worldwide; a number of them have been established from coast to coast in North America. The Chinese American community likewise has been offering sacrifices to Confucius from time to time since the 1920s, and such sacrifices now have become an annual ritual since 1982.

But the recognition of the importance of Confucius and Confucianism goes beyond academia and the Asian community. For example, in the year 2000 the governor of the California signed into law designating the birthday

(September 28) of the Master as Confucius Day. And on October 28, 2009, the U.S. House of Representatives overwhelmingly passed a resolution (H. Res. 784) honoring the 2560th anniversary of the birth of the Master and recognizing the invaluable contributions he made to philosophy and social and political thought. It was further pointed out that Confucianism has had tremendous influence on Japan, Korea, Vietnam, and the cultures of a number of Southeast Asian nations. Moreover, Confucianism has likewise made quite an impact on numerous American scholars as well as contributed to the multicultural reality in the United States. Such impact and contribution, in addition to those just mentioned above, bear significant meaning in the fields of science, law, medicine, engineering, music, art, and others.

How is Confucianism practiced in America by the Chinese and the people whom have been influenced by it? Being a defused spiritual tradition, it is practiced within the family. We can see this practice through parts of the wedding and ancestral sacrifice rites observed by the family, the family's emphasis on the ethical realm in the members' daily lives, and Confucianism's insistence on solidarity through the realization of the concept of filiality.

See also: Chinese Americans and LGBTQQI; Daoism; Religions

Further Reading

Lau, D. C., trans. 1992. *The Analects.* Hong Kong: The Chinese University Press.
Tu Wei-ming. 1989. *Confucianism in a Historical Perspective.* Singapore: The Institute of East Asian Philosophies.

Edmond Yee

DAOISM

Daoism has been called the most misunderstood of the world's major religions and thus understanding its role in Asian American religious culture is not easy. Like Hinduism and Shinto, it has no founder, credo, or single sacred text. Unlike Buddhism or Christianity, it is not a missionary faith, and thus has never found the need to express its teachings succinctly to outsiders.

Traditional Chinese Daoism is the indigenous religion of China and takes as its goal the realization of the Dao (perhaps better known as Tao), which means "way" and refers to the formless reality that forms all things. "Realizing the Dao" can be expressed through ritual, philosophy, biospiritual cultivation, or moral action. Historically, Daoism is the sum total of several lineages or denominations, most of which are based on textual revelations. Many of these lineages incorporate the teachings of previous groups. Thus Daoism's canon of sacred text is open.

Daoism is different from Chinese popular religion and in fact often defines itself in opposition to popular religion and local cults (and, in some ways, has manifested as a minority, elite religion). By the same token, "being a Daoist" is not simply a matter of accepting traditional Chinese cosmologies, theories of the body, or practicing longevity techniques. Nonetheless, there has been much mutual influence between Daoism and all these Chinese cultural practices.

Today, there are two main forms of Daoism: Zhengyi (Orthodox Unity), with married clergy acting as priest for the community, is most common in Taiwan and Southeast China; and Quanzhen (Perfect Truth or Complete Realization), which is monastically centered and is prevalent in the rest of China and, in a nonmonastic form, in Hong Kong. There are also several sublineages within each tradition.

Daoism in America has two separate aspects: as part of Chinese American religiosity and as "Popular Daoism"—a new American religion, a hybrid created by Chinese immigrants, who took on the role of "Daoist Masters," and their disciples.

Chinese Immigrant Daoism

The first recorded migration of Chinese people to the U.S. mainland came in 1848, the year gold was discovered at Sutter's Creek in California's Sacramento Valley. By 1854, an estimated 13,000 Chinese lived in the United States, most as gold miners or railroad workers, and in 1860, the first year that accurate statistics were kept, 34,933 Chinese were reported living in the continental United States. In 1880, that number had tripled to 105,613.

The Chinese brought their religion with them but not in the same way as other immigrants to North America did. Unlike Italian Catholic or Japanese Buddhist immigrants, the Chinese were neither accompanied by missionaries, nor were they supported by ecclesiastical structures that created branch churches in the new land. Unlike Jews in America, the Chinese did not set up independent temples as centers of learning. Rather, for the Chinese in America, organized religion remained in the hands of companies representing the interests of immigrants from particular clan villages or geographical areas in China. In San Francisco, for example, the six main companies (or lineage associations) known as the "Six Families," were in charge of funeral arrangements, financial security, and protection against outsider malefactors. They were also quick to build temples. What is generally considered to be the oldest temple in San Francisco's Chinatown, the Tian Hou Temple, was built by the Sze Yap Company in 1852, located on the fourth floor of a narrow building on a one-block street.

By the time of the 1882 Chinese Exclusion Act, there were countless Chinese temples across the western United States, probably numbering in the hundreds. Chinese temples were not just prevalent in San Francisco and other urban centers but in small towns as well. They were built and still exist in the towns of Marysville and Oroville in the Sacramento Valley, which had a large percentage of Chinese inhabitants.

Did Daoism exist in any form in early Chinese America? The standard answer, which can be found in any description of temples in Chinatowns, is that Daoism existed in blended, popularized form. Mariann Kaye Wells described the temples as "alloyed with some Taoist and Buddhist gods and beliefs." But using the stricter definition of Daoism presented in the introduction, with Daoism understood as opposed to and not equivalent to popular religion, there is no evidence that any Daoists were part of early Chinese America. As Daoist scholar Louis Komjathy put it, "the 'syncretic' or popular nature of the early Chinese temples makes it unlikely that individuals specifically identifying themselves as 'Daoists' inhabited the United States during the early phases of Chinese immigration." It seems unlikely that a Daoist religious professional, often tied to a particular location in China, would choose to emigrate.

By contrast, those in charge of the Chinatown temples were neither religious professionals nor monastics but were, in a sense, paid volunteers. A Daoist priest or temple custodian, who sold the incense and the candles, might or might not assist the worshipper, strike the drum and gong to announce him or her to the gods, or help in the divination procedure. He was not necessarily a cleric in the Western sense, and in America, at least, his position was purchased by him for the year, either outright or at a public auction. Even the gods enshrined in the temples were not Daoist. Tianhou, for example, made the transition from semihistorical figure to local deity to Empress of Heaven, not because of the petitions of Daoists but rather by imperial decree, since the government often "standardized" local cults in order to maintain better control over them. The gods and apotheosized figures one sees in Daoist temples in China (e.g., the Three Purities, the Eight Immortals, Zhang Daoling, Wang Chongyang) were not, so far as can be determined, visible in these temples. Thus, we know of no individual that identified himself or herself as a Daoist during the first century of the Chinese life in America (1849–1950).

Since the 1960s, several temples more readily identified as Daoist have opened in North America; most of them are offshoots of Hong Kong–based popular Quanzhen Daoist temples. A prominent example is Ching Chung Taoist Association in San Francisco, which is a branch temple of Qing Song Guan (Green Pine Temple), one of the most prominent Daoist temples in Hong Kong. (They also have branches in Canada and Australia.) For 25 years, the leader of this temple was the Rev. Wilson C. Lee (1931–2005). Lee was born in Guangdong, trained in Hong Kong, and arrived in the United States in 1981. Lee kept busy with liturgical duties but also functioned as a public exponent of Daoism. He often performed traditional Daoist ceremonies for public events in the Bay Area and occasionally in other parts of the United States and Canada.

Notably, Lee rededicated the 19th-century Chinese temples of Tian Hou in San Francisco's Chinatown and the "joss house" in Weaverville in the mountains of Northern California. One might see these actions of reconsecration of popular religious sites by a particular sectarian movement, with interests in promoting its own version of Daoism, as parallel to the process of local temples being taken over and "standardized" by larger organizations, a hallmark of Daoism in China for centuries.

Some Taiwanese sectarian movements founded in the early 20th century, such as Yiguandao and Tiandao, have branches in North America, and these temples sometimes promote themselves as being Daoist. But in general, among the religious preferences of Chinese Americans, Daoism would be ranked far behind Christianity, Buddhism, and nonaffiliated.

Popular American Daoism

From the 1850s on, Americans writing on the topic of Chinese religion—from Paul Carus to Thomas Merton—might have theoretically benefited from first-hand research without leaving the United States by visiting Chinese temples and talking with Chinese Americans about their religious life. These writers never did. The only Anglo-Americans to describe Chinese temples in America in the 19th and early 20th centuries were popular journalists looking for good stories. Instead, the narratives of the American discovery of Chinese religion and of Chinese religions in America, which occur roughly simultaneously, run parallel yet rarely meet for over 100 years. When they do meet in a series of cultural encounters, Popular American Daoism is born. One of the earliest examples of these cultural encounters is a short film made in 1948. The art film "Meditation on Violence," directed by the well-known avant-garde filmmaker Maya Deren, is probably the first American recorded image of Chinese martial arts, and was apparently shown in universities and art theatres throughout the country. The film opens with a title card stating it is "based on traditional training movements of the wu-tang and shao-lin schools of Chinese boxing." The sole actor is Chao-Li Chi, a young, well-built Chinese man, bare chested and wearing a white scarf around his waist. To the sounds of Japanese drumming, he performs a loose interpretation of *taiji*, then *kung fu*, and finally a sword form. The whole effect is stylized and theatrical. Deren, in her explanatory notes to the film, links the movements of *taiji* to the *Yijing*'s hexagrams.

Is this the symbolic birth of Popular American Daoism (even though Daoism is never mentioned)? It is certainly an example of a creative collaboration between two educated intellectuals. Deren brought her financial resources and artistic and metaphysical temperament. Chi brought the skills he acquired growing up in a privileged home in China, along with his desire to be a creative artist, mitigated by racial limitations imposed on him by being Chinese in America.

Chao-Li Chi was still teaching *taiji* as of the early 21st century and does not call himself a Daoist master. But, in 1970, he helped found one of the first Daoist organizations in North America, the Taoist Sanctuary of North Hollywood, California, along with Dr. Khigh Dhiegh and Master Share K. Lew.

Masters and Institutions

The 1970s saw the birth and growth of exclusively American Daoist organizations, led by Chinese masters. This development was due mainly to the 1965 changes in the immigration laws of the United States and Canada, which brought more Chinese to North America. A handful of these immigrants were experienced in various Chinese religio-physical techniques and eager to teach these skills to willing Americans. At approximately the same time, young North Americans' search for spirituality outside traditional institutions (often called "the new religious consciousness") led them to embrace teachers and practices from Asia. Thus, the situation was ripe for the creation of Popular American Daoist masters and organizations.

The immigrants who became Daoist teachers came from the well-educated and privileged classes of China who experienced a sense of displacement and of loss, a feeling of belonging to a nation and a culture that no longer exists as they remember it—not just the land of China that they left but also the social, educational, and cultural nexus of the Qing dynasty literati, which was torn about by civil war, invasions, revolutions, and communism—was an important factor in creating Popular American Daoism.

Daoism in America revolves around the figure of the teacher. If we compare American Daoism to American Buddhism, we find that Buddhism in North America has carried over its institutional forms from Asia to a vastly greater extent. This statement is not meant, of course, to underestimate the importance of the personality of the Asian Buddhist monk; teachers such as Shunryu Suzuki, Chogyam Trungpa, and, of course, the Dalai Lama have influenced the very identity of American Buddhism. But American Buddhism also has created a series of institutions (zendos, monasteries, and temples) that maintain continuity and permanence that American Daoism cannot match.

The first American Daoist organization officially recognized, as a tax-exempt religious institution in the United States was the Taoist Sanctuary, founded in North Hollywood, California in 1970. However, the founder of the Sanctuary was not Chinese—though he often played one on TV (most famously as the Red Chinese agent Wo Fat on "Hawaii 5-0"). Khigh Dhiegh was of Anglo-Egyptian descent and was born Kenneth Dickerson in New Jersey. Nonetheless, his Sanctuary was the first comprehensive Daoist organization in America, teaching *taiji*, martial arts, the *Daodejing* and the *Yijing*, and conducting seasonal Daoist rituals (albeit invented by Dhiegh himself). Dhiegh brought to the Sanctuary teachers who were from China, including one who had been trained at Daoist mountaintop monastery in Guangdong. The Taoist Sanctuary currently operates in San Diego, as directed by Bill Helm, a former student of Dhiegh's.

In 1976, three students of the Taoist Sanctuary, studying Chinese medicine in Taiwan, met a Chinese doctor whom they invited to the United States. Hua-Ching Ni settled in Malibu, California, opened a shrine called the Eternal Breath of Tao, and began teaching classes privately in a venue he named the College of Tao. Over the years, Ni-sponsored organizations have multiplied. His private acupuncture clinic was known as the Union of Tao and Man. He also founded Yo San University of Traditional Chinese Medicine in 1989, an accredited degree-granting college. His sons, Maoshing and Daoshing, now head both the clinic and the university while Master Ni lives in semiseclusion.

A Thai-born Chinese named Mantak Chia moved to New York City in 1979 and opened the Taoist Esoteric Yoga Center later renamed the Healing Tao Center. Today, Chia attracts an international clientele to his Tao Garden in Thailand, while the Healing Tao USA is headed by Chia's former student, Michael Winn. Chia's classes and books are best described as a popularized, streamlined system of *qigong* based on Chinese internal alchemy (*neidan*). Moy Lin-Shin founded the Taoist Tai Chi Society (TTCS) in 1970 in Toronto.

These are some of the major institutional forms of Popular American Daoism. They all teach practices through a combination of weekly classes and yearly, or seasonal, retreats or seminars. What all these practices have in common is they can be performed individually, not collectively, as a modular part of a daily regimen. This may well be inevitable in the American context.

Each practice has been radically recontextualized in North America: the *Daodejing* and the *Yijing* entered the American scene through the field of Sinology, which never imagined these texts would be construed as modern practice. Once *taiji* was in common circulation in the early 1970s and linked to the philosophy of the *Daodejing* and the *Yijing*, spiritual practice groups could offer courses in the study of these two texts as well as in *taiji*, linking them by a common vocabulary (*qi, yin-yang*).

See also: Bok Kai and Bok Kai Temple; Confucianism; Religions

Further Reading

Komjathy, Louis. 2004. "Tracing the Contours of Daoism in North America." *Nova Religio* 8 (2): 5–27.

Siegler, Elijah. 2010. "'Back to the Pristine': Identity Formation and Legitimation in Contemporary American Daoism." *Nova Religio* 14 (1): 45–66.

Towler, Solala. 1996. *A Gathering of Cranes: Bringing the Tao to the West.* Eugene, OR: Abode of the Eternal Tao.

Elijah Siegler

DYING AND DEATH RITUALS

For the traditional Chinese, death is the main life-passage event, surpassing birth and marriage. It is by dying that one can extend one's life as an ancestor, and funerals provide the ritual means for this transformation. In the United States, a Chinese funeral typically is structured into three main parts: the visitation, the formal service, and the burial. The visitation, which usually occurs on the evening before a funeral, is when family and friends keep the corpse company and perform their last rituals of caring, such as placing burial goods in the casket.

Though Christianity and Western customs dominate most Chinese American funerals today, a few traditional features persist that express some of the Chinese concepts of death and the afterlife. These concepts include (1) death pollution, (2) multiple aspects of the soul, (3) the spirit world mirroring the physical one, (4) reciprocity and exchange between the living and spirits, and (5) family continuity.

Death pollution has two aspects: the passive pollution of the decaying corpse and the active pollution of the deceased's volatile and confused spirit. Both are

Living descendants make offerings to ancestors at Manoa Chinese Cemetery in Honolulu, Oʻahu, Hawaiʻi, on April 1, 2000. Cooked foods are offered to ancestors and are considered blessed and to be eaten by living family members afterwards. Foods offered are usually the favorite dishes of the ancestors when living, which rekindle memories and familial bonds. Ancestral veneration is a core aspect of Chinese and Chinese American religiosity. (David Samuel Robbins/Corbis)

considered dangerous, evil, and unclean, and anything associated with them should be respectfully feared, avoided, and managed with countering talismans and rituals. Mortuary features dealing with pollution are in the form of (1) visual and audible announcements; (2) prophylactic elements that deflect, absorb, or counter death pollution; (3) the use of fire and water for purification; and (4) rituals to manage and give placement to the deceased's spirit. Together, they safeguard the living.

Off-white or natural-fiber mourning clothes are worn by the immediate family members to indicate their close relationship and polluting contact with the deceased. The clothes' lack of color pigmentation represents the lifelessness and putrefaction of the corpse. Black or dark blue are the colors of mourning and sadness worn by distant relatives and friends. Placards or cloth banners carried in the funeral procession announce the identity of the deceased and his or her family.

In the United States, where death often occurs in hospitals and the corpse is handled by a mortuary, pollution precautions are limited to the funeral and burial and are observed selectively by the family, often as a nod to tradition. Some Chinese families (usually the first generation in America), don off-white mourning clothes as a tradition during the funeral, though dark Western clothes are more frequently worn.

In major American Chinatowns such as San Francisco, Los Angeles, and New York (to a limited extent), where funeral processions are permitted as a tradition, a Western brass band (10–12 musicians) or (on occasion) a traditional Chinese funeral band may be hired to provide music to announce the presence of a corpse, to entice the deceased's spirit to stay close, and to add significance to the occasion. The funeral of a prominent person may include two or three brass bands to mark status and prestige. The Western band marches at the front of the procession; the Chinese band sits in the back of a pickup truck. The family and its entourage may elect to walk in the procession (the tradition in China), though most typically ride in limousines. In front of the hearse, in lieu of name placards or banners, may be a "picture car" in which a large wreathed photograph of the deceased is propped up in the convertible or the back of a pickup truck to inform the community of who died.

The most common prophylactic custom is the giving out of *li shi* (Cantonese) or *hung bao* (Mandarin)—money wrapped in red paper by the deceased's family to give to relatives and friends in attendance. Also known as "lucky money," the red color (symbolizing life) counters death; the money should be spent on something sweet to remind the living of the sweetness of life. Along with the red *li shi*, some families give a white (symbolizing death) *li shi* containing a coin and a piece of candy. The metal coin absorbs death airs (and therefore should be spent immediately); and the confection removes the bitterness of death. The giving of *li shi* is the most common funerary custom in the United States.

According to some shamanic and Daoist beliefs, blood from a sacrificial chicken is sometimes squirted around the grave to safeguard it once the corpse is buried. A symbol of the life force and with a red color indicative of good luck, blood is a potent ritual offering to the new ancestor that seals its spirit in the grave, imbuing it with continued life in the spirit world. Metal weapons such as a sword may also be wielded by the shaman to fend off evil spirits at the grave during the burial.

Certain plants are believed to deflect the bad luck from death pollution. A piece of bamboo, a pomelo leaf, or pine sprigs may be placed in the pocket of mourners and then discarded after a funeral. Pomelo or kaffir lime leaves are sometimes placed in the water used to wash the mourners' faces, hands, and legs prior to entering the home (followed by a complete bath). The use of such protective plant talismans varies according to regional customs and personal beliefs.

Along with water, fire is also used to cleanse and purify a person exposed to death pollution. Members of the deceased's immediate family may burn their off-white mourning clothes or step over a small fire to purify themselves from evil airs before entering the home after the funeral. Traditionally, anything to do with the corpse or funeral is considered bad luck and should be discarded or destroyed.

Rituals that serve to keep the deceased's spirit close to the corpse are critical until the spirit is safely situated in the grave. Until then, the mourning family is responsible for controlling the active pollution of a potentially dangerous spirit that poses a threat to the community. Wailing, food offerings, the aroma of incense, spirit flags, and music all keep the spirit attracted to remain nearby and are used extensively from the time of death until the corpse's burial. Wailing by the family begins at death to create a mournful mood and to invoke the spirit to return to the body because it is missed. Offerings of food and incense are immediately placed by the corpse to feed the spirit and to communicate with it. A spirit flag—a bamboo staff topped by frilly, white, paper-enwrapped loops attached with a dangling paper plaque naming the deceased—designed to "catch" the spirit is placed on the coffin. The eldest son (the main mourner) may be seen carrying the spirit flag and a giant incense stick during the procession along with a funeral band to keep the spirit entertained and in tow, and to alert passersby of an approaching corpse.

Cheap mock paper money is tossed out during the procession by assistants to distract malicious wandering hungry ghosts that are jealous of the ritually well-tended spirit of the deceased and tempt it to join them. This cheap mock money is made of thin, off-white paper with curved slits cut in it. When it is tossed, the hungry ghosts chase after it and slip through the curved slits. Since ghosts are known to travel only in straight lines, the ghosts become disoriented and are diverted away from the funeral cortege. This tradition, called *mai lu*, or "buying the road" (Mandarin), has its counterpart in imperial China, when beggars would block the road to bribe the passersby, who would then toss a handful of cheap copper coins to disperse the beggars and clear the road for passage.

Depending on the particular belief system, the number of soul aspects the Chinese believe in may vary. But basically, there are three soul aspects: one is imbued in the name tablet placed on the family altar or in a temple (why offerings are made there); one travels through hell and then resides in paradise; and one is placed in the grave (why offerings are also placed there). Unless the spirit is ritually situated, it may not go to paradise, and there would be no designated locale for "feeding" it with offerings, thereby dooming it as a wandering, hungry ghost.

In the Chinese cosmos, the spirit world mirrors the material one: spirits require the same sustenance as the living. Hence offerings of food are placed at the grave, and mock money and the paper replicas of goods needed for a comfortable life are burned there for the deceased's spirit. These goods may include a house, car, cellphone, chests of clothes and accessories, mountains of silver and gold, servants, boomboxes, mahjong sets, computers, and even Viagra. The spirit receives the essences of the food; and the value of the mock money and the paper goods is transmitted by smoke. Since corrupt bureaucrats demanding bribes rule the spirit world as they do that of the living, mock money is both burned (plain spirit money, gold and silver ingot papers) and placed in the casket (hell bank notes, gold and silver ingot papers) for such use in the spirit world, and a silver coin is placed between the corpse's lips to pay the guardian of the death realm.

To maintain a balance in matters concerning death and spirits, precautions are taken through monetary exchanges to neutralize pollution danger. Money is paid for services for the dead, and li shi is given to mourners. Spirit relationships are maintained through give-and-take transactions, and offerings to ancestors are expected to be reciprocated with prosperous blessings for the lineage. This is one reason why a family will spare no expense for a funeral and why visits to the grave to make offerings are regular family affairs. As among living people, the relationships between the living and spirits are maintained through reciprocal exchanges and gift-giving.

Special festivals such as ching ming in the spring and chung yung in the fall are major "grave cleaning" occasions for visiting family graves, cleaning them, and paying respects (bowing three times) to the dead with offerings of incense, flowers, food, drink, and the burning of mock money. In the United States, ching ming is the more popular festival, and is well observed as a Chinese memorial day. Chinese cemeteries, and some non-Chinese ones in areas with a large Chinese demographic, will organize programs and Buddhist or Taoist ceremonies, and provide refreshments.

The Chinese family consists of both living and dead members who continue to have an interactive, sustaining relationship. Funerals provide the ritual opportunity to create a beneficent ancestor who will protect the present family and its future members. Life and longevity elements at funerals refer to the long life and perpetuity of the lineage. Traditional Chinese burial clothes embroidered with longevity symbols (the crane, evergreen pines, the calligraphic symbol for longevity, etc.) signify an ancestor-to-be whose long life has produced sons who have had sons to extend the patrilineage (family lineage reckoned through the males).

Family caring and respect are demonstrated with the "blanket ceremony," a ritual common on the United States in which family members place lengths of fabric on the deceased during the wake or visitation. The color significances and symbolic explanations of the blankets vary. In San Francisco, for example, the eldest son and his wife place a white blanket (for death) on the dead parent, followed by a red one (for life). Subsequent blankets offered by the other children may be of any color, print, or number. In Boston, the red blanket is placed first; in New York, the first blanket for a deceased male is white or cream colored, while a female receives a pink one. The second blanket is always red, then any color or print after that.

Whenever a mourner approaches the casket, he bows to the deceased. If he makes adjustments to the corpse or places goods in the casket, he bows again after performing the task. In the traditional Chinese family, the Confucian order of patrilineal authority begins with the father, followed by the sons in order of seniority, and then the mother and daughters in order of seniority. At funerals, this order determines who the chief mourner will be to lead the processions and to perform the rituals.

Lineage perpetuity is highly valued, and the number of generations propagated by the deceased is shown off as a measure of a successful life. Each surviving generation may be represented by different-colored hair bows or sashes. While the color coding may vary according to individual and regional preferences, widows tend to wear white, daughters wear blue, and grandchildren and great-grandchildren wear green for fertility and their future propagation of the family.

Good fortune for the family lineage may be ensured with *fengshui*—a geomantic pseudoscience that believes the earth is a living entity with veins of positive energy running through it. A *fengshui*-determined grave calculated to be on or near such a vein will empower the hard bones of the ancestor and be transmitted to the lineage.

In recent years, Chinese immigrants in the United States have been able to realize their culture's mortuary ideals in a country with more economic opportunity and land. Many cemeteries have developed *fengshui*-designed memorial gardens to cater to Confucian traditions. With political instability, limited land and the push for cremation, and real estate developments using burial grounds in their ancestral homelands, there is a trend of Chinese families transporting their family corpses to their new home in the United States.

While burial in one's natal place is a traditional ideal, it is also important for a family to remain together in death as they were while alive. Full-body ground burials are still preferred over cremation, since an aspect of the soul resides at the grave and because one's life (and body) is a gift from one's ancestors that one should not disrespectfully destroy: one came into the world as a whole body and should leave the world in the same way.

See also: Chinatown Ghost Stories; Chinese Genealogy; Chinese Immigrant Cemeteries

Further Reading

Crowder, Linda Sun. 2002. *Mortuary Practices and the Construction of Chinatown Identity*. PhD diss., University of Hawai'i.
Crowder, Linda Sun. 2003. "The Taoist (Chinese) Way of Death." In *Handbook of Death and Dying*, edited by Clifton D. Bryant. Thousand Oaks, CA: Sage.

Linda Sun Crowder

FALUN DAFA/FALUN GONG

On May 13, 2012, the 20th anniversary of his first public speech promoting Falun Dafa, better known as Falun Gong, the new religious movement's founder and leader Li Hongzhi gave a speech to a packed audience of his "disciples" in New York. Those in attendance had travelled from around the country and across the world to get a glimpse of, hear a teaching from, and simply be in the presence of "Master" Li. The contents of Li's speech reflected upon the enormous shifts of fortune experienced by the movement in its brief history as well as looked forward with predictions of greater changes yet to come, changes that would affect not only Falun Gong and its practitioners, but also the whole world and indeed the entire cosmos.

Li Hongzhi first gave a lecture series on Falun Dafa to the public from May 13 to May 22, 1992, in a rented auditorium of a high school in Changchun, Jilin Province, China. The lecture series began on the date to which Li Hongzhi would, in 1994, officially change his birthday—a date that coincided with the celebration of the birthday of the Buddha in the altered year of Li's birth, 1951, according to the lunar calendar. Li claims to have, by this change, corrected the year and day of his birth, which had originally been recorded as July 27, 1952.

The initial workshops given by Li in May 1992, which were sponsored by the Changchun City Somatic Science Research Society, saw over 350 people sign up for participation. Subsequent workshops at the Changchun Army Club and the Provincial Party Commission drew some 800 attendees. Between June 1992 and March 1993, Li gave nine lecture series in Beijing.

Li would soon begin to distinguish between the broader world of *qigong* in China at that time—with the number of schools and techniques numbering in the hundreds—and the unique nature of Falun Gong. In 1995, his nine-day lecture series was edited into his second book, *Zhuan Falun*, or *Turning the Law (Dharma) Wheel*. In that book, and in numerous writings that would follow, Li drew connections between the teachings and practices of Falun Dafa and a variety of teachings and practices known most widely from Daoist and Buddhist traditions. Li even went beyond Chinese religious history, saying that the supposed founders of Buddhism, Daoism, and Christianity (Sakyamuni, Laozi, and Jesus, respectively) had taught not in order to establish religions, but to "guide cultivation practice." Finally, however, Li declared that the teachings that he presented in his system of Falun Gong go beyond all previous teachings.

Li Hongzhi's teachings build mainly upon the long history in China of transforming oneself through the cultivation of *qi*, but he distinguishes his Falun Dafa from these *qi*-based methods, and from the *qigong* craze of his own time in China, by asserting that his cultivation practice transforms the self/body through the accumulation of *gong* and the elimination of *qi*. More will be said on the matter of *gong* and *qi* below, but here we must take notice of the significance of Li's ever-growing reference to and deployment of overtly religious language and symbolism in the early years of Falun Gong to the fate of the movement in mainland China.

The Communist government of the People's Republic of China recognizes only five religions that citizens may freely practice: Daoism, Buddhism, Islam, and Catholic and Protestant Christianity. In the 1980s and 1990s, however, a social space was opened up by the Party allowing for the teaching and practice of various forms of *qigong*, which involve numerous practices centered upon breathing and bodily movement aimed at the achievement of physical and mental health and well-being. The allowance of what would become the aforementioned *qigong* craze of those decades was conditional on the separation of such practices from any religious elements that may have been traditionally intertwined with them, most notably in relation to Daoist and Buddhist teachings. As the new *qigong* schools grew increasingly religious in their rhetoric, Falun Gong chief among them, such movements drew increasing criticism in widely published newspapers, magazines, and television news broadcasts.

From as early as 1996, just a year after the publication of *Zhuan Falun*, Falun Gong found itself as the target of several such reports in the Chinese media. Whenever such a report would appear, the growing ranks of the Falun Gong faithful would rapidly rouse a response, mobilizing through means of modern social networking groups of protesters, who would show up at the sites of the offending newspaper offices or television stations, demanding retractions of media denunciations of the group. One such protest, now widely documented, was held in late April 1999 and would eventually lead to the outlawing of Falun Dafa in mainland China. In that instance, some 10,000 members of the movement chose to surround the headquarters compound of the Chinese Communist Party in Beijing to petition for specific demands. While those gathered dispersed after one day following a reportedly initially reassuring dialogue with Party members, within three months of the incident, on July 21, 1999, Falun Gong would find itself outlawed in China, a move apparently inspired by a fear of the group's ability to rapidly mobilize such prominent groups of protesters and its certainly exaggerated claims of 100 million followers in China. However, the ban on Falun Gong was officially reasoned as due to the group's and its leader's overstepping of the boundaries of religious freedom by engaging in illegal religious activities. Li Hongzhi, however, had left China in 1995, ultimately relocating to New York, where he remains in exile from his homeland to this day.

From New York, in the intervening years, Falun Gong has built up an impressive headquarters for global media outreach, including the newspaper and website *The Epoch Times* and the New Tang Dynasty Television network. While both organizations deliver a wide fare of news stories from around the world, each also gives extensive attention to mainland China's anti–Falun Gong campaigns since 1999, just as each is generally critical of the Chinese government. *The Epoch Times* has even issued a small book entitled *Nine Commentaries on the Chinese Communist Party*, which likens the Party to a "giant, evil possessing spirit" that is destined to soon perish due to its persecution of Falun Gong.

The New York–based television station, New Tang Dynasty TV, is related to Falun Gong in a fashion similar to *The Epoch Times*. Falun Dafa has never operated as an institution in which individuals can be said to have "membership," and no records of "members" are kept. Since early on in China, however, Falun Dafa has proclaimed 100 million practitioners, a number that it now touts as being a "worldwide" tally, but this claim is surely an immense exaggeration, to say the least. Still, in large U.S. cities, such as San Francisco, Los Angeles or New York, as well as others around the world, there may be hundreds and even thousands of practitioners, while the movement may also have at least a presence in smaller towns where one might never suspect them. In those places where they have a significant presence, like major U.S. cities, one often finds members in front of the Chinese embassy, both proselytizing for Falun Dafa and protesting the Chinese Communist Party over the continued outlawing of Falun Gong in mainland China and what practitioners understand to be an ongoing "persecution" of adherents in that country.

Falun Gong Fundamentals: Teachings

According to the practitioners, acceptance of Li's teachings is usually due to a combination of the persuasiveness of Li's writings and teachings as well as the almost universally reported experience of the supernatural power of Li through the healing of illness and/or injury. That is to say, Li's authority is granted legitimacy by virtue of his audience's culturally determined hopes of an enlightened and supernaturally gifted teacher who will transform their lives, their selves, and their world. This raises the significance of the aforementioned incident in which Li changed his birthday to coincide with that of the Buddha. It is also suggestive, to say the least, that the title of Li's central scripture, *Zhuan Falun*, translates to the equivalent of the Buddha's first sermon, "Setting in Motion the Wheel of the Dharma."

Practitioners' hopes are reinforced through the teachings of Li Hongzhi, who presents himself as a Buddha figure who has descended to earth from "higher levels" of the cosmos—indeed, the highest of innumerable levels—in order to save human beings in the Age of the End of the Dharma, which is characterized by worldwide social degeneration. Li claims also that he has dispatched to each individual practitioner one of his innumerable *fashen*, or "law bodies," which exist in another dimension, and that these serve each cultivator as a guide in both their practice and their daily lives, constantly arranging the student's cultivation by ensuring that the cultivator will meet trials to overcome in life, thereby transforming their *yeli*, or karma. By eliminating karma and cultivating *de*, or virtue, Master's Li's students are guided toward self-perfection. These goals are achieved through daily performance of five physical exercises as well as daily reading of *Zhuan Falun* and Master Li's numerous other texts. These activities serve to aid cultivators in their primary endeavor to raise the level of their *xinxing*, which is elevated in direct relation to the practitioner's accumulation of what Li calls *gong*.

The theory behind the production of *gong* is complex and involves an effort by Li to redefine some central concepts found variously in Buddhism, Daoism, and *qigong*. For *gong* "is developed through the transformation of the substance called virtue [*de*], and through the cultivation of *xinxing*." In Falun Dafa, "virtue" is a white physical substance that attaches to and surrounds the body, in another dimension. This substance exists in relation to another, "karma," which "is a type of black substance that surrounds the human body. It has physical existence in another dimension and can transform into sickness or misfortune." These two substances, virtue and karma, according to the teachings of Li, are the twin sources of pleasant and painful experiences in this life, respectively. One develops karma from committing negative acts, speaking negative words, or thinking negative thoughts just as, conversely, positive thoughts, words, and deeds result in the storing up of virtue, which in turn is transformed into *gong* once one has eliminated all of one's karma.

From *karma* and *de* to one's *xinxing*, one is obliged to transform these various aspects of oneself by means of the Falun Gong practices, discussed below. Aside from such formal practices, however, Li also teaches that one is cultivating oneself in every moment of one's life. Li teaches, for example, that a process of transformation takes place "after a conflict," referring to his understanding that people can transfer virtue and karma to one another while interacting in the course of everyday life. If, for instance, one were to shout insults at another, then virtue would flow from the insulter to the insulted and a reverse exchange of karma would take place. Naturally then, it is the intention of Falun Gong practitioners to rid themselves of karma and to obtain for themselves virtue and, subsequently, *gong*. The significance of the teaching in Falun Dafa that suffering hardships and tribulations in the midst of living a "normal life in society" is the primary mechanism for progressing toward enlightenment and developing *xinxing* and *gong*.

Falun Gong Fundamentals: Practices

For practitioners in North America, and indeed around the world, there are today four main components to Falun Gong practice: (1) Clarifying the Truth, (2) Sending Forth Righteous Thoughts, (3) the daily performance of the five physical exercises, and (4) the daily reading of Master Li's teachings. The practice known as "Clarifying the Truth" arose mainly as a response to the Chinese Communist Party's persecution of the movement since 1999. Engaging in this aspect of practice might mean volunteering to spend time at the entrance of popular tourist sites or the Chinese Embassy, if you happen to live near one. At these sites are displayed posters declaring both Falun Gong's "goodness" and its teachings of *Zhen, Shan Ren*, or "Truthfulness, Compassion, Tolerance/Forbearance," as well as other placards depicting images of tortures allegedly carried out by the Chinese Communist Party against mainland Chinese practitioners. Volunteers also engage passersby in conversation if possible and hand out literature that might either be the teachings of Master Li or the aforementioned *Nine Commentaries on the Chinese Communist Party* put out by *The Epoch Times*. Viewing Falun Gong as the repository of Chinese civilization's millennia-long history of self-cultivation technologies, and the Chinese Communist Party as the enemy of that history and its modern incarnation in Falun Dafa, practitioners of Chinese descent around the world may find their identities are reinforced as the standard-bearers of traditional Chinese culture, struggling against forces that would see that culture destroyed.

Another way that practitioners wage this ongoing battle with the Chinese Communist Party is through the world-traveling stage production Shen Yun. The costume and dance extravaganza began in New York in 2006 and today has three touring companies covering East and Southeast Asia, Europe, and the

Americas. Promoting the production and selling tickets has become one of the principal activities of Falun Gong adherents around the world, as they believe the show itself serves to "clarify the truth" of the situation between Falun Gong and the Chinese Communist Party. Indeed, aside from providing an artistic platform to make a political and religious statement, practitioners believe Shen Yun can have supernatural benefit in the lives of those who attend its performances.

Shen Yun claims to revive the 5,000-year-old Chinese civilization. In a series of 22 scenes, Chinese cultural heroes from throughout history are displayed triumphing over evil with their superior virtue, continuing a battle begun in the earliest emanations of time between the forces of heaven and the demonic forces led by an evil red dragon. In the end, though, the audience will also witness a re-creation of the persecution of Falun Gong practitioners in mainland China. As actors portraying Falun Gong adherents suffer beatings by actors portraying Chinese police officers, the world seems about to end. Indeed, in the 2012 version of the show, projected on a screen backdrop to the stage, the audience sees a comet explode in the sky, threatening all life on earth at the very moment that Falun Gong seems to have been eradicated in China by the police. In the final moments though, a Buddha-figure appears in the sky and with his giant palm he forestalls the comet, saving the planet and revivifying the Falun Gong practitioners who now rise to the heavens, becoming buddhas and goddesses themselves.

Another important practice for adherents of Falun Gong is that of Sending Forth Righteous Thoughts, which first appears in the writings of Li Hongzhi in 2001 and involves 15 minutes of meditation observed each day at 6:00 a.m., noon, 6:00 p.m., and midnight. One day a practitioner expanded on the significance of this practice, saying to me, "Because practitioners develop supernormal powers, doing 'sending forth righteous thoughts' really has enormous power to rectify the Fa and eliminate problems." "Rectifying the Fa" refers to the rectification of the universe by the Fa (Dharma), or Dafa (Great Dharma), taught by Li Hongzhi, which he says he is carrying out throughout the incalculable dimensions of the cosmos—a project to which his followers contribute through performance of the Dafa practices.

The remaining practices then are *liangong*, or daily performance of the five physical exercises of Falun Gong; and *xue fa*, or daily reading of Master Li's writings. To these third and fourth elements of Falun Gong practice we must add the already discussed cultivation of one's *xinxing* in daily life. Practitioners will often gather in local parks or at the home of an adherent to collectively do the slow, often perfectly still, Falun Gong exercises and to read together from *Zhuan Falun* and Li's other works. If a group is large enough and its members dedicated enough, practitioners might meet for this type of activity early every morning, or perhaps just once a week. When adherents gather to read and reflect upon the teachings of Master Li as a group, they call these meetings Fa Study. Large versions of these events, called Experience Sharing Conferences, which can attract thousands of Falun Gong practitioners, take place around the world. Master Li has appeared on a semiregular basis at conferences taking place within North America over the last several years, notably at the 20th anniversary Fa Teaching in New York.

Life for the Dafa practitioner is an opportunity to better oneself insofar as it is through Dafa that one endeavors to practice self-cultivation. Li's teachings revive and revise millennia-old teachings from Chinese tradition and, moreover, Li makes these "traditional teachings" relevant to the modern lives of his audience, and goes even further to identify his followers as the maintainers of traditional Chinese culture. This may be attractive to Chinese Americans and members of the worldwide Chinese diaspora, but the movement has now attracted followers of diverse backgrounds from around the world. The teachings of Li that are read during Fa Study spur the assembled practitioners to reflect upon both these traditions and their own merits in attempting to practice and uphold them, and further makes the merits of those traditions real for the group in that they see the teachings reflected in their own daily lives, week after week, as they attend to this method of Fa Study. Indeed, Fa Study can be said to consist of the twin activities of reflection upon the Master's teachings and the reflection upon one's efforts to practice those teachings in everyday life. Through this practice, and the others discussed above, practitioners of Falun Dafa firmly believe that they not only transform themselves, but that they aid their Master in transforming the world.

See also: Confucianism; Daoism; Religions

Further Reading

Li Hongzhi. 2000. *Essentials for Further Advancement*. 3rd translation ed. New York: Universe Publishing.

Li Hongzhi. 2001. *Falun Gong: Principles for Perfect Health and Enlightenment*. Gloucester, MA: Fair Winds Press.

Li Hongzhi. 2002. *Zhuan Falun*. 1st translation ed. Taipei: Yih Chyun Book Co.

Ownby, David. 2008. *Falun Gong and the Future of China*. New York: Oxford University Press.

Penny, Benjamin. 2012. *The Religion of Falun Gong*. Chicago, IL: University of Chicago Press.

Ryan J. T. Adams

FENGSHUI/GEOMANCY

In Chinese culture, *fengshui*, or geomancy, is a body of knowledge used to select and adjust building and gravesites. There are many schools of *fengshui* practice, but all have a common goal: to strategically align the living and the dead with the cosmos. For public spaces, such alignment is believed to protect the community from calamity and would bring prosperity to all. For homes and gravesites, proper alignments ensure prosperity of the residents (and their descendants) in all aspects of life. While *fengshui* embodies a generally Daoist worldview, it is rarely associated with religious institutions or taken as motivation for establishing formal religious affiliations or practices. Among Chinese Americans, levels of adherence to *fengshui* rules also vary greatly. Some hire professional *fengshui* consultants to oversee every aspect of their residential, office, and gravesite projects. Others take precautions with small, commonsense *fengshui* tips that circulate in their families and among friends. Still others consider these rules merely superstitious and unscientific.

There are many schools of *fengshui*, and most professional consultants use a combination from three major approaches: compass, form, and ritual. The compass approach involves aligning between the residents' astrological signs and the directions of the site, with meticulous calculations to help residents identify optimal direction that a site should face, and the arrangement of specific functional spaces within the site. For a home, a *fengshui* consultant who uses the compass approach is able to provide a precise grid of where major entrances and stairs should be, and also the best locations for master bedroom, bathroom, kitchen, living room, and ancestral altar. For a grave, the consultant finds the direction that the gravestone should face to bring most blessings upon the descendants of the deceased.

The form approach focuses on observing physical characteristics of the landscape. It determines the energetic quality of a site by looking at the shapes and positions of hills, valleys, and watercourses around it. Shapes of geographical features are corresponded with yin-yang and five elements categories, and an ideal site has features that match with the residents' astrological signs.

Finally, when structural alterations are not enough or not possible, the ritual approach is used to energetically transform a site so that it can be beneficial for the residents even without an astrological match of directions and forms. This approach is also an important last resort when a place is believed to be haunted or brings about misfortune.

In the Chinese American community, compass and form approaches are widely used by religious and nonreligious *fengshui* consultants alike, and are accepted by antisuperstition skeptics for being statistical and mathematical. On the other hand, the ritualistic approach is practiced mostly by religious specialists such as Taoist and other folk ritual masters, whose religious training requires them to cultivate themselves physically and psychically for safe and effective ritual performances. However, it was the ritual approach that first crossed ethnic boundaries and became the basis for the Americanized *fengshui* popularized by mainstream media.

See also: Religions

Further Reading

Bruun, Ole. 2008. *An Introduction to Feng Shui*. New York: Cambridge University Press.

Emily S. Wu

FIRST CHINESE BAPTIST CHURCH, SAN FRANCISCO

When gold was discovered in California in 1849, large number of Chinese from various districts near the city of Guangzhou came to the United States through the port of Hong Kong. Home Mission boards in the major denominations saw this as a God-given opportunity to reach the Chinese. The Presbyterians were the first to come to San Francisco Chinatown, establishing a church in 1853. Congregationalists and Methodists followed in 1878.

The First Chinese Baptist Church in San Francisco was organized in 1880 by Dr. J. B. Hartwell, a Southern Baptist missionary who had served in China. After several years, the church was turned over to the Northern Baptists (now American Baptist Churches USA).

The church was first located in Chinatown, in a rented store front on Washington Street across from Portsmouth Square. In 1888, through the support of the American Baptist Home Mission Society, the church was moved to a permanent location on the corner of Waverly Place and Sacramento Streets.

Missionary Janie Sandford came in 1884, the first of a long line of missionaries to serve the church. The missionaries worked with women and children and taught English to adults. The first Chinese pastor was the Rev. Tong Kit Hing, who came in 1886. He and those who followed him were responsible for Sunday worship, evangelistic outreach, and pastoral care. Trained in China, these early pastors generally did a tour of duty of several years here in the United States, after which they returned to China.

In 1906, a group of church members, feeling that the church should be independent from control of the Home Mission Board, left to form the Chinese Independent Baptist Church. The same year, the church building was destroyed by the earthquake and fire. For the next two years, the congregation met in Oakland, a city across the Bay. A denominational-wide effort raised 10,000 to construct a new building, completed in 1908. A third story was added to the church building in 1930.

In reaching out to the Chinese, the Home Mission Society had hoped that eventually the churches they established would become self-supporting. However, continuing discrimination against the Chinese limited their employment opportunities: working in laundries, restaurants, and domestic service were the main avenues of livelihood for many. The term "Chinaman's chance," which came into use during this period, meant you had no chance at all in terms of making it in America.

Faith Cheng, left, and Eva Wu learn to make red lanterns during a Year of the Monkey 2004 Chinese New Year weekend celebration at the First Chinese Baptist Church in the Chinatown section of San Francisco on January 25, 2004. Lisee (Cantonese), pronounced lay see, or hongbao (Mandarin), are the traditional red envelopes handed out for good luck during Chinese New Year. (AP Photo/Jeff Chiu)

In the early part of the 20th century, the Chinese population in the United States fell dramatically. In 1882, when the Chinese Exclusion Act was passed, the population stood at 132,000; by 1920, it had dropped to 60,000. Outreach to Chinese felt the impact of that change.

In the early 1930s, a young child named James Chuck (1929–) made initial contact with the church when he was sent by his parents to the church-sponsored nursery school. His parents had come to the United States in the late 1920s under business papers. Chuck was born in Oakland, California, but soon after the family moved to San Francisco, where they lived in one-bedroom apartment. At that time, many of the Chinatown family lived in rooming houses with shared kitchen and bath.

His father found work as a cook in a Chinatown butcher shop and a held a second job at night making noodles for a Chinatown teahouse. His mother found work as a seamstress in one of the many Chinatown sewing factories.

After attending nursery school, Chuck continued in the Sunday school, belonged to a club for boys, attended the Chinese-language school sponsored by the church, participated in the youth program, was baptized, and took an active part in the life and mission of the church.

In the 1930s and 1940s, there were few Chinese doing anything important: there were no Chinese policemen, judges, or public officials; and only a few professionals, whose practice was largely limited to Chinatown Chinese. Vocational choices available to Chinese were very limited.

World War II was a turning point for the Chinese. Employment opportunities opened up for the Chinese in Bay Area shipyards. Because China was an allied in the war effort, American society gradually saw Chinese people in a new light. Following World War II, many more opportunities for work opened up to Chinese Americans, but some discrimination continued in housing and other areas through the decade of the 1950s and early 1960s. Some church members reported that they were unable to buy homes in some of the new housing developments.

When Chuck graduated from the University of California at Berkeley in 1950, he began seminary studies at Berkeley Baptist Divinity School to prepare himself for Christian ministry. While he was in seminary, the church called him to join the church staff as Youth Director. Upon his graduation in 1953, in response to the increasing number of English-speaking young people in the church, the church called him to be the English-speaking pastor. When the Chinese-speaking pastor left for New York to start a new church in 1954, Chuck was called to be the pastor of the entire congregation, becoming the longest-serving pastor of the church until his retirement in 1991. He was followed by Dr. Jeff Sharp, who had been a missionary to Hong Kong and spoke fluent Cantonese. After his term of service, he was followed in 1998 by Dr. Don Ng, an U.S.-born Chinese who grew up in Boston, and who served for many years on the staff Educational Ministries of the American Baptist Churches USA.

In 1955, the National Council of Churches convened a meeting at the First Chinese Baptist Church to bring together pastors and lay leaders of Chinese churches from all across the country to discuss a study that they had commissioned regarding the status of Chinese churches in America. At that time, there were about 80–90 Chinese congregations in the country, almost all related to one of the mainline denominations. Fifteen of these congregations were in San Francisco and the East Bay. At the meeting, there was tension between the old-guard Chinese-speaking pastors and an emerging group of younger pastors who felt that more attention needed to be paid to the U.S.-born English-speaking constituents.

In the beginning of the 1950s, an increasing number of church members were able to find jobs following their graduation from college as teachers, accountants, engineers, and so on; some working for the government, others in the private sector. Because of this, the church was able to become financially self-supporting in 1955. The congregation assumed the salary of the one missionary that was still assigned to the church. The Home Mission Society, which held the deed to the church property, deeded the property to the church, stipulating only that if the property were ever sold, that the $35,000 or so that they had invested be returned to them.

The next few decades would be a period of transition for the congregation. The church members began to assume responsibility for all phases of the church's life and mission: in time, the ongoing program of the church would include English classes; church school for children, youth, and adults; leadership training programs; fellowship groups; youth camp; family camp; a six-week day camp; retreats; and short-term missions.

Prior to the 1950s, most church members lived in Chinatown and were able to walk to church. This began to change in the latter part of the 1950s, when long-time members and young married couples began to move out Chinatown proper. As a result, many church activities were concentrated on Sunday. The several adult fellowship groups met monthly on Saturdays, usually at the homes of members.

Beginning in the 1960s, a major change in the immigration laws allowed a large number of Chinese to immigrate to the United States. Ministry to these new arrivals, some of whom with church backgrounds, revitalized many Chinatown churches. First Chinese Baptist Church responded by adding a Chinese-speaking pastor to the staff. A Cantonese service was initiated, together with various programs for children, youth, and adults. The church program evolved into two parallel tracks, one for the English speaking, and the other for the Chinese speaking. Keeping the church united under these circumstances was a constant challenge for church leadership.

In 1978, a group of Chinese-speaking church members felt led to start a new church focused specifically for new immigrants. The new church—San Francisco Chinese Baptist Church—rented facilities about half a mile away in the North Beach area. The congregation has since grown, and in 2012 moved out to a new location in the Sunset district of San Francisco.

In 1998, a group of English-speaking young adults felt led to start a new church in the Sunset District of San Francisco. They called their new church "Sunset Ministry." It too has evolved into an active, thriving congregation.

Even with these departures, the congregation at the First Chinese Baptist Church remained strong. Over the years, the congregation has sent forth about a dozen or so people into Christian ministry. In 2005, the church celebrated its 125th anniversary with the completion of a major renovation and retrofit of the church facilities and reaffirmed their commitment to stay in Chinatown.

In the first decade of the 21st century, the church initiated a project to preserve and to share the life stories of persons connected with the church. Those participating in the project were asked to talk about parents, growing up, schooling, work, marriage and family, and faith and values. Their stories, together with photographs, were published in three volumes under the title, *Chinatown Stories of Life and Faith*: the first in 2002, the second in 2008, and the third in 2012. Collectively, the three volumes give a richly textured account of how the church showed them a new way to live, provided a place for them to belong, and gave them a vehicle for witness and service.

Now in its second century of service and witness, First Chinese Baptist Church in San Francisco remains an active and vital congregation, bringing the good news in an ever-changing environment that Jesus Christ can bring healing and wholeness to human life.

See also: Chinese Christians in America; Watchman Nee and Witness Lee

Further Reading

First Chinese Baptist Church, San Francisco. 2015. Accessed July 16, 2015. http://www.fcbc-sf.org/.

Yang, Fenggang. 1999. *Chinese Christians in America: Conversion, Assimilation, and Adhesive Identities*. University Park: Penn State University Press.

James Chuck

GUANYIN

The concept of the "bodhisattva" is a very important one in Mahāyāna Buddhism. Bodhisattvas are compassionate divine beings who are dedicated to the universal awakening, enlightenment, and/or salvation of all sentient beings. They exist as guides and providers of succor to suffering beings and offer everyone an approach to meaningful spiritual life. Avalokiteśvara is the most popular and important of all the Mahāyāna bodhisattvas because of his many unique virtues, especially his compassion for all sentient beings and his deep involvement in their welfare. He took a vow that he would not attain final *Nirvāṇa* until all sentient beings are delivered and saved from suffering or, rather, saved from *samsāra*, the cycle of death and rebirth characterized by suffering. According to Mahāyāna tradition, he is to look after the benefit of humankind during the *Bhadrakalpa*, between the death of the historical Gautama Buddha and the advent of the future Buddha Maitreya.

It is generally agreed that the cult of the Bodhisattva Avalokiteśvara originated in the northwestern borderland of a unified India. In Buddhist mythological texts it is narrated that once upon a time, Amitabha (Bodhisattva Unlimited Light) while in meditation emitted a white ray of light from his right eye, which brought Padmapani Avalokiteśvara into existence. Amitabha blessed him, whereupon the Bodhisattva uttered the prayers *Om Mani Padme Hum*, thus Avalokiteśvara is regarded as the spiritual "son" of Amitabha. Avalokiteśvara's connection to Amitabha, his spiritual father, is so intimate that the bodhisattva carries a small Amitabha image on his crown. This iconographic clue clearly indicates this bodhisattva as Avalokiteśvara who otherwise would look no different from other bodhisattvas. Some scholars suggest that Avalokiteśvara came into existence as a result of Sakyamuni Buddha's compassionate gaze, therefore explaining the name, which means "He Who Looks Down from on High." Avalokiteśvara plays the role of saving all sentient beings from their afflictions during the *Bhadrakalpa*. He is the Bodhisattva possessed of all the qualities of the Buddha—especially his compassion and skill in means, *upāya*. He is the eternal outpouring of the compassion, which is wisdom; and the wisdom, which is compassion. The idea of compassion or *karuna*, which was an ancient Buddhist concept, was thus concretized in the person of the Bodhisattva who would sacrifice everything, his own personal happiness and his own merit, for the suffering humanity. More importantly, with Avalokiteśvara the Buddhists obtained what they had previously lacked—a personal savior whom they could invoke and in whom they could take refuge.

Avalokiteśvara Becomes Guanyin

The Bodhisattva Guanyin (Perceiver of Sounds), or Guan-shih-yin (Perceiver of the World's Sounds), is the Chinese name for the Indian-based Mahāyāna Bodhisattva Avalokiteśvara (He Who Looks Down from on High). Guanyin is the best-known Buddhist "deity" in China, and by extension, Chinese America, where, for at least the last 1,000 years of Chinese religious history, she has been generally depicted and represented in the feminine form. The Indian Avalokiteśvara was not originally depicted popularly and/or represented in female form. Usually he was depicted as a handsome young prince in India, Tibet, Southeast Asia, and even in China before and during the Tang Dynasty (618–907). Guanyin's female form became popular during the later Tang Dynasty and the Song Dynasty (960–1279) as evident by literary, epigraphic, and artistic artifacts. Scholars of Chinese Buddhism argue that the making of Guanyin in China is an example of the "domestication" or the Chinese "transformation" of Avalokiteśvara.

The process of domesticating Avalokiteśvara in China can otherwise be viewed as the "sinification" of the Indian Avalokiteśvara. Although this differentiation is useful, I suggest another perspective: introducing the concept of examining the gender "transformation" not so much as a "transformation" or "domestication," but as the "popularization" of the female image of Avalokiteśvara. This creation of a female Guanyin was revolutionary. The Chinese had taken a male deity, albeit an androgynous one with "feminine" attributes such as compassion, and turned this around to create a female deity. From there, they created entirely new representations of the deity in statues, depicting her with gentle femininity. After the female Avalokiteśvara/Guanyin was established, increasing centralization and consolidation of China under the Tang and Song dynasties underscored the importance of having a national religious structure. Popular Daoism and popular Buddhism offered an umbrella structure under which they were able to absorb ancient local deities—both female and male—by incorporating them into their respective celestial pantheons. As this occurred, Guanyin's already-diverse sources of origin took on Daoist and even shamanistic hues, making her identity as a purely Buddhist deity in China somewhat inaccurate. Guanyin's success in China is a direct result of her ability to transcend barriers of specific nomenclature. This is also the case in Guanyin's American experience. Guanyin can be found not only in Chinese Buddhists temples, but also in Japanese Buddhist home shrines, Vietnamese American restaurant altars, non-Asian women converts' homes, and neo-pagan shrines as well.

Guanyin in America

Long before the first Chinese gold miner and or laborer migrated to the United States in the late 1840s, Guanyin devotion in China, Korea, Japan, and Vietnam was well established. Dating back to the early 19th century, there is material evidence of Guanyin veneration among the first waves of Chinese immigrants to the United States. They are found on the altars of historic Chinese Buddho-Daoist temples throughout California's gold-mining towns (Oroville, Weaverville, and Auburn, California), as well in San Francisco's Chinatown (Tin Hau Temple). Like migrants the world over, the Chinese brought their religious rituals and beliefs with them.

The veneration of Guanyin develops in the United States (and Europe) as several cultural and political forces converge: feminism, 19th-century geopolitical events in Asia since World War II, and the immigration of Buddhist teachers to the West. When China became Communist in 1949, many Chinese monks escaped to Hong Kong, Taiwan, Singapore, and the United States. Similarly, while most Tibetan lamas escaped to India, some came to the United States when Tibet was occupied by China in 1959. With the end of the Vietnam War in 1975 and the arrival of new immigrants from Vietnam and other Southeast Asian countries since the 1980s, people in the United States have been exposed to many forms of Buddhism as well as to the different names and identities of the bodhisattva.

From 1848 to 1965 the veneration of Guanyin was limited to Asian immigrants. The liberalization of immigrant policy after 1965 parallels the changing mainstream attitude and belief in American culture. This period witnessed a spiritual search among Euro-Americans who were disenchanted by Judeo-Christian spiritualties. Their gaze was focused on Asia, primarily on India and China—Hinduism, Buddhism, and Daoism. The initial reaction to Guanyin veneration was not very positive because non-Asian converts approached Buddhist practices with a "reformation style" focus that emphasized quiet seated meditation (i.e., *zazen*), a nonritualistic and nondevotional style of Buddhist practice.

As more non-Asians converted to Buddhism, and as more and more Asian immigrants began to openly practice Guanyin Buddhism in America, coinciding with the rise of the feminist movement—expressed in goddess worship and neopaganism—Guanyin veneration became more popular. Similar to the process by which Guanyin veneration developed in China, Guanyin was popularized in America through publications that focused on Guanyin devotion and rituals, as well as through material representations of Guanyin from mundane garden art, to new depictions of Guanyin as a mother goddess to the world.

The way Avalokiteśvara became Chinese is slightly different to the way she became American. Locally produced art and representations played a key role in the Chinese transformation of Avalokiteśvara. In America, Guanyin did not become "American." Instead, Americans appropriate her in their religious practice because she represents an available source of cosmic compassion. Changes in the social consciousness of people in the 1960s–1990s also played an important part in the transplantation of Avalokiteśvara veneration in the United States outside of Asian/Asian American communities.

Guanyin in the Lives of Asian Americans

Today, Guanyin is the single most popular deity in all of Asia and Asian America, where she is worshipped in her many manifestations as Kannon or Kanzeon by Japanese/Japanese Americans, Kwanse'um by Koreans/Korean Americans, and Quan-am by Vietnamese/Vietnamese Americans. Among Tibetans, the Dalai Lama is believed to be the living personification of Avalokiteśvara. Guayin altars are located in homes of Buddhist Chinese, Japanese, Korean, Vietnamese, Tibetan, and some Indian American families. Many elderly Chinese and Vietnamese grandmothers will wear a jade pendant of Guanyin as a way to ward off evil and as a reminder to be compassionate to all sentient beings they encounter. Newly married young female devotees of Guanyin will visit her temple to request a baby, ideally a son. Vietnamese refugees, and Sino-Cambodian and other Sino-Southeast Asians make offerings to Guanyin at their homes and at community temples to create merit for family members and loved ones who died during the Vietnam War. For early and new immigrants, Guanyin provides security and comfort during the immigration and relocation process.

See also: Religions

Further Reading

Hurvitz, Leon, trans. 1976. *Scripture of the Lotus Blossom of the Fine Dharma (The Lotus Sutra)*. New York: Columbia University Press.

Palmer, Martin, Jay Ramsay, and Man-Ho Kwok. 1995. *Kuan Yin: Myths and Prophecies of the Chinese Goddess of Compassion*. London: Thorsons.

Yü, Chün-fang. 2001. *Kuan-yin: The Chinese Transformation of Avalokitesvara*. New York: Columbia University Press.

Jonathan H. X. Lee

HONG FOOK TONG

Hong Fook Tong, also called Tong Hook Tong or Hong Took Tong, is the first legitimate Chinese theatrical troupe to stage full-scale Chinese opera performances—Cantonese opera, in particular—in the United States. The troupe, from the Guangdong Province in China, arrived at San Francisco in 1952 and premiered at the American Theater on Sansome Street on October 18. The occasion also marked the first time that *Liu Guo Da Feng Xiang* (The Joint Investiture of a Prime Minister by Six Warlords), a folkloric ritual opera played as preopening show for any significant, festive occasions, was staged in the United States.

The opera, featuring a large cast and displaying elaborate acrobatic acts, would be performed hundreds of times before the century's end. Its staging aims to ask for blessings from the deities and bring good luck to the theater, events, community, and so on. It has become an important part of the performing tradition in the Chinese American community. The newspaper *Alta California*, which included many reports and advertisements of the troupe, noted that it consisted of 123 performers, including singers, musicians, and stagehands, as well as extraordinarily elaborate folk costumes. Merchants in Guangzhou City reportedly paid £2,000 (one Chinese yuan was equivalent to $288 USD in 1952) for the expenses of the troupe. On December 23, 1952, the troupe moved to a theater of its own construction on Dupont Street, the New Chinese Theater, and performed there until the following March, giving two daily performances—11:00 a.m. and 7:00 p.m., seven days a week. It was very popular among both Chinese and other Americans.

In March, the troupe sold its theater and was contracted by American impresarios to perform in New York City. A reduced group of performers went on the steamship *Corter*, bound via Panama for New York. Upon arrival in New York City, the troupe found the sponsors had backed out and itself in deep debt for the passage, the beginning of a series of disasters. Though the troupe was soon booked to perform at Niblo's Garden on May 20, the ticket price was as low as 50 cents. Its performances proved too alien for the New York audiences, who were more accustomed to the highly Westernized staging of Chinese music theater, and the show folded after only a week. Critics praised the acrobatic movements, fighting scenes, and gorgeous costumes, but they made little attempt to understand the art and were dismissive about the performance, music, and singing. Though another performance was staged at the Castle Garden on July 4, the troupe was not successful and was again cheated by the impresario.

The troupe dissolved quickly, and the performers had to rely on charity to leave New York. Though the troupe flopped disastrously at the end, it nevertheless constitutes the beginning of professional Chinese opera troupes in the United States. Through these opera performances, much Chinese folklore was presented onstage, and over the years became part of the community's identity.

See also: Chinese Operas

Further Reading

Lei, Daphne P. 2006. *Operatic China: Staging Chinese Identity Across the Pacific.* New York: Palgrave Macmillan.

Moon, Krystyn R. 2005. *Yellowface: Creating the Chinese in American Popular Music and Performance, 1850s–1920s.* New Brunswick, NJ: Rutgers University Press.

Riddle, Ronald. 1983. *Flying Dragons, Flowing Streams: Music in the Life of San Francisco's Chinese.* Westport, CT: Greenwood Press.

Rodecape, Lois. 1944. "Celestial Drama in the Golden Hills: The Chinese Theater in California, 1849–1869." *California Historical Society Quarterly* 23 (2): 97–116.

Wei Tchen, and John Kuo. 1999. *New York Before Chinatown: Orientalism and the Shaping of American Culture, 1776–1882.* Baltimore, MD: The Johns Hopkins University Press.

Nancy Yunhwa Rao

LUNAR NEW YEAR

People throughout China, Korea, Japan, Singapore, Taiwan, Vietnam, and diasporic communities worldwide will celebrate the Lunar New Year during the first 15 days. The Lunar calendar is based on the cycles of the moon, which is different than the Western Gregorian calendar based on the cycle of the sun. Lunar New Year always corresponds to the last two weeks of January or the first two weeks of February.

The dragon is the fifth sign of the Chinese zodiac. It is considered to be the most auspicious sign; thus, in the year of the dragon, people born under this sign will benefit greatly from the forces of the dragon. Since the year of the dragon is an auspicious year, many will want to get married during this year. Family will want a baby born in the year of the dragon because dragons are a lucky sign; dragon people tend to be successful in life, and may potentially bring prosperity to the family. As such, women in China, Hong Kong, Singapore, Taiwan, Vietnam, and Chinese diasporic communities worldwide will visit fertility clinics and doctors in order to ensure the birth of a dragon baby. Toward the end of the dragon year, pregnant women may also ask their doctors to induce birth if it is safe. These activities speak to the value and importance Chinese people put into the year of the dragon.

A Chinese American wears his best clothes to celebrate Chinese New Year in New York on February 2, 1916. Chinese Lunar New Year is still the most important holiday in Chinese culture worldwide. (Library of Congress)

In Asia, young people who have moved away from their parental homes and villages pack buses, trains, and planes to go back to celebrate the Lunar New Year with their families. Businesses, such as restaurants and shops, shut down. For a brief moment, big cities such as Beijing, China, and Taipei, Taiwan, become quiet.

Planning for the celebration starts well before New Year's Day. Families are busy cleaning their homes, decorating it with freshly cut flowers, such as narcissus, water lilies, peonies, and azaleas, representing beauty and new growth for the new year; fruits, especially oranges and tangerines, are displayed and given as gifts to visitors and friends, as they symbolize wealth and money. During the New Year season, red is the preferred color for dress, as it symbolizes health and life, as blood runs through a living healthy body. Other bright colors are worn to keep the mood festive and jovial. A home that has a blooming plant on New Year's Day is believed to prosper during the year. The color white is avoided as it represents death, as a dead body turns "white" when blood no longer runs through the body.

On New Year's Day, it is taboo to sweep the house, as it would be sweeping away one's prosperity for the coming year. One cannot use a knife or scissors either, as it would be akin to cutting away one's prosperity in the New Year.

The number four is avoided because in all dialects of Chinese, the sound for the number "four" sounds like the word for "death." Similarly, death and dying are taboo subjects and should be avoided. Because the New Year sets the tone for developments during the entire year, parents will not spank their children for being mischievous. Instead, they are tolerated with smiles and a positive attitude.

Traditionally, Lunar New Year in China and in Chinese communities worldwide is celebrated for 15 days. However, due to common constraints on time and resources the 15-day celebration may be shortened, or all activities for all 15 days may not be observed.

On day 1, rituals are performed and offerings are made to the gods of heaven and earth.

On day 2, extended family members come together to make offerings and perform rituals for the ancestors. This includes cooking their favorite dishes when they were alive and sharing in the memories of their lives. All dinners will serve a whole fish, a homonym for "abundance"; a whole chicken to represent wholeness and completeness; seaweed, a homonym for "wealth"; and lotus seeds, which symbolize fertility and a male child. Families with dogs treat their pets with extra special attention, as it is considered the birthday of the dog.

On days 3 and 4, children will offer tea and well-wishes to their parents, which includes in-laws. Parents will then give their children red envelopes, known as "hong bao" in Mandarin Chinese or "lai see" in Cantonese, which will contain some money.

On day 5, everyone stays in their own home to welcome the visit from the God of Wealth. It is taboo to go out on this day.

From day 6 to day 12, people will visit families, extended families, and good friends. At each visit, visitors present their host with oranges, tangerines, and flowers, and more red envelopes are given to children of the house. During this period, day 9 is reserved for rituals and offerings to the Jade Emperor, the highest-ranking deity in the Chinese celestial pantheon.

On day 13, people will eat a simple dinner of rice porridge and mustard greens. On day 14, people will prepare for the celebration of the Lantern Festival by making lanterns. On day 15, people celebrate the Lantern Festival at night, writing wishes on their lanterns, lighting them up, and seeing them slowly rise to heaven. The Lantern Festival marks the end of the Lunar New Year celebrations.

While this celebration is important to people in Asia, it is also very important to Asian Americans. Cities throughout North America with large Chinese, Korean, and Vietnamese communities hold public celebrations and parades in honor of Lunar New Year. The annual San Francisco Chinese New Year Parade is the largest celebration of its kind outside of Asia. Many Asian Americans close their shops or take a day off work to observe Lunar New Year.

Further Reading

Lee, Jonathan H. X., and Kathleen Nadeau. 2011. *Encyclopedia of Asian American Folklore and Folklife.* 3 vols. Santa Barbara, CA: ABC-CLIO.

Jonathan H. X. Lee

NARCISSUS FESTIVAL AND QUEEN PAGEANT (HONOLULU)

The Narcissus Festival and Queen Pageant in Honolulu, Hawai'i, is an annual chain of festivities surrounding Chinese Lunar New Year that was first held in 1950. Organized by the Chinese Chamber of Commerce to stimulate Chinatown's commerce and create a modern, prodemocracy image of Chinese Americans while showcasing traditional Chinese culture, the festival was designed to attract broad appeal. Over the years, it has included parades, exhibits, demonstrations, contests, and concerts for things Chinese (arts, crafts, martial arts, cooking, cultural performances, fashion); and various sport tournaments. The Kick-Off Reception, the "Night in Chinatown" street fair, and the Narcissus Queen's Coronation Ball and Goodwill Tour to China are highlights, but the core feature around which the festival was organized remains the Narcissus Queen Pageant.

The festival was created during a time when the Hawai'i Chinese community felt threatened by the ascension of the Japanese into island politics, disturbed by the derogatory Cold War image of Mao's communist China, troubled by Chinatown's commercial decline, and self-conscious of their invisibility as an ethnic group. By repackaging a traditionally family-centered celebration of the Chinese Lunar New Year into a modern ethnic spectacle, its organizers proactively steered the public gaze on the Chinese presence as traditional yet progressive, and established a distinctive Chinese *American* identity.

The two key symbols consciously selected to link the past with the present into a Chinese American representation were the narcissus flower and the Narcissus Queen. A spring flower popular in Canton and Fujian provinces and imported yearly to the islands for the festival, the narcissus was interpreted to symbolize the hope and prosperity of the Chinese renaissance in Hawai'i. Its white, fragrant, delicate blossom emerging from a bulb evoked a positive image of purity, elegance, and rarity, and by association projected the Chinese community as a loyal, peace-loving, upstanding, but stably rooted contributor to Hawai'i's future.

The other symbol that personified this duality of Chinese tradition with American modernity was the Narcissus Queen. To draw a crowd and ensure sufficient fund-raising, the first Narcissus Festival was jump-started by a beauty contest with swimsuit competition. Contestants had to speak Chinese, be full-blooded Chinese, and demonstrate a talent. By displaying female bodies in a way that was antithetical to Chinese tradition and framing them in an American institution (a beauty pageant), Chinese women were shown to be progressive, contemporary Americans of Chinese ethnicity (blood quantum) and culture (language fluency).

To engage more participants and to better represent the increasingly diverse Chinese community, the blood quantum (the degree of ancestry for a member of a racial or ethnic group) for contestants was reduced to 50 percent in the mid-1990s. Contestants are judged on their speech, poise, talent, beauty, personality, and wit—attributes for success as a goodwill ambassador for the Chinese Chamber of Commerce and the Chinese community. Because the Narcissus Queen solely represents the Hawai'i Chinese community, the pageant is a locally contained one and not a forerunner for national pageants such as Miss Chinatown USA. (The Miss Chinatown Hawai'i pageant produces a candidate for this competition.)

See also: Chinese in Hawai'i; Miss Chinatown USA Pageant

Further Reading

"Chinese Chamber of Commerce of Hawaii Narcissus Festival." 2009. Accessed July 16, 2015. http://www.narcissusfestival.com.

Goo, Miri, interview by Linda Sun Crowder, April 23, 2009, Honolulu, Hawai'i.

Li, Jinzhao. 2005. "Constructing Chinese America in Hawai'i: The Narcissus Festival, Ethnic Identity, and Community Transformation, 1949–2005." PhD diss., University of Hawai'i.

Linda Sun Crowder

RELIGIONS

As the largest and one of the oldest Asian ethnic groups in the United States, Chinese in America are religiously pluralistic, yet hold certain spiritual values and practices in common. According to the National Asian American Survey conducted in 2008, no one religious tradition served the majority of Chinese Americans. Instead, 19.7 percent affiliated as Protestant Christians, followed by Buddhists (13.8 percent); Catholics (1.7 percent); and other (1.0 percent). In fact, Chinese in the United States have the highest rate of having no religious affiliation, at 52.0 percent. In addition, 4.5 percent identified as Agnostic/Atheist and 4.1 percent said they did not know their religious affiliation. However, these latter percentages are deceptive, as many Chinese Americans venerate their ancestors and adhere to popular religious practices, and may identify with no religion or, sometimes, more than one. This essay describes different Chinese American religious traditions as well as some of the religious features that most Chinese share.

Bishop Ignatius Wang, right, poses for pictures outside St. Mary's Cathedral prior to his ordination in San Francisco on January 30, 2003. Wang is the first Catholic Bishop of Chinese or Asian ancestry to be appointed in the U.S. Wang is a native of Beijing and has served in the Archdiocese of San Francisco since 1974. (AP Photo/Eric Risberg)

Chinese American Protestant Christianity

Chinese American Protestantism has a long history of missionary evangelism, transnational political involvement, immigrant ministries, and ethnic activism. The oldest Asian American Christian congregation is San Francisco's Presbyterian Church in Chinatown, which was founded in 1853. By the beginning of the 20th century, eight different denominations established churches among the San Francisco Chinese. Along with Bible studies and worship services, these churches developed English-language classes and other ministries to assist their members. Christian religious organizations, such as the Young Men's Christian Association and the Young Women's Christian Association, also sponsored sports and music programs to help Chinese Americans adapt.

By the 1950s, most Chinese American congregations were family oriented and catered to the second generation in English. The civil rights movement in the 1960s and 1970s spurred a rise in ethnic activism that also shaped local congregations. As a result, many local churches helped to start denominational caucuses and social service programs, some of which became independent non-profit organizations. For example, the San Francisco's Asian Women's Resource

Center in San Francisco and Oakland's Oakland Asian Cultural Center both were church-initiated efforts.

With the passage of the 1965 Immigration Act, the end of the Vietnam War, and the 1989 Tiananmen Square protest, Chinese immigrated to the United States from different countries in increasing numbers. This immigration revitalized Chinese American churches, such that the number of Chinese American churches grew from 62 in 1950 to over 1,000 by 2000.

Sociologists of religions have identified different contextual factors as to why the immigrant generation and the 1.5/second generation of Chinese Americans have seen large-scale conversion to Christianity. Many of the Chinese churches are now receiving scholars from the People's Republic of China, who are adopting Christianity as a response to political and religious factors in China. They observe that converts often view the materialism of today's China as a reflection of its moral crisis. They become Christians not only for its spiritual beliefs, but also to reclaim traditional Chinese values. In contrast, others suggest that Chinese American college students are more likely to join Christian churches for an American group identity. Increasingly distant from Chinese traditions, but not belonging fully in mainstream America, Christians found kindred values, peer community, and ethnic identity in Chinese American or Asian American Christian fellowships.

Chinese American Buddhism

The Sze Yup Association in San Francisco, founded by immigrants from the Xinhui, Xinning, Kaiping, Heshan, and Enping districts of Guangdong, China in 1851, installed shrines on its top floor "to be as near the gods as possible." Now called the Kong Chow Temple, its chief deity is Kuan Ti (Guan Di) or Kuan Kung (Guan Gong), revered as a god of war, as well as a Buddhist Bodhisattva and exemplar of Confucian virtue. Yet this temple also housed the first Buddhist shrine in the United States, as Kuan Yin (Guan Yin), the Buddhist goddess, and Bodhisattva of compassion, is revered there. With a plurality of gods, this temple illustrates how Chinese popular religion, or folk religion, incorporates Buddhist deities as well. By 1875 eight such temples existed, and by 1900, approximately 400 Chinese temples were established on the West Coast, with most of them hosting Buddhist shrines and altars to Chinese deities.

Like the Chinese Christian churches, older Chinese Buddhist temples have been revived and new ones built since 1965. Beyond the Buddhism integrated into Chinese popular religion, three schools of Buddhist teachings now also represent Chinese Buddhism. In the 1960s, Venerable Master Hsuan Hua sought to introduce the dharma to the West and established what would become the Dharma Realm Buddhist Association, teaching the Pure Land form of Buddhism. This school focuses on reciting the name of Amitabha Buddha, cultivating one's single-minded vow, and developing a strong faith in this other-power. He founded the Gold Mountain Monastery in San Francisco in 1970 and in 1976 built a large retreat center near Ukiah, California called the City of Ten Thousand Buddhas.

The second main school of thought is taught at the Hsi Lai Temple in Hacienda Heights, California. Founded by the Venerable Master Hsing Yun, it propagates the Fo Guang Shan, "humanistic Buddhism," which affirms that nirvana can be experienced through the cultivation of wisdom and compassion. Rather than seeking nirvana or pure land in another world, humanistic Buddhism focuses on the establishment of a pure land in this world.

The Tzu Chi Compassionate Relief Society, the third example of Chinese Buddhism, is a lay organization that emphasizes charitable actions. Established in 1966 by Dharma Master Cheng Yen in Taiwan, the organization established a U.S. branch in 1989. According to its organizational website, it now has over 80 offices and facilities in the United States and over 100,000 volunteers who assist in disaster relief and community service. It states "Not only do the volunteers endeavor to promote the universal value of 'Great Love,' they also fully employ the humanitarian spirit of Chinese culture to its utmost."

Chinese American Catholicism

Catholic missionary work with Chinese in San Francisco began as early as 1856, and in 1884 Paulist fathers initiated a Chinese apostolate at Old Saint Mary's Cathedral. Immediately after the 1906 earthquake, the Society of Helpers sent sisters to meet the urgent needs in the Chinese section of the refugee tent villages. There they met Francis Low, the first Chinese Catholic convert who then introduced many friends to Catholicism. Holy Family Church became the title of the mission that was established as a national parish for the Chinese in San Francisco.

Today about 12.3 percent of Chinese Americans, or about 300,000 individuals, are Catholic. They generally belong to personal parishes, which are established to meet particular needs of specific communities by reason of language, nationality, or liturgical rite. These parishes exhibit a "close identification between faith, ethnicity, and culture" through their leadership, popular devotions, and congregational practices. For instance, Lunar New Year and mid-Autumn Festival traditions are observed, and Chinese-language classes are often offered to students.

Chinese American Nonreligious

The percentage of Chinese Americans who affiliate with no religion is the highest rate of any ethnic group in the United States. However, this number may be inaccurate, as many Chinese Americans may identify with Chinese popular religions or venerate their ancestors, but this type of religious practice is not measured by surveys. Another reason why Chinese Americans may not identify any religious affiliation is that they may identify with more than one religious tradition. For example, they may venerate not only ancestors and deities of Chinese popular religions, but also of Buddhism, Taoism, and even Christianity.

The accuracy of these statistics notwithstanding, many Chinese Americans do hold secularized worldviews so that they identify with no religion. About 60 percent of Chinese immigrants to the United States come from the People's Republic of China, where the government is officially atheist. Consequently, few of these households would list a religion. In addition, about one in five Chinese Americans work in the computer, science, or engineering fields, and those in these occupations are much less likely to affiliate with a religion.

Chinese Popular Religions

As stated above, many of the Chinese Americans categorized as nonreligious still hold to practices of Chinese popular religions. Here, they "engage in religious acts that assume a vast array of gods and spirits, and also assume the efficacy of these beings in intervening in this world." Also termed Shenism or Chinese Folk Religion, these traditions incorporate the veneration of ancestors, spirits, and deities. They also include practices to influence one's luck, *qi* (life force), and *fengshui* (spatial arrangements of qi).

Chinese popular religious customs are best exemplified during Lunar New Year, when the majority of Chinese Americans eat special foods, display couplets for fortune, and bai-bai (bow in reverence) to ancestors and spirits. Some households, especially those who from Guangdong, maintain taboos for blessings in the new year.

Chinese American health practices are also influenced by Chinese popular religions. The use of acupuncture, as well as the exercise of tai-chi and qi gong, is based on principles drawn from Chinese popular religions.

Chinese American Confucianism

Confucianism is a cultural orientation deeply embedded in China and in the lives of some Chinese Americans. As a system of ethical values, it shapes how many Chinese would answer the question about human relations, "To whom do you sacrifice?" Originating in China's pluralistic ethical-spiritual culture, Confucianism joins familial, ethical, spiritual, philosophical, educational, and sometimes political ways of life into a shared Chinese American cultural orientation. Immigrant families most strongly maintain Confucian ethical ways of life, though the U.S.-born may also practice some Confucian values. Common

Confucian practices include filial piety of children toward their parents, reverence for education, benevolence toward others, and veneration of ancestors. Many Chinese Americans also often combine Confucian influences with Buddhism, Daoism, Christianity, and Chinese popular religion.

Since at least the 19th century, Chinese Americans themselves also have debated about whether Confucian ethics were religious or secular. By the early 20th century, China's culture became more secular, so more Chinese Americans treated Confucianism as nonreligious. Chinese American Confucianism also interacted extensively with Christianity. At times, Christian conversion could "liberate" individuals from traditional Confucian family expectations, and at other times Christians fused their faith with Confucian culture. Confucianism also influenced Chinese American civic ideology and rituals within language schools and other community organizations. Further, subtle Confucian influences may contribute to Chinese American worldviews, often present in Chinese American literature.

See also: Chinese Temples in America; Confucianism; Daoism; Guanyin; Taiwanese American Religions

Further Reading

Chen, Carolyn. 2008. *Getting Saved in America: Taiwanese Immigration and Religious Experience.* Princeton, NJ: Princeton University Press.

Jeung, Russell. 2012. "Second-Generation Chinese Americans: The Familism of the Nonreligious." In *Sustaining Faith Traditions: Race, Ethnicity, and Religion Among the Latino and Asian American Second Generation*, edited by Carolyn Chen and Russell Jeung, 197–200. New York: New York University Press.

Tan, Jonathan. 2005. "Asian American Catholics: Diversity Within Diversity." *New Theology Review* 18 (2): 36–47.

United States Conference of Catholic Bishops. 2001. "Asian and Pacific Presence: Harmony in Faith." Accessed July 16, 2015. http://www.usccb.org.

Wang, Yuting, and Fenggang Yang. 2006. "More Than Evangelical and Ethnic: The Ecological Factor in Chinese Conversion to Christianity in the United States." *Sociology of Religion* 67 (2): 179–92.

Yang, Fenggang. 1999. *Chinese Christians in America: Conversion, Assimilation, and Adhesive Identities.* University Park: Penn State University Press.

Russell Jeung and Lisa Rose Mar

TAIWANESE AMERICAN HERITAGE WEEK

In 1992, President George H. W. Bush signed H.R. 5572, declaring May to be Asian Pacific American Heritage Month. On May 2010, the U.S. Congress passed a resolution declaring Taiwanese American Heritage Week, which is celebrated in mid-May. Oregon Democrat David Wu, the first Taiwan-born

U.S. member of Congress in the House of Representative introduced the resolution that was supported by 26 cosponsors. Taiwanese American Heritage Week was created by the Formosan Association for Public Affairs (FAPA) in 1999. During the first Taiwanese American Heritage Week celebration, former U.S. President William Jefferson Clinton stated in a letter addressed to FAPA: "Americans of Taiwan descent can be proud of their roots and of their vital role in the continued growth of our nation. This observance offers us an opportunity to learn more about the outstanding contributions that men and women from Taiwan have made to our nation and the world." While speaking to the House of Representative on his resolution, Representative Wu said, "Taiwanese Americans have greatly enriched the fabric of American society and the mutual understanding between the peoples of the United States and Taiwan. I encourage Congress and the American people to absorb the legacy, culture and achievements of the Taiwanese American community." As a result, cities with sizable Taiwanese American populations such as San Francisco, Orlando, and New York hold organized Taiwanese American Cultural Festivals annually in mid-May.

See also: Taiwan; Taiwanese Food in America; Taiwanese Immigration History

Further Reading

Chee, Maria W. L. 2012. *Taiwanese American Transnational Families: Women and Kin Work*. New York: Routledge.

Ng, Franklin. 1998. *Taiwanese Americans*. Westport, CT: Greenwood Press.

Jonathan H. X. Lee

TAIWANESE AMERICAN RELIGIONS

Although the "Taiwanese American" can be subsumed in the category of "Chinese American," there are various Taiwanese ethnic groups (Hakka, Zhangzhou, Quanzhou, and other Fujianese "Taiwanese") to distinguish from the "mainlanders" who fled to Taiwan in the wake of the Communist victory. Hence, the cultural, social, economic, and political background of the Taiwanese makes their experience different from other Chinese immigrants. Taiwanese American immigrants arrive to the United States armed with increasing technology and wealth; Taiwanese nationals lived across ocean and nation, markedly changing their experience in America. The experience of religion in mainland Chinese versus Taiwanese societies was drastically different; Taiwan fostered religious communities, rituals, and temples, benefiting from the great wealth produced during the 1970s and 1980s. On the other hand, programs of socialist state secularization marked the religious experience in China, which only recently has been able to appear in public as "religion." The majority of Taiwanese

Americans practice Buddhism, Daoism, Confucianism, and folk religious traditions. Some will identity strictly as Buddhist, such as Tzu Chi volunteers, but this does not mean that they will not visit Daoist temples. Confucian morals and ethics are transmitted primarily through the home, expressed in relationships between elder and young. Taiwanese American religious life in contemporary America is unique in that it is transforming due to the forces of globalization and modernization. The shifting composition and trend in Chinese emigration to the United States—in terms of establishing a transnational citizenry and, by extension, a transnational community between Taiwan and the United States—is reflected in the establishment of uniquely global Taiwanese religious communities. These communities have also adapted to American civic culture and society in offering social and medical services to the border communities in which they operate.

Taiwanese Buddhist organizations and temples from Taiwan have enjoyed rapid global growth in recent years. The Hsi Lai Temple, the largest Buddhist monastery in North America, completed in 1988 at a cost of $26 million, is situated on 15 acres of a hillside at Hacienda Heights in Los Angeles, near "Little Taipei," a rapidly growing community populated mostly by Taiwanese Americans. Hsi Lai is a satellite community of the mother temple, Foguangshan "Buddha Light Mountain," located at Kaohsiung (Gaoxiong) in southern Taiwan. Foguangshan was founded by Master Xingyun, who is the 48th patriarch of the Linzhi School of Chan (Zen) Buddhism. Foguangshan has branches across America, including Denver, New York, San Francisco, and San Diego, as well as in other major cities worldwide. Hsi Lai Temple has also established the Hsi Lai University, offering undergraduate and graduate degrees.

Another global Buddhist organization has left an influential footprint in the American religious landscape, the Tzu Chi Compassion Relief Society (Tzu ChiGongdehui), a worldwide network with centers throughout Europe, Latin America, Southeast Asia, and North America. The headquarters of Tzu Chi in the United States is located in Los Angeles, in a predominately Chinese-immigrant community of Monrovia. Tzu Chi has established itself in the new American religious landscape through the promotion of social services, primarily through its free clinic program. Dharma Master Zhengyan, along with a group of 30 followers, founded Tzu Chi in Hualian, Taiwan in 1966. Currently, Tzu Chi is the largest civil organization in Taiwan. In 1993, the Tzu Chi Foundation established its Free Clinic in Alhambra, CA. The clinic is a general health-care facility providing medical assistance to financially disadvantaged residents in Los Angeles. It incorporates traditional Chinese healing with Western medicine and Buddhist philosophies of compassion to serve clients without regard to age, sex, race, class, or religious affiliation.

In addition to these two major global Taiwanese Buddhist communities, there is Zhuangyen Monastery located at Carmel, New York, and serving New

York, New Jersey, and Connecticut. Another major center is the Jade Buddha Temple, associated with the Texas Buddhist Association in Houston, Texas.

Taiwanese Daoist or Buddho-Daoist temples have also appeared in the American religious landscape. The worship of the Empress of the Heaven, Goddess of the Sea, known in Taiwan as "Mazu"—an affectionate kinship term denoting "Granny," otherwise known as Tianhou—is the most popular female object of devotion within Taiwanese communities. The first Tianhou/Mazu temple was, not surprisingly, founded in San Francisco's Chinatown in 1852, as immigrants who landed there immediately wanted to return thanks to her for safely guiding their ships on the arduous three-week journey across the Pacific Ocean. Today, Tianhou/Mazu travels to America by plane. She is no longer solely venerated as a sea goddess: she is protector of women and children, listener of prayers and illnesses, giver of prosperity, and protector of family and community. In 1986, the growing Taiwanese community established the Ma-tsu Temple U.S.A. with links to the mother temple in Beigang, Taiwan. From the beginning, the Ma-tsu Temple U.S.A. has adopted to American civic culture by participating in the annual San Francisco Chinese New Year Parade, which also doubles as the traditional celestial inspection tour to be performed later on her birthday. Taiwanese temples will differ from other Chinese temples found in America in that they will house other deities, popular to people from Taiwan, such as Qingshui Zushi, who is popularly venerated in San-hsia north of Taipei.

The Taiwanese Christian community is also vibrant. Christianity came to Taiwan in the 17th century with the Europeans, the Dutch introducing Protestantism, and the Portuguese introducing Catholicism. Compared to Taiwan, a larger percentage of Taiwanese Americans attend churches in America, perhaps because many of the educated Taiwanese immigrants were Christian even before immigration. In America, Taiwanese Christian communities are places for religious fellowship, as well as Taiwanese solidarity.

Taiwanese Americans will celebrate and observe all the major Chinese festivals and holidays, such as Chinese Lunar New Year, spring and autumn festivals, and the Lantern Festival. During the Chingming Festival (Tomb-Sweeping Day), Taiwanese Americans will travel back to Taiwan to visit the graves and tombs of their ancestors. However, there are some festivals that are unique to Taiwanese religiosity. For example, since the Empress of Heaven is a major cult in Taiwan, her birthday celebrated in March calls for big fanfare in America at local temples where she is enshrined, such as the Ma-tsu Temple U.S.A. Taiwanese Americans, like other Chinese Americans, will also practice *fengshui*, the science of placing things in the home and in business sittings to enhance wealth. Taiwanese Americans will also frequent fortune tellers during Chinese Lunar New Year. Grandmothers and mothers will burn incense in the morning and in the evening at their home altars for the health and well-being of their families.

Taiwanese Americans and their religions, like their identity, is increasingly global and transnational in scope, utilizing the latest technology—the Internet—to establish imagined communities across borders and oceans. Taiwanese Americans find fertile grounds in the pluralistic religious landscape of America to transplant their religions while creatively adapting to their new life.

See also: Taiwan; Taiwanese American Heritage Week; Taiwanese Food in America; Taiwanese Immigration History

Further Reading

Chen, Carolyn. 2009. *Getting Saved in America: Taiwanese Immigration and Religious Experience.* Princeton, NJ: Princeton University Press.

Huang, Chieng-Yu Julia, and Robert P. Weller. 1998. "Merit and Mothering: Women and Social Welfare in Taiwanese Buddhism." *The Journal of Asian Studies* 57 (2): 379–96.

Jonathan H. X. Lee

TAIWANESE FOOD IN AMERICA

Taiwanese have brought their unique Taiwan style cuisine to the United States. The milk tea with tapioca balls (*zhenzhu naicha*) is available at many Chinese restaurants and delis in the United States. Popularly called "bubble tea" or tapioca tea or "boba milk tea" in the United States, zhenzhu naicha was invented in Taiwan in the 1980s. It is a drink that is a blend of ice tea with a flavoring (e.g., taro, coffee, cantaloupe melon). The tapioca balls are chewy and made of starch. These drinks first spread to nearby Asian countries, then to Canada, then to the United States and Europe in the 1990s. It is popular among West Coast college towns (Berkeley, Santa Barbara, Los Angeles) and available at the Quickly Tea Café located in nearly all Chinatown communities across the United States, new and old. It is also found in other Asian ethnic enclaves such as the Vietnamese American Little Saigon, and in Japantowns.

Another notable Taiwanese food that is popular and successful in the United States is Din Tai Fung, a Shanghai-style dumpling restaurant founded in Taipei. In 2000, Guohua "Frank" Yang opened a Din Tai Fung in Arcadia, California. The restaurant became an immediate success because of the notoriety of Din Tai Fung in Taipei, Taiwan. Besides local Taiwanese Americans, other Chinese and non-Asian foodies from all over frequent the restaurant. It serves roughly 2,000 dumplings a day. Among some Taiwanese American patrons, Din Tai Fung in Arcadia reminds them of life and family back in Taiwan. In Taiwan, the restaurant uses bamboo steamers, which was not allowed in Los Angeles because of health issues. The owner, Frank Yang, was concerned that using steel streamers would compromise the flavor profile of his dumplings. Even so, Din Tai Fung is one of the most popular Taiwanese dumpling houses in Southern California.

A local favorite of many Taiwanese is stinky tofu or *chou doufu*. In Taiwan, the smell of stinky tofu can be picked up miles away from a stinky tofu stand or shop. Stinky tofu is a fermented tofu that is appreciated for its pungent stinkiness. As the saying goes, "the stinkier the better." Stinky tofu can be eaten cold, steamed, or stewed but is most commonly deep fried. It is often served with pickled cabbage and red chili paste. Little Taipei commercial areas are known for serving stinky tofu, but many Taiwanese Americans will complain that it is not as stinky as stinky tofu in Taiwan.

See also: Chinese Foods; Taiwan; Taiwanese American Heritage Week; Taiwanese Immigration History

Further Reading

Anderson, Eugene. 1988. *The Food of China*. New Haven, CT: Yale University Press.

Jonathan H. X. Lee

TIANHOU—EMPRESS OF HEAVEN
See: Taiwanese American Religions

TZU CHI FOUNDATION USA
See: Chinese Temples in America; Religions; Taiwanese American Religions

WATCHMAN NEE (1903–1972) AND WITNESS LEE (1905–1997)

Watchman Nee (1903–1972) and Witness Lee (1905–1997) were Chinese Christian leaders whose ministry began in mainland China in the 1920s. They labored closely together for 17 years until they were separated after the Communist takeover in China in 1949. Following their separation, Lee continued Nee's ministry until his own death in 1997.

Watchman Nee (*Ni Tuosheng*), was one of the most influential Christian figures in China in the 20th century, and his influence has continued into the 21st century. He is regarded as one of three of China's mightiest men and one of the 70 greatest Christians in the history of the church. As a Chinese Christian author and church leader, Nee ministered for 30 years, beginning in 1922, and spent the last 20 years of his life in prison. Through the spread of his ministry, churches were established in different cities in China. In 1928 he began to hold Christian conferences and trainings in Shanghai. In 1952 he was imprisoned for his faith and remained in prison until his death in 1972. He is the author of more than 50 Christian books, which have been widely published and translated for readers all over the world, including his most famous work, *The Normal Christian Life*.

Watchman Nee, whose English name was Henry Nee, was born into a Methodist family in Fujian Province, China in 1903. His paternal grandfather studied at the American Congregational College in Fuzhou and served as a Congregationalist minister; his parents were faithful Methodists. Nee was consecrated to the Lord before his birth. Desiring a son, his mother prayed to the Lord, saying, "If I have a boy, I will present him to You." Her prayer was answered. His father later impressed this point upon him, saying, "Before you were born, your mother promised to present you to the Lord."

Nee was exceptionally intelligent. From his entrance into elementary school through his graduation from the Anglican Trinity College in Fuzhou, he ranked first in his class. With many grand dreams and plans for his future, he could have been a great success in the world. In 1920 at the age of 17 and after considerable struggle, he was converted by Dora Yu, a Methodist evangelist. At the moment of his salvation, Nee's plans for his future were entirely abandoned. He felt that he experienced a spiritual revival and testified, "From the evening I was saved, I began to live a new life, for the life of the eternal God had entered into me." Later, when he was called by the Lord to carry out His commission, he adopted the English name *Watchman* and the Chinese name *Tuo-sheng*, which means "the sound of a watchman's rattle," because he considered himself to be a watchman raised up to sound out a warning call in the dark night.

In 1922, at the age of 19, Nee began his literary work in his home city. By 1928 he had completed the final chapters of *The Spiritual Man*. Many of his Bible study practices are included in his book *How to Study the Bible*. He did not attend seminary. He read great works by many Christian authors from throughout the history of the church. He claims his wealth of knowledge concerning God's purpose, Christ, the Spirit, and the church was acquired through studying the Bible, reading spiritual books, and pursuing spiritual matters. The influences on his theological formation came "from the Brethren tradition of Radical Reformation, the Holiness and Keswick revival movements, the Quietist mystics (e.g., Miguel de Molinos, Jeanne Guyon, and Francois Fenelon), and patristic allegorical interpretation of the bible." His development was strengthened by the influence of Jessie Penn-Lewis, Robert Govett, D. M. Panton, G. H. Pember, John Nelson Darby, Theodore Austin-Sparks, Andrew Murray, mystic Madame Guyon, and many others. In 1921, he met the British missionary M. E. Barber, who was a great influence on him. During Nee's college years, Miss Barber, an independent British missionary was his teacher and mentor.

She treated him as a young learner and frequently administered strict discipline. Miss Barber died in 1930 and left all her belongings to Watchman Nee. She introduced him to many Christian writings, among which were the writings of John Nelson Darby and the Plymouth Brethren. Nee adopted Darby's nondenominational view of Christian assembly. Such Christian writings had a profound influence on Nee and his teachings. In the early days of his ministry, he spent a third of his income on his personal needs, a third on helping others, and the remaining third on spiritual books. He acquired a collection of more than 3,000 Christian books, including nearly all the classical Christian writings from the first century onward. Nee received much enlightenment and help from Christian writers related to points of truth. He read widely and was able to glean from his reading the important scriptural truths and principles from Christian writers throughout the centuries and to incorporate these into his Christian life and church experience.

From the very beginning of his ministry, Nee viewed his situations as opportunities to experience the resurrection life of Christ. He taught that believers had not only died with Christ but were also raised with Him (Rom. 6:4–5, 8). For the first 11 years of his ministry, Nee suffered from tuberculosis. In later years he was also stricken with a chronic stomach disorder as well as angina pectoris, a serious heart ailment. He was never cured of the heart disease; thus, he believed that his ministry was sustained by his faith in the resurrection life of Christ and not by physical strength.

Nee's teaching that there should be only one church in a city was often criticized and opposed by the Christian denominations. He was the frequent subject of false rumors. The misrepresentations of his ministry were so strong that he once responded, "The Watchman Nee portrayed by them I would also condemn." In 1924 Nee was "excommunicated" by some of the leaders in his home church because he protested the ordination of a church worker by a denominational mission board. In the midst of such opposition, Nee would not defend himself.

Nee believed that the church as the Body of Christ is the enlargement, expansion, and expression of the resurrected Christ. He identified a universal aspect of the Body of Christ in the book *The Glorious Church* and a local expression of the Body of Christ in the books *The Assembly Life*, *The Normal Christian Church Life*, and *Further Talks on the Church Life*. Nee felt that his ultimate commission was to build up the practical expression of Christ in local churches according to what he understood to be the God-ordained pattern revealed in the New Testament (Acts 11:22; Rom. 16:1; 1 Cor. 1:2; Rev. 2:1, 8, 12, 18; 3:1, 7, 14).

Nee worked with others, including Witness Lee (*Li Changshou*), his close coworker. Lee was raised as a Southern Baptist and was saved in 1925 at the age of 19. In his seeking to know the Bible, Lee came to regard Nee's articles and publications as being the most accurate in presenting the truth contained in the Bible. When he began to correspond with Nee, he was surprised to learn that someone only two years older than himself could teach the Bible so well. In 1932 Lee invited Nee to Chefoo (today's Yantai, Shandong Province), and the two had their first personal contact. During the time they spent together, Lee's relationship with the Lord deepened and grew more intimate. In the same year believers began meeting in Lee's hometown, and by the following year this meeting was thriving. In 1934 they began working together in Shanghai. They labored, suffered, spread their ministry, and raised up local churches. Under Nee's training and fellowship, Lee became the editor in chief of Nee's publication *The Christian* from 1934 to 1940 in the Shanghai Gospel Book Room, and he later oversaw the Taiwan Gospel Book Room.

Uncertain about their ministry in China following the collapse of the nationalist government, Nee sent Lee to Taiwan in 1949, where the church was to flourish and spread around the Pacific Basin. The last contact between Nee and Lee was in Hong Kong in March 1950. At that time, they had extensive fellowship about Nee's return to the mainland. Nee told Lee, "What shall we do with so many churches on the mainland? I must return to take care of them and stand with them for the Lord's testimony."

Following the Communist takeover of China, the government regarded the spreading of local churches and Nee's ministry as a threat. In February 1952 Nee was arrested, and in 1956 he was sentenced to 15 years' imprisonment. During this time, only his wife was allowed to visit him. Though Nee was not allowed to communicate with the outside world, his last eight letters provide a glimpse into his suffering, feeling, and expectation during his confinement. The prison censors did not allow him to mention the name of Jesus in his letters. In his final letter, written on the day of his death, Nee alluded to Philippians 4:4 ("Rejoice in the Lord always") when he wrote: "In my sickness, I still remain joyful at heart." He died in confinement on May 30, 1972. Not one relative or fellow Christian was with him. There was no proper notification of his death and no funeral. He was cremated on June 1, 1972. Because his wife had died six months earlier, her eldest sister was informed of his death and cremation. She retrieved his ashes, which were then buried alongside those of his wife in Guangchao, in the county of Haining, Zhejiang Province. In May 1989 the ashes of Watchman Nee and his wife were transferred to and buried in "The Christian Cemetery" in Xiangshan in the city of Suzhou, Jiangsu Province.

Although Nee was not aware of it, his ministry continued to spread after his imprisonment. Approximately 55 of his books have been published in English. *The Collected Works of Watchman Nee*, a 62-volume set, is published by Living Stream Ministry in Anaheim, California.

By the time Nee was arrested in 1952, approximately 400 local churches had been raised up in China. In addition, over 30 local churches had been raised up in the Philippines, Singapore, Malaysia, Thailand, and Indonesia.

In December 1962, Witness Lee and a few brothers spent 21 days of prayer and began to work in the United States, continuing the teaching and practice he had learned from Nee. In 1965 he founded Stream Publishers. In 1974 he relocated to Anaheim, California, and Stream Publishers became Living Stream Ministry. From 1974 to 1995 Lee conducted live training in which he expounded every book of the Bible from the perspective of the believers' experience of Christ as life for the building up of the Body of Christ. The spoken messages given in those gatherings were edited for print and now comprise over 25,000 pages (1,983 messages) in *The Life-Study of the Bible* collection published by Living Stream Ministry.

During the period in which he conducted the Life-Study trainings, Lee also wrote outlines, footnotes, and cross-references for every book of the *New Testament*. These were later included in *The New Testament: Recovery Version*, published in Chinese in 1987 and in English in 1991. *Holy Bible: Recovery Version* was published in 2003, after Lee's death in 1997, in Anaheim, and it included Old Testament outlines, footnotes, and cross-references compiled from his ministry by the editorial section of LSM.

The ministry of Watchman Nee and Witness Lee continues to gain recognition from Christian leaders in the United States. In July 2009 Representative Christopher H. Smith of New Jersey read into the Congressional Record a statement recognizing "the immense spiritual achievement of Watchman Nee" and Nee's contribution to global Christianity. In September 2010 Hank Hanegraaff of the Christian Research Institute (CRI) devoted two sessions of his *Bible Answer Man* radio program to discussing the impact of Nee's *The Normal Christian Life* with representatives of Living Stream Ministry. Hanegraaff has also voiced public support for the ministry of Witness Lee on the air and in the *Christian Research Journal*, CRI's flagship publication. Other prominent Christian leaders have likewise expressed their appreciation for the ministry of Watchman Nee and Witness Lee and have offered public affirmations of their ministry in print, broadcast, and Internet media.

Today in Taiwan there are more than 200 local Christian churches with 80,000 members. In the United States, there are more than over 250 local churches. Local churches have been planted in Europe including England, France, Russia, Middle East, South Asian, Africa, Australia, and New Zealand, as well as in mainland China.

See also: Chinese Christians in America; First Chinese Baptist Church, San Francisco; Religions

Further Reading

Lee, Witness. 1991. *Watchman Nee—A Seer of the Divine Revelation in the Present Age*. Anaheim, CA: Living Stream Ministry.

Nee, Watchman. 1974. *Watchman Nee's Testimony*, Anaheim, CA: Living Stream Ministry.

Wu, Dongsheng John. 2012. *Understanding Watchman Nee: Spirituality, Knowledge, and Formation*. Eugene, OR: Wipf & Stock.

Wei Shao

YEE, JAMES J. (CA. 1968–)

James J. Yee (ca. 1968–) is a third-generation Chinese American. Yee was born in New Jersey and grew up Lutheran in the small town of Springfield Township. After attending Jonathan Dayton High School, Yee enrolled at West Point and graduated in 1900. In April 1991, Yee converted to Islam and took the

Army Captain James Yee holds his daughter Sarah, 3, as he stands with his wife Huda and listens to reporters' questions prior to his military hearing at Fort Benning in Fort Benning, Georgia, on December 9, 2003. Yee wrote the book *For God and Country*, which offered the public its first glimpse into the West Point graduate's ordeal of being arrested on suspicion of espionage and held in solitary confinement for 76 days. He was later cleared in the investigation, but said his case should be a warning to others. (AP Photo/ Dave Martin)

Arabic name Yusuf Yee. In 1995, Yee went to the Abu Nour Islamic foundation in Damascus, Syria to study the Arabic language and the traditional Islamic sciences with Muslim clerics. While in Syria, Yee met his wife Huda Suboh, a 22-year-old Palestinian. Together, they have one daughter. After four years of intensive study, Yee received a Certificate of Islamic Studies, which is equivalent to a graduate degree. In January 2001, Yee took a position as U.S. Army Muslim Chaplain with an endorsement from the American Muslim Armed Forces and Veterans Affairs Council.

Yee served as a U.S. Army Chaplain for the U.S. prison camp at the Marine base in Guantanamo Bay, Cuba. Guantanamo Bay is a controversial prison for its treatment of detainees designated as "enemy combatants" by the U.S. government. Many critics argue it is a site of torture and goes against the founding principles of American liberty and justice. While ministering at Guantanamo Bay, Chaplain Yee advised camp commanders on Muslim religious practices and beliefs, and objected to the cruel, dehumanizing, and degrading abuses taking place there.

Yee was promoted to captain for outstanding performance, but on September 10, 2013, he was arrested when returning to the States for a two-week leave with his wife and daughter. Yee was arrested by the FBI at the Jacksonville, Florida, Naval Air Station and whisked away in shackles, blackened eye goggles, and soundproof earmuffs to an isolation cell in the U.S. Navy brig in Charleston, South Carolina, where he was kept for 76 days. Yee was charged with five offenses: sedition, spying, espionage, aiding the alleged Taliban and al-Qaeda prisoners, and failure to obey general orders. After months of government investigation, all criminal charges against Yee were dropped. Yee was then reinstated to full duty at Fort Lewis, Washington. Even though he was assured that his record would be wiped clean, Yee sensed his superiors and his fellow chaplains maintained doubts about his loyalty. On January 7, 2005, Yee received an Honorable Discharge from the U.S. Army. Upon separation, Yee received an Army Commendation Medal for "exceptionally meritorious service."

Captain Yee's defense fund has been organized by Justice for New Americans, first formed during the case of Wen Ho Lee, the Taiwan-born Los Alamos National Laboratory scientist who was arrested by the FBI in 1999 and found not guilty after 10 months in solitary confinement and the ruination of his career. The FBI had initially investigated Lee as a potential Chinese spy but never had any evidence to back up the charge.

Yee shared his account of his work at Guantanamo Bay and his arrest and incarnation in a biography entitled *For God and Country: Faith and Patriotism Under Fire* (2005). Yee received the Exceptional Communicator Award from New America Media in January 2006. In June 2006, Yee earned his master's degree in international relations. He now lectures about his harrowing ordeal,

Guantanamo Bay, Islam, Asian American and religious diversity issues, and the challenges of protecting both national security and civil liberties.

See also: Lee, Wen-Ho

Further Reading

"Justice For Yee." 2014. Accessed July 16, 2015. http://www.justiceforyee.com.

Yee, James. 2005. *For God and Country: Faith and Patriotism Under Fire*. New York: PublicAffairs Books.

Jonathan H. X. Lee

PART IV

LITERATURE, THE ARTS, POPULAR CULTURE, AND SPORTS: PEOPLE, MOVEMENTS, AND EXPRESSIONS OF IDENTITY

HISTORICAL OVERVIEW

Among Chinese Americans, the expression of Chinese identity through literature, the arts, popular culture, social movements, and film have been the fuel for many. Historically—and unfortunately, even today—Chinese Americans have been stereotypically represented in entertainment and mainstream popular culture. Chinese American men are represented as being mousy, untrustworthy, weak, and effeminate, whereas, Chinese American women are represented as immoral, hypersexual, and seductive. Moreover, early on, Chinese American actors and actresses were not hired to play Chinese roles; instead, white actors, in "yellow-face" make-up and wearing fake queues and traditional Chinese clothes, were hired. Chinese American cultural producers and their expressions of identity span several decades and continue to flourish as they reimagine and take ownership of their own identity and, by extension, their own portrayal. For instance, *Flower Drum Song* (1961) was made into a motion picture, and although the cast was not all Chinese, it was the first musical and motion picture to be about a Chinese American family in Chinatown. Bruce Lee became a big international *kongfu* superstar, and his fame among Chinese Americans remains strong, in large part because he embodies the image that counters negative Chinese male stereotypes. To combat the negative stereotypes and racialized images of Chinese Americans in entertainment, Chinese American filmmakers, such as Wayne Wang, make their own films. Wang's best known film is the 1993 adaptation of the best-selling novel *The Joy Luck Club* by Chinese American author Amy Tan. Seeking to break racial stereotypes of Chinese American youth as "model minorities," Justin Lin, a Taiwanese American filmmaker, independently funded and directed *Better Luck Tomorrow* (2002), which was very popular among Asian American youths because it portrayed Asian American overachievers who were involved in petty crime and material excess.

A rich body of Chinese American cultural producers includes Maya Ying Lin, architect and sculptor, who is best known for designing the Vietnam Veterans Memorial on the National Mall in Washington, D.C. I. M. Pei is another world-famous Chinese American architect, best known for his sleek, modernist steel-and-glass skyscrapers. Vera Wang is a popular fashion designer based in New York who became popular with her luxurious high-end wedding dresses. In addition, there are a lot of great Chinese American literary works: Jade Snow Wong's *Fifth Chinese Daughter* (1950), Maxine Hong Kingston's *The Woman Warrior: Memoirs of a Girlhood Among Ghosts* (1976), Amy Tan's *The Joy Luck Club* (1989), and Shawn Wong's *Homebase* (1979), just to name a few. All have explored the meaning of being Chinese in America and complex issues of cultural identity and generational conflicts.

Second and subsequent generations of Chinese Americans have less political interest in China, Hong Kong, Taiwan, and Singapore, because they identify themselves as American and consider the United States their homeland. Chinese American integration into American society has faced many barriers. While some Chinese Americans have established themselves and achieved their own versions of the "American dream" of home ownership, a comfortable family life, and financial stability, discrimination has prevented many from achieving personal and career goals. Historically, Chinese immigrants were prevented from owning land and acquiring citizenship through naturalization because they were not "white." While there are no such laws today, there are still unofficial barriers to success. A "bamboo ceiling" prevents many Chinese Americans from reaching upper levels of management and they are underrepresented in certain industries. Portrayals of Chinese Americans in the media have also drawn upon racist and stereotypical caricatures, such as the evil Fu Manchu, domineering Dragon Lady, and submissive Madame Butterfly.

Even though the majority of Chinese Americans are foreign-born first-generation immigrants, the preponderance of them have grown up in two-parent nuclear families, with only a small number raised in extended families, and even fewer in transnationally "split families." Exposed to two different cultures, Chinese and American, Eastern and Western, these Chinese Americans must negotiate their two worlds. Chinese immigrant families play an important role in socializing and transmitting Chinese values, norms, and ideals to the younger generation. In these households, immigrant parents expect their children to behave in accordance with the Confucian virtues that emphasize filial piety, respect for elders, self-discipline, studiousness, sacrifice, and hard work. Many Chinese immigrants attach great significance to their children's educational achievements and expect them to move up socioeconomically through determined efforts, with the hope that their next generation will bring honor to the family and take care of them in old age. Failure to live up to their parents' cultural expectations are attributed to the flaws of American and Western norms and values, in addition to laziness and a lack of self-discipline.

Structural and institutional obstacles also exist in U.S. society that limit the ability of U.S.-born and -raised Chinese American youths from acculturating and assimilating fully into the mainstream American culture. The stereotypical representation of Chinese Americans and other Asian Americans as a racialized "model minority" artificially homogenizes all Asian American communities as being the same, and is employed as a weapon to incite interethnic racial conflicts. The model-minority stereotype unfairly lays blame on African Americans, Latinos, and Native Americans for not succeeding educationally and socioeconomically as well as the Asian Americans because their cultural values do not focus on education. This line of thinking leads to racial divisions and heightens racial conflicts among ethnic minorities in the United States.

With multiple institutional forces operating simultaneously to pull in or push out their second and subsequent generations, Chinese Americans find themselves in the ongoing process of defining who they are. Accordingly, they have developed a continuum of identities, ranging from a complete identification with mainstream European America to an adherence to the panethnic Asian American identity. This process of self-definition is full of conflicts, contradictions, and reconciliations. Navigating two different worlds, Chinese American children and youths have already noted that there is a cultural gap between themselves and their immigrant parents, which has translated into intergenerational conflicts and arguments over some issues, such as consumption behavior, dating, marriage, education, career, and cultural expressions.

The majority of first-generation Chinese American youth will be bilingual, speaking English as well as some dialect of Chinese: Cantonese, Mandarin, or Taiwanese. Language barriers between first- and second-generation Chinese Americans are the primary cause of generational conflicts. Many Chinese American parents, especially recent immigrants, will demand that their children only speak Chinese at home. In addition, children are required to attend Chinese-language schools on the weekends. Second- and third-generation Chinese Americans are more likely to not be able to speak, read, or write Chinese. For some, this may cause an identity crisis.

ADRIAN, NATHAN GHAR JUN (1988-)

Nathan Ghar Jun Adrian, the third child of James and Cecilia Adrian, was born on December 7, 1988, in Bremerton, Washington. His father is a retired nuclear engineer for the Puget Sound Naval Shipyard, and his mother is a nurse for the Bremerton School District. His mother is Chinese and was born and raised in Hong Kong. Following the examples of his older siblings, Adrian began swimming at the age of five. As a senior at Bremerton High School in 2006, he established a high school state record in the 200-meter freestyle of 1:37.17. After graduating from high school, Adrian accepted an athletic scholarship to swim at the University of California in Los Angeles (UCLA). His older sister, Donella, swam at Arizona State University, and his older brother, Justin, swam at the University of Washington.

Although he entered the UCLA in the fall of 2006, Adrian swam unattached to prepare for the 2008 Olympic Games. At the 2007 U.S. Short Course National Championships, he finished third in the 100-meter freestyle and sixth in both the 50- and 200-meter freestyles. Representing the United States at the 2008 World Short Course Championships in Manchester, England, Adrian won gold medals in the 100-meter freestyle and the 4×100-meter freestyle relay and a silver medal in the 4×100-meter medley relay. His winning time of 46.67 in the 100-meter freestyle established the championship meet record, and the U.S.'s winning time of 3:08.44 marked a new world record. Adrian qualified for the 2008 Olympic team in the 4×100-meter freestyle relay by finishing fourth in the 100-meter freestyle at the U.S. Olympic Trials/Long Course National Championships. At the 2008 Olympic Games in Beijing, China, he won a gold medal in the 4×100-meter freestyle relay, swimming in the preliminary heats, in which the United States established a world record of 3:12.23. The United States won the final, improving the world record to 3:08.24.

In 2009, Adrian embarked on becoming one of the most accomplished swimmers in UCLA history. In that year, he won Pacific Athletic Conference (PAC-10) titles in the 50-, 100-, and 200-yard freestyles, and swam on the PAC-10 championship 4×50- and 4×100-yard medley relay teams. In 2010, he swam on the NCAA championship 4×50- and 4×100-yard freestyle relay teams and the 4×100-yard medley relay team. In 2011, UCLA, led by Adrian, defended its NCAA titles in the 4×100 freestyle and the 4×100-yard medley relays, won the 4×50-yard medley relay, and finished second in the 4×50-yard medley relay.

After graduating from UCLA in 2012, Adrian turned his attention to the Olympic Games. At the U.S. Olympic Trials/Long Course National Championships, he finished first in the 100-meter freestyle and third in the 50-meter freestyle. At the 2012 Olympic Games in London, England, Adrian won gold medals in the 100-meter freestyle and the 4×100-meter medley relay and a silver medal in the 4×100-meter freestyle relay. At the U.S. Long Course National Championships in 2013, he won the 50- and 100-meter freestyles. At the World Long Course Championships that year, Adrian finished fourth in the

50-meter freestyle and third in the 100-meter freestyle. He won a silver medal in the 4×100-meter freestyle relay. Adrian won both the 50- and 100-yard freestyles at the U.S. Short Course National Championships. At the 2014 U.S Long Course National Championships, he finished second in the 50-meter freestyle and won the 100-meter freestyle. At the 2014 Pan Pacific Championships in Gold Coast, Australia, Adrian won a gold medal in the 4×100-meter medley relay, silver medals in the 100-meter freestyle and 4×100-meter freestyle relay, and a bronze medal in the 50-meter freestyle.

See also: Chinese Americans in Sports

Further Reading

"Nathan Adrian." n.d. Accessed July 16, 2015. http://www.nathanadrian.com/.
USA Swimming. 2010. "Nathan Adrian." Accessed July 16, 2015. http://www.usaswimming.org/.

Adam R. Hornbuckle

AU-YEUNG, JIN (1982–)
See: Chinese American Hip-Hop

CHANG, APANA (1871–1933)

The acknowledged inspiration for the fictional Asian detective, the "honorable" Charlie Chan, as a Chinese Hawaiian member of the Honolulu Police Department, first as an officer, then as a detective, Apana Chang's feats of bravery as he dealt with the criminal element made him something of a local folk hero during his own lifetime.

Born Chang Ah Ping (Apana being the Hawaiian version of the Chinese Ah Ping) on December 26, 1871, in Waipio, Oahu, Hawai'i, he returned to his father's native village just outside of Guangzhou, China, at the age of three. He returned to Hawai'i at the age of 10 to live with his uncle. Chang began working in 1891 as a *paniolo*, or "Hawaiian cowboy," and customarily carried a bullwhip as a part of his attire. Three years later, he found work with the Hawai'i Humane Society, at the time under the auspices of the police department. In 1898, he moved to Honolulu to join the Honolulu Police Department. Among a force of over 200 men, where the officers were Hawaiian and the chiefs were Caucasian, he stood alone as the only Chinese member of the department. Given his circumstances, he became fluent in spoken Hawaiian and knew Hawaiian Pidgin and Chinese as well. However, he never learned to read. He was, predictably, assigned to patrol "Blood Town" and "Hell's Half Acre," the most notorious areas of Chinatown, and eventually found himself working on the most dangerous of cases involving gambling and smuggling of opium. In place of a gun, he continued to carry his bullwhip.

Opium pipes valued at several thousand dollars are burned at a public dumping ground under the supervision of (left to right) the governor's secretary, John Stone; ex-sheriff Charles H. Rose; Acting Governor Raymond C. Brown; former captain of detectives Arthur McDuffie; and Detective Chang Apana in Honolulu, O'ahu, Hawai'i. The pipe burning was the result of a housecleaning conducted at police headquarters at the beginning of a new administration. Almost 1,000 pipes were burned, all of which had accumulated in the evidence room over six years. Among the lot were opium burners valued at $100 each, which were richly carved and inlaid with mother of pearl. Many were ordinary bamboo variety, but all of them showed evidence of use when seized by the police. (Underwood & Underwood/Corbis)

From 1916 onward, Chang was regularly assigned to investigate cases of opium-smuggling and illegal gambling. Due in part to his fluency in several languages, wide network of informants, and shrewd and meticulous investigative style, he was successful in solving many such cases, so much so that his career quickly became the stuff of local legend. Whether he was being attacked by a sword-wielding leper, taking his "lumps" as he was thrown from a second-story window by drug fiends—only to land, in characteristic fashion, on his feet—or marching some 70 gamblers down the dark streets and parading them, single file, into the jailhouse, tales of his prowess and escapades grew almost nightly. By the time Earl Derr Biggers arrived in Hawai'i on vacation in 1919, Chang had become the talk of the town, but it was not until 1924, while reading from among the Honolulu newspapers in the New York City Library, that Biggers came across these larger-than-life exploits. The New York writer created a new character based on Chang and made him the basis for "Enter Charlie Chan," the title given to Chapter 7 of The House Without a Key. This novel was published serially in the Saturday Evening Post in 1925. Immensely popular with the

American reading public, the distinctive Chan would become central to Biggers's later novels. In the summer of 1928, Chang encountered the author at the Royal Hawaiian Hotel in the briefest of meetings; in characteristic fashion, he never related details of the event to others. Whereas people on the streets had already taken to addressing Chang as Charlie Chan, it would take the release of several more financially lucrative novels before the author would publicly acknowledge that Chang had been his sole inspiration—tellingly so—in a letter to the *Honolulu Advertiser* dated June 28, 1932. So popular was the fictional character that Charlie Chan soon appeared on the Hollywood silver screen, where the awkwardly effeminate and circumspect caricature commanded huge audiences in the 1930s. Over time, these same images gained notoriety as they were recognized as perpetuating the very anti-Asian racism so prevalent across white America.

Compounding the obvious overt racism, in spite of there being many professional and widely acclaimed Asian actors, the redoubtable detective was almost exclusively portrayed by their Caucasian counterparts. Warner Oland held the role in *Charlie Chan Carries On* (1931) through *Charlie Chan at Monte Carlo* (1937). Sidney Toler stepped into the role in *Charlie Chan in Honolulu* (1938) and remained there at least through *Shadows Over Chinatown* (1946). Roland Winters assumed the role in *Sky Dragon* (1949), and Peter Ustinov took his place in *Charlie Chan and the Dragon Queen* (1981).

On December 8, 1933, after having sustained a serious injury to his left leg, Chang contracted gangrene and died. He was buried in the Mānoa Chinese Cemetery in Honolulu. Over 70 years later, in May 2009, the short film *The Legend of Chang Apana*, directed by Jon Brekke and Michael Wurth, debuted at the Honolulu International Film Festival. Reflecting an increased social awareness of issues of representation and racist subtexts behind previous depictions, Asian American actor Cary Hiroyuki Tagawa led the cast as the real-life detective.

See also: Chinese American Literature; Chinese in Hawai'i; Fu Manchu and Charlie Chan

Further Reading

Huang, Yunte. 2010. *Charlie Chan: The Untold Story of the Honorable Detective and His Rendezvous with American History*. New York: W. W. Norton.

Kim, Hyung-chan, ed. 1999. "Chang Apana." In *Distinguished Asian Americans: A Biographical Dictionary*, 18–20. Westport, CT: Greenwood Press.

James A. Wren

CHANG, MICHAEL TE-PEI (1972–)

Michael Te-Pei Chang was born February 22, 1972, in Hoboken, New Jersey, the second of two sons of Joe and Betty (née Tung) Chang, both chemists, who had emigrated from Taiwan in 1959 and 1966, respectively. His father, born in Chaozhou, China, had moved to Taiwan at age seven; his mother was born in Delhi, India, where her father, Michael Tung, served as a diplomat of the Republic of China.

Joe Chang introduced Michael and his brother Carl to tennis after the Chang family moved to St. Paul, Minnesota. As the boys' skills improved, the Changs moved to California, first Placentia, and then Encinitas, to increase the tennis opportunities for their sons. In 1984, at the age of 12, Michael won his first national title, the United States Tennis Association (USTA) Junior Hard Court singles. Next year, he won the Fiesta Bowl Singles title for 16-year-olds. In 1987, Chang won the USTA Boys Hard Court Singles and the Boys Nationals Single titles. At the U.S. Open that year, he became the youngest player, at the age of 15, to win a main draw match when he defeated Paul McNamee of Australia in four sets in the first round. Later that year, Chang become the youngest player to reach the semifinals of a major tournament, in Scottsdale, Arizona. After ranking 163rd as an amateur in 1987, he obtained a General Educational Development (GED) diploma and dropped out of 10th grade at San Dieguito High School in Encinitas to pursue a professional tennis career.

From 1988 to 1991, Chang showed great promise as a professional tennis player. He won 153 of 224 singles matches, including five victories and four runner-up finishes in Association of Tennis Professional (ATP) tournaments. At the age of 17, Chang became the youngest male player to win a Grand Slam tournament by defeating Stefan Edberg of Sweden in five sets to win the French Open in 1989. En route to the final, he defeated Ivan Lendl, of then Czechoslovakia, in five sets in the fourth round. Lendl had won the men's singles title in the French Open in 1984, 1986, and 1987. Chang's play at the French Open moved him to number five in the men's singles rankings. In the 1990 Davis Cup final, Chang contributed to the U.S.'s 3-2 victory over Australia by defeating Darren Cahill in three sets in the second singles match of the tournament.

In 1992, Chang began a six-year interval of consecutive top-10 rankings. Ranked sixth in 1992, he reached the finals of five ATP tournaments, winning three. A semifinalist the U.S. Open in 1992, Chang defeated Alberto Mancini of Argentina in four sets in the first round but lost to Jaime Oncins of Brazil in four sets in the second round of the Olympic Games that year. Ranked as high as eighth in 1993, he won five and finished second in ATP competition, and advanced to the quarterfinals of the U.S. Open. The following year, Chang, who ranked sixth, reached the finals of nine ATP tournaments, winning six, and advanced to the quarterfinals of Wimbledon, his best performance in that Grand Slam event. Ranked fifth in 1995, he won four of six ATP tournaments, reached the quarterfinals of the U.S. Open and the semifinals of Australian Open, and advanced to the finals of the French Open, losing to Thomas Muster of Austria in three sets.

Chang enjoyed his best years as a professional in 1996 and 1997. He won three of six ATP tournaments in 1996 and reached the finals of the Australian Open but lost to Boris Becker of Germany in four sets. He passed on competing in the 1996 Olympic Games to concentrate on the U.S. Open, where he lost to Pete Sampras in the final in three sets. In 1996, he ranked as high number two among men's singles players. Undefeated in five ATP tournaments in 1997, he reached the semifinals of the Australian Open and the U.S. Open and ranked as high as third among men's singles performers.

After 1997, Chang declined as a force in men's tennis. From 1998 to 2000, he advanced to the finals of six ATP tournaments, winning three. In 1999, Chang began to venture into other vocations, including the establishing the Chang Family Foundation, which integrates tennis, family, and Christian faith. He retired from professional tennis in 2003, after having won 662 matches and losing 312 and earning $19,145,632. Married to Amber Liu, a professional tennis player whom he once coached, since October 2008, Chang is the father of two daughters, Lani and Maile. He was inducted into the International Tennis Hall of Fame in 2008.

See also: Chinese Americans in Sports

Further Reading

The Chang Family Foundation. 2015. Accessed July 16, 2015. http://mchang.com/.

Chang, Michael, and Mike Yorkey. 2008. *Holding Serve: Persevering On and Off the Court.* Nashville, TN: Thomas Nelson.

Adam R. Hornbuckle

CHIN, FRANK JIANXIU (1940–)

Widely heralded American author, musician, and playwright, Frank Jianxiu Chin first gained national recognition as a pioneer in Asian American theatre. Shortly thereafter, the release of his anthology, *Aiiieeeee! An Anthology of Asian-American Writers* (1974, coedited with Jeffrey Paul Chan, Lawson Fusao Inada, and Shawn Wong), served to bring the field of Asian American studies to the fore. Additionally, since that time, Chin has remained active with those issues he feels most relevant to the field, framed as they are in his often-outspoken criticism of Asian American female writers and the egregious treatment experienced by Japanese Americans who had dared resist conscription during World War II. He is widely seen as the most influential Asian American dramatist and novelist, and his unabashed depictions of Asian American stereotypes alongside his iterations of traditional Chinese folklore, as well as his redoubtable master of the essay, have made him the most significant voice for Asian American social activism to this day.

Chin was born in Berkeley, California, on February 25, 1940, but remained until the age of six under the care of a retired vaudeville couple in Placerville, California. At that time, his mother brought him back to the San Francisco Bay Area, and thereafter he grew up in Oakland Chinatown. He attended the University of California, Berkeley, and graduated from UC Santa Barbara in 1965. With *The Chickencoop Chinaman* (1971), be became the first Asian American playwright produced in New York City on a mainstream stage. Thereafter, in 1973, he founded the Asian American Theatre Workshop that evolved into the Asian American Theater Company (AATC). He followed his initial success with *The Year of the Dragon* in 1974. An adaptation starring George Takei was first televised a year later to critical acclaim as part of the PBS Great Performances series.

Chin later turned his attentions to the larger-than-life myths repeated time and again among members of the Chinese diaspora, especially in his *The Chinaman Pacific and Frisco R.R. Co.* (1988), *Donald Duk* (1991), *Gunga Din Highway* (1994), and *Bulletproof Buddhists* (1998). His newest work, *The Confessions of a Number One Son: The Great Chinese American Novel*, scheduled for release in March 2015, represents a "forgotten" novel written as a sequel to *The Chickencoop Chinaman*. Critics are already suggesting that, had it been published in the 1970s as originally intended, it would have redefined changed the face of Asian American literature. Nonetheless, it does hold its own as perhaps the funniest and most powerful—certainly most poignant—work to date.

During the same period, his role as a social actionist became far more apparent. Consider, for example, the biting criticism he levels in his 1978 discussion with Jeff Chan, Al Wong, and Sandra Lee on *Flower Drum Song*. Or later, he pens *Born in the USA: A Story of Japanese America, 1889–1947* (2002), a novel that grew out of his long-time work with the Japanese American community. In Jeff Adachi's documentary, *The Slanted Screen* (2006), he draws public attention to the sad state of current visual and literary representations given currency in Hollywood of Asians in general and Asian American men in particular. Since 2012, he has been consistent with his criticism of George Takei's *Allegiance*, in large part for what he sees as an unmistakable erasure of the very sense of race and cultural difference defining Asian American experiences. But his often-outspoken commentary has not gone without notice. Certainly, he has remained quite vocal in his accusations against other Asian American writers, most notably Maxine Hong Kingston, Amy Tan, and David Henry Hwang, for what he sees as their complicity in perpetuating racial stereotypes and misrepresentations as well as gross inaccuracies in recalling details of the Chinese cultural heritage.

In 1989, Chin received an American Book Award and a Lifetime Achievement Award in 2000, and became the subject of the 2005 biographical documentary, *What's Wrong with Frank Chin*, directed by Curtis Choy. The Frank Chin Papers are now available in the California Ethnic and Multicultural Archives, as a part of then Special Collections of the Library of University of California, Santa Barbara.

Chin currently resides in Los Angeles, California, where he remains an active voice striving toward the accurate representation of gender and ethnicity of nonwhite voices in the American literary scene.

See also: Chinese American Literature

Further Reading

Kim, Daniel Y. 2005. *Writing Manhood in Black and Yellow: Ralph Ellison, Frank Chin, and the Literary Politics of Identity.* Palo Alto, CA: Stanford University Press.

Kim, Elaine H. 1978. "Frank Chin: The Chinatown Cowboy and His Backtalk." *Midwest Quarterly: A Journal of Contemporary Thought* 20: 78–91.

James A. Wren

CHINESE AMERICAN BASEBALL

Chinese Americans have used baseball as a means of developing and maintaining a sense of community. Through baseball, they have crossed often-treacherous cultural boundaries to play with and against people of varied racial and ethnic identities. Some American ballplayers of Chinese ancestry have competed effectively at the highest levels of professional baseball.

In the late 1800s, "all-Chinese" teams surfaced occasionally on the U.S. mainland. It is hard to gauge whether such teams were organized to allow Chinese-immigrant young men a chance to bond together in a country that supported Chinese exclusion or whether they were assembled by white entrepreneurs hoping to profit from the supposed novelty of Chinese playing the "American National Pastime." However, by the early 20th century, legitimate community teams emerged in Chicago and the San Francisco Bay Area. In Los Angeles, a Chinese American team, often known as the Los Angeles Chinese, played some of the best semiprofessional teams in the region during the 1920s. Likewise, in the 1930s, Oakland's Wa Sung team frequently dominated its semiprofessional competition. After World War II, Chinese American teams showed up briefly in San Francisco and Oakland.

Meanwhile, Honolulu had become a hotbed of Chinese American community baseball. In the early 1900s, the Chinese Athletic Club (CAC) team and the Chinese Alohas called on the services of some of the best ballplayers in the city. In 1912, the CAC, with the financial help of Chinatown merchants and *haole* boosters anxious to promote Honolulu on the mainland, assembled an "all-Chinese" team that journeyed across the Pacific and engaged in over 100 games against college, community, semiprofessional, and professional teams. In 1914, the Chinese Athletic Union (CAU) established a team that would, in

New York Mets pitcher Ron Darling shows his winning form during a St. Louis Cardinals-New York Mets baseball game in St. Louis on June 14, 1984. Darling shut out the Cardinals by the score of 6-0, recording his first career shut out. (AP Photo)

1915, effectively represent Hawai'i in the Far Eastern Games as well as compete in the Philippines. For several decades thereafter Hawaiian Chinese organized their own leagues while supporting a team called the Chinese Tigers that competed in the Hawai'i Baseball League.

Despite its troubling relationship with institutionalized discrimination in the United States, baseball has drawn people across often dangerously shifting cultural borderlands. As it turned out, Hawai'i proved more receptive than the mainland to constructing flexible cultural boundaries on its many baseball diamonds. One important reason was demographics. Because haoles were a numerical minority on the islands, it was foolish for white baseball coaches to cut talented Asian Hawaiian athletes if they wished to win. Thus, superb Hawaiian Chinese ballplayers of the early 20th century, such as En Sue Pung, Lai Tin, and Vernon Ayau, not only played for Chinese nines but also teams populated by non-Chinese. Lang Akana, who claimed Chinese and indigenous Hawaiian ancestry, competed for several diverse Hawaiian teams from the 1900s to the 1920s. When Akana's playing career ended, he managed the "Hawai'is" in the Hawai'i Baseball League—a team supposedly comprising ballplayers of indigenous Hawaiian descent.

The U.S. mainland, at the same time, witnessed fewer such interactions, but they were not unknown or necessarily unwelcomed. In the 1910s, the University of Chicago fielded a Hawaiian Chinese named William Achi, and Lehigh University suited up first baseman Al Yap, another Hawaiian who would play semiprofessional baseball in and around Philadelphia during the late 1910s and early 1920s. Lee Gum Hong, a hard-throwing pitcher, competed for Oakland High School in the 1920s. Al Wong, who teamed with Lee Gum Hong on the Wa Sung nine, stood out on predominantly European American semipro teams in the San Francisco Bay Area.

Indeed, semiprofessional baseball on the early-20th-century mainland deserves special attention. Frequently just as talented as minor league and organized baseball teams, the more famous semipro teams offered athletes opportunities to compete against top-notch white, Latino, and African American ballplayers. At the same time, these semipros could find in baseball the means to supplement their incomes as factory workers, office clerks, or shopkeepers.

The aforementioned Al Yap was one of these ballplayers. Yap arrived on the mainland in 1915 as a member of the then-famous and often misnamed "Chinese University of Hawai'i" baseball team originally representing the CAC and that barnstormed the mainland from 1912 to 1916. A scion of a prominent Hawaiian Chinese family, Yap decided to attend Lehigh rather than return to the islands after the 1915 tour ended. He then spent several years as an itinerant amateur and semiprofessional baseball in eastern Pennsylvania. Within a year, Yap was joined on the East Coast by "Chinese University of Hawai'i" teammates Lai Tin, Vernon Ayau, Apau Kau, Andy Yim (who was really a Japanese Hawaiian named Andy Yamashiro), and part-Hawaiian Fred Markham. All of these young men prospered on semipro teams on the East Coast. Lai Tin, later known as Buck Lai, particularly stood out as a semiprofessional luminary for several East Coast teams, most prominently the famed Brooklyn Bushwicks.

Starting out as an ostensibly amateur traveling team, the "Chinese University of Hawai'i" eventually blurred whatever distinctions that might have existed between amateur, semiprofessional, and professional. Sharing the gate receipts, the Hawaiians played—and usually won—well over 100 games a year against college, commercial, semiprofessional, and professional teams. In 1912, the team was entirely composed of young men of Chinese ancestry. In 1913, Fred Markham joined the team most appropriately described as the Travelers. From 1914 through 1916, more non-Hawaiian Chinese joined the club, including Hawaiian Japanese such as Yamashiro and the talented Moriyama brothers. As the Travelers came to have fewer Chinese players, Hawai'i's Chinese community distanced itself from them and assembled the aforementioned CAU nine.

Several of these Hawaiian ballplayers attracted interest from mainland professional teams. Outfielder Lang Akana was signed by the Pacific Coast League's (PCL) Portland Beavers for the 1915 season, but a threatened boycott by white

PCL players moved the team owner to release the outfielder. Lai Tin was inked as well by the Chicago White Sox of the American League. At this time, he, too, remained outside of organized baseball's fold, either because, according to the press, he was not good enough for the major leagues or he did not want to play with a team of *haoles*.

However, a few of the Travelers did make it into organized baseball. Vernon Ayau, a deft shortstop, played in the Pacific Northwest League in 1917, and Andy Yamashiro (curiously competing as Andy Yim) did fine as an outfielder in the Blue Ridge League. Getting another chance to play organized baseball in 1918, Buck Lai started as a third baseman for the Bridgeport Americans of the Eastern League after the Philadelphia Phillies cut him. Lai would have one more shot at the big leagues when the New York Giants invited him to camp in 1928. Once again, Lai was not seen as big league material.

Apau Kau was an often dominating pitcher for the Travelers. Organized baseball teams expressed interest in obtaining his talents. As mentioned earlier, he did decide to linger on the East Coast after the last trek of the Travelers in 1916. He pitched semiprofessionally for a Philadelphia department store in 1917 and subsequently joined the U.S. military when World War I flared for Americans. In the fall of 1918, Sergeant Apau Kau lost his life on a European battlefield.

Other ballplayers of Chinese descent would find their way into organized baseball. Pitcher Lee Gum Hong appeared for the PCL's Oakland Oaks in 1932, seemingly more out of an effort to lure fans to watch a mediocre team in the throes of the Great Depression. In the 1940s, George Ho was a peripatetic minor leaguer from New York City. More recently, Ray Chang has played minor league baseball for organizations such as the Boston Red Sox and Pittsburgh Pirates. Significantly, since his parents were born in China, he competed for China in the World Baseball Championship in 2009.

Pitcher Ron Darling remains the most famous ballplayer of Chinese ancestry. The Hawaiian-born Darling became a stalwart member of the New York Mets' pitching staff in the 1980s, winning 17 games for the team in 1988. Darling subsequently took the mound for the Toronto Blue Jays and the Oakland Athletics. He presently does baseball commentary for TBS and the Mets.

Encountering racial and gender barriers, Kim Ng has served as assistant general manager for both the New York Yankees and the Los Angeles Dodgers. In the process, the former college softball player experienced ethnic taunts from a member of the New York Mets' front office. Moreover, she has been interviewed but not yet hired for general manager positions. Even the Dodgers passed over her and hired an assistant general manager from the rival San Francisco Giants.

As Ng's career suggests, the Chinese American experience with baseball has been ambivalent. Undoubtedly, baseball has offered them joy and chances to represent their communities, cross-cultural borders, and achieve fame and, in

Darling's case, a relative fortune. But it would be understandable to wonder if the sport could not have been more generous to the likes of Lang Akana, Buck Lai, and Kim Ng.

See also: Adrian, Nathan Ghar Jun; Chang, Michael Te-Pei; Chinese Americans in Sports; Chinese Martial Arts; Chow, Norm Yew Heen; Kwan, Michelle Wing Shan

Further Reading

Franks, Joel S. 2002. *Hawaiian Sports in the Twentieth Century.* Lewiston, NY: Edwin Mellen Press.

Franks, Joel S. 2008. *Asian Pacific Americans and Baseball: A History.* Jefferson, NC: McFarland.

Franks, Joel S. 2008. "From Honolulu to Brooklyn: Some of the Journeys of the Hawaiian Travelers." *Base Ball: A Journal of the Early Game* 2 (1): 5–16.

Ma, Eve Armentrout, and Jeong Hui Ma. 1982. *The Chinese of Oakland: Unsung Builders.* Oakland, CA: Oakland Chinese Research Committee.

Nagata, Yoichi. 1992. "The First All-Asian Pitching Duel in Organized Baseball." *Baseball Research Journal* (21): 13–14.

"Ray Chang." 2012. Baseball Cube. Accessed October 26, 2015. http://www.thebase ballcube.com/players/C/ray-chang.shtml.

"Ron Darling." 2012. Baseball-Reference.com. Accessed October 26. http://www.baseball -reference.com/players/d/darliro01.shtml.

Yee, George, and Elise Yee. 1986. "The 1927 Chinese Ball Team." *Gam Saan Journal* 10

Zieff, Susan G. 2000. "From Badminton to the Bolero: Sport and Recreation in San Francisco's Chinatown, 1895–1950." *Journal of Sport History* 27 (1): 1–29.

Joel S. Franks

CHINESE AMERICAN HIP-HOP

Chinese American hip-hop is part of Asian American hip-hop and is a cultural form that gives voice to Asian American youth expressions. Since the early development of Asian American hip-hop, Asian Americans across ethnicities have often collaborated in the making of hip-hop music. Their collaborations, practices, and ideals form a panethnic identity and political alliance that empowers Asian Americans. Even if a group is composed of a single ethnicity or a single rapper, it often identifies as being "Asian American" for the collective identity that is more powerful. Before the development of Asian American hip-hop, folk-style music served as political forum during the Asian American Movement.

Inspired by movements such as the 1960s Black Power Movement and the emergence of politicized rap groups like Public Enemy and Boogie Down Productions in the 1980s, Asian American college students began to form groups like Seoul Brothers (Korean) from the University of Washington, Asiatic

Apostles (Chinese and Filipino) from the University of California Davis, Yellow Peril (Chinese) from Rutgers University, Fists of Fury (Korean) from San Francisco, and Art Hirahara (Japanese) from Oberlin College in the early 1990s. These groups were social activists who turned to hip-hop as a means to reach the public with their social criticism, and their songs' content was highly politicized. These groups rapped about their experiences of being Asian Americans. They attacked stereotypes and white supremacy and encouraged dialogues on social issues such as interracial tensions, interracial dating, anti-Asian discrimination, misogyny and sexism, and black-Korean tensions in the inner city. Essentially, the adaptation of black culture is political as it goes against assimilation into the mainstream white culture. While using hip-hop as their tool for political expressions, these groups highlighted their racial identity and favored the rhetoric of hip-hop over its aesthetics and musical craft. They performed mostly at Asian American collegiate and community events and targeted Asian Americans as their main audiences. The fact that these early-1990s' Asian American rappers sought to dialogue specifically (though not necessarily solely) with Asian American listeners hindered their appeal and potential to succeed in the competitive music industry. Since there is no commercial viability and financial sustainability in making rapping a careers, very few of these rappers continue their rapping careers after their college years.

In the mid-1990s, more groups, such as the Los Angeles's Key Kool (Japanese), Philadelphia's Mountain Brothers (Chinese), Chicago's duo Pacifics (Filipino), Orlando's Southstar (Chinese/Filipino), and the San Francisco's Lyric Born (Japanese), were formed. In contrast to the earlier wave of Asian American rappers, these artists were more "underground" and believed that race could be a commercial liability. They downplayed their racial pride and focused more on race-neutral values such as "skills," "talent," "aesthetics," and "personal expressions" as being the marker of authenticity rather than racial origin. They believed that racial authenticity in hip-hop is a factor of how listeners actually "hear" the music, as listeners are most likely to be biased if they knew the artists are not African Americans, despite the fact that African American hip-hop artists have been outspoken about their racial pride. By downplaying their racial identities, these artists tried to attract a wider and multiethnic audience in an attempt to succeed in the record industry.

By the late 1990s, groups like "AZNs" appeared that are active almost exclusively on the Internet. They began with putting new lyrics on existing popular hip-hop songs, expressing racial pride and superiority. One example is their song "Got Rice?" Other groups (not Internet exclusive) that were also active around this time were Neptunes' Chad Hugo (Filipino), Linkin's Park Mike Shinoda (Japanese), and the Black Eyed Peas' Allan Pineda (a.k.a. Apl.de.ap) (Filipino).

The best-known Asian American rapper is probably Jin. Performing with the stage name MC Jin, Jin (Jin Au-Yeung) is a Chinese American who grew up in

Miami and later relocated to Flushing, New York. In 2002 he became one of the only two rappers in history to win seven consecutive weekly freestyle rap battles on the BET (Black Entertainment Television) network's program *106 & Park* and was inducted to the Freestyle Friday Hall of Fame for his victories. At the same year, he became the first Asian American rapper to sign with a major record label—Ruff Ryders (part of Virgin Records)—and released his debut album, *The Rest Is History*, in 2004. Unlike some of the earlier "underground" Asian American rap groups, Jin made race as prominent as possible in order to deny his potential detractors from raising it as an issue against him. For example, his first single, "Learn Chinese," opens with Jin proclaiming, "Yeah, I'm Chinese. And what?" His strategy was to draw attention to his race in an attempt to get his potential audience to look past his race and focus on his talent since he knew that his audience could not ignore his racial difference in the black hip-hop world.

The visibility of Jin brought public attention to the authenticity and owner-ship of "black" hip-hop. Questions of cultural exploitation and appropriation of hip-hop are raised as critics heavily criticized Asian American rappers' practices and adaptation of hip-hop. It is difficult for the black hip-hop world to accept Asian American hip-hop because they do not identify themselves with the also-marginalized Asian Americans. They do not think Asian Americans under-stand the historical struggles and disadvantages that African Americans have suffered, even though Asian Americans think they share commonalities in his-torical struggles and can identify and understand each other. Race is one issue that Jin can never escape, and he has noted that it is a lose-lose situation for him. As he describes in 2004, if he talks about being Asian, the critics would say he is exploiting his background to get attention, and if he doesn't, they say, "He thinks he's black." Moreover, like many Asian American hip-hop groups/artists that preceded him, Jin's most powerful antagonists are hip-hop consum-ers and the record executives who put marketability and commercial viability as priority above talent. Nonblack rappers, especially Asian Americans, face a racial dilemma since the racial difference does not meet the standard of black authenticity held by rap fans and music executives alike. Jin's debut album, *The Rest Is History*, received a modest sale of 100,000 units, and shortly after he announced his retirement in 2005. Despite the retirement announcement, Jin appeared to have come back and is currently active in hip-hop, as he continues to produce rap albums and collaborates with several other Asian and Asian American rap artists.

In late 2000s, newer groups like Far East Movement (Korean and Chinese/Japanese) started to receive success with their works. Far East Movement began by playing in small Los Angeles-area venues and using social networking web-site MySpace to cultivate a committed local fan base. In 2010, Far East Move-ment signed a record deal with Cherrytree Records, a major record label, and went on to become the first Asian American rap group to score a number one hit on the *Billboard* charts with their single, "Like a G6" (2010). Other noteworthy groups are Dumbfoundead (Korean), Bambu (Filipino), Roscoe Umali (Filipino), Blue Scholars (Filipino), Chan aka Snacky Chan (Korean), and Model Minority (Chinese). Although the themes of their songs vary from group to group, they cover topics such as race, stereotypes, politics, global issues, social commentaries, lifestyles of young Asian Americans, academic pressure from parents, parents' perception of highbrow or lowbrow culture, Asian food and culture, and romance.

See also: Chinese American Jazz

Further Reading

Chang, Jeff. 2005. *Can't Stop, Won't Stop: A History of the Hip Hop Generation*. New York, Picador.

Wang, Oliver. 2006. "These Are the Breaks: Hip-Hop and AfroAsian Cultural (Dis) Connections." In *AfroAsian Encounters: Culture, History, Politics*, edited by Heike Raphael-Hernandez and Shannon Steen, 146–164. New York: New York University Press.

May May Chiang

CHINESE AMERICAN JAZZ

Chinese American jazz is part of Asian American jazz. Since the early 1980s, Asian American musicians and social activists across ethnicities have collaborated in the making of jazz music that highlights racial identity and political expressions. The demographic of the first wave of Asian American jazz musicians were mainly Chinese and Japanese Americans born in the 1950s and they frequently incorporated Asian music elements with jazz. Although Chinese/ Asian American jazz is best known for its activism starting in the 1980s, earlier attempts to use Chinese musical instruments in a jazz band can be traced back to the 1920s, when the "Honorable Wu" (Harry Haw) directed his Chinese Showboat Revue in their shows. Then during the 1930s swing era, a Chinese American saxophonist, Willie Mae Wong, participated in the all-female jazz band International Sweethearts of Rhythm. Around the same time, The Chinatown Knights and the Cathayans in Watsonville were two dance orchestras playing jazz and swing compositions in San Francisco's Chinatown. Besides these early activities in the United States, expatriate Asian Americans were also involved with jazz in Shanghai (known as the "Asian jazz Mecca" in the 1930s) and Tokyo during the 1920s and 1930s.

The development of Asian American jazz coincided with the Asian American movement of the 1970s and 1980s that sought an official apology and financial compensation for the Japanese Americans who suffered preemptive incarceration during World War II. The issue of redress as well as cases of anti-Asian violence such as the Vincent Chin incident in 1982 provoked Asian American activists and encouraged them to form a variety of coalitions. Consequently, Asian American jazz musicians and activists formed one of those groups. The musicians and activists during this time include Anthony Brown, Glenn Horiuchi, Fred Ho, Jason Kao Hwang, Mark Izu, Jon Jang, Miya Masaoka, and Francis Wong. They saw their work as an integral part of the growing Asian American movement, and many early performances and recordings, such as Horiuchi's *Manzanar Voices* (1989), Ho's *Tomorrow Is Now!* (1985), and Jang's *Are You Chinese or Charlie Chan?* (1983), addressed the issues raised in the movement.

Asian American jazz musicians view jazz as an oppositional musical expression distinguished from white mainstream culture and a cultural identity that could potentially empower them. American-born Asian musicians identify with black culture and jazz because of the similar marginalized history, experience, and struggles. Moreover, they are attracted to the characteristic of freedom in jazz. Inspired by the black liberation movement in the 1960s, many Asian American jazz musicians studied texts such as *The Autobiography of Malcolm X* and the poetry and essays of Amiri Baraka, as well as listening closely to "freedom jazz" albums such as Max Roach and Abbey Lincoln's *We Insist! Freedom Now Suite* (1960). They frequently collaborated with African American musicians and drew inspirations from avant-garde jazz musicians like John Coltrane. The experimentalism and freedom implicit in avant-garde jazz attracted Asian American jazz musicians and provided them an ideal outlet for forging and improvising new musical identities. By creating new forms of expression, Asian American musicians hoped to open a new front for the Asian American movement and help their fellow Asian Americans move beyond demeaning stereotypes at the margins of U.S. society. In a way, jazz has provided Asian American musicians the opportunity to become part of the American social fabric.

Nevertheless, Asian American jazz musicians encountered many challenges in jazz due to their racial identities, preference in avant-garde jazz, and political agenda. First, the racial identities of Asian Americans have posited them as "foreigners" in the American culture as well as in the jazz world. For example, in one of the jazz discourses, jazz scholar Scott DeVeaux describes jazz as an exemplar of racial harmony, a rare and privileged arena, in which black and white musicians compete and cooperate in an atmosphere of mutual respect with the support of a multiracial audience. Asian Americans, being neither black nor white, are excluded from such a jazz discourse. DeVeaux's comment is just one example that shows that race in jazz, as well as in American culture, is still a binary, "black and white" affair. Furthermore, Asian American males are often stereotyped as not masculine, passive, and feminine, and Asian Americans of both genders suffer from being the noncreative "nerdy" type. Since jazz has a certain masculine quality, and being creative is essential in jazz, these stereotypes have made others suspicious and skeptical about the ability and work of Asian American jazz musicians. Second, the decade in which Asian American jazz flourished witnessed the rise of a neotraditionalist wing of jazz criticism led by famous jazz musician Wynton Marsalis. The neotraditionalists criticize the excess of 1960s' avant-garde jazz and how it has taken jazz away from its roots. Marsalis and critic Stanley Crouch were concerned that by adopting a nationalist stance that equated jazz authenticity with the direct expression of struggle and protest, the avant-garde had unwittingly bought into a "noble savage" stereotype that cast jazz as an untutored expression of black emotion requiring little work or artistic ingenuity. Finally, the political agenda and mission of Asian American jazz musicians have largely limited their audience to the Asian American community and hindered the marketability of their work.

Since mainstream music companies are not interested in the political and avant-garde work of Asian American jazz musicians, Asian American jazz musicians used "Asian American" as a rubric to promote, present, document, and distribute their work. They have consequently established a nationwide network of artists and organizations with branches in major U.S. metropolitan areas such as San Francisco. One of the first modern Asian American jazz bands in the early 1970s was Hiroshima, a popular band based in Los Angeles that incorporated Japanese instruments. Then came the Asian American Jazz Festival (AAJF), cofounded by Paul Yamazaki, George Leong, and Mark Izu, now the longest ongoing jazz festival in San Francisco, held annually in the Bay Area since 1981. It later influenced the establishments of other Asian American Jazz Festivals in cities such as Chicago in 1996 and in Boston (the Boston Asian American Creative Music Festival) in 1997. Asian American musicians produced their own recordings as a way to maintain creative control and reach target audiences. Pianist Jon Jang's first album was released on RPM Records, an independent label created to record the avant-garde Afro-Asian quartet United Front, consisting of Brown, Izu, Lewis Jordan, and George Sams. In 1987, Jon Jang, saxophonist Francis Wong, and Fred Ho founded the independent Asian Improv Records (AIR) in the Bay Area, which has helped to promote Asian American jazz musicians nationwide. Asian American jazz musicians expressed solidarity with political struggles through recordings inspired by and dedicated to these movements as well as by playing benefit concerts and political demonstrations. Many Asian American jazz musicians have risked family opprobrium and financial instability in order to commit themselves fully to their music and political organizing.

New York-based baritone saxophonist Fred Wei-han Ho and San Francisco-based pianist Jon Jang, both American-born Chinese, are two highly regarded Asian American jazz musicians. As an important figure in the Asian American jazz development, Fred Ho is a baritone saxophonist, composer, acclaimed recording artist, proficient writer, and activist in Asian American radical politics.

Like many other Chinese Americans growing up in the United States, he went through a journey of rejecting traditional Chinese culture, feeling alienated in the mainstream American culture and system, and searching for a "voice" or path that he could thrive in. After graduating from Harvard University with a sociology degree in 1979, he went to New York and in 1982 established the Brooklyn-based multiracial Afro Asian Music Ensemble. In 1987, he cofounded a record label to help promoting Asian American jazz. In 1988, he became the first Asian American to receive the Duke Ellington Distinguished Artist Lifetime Achievement Award from the Black Musicians Conference.

Fred Ho calls his music "an Afro-Asian new American multicultural music" or "new Chinese American multicultural music." He has committed his compositions to a broad spectrum of political and social concerns, ranging from the Chinese immigrant experience in America, Filipino bachelor immigrant workers' struggles, and strikes by black and Latina women hotel workers in New York City, to critiques of orientalist, stereotyped Chinese images, social issues (such as AIDS, drug abuse, and sexual responsibility), progressive politics, panethnic coalition, and commentaries (on radical political ideas, economic oppressions, and oppression of Asian and Asian American women). In his opinion, jazz is the "music of an American oppressed nationality," and for Asian Americans to "choose 'black' over 'white' reflects and strengthens a potential anti-imperialist bond." He believes that "a common identification as oppressed peoples" produces "free and voluntary intermingling, cultural synthesis, and crossfertilization" that leads to "new cultural forms." He frequently incorporates Chinese instruments, Chinese musical elements, Chinese musicians, Chinese-language lyrics, Chinese literature, and Chinese historical or mythical figures with jazz musical idioms and American social consciousness, forging a strong diasporic cultural identity. His work *Havoc in Gold Mountain* (1992) is one such example that directly addresses Chinese American immigration history and experience, psychological wounds, identity crises, and social awareness wrapped in a collage of complex jazz rhythms, chords progressions, Chinese timbre and melody, and improvisations on Chinese traditional musical instruments. Such incorporation of Chinese musical idioms into American jazz music has helped Chinese and Chinese American musicians who play traditional instruments to break through the ethnic cultural barriers and to develop their careers as professional musicians in the United States. For example, *pipa* players such as Wu Man, Tang Liangxing, and Min Xiaofen, have successfully established themselves as professional musicians among the Chinese traditional instrumentalist in the East Coast through various gigs and recording sessions with jazz ensembles.

Similar to Fred Ho, compositions by Jon Jang are committed to a broad spectrum of social and political concerns, ranging from the Asian immigrant experience in America to criticism on Eurocentrism, oriental stereotyped Chinese images, progressive politics, and panethnic coalitions. Jang attended the Oberlin Conservatory from 1974 to 1978, studying piano performance and composition with Wendell Logan, an African American professor. He has collaborated frequently with Chinese immigrant musicians in their compositions and performances, employing Chinese instruments, musical elements, and language and relating their compositions to Chinese classical literature and contemporary events. Jang's Pan-Asian Arkestra was a multiracial affair, inspired by the Pan African People's Arkestra led by Horace Tapscott.

It is difficult to define the style of Asian American jazz since many musicians have ventured and experimented with different possibilities in jazz. Although the trait to combine traditional Asian music and improvised jazz was prominent among the first wave of Asian American jazz musicians, many changes in political and musical outlook have occurred since the 1980s. No matter how the development of Asian American jazz unfolds in the future, it is certain that Asian American jazz musicians have benefited from uniting as Asian Americans. For example, later-wave musicians like Tatsu Aoki, Jeff Chan, Vijay Iyer, Kuni Mikami, Hafez Modirzadeh, and Jeff Song were provided the opportunity to produce their own recordings on the Asian Improv label, benefiting from the legacies of the early Asian American jazz movement.

See also: Chinese American Hip-Hop

Further Reading

Fellezs, Kevin. 2007. "Silenced But Not Silent: Asian Americans and Jazz." In *Alien Encounters: Popular Culture in Asian America*, edited by Mimi Thi Nguyen and Thuy Linh Nguyen Tu, 69–110. Durham, NC: Duke University Press.

Kajikawa, Loren. 2015. "Asian American Jazz." *Grove Music Online*. Accessed July 16, 2015. http://oxfordmusiconline.com

Zheng, Su. 2010. *Claiming Diaspora: Music, Transnationalism, and Cultural Politics in Asian/Chinese America*. New York: Oxford University Press.

May May Chiang

CHINESE AMERICAN LITERATURE

Chinese American literature is poetry, fiction, nonfiction, drama, and other writings written by those of Chinese descent living in the United States.

Early Pleas for Tolerance

The earliest known Chinese American writings were written by Chinese immigrants in the 19th century who were protesting unfair treatment and

Author Amy Tan, left, poses with Actress Annette Bening and director Wayne Wang after a screening of the motion picture *The Joy Luck Club* in the Westwood section of Los Angeles, California, on August 28, 1993. The film was based on Tan's bestselling novel of the same name. (AP Photo)

discrimination. Much of early Chinese American writing could be described as realist descriptions of social conditions within Chinese American communities. As the number of Chinese living and working in North America increased dramatically after the 1850s, mainstream American society's views of Chinese immigrants became much more hostile. Much writing on the Chinese by non-Chinese published in American newspapers reflected this negative attitude and appealed to white fears of a "Yellow Peril," a fear by white Americans that an overwhelming number of Chinese immigrants would overwhelm America. In addition, legislation targeting the Chinese began to be enacted, culminating in the passage of the 1882 Chinese Exclusion Act. The Chinese Exclusion Act was the first law preventing a specific group from immigrating to the United States based on ethnicity, which ultimately resulted in prohibiting immigration of all Chinese laborers.

Early Chinese immigrants saw such punitive laws and regulations as discriminatory. Those who were educated, such as the Chinese merchants associated with the Chinese Consolidated Benevolent Association (CCBA), viewed themselves as spokesmen for Chinese immigrants and wrote complaints to government officials. The earliest and most influential of these letters is "Letter of the Chinamen to His Excellency, Governor Bigler," a five-page essay written by Hab Wa and Tong K. Achick, two merchants associated with Chinese trading companies in San Francisco. The letter was written in response to two anti-Chinese propositions that John Bigler, who was the governor of California at that time, had submitted to the California legislature. Published on April 29, 1852, in both of San Francisco's mainstream newspapers, the *Daily Alta California* and *San Francisco Herald*, the letter argued against Bigler's claims that the Chinese made no financial contributions to America. Instead, the letter claimed that San Francisco's business profited from Chinese customers and imports and provided evidence of Chinese immigrants' willingness to assimilate into American society. Many subsequent writings modeled the accomodationist tone of the letter and plea for tolerance of the Chinese.

Angel Island Poetry

The two-volume *Songs from Gold Mountain* and the poems written by Chinese detainees at the Angel Island immigration center depict a collective experience of the hardships of Chinese American life. The Angel Island immigration center became a processing center to hold Asian immigrants, mostly Chinese, until they could be verified as having a valid claim to enter the United States. After the 1906 San Francisco earthquake and fire destroyed local citizenship records, some Chinese took the opportunity to bypass the restrictions of the Chinese Exclusion Act. By using the right of derivative citizenship, those who claimed to be children of Chinese who were American citizens could claim citizenship themselves, even if they were born outside of the United States. Some Chinese American citizens sold their citizenship "slots" to boys who had no family relationships in the United States, which would allow them to enter the country. These "sons" who bought the slots were known as "paper sons." At Angel Island, an interrogation system was set up to screen applicants, who were considered guilty of attempting to enter the United States under false documents unless proven innocent. While detained at Angel Island, many documented their experiences by writing Chinese-language poems on the walls of the immigration station. The poems, of which more than 135 survive, often dealt with bitter and angry feelings about the discriminatory interrogation system and the terrible living conditions.

The Angel Island poems and prose express their longing and memories of home, family, and dreams and frustrations with America. They were also written in Chinese, not English. Similarly written in Chinese are Cantonese rhymes that Marlon Hom calls "Chinatown songs," published during the early 20th century as well. These songs address an array of subjects that include sex, frustration with the American government, bureaucracy, poverty, alienation, and concerns of the old generation for the values and morals of the younger generation of Chinese Americans. They were personal as well as outspoken. These early literary works are classified as Chinese American because they were written by early Chinese Americans, or Chinese in America, and their subjects and topics are universally addressed through the decades as a source of muse and "inspiration." Among the early Chinese American writers are Lee Yan Phou (1861–ca. 1938), who published *When I Was a Boy in China* (1887), an autobiographical works geared toward countering negative portrayals of the Chinese in popular American culture in the late 19th century; and Yung Wing (1828–1912), the first Chinese student to graduate from an American university—then known as Yale College—in 1854. Yung's memoir, *My Life in China and America* (1909), narrates his education in both China and the United States, reintroduction to Chinese society, and steadfast love for China.

Early Chinese American Literature

Chinese American literature written in the 20th century is written exclusively in English. Several early works are by Eurasian Chinese, such as Edith Maude Eaton (1865–1914), who wrote under the pen name Sui Sin Far, is known as the first Chinese woman writer in North America and was one of the first Chinese American writers to write in English. In addition, Far's Eurasian identity gave her access to white American society and allowed her much more access to European Americans than other Chinese American authors. Because of this, Far was one of the first Chinese American writers to incorporate both Chinese American immigrant characters and white American characters in her work. Far is credited with coining the term "Chinese American." *Mrs. Spring Fragrance* (1912), her last collection of short stories, was rediscovered and republished in 1995. In contrast, Far's younger sister, Winnifred Eaton, adopted a Japanese pen name, "Onoto Watanna," and chose to focus on Japanese American themes instead. Han Suyin (1916–2012) (pen name Elizabeth Comber and birth name Rosalie Matilda Kuanghu Chou) published *A Many-Splendoured Thing* (1952), about a British foreign correspondent who marries a Eurasian doctor in Singapore. Han Suyin's works are often set in China and Southeast Asia. Her best known work was made into a film entitled *Love Is a Many-Splendored Thing* (1955), with the same titled theme song that won the Academy Award for Best Original Song. Later, the movie was made into a daytime soap opera that ran from 1967 to 1973 on American television. Diana Chang, novelist and poet is considered to be the first American-born Chinese American to publish a novel in the United States. Her father is Chinese and her mother Eurasian. Her best known novel, *Frontiers of Love* (1956), is set in Japanese-occupied Shanghai in 1945 and deals with cultural expressions and identities vis-à-vis colonial forces—Japanese and Western.

As was the case with earlier Chinese American writers, Chinese American writing reflected the material conditions of Chinese American communities. In the 1930s, Lin Yutang (1895–1976) published *My Country and My People* (1935) and *The Importance of Living* (1937). Lin Yutang's many works represent an attempt to bridge the cultural gap between the East and the West. During and after World War II, sentiment toward the Chinese American community shifted in relation to China's status as an ally, and the Chinese Exclusion Act was lifted. This was a period that saw more publication and success for Chinese American writers. In the 1950s, C. Y. Lee (1917–) achieved great success with *Flower Drum Song* (1957), a novel that tells the story of Chinese immigrants in San Francisco, which was made into a Rodgers and Hammerstein musical in 1958 and a film version in 1961. Jade Snow Wong (1922–2006) published *Fifth Chinese Daughter* (1945, revised 1950), a memoir about generational conflicts, gender, and balancing her identity as a Chinese American woman with Chinese traditions. Chinese American literature published in this period reflected the experiences of second-generation American-born Chinese (or ABCs). In this time period, these Chinese American writers were more concerned about belonging in American culture, which is reflected in themes such as conflicts between generations and cultural values between East and West, the American Dream, alienation from the Chinese community, and a concern with "loyalty" to America. In addition, some of these books were published by major commercial publishers and received well by mainstream audiences.

Rebellion

The new 1965 immigration law transformed the Chinese American community in the United States, resulting in a much larger and diverse community. In addition, the activism in the 1960s (for racial equality and against the war) created a new direction for Chinese American literature with a new sensibility.

In the 1970s, a group of young male Asian American writers, which included Chinese American writers Frank Chin (1940–), Jeffrey Paul Chan (1942–), and Shawn Hsu Wong (1949–), rebelled against what they perceived as their predecessors' conformity to assimilationist values. Chin, Chan, and Wong, along with Lawson Fusao Inada, would coedit the ground-breaking Asian American anthology, *Aiiieeeee!*, in 1974.

During this period, playwright Frank Chin's play, *The Chickencoop Chinaman* (1971), became the first play by a Chinese American (and, by extension, Asian American) to be produced as a major New York production. Shawn Wong published a short novel, *Homebase* (1979), about a young Chinese American caught in two cultures—Chinese and American. Maxine Hong Kingston's first memoir, *The Woman Warrior: Memoir of a Childhood Among Ghosts* (1976), received the National Book Critics Circle Award. Chin also became known as a critic of Maxine Hong Kingston, charging she perpetuated negative stereotypes of Chinese culture and, by extension, Chinese Americans, and misrepresented traditional Chinese stories. Later, Chin lauded similar critiques on Amy Tan. Fans of Kingston's *Woman Warrior* and her subsequent *China Men* (1980) highlight how she incorporated feminist concerns and a historical consciousness into Chinese American literature.

In the 1980s, playwright David Henry Hwang (1957–) was awarded an 1980 Obie Award for his play *FOB* (1979) that depicts the conflicts and contrasts between established Asian Americans and "fresh off the boat" newcomer Asian immigrants. Hwang received a 1988 Tony Award for Best Play for *M. Butterfly* (1988) that deals with the subject of orientalism and sexuality. Bette Bao Lord (1938–) published *Spring Moon* (1981), an international best seller that spans the time period of prerevolutionary China to President Richard Nixon's visit. One of the most prolific Chinese American writers, Amy Tan published the best-selling novel *The Joy Luck Club* (1989), about the relationships between Chinese American mothers and daughters, which won the National Book Award and made into a major Hollywood motion picture in 1993.

According to scholar William Wei, the emergence of the Asian American movement in the 1960s created two competing but interrelated approaches to Chinese American creative writing. One emphasizes the social responsibility of Chinese American writers as members of a racial and ethnic group that has been discriminated against; the other emphasizes aesthetic and individual freedom.

Wider Recognition and Acceptance

In the late 1980s, Amy Tan published the best-selling novel, *The Joy Luck Club* (1989), about the relationships between Chinese American mothers and daughters, which won the National Book Award. *The Joy Luck Club* was embraced by the American literary community and was made into a major Hollywood motion picture in 1993 with a largely Asian cast. Tan's success signaled a shift in Chinese American publishing because Tan was heralded as a writer with more universal themes than her predecessors. In a sense, Tan's success also ushered in a new era for Chinese American writing, which is more diverse than in the past and covers a wide range of themes, aesthetics, and concerns.

Several Chinese American writers have received success throughout the 1990s to today. Among them are David Wong Louie's (1954–) short stories, *Pangs of Love* (1991); Eric Liu's (1968–) collected memoirs and essays in *The Accidental Asian: Notes of a Native Speaker* (1997); Gish Jen's (1955–) *Tiger Writing: Art, Culture, and the Interdependent Self* (2013); Jean Kwok's *Girl in Translation* (2010) and *Mambo in Chinatown* (2014); and Shirley Geok-lin Lim's (1944–) collection of poems, *Crossing The Peninsula* (1980). Writing for young adults, Laurence M. Yep (1948–) has published 10 *Golden Mountain Chronicles* that spans the period of 1835 to the present, four Dragon fantasies, three Chinatown mysteries, and much more. Gene Luen Yang (1973–) published the graphic novel, *American Born Chinese* (2008), which employs the popular Chinese Buddhist folklore of the Monkey King and the relationship between an American-born Chinese American and a Taiwan-born Chinese classmate. Central to all these works is the issue of identity across cultural landscapes and time.

Although early Chinese American literature was primarily set in Chinatown, the cultural tussles of being both Chinese and American continue to be a muse for current writers and, by extension, future writers. The expressions of identities will continue to be a universal theme that resonates with other immigrants and reflects an archetypical life experience of being an immigrant in America, which for Chinese Americans is the multiple dimensions and expressions of self, community, and history through writing.

See also: Angel Island Immigration Station; Folklore in Children's Literature

Further Reading

Chang, Joan Chiung-Heui. 2000. *Transforming Chinese American Literature: A Study of History, Sexuality, and Ethnicity.* New York: Peter Lang.

Lai, Him Mark, Genny Lim, and Judy Yung, eds. 1991. *Island: Poetry and History of Chinese Immigrants on Angel Island, 1910–1940.* Seattle: University of Washington Press.

Yin, Xiao-huang. 2006. *Chinese American Literature Since the 1850s.* Urbana: University of Illinois Press.

Ching-In Chen and Jonathan H. X. Lee

CHINESE AMERICANS AND LGBTQQI

Much has been written on the topic of Chinese American history, literature, arts, and notable Chinese Americans in politics, science, medicine, film, and even sports. However, in the arena of Chinese Americans and Lesbian, Gay, Bisexual, Transgender, Queer, Questioning, and Intersex (LGBTQQI) issues, there are very few published works—and miniscule research. The absence of Chinese American LGBTQQI research is emblematic of larger issues that surround Chinese Americans who are LGBTQQI; namely, the lack of Chinese American LGBTQQI individuals in public life and entertainment and cross-cultural misunderstandings about Chinese versus American views, assumptions, and openness to LGBTQQI individuals and communities. The infectious racialized image of Chinese Americans as a "model minority" encapsulates Chinese American subjectivity in heteronormative standards as indicated by success and achievement in education and socioeconomic status and conformity to mainstream discourses of "normal" that do not include same-sex marriage or relationships that do not conform to heterosexual normativity.

Chinese American LGBTQQI sexuality and gender identities intersect with the ways that Chinese American identities—and, by extension, Asian American identities—have been constructed via dominant society's ideologies of race, gender, and sexuality. Chinese American communities have often been portrayed as conformist, conservative, and unaccepting of their LGBTQQI members. As Russell Leong argues, "the myth of Asian Americans as a homogenous, heterosexual 'model minority' population since the 1960s has worked against exploration into the varied nature of our sexual drives and gendered diversity." Simultaneously, Chinese American bodies have been "Otherized" through the way that dominant American society constructs their sexualities. Early Chinese American communities were shaped by legislation that restricted Chinese American women from entering the United States, labeling Chinese women as prostitutes. In contrast, early Chinese American society was a "bachelor society" in which men greatly outnumbered women. Though some of the so-called bachelors may have found companionship outside of the Chinese American community, some also found intimacy within the largely homosocial communities of

Hawaiʻi state Rep. Chris Lee speaks with faith leaders about gay marriage at the First Unitarian Church of Honolulu in Honolulu on August 19, 2013. More than two dozen Hawaiʻi faith leaders of various religions signed a resolution calling for the state to pass a law legalizing gay marriage. (AP Photo/Oskar Garcia)

Chinatown. This pathologization of Chinese American sexualities impacted the way that some Chinese American men, especially during the cultural nationalist 1970s, constructed their own sexual identities around an investment in heteronormative constructions of masculinity. This was a reaction to Chinese American emasculation, a phenomenon that David L. Eng has termed "racial castration." Whitney McNally's controversial 2004 piece entitled "Gay or Asian," printed as part of the "Anthropology" page of *Details*, drew much criticism from Asian American and LGBTQQI community organizations and highlights the way that the model minority discourse continues to reconstruct Chinese and Asian American men as sexually deviant.

General and popular assumptions illustrate inherent tensions and conflicts between being LGBTQQI and the Chinese family, cultural, and religious values. In particular, it paints an image of a patriarchal and domineering heteronormative Confucian ideological system and practice that is embedded in Chinese and Chinese American societies that firmly expect Chinese and Chinese American children to marry the opposite sex and have babies to continue the family lineage and name. This Confucian expectation is considered one of the heaviest obstacle for gay Chinese Americans to accept their authentic self and to be truthful about their sexual orientation with their families, in particular their parents. According to a Chinese state media estimate, in China, the pressure to marry has made it difficult for many gay men to be open about their sexual orientation and has resulted in as many as 10 million to marry straight women just to placate their parents. This heterosexual expectation is also present among Chinese Americans, especially among first-generation Chinese American families and Chinese-speaking American parents.

Among Chinese Americans, there are complex and nuanced differences in perceptions and attitudes toward LGBTQQI people that is split between English-speaking versus Chinese-speaking Chinese Americans, and younger (under 35 years old) versus older (over 35 years old) Chinese Americans. According to a study by API Equality-LA, "Talking to Chinese Americans About LGBT Issues," for Chinese-speaking Americans, gender norms and expectations are employed to define, perceive, and form attitudes toward LGBTQQI people. Moreover, gender is also a foundational lens through which Chinese-speaking Americans form their attitudes toward LGBTQQI people in relation to LGBTQQI families—raising children and parenting—marriage equality, and culture. The study concludes that a vast majority of Chinese-speaking Americans describe LGBTQQI people as people whose gender—appearance, roles in relationship, and behavior—do not conform to heterosexual gender norms. Gender non-conformity was the most cited definition for being LGBTQQI and the strongest source of discomfort with LGBTQQI people. In fact, Chinese gender roles are embedded in traditional Chinese religious conceptions, in particular, in the cosmological system of yin and yang: yin represents dark, wet, decay, and by extension, women and femininity; whereas yang represents light, dry, growth, and by extension, men and masculinity. The study found that a majority of Chinese-speaking Americans described LGBTQQI men when asked to explain their perceptions of LGBTQQI people. In addition, many Chinese-speaking Americans cited extreme discomfort toward LGBTQQI people who are neither masculine nor feminine. They also describe LGBTQQI people as confused about their gender identity. The bias that Chinese-speaking Americans maintain is partially unconscious and partially informed by misunderstanding and misrepresentation of Confucianism and yin-yang cosmology.

Among Chinese-speaking immigrant parents whose knowledge of Chinese culture is strong, having LGBTQQI children results in social shame and loss of face. Parents of LGBTQQI children are concerned that other family members, friends, and their community will ridicule and label them ineffective parents who have failed in raising their children. Additionally, Chinese-speaking parents will blame both American culture and values and blame themselves for having children who turned out LGBTQQI.

In general, English-speaking Chinese Americans, especially those who are younger, express more openness and acceptance of LGBTQQI people. However, the study by API Equality-LA found that a majority do not support same-sex marriage and express their strong reservations about it. The antimarriage equality attitudes can be divided into three categories: first, LGBTQQI people should be able to have the same marriage rights but not call it "marriage"; second, the function of marriage is strictly coupled with reproduction and, by extension, continuation of the family name; and third, same-sex marriage is a violation of traditional values. For many second-generation or American-raised Chinese Americans, being able to communicate with their Chinese-speaking parents is difficult, which magnifies the tension and gap around issues of LGBTQQI issues.

The overall situation for LGBTQQI Chinese Americans may seem bleak and nearly impossible to negotiate. However, some have selected to live "double" lives: out with friends, peers, possibly even siblings, but in the closet to their parents. The risk is being constantly pressured by their parents to get married and bear children. Due to the lack of cultural knowledge and familiarity with Chinese culture, especially Confucianism, many Chinese Americans appropriate the Western interpretation of Confucianism that reinforces patriarchy and domination of women. However, a critical examination reveals that there are no prohibitions against same-sex relationships in the Confucian cannon. Instead, the focus of Confucian discourse is on fulfilling duties, especially those that are required by filial piety. Confucian relationships are reciprocal and interdependent. Therefore, Chinese and Chinese American parents will value their LGBTQQI children so long as they fulfill their duties, which include caring for them in their old age, and perhaps having children, which is possible through in vitro fertilization and adoption.

The situation for LGBTQQI people in China and Taiwan may indicate changes on this issue for all Chinese and Chinese Americans. Although homosexuality was classified as a "mental illness," it has been "legal" in China since the 1990s. But, as business interests guide changes in the market place for LGBTQQI products, the profitable "gay market" may pave the path to making LGBTQQI people and cultures "more acceptable." For example, in 2013–2015, Blued, a gay dating app that is mainly used in Beijing, raised $30 million from a U.S. venture capital firm and captured over 15 million users in two years. Another example is Taobao, a Chinese online marketplace, which launched a campaigned called "We Do" to send gay couples to Western countries with legalized same-sex marriage. Across the strait, over in Taiwan, LGBTQQI marriage equality has been an issue of debate for nearly a decade. Lawmakers have tried to legalize same-sex marriage since 2003. On August 2012, two women exchanged marriage vows in what the media referred to as Taiwan's first same-sex marriage ceremony. According to gay travel guides, Shanghai, Hong Kong, and Taipei are 3 of the top 10 Asian countries that are "gay-friendly" travel destinations.

Two popular films have explored the intersection of queer subjectivities and Confucian ideologies among Chinese Americans: Ang Lee's *The Wedding Banquet*

Though there have been prominent LGBTQQI Chinese Americans involved in both the Asian American and gay and lesbian rights movements since the 1970s, many LGBTQQI Chinese Americans have also felt marginalized within both the LGBTQQI movement and Asian American communities. There have been some ethnic-specific projects, such as the Mandarin-speaking Asian Pacific Lesbian Bisexual Network (MAPLBN). Cofounded by Koko Lin, MAPLBN is best known for creating the "Beloved Daughter" booklet, a 40-page collection of letters from Chinese mothers, fathers, brothers, and sisters to their lesbian and bisexual daughters and/or sisters about their "coming-out" stories, translated into both Chinese and English. Groups such as the Lesbian and Gay Asian Collective organized during the first National Third World Lesbian and Gay Conference on October 12, 1979. In the 1980s, activists founded local, national, and international organizations serving Asian American LGBTQQI communities, such as the Asian/Pacific Lesbian Network (1988), the Gay Asian Pacific Alliance (1988), and the Asian Lesbian Network (1989). In 1987, the first national meeting of lesbian and gay Asian Americans, "Breaking the Silence: Beginning the Dialogue," was organized in California.

In recent years, there has been more LGBTQQI Chinese American visibility with increased production of creative work that focuses on LGBTQQI Chinese American experiences by prominent writers, playwrights, and filmmakers, including Richard Fung, Justin Chin, David Henry Hwang, Chaw Yew, Helen Zia, Kitty Tsui, Merle Woo, Christopher Lee, Norman Wong, and Alice Lu. There has also been more visibility of transidentified Chinese Americans, such as Chinese American spoken-word artist Kit Yan and Alexander Lee, former director of the Transgender Gender Variant and Intersex Justice Project.

Ching-In Chen

(1993) and Alice Wu's *Saving Face* (2004). *The Wedding Banquet* is about a gay Taiwanese American who lives with his white American lover in Manhattan and a complicated plot by his father to get a grandson that involves a fake-visa marriage to a Chinese artist. In the end, the Confucian father expresses his joy of having a grandson as well as symbolically communicates his acceptance of his son's homosexuality and gay relationship by giving Simon, his son's white partner, a *hongbao* (red envelope). In *Saving Face*, three generations come to terms with filial responsibility and duties. In this film, a Chinese American surgeon struggles to come out to her Chinese-speaking mother and grandfather. The film illustrates the reciprocal dynamics of Chinese-cum-Confucian relationships and ends with the grandfather accepting his daughter's love of a younger man and the mother accepting her daughter's lesbian identity and relationship. It ends with the mother asking whether her lesbian daughter will give her a grandchild. Both films portray Confucian humanism and the embodiment of filial piety as a debate about family and the (re)definition of family, not queer sexuality versus heterosexuality. Unlike Christianity's proscription and declaration that homosexuality is an abomination and sin, Confucianism ideologies and Chinese/Chinese American subjectivity emphasizes the reproduction of family. As such, *The Wedding Banquet* and *Saving Face* reveal the shifting contours and definitions of the Chinese/Chinese American family and, therefore, accept queer relationships and subjectivities because family lineage can be continued by other means, not just by heterosexual intercourse.

For Chinese American LGBTQQI people, the lack of visibility within the LGBTQQI community presents obstacles and challenges. An absence of positive images of LGBTQQI Chinese Americans in popular culture, entertainment, and mainstream media can also make acknowledging one's orientation or gender identity more difficult. In addition, LGBTQQI Chinese Americans also encounter racism in society at large and within the LGBTQQI community. The tides are changing for LGBTQQI Americans overall, and there is strong effort to push the LGBTQQI movement to become more inclusive of communities of people of color. The historic and present failures to meaningfully include people of color have prevented the LGBTQQI movement from realizing its full potential.

See also: Lee, Ang; Low, Evan

Further Reading

Leong, Russell, ed. 1996. *Asian American Sexualities: Dimensions of the Gay and Lesbian Experience*. New York: Routledge.

Masequesmay, Gina, and Sean Metzer, eds. 2009. *Embodying Asian American Sexualities*. New York: Rowman & Littlefield.

PFLAG—San Gabriel Valley Asian Pacific Islander. 2015. Accessed July 16, 2015. http://www.sangabrielvalleyapipflag.com/.

Jonathan H. X. Lee and Ching-In Chen

CHINESE AMERICANS IN MOTION PICTURES

The stereotype image of Chinese influenced the roles that Chinese American actors and actresses could play in motion pictures. This image of Chinese figures in movies also shaped the Western image of Chinese Americans. Historical circumstances helped create this stereotype image. The producers created characters for movie based on information and images already touted by the press and other written materials and already imbedded in the American consciousness. A stereotype of Chinese then emerged in American movies as movie producers sought to portray Chinese figures.

In the early 1850s, the Chinese image changed from positive to negative, and the aliens easily sank in the social hierarchy. The fear of the Chinese immigrants' negative influence on Americans created a negative image for Chinese. There were several elements, such as the increase of Chinese population in the United States, economic competition, cultural difference, and lifestyle, contributing to the shift of American attitudes toward Chinese immigrants. The negative image of Chinese soon became a stereotype for all Chinese immigrants. They were lumped into one single group with little chance of breaking free from the mold. This group identity replaced individual identity. Almost without exception, white Americans saw the Chinese group as subservient and inferior.

In the early 20th century, the Chinese image in motion pictures did not change significantly. The Chinese figures in movies were always represented as lower-class domestic servants, laundrymen, cheap labor, opium smokers, and other unsavory and vicious characters. American movies in the early 20th century contained Chinese characters, but only in very minor roles. Chinese played either domestic servants or laundrymen. They all belonged to the lower-class stereotype. For example, Chinese laundrymen appeared in *The Chinese Rubbernecks* (1903), *Chinese Laundry: At Work* (1904), and *Chink at Golden Gulch* (1910). There was a Chinese domestic servant in *The Yellow Peril* (1908).

Chinese characters were also depicted as villains and vicious invaders in films. In the 1920s and 1930s, Sax Rohmer's Fu Manchu became American Film Company's target. Sax Rohmer, a British writer, created Fu Manchu in the novel *The Insidious Dr. Fu Manchu* (1913). After this novel, Rohmer published a series of Fu Manchu novels between 1918 and the 1930s. Paramount Studios released a series of Fu Manchu films between 1929 and 1932. Republic Studios released *The Drums of Fu Manchu* as a serial. In these Fu Manchu movies, the American movie audience saw the negative Chinese stereotypes continue to reinforce existing public opinion. Fu Manchu was a Chinese villain and ambitious. Paramount Studios released *The Mysterious Dr. Fu Manchu* in 1929; *The Return of Dr. Fu Manchu* was released in 1930. The portrayal affected the perception of Chinese Americans.

Since the perception of Chinese had been ingrained, it did restrict how Chinese Americans could be starred in films. Anna May Wong was a popular Chinese American actress in the United States from 1919 through 1961. Wong was interviewed many times. She expressed she was tired of playing villains in movies. She asked that why Chinese were always villains in movies. In some films, Wong played slave girls, prostitutes, and villains. In *The Thief of Bagdad* (1924), Wong's character was a Mongol slave girl. In *Daughter of the Dragon* (1931), Wong's character, Princess Ling Moy, was a Chinese dancer. She attempted to kill her white love interest and his fiancée, but Wong's character was killed by the police. There is no doubt that such stories served to alert the white viewers to the consequences of improper contact with Chinese people. In *Shanghai Express* (1932), Wong's character, Hui Fei, was a prostitute who killed the villainous Chinese warlord. As a Chinese American actress, Wong never received a leading role. Due to the anti-miscegenation law in the United States, she could not even kiss white actors on screen. Therefore, Wong's development in Hollywood was limited to supporting roles.

A close look at fictional representation movies showed that two particular extremes developed in the Chinese image. One was the servant and the other was the vicious invader and villain. While the menial servants working for whites implied Chinese intellectual inferiority and lower status, the invaders represented a hidden threat of conquest and destruction, the "yellow peril." These opposite representations seemed to have a stranglehold, but change was on the way. Writer Earl Derr Biggers created a new Chinese image in the 1920s. Enter the sharp, witty detective Charlie Chan. From the 1930s through the 1940s, Hollywood made a series of Charlie Chan movies based upon Biggers's creation. Instead of using Chinese Americans to play Charlie Chan, film companies used white actors. The series was a success. Audiences liked Charlie Chan, and thus began the redefinition of the Chinese image among white America. Although Hollywood based Chan on Biggers's character, the producers saw fit to change the physical appearance, transforming Chan from a clean-shaven sleuth to one with a mustache and a little beard. Both the mustache and beard reminded moviegoers of traditional Chinese male images as already seen in photographs and other visuals. Plus, the mustache and beard helped disguise the fact that the actor playing Charlie Chan was not Chinese. The Chan character himself evolved, from a humble detective in the 1930s to a sharper, more commanding sleuth in the 1940s, who was on top of the case whether it be helping the U.S. government catch thieves who stole top-secret plans or catching everyday murderers or resolving tough cases.

Chan's movies introduced the new image of Chinese Americans. The children of Charlie Chan spoke fluent English with no trace of a Chinese accent. They all received an American college education and were consummately more Americanized than Charlie Chan himself. Film companies used Chinese American actors and actresses to play Charlie Chan's offspring. Keye Luke played Lee Chan, the Number One Son of Charlie Chan. Sen Yung played James Chan, the Number Two Son. Benson Fong played Tommy Chan, the Number Three Son. Marianne Quon played Iris Chan, Charlie Chan's daughter. This was very positive compared to other movie portrayals of Chinese, and it persuaded contemporary white Americans to reconstruct their understanding of Chinese immigrants and the second generation of Chinese Americans.

At that time, it was not uncommon to have white actors and actresses play leading Chinese roles. Like Fu Manchu movies and Charlie Chan movies, *The Good Earth* (1937) also used white actors and actresses to play leading Chinese roles. In *The Good Earth*, Paul Muni was cast as a Chinese farmer, Wang Lung, and Luise Rainer was cast as Wang's wife, O-Lan. Like the Charlie Chan movies, this film's other supporting roles were played by Chinese American actors and actresses. Anna May Wong was offered to test for a supporting role of a Chinese concubine, Lotus. Wong turned down the offer.

Toward the end of the 1930s, Americans began to be more sympathetic to Chinese people as Japanese invaded China. During World War II, China became an American ally. Chinese and Americans had the fight against Japan in common. The Chinese image shifted from vicious to heroic. The Chinese image became far more positive in Hollywood war films. For example, Monogram's *Dragon Seed* (1944) portrayed Chinese who were heroic as they fought against the Japanese invaders. China was no longer the feared yellow peril but was itself the victim of invasion. However, leading and supporting Chinese roles were still played by white actors and actresses. Katharine Hepburn was cast as Jade, a Chinese woman. Walter Huston was cast as Ling Tang. Although there were several war films focusing on Chinese, the positive, sympathetic image of Chinese helped improve race relations between Chinese and white Americans during the wartime.

In the 1970s, Bruce Lee's Chinese Kung Fu forms changed how Chinese Americans were viewed in motion pictures. Lee represented a new image and role that Chinese American actors could play in films. In the 1960s, Lee tried to develop in Hollywood but he was not successful. In 1971, Lee collaborated with Warner Brothers and developed a new television series. Lee expected himself to play a leading role. However, the producer worried that American audiences might not accept a Chinese American actor in a leading role. A Caucasian actor was chosen instead of Lee. Lee then went to Hong Kong and made several Chinese Kung Fu films that made him famous in Asia. Meanwhile, in 1972, President Nixon visited China. His visit drew a lot of attention in the world. More Americans wanted to know China and its culture. This also helped Americans to look at Chinese Americans differently. In 1973, Lee went back to Hollywood. He played a leading role in *Enter the Dragon*, a Chinese martial arts action movie coproduced by Warner Brothers, Golden Harvest Studio, and Lee's production company. This film was a big success. This movie was not only the first English-language martial arts film but also introduced a new style of fighting that had never been seen onscreen.

The success of *Enter the Dragon* did not totally change the stereotype image of Chinese Americans; the perception still existed in Hollywood movies in the 1980s. In *Year of the Dragon* (1985), John Lone played one of the leading roles and was cast as Joey Tai, the head of a Chinese triad society in New York

Chinatown. He was portrayed as a villain, murderer, and rapist. He killed himself at the end.

It was always a risky move when Asian American actors and actresses played leading roles in an American movie. For instance, *The Joy Luck Club* (1993) was based on a best-selling book written by Amy Tan, a Chinese American writer. The movie is about four Chinese American women and their families in the United States. This film used a number of Asian American actors and actresses. The budget of this film was about $10.5 million, but the film brought in $33 million. As a film with an Asian theme, this was a success. In addition, this film showed the other side of Chinese Americans that was different from what was seen in the early 20th century.

The Wedding Banquet (1993) was another movie that gave a different image to Chinese Americans in motion pictures. This film was coproduced by American and Taiwanese companies. The film was about Wai-Tung Gao, a Chinese American, and his Caucasian gay partner, Simon. This kind of storyline would never have been allowed if this movie had been made in the early 20th century. In *Saving Face* (2004), two Chinese American women, Vivian Shing and Wilhelmina Pang, fell in love. Pang revealed her love to Shing by kissing her in public. Pang's mother, Hwei-lang Gao, was pregnant. The baby's father was the son of Gao's friend. The portrayals of Chinese Americans in these two movies were not the stereotype image that Chinese characters used to have.

When compared to Anna May Wong, Chinese American actresses did have more opportunities. They were not just cast as villains, prostitutes, and slave girls. Like Anna May Wong, Lucy Liu also played some stereotype and supporting roles in motion pictures. In *Kill Bill* (2003), Liu was cast as O-Ren Ishhi, who was a half-Chinese American and half-Japanese American assassin and villain. She was killed in the film. But Liu did have a chance to play leading roles. In *Charlie's Angels* (2000) and *Charlie's Angels: Full Throttle* (2003), Liu's character was one of the three Charlie's angels working for a private investigation company. Liu also got the leading role in *Rise: Blood Hunter* (2007). She was cast as a reporter.

Sometimes Chinese American actors and actresses were not cast as Chinese characters in films. For example, Richard Loo, a Chinese American actor, was cast as a Japanese general in *The Purple Heart* (1944) and a Thai millionaire in *The Man with the Golden Sun* (1974); and Soo Yong, a Chinese American actress, played the supporting role of a Japanese woman in *Sayonara* (1957). In *On Deadly Ground* (1994), Joan Chen, a Chinese American actress, played a role of the daughter of an Eskimo tribe chief.

The image of Chinese Americans in motion pictures evolved over time. The roles that Chinese Americans could play also changed. Although some Chinese American actors and actresses successfully landed leading roles, most of them still played supporting or minor roles in Hollywood movies.

See also: Fu Manchu and Charlie Chan; Lee, Ang; Lee, Bruce; Liu, Lucy

Further Reading

Chan, Jachinson. 2001. *Chinese American Masculinities: From Fu Manchu to Bruce Lee*. New York: Routledge.

Hanke, Ken. 1989. *Charlie Chan at the Movies: History, Filmography, and Criticism*. Jefferson, NC: McFarland.

Richardson, Michael. 2010. *Otherness in Hollywood Cinema*. New York: The Continuum International.

Edy Parsons

CHINESE AMERICANS IN SPORTS

Sports have been an integral part of Chinese American life since the late 19th and early 20th centuries. In the 1880s, Chinese immigrants participated in sports such as baseball, cycling, prizefighting, and racewalking, but their participation was limited by insufficient leisure time, social prejudice and ridicule, access to facilities, and federal immigration policy. By the late 1910s and 1920s, interest and participation in sports spread throughout Chinese American communities on the West Coast, particularly in the San Francisco Bay Area, as stable family life replaced the itinerant bachelor culture of first-time

A Chinese American baseball team from Hawai'i that came to the United States to play against university teams. The Chinese team played Columbia University on May 31, 1914. (Library of Congress)

immigrants. At that time, organizations such as the Young Men's and Women's Christian Associations (YMCA and YWCA), children's homes, athletic and social clubs, and high schools and colleges organized team sports and held and sponsored tournaments and other competitions. With the onset of hostilities between China and Japan in the late 1930s and America's entrance in World War II in the 1940s, Chinese American sporting activities leveled off as communities focused their attention on more serious concerns. After the war, interest in sports rejuvenated in the late 1940s, and by the end of the 20th century and into the 21st century, Chinese American athletes excelled at national and international levels.

Although Chinese American participation in sports was not extensive in the late 19th and early 20th centuries, newspaper accounts from the 1880s and 1890s provide some examples. In 1880, the *San Francisco Examiner* noted that two Chinese men, who competed in a racewalking marathon, did not finish, raising speculation of Chinese athletic ability. In the 1890s, Ah Sam, a member of the Los Angeles Fowler Bicycle Racing Club, raced against an unnamed Chinese rider in Oakland. In 1885, the *Examiner* reported a prizefight, in the most complimentary words, between Jim Bung and Ah Fat. In the early 1900s, however, Ah Wing gained notoriety and respect in the boxing ring. Described by the *San Francisco Chronicle* as "America's only Chinese boxer," Ah Wing knocked out Manuel Toores in a much-publicized fight in 1905. Participation in sports like boxing conflicted Chinese culture, which emphasized kinship ties rather than man-to-man and team-to-team contests over competition between groups and individuals. In the 1880s, Chinese students in American universities formed baseball teams, as did one group at Yale who were quite skilled at the game. The Chinese Educational Mission in Hartford, Connecticut, organized a baseball team called "The Orientals." In 1881, as anti-Chinese sentiment grew in the United States, culminating in the Chinese Exclusion Act (1882), members of the Chinese Educational Mission returned to China, but during their stopover in San Francisco, The Orientals played a Caucasian team from Oakland, whom they soundly defeated.

Anti-Chinese sentiment in late 19th- and early 20th-century America, enforced by federal immigration policy, profoundly affected the Chinese American community. As immigration halted and many Chinese returned to China, the remaining populations formed close-knit communities, known as China-towns, with the most known and influential being in San Francisco. With the increase of the native-born population, stable family life gradually replaced the bachelor culture of peripatetic laborers. Families emphasized traditional cultural values, stressing duty, obligation, obedience, and respect. To instill an appreciation of Chinese culture, students attended Chinese school daily for two or more hours after public school, where they studied the Chinese language, Confucianism, and history. Pleased that their children had the opportunity for a good education and the freedom to choose what they would want to do later in life, many Chinese parents found it difficult to imagine their offspring embracing a lifestyle independent from the family, with its emphasis upon leisure. Parental reservations aside, second- and third-generation Chinese American youngsters embraced the activities and social patterns practiced by their white classmates, such as dating, wearing fashionable clothes, driving nice cars, listening to popular music, and participating in sports.

Within the burgeoning Chinese American youth culture in early 20th-century San Francisco Chinatown, interest and participation in sports took root and flourished. Organizations such as the Chinese YMCA and YWCA, children's homes, churches, and social and athletic clubs facilitated the growth of sports. Established in 1911, the Chinese YMCA offered opportunities for boys and young men to play basketball, softball, table tennis, and pool; practice gymnastics and swimming; and pursue outdoor activities of camping, hiking, and horseback riding. The Chinese YWCA, established in 1916, provided opportunities for women to participate in badminton, table, tennis, basketball, volleyball, and gymnastics. In 1933, the YMCA granted YWCA members access to the swimming pool. The Ming Quong Home for girls, in 1915, and the Chung Mei Home of boys, in 1923, encouraged participation in team sports and field days to promote a "spirit of keen, clean competition and good sportsmanship." Founded in 1920 by the Chinese Congregational Church, the Yoke Choy (Disseminate Knowledge) Club promoted Christianity, music, and participation in track and field, tackle football, basketball, and lawn tennis. Similarly, the Cathay Club, which evolved from the Chinese Boys Band, originally organized in 1911, promoted sports and organized a basketball team in 1918.

Although Chinese Americans had been interested in baseball since the 1880s, they did not begin organizing teams until the late 1910s. In 1918, the Chinese Athletic Club in San Francisco formed a baseball team. According to the *San Jose Mercury*, a semipro team from San Jose defeated the Sing Fats, a team of Chinese students from the University of California in Berkeley. In the 1920s, Al Bowen, a former Oakland Oaks player in the Pacific Coast League (PCL), organized the Wah Sungs, which earned a reputation as a good semipro baseball team through the 1930s. Allie Wong, a Wah Sung standout, was recruited by PCL teams. Joe Lee, another standout player on the Wah Sungs in the 1930s, had played for San Francisco State University. Hawaiian-born Chinese surpassed their mainland counterparts in baseball. From 1910 to 1916 the University of Hawai'i's Chinese team toured the continental United States, playing college, semipro, and professional African American teams. In 1914, the Portland Beavers of the PCL signed Lang Akena, a Hawaiian of Chinese descent, but quickly released him because white players would not play against him because of his dark skin. That year, the Chicago White Sox signed Isi Tim, a Hawaiian Chinese, who soon left the team. Hawaiian Chinese "Buck" Lai Tin, who played for the semipro Brooklyn Bushwicks, earned a tryout with the New York Giants. A good fielder, Tim's hitting failed to impress John McGraw, the Giant's manager, who did not sign him.

Beginning in 1919, Chinese Americans began to show interest in football. In that year, Son Kai Kee, who had played football at the University of California in Berkeley, organized teams of players averaging 145 pounds in weight. In the 1920s, the Yoke Choy Club sponsored a football team. Throughout the 1930s, many Chinese American football teams and leagues formed in San Francisco and Southern California. In 1935, the Chung Mei Home organized a 100-pound team and the Chinese Crusaders organized in Oakland. The Chinese YMCA football team enjoyed much success against non-Chinese teams and instilled much pride in the community. In 1937, the Unknown Packers, sponsored by St. Mary's Church, enjoyed an undefeated season against other lightweight teams. In 1940, the Unknown Packers and two other San Francisco teams, Hip Wo and the Dragoneers, joined Sacramento's Black Panthers and Oakland's Young Chinese Athletic Club to form the lightweight Northern California Chinese Football League. In 1941, the League swelled to nine teams.

In the late 1930s and 1940s, the Rice Bowl showcased the best in Chinese American football. Usually played between teams representing San Francisco and Los Angeles, the Rice Bowl evolved out of local efforts by San Francisco's Chinese Consolidated Benevolent Association and national efforts by the United Council for Civilian Relief for China and the American Bureau for Medical Aid to China to raise money to assist victims of Japan's attack on Shanghai in 1937. By 1940, Chinese communities in 39 states held Rice Bowl celebrations. In 1938, the *San Francisco Chronicle* reported that 300,000 participated in the Rice Bowl celebrations. That year, the celebration began with a parade in which the St. Mary's Drill Team, the Chung Mei Drum Corps, three Boy Scout troops, and Locke's Chinese School marched, followed by the football game at San Francisco's Ewing Field. Up to 2,000 spectators watched the games. In 1939, San Francisco entrant in the Rice Bowl, which won for third consecutive time, featured Marshall Leong, who had played for three years on the Mission High School varsity. The six-foot, 200-pound fullback won praise from local sports writers as "the best Chinese football player of the season." Selected to play in the 1939 East-West DeMolay All-Star game, Leong accepted an athletic scholarship to then Oregon State College.

Before World War II, basketball became the most widely played sport throughout Chinese American communities. Invented by Dr. James Naismith at the YMCA training school in Springfield, Massachusetts in 1892, basketball spread across the nation through the YMCAs. Groups such as the YMCA and Catholic Youth Organization (CYO) used the sport to introduce urban immigrant youngsters to American values of teamwork and sportsmanship. Both the Chinese YMCA and YWCA promoted basketball among its memberships.

Male and female students in the San Francisco public schools and colleges formed the Chi Hi Basketball League in the 1930s, and the boys played most of their games at the Chinese YMCA, while the girls played most of their games at the Chinese YWCA. In 1935, the Mei Wah Girls' Club won the basketball tournament sponsored the City of San Francisco Recreation League. Coached by Erline Lowe, Chinatown's "foremost all-around girl athlete," two Catholic Daughters of America (CDA) teams won their divisions in the San Francisco Girls Basketball League in 1938. In 1940, the Wah Kue Basketball Club of San Francisco traveled throughout the Pacific Northwest, Utah, Montana, Idaho, and North Dakota, playing against Chinese and other local teams. During the 1940s, the St. Mary's Saints dominated CYO girls' tournaments.

Beginning in the 1920s, track and field became one of the most popular sports among Chinese American youth. In 1920, the Chinese YMCA held its first track and field meet at Golden Gate Park. The first Athletic Carnival, as the YMCA track meet came to be known, expanded in 1921 to include athletes from Oakland, San Rafael, and Berkeley's Chinese Athletic Club. In 1922, the YMCA added a "marathon," a two-mile run through the streets of Chinatown, to the Athletic Carnival agenda. Cheung S. Lee, who represented the Yoke Choy Club, won the race. The Yoke Choy Club came to dominate track and field, winning the 1921 and 1922 Chinese YMCA meets. In 1930, the Cathay Club held the first Cathay Relay Carnival, which attracted participants from Sacramento and Stockton. Girls participated in the 1933 Cathay Relay Carnival. In 1941, the Young Men's Division Invitational, commemorating the Chinese YMCA's 30th anniversary, was Chinatown's first statewide track and field meet. That year, the San Francisco held a citywide YMCA track meet, which the Chinese branch won, doubling the score of its closest competitor, the Central San Francisco branch.

In the 1920s, Chinese Americans began playing tennis and was, by 1935, as the *Chinese Digest* noted, "a sport considered a silly game a few short years ago by many young Chinese, is one of their most popular games today." In that year, tennis enthusiasts formed the Chinese Tennis Association of San Francisco, known as Chitena, which conducted local, state, and regional tournaments and held stylish annual award banquets, dances, and other social events. In 1935, Henrietta Jung, at 11 years of age, received much attention at San Francisco tennis exhibitions. In the inaugural Amateur Tennis Tournament sponsored by the *San Francisco Examiner* in 1936, Jung lost to Jennie Chew in the semifinals of the Girls' Division before defeating Susan Tivol in the finals. In 1936, Tahmie Chinn and Erline Lowe won the singles titles in the First Chinese Pacific Coast Tennis Championships, jointly sponsored by Chitena and the San Francisco Lodge of the Chinese American Citizens Alliance. Peter Gee won the Chinese Pacific Coast Tennis Championships men's single titles in 1937 and 1940, and Jung won the women's singles title from 1938 to 1940. In 1940, an exhibition between Gee and W. C. Choy, Chinese Davis Cup player, drew huge crowds. A graduate of Cambridge University, Choy was the first Chinese on the tennis team. His appearances in Los Angeles and San Francisco were part of a tour to raise funds for war-ravaged China.

Other sports attracted Chinese American interest and participation from the 1920s to the early 1940s. Beginning in the late 1920s, the Chinese Golfers Association of America in San Francisco began to sponsor tournaments. In 1935, the Chinese YMCA held the first citywide billiard tournament. From 1938 to 1939, James Lee, a member of the Oakland YMCA weightlifting team, won the Northern California 132-pound championship. For those less interested in rigorous physical exertion, the Chinese Sportsmen's Club organized fishing excursions and fishing derbies. In 1935, Sammy Fooey competed in the flyweight division of the Northern California Golden Gloves Tournament. Harry Jung won the Northern California and Pacific Athletic Association 105-pound championships. In 1941, Hawaiian-born Kui Kong Young defeated Lou Salica, the defending bantamweight champion, in the Golden Gloves tournament. In 1940, Bakersfield hosted the First Annual Pacific Coast Chinese Bowling Tournament and, in 1941, 11 cities participated in the Second Annual Tournament, held at San Francisco's Chinese Bowling Alley.

Following the Japanese attack on Pearl Harbor and America's entry into World War II in 1941, sports became a secondary consideration for most Chinese Americans. The Seventh Wah Ying Basketball Tournament, held before December 7, would be the last. After 1942, the Chinese YMCA canceled its annual track meet and marathon for the duration of the war. Despite losing several of its star players to military service, the Chitena traveled to Southern California for matches against the Los Angeles Tennis Club in 1942. Men who once participated on teams of the various organizations that facilitated sports participation, such as 135 who grew up in the Chung Mei Home, now served in the military. The Chinese YMCA offered its showers and swimming pool to Chinese servicemen, and the Chinese YWCA organized a fitness program, assisted the Red Cross, gathered clothing for war refugees, and organized dances for Chinese servicemen. The Chinese American community reaped great benefits during the war, including the limited repeal of the 1882 Chinese Exclusion Act in 1943. Chinese Americans obtained employment in the shipyards and in other wartime industries, which opened up opportunities for careers outside Chinatown after the war. Women as well as men gained access, albeit limited, to professional fields and trades otherwise unavailable to them.

After the war, Chinese Americans returned to participating in sports with greater interest than in previous decades. The YMCA resumed its track and marathon in 1946. Frank Chow, a World War II gunnery instructor, represented the United States in the rapid fire pistol event at the 1948 Olympic Games in London. The Chinatown Veterans of Foreign Wars, founded in 1945, as well as the Chinese Optimist Club, organized basketball tournaments to replace the defunct Wah Ying Club's basketball tournament. The Chinese Optimist Club also started a youth amateur boxing group coached by Tommy Chew, who learned how to box in college. The San Francisco Clippers was one of a half-dozen Chinese football teams in Northern California following the war. In 1948, the San Francisco Chinese Basketball team, paced by 21-year-old Willie "Woo Woo" Wong, defeated Berkeley Nisei, 49-45, in Seattle, to capture its second crown at the National Oriental Basketball Tournament. Wong, who also played on the University of San Francisco basketball team, led the Dons to the New York Invitational Basketball Tournament title in 1949.

From the 1950s through the 1970s, Chinese Americans continued their pursuit of sports. During the 1950s, participation in tennis and golf exceeded levels before the war. Although not a Chinese American, Yang Chuan Kwang (or C. K. Yang) of Taiwan, who competed in track and field for the University of California in Los Angeles in the late 1950s and won the silver medal in the Olympic decathlon in 1960, inspired the Chinese American community. After passage of the 1965 Immigration and Naturalization Act, which abolished the limits set forth in the 1943 repeal of the 1882 Chinese Exclusion Act of 1882, tens of thousands of immigrants now arrived annually, promoting organizations such as the East Bay Chinese Youth Council to established programs in "tutoring, employment, counseling, legal assistance, and recreation." With the influx of Chinese immigrants came a renewed sense of ethnic pride and appreciation of Chinese traditions. A youth culture, similar to that of the early 20th century, shaped the Chinese American community. The enactment of Title IX in 1972 led to increased opportunities for women in sports. By the late 1970s, Chitena cosponsored the First Annual Community Tennis Championship and organized a benefit tournament for Chinese for Affirmative Action. In 1978, the YMCA Marathon, the first to be run since 1949, attracted 381 female and male runners, of which only 71 were Chinese Americans. In that year, Chitena and the Chinatown Savings and Loan sponsored the Chinese tennis championships, then in its 43th consecutive season.

Since the late 20th century, Chinese American athletes have excelled at both the national and international levels in a variety of sports. In 1989, tennis player Michael Chang, age 17, won the French Open, to become became the youngest male player to win a Grand Slam tournament. During the 1990s through the 2000s, Michelle Kwan dominated figure skating, winning nine U.S. titles, five world titles, and two Olympic medals. From 2002 to 2014, Julie Chu represented the United States in Olympic ice hockey, winning one bronze and three silver medals. From 2008 to 2014, Nathan Adrian represented the United States in swimming, winning 21 medals in international competition, including one silver and three gold medals in the Olympic Games. In 2010, Jeremy Lin became the first Chinese American to play in the National Basketball Association.

See also: Adrian, Nathan Ghar Jun; Chang, Michael Te-Pei; Chinese American Baseball; Chow, Norm Yew Heen; Kwan, Michelle Wing Shan; Lin, Jeremy

Further Reading

Choy, Philip P. et al., eds. 1996. *A Celebration of Roots: Chinese Americans in Sports.* San Francisco, CA: Chinese Historical Society of America.

Emery, Lynne. 1984. "Games and Sport of Southern California's Chinese-Americans." Paper presented at the annual convention of the American Alliance for Health, Physical Education, Recreation, and Dance, Anaheim, CA, March 30–April 2.

Frank, Joel S. 1996. "Chinese Americans and American Sports, 1880–1940." *Chinese America: History & Perspectives* 10: 133–47.

Park, Roberta J. 2000. "Sport and Recreation Among Chinese American Communities of the Pacific Coast from Time of Arrival to the 'Quiet Decade' of the 1950s." *Journal of Sport History* 27 (3): 445–80.

Adam R. Hornbuckle

CHINESE MARTIAL ARTS

Kung Fu is widely known around the globe and especially in the United States as a common expression for Chinese martial arts, combining hand fighting and the ability to use different weapons (e.g., swords or lances). What is definitely a part of American culture today was brought to North America by Chinese immigrants and belonged to part of the Chinese diaspora in the United States, being part of its cultural heritage for a long time. It was Hollywood that finally made the public aware of this aspect of Chinese tradition, long after karate had become part of martial arts in the United States. The martial arts from China reached the shores of California with the first immigrants in the first half of the 19th century, but it took almost 100 years for them to become commonly accepted. Especially Bruce Lee, and his appearance in action movies, created a hype for martial arts, which later U.S. movie stars would benefit from. But even in China, the history of martial arts is a diverse one.

Martial arts in the Middle Kingdom seems to have been connected mainly to the temple of the legendary Shaolin monks, who would lead the resistance against the Manchu rule, as has often been depicted in Chinese martial arts movies through the decades. However, martial arts in China could simply consist of common exercises that are very often connected to arcane religious beliefs. These religious aspects of Kung Fu, for example, are often forgotten when the Chinese martial arts become reinterpreted in the North American setting. In this specific environment a version of martial arts is created that is far away from gymnastics or religious beliefs; rather, it becomes an artistic way of fighting with or without weapons in an extremely masculine and powerful way.

Kung Fu was originally just translated as *ability*; it never had this martial character before it became a famous term in American movie culture. In general, the term originally had no implication with regard to fighting skills, but it developed step by step to become an emblem for martial fighting, which was depicted in Hong Kong and later in Hollywood. During the late imperial history of China, Kung Fu described special techniques of concentration by which people were able to let their power—or chi—flow throughout their bodies. It still did not specifically describe a skill that was related to man-to-man fighting.

Kung Fu in China was very often connected to secret societies, whose members trained in it to defend themselves against corrupt state officials, but the government seemed to depict the fighting skills in general as something that belonged to the illiterate masses of the lower class. The social inferiority of the martial arts remained, especially when the martial arts became connected to the secret societies, which developed criminal networks and activities in late 19th and early 20th-century China. Those who performed martial arts were not rarely seen to be criminals. This image became promoted by the ruling Ching Dynasty. The Manchu rulers, who had taken power in China during the 17th century and erected this dynasty, were eager to stay in power by prohibiting boxing associations, because they feared the organization of rebellious forces. Combined with the rather bad image of the martial arts and the restrictions by the Chinese government, martial arts remained rather superficial in many parts of the country, and just some immigrants who left for the United States were still performing it for religious reasons or gymnastics.

However, the image would change around 1900, when the Boxer Rebellion, which was highly connected to martial arts groups in China, tried to get rid of the government as well as the Western imperial penetration of the country. Although the Ching rulers tried to restrict the spread of fighting abilities in the population, the Boxer movement was able to attract countless young men, who also belonged to Chinese secret societies. Despite the fact that the Boxer Rebellion was suppressed by an international expeditionary force, a higher interest in martial arts remained in China, and those who left their country to settle in North America brought their skills and a higher interest with them. However, the Chinese martial arts mainly remained a part of the Chinese subculture in the United States. While karate became quite well known as a consequence of World War II and the American occupation of Japan after 1945, Kung Fu remained something rather Chinese. This fact seems to be a simple consequence of the anti-Chinese sentiments of the American public until the end of the World War II. In Canada, due to China's fight against Japan, the sympathies had grown, but there was still not sufficient interest in the martial arts styles of China—a fact that would finally be changed by the movie industry, which transported the image to a wider American public and helped Chinese martial arts to become an essential part of the U.S. public image.

Modern wars did not need a heroic form of individual fighting, but for the movie industry, the heroic stories of capable men who became even more masculine by using their hands and feet to defeat an enemy, thereby making their own body into a weapon, would be able to attract a larger audience. However, Chinese martial arts were not the first to be presented to an American audience. Sword fights by Japanese samurai were shown in Akira Kurosawa's movies *Seven Samurai* (1954) and *Yojimbo* (1961). Japan seemed to be the first focus of interest, as those sword fights also impacted Western cinema (e.g., the light-saber fights of *Star Wars*). As mentioned above, karate was also already established, as U.S. soldiers had come into contact with this martial art in Okinawa during the occupation of Japan. The term was already part of English dictionaries in the mid-1950s, a time during which a wider public did not even know about the existence of Chinese martial arts. As karate was also shown in the James Bond movie *You Live Only Twice* (1967), it seemed to dominate the U.S. public knowledge of Asian martial arts.

It was the movies of Bruce Lee that changed this situation. He was responsible for the international success story of the Chinese martial arts movie. These movies had been very successful in China, where they depicted the prerevolutionary fight of the people against the Manchu tyrants, who were depicted as the archenemy of the Chinese Revolution by the communist filmmakers. However, the amazing martial arts skills of Bruce Lee brought moviemaking to another level, one that was also recognized by the American movie industry. Bruce Lee, who was Chinese American, left the United States, where he had to face racial discrimination, to work in Hong Kong. There he starred in and produced the blockbusters *The Big Boss* (1971) and *Fist of Fury* (1972). These movies would not only create box office sales records in Hong Kong, but would also strengthen the international interest in such movies, showing tremendously amazing Chinese martial arts skills.

Despite the fact that Lee died too early to develop a full international career, even his incomplete movie *Game of Death* (1972) had a large impact on the image of Chinese martial arts in the United States. Bruce Lee became a symbol of Kung Fu skills, and many young Americans were so impressed by his skills that martial arts studios spread throughout the country, where people were starting to study traditional Chinese martial arts skills. The wave of interest did not end with the death of Bruce Lee. Other martial arts figures emerged, such as David Carradine, Samo Hung, and Chuck Norris, who starred in martial arts movies and series over the following decades. The borders between Chinese, Korean, and Japanese martial arts increasingly vanished, but a second generation of Chinese movie stars (e.g., Jet Li) proceeded with the legacy of Bruce Lee. Large productions not only depicted Chinese history, and were thereby able to act as intercultural exchange tools, but were also able to continue the depiction of Chinese martial arts in American popular culture.

But this was not the only achievement of Bruce Lee. He also constructed an image of Asian masculinity that was based on morality and supreme body skills. He thereby paved the way to ending the image of white racial superiority over the Chinese immigrant community. White American students met their Chinese martial arts teachers on a level where respect and a wish for understanding dominated. Such images became also depicted on the screen, for example, in *American Shaolin* (1992). Today, the United States is experiencing a specific martial arts fusion, as many studios offer a larger variety of different martial arts styles. The Chinese techniques have thereby become integrated into a broader image or repertoire of Asian skills in hand-to-hand combat.

All in all, the history of the Chinese martial arts in the United States resembles not only the history of racial discrimination during the Chinese diaspora abroad, but it also resembles the history of martial arts in China. Connected to revolutionary secret societies in late imperial China, it continued until the image of martial arts was reversed and more immigrants practiced what had been a gymnastic training connected to religious beliefs. For a greater interest in Chinese abilities it needed the events of the first half of the 20th century, which finally led to a partial abolishment of racially motivated stereotypes and prejudices. It also needed a public depiction, which was pioneered by the Chinese American Bruce Lee, who created a hype for Chinese martial arts in both China and the United States. Further generations of action movie stars surfed on this wave of interest and further stimulated a growing martial arts movement in America.

With more and more people becoming interested in martial arts training, the cultural exchange rate between the Chinese diaspora community and its environment grew, even if the abolishment of the old stereotype of Chinese weakness and servant status had been partially exchanged for another one of martial arts masculinity. However, the role martial arts played in American as well as Chinese American history should never be underestimated; it needs more detailed studies, which would focus on different parts of the moving history of Kung Fu and other martial arts forms of Chinese origin in the United States.

See also: Lee, Bruce

Further Reading

Farkas, Emil, and John Corcoran. 1987. *Martial Arts: Tradition, History, People.* New York: Gallery Books.

Nitta, Keiko. 2010. "An Equivocal Space for the Protestant Ethnic: US Popular Culture and Martial Arts Fantasia." *Social Semiotics* 20 (4): 377–92.

Frank Jacob

CHINESE NIGHTCLUBS (1920s–1940s)

When Chinese immigrants arrived on the shores of the United States during the gold rushes, the railway building periods, and the eras in which they had to face dangers and insecurities in China as a consequence of rebellions such as the Taiping Rebellion, revolutions such as the Chinese Revolution of 1911, or civil wars, they brought not only their labor force, but also their specific Chinese culture to the United States. America, which had always been a target for immigration, faced a growing number of Chinese settlers, who founded Chinatowns in the major U.S. cities. A tremendously important part of this culture was the Chinese nightlife, especially during the years from 1920 until the end of the 1940s, when it became a resemblance of a rather unconventional perspective of the lives of Asians in America. Chinese nightclubs, like Charlie Low's Forbidden City in San Francisco, became emblematic of the success of this specific kind of Asian nightlife in the United States, especially since these places provided the rare opportunity for Asian American performers to show their real talents, without being pushed into racial stereotypes.

Chinese immigration to the United States might have been determined by changing historical factors, but it always created spheres of a Chinese diaspora in North America, especially in the metropolitan areas of the country. Like many other immigration groups in the United States, the Chinese people brought their cultural heritage with them, but also developed a new cultural diversity, which would mix Chinese as well as American experiences. Consequently, Chinese nightlife could resemble Asian exotic aspects as well as quite common Western ones. The white middle classes in the country developed a nightlife between the 1880s and the 1930s by "slumming," meaning to tour immigrant enclaves of metropolitan areas, and thereby overcoming sexual, racial, and socioeconomic prejudices to create a new common consciousness, namely, for a new form of identity. Meanwhile, the Chinese immigrants also tried to establish their changed consciousness by combining an American-style nightlife with their cultural and social heritage. Consequently, nightlife experiences led to a further development of cultural diversity and cultural exchange, and to a redefinition of the norms of popular culture itself.

Due to the process of exchange between U.S. popular culture and Chinese traditional values, civilizational clashes also arose. Those Chinese Americans who had decided to work in the show business of a newly established and vibrant nightlife in the urban centers of San Francisco or New York also had to face severe problems. First, they might have been ostracized by their own communities, whose older generations still lived in a traditional Chinese setting, which followed a Chinese self-imagination. Second, those early Chinese American entertainers also had to face racism and stereotypes, which were quite widespread in U.S. society. However, some decided for a career in American-style nightclubs, where they would perform as a bias of Chinese and American culture, even if such a choice was an extremely radical one during the 1930s and 1940s, when many entertainers had a hard life in such a white-dominated industry. Despite the harsh situation, these men and women wanted to become entertainers, and therefore, willingly or not, they played their role in bridging the cultural gaps between the Chinese immigrant community and the white American audience.

It was the Chinese American performers, such as Larry Ching and Frances Chung, who attracted the white audiences at such clubs; these people were searching for an exotic but at the same time quite common experience in the nightclubs. There were seven well-known nightclubs in San Francisco, while New York had only one large and well-received club for Chinese American performers—the *China Doll*, which opened between 1920 and 1950. Tom Ball, a white stage producer, owned the New Yorker club, which played the Asian card to attract the party audience of the Roaring Twenties by overemphasizing Chineseness, especially so-called "pagoda punches," for the indulgence of the guests. In contrast to this setting, the facilities in San Francisco were all Chinese owned; the performances here dealt with the Gold Rush or other topics of Chinese American history. During the 1940s, especially, the Forbidden City became a star of the Chinese nightclubs in America, attracting full houses of audiences that were attracted by its exotic tapestries and Mandarin-collared bartenders who provided drinks during the shows. A huge golden Buddha surveyed the audience from its bar stand and many celebrities of that time, including Bob Hope and Lauren Bacall, were attracted by the atmosphere in the Forbidden City. However, it was not only the stars who visited the pulsing nightclub, but also tourists from other parts of the country who were eager to experience the exotic atmosphere as well as the special shows starring Chinese performers.

It was young Chinese American dancers who performed American dances like the Charleston or the shim sham. Furthermore, Larry Ching, who was known as the "Chinese Frank Sinatra," performed well-known pop tunes and Broadway songs. The exotic aspect was consequently not provided by the content, but by the image of a Chinese performer who sang well-established Western songs. Another image that could be seen in the Chinese nightclub was a mix of both cultural settings. While dancers started their shows in Chinese robes, they slipped them off to appear in showgirl outfits when dancing to American music tunes. These could include Bing Crosby songs, Latin American Sambas, or European Polkas. Consequently, the Asian American dancers delivered a stereotyped content that was "exoticized" simply by their own appearance as Chinese Americans.

They simply added an exotic air of mystery to existing American routines, thereby attracting the mainly white audience. Despite the fact that the performers used the racially determined exoticism of their cultural background to make a career, this seemed to be the only chance to perform at all in the field of their interest. Consequently, it was their ambition to perform that created the pulsing nightlife of the Chinese clubs, which not only attracted the white audience but at the same time antagonized the conservative Asian communities in the United States. Furthermore, even if the Chinese American performers could be described as stars or idols, they were also confronted with racial discrimination, a problem that was common in the early American entertainment industry, whether in the nightclub scene or in Hollywood.

That this kind of discrimination continued in the nightclubs is also visible through the fact that not only Chinese Americans could perform there, but also Japanese Americans such as Pat Morita, who would later star in *Karate Kid* (1984), could appear without destroying the Chinese exoticism for the white audience; it seems an Asian was an Asian, regardless of country of origin. Jimmy Borges, who had a Portuguese father and a Hawaiian Chinese mother, even had to change his stage name to Jimmy Jay, to sound more Chinese for the audience when he began to perform at the Forbidden City in 1958. The memorabilia of these decades highlight the depiction of a Chinese American exoticism that was based on the faces of the performers, but not the content that had been staged. What they do not show is the daily racism, the criticism from home, and the prejudices from the Hollywood-based entertainment industry that these performers, who simply wanted to live their dreams, had to face.

But due to their performances, the stars of the Chinese American nightclub scene helped to overcome racial stereotypes. The white audiences began to find out that myths about bowlegged Asian girls or Asians' lack of talent in performing Western music were simply not true. The same prejudices existed in the entertainment industry itself for quite a long time, as Asian performers were denied because producers thought them unable to perform in a theatrical way, for which they were supposed to have no talent at all. Although they had U.S. citizenship, the Chinese American performers were often reduced to roles that underlined the stereotypes of an Asian orientalism, which white audiences expected to see.

Despite the fact that the Chinese American, Japanese American, and even Korean American performers were not intending to change the course of history, they definitely did. While they followed their dreams of a career as a performer in the entertainment industry, they helped overcome the racially motivated stereotypes of Western supremacy, especially with regard to talent and cultural performance abilities. By fighting for an opportunity to perform, whether dancing or singing, they also crossed cultural borders. They helped to spread the understanding of Chinese Americans, not only as victims of American racism but also of talented and even sexually attractive human beings, who were part of American society in general and the American entertainment industry, represented in the Chinese American nightclubs between the 1920s and 1940s, in particular.

See also: Chinese American Hip-Hop; Chinese American Jazz

Further Reading

Dong, Arthur, and Lisa Lee. 2014. *Forbidden City, USA: Chinese American Nightclubs, 1936–1970*. Los Angeles, CA: Deep Focus.

Lee, Esther Kim. 2006. *A History of Asian American Theatre*. Cambridge, UK: Cambridge University Press.

Frank Jacob

CHOW, NORM YEW HEEN (1946–)

Born on May 3, 1946, in Honolulu, Hawai'i, Norman Yew Heen Chow is of Chinese, Hawaiian, and Portuguese lineage. His mother is a native Hawaiian, while his father is the son of Chinese emigrant. Chow was a graduate of the Punahou School, a private college preparatory school on Honolulu, where he played on the football team as an offensive lineman.

After graduating from high school in 1964, Chow accepted an athletic scholarship to play football at the University of Utah. A three-year letterman and a two-year starter as an offensive guard, he was named to the All-WAC (Western Athletic Conference) team and earned All-American honorable mention honors in his senior season in 1967. After graduating with a bachelor's degree in physical education in 1968, Chow played professional football for the Saskatchewan Rough Riders of the Canadian Football League until an injury ended his professional career. Upon returning to Hawai'i, he started coaching high school football and, from 1970 to 1972, served as the head coach at Waialua High and Intermediate School in Honolulu.

In 1973 Chow entered graduate school at Brigham Young University (BYU) and became a graduate assistant on the football team under coach LaVell Edwards. After coaching freshmen in 1975, he became the wide receivers' coach in 1976. Except for a year as the running backs' coach in 1978, he remained the wide receivers' coach until 1982. In that year, Chow became the offensive player caller and continued in that role until leaving BYU in 2000. In the meantime, he had earned a master's degree in special education and a doctorate in educational psychology from BYU.

In 1983, Chow became the Assistant Offensive Coordinator and quarterbacks' coach at BYU. That year, he coached Steve Young, who established a National Collegiate Athletic Association (NCAA) single-season records for pass completion percentage (71.3 percent) and total yards per game (584.2) and finished second in the Heisman Trophy balloting. In 1984, BYU enjoyed an undefeated season and won the consensus national championship. Quarterback Robbie Bosco, under Chow's guidance, finished second in the nation in total passing and third in the Heisman vote.

Chow became the Assistant Head Coach and retained the position of Assistant Offensive Coordinator at BYU in 1990. In that year, BYU upset number-one University of Miami, 28-21, the defending national champion, posting nearly 500 offensive yards. Brigham Young quarterback, Ty Detmer, won the Heisman Trophy. Maintaining the position of Assistant Head Coach, Chow was promoted to Offensive Coordinator in 1996. That year, BYU won the WAC and defeated Kansas State, 19-15, in the Cotton Bowl, finished the season ranked fifth in the nation with a 14-1 record, the most wins in a season by Division I football team. Quarterback Steve Sarkisian finished the season with a quarterback rating of 162.0, the third highest in the country.

After a career spanning 27 years at BYU, Chow spent the next decade serving as the offensive coordinator for several college teams and a professional team. In 2000, he joined North Carolina State University. That year, the Wolfpack finished second in total offense in the Atlantic Coast Conference and defeated the University of Minnesota, 38-30, in the Micron PC Bowl, for its first bowl win in five years. In 2001, Chow became the offensive coordinator at the University of Southern California (USC). After posting a 12-1 record in 2002, the Associated Press ranked USC first in the nation. That year, he coached quarterback Carson Palmer, who won the Heisman Trophy. Chow, who received the Broyles Award as the nation's top assistant coach, turned down an offer from the University of Kentucky to become its head coach. In 2004, USC defeated the University of Oklahoma, 55-19, in the Orange Bowl for the BCS National Championship. That year, quarterback Matt Leinart, coached by Chow, won the Heisman Trophy.

Beginning in 2005, Chow served as the offensive coordinator of the Tennessee Titans of the National Football League. Under his leadership, Vince Young, the Offensive Rookie of the Year in 2006, became the first rookie quarterback to play in the Pro Bowl. During Chow's tenure at Tennessee, the Titans won 24 and lost 26 games, and qualified the playoffs in 2007. In 2008, Chow returned to the college ranks as the offensive coordinator at the University California, Los Angeles. In 2011, Chow joined his undergraduate alma mater, the University of Utah.

At the end of the 2011 season, Chow became the head coach at the University of Hawai'i at Mānoa. Under his tutelage, the Warriors won 8 out of 37 games. Married since 1974, Chow is the father of four children.

See also: Chinese Americans in Sports

Further Reading

"Norm Chow." 2015. Accessed July 16, 2015. http://www.sports-reference.com/.
"Norm Chow." 2013. Accessed July 16, 2015. http://hawaiiathletics.com/.

Adam R. Hornbuckle

DONG, ARTHUR (1953–)

Born in San Francisco, California, on October 30, 1953, screenwriter, director, and producer Arthur Dong is perhaps best known for his work with documentary films. Making full use of the visual nature and form of film, his investigative style allows him to tackle a myriad of difficult issues such as of ethnic identity, modern Asian American history, and gender oppression. As a member of the Academy of Television Arts and Sciences, he boasts a distinguished career of service to the industry. For example, from 2000 to 2003, he served on the Board of Directors of Film Independent, and from 2002 to 2006, on the Board of Governors of the Academy of Motion Picture Arts and Sciences. He currently serves on the National Film Preservation Board.

Dong began making films at Galileo High School (now the Galileo Academy of Science and Technology) as the Vietnam War was coming to a close. With the debut in 1970 of *Public*, a five-minute animated short based on a poem he had earlier written and shot on his bedroom floor, he took first prize at the California High School Film Festival. Of equal importance, his intense exploration of the visceral responses of a child to violence demonstrated to him the efficacy of the visual image to promote social awareness and bring about change. Over the next decade he developed his craft. With his *Living Music for Golden Mountains* (1981) and its profile of his Chinese music teacher, Dong made his professional debut as a documentary filmmaker. He soon found gainful employment as an associate producer for KGO-TV in San Francisco from 1981 to 1982, and concurrently received his B.A. in film studies (*summa cum laude*) from San Francisco State University. Shortly thereafter, he founded DeepFocus Productions, where he continues to serve as producer, director, and writer.

He received a nomination for an Academy Award for Documentary Short Subject in 1984 for his undergraduate project, *Sewing Woman*, a documentary about his mother's immigration from China to America. A year later, in 1985, he completed a Director's Fellowship with the American Film Institute Center for Advanced Film Studies. Thereafter he produced *Lotus* (1988), a half-hour drama forcefully exposing the feudal practice of foot-binding among Chinese women. *Forbidden City, U.S.A.* (1989), his musical tribute to the plight of Asian American nightclub performers in the 1940s, and *Claiming a Voice: The Visual Communications Story* (1990) followed. From 1991 to 1992, he produced 12 emotionally charged installments for the Emmy-Award-winning *Life and Times* at KCET in Los Angeles. He received a Peabody Award in 1995 for *Coming Out Under Fire*, his historical investigation of gay and lesbian soldiers during World War II, at a time when the military established its first explicit antigay policy. He continued the exploration of this issue with *The Question of Equality* (1995), the first public television series to cover the modern gay and lesbian civil rights movement following the Stonewall Riots. His *Licensed to Kill* (1997) went a step further with its vividly brutal depiction of the minds of murderers who had killed gay men. And his *Family Fundamentals* (2002) pushed the envelope still further, as he explored the cultural wars over homosexuality through the specific experiences of three fundamentalist American families coming to grips with their gay adult children.

As prolific and fluid as he is profound, the succinct nature of his works have not escaped critical attention. He counts among his many recognitions three Sundance Film Festival Awards, the Teddy Award from the Berlin Film Festival, and the Golden Horse Award from the Taiwan film industry. Additionally, he has been nominated for no less than five Emmy Awards. So very appealing was his 2007 documentary *Hollywood Chinese* that it was rebroadcast two years later as a part of the PBS series, *American Masters*. Tellingly, at precisely the same time that Dong was working on this subject, he, too, was fighting against the ravages of time to preserve and restore *The Curse of Quon Gwon* (1916), the earliest known Chinese American feature film.

His work in documentary film has simultaneously provided him a substantial platform from which he continues to work as a community activist and leader. Among his many recognitions are the George Foster Peabody Award and the James Wong Howe Award, presented to him by the Association of Asian Pacific American Artists, the Steve Tatsukawa Award for excellence in visual communications, the Asian American Media Award from Asian CineVision, the Historian Award from the Chinese Historical Society of America, and the Historymakers Award from the Chinese American Museum.

His significant passion for and long-term dedication toward the fight for recognition, respect, and equal rights for the LGBT community have also garnered him considerable attention. In addition to having received two prestigious GLAAD Media Awards and the San Francisco Foundation James D. Phelan Award in Filmmaking, he is the recipient of the Paul Monette Award and the Out 100 Award, presented by *Out Magazine*.

Dong's feature-length documentaries have found distribution throughout the United States, and his films continue to be featured in hundreds of festivals worldwide. The Human Rights International Film Festival in Warsaw, Poland, the Walker Art Center in Minneapolis, the Hawai'i International Film Festival, Taipei's CNEX Documentary Film Festival, and Outfest in Los Angeles have each featured significant and moving retrospectives of his works. His curatorial exhibition in April 2014, at the San Francisco Main Public Library both showcased his extensive personal collection of Chinese American nightclub ephemera and launched the publication of his book, *Forbidden City, USA: Illustrated Histories of Chinese American Nightclubs, 1936–1965*, a scholarly document of the research underpinning his award-winning 1989 film on the topic.

Dong has taught documentary film classes at the University of California, Santa Barbara; the University of North Texas; the University of Texas at Austin;

the University of Hawai'i at Mānoa; Emory University at Atlanta; and the Sundance/CNEX Documentary Workshop in Beijing. More recently, he has been named twice as a Rockefeller Fellow in Media Arts and has held a Guggenheim Fellow in Film. He currently teaches at Loyola Marymount University's School of Film and Television. His newest film, *The Killing Fields of Dr. Haing S. Ngor*, debuted in spring 2015 at CAAMFest (formerly the San Francisco International Asian American Film Festival). Chronicling the life, times, and murder of Ngor, it stands as an appropriate and sincere homage to the first-time Cambodian Chinese actor who had translated the horrific experiences of his four-year internment in Khmer Rouge prison camps to create an Oscar-winning performance in *The Killing Fields*.

See also: Chinese Americans and LGBTQQI; Chinese Americans in Motion Pictures; Ngor, Haing S.

Further Reading

Hamamoto, Darrell. 2000. *Countervisions: Asian American Film Criticism*. Philadelphia, PA: Temple University Press.
Miura, Glen M. 2009. *Ghostlife of Third Cinema: Asian American Film and Video*. St. Paul: University of Minnesota Press.

James A. Wren

EATON, EDITH MAUDE (SUI SIN FAR) (1865–1914)

See: Chinese American Literature

FA MU LAN

Fa Mu Lan is a Chinese American folk heroine who became familiar to many English speakers as a result of Maxine Hong Kingston's bestselling book, *The Woman Warrior: Memoirs of a Girlhood Among Ghosts* (1976). Kingston's work draws inspiration from the legendary Chinese character, commonly known as Hua Mulan among Chinese speakers. This heroine has a long tradition and remains well known in China. It is believed that the poem "Ballad of Mulan" (ca. fourth–sixth century CE) is the earliest written account of her legend. The basic storyline portrays how, to save her father from going to war, the daughter Mulan impersonates a young man, joins the army, and serves her country for years. After her troops' triumph, Mulan turns down the official rank and welfare bestowed on her and returns home to her womanly life.

Kingston's writing transforms Mulan into a Chinese American heroine. Published as a memoir, her controversial work adapts the Chinese folk story that the narrator acquired through her mother's "talk-story" and recounts how the narrator constructs her identity as she comes of age. Instead of literally translating the Chinese legend, Kingston rewrites Mulan into a Chinese American woman warrior whose image is enriched by a bicultural legacy and a conscious female empowerment. Kingston's book has appealed to many readers and has had far-reaching influence on Asian American communities. Her reconfigured heroine Fa Mu Lan has incurred debate among readers and scholars about cultural authenticity. For example, Chinese American writer Frank Chin has criticized Kingston's rewriting as a distortion of the "real" Chinese folktale. The enduring critical pen war between Chin and Kingston, along with their supporters, has become a historical milestone in Asian American studies. The debate reflects a number of the critical issues that have helped shape Asian American literary studies and continue to influence the emerging field of Asian American folklore.

Originating in Chinese folklore, the character of Fa Mu Lan also has appeared in a number of picture books for children in the United States. Disney Studio's animated features *Mulan* (1998) and *Mulan II* (2005) have further expanded the heroine's fame and introduced her to an international audience. Her story has become an important part of Chinese American folklore and continues to play a significant role in Asian American literature.

See also: Folklore in Children's Literature; Kingston, Maxine Hong

Further Reading

Chin, Frank. 1991. "Come All Ye Asian American Writers of the Real and the Fake." In *The Big Aiiieeeee! An Anthology of Chinese American and Japanese American Literature*, edited by Jeffery Paul Chan et al., 1-93. New York: Meridian.

Dong, Lan. 2006. "Writing Chinese America into Words and Images: Storytelling and Retelling of *The Song of Mu Lan*." *The Lion and the Unicorn* 30 (2): 218–33.

Frankel, Hans, trans. 1976. "Mu-lan." In *The Flowering Plum and the Palace Lady: Interpretations of Chinese Poetry*, 68–70. New Haven, CT: Yale University Press.

Wong, Sau-ling Cynthia, ed. 1999. *Maxine Hong Kingston's The Woman Warrior: A Casebook*. New York: Oxford University Press.

Lan Dong

FOLKLORE IN CHILDREN'S LITERATURE

In addition to Eurocentric folklore, there are two other types of folklore that can be found in Chinese American children's picture books. The first originates from China, and the second has its roots in Chinese America.

Chinese folklore has been translated and retold often in English storybooks, sometimes by Chinese American writers like Laurence Yep and Ed Young. Among the most popular Chinese stories published for American children is the story of Mulan. As with other Chinese folklore, her legend has been trans-lated verbatim into English as well as adapted and retold variously from the original Chinese "Ballad of Mulan" (fourth–sixth century CE).

So-called Chinese folklore created by American writers has questionable authenticity. A children's short story by Palmer Cox entitled "The Curious Case of Ah-Top" (1898) describes how the top, a toy, got its name from a Chinese man named Ah-Top. *Tikki Tikki Tembo* (1968) is a story retold by Arlene Mosel about the origin of monosyllabic or short Chinese names. Another author, David Bouchard, explains two Chinese holidays. In *The Dragon New Year* (1999), a Chinese American grandmother tells her granddaughter a New Year origin story in which an evil sea dragon kills a young man, and whose mother seeks revenge and learns from Buddha how to defeat the dragon. In *The Mermaid's Muse* (1999), a Chinese American grandmother tells her grandson the origin of the Dragon Boat Festival that involves an intimate friendship between poet-scholar-minister Qu Yuan and a beautiful mermaid, who is a sea dragon in disguise.

A common literary technique among children's storywriters is to insert Chi-nese folklore into an American setting by creating a Chinese American storyteller, usually an immigrant elder, whose function is to educate the United States about China. These stories serve as cultural ambassadors, with no character develop-ment on the part of the narrator. They also provide Chinese cultural maintenance and transmission for American-born Chinese children who have supposedly "lost their roots" in the United States. In these stories, Chinese folklore becomes Chi-nese American by its transnational association with a Chinese American setting.

Folklore that is uniquely Chinese American can be found in origin stories that have been published for children to historically explain Chinese America. *Dragon Parade* (1993), by Steven A. Chin, fictionalizes the first Chinese Lunar New Year celebration and parade in the United States, if not the world. *Pie Biter* (1983), by Ruthanne Lum McCunn, recounts how pie was introduced to China by a Chinese American laborer named Hoi. *The Story of Chinaman's Hat* (1990), by Dean Howell, tells how a Hawaiian tourist attraction got its name from Lick Bean, who floated from Xinhui, China. Also explaining Chinese American origins are a few biographical picture books depicting legendary figures. Allen Say's picture book *El Chino* (1996) shows how Arizona-born Bong Way "Billy" Wong became Spain's first matador of Chinese descent; Ken Mochizuki's *Be Water, My Friend* (2006) describes the early years of San Francisco-born Bruce Lee before his mar-tial arts and acting days; and Paula Yoo's *Shining Star* (2009) tells the story of Los Angeles-born Anna May Wong, Hollywood's first major Chinese American actress.

Chinese Americans have more presence in stories about America's railroads. *Coolies* (2001), by Yin, begins with a Chinese American grandmother practicing the ancestral rituals of the Qing Ming Festival with her grandson and, in doing so, narrates the family's history from China to the United States. By exten-sion this becomes an origin story of Chinese American workers who built the

Transcontinental Railroad during the 1860s. There are also two ghost stories based on the railroad experience: *The Iron Moonhunter* (1977) by Kathleen Chang and *Ghost Train* (1996) by Paul Yee, where ghosts of Chinese American railroad workers recall their oppression. These storybooks contribute to making Chinese Americans an integral part of America's railroad folklore.

Fairy tales have also been published with Chinese American characters. Grace Lin wrote and illustrated *The Red Thread* (2007) to explain the adoption of Chinese girls in the United States. The story begins with the Caucasian adoptive parents telling their Chinese daughter that "once upon a time," a Caucasian king and queen found their Chinese princess by following a red thread to China and they "lived happily ever after." In *The Prince and the Li Hing Mui* (1998), Sandi Takayama adapts Hans Christian Andersen's "The Princess and the Pea" and has a Pacific Islander princess test a Chinese commoner. Instead of a pea, she places under the stack of mattresses a Chinese preserved plum known as *li hing mu* (the Zhongshan dialectal pronunciation for *lüxing mei*).

Folklore that originated from China and is deemed the ancestral heritage of Chinese America serves as a cultural ambassador and transmitter but has varying degrees of authenticity in its transference. Folklore that is based on the Chinese American experience transmits stories that may not come from the oral tradition of the community, but it is uniquely rooted in the United States. Together, the two bodies of stories provide a glimpse into Chinese American folklore that has been mostly ignored and not studied in American children's literature.

See also: Fa Mu Lan; Yep, Laurence Michael

Further Reading

Cai, Mingshui. 1994. "Images of Chinese and Chinese Americans Mirrored in Picture Books." *Children's Literature in Education* 25 (3): 169–91.

Dong, Lorraine. 2009. "Mulan Leaves China." In *At 40: Asian American Studies @ San Francisco State*, edited by Jeffery Paul Chan et al., 179–89. San Francisco, CA: AAS Department, San Francisco State University.

Dong, Lorraine. 2014. "Once Upon a Time in Chinese America: Literary Folktales in American Picture Books." In *Asian American Identities and Practices: Folkloric Expressions in Everyday Life*, edited by Jonathan H. X. Lee and Kathleen Nadeau, 49–68. Lanham, MD: Lexington Books.

Fox, Dana L., and Kathy G. Short, eds. 2003. *Stories Matter: The Complexity of Cultural Authenticity in Children's Literature*. Urbana, IL: National Council of Teachers of English.

Yokota, Junko, and Ann Bates. 2005. "Asian American Literature: Voices and Images of Authenticity." In *Exploring Culturally Diverse Literature for Children and Adolescents: Learning to Listen in New Ways*, edited by Darwin L. Henderson and Jill P. May, 323–55. Boston, MA: Pearson.

Lorraine Dong

FU MANCHU AND CHARLIE CHAN

Fu Manchu and Charlie Chan are well-known Asian male characters in the early to mid-20th century whose stories are of importance in the studies of Orientalism and Asian American folklore. Being portrayed as an evil genius who personifies the Asian threat, the Fu Manchu character in British literature preceded his film and television embodiment in the United States. In 1913, British writer Sax Rohmer (pseudonym of Arthur Henry Sarsfield Ward, 1883–1959) published *The Mystery of Dr. Fu Manchu* in London, which was published as *The Insidious Dr. Fu Manchu* in New York in the same year and later was adapted into a film by Rowland V. Lee and released by Paramount Pictures in 1929. From 1913 to 1959, Rohmer continued to publish novels and novellas that featured the villainous doctor. These works won Rohmer prestige both in Britain and abroad and introduced the vicious and mysterious Dr. Fu Manchu to a broad readership. A number of his works were adapted into films from the 1920s to the 1960s. In 1956, a television series based on the character of Fu Manchu was created. Through these literary and media incarnations, Fu Manchu became a popular Asian character who embodies evilness.

Warner Oland (October 3, 1879 – August 6, 1938) in a scene from the 1929 film *The Mysterious Dr. Fu Manchu.* Oland was a Swedish American actor most remembered for his screen role as the detective Charlie Chan. Oland's role as Charlie Chan is an example of yellowface, when a non-Asian actor wears makeup to appear Asian. Yellowface is not a thing of the past, as evidenced by *Cloud Atlas* (2012), a film in which an English actor, James D'Arcy, portrays an East Asian character. Asian American critics called it "racist." (John Springer Collection/Corbis)

Charlie Chan was the main character in American writer Earl Derr Biggers's (1884–1933) mystery novel series published between 1925 and 1933, beginning with *The House Without a Key* (1925). Charlie Chan attracted much attention from general readers and audiences as a result of

Biggers's works as well as many film, television, and comic series based on his writing in the 1930s and 1940s. Perceived as a contravention of Fu Manchu, the detective Charlie Chan symbolizes the tamed and desexualized Asian man who has been assimilated.

Edward Said's groundbreaking work *Orientalism* (1979) questions the demarcation between the Orient and the Occident as discursive constructions. According to Said, the concepts of Orient and Orientalism are social constructs invented, standardized, and reiterated by the European and American ideology. The characters of Fu Manchu and Charlie Chan, both creations of the Occident, reflect Orientalism in American popular culture and films in the 20th century. Fu Manchu and Charlie Chan, respectively, represent the two major stereotypes of Asian men in British and American imagination: on the one hand, the notorious villain who endangers Euro-American society and embodies evil spirit and actions; and on the other hand, the docile, emasculated detective who has been domesticated to serve the mainstream.

See also: Chang, Apana; Chinese Americans in Motion Pictures

Further Reading

Chen, Tina. 2002. "Dissecting the 'Devil Doctor': Stereotypes and Sensationalism in Sax Rohmer's Fu Manchu." In *Re/Collecting Early Asian America: Essays in Cultural History*, edited by Josephine Lee, Imogene Lim, and Yuko Matsukawa, 218-237. Philadelphia, PA: Temple University Press.

Lahusen, Thomas. 2000. "Dr. Fu Manchu in Harbin: Cinema and Moviegoer of the 1930s." *The South Atlantic Quarterly* 99 (1): 143–61.

Rzepka, Charles J. 2007. "Race, Region, Rule: Genre and the Case of Charlie Chan." *PMLA* 122 (5): 1463–81.

Lan Dong

HO, FRED WEI-HAN (1957–2014)

See: Chinese American Jazz

HUANG, EDDIE (1982–)

Eddie Huang was born on March 1, 1982 in Washington, D.C., to Louis and Jessica Huang, immigrants from Taiwan. He is one of three sons. His family relocated to Orlando, Florida, where his father managed a successful group of steak and seafood restaurants.

Huang went to The University of Pittsburgh and Rollins College and graduated with a bachelor's degree. He then attended Cardozo School of Law at Yeshiva University, and after graduating practiced law for a brief period before

Chef/writer Eddie Huang rings the NASDAQ opening bell at NASDAQ MarketSite in New York City on February 26, 2015. (Slaven Vlasic/Getty Images)

changing careers to become a stand-up comic and, later, a successful restaurateur.

Huang's first restaurant was BaoHaus, located on the Lower East Side of New York, which he opened in December 2009, serving Taiwanese braised pork belly buns, known as gua-bao. Later, he relocated to the East Village and expanded his menu. He opened another restaurant, Xiao Ye, which was less successful and received negative reviews from critics, and which eventually closed due to controversy over selling Four Loko, a drink that contains alcohol, caffeine, taurine, and guarana.

Huang is best known for his memoir, Fresh Off the Boat, which started as a popular blog, and later published by Spiegel & Grau (an imprint of Random House) in 2013. His memoir relates his early life, his Taiwanese (and, by extension, Asian) heritage, and rise in the New York food celebrity scene hosting food-themed programs for the Food Network and Vice TV. He deals with the struggle to form his identity growing up as an "other" in America and his identification with hip-hop and black culture. Huang was exposed to cooking through his parents; he learned how to prepare Taiwanese dishes at home from his mother and learned American regional cuisines through cooking at his father's Orlando, Florida steak and seafood restaurants. He also talks about his days in college, his short stint as a lawyer and stand-up comic, and his various forays into pornography and marijuana dealing.

Huang's memoir was adapted into an ABC comedy sitcom of the same name in 2014. The show made its national primetime debut in February 2015. Huang's TV show feeds a hungry Asian American audience that wants cultural recognition, but in an interview with The New York Times Magazine, he comments that he worries about the show changing his characters in the pursuit of universal appeal, which he calls "reverse yellowface," telling white American stories with Chinese faces.

See also: Chinese Americans in Motion Pictures; Model Minority

Further Reading

Huang, Eddie. 2013. *Fresh Off the Boat*. New York: Spiegel & Grau.

Jonathan H. X. Lee

HWANG, DAVID HENRY (1957–)

David Henry Hwang is one of the most prominent Asian American playwrights working in the theater today. Born in Los Angeles, California, Hwang was the son of a Chinese banker and a Chinese piano teacher, both immigrants to the United States. Hwang received his B.A. in English from Stanford University, took literature classes at the Yale School of Drama, and is currently Columbia University's Director of the Theatre Program's Playwriting Concentration. He is known for the plays *FOB* (1980), *The Dance and the Railroad* (1981), *M. Butterfly* (1988), *Golden Child* (1998), *Yellow Face* (2007), *Chinglish* (2011), and *Kung Fu* (2014); the Broadway musicals *Disney's Tarzan* (2000), *Aida* (2000, with music and lyrics by Elton John and Tim Rice), and *Flower Drum Song* (2002, revised version); and the screenplays *M. Butterfly* (1993), *Golden Gate* (1994), and *Possession* (2002, coauthored with Laura Jones and Neil LaBute). He is also America's most-produced living opera librettist and has collaborated with world-renowned composers, including Philip Glass, Osvaldo Golijov, Bright

Tony-Award winning playwright David Henry Hwang at The Public Theater in New York on November 29, 2007. His play, *Yellow Face*, was Hwang's first in ten years, and is in many ways his most personal, most autobiographical, and most confessional piece to date. (AP Photo/ Jim Cooper)

Sheng, Unsuk Chin, Huang Ruo, and Howard Shore. Hwang has written on the themes of Asian immigrants in America, the conflicts between tradition and change in Chinese society, and the fluidity of identity. He is also an advocate of racial diversity in theatre and openly supports minority actors on stage. According to Hwang, plays are his most personal form, and probably his most universally recognized work to date is the Tony Award-winning play *M. Butterfly* (1988), which is inspired by Puccini's opera *Madame Butterfly* and loosely based on the true romantic story of the French diplomat Bernard Boursicot and the male Beijing opera singer and spy Shi Pei Pu. For his theatre work, Hwang has received a Tony Award (*M. Butterfly*) and an OBIE Award three times (*FOB, Golden Child, Yellow Face*). He has also been a three-time finalist for the Pulitzer Prize in Drama (*The Dance and the Railroad, M. Butterfly, Yellow Face*). In 2015, Hwang was one of the recipients of the Distinguished Artist Award at the International Society for the Performing Arts Congress.

See also: Chinese American Literature; Chinese Americans in Motion Pictures

Further Reading

Boles, William. 2013. *Understanding David Henry Hwang.* Columbia: University of South Carolina Press.

Tammy Ho Lai-Ming

KINGSTON, MAXINE HONG (1940–)
See: Chinese American Literature

KWAN, MICHELLE WING SHAN (1980–)

Born on July 7, 1980, in Torrance, California, Michelle Wing Shan Kwan is the third child of Danny and Estella Kwan, both of whom are immigrants from Hong Kong. Influenced by her older siblings, Ron, a hockey player, and Karen, a figure skater, Kwan became interested in skating at the age of five. By 1988, she and her sister began training seriously, skating three to four hours a day, before and after school. Supported by the Los Angeles Figure Skating Club, Kwan and her sister began training at the Ice Castle International Training Center in Lake Arrowhead, California.

Coached by Frank Carroll, Michelle quickly became an international competitor. At the age of 11, she placed ninth in the junior competition at the 1992 U.S. Figure Skating Championships. That year, Kwan surpassed the gold standard necessary to compete at the senior level and, in 1993, finished sixth in the senior competition at the U.S. Championships. After winning the junior title at the 1994 World Championships, she finished second in the U.S.

Championships that year. In 1994, the U.S. Championships served as the U.S. Olympic Trials, and Kwan qualified for the Olympic team with her second-place finish, but she was named as an alternate to the squad instead. Nancy Kerrigan, a strong favorite to win the gold medal, was placed on the team, since she had been unable to compete following a vicious attack by the ex-husband of competition-winner Tanya Harding. Kwan did not skate in the Olympic Games in Lillehammer, Norway, but finished eighth in the World Championships, second in the Goodwill Games, and third in the Trophée de France.

Michelle Kwan waves as she holds a World Figure Skating Hall of Fame plaque during a ceremony at the U.S. Figure Skating Championships in Boston, Massacusetts, January, 2014. (AP Photo/Steven Senne)

From 1995 to 1998, Kwan emerged as a serious contender in international figure skating. She won two U.S. Championship titles in 1996 and 1998 and two World Championship titles in 1996 and 1998. Kwan finished second to Nicole Bobek in the 1995 U.S. Championships and second to Tara Lipinski in 1997. In 1995, she finished fourth in the World Championships and second to Lipinski in 1997. Other victories included the Goodwill Games in 1995, Grand Prix Final in 1996 and 1998, Grand Prix Nation's Cup in 1995, Skate America from 1995 to 1997, Skate Canada in 1995 and 1997, and the Trophée de France in 1996. At the 1998 Olympic Games in Nagano, Japan, she won the silver medal behind Lipinski.

After the 1998 Olympic Games, Kwan dominated women's figure skating in the United Sates, winning seven consecutive U.S. Championship titles from 1999 to 2005. With a total of nine U.S. titles, she matched Maribel Vinson-Owen, who claimed nine U.S. titles in the 1920s and 1930s. During this time, Kwan won the three World Championships in 2000, 2001, and 2003, finished second in 1999 and 2002, and claimed third and fourth in 2004 and 2005, respectively. At the 2002 Olympic Games in Salt Lake City, Utah, she garnered the bronze medal. Injury forced Kwan to withdraw from the 2006 U.S. Championships, which also served as the U.S. Olympic Trials. She petitioned the U.S. Figure Skating Association (USFSA) for a medical waiver to be placed on the 2006 Olympic figure skating team. On January 14, 2006, after the U.S. ladies' figure skating event, the USFSA's International Committee met and in a 20-3 vote approved Kwan's petition under the stipulation that she show her physical and competitive readiness to a five-member monitoring panel by January 27. Kwan performed her long and short programs for the panel on the scheduled day and confirmed her place on the Olympic team. On February 12, 2006, however, she withdrew from the Games after suffering a new groin injury in her first practice in Turin, Italy.

After the 2006 Olympic Games, Kwan did not return to competitive figure skating but rather pursued educational and vocational goals. In fall 2006, she entered the University of Denver, transferring a year of course work completed at the University of California, Los Angeles after graduating from Rim of the World High School in Lake Arrowhead, California, in 1998. While studying international studies and political science at Denver, Secretary of State Condoleezza Rice named Kwan an ambassador of public diplomacy in 2006, a position she continued to hold in the Obama Administration. In this capacity, Kwan visited Argentina, China, Russia, South Korea, Singapore, and Ukraine. After graduating from Denver in 2009, she entered the Fletcher School of Law and Diplomacy at Tufts University in Medford, Massachusetts, and graduated with a master's degree in international relations in 2011. That year, she served as an adviser to the U.S.-China Women's Leadership Exchange and Dialogue. In 2012, Kwan became a U.S. State Department senior adviser for public diplomacy and public affairs.

A member of the President's Council on Physical Fitness and Sports since 2009, Kwan married Clay Pell, an American lawyer, military officer, and director for strategic planning on the National Security Staff at the White House, in 2013.

See also: Chinese Americans in Sports

Further Reading

Kwan, Michelle. 1998. *Michelle Kwan: Heart of a Champion.* Madison, WI: Demco Media.

Stewart, Mark, and Mike Kennedy. 2002. *Michelle Kwan: Quest for Gold.* Brookfield, CT: The Millbrook Press.

Adam R. Hornbuckle

LAM, WIFREDO (1902–1982)

Wifredo Lam (1902–1982) is considered by many to be the greatest of the Caribbean's modern artists. While predominantly a painter, Lam also worked with sculpture, ceramics, and printmaking. Throughout his life Lam contemplated his multiracial and multicultural ancestry, producing work that attests to his contributions to important dialogues about art and politics.

Lam, who had the Chinese name Lín Fēilóng, was born and raised in the Sagua La Grande, a city located on the north coast of Cuba's Villa Clara province. His father was Yam Lam, a first-generation Chinese immigrant, and his mother, Ana Serafina Castilla, of mixed African and European ancestry. The senior Lam, purportedly in his eighties at the time of his son's birth, is thought to have been of Hakka origin.

The Hakka were one of the groups represented in the 19th-century Chinese migration to Cuba. Most worked on plantations as indentured laborers, often alongside enslaved Africans. The majority of these men arrived between the years of 1847 and 1874.

The young Lam grew up frequently interacting with people of Afro-Cuban heritage. His family, like many others, practiced Catholicism alongside their Afro-Cuban traditions. His godmother, Matonica Wilson, a priestess and healer, taught him about the rites of spirits in the Yoruba spiritual or religious tradition known as Santería, themes he later explored in his visual art.

Lam's family initially encouraged him to study law. But in 1923, after studying art in Havana's Academy of San Alejandro, he moved to Madrid, Spain. Lam worked with the influential painter Fernando Álvarez Sotomayor, curator of the Prado Museum and teacher of Salvador Dalí. He produced work directly influenced by Spanish Surrealism.

In 1929, he married Eva Piriz, but both she and their young son died in 1931. This loss probably contributed to the dark aura of much of Lam's work. His artistic production was also shaped by politics. He supported the Republicans in the Spanish Civil War and created posters to support their cause.

In 1938 Lam moved to Paris, where he met Pablo Picasso. Picasso encouraged Lam to develop his own style, and together they exhibited their work in New York. Influenced by Picasso and other avant-garde artists, Lam's work grew to incorporate a stronger African influence. Some paintings from this period also reflect Chinese tradition, such as elements of calligraphy.

Lam returned to Cuba in 1941, following the outbreak of World War II. Two years later he produced his triumphant masterpiece, "The Jungle." Reactions to the painting contributed to his growing international acclaim as a key figure in "New World Modernism." Throughout the 1940s, he exhibited frequently in North American, Europe, and the Caribbean. He traveled to Haiti and New York, meeting with leading artists, intellectuals, and political activists.

As he grew older, Lam promoted the idea that art should have a social aim but shied away from direct involvement in politics. He closely followed Mao Zedong's declaration of the People's Republic of China in 1949 and in the mid-1950s supported student protests against Cuba's Batista dictatorship. However,

Lam left Cuba just before Fidel Castro took power in 1959, and three years later he rejected Castro's invitation to work as Minister of Culture. However, in 1965 he expressed solidarity with the socialist revolution by painting "The Third World" for Cuba's presidential palace.

Lam died on September 11, 1982, in Paris. His third wife, Lou Larin, and three sons survived him.

See also: Chinese in Cuba

Further Reading

Balderrama, Maria R., ed. 1992. *Wifredo Lam and His Contemporaries 1938–1952*. New York: The Studio Museum in Harlem.

Richards, Paulette. 1988. "Wifredo Lam: A Sketch." *Callaloo* 11 (1): 90–92.

Sims, Lowery S. 2002. *Wifredo Lam and the International Avant-Garde, 1923–1982*. Austin: University of Texas Press.

Don E. Walicek

LEE, ANG (1954–)

Ang Lee was born an agricultural town of Chaochou in Pingtung, Taiwan. Both of Lee's parents moved to Taiwan from China following the Chinese Nationalists' defeat in the Chinese Civil War in 1949. Growing up, Lee's parents emphasized studying the Chinese classics, Chinese culture, art, and calligraphy. Lee attended the Provincial Tainan First Senior High School (now National Tainan First Senior High School), where his father served as principal. Lee failed the Joint College/University Entrance Examination twice, and subsequently enrolled in a three-year college, the National Arts School (now National Taiwan University of Arts). Lee graduated in 1975 and then served his mandatory military service. Afterwards, he enrolled at the University of Illinois at Urbana-Champaign and graduated with a bachelor's degree in theater in 1980. Lee went on to graduate school and earned a master of fine arts from Tisch School of the Arts in New York. While in graduate school, Lee completed a 16mm short film, *Shades of the Lake* (1982), which won the Best Drama Award in Short Film in Taiwan. Two years later, he completed his M.F.A. thesis, a 43-minute drama, *Fine Line* (1984), which won New York University's Wasserman Award for Outstanding Direction and was later selected for the Public Broadcasting Service. This success caught the interest of the William Morris Agency, the renowned talent and literary agency that would represent Lee. For the first six years, Lee did not have much opportunity as a filmmaker. During this time, his wife, Jane Lin, whom he met while studying at University of Illinois at Urbana-Champaign, was the sole breadwinner. They lived in New York, together with their two sons. Lee was a stay-at-home dad and husband, but with his wife's support, he completed several screenplays.

In 1990, Lee entered a screenplay competition sponsored by Taiwan's Government Information Office. His screenplays, *Pushing Hands* and *The Wedding Banquet*, received first and second place, respectively. This success garnered the attention of Hsu Li-Kong (pinyin, *Xu Ligong*) who was just recently promoted to senior manager in a major studio. Hsu was very interested in Lee's approach and idea and invited him to direct *Pushing Hands* (1992) into a full-length feature film, which debuted in Taiwan. *Pushing Hands* was very successful, receiving eight Golden Horse Film Festival nominations. Following this success, Hsu collaborated with Lee on their second film, *The Wedding Banquet* (1993), which won the Golden Bear Award at the 43rd Berlin International Film Festival, and was nominated for both the Golden Globe and Academy Awards as the Best Foreign Language Film. *Pushing Hands* and *The Wedding Banquet* are both based on Chinese Americans and filmed in the United States. Lee worked with Hsu again in 1995 when he was invited back to Taiwan to film *Eat Drink Man Woman*, which is about the intersection of modern relationships and traditional values within a family in Taipei. *Eat Drink Man Woman* was a major box office hit and Lee received a second Best Foreign Language Film from both the Golden Globe and Academy Awards. These three films all depict the "Confucian family" that struggles with modernity and is known as Lee's "Father Knows Best" trilogy.

Lee's success in Taiwan opened the door to him in Hollywood. In 1995, he directed *Sense and Sensibility* for Columbia TriStar, which was nominated for seven Academy Awards, and won the Golden Globe Award for Best Motion Picture Drama. After this, he worked with Hsu again on *Crouching Tiger, Hidden Dragon* (2000), a film about "wuxia" (Chinese martial arts and chivalry). *Crouching Tiger, Hidden Dragon* received 10 Academy Awards nominations, including Best Picture, Best Foreign Language Film, and Best Director. In addition, it was the highest growing foreign film in many countries, including the United States and the United Kingdom. In 2003, Lee direct *Hulk*, which was moderately successful at the box office and received mixed reviews. The film that the LGBTQQI community knows Lee for is *Brokeback Mountain* (2005), about gay ranch hands in Wyoming. Unlike *Hulk*, a big-budget film, *Brokeback Mountain* was a small-budget, low-profile independent film based on Annie Proulx's Pulitzer Prize–finalist short story. This was Lee's second gay theme film; the first was *The Wedding Banquet*. *Brokeback Mountain* received critical acclaim, winning 71 awards, receiving the Golden Globe Award for Best Director and Best Motion Picture, and was nominated for eight Oscars. Lee was the first Chinese American (first Asian American) to win Best Director at the Academy Awards. In 2006, Lee was given the second highest civilian honor by the Taiwanese government when he was bestowed with the Order of Brilliant Star with Grand Cordon. Lee's success continued with *Lust, Caution* (2007) and *The Life of Pi* (2012).

Lee's Chinese–Taiwanese American films *Pushing Hands*, *The Wedding Banquet*, and *Eat Drink Man Woman* resonate with the Chinese American and

Confucian-influenced Asian American communities because they probe the dynamics of generational conflicts, shifting identities between East and West, modernity versus tradition, and the complexity of family relationships among transnational Chinese and Chinese American families, in particular among Taiwanese and Taiwanese Americans. These themes of identity, tradition, family relationships, and even queerness appeal to a universal audience as they cut across geographic and cultural boundaries.

See also: Chinese Americans and LGBTQQI; Chinese Americans in Motion Pictures; Confucianism; Taiwanese Americans

Further Reading

Arp, Robert, Adam Barkman, and James McRae, eds. 2013. *The Philosophy of Ang Lee.* Lexington: The University Press of Kentucky.
Dilley, Whitney. 2015. *The Cinema of Ang Lee: The Other Side of the Screen.* New York: Wallflower Press.

Jonathan H. X. Lee

THE WEDDING BANQUET (1993)

The Wedding Banquet is one of the first Chinese American films to deal with queer identity and relationship within a Chinese American family. It is a film about Wai-Tung Goa, a gay Taiwanese American who marries a mainland Chinese woman, Wei-wei who is a penniless artist, to placate his parents' Confucian expectations. Wai-Tung, however, is in a relationship with Simon, a Euro-American, and they live together in Manhattan but is not out to his parents. Wai-Tung's parents, Mr. and Mrs. Gao, visit New York with $30,000 to hold his fake wedding. The fake marriage takes place and the banquet follows. After the banquet, Wai-Tung sleeps with Wei-wei and she becomes pregnant. Conflicts and drama grows as Wai-Tung tells Simone, his lover and partner, about Wei-wei, and Mr. Gao suffers a stroke. Wai-Tung finally shares his secret with his mother, and she is shocked and asked that they keep the secret from his father. However, Mr. Gao meets with Simon and tells him that he is aware of their relationship and that he appreciates the considerable sacrifices he has made for his son. Mr. Gao gives him a *hongbao* (red envelope) that symbolizes their relationship as son and father-in-law, but Mr. Gao asked that Simone not tell anyone. Mr. Gao tells Simone that if everyone did not try to lie to him, he would not be getting a grandson. In their complex relationships, kinship bonds are tested, affirmed, and Confucian ideals and values are reconfigured for a modern 20th- (and 21st-) century Chinese American family.

LEE, BRUCE (1940–1973)

Born on November 27, 1940, in San Francisco, California, Bruce Lee was the fourth of five children of Lee Hoi Chuen and Grace Ho, both of Hong Kong. While his parents named him Lee Jun Fan, the English name of Bruce was given to him by either a nurse or the attending physician at the Chinese Hospital in San Francisco's Chinatown. His father was a film actor and a performer with the Cantonese Opera Company, which was on a tour of the United States at the time of Lee's birth. His mother, purportedly of German and Chinese descent, was the adopted niece of Sir Robert Ho Tung, the patriarch of a wealthy Hong Kong family, who claimed Dutch and Chinese parentage.

Late martial artist and actor Bruce Lee (1940–1973). Lee was best known for his cult action movies such as *Enter the Dragon* (1973). (AP Photo/Colombia Pictures)

In 1941, when Lee was three months old, his family returned to Hong Kong, taking residence in an apartment on Nathan Drive in the Kowloon district. On December 8, 1941, less than a year after the Lee's return home, Japanese forces invaded Hong Kong. After the British surrendered on December 25, 1941, the Japanese occupied Hong Kong until August 1945. A young but defiant Bruce Lee would stand on the balcony of his family's apartment overlooking Nathan Drive and shake his fist at the Japanese warplanes flying above and the troops garrisoned across the street. In 1946, he entered the Tak Sun School in Kowloon and appeared in three movies, *The Beginning of a Boy*, *The Birth of Mankind*, and *My Son, Ah Cheun*, released in the United States as *The Kid*. Lee, who would eventually perform in 20 more films as a child and teenager in Hong Kong, made his acting debut as an infant in the *Golden Gate Girl*, filmed in San Francisco in 1941.

After completing his primary education at the Tak Sun School in 1952, Lee transferred to La Salle College, a Catholic boys' secondary school in Kowloon. At this time, his growing participation in street fights led his father to introduce him to the fundamentals of t'ai chi ch'uan. In 1953, Lee became a student of the Wing Chun style of Kung Fu under grandmaster Yip Man. After training with Yip for nearly a year, many students refused to train with him after they learned of his mixed ancestry, as many Chinese opposed teaching martial arts techniques to individuals with mixed ancestry. After 1955, Lee trained privately with Yip and Wong Shun Leung. While Yip encouraged his students to compete in organized tournaments, Wong preferred and participated in illegal semiorganized bare-knuckle challenge fights, known as *beimo*, conducted secretively in the backrooms and alleys of Hong Kong. According to Wan Kam Leung, another of Wong's students, Wong could not match Lee's speed and precision.

Misconduct and poor academic performance caused Lee to transfer to St. Francis Xavier's College, another Catholic boys' secondary school in Kowloon in 1956. There he took up boxing and, in 1958, won the Hong Kong Boxing Championship. That year, Lee also won the Crown Colony Cha-Cha Championship; he had been practicing the cha-cha, a Cuban form of ballroom dancing, since the age of 14. In 1958, Lee made his final movie in Hong Kong, *The Orphan*. However, he continued to participate in street fights, sometimes against members of underground organized criminal syndicates known as triads, which involved police intervention. In part to protect their son from triad retaliation, Lee's parents sent him to live with his older sister, Agnes Lee, in San Francisco in 1959. Later that year, he moved to Seattle, Washington, and worked as a waiter in a Chinese restaurant owned by Ruby Chow, whose husband Ping Chow was a friend of Lee's father. Lee, who lived in a room above the restaurant, completed his high school education at Edison Technical School (now Seattle Community College) and, in 1961, enrolled at the University of Washington to study drama.

After arriving in Seattle, Lee began teaching martial arts to friends and fellow students. He taught his own interpretation of Wing Chun, called Jun Fan Kung Fu, or "Bruce Lee's Kung Fu." First holding informal classes, Lee opened the Lee Jun Fan Kung Fu Institute near the campus of the University of Washington in 1963. One of his first students, Taky Kimura, became Lee's assistant instructor. That year, at Garfield High School, Lee demonstrated the "one-inch punch," which he developed with James DeMile, another student. To execute the punch, Lee would hold his arm straight out, with his fist one inch from an opponent's chest, and with a shrug of his shoulder, knock the individual across the floor. Placing Kimura in charge of the institute in 1964, Lee moved to Oakland, California, where he opened the second Lee Jun Fan Kung Fu Institute with James Yimm Lee, a well-known Chinese martial artist in the area. That year, Ed Parker, an American martial arts specialist, invited Lee to perform in the Long Beach International Karate Championships. He demonstrated the "one-inch punch" and the "two-finger push-ups," in which he used only the thumb and the index finger of one hand to push himself up from the floor.

There, Lee met Korean Taekwondo master Jhoon Goo Rhee, who would teach Lee the "side kick," and with whom Lee shared the "non-telegraphic punch."

Within a year after opening the Lee Jun Fan Kung Fu Institute in Oakland, Lee received a challenge from Jack Man Wong, a leading Kung Fu specialist in the Oakland Chinese community, who opposed Lee teaching martial arts to non-Asians. He accepted Wong's challenge and agreed to close his school and stop teaching whites if he lost. Lee defeated Wong in a fight that lasted more than 20 minutes. Concerned over the length of the bout, he reevaluated his fighting style, concluding that the traditional martial arts styles were too formal and rigid. Lee developed new a martial arts style that borrowed techniques from a host of fighting disciplines, including kung fu, boxing, karate, taekwondo, and fencing. He described his new eclectic and hybrid martial art as "a style with no style," naming it Jeet Kune Do, or "the art of the intercepting fist." Lee also incorporated other forms of physical training, such as running and weight lifting as well as proper nutrition, into the practice, making Jeet Kune Do more than a system of combat, but a broader approach to life that stressed efficiency and simplicity.

Upon his return to the United Sates in 1959, Lee did not resume the acting career but his exhibition at the 1964 Long Beach International Karate Championships caught the attention of television executives. Impressed by his physical skill and strength, William Dozier, the executive producer of the *Batman* television series, invited Lee to audition for a part in the pilot for a new television show, *Number One Son*. Although the show never aired, he obtained the role of Kato in *The Green Hornet*, another Dozier television production, which ran from 1966 to 1967. Appearing as Kato three times in *Batman* in 1967, Lee played the character Leon Soo in an episode of the crime drama *Ironsides* that year. In 1969, he played a martial arts instructor in an episode of *Blondie* and a character named Lin in an episode of *Here Come the Brides*.

In 1969, Lee ventured back into the film industry through script writing, acting, and directing. That year he joined screen writer Stirling Silliphant and actor James Coburn, two of his students, in developing a script for a film called *The Silent Flute*, which did not go into production. In 1969, Lee made his first film appearance in 10 years in *Marlowe*, playing a henchman hired to threaten private detective Philip Marlowe, played by James Garner. That year, he choreographed the fight scenes for *The Wrecking Crew* and *A Walk in the Spring Rain*. In 1971, Lee appeared in four episodes of the television series *Longstreet* as Li Tsung, the martial arts instructor of the title character Mike Longstreet, played by James Franciscus. Written by Silliphant, *Longstreet* incorporated aspects of Lee's martial arts philosophy into the script. Early in 1971, Lee had proposed a television series to Warner Brothers Studio about a Shaolin monk who wandered the postbellum American West in search of his brother. Although the studio initially dismissed the idea, he learned later that year, after he had returned to Hong Kong, that Warner Brothers planned to develop such a show, but without attribution to him. The series, which became known as *Kung Fu*, ran from 1972 to 1975, with David Carradine, rather than Lee, starring as Kawai Chang Caine, the Shaolin monk.

Dissatisfied with minor television roles, Lee returned to Hong Kong to rejuvenate his acting career in 1971. Upon his return, people immediately recognized him as the star of *The Kato Show*, as *The Green Hornet* was known in Hong Kong. Lee signed a contract to play the leading role in several martial arts films proposed by the Golden Harvest production company. In 1971, he starred in *The Big Boss*, which became an enormous box office success across Asia and catapulted him to stardom. Next year, Lee appeared in *Fist of Fury*, which broke the box office records established by *The Big Boss*. In the *Way of the Dragon*, in 1972, he not only starred in the film, but wrote, directed, and choreographed the fight scenes. Lee introduced Asian audiences to American martial arts champion, Chuck Norris, who played his opponent in the film's final fight scene. Late in 1972, he began work on the *Game of Death*, his fourth Golden Harvest film. Production of the film, however, ceased when Warner Brothers offered Lee the opportunity to star in *Enter the Dragon*, a film to be produced jointly by Golden Harvest and Warner Brothers.

Toward the completion of *Enter the Dragon* in 1973, Lee began experiencing severe headaches and, on one occasion, collapsed unconscious at the Golden Harvest studio. Doctors determined that cerebral edema, or swelling of the brain, caused the headaches and his subsequent collapse. On July 20, 1973, Lee met with Raymond Chow, of Golden Harvest, and Betty Ting Pei, a Taiwanese actress, to discuss completing the *Game of Death*. He complained of headaches and Ting gave him a painkiller called Equagesic, which contained aspirin and mepobamate, a muscle relaxer. Lee lay down to take a nap but did not wake up despite attempts to revive him. Physicians who arrived on the scene pronounced him dead. An autopsy revealed that his brain had swollen by 13 percent; the coroner deemed cerebral edema precipitated by the painkiller caused Lee's death.

Released six days after Lee's death, *Enter the Dragon* cemented Lee's legacy as a martial arts icon. Arguably the most successful martial arts film history, *Enter the Dragon* has earned $200 million. Lee's martial arts films raised the genre to a new level of popularity and acclaim and fueled a surge of interest in Chinese martial arts in the West. His portrayal of strong and confident characters changed the way Asians were presented in American films. Married to the former Lee Emery since 1964, Lee was the father of a son, Brandon, and daughter, Shannon.

See also: Chinese Americans in Motion Pictures; Chinese Americans in Sports; Chinese Martial Arts

Further Reading

All About Bruce Lee. 2001–2009. "Chronology." Accessed July 16, 2015. http://www
.allbrucelee.com/.

Bruce Lee Foundation. 2008. Accessed July 16, 2015. http://www.bruceleefoundation
.com/.

Lee, Linda. 1989. *The Bruce Lee Story*. Berkeley, CA: Ohara Publications.

Adam R. Hornbuckle

LEE, C. Y. (1917–), AND *FLOWER DRUM SONG*

C. Y. (Chin Yang) Lee is a Chinese American novelist and writer. He was born in December 23, 1917, in Hunan Province, China, the youngest of 11 children. His family moved to Beijing when he was 10. Not long after Lee enrolled at Jinan's Shandong University, he had to flee to Yunnan when Japan invaded China. He completed his bachelor's degree in comparative literature at Southwest Associated University (a wartime refuge college in Kunming, Yunnan Province) in 1942. Due to the continued turbulence in China, he decided to flee the war-torn China and enrolled in a graduate comparative literature program at the Columbia University on a student visa later that year. In less than a year, he transferred to Yale University to study drama with Walter Pritchard Eaton (Eugene O'Neill's mentor) and completed his MFA in 1947. In 1949, his "Forbidden Dollar" won the Best Original Short Stories contest sponsored by *Writer's Digest*. The award encouraged and enabled Lee, who was a struggling writer at the time, to gain his permanent residency and later become the citizen of the United States.

Lee is the author of 11 novels and a collection of short stories, many of which have been translated into other languages. His stories are informed by wit, humor, and a canny knowledge of Chinese and American culture. He is probably best known for *Flower Drum Song* (originally titled *Grant Avenue*), published in 1957, a *New York Times* best-selling novel that was later adapted into a Broadway musical by Rodgers and Hammerstein in 1958. Through telling the story about a family trying to find a wife for the eldest son in San Francisco's Chinatown during the 1950s, the novel describes the cultural and generational conflicts between Old Master Wang Chi-yang and his American-born son Wang Ta. Other themes include familial strife and misunderstandings, callous dames on the make, youthful rebellion, striptease, forced marriages, chop suey jokes, wife beating, suicide, and a discriminatory job market not open to the young Chinese males. The Broadway adaptation was much more lighthearted than the original novel; it focused more on the assimilation to the American culture and romantic relationships. For example, the song "The Other Generation" talks about the generation gap between parents and children, "A Hundred Million Miracles" talks about cultural traditions, and "Chop Suey" is a metaphor for ethnic pluralism that celebrates assimilation. Rodgers and Hammerstein's original production of *Flower Drum Song* was the first Broadway show to feature Asian Americans. Its 1961 film version also inaugurated the careers of the first generation of Chinese American actors such as Nancy Kwan and Jack Soo.

Behind the success of the Broadway production are controversies on Orientalism and the stereotyping of Asian Americans. For many following years, Asian American activists have examined and criticized the Broadway production of *Flower Drum Song*. For example, during the 1983 revival of *Flower Drum Song* musical by David Plotkin and George Costomiris, the production received much criticisms, protests, resistance, and threats from Asian American activists and groups long before its opening night at the theatre, despite the fact that the producers had made efforts to cut out all hints of stereotypes and racism in the show. Not surprisingly, the production didn't last out its scheduled three-week run at the Palace Theatre in San Francisco. The original novel received less criticism, but when being criticized, C. Y. Lee argued that the portrayals of the Chinese American characters in the novel were appropriate for its time. In 2001, David Henry Hwang (a Chinese American playwright) produced a new adaptation of *Flower Drum Song*. It had a successful run in Los Angeles but was not well received on Broadway. The controversy on stereotypes continued despite Hwang's effort. As he discovered when revising *Flower Drum Song*, "I began to realize that one generation's breakthroughs often become the next generation's stereotypes". Nevertheless, *Flower Drum Song* remains significant as the first and only Broadway musical that focuses on Chinese and Asian Americans. Whether the reactions toward *Flower Drum Song* are positive or negative, it has brought Chinese and Asian Americans and cultures to the much-needed spotlight, and it has opened "doors" for Asian American performers and artists in the U.S. performing world.

See also: Chinese American Literature; Chinese Americans in Motion Pictures

Further Reading

Brantley, Ben. 2002. "New Coat of Paint for Old Pagoda." *New York Times*, October 18: E1.

Kim, Chang-Hee. 2013. "Asian Performance of the Stage of American Empire in *Flower Drum Song*." *Cultural Critique* 85 (1): 1–37.

Lewis, David. 2006. *Flower Drum Songs: The Story of Two Musicals*. Jefferson, NC: McFarland.

May May Chiang

LIN, JEREMY (1988–)

Born on August 23, 1988, in Torrance, California, Jeremy Shu How Lin is the second of three sons of Lin Gie Ming, an electrical and mechanical engineer, and Shirley Lin (formerly Wu Xinxin), a computer scientist. His parents, who migrated to the United States from Taiwan in the late 1970s, met as students at Old Dominion University in Norfolk, Virginia. They married and moved to Lafayette, Indiana, to earn advanced degrees at Purdue University. After completing their degrees, the Lins pursued careers and in Los Angeles and later Palo Alto, California.

In Palo Alto, Gie Ming introduced his sons to basketball, teaching them how to play at the local YMCA and by watching National Basketball Association (NBA) games he had taped on the VCR. The Lin sons, especially Jeremy, showed exceptional talent for the game, but there was no elite-level program for them and other talented youngsters to develop and showcase their skills. Shirley Lin, who enthusiastically supported her sons' interest in basketball, helped organize a National Junior Basketball program in Palo Alto, which sponsored teams to play in Amateur Athletic Union (AAU) leagues and tournaments. Criticized by her friends for letting her sons play so much basketball, Lin made certain they struck a balance between basketball and education and intervened when one overwhelmed the other.

Lin played guard on the Palo Alto High School basketball team. Coached by Peter Diepenbrock, he started three years in that position beginning as a sophomore. Lin led the Vikings to a 25-4 record during his sophomore year, a 32-2 record his junior year, and a 32-1 his senior year. In 2006, he captained Palo Alto's 51-47 upset of nationally ranked Mater Dei in the California Interscholastic Federation (CIF) Division II State Championship. Three times Lin made the All-Santa Clara Athletic League First Team and twice earned recognition as the League's Most Valuable Player. Named the Northern California District II Player of the Year in 2006, he also earned recognition as Northern California Scholar Athlete of the Year and First Team All-State. In 2006, the San Francisco Chronicle and the San Jose Mercury News named Lin as Boys Player of the Year. Apart from basketball, he served as editor of the school newspaper, worked as a summer intern in office of California State Senator, Joe Simitian, and graduated with a 4.2 grade point average.

After graduating from high school in 2006, Lin entered Harvard University in Cambridge, Massachusetts. Despite his basketball ability and accomplishments, no colleges and universities recruited him for their teams. Lin marketed his talents to the University of California, Berkeley, the University of California, Los Angeles, Stanford University, and all the schools in the Ivy League. While Stanford and UCLA encouraged him to walk on, Harvard and Brown guaranteed him a place on their teams. As Ivy League institutions, neither Harvard nor Brown offered athletic scholarships, but Lin chose to attend and play for Harvard. Named to the All-Ivy League Second Team as a sophomore, he earned recognition as a consensus All-Ivy League First Team Selection as a junior and a senior. Lin, who led the league in steals in his sophomore, junior, and senior years, and in free throws his junior and senior years, completed his college career as the first player in the history of the Ivy League to record over 1,450 points (1,483), 450 rebounds (487), 300 assists (406), and 200 steals (220).

After graduating from Harvard with a degree in economics in 2010, several NBA teams invited Lin to participate in pre-draft workouts, but none of them selected him in the actual draft. The Dallas Mavericks, however, invited him to its mini-camp. Lin, who played for Dallas's Summer League team in Las Vegas, led the team with a 54.5 field goal percentage, averaged 9.8 points, 3.2 rebounds, 1.8 assists, and 1.2 steals per game. After the conclusion of the Summer League, Lin received offers to play for several NBA teams, including the Mavericks, Los Angeles Lakers, and Gold State Warriors.

Lin signed a two-year contract with the Golden State Warriors, thus becoming the first American of Chinese descent to join an NBA team. However he was not the first American of Asian descent to become part of the NBA, as several (mainly of Japanese) descent—including Wataru Misaka, Raymond Townsend, Corey Gaines, Rex Walters, and Robert Swift—had played in the NBA. Lin's regular season debut came on October 29, 2010, in Golden State's 109-91 victory over the Los Angeles Clippers. Lin played one season for the Warriors, appearing in 28 games, shooting 38.9 percent from the floor, and scoring 76 points. Three times during the season, Golden State assigned him to the Reno Bighorns, Golden State's Development League (D-League) team. In 20 games for Reno, Lin averaged 18 points, 5.8 rebounds, and 4.4 assists per game. He scored a career high of 27 points in the Bighorns' 107-103 win over the Utah Flash on March 18, 2011, and led Reno to a record of 2-0 in the D-League Showcase Tournament, averaging 21.5 points, 6.0 rebounds, 5.5 steals, and 3.5 steals per game.

A labor dispute between NBA owners and players delayed the start of the 2011–2012 basketball season. In September 2011, Lin played for Dongguan Leopards in the Chinese Basketball Association (CBA) Championship in Guangzhou, China, in which he received recognition as the tournament's MVP. Former NBA star Yao Ming, the President of the Shanghai Sharks, tried unsuccessfully to recruit Lin for the upcoming CBA season. In the meantime, the Warriors had placed Lin on waivers. Following the conclusion of the labor lockout, the Houston Rockets claimed Lin, but within two weeks placed him back on waivers to sign other players. Picked up by the New York Knicks, he debuted for his new team two days later on December 29, 2011, in the Knicks' 97-78 loss to Golden State in Oakland. On January 17, 2012, the Knicks assigned Lin to the Erie Bay Hawks of the D-League. Three days later, he produced a triple-double with 28 points, 11 rebounds, and 12 assists in the Bay Hawks' 122-113 victory over the Maine Red Claws.

Although Lin returned to the Knicks in late January, he saw little playing time until February 4, 2011, when he came off the bench to lead all scorers

A devout Christian, Lin led the Asian American Christian Fellowship as a student at Harvard. He attributes his success as a professional basketball player as being able to play without pressure, as he has "surrendered that to God" and is no longer "in a battle with what everybody else thinks anymore." Looking to become a pastor, Lin hopes to lead a nonprofit organization to help disadvantaged communities. His younger brother, Joseph, followed him as a basketball player at Hamilton College in Clinton, New York, and his older brother, Josh, studied dentistry at New York University.

with 25 points in New York's 99-92 victory over the New Jersey Nets. Two days later, against the Utah Jazz, Lin made his first professional start, scoring 28 points, and leading the Knicks to a 99-88 win. He started the next 25 games until a knee injury ended his season on March 24, 2011. When Lin took over as point guard, the Knicks had a record of 8-15 but improved to 24-25 under his leadership. As a starter, he scored in double figures 23 times, including 11 games with over 20 points, and posted a career high of 38 points against the Los Angeles Lakers on February 12, 2012. Since the end of the 2012 season, Lin has continued to play basketball in the NBA, with the Houston Rockets from 2012 to 2014, and the Los Angeles Lakers since 2014. With the Rockets, Lin started all 82 games in his first season and matched his career-scoring high with 38 points in a 134-126 overtime loss to the San Antonio Spurs.

During his brief period as a starter for the Knicks, Lin generated a worldwide discussion over the role of Asian Americans in sport. The media coined the word, "Linsanity," to describe the world's almost insane fascination with him, as he defied the American stereotype of the nonathletic effete Asian. "By making it to the NBA," observed David Jiang, of the New England Sports Network, "he is helping break Asian American stereotypes and setting an example for aspiring Asian athletes in America who rarely get a chance to see Asian Americans playing on their favorite teams." Rex Walters, the coach of the University of San Francisco Dons, whose mother is Japanese, affirmed Jiang's observation, noting that although Lin may not look Asian, when aspiring Asian American athletes see him, they see themselves. In an interview with the *San Francisco Chronicle* shortly after joining the Warriors, Lin expressed hope that he could "help break the stereotype."

See also: Chinese Americans in Sports

Further Reading

Jiang, David. 2010. "Jeremy Lin Making History As Rare Asian-American, Ivy Leaguer in NBA." New England Sports Network, July 21. Accessed August 13, 2015. http://nesn.com/2010/07/jeremy-lin-represents-asianamericans-ivy-leaguers-in-nba/.

"Lin-sanity Accepted into English Lexicon . . . Lin-ough already!?" 2012. *The Global Language Monitor*, February 24. Accessed August 13, 2015. http://www.language monitor.com/sports/lin-sanity-accepted-into-english-lexicon-lin-ough-already/.

Adam R. Hornbuckle

LIU, LUCY (1968–)

Lucy Liu is a Chinese American best known for her accomplishments in acting, painting, and photography. The youngest of three children, she was born on December 2, 1968, in Jackson Heights, Queens, New York. Her parents were originally from Beijing and Shanghai, China. She graduated from Stuyvesant High School in 1986 and later earned a bachelor of arts degree in Asian languages and cultures from the University of Michigan (UM).

Liu has enjoyed a successful career as an actress. As a senior at UM, she auditioned for a small part in a rendition of *Alice in Wonderland* but was given the lead role. After scoring many walk on parts in several hit television shows and a reoccurring role on the sitcom *Pearl*, Lucy Liu became a household name (in the United States) when she began portraying Ling Woo, a formidable Chinese American lawyer, on the hit U.S. comedy-drama *Ally McBeal*. As arguably the most visible Asian female character in the United States at the time, the character Ling Woo attracted much scholarly attention. Much of this attention was focused on a change in the stereotype of Asian American women from the submissive, quiet "China doll" who struggles with English to the intelligent, aggressive, articulate, and sexually open and confident "Dragon lady." Subsequently, Liu continued to depict strong, intelligent, female Asian characters in her prolific film and television career. She has also had success as a voice-over artist, narrator, and actress on Broadway. Some notable films Lucy worked on include *Charlie's Angels*, *Charlie's Angels: Full Throttle*, *Chicago*, *Detachment*, *Kill Bill*, *Kung Fu Panda*, *Kung Fu Panda 2*, *Shanghai Noon*, and *Shanghai Knights*.

As a visual artist, Liu has had many gallery events showcasing her paintings and photography. She attended the New York Studio School from 2004 to 2006 for drawing, painting, and sculpture. Liu donates her share of exhibit profits to The United Nations Children's Fund (UNICEF). A portion of the profits from her book *72*, a collection of 72 paintings, were also shared with UNICEF.

Liu received the distinction of UNICEF Goodwill Ambassador in 2005 and became a spokeswomen for the Human Rights Campaign in 2011. As a UNICEF ambassador, she has traveled around the world in effort to highlight the needs of impoverished children and works to raise awareness of child trafficking.

See also: Chinese Americans in Motion Pictures; Fu Manchu and Charlie Chan; Huang, Eddie

Further Reading

"Lucy Liu." 2015. Accessed July 16, 2015. http://www.imdb.com.

Sun, Chyng Feng. 2002. "Ling Woo in Historical Context: The New Face of Asian American Stereotypes on Television." In *Gender, Race, and Class in Media: A Text-Reader*, 2nd ed., edited by Gail Dines and Jean McMahon Humez, 656–64. Thousand Oaks, CA: Sage.

Ryan W. Higgins

MA, YO-YO (1955–)

Yo-Yo Ma is a world-renowned American cellist of Chinese birth. He was born in Paris, France, on October 7, 1955. His mother, Marina, was a mezzo-soprano from Hong Kong, and his father, Hiao-Tsiun Ma, was a composer, violinist, musicologist, and a teacher for musically gifted children. He studied the violin with his father briefly, then he decided to switch to the cello at age 4. Since Ma's father was specialized in the musical education of gifted children, he had Ma memorized two measures of a Bach suite for unaccompanied cello each day. He had learned three Bach cello suites by the time he was five, and at age six, he played one of them in his first recital at the Institute of Art and Archeology at the University of Paris.

At age seven, Ma's whole family moved to New York and his father began teaching at a school for musically gifted children in the city. World-famous violinist Isaac Stern, whose children attended the school, heard Ma playing the cello one day and was impressed by his talent. He recommended him to cellist Leonard Rose at The Juilliard School. Pablo Casals, who also heard Ma play, convinced conductor Leonard Bernstein to include Ma in the "American Pageant of the Arts," a fund-raising program at Washington D.C., which was nationally televised in 1963. Ma attracted international attention

President Barack Obama awards cellist Yo-Yo Ma the 2010 Medal of Freedom during a ceremony in the East Room of the White House in Washington, D.C., on February 15, 2011. (AP Photo/Charles Dharapak)

after appearing in the program. He made his New York City debut at age nine at Carnegie Hall in 1964. He later gave his first professional recital at the same venue in 1971.

Ma studied with Leonard Rose and Janos Scholz at Juilliard from the ages of 9 to 16. He attended the Professional Children's School in New York City and graduated when he was 15 years old. When Ma was nine, he began to realize that he lived in two contradictory worlds. His Chinese heritage and parents demanded strict obedience, discipline, and structure, while the American society valued freedom and self-expression. Growing up in such environments, Ma was struggling to find his place. During his teenage years, he cut classes and wandered on the street alone, acquired a fake I.D. and drank alcohol while underage. When he was 16, Ma made an important decision to enroll at Harvard University and sought out a traditional liberal arts education to expand upon his musical training. During his Harvard years, he developed a more mature integration between his intuitive ability and analytic understanding of music. He continued to perform music while in Harvard and his commitment to music deepened. He graduated with a bachelor of arts degree in humanities in 1976. In 1991, Harvard awarded Ma an honorary doctorate in music.

Since winning the prestigious Avery Fisher Prize in 1978, Ma has appeared with nearly all of the world's great orchestras and conductors, establishing himself as one of the superstars in classical music. In 1982, Ma was invited to play with the London Symphony Orchestra in London at the Barbican Centre in the presence of Queen Elizabeth II. Inspired by his curiosity about the world and eager to forge connections across cultures, disciplines, and generations, he founded the nonprofit organization Silkroad and The Silk Road Project in 1998. The Silk Road Project explores the exchange of musical ideas that occurred along the trade route. In 2002, Ma was appointed as a Culture Connect Ambassador by the U.S. Department of State. In 2011, Ma was recognized as a Kennedy Center Honoree. Ma has produced more than 90 albums and has won more than 17 Grammy Awards with his recordings in wide-ranging musical genres such as classical music, Brazilian bossa nova, Argentine tango, American roots and bluegrass, and the soundtrack for *Crouching Tiger, Hidden Dragon*. He received the Glenn Gould Prize (1999), the National Medal of Arts (2001), the Dan David Prize (2006), the Sonning Prize (2006), the World Economic Forum's Crystal Award (2008), the Presidential Medal of Freedom (2010), the Polar Music Prize (2012), the Vilcek Prize in Contemporary Music (2013), and the Fred Rogers Legacy Award (2014). Ma serves as a UN Messenger of Peace and a member of the President's Committee on the Arts & the Humanities. He has performed for eight American presidents and, most recently, at the invitation of President Obama on the occasion of the 56th Inaugural Ceremony. Ma plays a Montagnana cello (dated 1733) and the "Davidov" Stradivari (dated 1712). Ma married Jill Hornor in 1978 and they have two children.

See also: Chinese American Hip-Hop; Chinese American Jazz

Further Reading

Ma, Marina. 1995. *My Son, Yo Yo*. Hong Kong: The Chinese University Press.
Weatherly, Myra. 2007. *Yo-Yo Ma: Internationally Acclaimed Cellist*. Minneapolis, MN: Compass Point Books.

May May Chiang

MISS CHINATOWN USA PAGEANT

The Miss Chinatown USA Pageant is a beauty contest held in San Francisco, California. The contest is exclusively for Chinese American women, and the winners become goodwill ambassadors for the Chinese community throughout the new year. All candidates must be citizens of the United States, single, never married, and never had any children. The candidate must have Chinese heritage, as measured through her father's side. In addition, there is an age requirement. A perspective candidate may not be younger than 17, nor older than 26. The winner of the competition has an obligation to promote Chinese American culture and heritage. The pageant is sponsored by Southwest Airlines.

The Miss Chinatown competition has its origins in the period following World War II. In 1948, during a Fourth of July picnic, a Chinese organization sponsored a bathing suit competition. The bathing suit competition was an annual event that lasted four years, evolving into the beginnings of a Miss Chinatown beauty contest. However, the original beauty contest was a local event, limited to residents of San Francisco's Chinatown. The event has occurred during Chinese New Year every year since 1953. Chinese Lunar New Year falls on the first lunar moon, typically between the end of January and early February.

Six winners of Miss Chinatown have went on to win Miss China International, an international beauty contest for Chinese ex-nationals. Miss China International is open to any woman of Chinese background, though she may not be a resident of China. She must also be a winner of a national beauty contest. Winners of Miss Chinatown have gone on to become models as well as film and television actresses.

Further Reading

"Miss Chinatown U.S.A. Pageant." 2008–2015. The Southwest Airlines Chinese New Year Parade. Accessed July 16, 2015. http://www.chineseparade.com/pageant.asp.
Yeh, Chiou-ling. 2008. *Making an American Festival: Chinese New Year in San Francisco's Chinatown*. Berkeley: University of California Press.

Douglas R. Jordan

MODEL MINORITY

Asians in the United States, regardless of their economic, social, political, and cultural statuses are imagined as a "model minority." This imagination exerts a wholesale, totalizing image of Asians living in America, an image that conjures up hardworking immigrants who cherish the educational opportunities not available in their homelands, to become successful in the land of "equal opportunity." It is an image that is deeply engrained in American popular cultures and reinforced by popular media. Although Asian American studies scholars and activists have critiqued the model minority image as a racialized stereotype that fuels ethnic antagonism, the statistical data that measures success, such as median family income, or postbaccalaureate professional degrees indicate that this so-called stereotype might indeed bear witness to truth. It is important to discuss the historical development of the model minority image, as it foregrounds the discourse, both negative and positive, surrounding the stereotype.

The image of model minority was conjured by Sociologist William Petersen on January 9, 1966, when he published "Success Story, Japanese-American Style" in *The New York Times Magazine*. This article is one of the most influential articles about an Asian American group. Petersen did not employ the phrase "model minority" but his article alluded to it. Peterson documented the Japanese American experience after World War II, when anti-Asian (in particular, anti-Japanese) sentiments were still strong. During World War II, Japanese Americans were interned and lost most of their livelihood. He was concerned that the history of racial and ethnic discrimination and prejudice experienced by the Japanese Americans would result in them becoming a "problem minority" like the African American communities. A "problem minority" refers to a community of people, minorities, whose socioeconomic indicators of success are low, such as generally having "poor health," "poor education," "low income," "high crime rates," "unstable family patterns," and so on. Instead of finding a community that reflects the indictors of being a "problem minority," Petersen observed that Japanese Americans of that period challenged their historical experiences. He stated, "the history of Japanese Americans, however, challenges every such generalization about ethnic minorities." More important, "even in a country whose patron saint is the Horatio Alger hero, there is no parallel to this success story." According to him, the key to Japanese American success lies in its "traditional culture." He argued that Japanese immigrants brought with them a strong "work ethic" and an ethic of "frugality" similar to the white Protestant work ethic, which was associated with their success even in the face of racial, political, economic, and social adversities.

Eleven months after the publication of Petersen's article, a similar article was published in *U.S. News and World Report* on December 26, 1966, "Success Story of One Minority Group in the U.S." Supporting Petersen's claims with empirical data, this article described the nation's 300,000 upwardly mobile Chinese Americans. It compared the Chinese Americans to the African Americans who needed "uplifting" and "support" by the government. It employed census data and made a conclusion that surprised the general public, who did not expect the Chinese Americans to have higher educational attainment and higher percentage of representation in professional fields than the national average, even higher than white Americans. It argued that like the Japanese Americans, Chinese Americans faced and experienced violent racism and prejudice, but they were able to "pull" themselves up from the hardship and discrimination to become a "model" of self-respect and personal achievement. The phrase "model minority" was not used, but the article considered Chinese Americans a "model" of achievement in American society. Furthermore, its anonymous author suggested that the African Americans can learn something from the Chinese Americans, as their community represented an example of the true American way. Such a conclusion flamed and fed American resentment for the African American communities and placed the blame for all their "failures" on African Americans and their cultural values (or lack thereof).

Similar to Petersen's article, "Success Story of One Minority Group in the U.S." concluded that Chinese cultural values are key to Chinese Americans' success. In explaining how the "Chinese get ahead," it argued that Chinese immigrants brought with them "the traditional virtues of hard work, thrift, and morality." Moreover, Chinese culture has strong family values, so strong that the streets of New York Chinatown are the safest streets around. Both articles, one documenting Japanese American success and the other documenting Chinese American success, argued that both communities historically faced racism and discrimination but were able to overcome these obstacles. This proves that American society is a land of equal opportunity. Success is therefore only available and attainable if one's cultural values reflect and mirror that of white American mainstream values. Failure, poverty, and literacy are neither historical byproducts nor indicators of institutional inequality; rather, they are indicators of some cultural pathology within said community. "Success Story of One Minority Group in the U.S." notes, "it must be recognized that the Chinese and other Orientals in California were faced with even more prejudice than faces the Negro today. We haven't stuck Negroes in concentration camps, for instance, as we did the Japanese during World War II. The Orientals came back, and today they have established themselves as strong contributors to the health of the whole community."

The popular media consumed the success stories of the Japanese and Chinese Americans wholeheartedly. These two case studies affirmed that America is a land of opportunity. Otherwise, how could the Japanese and Chinese Americans attain success in a relatively short period of time after World War II? How would they have been able to pull themselves up by their bootstraps,

out of the slums and out of poverty, over racial prejudice, and doing so without government support (i.e., welfare)? The Chinese Americans went from
being "coolies" to "engineers, doctors, and research scientists." Throughout the
1990s, the image of Asian Americans as a "model minority" flourished, especially due to conservatives who wanted to cut government social programs and
affirmative action policies.

Contemporary Forms and Impact

Conservatives were quick to employ the model minority stereotype to argue
against the progress of the Civil Rights movement, as it critiqued the demands
of the "black," "brown," "red," and "yellow" power movements by arguing that
American society and institutions are, in fact, equal. The model minority stereotype was employed to fuel the flames of ethnic antagonism, whereby minority groups fight each other, instead of the structures and historical conditions
that limit their access to resources. By the 1980s, the model minority image had
spread to include Koreans, Indians, and new refugees from Vietnam, Cambodia, and Laos. This period also witnessed an increasing number of publications
documenting Asian Americans as a model minority as seen in "Indochinese
Refugee Families and Academic Achievement" (*Scientific American*, February
1992), Dennis Williams's "A Formula for Success" (*Newsweek*, April 23, 1984),
and David Brand's article "The New Whiz Kids" (*Time*, August 31, 1987). These
popular media accounts document young Asian Americans' academic drive
and achievements from elementary to college; all conclude that their cultural
work ethic and value of schooling are key to their success.

The model minority stereotype has been cast upon Asian Americans, in particular Chinese Americans, as hardworking, persevering overachievers. This stereotype posits that good work ethic determines the success of most Asian American
ethnic groups. Upholding this concept is the belief that other racial groups can
also reach high academic attainment leading to upward social mobility if only
they would simply emulate Asian Americans' Confucian ethics. Underlying this
premise is that other racial groups are not succeeding because they are lazy,
unmotivated, or culturally deficient. This viewpoint has been asserted to refute
systemic racism and discrimination in the United States and places the responsibility fully on the individual and racial group(s). The model minority stereotype is significant to Asian Americans because it has denied public assistance to
other ethnic Asian American groups in need, such as Hmong, Cambodian, and
Vietnamese. Furthermore, the model minority myth creates a racial hierarchy
with whites on top, followed by Asian Americans, with the remainder of the
racial groups in the United States at the lower rungs of society. This hierarchy
creates interracial tensions between Asian Americans and other racial groups
(which have often led to anti-Asian violence) while maintaining white supremacy.

"THE RISE OF ASIAN AMERICANS"

Despite the widespread scholarship to correct faulty practices regarding the model minority stereotype, in 2012, the Pew Research Center used the U.S. Census data from 2010 and made the same mistakes in its evaluation of Asian Americans as model minorities in its report entitled "The Rise of Asian Americans." The Pew report upset the Asian American communities and organizations; the Association for Asian American Studies (AAAS) was one of many associations that wrote a response expressing its disappointment of the generalizations and misrepresentations that were made about the ascension of Asian American communities. One of the many concerns addressed include public policy makers using this report to cut back on necessary resources from vulnerable Asian American subgroups. Another apprehension that was expressed in the letter is the fear that during this challenged economy in the United States, anti-Asian sentiments and violence will be incited because of the perceived unfair advantage of Asian Americans over other minority groups.

Further Reading

Rise of Asian Americans, The. 2012. Released June 19, rev. July 12. Washington, DC: Pew Research Center.

See also: Lee, Wen-Ho; Wong, Jade Snow; Yee, James J.

Further Reading

Chou, Rosalind S., and Joe R. Feagin. 2008. *The Myth of the Model Minority: Asian Americans Facing Racism.* Boulder, CO: Paradigm.

Danico, Mary Yu, and Franklin Ng. 2004. *Asian American Issues.* Westport, CT: Greenwood Press.

Petersen, William. 1966. "Success Story: Japanese American Style." *The New York Times,* January 9.

"Success Story of One Minority Group in U.S." 1966. *U.S. News & World Report,* December 26.

Mary Thi Pham and Jonathan H. X. Lee

NG POON CHEW (1867–1931)

Ng Poon Chew (Wu Panzhao), born in Taishan in Guangdong Province, came to California in 1881 as a boy of 14 and lived there until his death in 1931.

His story is that of service to his countrymen as a preacher, journalist, popular lecturer, and even diplomat.

Like a number of other young ambitious Chinese immigrants in those days, he decided to work as a houseboy for a European American family. He chose the right employers, a couple in San Jose. They taught him English and other American skills while attending a local Sunday school. He became an ardent Christian as well as a capable speaker and writer of English, which helped facilitate his desire to become to enter the religious profession. In 1892, at the age of 23, he graduated from the San Anselmo Theological Seminary north of San Francisco and was ordained, becoming the first Chinese Presbyterian Minister on the west coast. He began preaching in Los Angeles, where he also taught at a local mission school. Branching out, in 1898 he founded a newspaper, the weekly *Chinese-American News* or *Wa Mi San Po* (*Huamei xinbao*). The 1899 Chinatown fire in Los Angeles ended these ventures and may have persuaded him to return to the Bay Area.

When he and his family reached San Francisco in 1900, he changed career directions. Putting his ministry on hold, he focused instead on recording, educating, and shaping the Chinese of the United States through a much more ambitious newspaper, the *Chung Sai Yat Po* (*CSYP*) (*Zhongxi ribao*, or *Chinese American Daily News*). The first issue of the *CSYP* appeared in February of the same year. It was the first daily in the United States to be entirely in Chinese, and the first to be produced by typesetting rather than by lithograph or by cutting the text onto wooden blocks. Ng's guiding hand was evident in the newspaper's objectivity and willingness to risk controversy as well as in its downplaying of obituary announcements, traditional temple festivals, and anything else that involved non-Christian religious beliefs. In spite of this limitation, the *CSYP* enjoyed a wide readership, as again and again it took the lead in addressing immigration, civic, and social issues for Chinese in America and in China. Distributed as far north as Canada and all over the western United States, the paper became the most influential Chinese-language periodical in the Americas and remained so until the World War II.

Ng himself soon became a celebrity, a spokesman for Chinese Americans, and a popular lecturer to European American audiences. Seen by the English-language press as an editor, lecturer, essayist, and even "the Chinese Mark Twain," he traveled widely, speaking on topical Chinese issues to a variety of religious and secular audiences. In 1905 he was received by President Theodore Roosevelt, while various Chinese political factions competed for his goodwill. He became an official consultant to the imperial Consul General in San Francisco, was befriended by the leaders of the Chinese Empire Reform Association shortly after the Chung Sai Yat Po first appeared, and later was courted by supporters of the revolutionist Sun Yat-sen. The subsequent endorsement of the revolutionary movement by Ng and his newspaper was an important factor in Sun's success in attracting the support of Chinese in North America.

Ng returned to China in 1911, for the first time in 30 years, just before the fall of the Manchu Empire and Sun's installation as the president of the new Chinese Republic. Visiting his hometown, he was supposed to have convinced his fellow villagers to burn their pagan idols and join the modern age, while he himself laid plans to develop a Western-style newspaper syndicate in China. Although those plans did not materialize, Ng was recognized as a key supporter of progress by the revolutionary government. In 1912 he became the Vice Consul of China in San Francisco. A year later the University of Pittsburgh honored him with a doctor of letters degree. He continued to lecture, preach, and promote civil rights for Chinese Americans until 1931, when he died of a heart attack at a dinner reception in Oakland. His newspaper, *Chung Sai Yat Po*, lived on until 1951.

See also: Chinese-Language Newspapers in America

Further Reading

"Chinese American Philanthropist: Ng Poon Chew." 2009. *Asian Week*, July 21. Accessed July 16, 2015. http://www.asianweek.com/2009/07/31/chinese-american-philanthropist-ng-poon-chew/.

Wandering Lizard History. (2010). "Biographical Notes: Ng Poon Chew." Accessed July 16, 2015. http://www.inn-california.com/articles/biographic/ngpoonchewbiono tes1.html.

Bennet Bronson and Chuimei Ho

NGOR, HAING S. (1940–1996)

Chinese Cambodian Haing S. Ngor was born in Samrong Young, Cambodia, on March 22, 1940. Before the Khmer Rouge captured control of Cambodia on April 17, 1975, Ngor was a middle-class skilled surgeon and gynecologist in Phnom Penh. Shortly afterward, Ngor, along with two million other inhabitants, were forced into labor camps and forced to endure systematic inhumane torture. While in the camps, his wife, My-Huoy, died after giving birth. Although a gynecologist, Ngor was unable to treat his wife because he would have been exposed and killed. For three years, eight months, and 20 days, between 1975 and 1979, nearly two million Cambodians perished from mass starvation, forced labor, torture, slavery, ethnic cleansing, and senseless killing. After four years in the "death camps," Ngor and his niece Sophia Ngor took refuge in Thailand, where he worked as a medical doctor until resettling in the United States on August 30, 1980. Ngor did not resume his medical career in the United States and did not remarry.

Ngor was cast to play the role of journalist Dith Pran in the film, *The Killing Fields* (1984), arguably the first major international call for attention to the Cambodian situation. In his debut role, Ngor won a Golden Globe Award and an Academy Award for Best Supporting Actor. He is the first Asian American male actor to win the Academy Award for a supporting performance. Overnight, Ngor became the face of Cambodia to the world. In 1988, he published his memoir, *Haing Ngor: A Cambodian Odyssey*, describing his life under the Khmer Rouge. Ngor's Hollywood career includes roles in Oliver Stone's *Heaven & Earth* (1993) and appearances in the miniseries *Vanishing Son*, *China Beach*, and *Miami Vice*.

The money Ngor earned as an actor provided a means for him to continue his humanitarian work. Ngor says, "Nothing has shaped my life as much as surviving the Pol Pot regime. I am a survivor of the Cambodian holocaust. That's who I am." For years, Ngor returned to Cambodia and Thai border refugee camps to help build a medical center, a school, and several orphanages. While doing so, he openly condemned and challenged Pol Pot and Khmer Rouge leaders who were attempting to reestablish forces in Thailand, putting himself in harm's way for possible revenge. In 1990, Ngor and Jack Ong established the Dr. Haing S. Ngor Foundation. The foundation's mission include preserving the legacy of Ngor's accomplishments and human rights' endeavors as well as promotion of Cambodia's dark history through education, arts, and activism. Haing Ngor was an early advocate for a tribunal to bring the Khmer Rouge to justice, a process that the United Nations finally helped bring to fruition in 2009.

On February 25, 1996, Ngor was murdered in a dark alley outside his apartment in Los Angeles Chinatown. It is unknown whether his murder was a botched robbery or an international conspiracy. Two years after his death, in 1998, a Los Angeles jury found three Chinese American gang members guilty of murder on the same day Pol Pot died quietly in a tiny jungle village, never having faced charges for his heinous crimes.

His is an inspiring survivor's story of reconciliation with the horrors of genocide, a story that ends mysteriously with his murder in 1996. His legacy in making public the horrific acts of senseless murder continues to assist the reconciliation and collective healing for Cambodia and Cambodians today.

See also: Chinese Americans in Motion Pictures; Chinese Cambodians

Further Reading

Dr. Haing S. Ngor Foundation, The. 2014. Accessed July 16, 2015. http://www.haing ngorfoundation.org.

Ngor, Haing S. 2003. *Survival in the Killing Fields*. New York: Carroll & Graf. First published in 1987 under the title, *A Cambodian Odyssey*.

Jonathan H. X. Lee

PEI, I. M. (IEOH MING) (1917–)

I. M. Pei is one of the world's most recognizable modern architects, whose creations can be seen in many cities around the world. Ieoh Ming (or I. M.) Pei was born in 1917 to an upper-class family in the Chinese city of Suzhou, near Shanghai. In 1940, Pei completed a degree in architecture at the Massachusetts Institute of Technology. He continued his education at the Graduate School of Design at Harvard University, where he both studied and taught architecture. Under the tutelage of Walter Gropius, founder of the Bauhaus School, Pei completed a master's degree in 1946. Shortly after completing his studies, Pei accepted a position at Webb and Knapp, a New York architectural firm owned by the wealthy property developer William Zeckendorf. In 1960, Pei established his own firm and was asked to design several important buildings, including the John F. Kennedy Library on Columbus Point in Boston. The political challenges and complications that surrounded the building of the John F. Kennedy Library would help prepare Pei for another politicized creation. In 1984, President François Mitterrand of France asked Pei to revitalize Paris's Louvre Museum. The highlight of Pei's renovation is the ultramodern glass pyramid in the center of the courtyard. The pyramid provoked a backlash

Architect I.M. Pei gestures as he speaks after receiving a 2004 Ellis Island Family Heritage award in New York on April 21, 2004. Pei, born in China, came to America from Shanghai in 1935 to attend the Massachuesetts Institute of Technology. He entered the United States aboad the S.S. *President Coolidge* from San Francisco. Ellis Island was the main East Coast entry point for immigrants from 1897 and 1938. (AP Photo/Kathy Willens)

from the French pubic that was largely directed at Pei. Despite the resistance, Pei's Louvre pyramid was completed in 1989. Throughout the remainder of the 20th century and into the 21st century, Pei continued to design major projects, including the Meyerson Symphony Center in Dallas, Texas, the Bank of China Tower in Hong Kong, the Four Seasons Hotel in New York, the Rock and Roll Hall of Fame in Cleveland, Ohio, and the Grand Duke Jean Museum of Modern Art in Luxembourg. The work that Pei has completed in his seven decades as an architect has left a lasting impact on modern architecture that will ensure his legacy into the future.

Further Reading

Cannell, Michael. 1995. *I. M. Pei: Mandarin of Modernism*. New York: Carol Southern Books.

Jodidio, Philip, and Janet Adams Strong. 2008. *I. M. Pei: Complete Works*. New York: Rizzoli.

Wiseman, Carter. 2001. *I. M. Pei: A Profile in American Architecture*. Rev. ed. New York: Harry N. Abrams.

John Cappucci

TAM, VIVIENNE (1957–)

Vivienne Tam has gained fame as a fashion designer known for her "East meets West" style. Born Yin Yok Tam in Guangzhou, China, in 1957, Vivienne Tam graduated from Hong Kong Polytechnic University and also studied in London. She moved to New York in 1982 and established East Wind Code, a women's, children's, and infants' clothing and accessories wholesaler.

Vivienne Tam's earliest memory of fashion was her mother's cheongsam, and her original designs experimented with its elements: the sleeves, collars, darts, and slits. When a woman wears a cheongsam, "a metamorphosis takes place—she's taller, more elegant, in a state of grace." Tam launched her signature collection of Eastern-inspired clothes in New York in 1994. The next year she introduced her "Mao" collection, which crossed the lines from the fashion to the art world. Tam's inspiration for the Mao collection came from her association with Zhang Hongtu, one of the first Chinese artists to use images of Mao in his work. In 1997 she launched her venerable Buddha collection. Tam observed that Buddhist villagers would visit the temple on festival days and decorate statues of Buddha and Kuanyin with silks and flowers, and she sought to incorporate these images into her fashion. Pieces of her collections have been included in the Andy Warhol Museum in Pittsburgh, Pennsylvania, the museum of the Fashion Institute of Technology and Metropolitan Museum in New York, and the Victoria and Albert Museum in London. In 2010, Tam moved beyond textile design. In conjunction with the electronics firm Monster, she introduced her Butterfly-shaped headphones, designed specifically for listening to string and orchestral instruments. During the rollout, Tam noted the strong symbolism that the butterfly holds for Asian people.

Vivienne Tam has received many awards, including being listed in *People* magazine's 50 Most Beautiful People (1995) and Outstanding Alumnus, Hong Kong Polytechnic University (1997). The Council of Fashion Designers of America nominated her for the Perry Ellis Award in 1997.

See also: Wang, Vera

Further Reading

Tam, Vivienne. 2000. *China Chic*. New York: ReganBooks.
"The 50 Most Beautiful People in the World." 1995. *People* 43 (18): 66.

Wendell G. Johnson

TAN, AMY (1952–)
See: Chinese American Literature; Chinese Americans in Motion Pictures

WANG, ANNA MAY (1905–1961)
See: Chinese Americans in Motion Pictures

WANG, VERA (1949–)
Born in New York City in 1949, Vera Ellen Wang, former figure skater turned fashion designer, was the daughter of Chinese immigrants. Her father made his fortune in the pharmaceutical industry and her mother served as a translator to the United Nations. Wang's father played a role in the development of her business prowess, while her mother first introduced her to the world of couture fashion. Wang enjoyed an elite education at the Chapin School and studied at the School of American Ballet before earning her degree in art history from Sarah Lawrence College. Inspiration abounded for Wang as she grew up in vibrant Manhattan, attending Yves St. Laurent couture shows with her mother. She has drawn inspiration for her collections from Flemish paintings to French designer Paul Poiret. A year in Paris in the family's apartment with her mother as she studied at the Sorbonne became influential in her early work and fueled her passion for couture fashion. After returning to the United States, Wang began working at the Yves St. Laurent boutique in Manhattan, where fate brought Frances Patiky Stein, *Vogue's* fashion director, into her path. Wang was promptly told to give her a call after graduation, and did.

Acclaimed fashion designer Vera Wang arrives at a Vanity Fair fashion event in Los Angeles on February 26, 2012. (Carrienelson1/Dreamstime.com)

Wang's career began in earnest at *Vogue*. She was initially hired as a temporary assistant and through determination and effort worked her way through the ranks to become one of the youngest ever fashion editors. She was eventually passed over for the editor in chief position at *Vogue*, which was a crushing blow. Ralph Lauren then hired her as a design director for accessories.

Wang's first adventure into fashion design was her own wedding dress in 1989, her only design experience coming from designing her own skating ensembles for her short-lived professional career in the late 1960s. After securing financial support, she opened a bridal boutique located in the Carlyle Hotel in New York City. Though she initially carried haute gowns by other renowned designers, she eventually launched her own line of bridal wear. Pushing her skills even further, she designed an original ensemble for Nancy Kerrigan during the 1994 Olympics that won her international acclaim. The attention from this secured her place as a couture designer, as she branched out into evening wear and an exclusive line, Vera Wang Made to Order. Characterized by classic lines and sophisticated minimalism, Wang's designs have cultivated a following in celebrity circles that is unparalleled.

Wang's empire now includes engagement jewelry and lines of fragrance, lingerie, and home products, and has exclusive contracts with Men's Wearhouse, Zales, and the department store Kohl's, for which she developed a more affordable line of clothing dubbed Simply Vera. This move allowed Wang to become a household name by allowing women at all price points and demographics access to her label. Though the focus of her business is in high-end fashion, she has become a cultural icon and household name by including ready-to-wear items in her brand. Once a distributor of Christian Dior, Carolina Herrera, and other high-end bridal wear, her lines are now considered to be a major competitor of the very fashion houses she once sold.

See also: Tam, Vivienne

Further Reading

Krohn, Katherine. 2007. *Vera Wang.* Minneapolis, MN: Twenty-First Century Books.
Louie, Ai-Ling. 2007. *Vera Wang Queen of Fashion.* Bethesda, MD: Dragoneagle Press.
Todd, Anne. 2009. *Vera Wang.* New York: Chelsea House.

Carlise Womack Wynne

WANG, WAYNE (1949–)

Wayne Wang is a Hong Kong-born American filmmaker, best known for *Dim Sum* (1985), *The Joy Luck Club* (1993), and *Smoke* (1995). He moved to California at the age of 17 to study film and television. After working in television in Hong Kong for a few years, he returned to the United States, where he directed his first feature *Chan Is Missing* (1982), set in San Francisco's Chinatown. *Dim Sum*, which followed three years later, similarly explored the Chinese immigrant experience in America and generational issues between first- and second-generation Chinese Americans in San Francisco.

His adaptation of Amy Tan's best-selling novel, *The Joy Luck Club*, in 1993 opened to critical acclaim and was a box-office success. The film continues in the vein of much of Wang's work, focusing on four Chinese immigrant families in San Francisco, who set up a Mahjong club. In 1995 Wang collaborated with the American author Paul Auster on *Smoke* and *Blue in the Face*, two films centered on a tobacco shop in Brooklyn. The film won Wang the Silver Bear for best direction at the Berlin Film Festival and was another critical and commercial success. In *Chinese Box* (1998), set during the Hong Kong handover, Wang worked with Asian stars Gong Li and Maggie Cheung for the first time.

After making a string of Hollywood films as a hired hand, including the 2002 Jennifer Lopez vehicle *Maid in Manhattan*, he returned to Asian American themes in 2007 with two adaptations from the Chinese American writer Yiyun Li, *The Princess of Nebraska* and *A Thousand Years of Good Prayers*. These once again dealt with Chinese immigrant communities, particularly generational difficulties among them. He turned his hand to historical cinema for the first time with *Snow Flower and the Secret Fan* (2011) and to documentary in *Soul of a Banquet* (2014), about Cecilia Chiang, who popularized Chinese cuisine in the United States in the 1960s.

See also: Chinese Americans in Motion Pictures

Further Reading

Lim, Dennis. 2008. "Wayne Wang, Bridging Generations and Hemispheres." *The New York Times*, September 12.

Wolz, Silke. 1998. *The Chinese American Films of Wayne Wang*. Berlin: John-F.-Kennedy Institut für Nordamerikastudien.

Tammy Ho Lai-Ming

WONG CHIN FOO (1847–1898)

Wong Chin Foo (Wang Qinfu) lived in America twice, the first time from 1867 to 1870 as a teenager being educated in Washington D.C, and Pennsylvania, and the second time from 1874 to 1898 as a self-exiled political refugee. It was during his second stay that he made an indelible mark on Chinese American history. Wong is known as one of the most prolific Chinese American writers in the San Francisco press during the 19th century. In addition, he was an activist, journalist, and lecturer. Wong was born in Jimo Shandong Province China and was among the first Chinese immigrants to be naturalized in 1873. During the Chinese Exclusion period, Wong was dedicated to fighting for equal and civil rights for Chinese Americans.

Wong published an article about Chinese food in the *Brooklyn Eagle* in 1884, which included the first description of "chop suey" anywhere. His newspapers, both called *The Chinese American* in English but with slightly different names in Chinese (*Huamei Xinbao* and *Huayang Xinbao*), begun in New York in 1883 and revived in Chicago a decade later, were the first bilingual Chinese-English periodicals east of San Francisco. His newspapers' English names marked the first known use of the term "Chinese American." Chinese in the United States call themselves by that name partly because of Wong Chin Foo.

His Chinese Equal Rights League, founded in Chicago in 1892, was the first rights-oriented Chinese association in American history. Widely publicized at that time, the League stimulated the formation of other Chinese civil rights organizations, including the Native Sons of the Golden State (later to become the Chinese American Citizens' Alliance) in California in 1895 and the American Born Chinese Brigade in Oregon in 1900.

With an unusually clear view of the issues involved in attempts to exclude Chinese from the United States, Wong managed to get himself naturalized in Michigan on the first Saturday of April in 1874, in spite of the anti-Chinese Naturalization Act of 1870. He fought determinedly against the various Chinese Exclusion Acts, even testifying before Congress against the Geary Act of 1892. He was a constant and amusing critic of the arch-racist Denis Kearney, on one occasion beating him badly in a debate in a New York newspaper office and later challenging him to a duel with potatoes, chopsticks, or Krupp cannon.

It is not clear how Wong made his living. He was a close friend of the Theosophist leader Madame Blavatsky and may have received financial help from her. Moreover, he was an immensely successful paid speaker in an age when traveling lecturers were real stars, pulling down substantial fees. Most of his lectures to non-Chinese audiences treated serious subjects like ethnicity or civil rights with courage and humor. Perhaps his most successful lecture was his sensational, frequently reprinted essay, "Why Am I a Heathen?" in which he offered a sharp, amusing critique of Christian hypocrisy. Interestingly, Protestant churches often invited him to speak on that subject to their congregations. Despite the general anti-Chinese atmosphere in the United States, Wong himself was popular among European Americans. English-language newspapers called him "interesting," "entertaining," "humorous," and "a witty genius."

He was not so popular with everyone in America's Chinatowns, however. Some saw him as an outsider, a native of Shandong province who had difficulty speaking Cantonese, the language of most American Chinese, and as a disturbing influence with alien ideas. Upon his arrival in San Francisco in 1874, he promptly became an enemy to local Chinese gangs by reporting to American authorities that some of his fellow passengers were not respectable immigrants but female "slaves"—indentured prostitutes. He did not make himself popular in Chicago and New York either, due to his continuing campaign against opium and gambling. Several attempts have been made to harm or assassinate him, a contemporary article in the *New York Times*.

He may have been more comfortable in Chicago than New York. In 1892 he moved there and became involved in helping the Wong Clan Association in legal quarrels with other clans. An apparent connection with the spectacular, commercially oriented Chinese Village at the great World's Columbian Exposition of 1893 made him an enthusiast for such fairs, partly for their possibilities in showing Chinese to other Americans in a favorable light and partly for their potential for making money. This may be why he became involved with Omaha's Trans-Mississippi Exposition of 1898, for which he agreed to become a commissioner and to finance several theatrical troupes to come to the fair from China.

This proved to be a serious mistake. Something went wrong with the plans and he found himself seriously in debt. It may have been to avoid his creditors that Wong decided, without publicity or notice by the press, to return to China right away, perhaps before the fair closed in the fall of 1898. He died in China shortly afterward. Even though the Chinese government may have regarded him as a dangerous subversive, his death, about which no details have survived, may have been due to natural causes. No one has managed to locate his grave, a sad coda to the end of one of history's most colorful—and one of its greatest—Chinese Americans.

See also: Ng Poon Chew; Wu Tingfang; Yung Wing

Further Reading

Bronson, Bennet, and Chuimei Ho. 2015. *Coming Home in Brocade: Chinese in the Early American Northwest*. Seattle, WA: Chinese in Northwest America Research Committee.

Seligman, Scott D. 2013. *The First Chinese American—the Remarkable Life of Wong Chin Foo*. Hong Kong: Hong Kong University Press.

Bennet Bronson and Chuimei Ho

WONG, JADE SNOW (1922–2006)

Jade Snow Wong, author and ceramicist, is known primarily for her 1950 memoir, *Fifth Chinese Daughter*. Published in an era when Chinese Americans were working for white acceptance in the United States, and the United States

Jade Snow Wong of San Francisco, California, shows a pair of quartz jewel bowls which she made by her own secret process in 1953. Wong described the bowls as having bottom sections with the firmness of porcelain but the transparency of patterned glass. (AP Photo/Ernest K. Bennett)

sought to project its image abroad as inclusive and egalitarian, the book portrayed her family as ethnically distinctive, self-sufficient, and devoted to education, family, hard work, and Christian values, and her white teachers and employers as liberal and supportive of Wong herself. *Fifth Chinese Daughter* was chosen as a Book of the Month, published in England and Germany, and translated into numerous Asian languages by the U.S. State Department, which sent Wong on a speaking tour through Asia in 1953. Reprinted in 1989, the book has been the most enduring of several early works by Asian American writers acting as cultural tour guides, despite criticism of its optimistic "model minority" stance. Over decades, readers have responded to Wong's lively voice, her vivid depictions of Chinatown family life, and the familiar plot of the hardworking daughter who gains agency by leaving home. The book is still taught on college campuses today.

Jade Snow Wong is the pseudonym of Constance Wong Ong, born on January 21, 1922, the sixth of nine children. Her father, a garment factory owner, minister, and community leader in San Francisco's Chinatown, instructed her in Chinese language and culture, and sent her to Chinese school for nine years, but his plan to prepare her for study and work in China was rendered impractical by Japan's invasion of China. At 11, Jade Snow assumed about half her family's housework so that her mother could earn more money for the family; at 12 she was also given a Sunday school class to teach. When Wong's parents declined to send her to college, she worked her way through San Francisco Junior College and Mills College, graduating in 1942, then crossed racial boundaries and showcased her patriotism as a secretary at the wartime U.S. Navy shipyards. Later, she decided to promote intercultural understanding by writing and to support herself by making and selling pottery. She rented a small workspace in the window of a Chinatown shop (wryly illustrated by Katheryn Uhl), where in 1945 she installed herself as a potter, turning heads, attracting enough customers to become a local celebrity and buy "the first postwar automobile" in Chinatown, and winning her father's approval. Wong married Woodrow Ong in 1950; they supported themselves and their four children by making and selling their distinctive pottery and enamelware and guiding tours to Asia, as depicted in her 1975 memoir, *No Chinese Stranger*. That memoir also gives a more complete portrait of her father within a transpacific context, including anti-Chinese discrimination in the United States and abroad. After a distinguished career as a writer and ceramicist, Wong died of cancer in 2006.

Fifth Chinese Daughter was published in 1950, but some sources erroneously list the publication date as 1945 due to the multiple copyright dates of the first edition. In fact, Wong published two essays in *Common Ground* (1945, 1948), one of which was incorporated into the memoir. The memoir, which ends with the establishment of her pottery business in 1945, invites competing readings. It presents Wong as a protofeminist rebel claiming individual rights in contrast to her parents' Confucian family values. Conversely, it also shows that her family combines Chinese customs and a Confucian family hierarchy with the Methodist faith, the Protestant work ethic, and "American" ingenuity. While portraying her parents as remote, frugal, strict, and biased toward sons, she also depicts them as model Americans: hardworking, self-supporting, resourceful small-business operators, devoted parents, and community leaders. Written in the author's twenties, the memoir portrays Wong's parents as traditional Chinese, demanding diligence, obedience, self-sacrifice, and loyalty to family and community. Jade Snow both exemplifies and challenges these values when she leaves her home to work for white families, attend Mills College, work in a U.S. Navy shipyard, and open her own business in Chinatown. Wong reconciles her need for individual expression and recognition with her loyalty to family and community by winning white recognition for her writing and her pottery but establishing her pottery business within Chinatown. Studded with references to obstacles overcome and honors achieved, the book explicitly refutes claims that whites would not hire Chinese, citing many instances of whites' acceptance and support for Wong. Yet it also makes clear that her career was exceptional: few of her Chinatown classmates entered college. Hence, the book is both a model minority success story and a more complex community portrait.

In the 1970s, ethnic studies scholars found fault with Wong for valuing white standards and ideals too highly over those of her parents and relying on her publisher's and instructor's editing for her first book. Elaine H. Kim criticized Wong even for valuing Chinese culture, claiming this was a "defensive reaction" that represented "withdrawal from conflict rather than militant challenge." Literary critic Xiao-huang Yin was more sympathetic, noting the Wongs' extreme poverty, the generous support of Wong's white benefactors and mentors, and her text's progressiveness for its time. Cultural critic Christina Klein suggested that Wong was one of a group of ethnic writers and artists whose efforts to promote America's influence abroad were valued, so long as they asserted and embodied the presence of opportunity for minorities.

See also: Chinese American Literature

Further Reading

Kim, Elaine H. 1982. *Asian American Literature: An Introduction to the Writings and Their Social Context.* Philadelphia, PA: Temple University Press.

Klein, Christina. 2003. *Cold War Orientalism: Asia in the Middlebrow Imagination, 1945–1961.* Berkeley: University of California Press.

Wong, Jade Snow. 1945. "Daddy." *Common Ground* (Winter): 25–29.

Wong, Jade Snow. 1948. "The Sanctum of Harmonious Spring." *Common Ground* (Winter): 84–91.

Wong, Jade Snow. 1975. *No Chinese Stranger.* New York: Harper & Row.

Wong, Jade Snow. 1989. *Fifth Chinese Daughter.* Seattle: University of Washington Press.

Yin Xiao-huang. 2000. *Chinese American Literature Since the 1850s.* Champaign: University of Illinois Press.

*Patricia P. Chu**

* Patricia P. Chu, "Jade Snow Wong" is excerpted from "Chinatown Life: H. T. Chiang, Jade Snow Wong, and C. Y. Lee" in *The Cambridge History of Asian-American Literature*, ed. Min Hyoung Song and Rajini Srikanth, copyright 2015 Cambridge University Press; reprinted by permission.

WONG, SHAWN (1949–)

Chinese American novelist and pioneer of Asian American studies Shawn Hsu Wong was born in Oakland, California, in 1949. For a second-generation Chinese American like Wong, the 1960s proved a formative time, as many began to question the evolving nature of cultural difference and ethnic identity. He received his undergraduate degree in English at the University of California at Berkeley in 1971 and his master's degree in creative writing at San Francisco State University in 1974. Wong specialized in creative writing and Asian American studies and from 1972 onward taught at Mills College, University of California at Santa Cruz, and San Francisco State University. He joined the faculty of the University of Washington in 1984, was Director of the Creative Writing Program from 1995 to 1997, Chair of the Department of English from 1997 to 2002, and Director of the University Honors Program from 2003 to 2006. Still an active member of the Washington faculty in English and comparative literature, he has also found time to lecture at Universität Tübingen (Germany), Jean Moulin Université (Lyon), and the University of Washington Rome Center in Italy.

Wong's first novel *Homebase* (1979) is the coming-of-age story of a fourth-generation Chinese American, Rainsford Chan, growing up in 1950s' and 1960s' California. Named after the town where his great-grandfather had found employment during the Great Gold Rush and orphaned at 15, he can do no more than stake his own claim, in this instance in America as his "home base." His personal history becomes a tapestry interwoven with dreams, stories, and letters of his family's life in America. Moving through time and place, his emerging story allows us as readers to discover the past as Rainsford does, to grasp and bear witness to the world through his eyes, and to learn the truth about the Chinese American experience. Wong's first novel would win for him the Pacific Northwest Booksellers Association Award and the 15th Annual Governor's Writers Day Award of Washington.

His second novel, *American Knees* (1996), is as much a thought-provoking romantic comedy, as it is a witty exploration of cultural and ethnic difference as they play in and out of the bedroom. The novel was adapted into an independent feature film entitled *Americanese* (2010), written and directed by Eric Byler and produced by Lisa Onodera.

Excerpts of his anticipated novel, *From the Ancient and Occupied Heart of Greg Li* (2012), have appeared in *Hot Metal Bridge*, the literary magazine of the University of Pittsburgh. The short film *Dolci* (2011), directed by Paula Benett, is based in part from a scene in Wong's third novel. A film of love and loss certainly, it is also about the potential, the promise of hope, to be found in a beautiful garden springing to life in early spring.

In addition to his creative endeavors, Wong has demonstrated a prolific bent toward academic writing. He is coeditor of six multicultural literary anthologies, including the pioneering anthology *Aiiieeeee! An Anthology of Asian-American*

Writers, Literary Mosaic: Asian American and Asian Diasporas, Cultures, Identities, Representations, and *The Big Aiiieeeee!* Additionally, he serves as consulting and contributing editor for *Transtext(e)s-Transcultures: A Journal of Global Cultural Studies*. He has been awarded a National Endowment for the Arts Creative Writing Fellowship and a Rockefeller Foundation residency in Italy. He is featured in the 1997 PBS documentary *Shattering the Silences*, in the Bill Moyers' 2003 PBS documentary *Becoming American: The Chinese Experience*, and in the 2005 documentary *What's Wrong with Frank Chin?*

See also: Chinese American Literature

Further Reading

Wong, Shawn. 2005. *American Knees*. Seattle: University of Washington Press.
Wong, Shawn. 2008. *Homebase*. Seattle: University of Washington Press.

James A. Wren

WU, DANIEL (1974–)

Daniel Wu has achieved success as a film star both in China and the United States. He was born September 30, 1974, in San Francisco, California. His parents immigrated to the United States from Shanghai after the Communist Revolution in 1949. His father worked as an engineer at Bechtel and his mother taught at St. Mary's College. Wu majored in architecture at the University of Oregon where he also coached the university's Wushu club. While at Oregon, he took film classes and developed an appreciation for the work of filmmakers Luc Besson and Akira Kurosawa. Upon graduation from the University of Oregon, he moved to Hong Kong in 1997, where he witnessed the former British colony's handover to China. Wu tried his hand at modeling and was discovered by a Hong Kong director during a photo shoot. He became one of the Chinese-language industry's biggest stars. According to the Hong Kong Movie Database, Daniel Wu acted in over 60 films and produced 5 films. His debut as a director, *The Heavenly Kings* (a mockumentary about the Hong Kong musical industry) was nominated for the Best New Director category of the 26th Hong Kong Film Awards.

Having achieved success in Hong Kong, Wu hoped to make it in Hollywood. As a youngster, he noticed there were few Asian faces on the big screen and wanted to leverage his reputation in Hong Kong to correct the cinematic prejudices he found in the United States. He felt, in particular, that America TV and films emasculated Asia men. Wu worked with Kevin Spacey in *Inseparable* and found it an amazing experience to film with someone who had won two Oscars. In his latest movie, *That Demon Within* (2014), Wu plays a film noir police detective (Dave Wong) who identifies with his evil counterpart.

Daniel Wu married Lisa Selesner in 2010. The couple has a daughter, Raven Wu.

See also: Chinese Americans in Motion Pictures

Further Reading

McDonald, Katherine. 2000. "American Wu Finds Stardom in Hong Kong." *Variety* 380 (13): 86–87.

Wang, Chih-ming. 2007. "Thinking and Feeling Asian America in Taiwan." *American Quarterly* 59 (1): 135–55.

Wendell G. Johnson

YANG, GENE LUEN (1973–)

See: Chinese American Literature

YEP, LAURENCE MICHAEL (1948–)

Born on July 14, 1948, Laurence Michael (Xiangtian) Yep is a prolific Chinese American writer, best known for his children's books. A recurring topic across his works involves individuals who are alone or who do not belong, and as such, many of his characters undergo journeys of self-discovery as they learn who they are and where they belong. In 2005 he received the biennial Laura Ingalls Wilder Medal from the professional children's librarians for his "substantial and lasting contribution to literature for children." The committee noted that "Yep explores the dilemma of the cultural outsider" with "attention to the complexity and conflict within and across cultures."

Yep was born in San Francisco to Yep Gim Lew and Franche, Chinese immigrants who insisted on speaking English at home. As a result, young Yep identified himself as Chinese in Chinatown but as Chinese without the benefit of a Chinese voice. Adding to his disenfranchisement, he grew up in an African American neighborhood. Reflecting the precarious nature of his early years, for most of his life he experienced the feeling of being out of place. This sense only intensified as he entered a Catholic high school in the heart of San Francisco's Chinatown. There he attempted to balance his interest in chemistry with a newfound love for writing. Encouraged by his teacher, a priest, to write with the expressed idea of being published, he embarked on what would eventually lead him toward a career in writing.

Following graduation, Yep attended Marquette University. When he arrived there, he found himself to be one of the very few Asian faces on campus. But from an uneventful beginning, he set about learning the history and culture of the Chinese people and quickly realized that their story had not been fully told in American literature. At the same time, he befriended literary magazine editor, Joanne Ryder, who introduced him to children's literature and who would later, when she was working at a major publishing house, ask him to write a book for children. The result was his first science fiction novel, *Sweetwater* (1973). After Marquette, he would undertake his M.A. at the University of California, Santa Cruz, and his PhD in English at the State University of New York at Buffalo. According to Yep, his relationship with Joanne progressed with time from one of friendship to intimacy and eventual marriage.

Yep's most notable work is the *Golden Mountain Chronicles*, documenting the fictional Young family from 1849 in China to 1995 in America. Two of the series are Newbery Honor Books (runners-up for the annual Newbery Medal): *Dragonwings* (1975) and *Dragon's Gate* (1993). *Dragonwings* won the Phoenix Award from the Children's Literature Association in 1995, recognizing the best children's book published 20 years earlier that did not win a major award. Another of the *Chronicles*, *Child of the Owl* won the Boston Globe-Horn Book Award for children's fiction in 1977. Yep wrote two other notable series, *Chinatown Mysteries* and *Dragon* (1982 to 1992). The latter is an adaptation of Chinese mythology as four fantasy novels. *The Rainbow People*, his collection of short stories based on Chinese folktales and legends, was a runner-up to the Horn Book Prize in 1989.

See also: Chinese American Literature; Folklore in Children's Literature

Further Reading

Lawrence, Katherine. 2004. *Laurence Yep*. New York: Rosen Publishing.
Marcovitz, Hal. 2008. *Laurence Yep (Who Wrote That?)*. New York: Chelsea Park Publishing.

James A. Wren

YEW, CHAY (1965–)

Born in Singapore in 1965, Yew Chay first came to California for his university studies in the 1980s and has with few exceptions remained there since. An accomplished and widely respected playwright, in 1989, the government in Singapore banned his first play, *As If He Hears*, because the gay character was depicted as "too sympathetic and too straight-looking." Thereafter, he took his works to stages across America and abroad, exploring the battlegrounds, be they internal or external, where psychological conflict meets physical barriers of race and sexuality, as he consistently addresses issues of racism, homophobia, and censorship. Hailed as "a promising new voice in American theater," he remains, as do many immigrants writers, caught in a precarious balance betwixt and between, hovering as he does in a limbo that is both psychological and cultural. As a result, he stands both as an activist as well as a leading artist in the theatre.

During his youth in Singapore, Yew became entranced with the American popular culture and moved to the United States when he was 16 to begin undergraduate studies at Pepperdine University in Malibu, California. There, he learned one of his first lessons about racial biases in American theater productions, having auditioned for a role and being summarily rejected solely because he was Asian. He would eventually move to Boston University for his M.F.A. in communications. After reading a newspaper article about arrests of men having sex in campus rest rooms, he adapted specific details from those reported events into a television script for his thesis. Telling of the times and of the subject matter, not a single actor showed up for his casting call.

Returning to Singapore in 1988, Yew wrote his first play for TheatreWorks. By all accounts topically relevant and objective, *As If He Hears* explores the relationship between a heterosexual businessman with HIV and a gay Malaysian social worker who comes to his assistance. Government censors immediately stepped in and banned it from production. In spite of the frequent confrontations with racism, homophobia, and censorship, Yew remained true to his ideals. As a playwright-in-residence at Mu-Lan Theatre in London in the early 1990s, for example, he rewrote his Boston thesis as a play for the British stage.

Yew followed the success of his thesis with *Porcelain* (1992), the recounting of those events leading up to a crime of passion, as a 19-year-old Chinese student shoots his working-class Caucasian lover in the same public toilet where they first met and began their sexual relationship. Desperate for acceptance, he seeks a sense of salvation in casual—doomed—sexual exploits that promise nothing permanent, and in the absence of commitment, desperation gives way to murderous rage. The play earned Yew his first widespread critical recognition and sold-out houses. He was awarded the 1993 London Fringe Award for Best Play.

His next success, *A Language of Their Own* (1995), deconstructs the nature of love, desire, sexuality, and identity as four men meet and partner, split, and reconnect in the age of AIDS. Built upon the doomed affair of Ming, an assimilated Chinese American, and his Chinese-born lover Oscar, who is older and HIV-positive, the work simultaneously lays bare the difficulties of love between individuals who are multiply marginalized, as it mounts a scathing criticism of the importance of youth and physical beauty that preoccupy gay male culture, be it in the States, Europe, or Singapore. At the invitation of George C. Wolfe, the play moved to New York City for a successful run at the Joseph Papp Public Theater later in 1995, under the direction of Keng-Sen Ong and starring Francis Jue, Alec Mapa, and B. D. Wong. Yew's stereotype-breaking storyline provided an extraordinary vehicle to the talents of these three fine actors, and as a result the play was rewarded the GLAAD Media Award for Best Play and the George and Elizabeth Marton Playwriting Award.

In 1995, Yew became the Director of the Asian Theatre Workshop at the Mark Taper Forum in Los Angeles (a position he held until 2005). Soon after, he began working as resident playwright and director with the East West Players in Los Angeles. These institutions have provided Yew the possibility of developing projects that expand opportunities and new kinds of roles for Asian American theatrical artists.

The prolific Yew has continued to write his own plays. Some of his recent works include *Half Lives* (1996), in which an Asian American goes to Singapore on business, marries his pregnant girlfriend, and brings her to America, where their son grows up and eventually comes to terms with his homosexuality; *Red* (1998), which explores the crackdown on artists during China's Cultural Revolution, but which was inspired by the American attempt to censor artists by reducing funding for the National Endowment for the Arts; *A Beautiful Country* (1998), which is narrated by drag queen Miss Visa Denied and explores the experiences of Asian Americans over the last 160 years; *Wonderland* (1999), about an Asian American family's struggle to realize the American dream; *Here and Now* (2002), about an elderly couple; and *A Distant Shore* (2005), a sprawling history of Asian and Caucasian interaction from the 1920s to the present. What unifies nearly all his diverse projects is his concern with the experiences of sexual and ethnic outsiders and his commitment to expanding the scope and breadth of Asian American theater.

Yew served as the director of the Mark Taper Forum's Asian Theatre Workshop for 10 years and has directed works at the Public Theater, New York Theatre Workshop, American Conservatory Theatre, Kennedy Center, Long Wharf Theatre, East West Players, Actors Theatre of Louisville, Goodman Theatre, Cincinnati Playhouse, Portland Center Stage, Geva Theatre Center, Empty Space, National Asian American Theatre Company, Laguna Playhouse, Theatre at Boston Court, Gala Hispanic Theatre, Singapore Repertory Theatre, Ma-Yi Theatre Company, Cornerstone Theatre Company, Northwest Asian American Theatre, Walk and Squawk, Highways Performance Space, Pillsbury Playhouse, Smithsonian Institution, and Theatre Rhinoceros. In 2007 he received the OBIE Award for Direction and took over the board of directors of Theatre Communications Group. He has also served on the executive board of the Stage Directors and Choreographers Society. In July 2011, he joined the Chicago-based Victory Gardens Theater in July 2011 as its first new artistic director in 34 years. At that time, he reaffirmed his ongoing commitment toward "providing an artistic home for emerging and established theater artists in Chicago and around the country . . . [and] . . . to refine and amplify Victory Gardens' mission of championing new plays and diversity as the mission remains close to my heart and everything I've done in American Theatre."

See also: Chinese American Literature

Further Reading

Lee, Ester Kim. 2011. *A History of Asian American Theatre*. Cambridge, UK: Cambridge University Press.

Yew, Chay. 1997. *Porcelain and a Language of Their Own: Two Plays*. New York: Grove Press.

Yew, Chay. 2002. *The Hyphenated American: Four Plays: Red, Scissors, A Beautiful Country, and Wonderland*. New York: Grove Press.

Yew, Chay, ed. 2011. *Version 3.0: Contemporary Asian American Plays*. New York: Theatre Communications Group.

James A. Wren

PRIMARY DOCUMENTS

Document 1
1854 THE PEOPLE, RESPONDENT, V. GEORGE W. HALL, APPELLANT.

People v. Hall (1854) *made it illegal for Chinese to testify against a white person in court. On August 9, 1853, George Hall, a white miner, accompanied by his brother and one other man, assaulted and robbed a Chinese placer miner on the Bear River in Nevada County, California. Ling Sing left his tent after hearing the sound of gunfire and was shot and killed by Hall. The sheriff arrested Hall and his companions. Hall was later tried and found guilty based on the testimony of three Chinese witnesses. The judge sentenced Hall to death by hanging. However, California Supreme Court Chief Justice Hugh Murray overturned the conviction on the basis that "Asiatics" were "Indians" and therefore unable to testify against a white man in court. Murray argued that "Asiatics" long ago traveled over the Bering Strait and "descended" into Indians. Indians were not allowed to testify in court against a white man, so since "Asiatics" (in this case, the Chinese eye-witnesses) were Indians, they too, cannot testify in court against a white man.*

Mr. Ch. J. Murray delivered the opinion of the Court. Mr. J. Heydenfeldt concurred.

The appellant, a free white citizen of this State, was convicted of murder upon the testimony of Chinese witnesses. . . .

The 394th section of the Act Concerning Civil Cases provides that no Indian or Negro shall be allowed to testify as a witness in any action or proceeding in which a white person is a party.

The 14th section of the Act of April 16th, 1850, regulating Criminal Proceedings, provides that "No black or mulatto person, or Indian, shall be allowed to give evidence in favor of, or against a white man."

The true point at which we are anxious to arrive is, the legal signification of the words, "black, mulatto, Indian, and white person," and whether the Legislature adopted them as generic terms, or intended to limit their application to specific types of the human species. . . .

The Act of Congress, in defining that description of aliens may become naturalized citizens, provides that every "free white citizen". . . .

If the term "white," as used in the Constitution, was not understood in its generic sense as including the Caucasian race, and necessarily excluding all others. . . .

We are of the opinion that the words "white," "Negro," "mulatto," "Indian," and "black person," wherever they occur in our Constitution and laws, must be taken in their generic sense, and that, even admitting the Indian of this continent is not of the Mongolian type, that the words "black person," in the

14th section, must be taken as contradistinguished from white, and necessary excludes all races other than the Caucasian. . . .

The same rule which would admit them to testify, would admit them to all the equal rights of citizenship, and we might soon see them at the polls, in the jury box, upon the bench, and in our legislative halls.

This is not a speculation which exists in the excited and overheated imagination of the patriot and statesman, but it is an actual and present danger. . . .

The anomalous spectacle of a distinct people, living in our community, recognizing no laws of this State, except through necessity, bringing with them their prejudices and national feuds, in which they indulge in open violation of law; whose mendacity is proverbial; a race of people whom nature has marked as inferior, and who are incapable of progress or intellectual development beyond a certain point, as their history has shown; differing in language, opinions, color, and physical conformation; between whom and ourselves nature has placed an impassable difference, is now presented, and for them is claims, not only the right to swear away the life of a citizen, but the further privilege of participating with us in administering the affairs of our Government.

These facts were before the Legislature that framed this Act, and have been known as matters of public history to every subsequent Legislature.

There can be no doubt as to the intention of Legislature, and that if it had ever been anticipated that this class of people were not embraced in the prohibition, then such specific words would have been employed as would have put the matter beyond any possible controversy.

For these reasons, we are of opinion that the testimony was inadmissible.

The judgment is reversed and the cause remanded.

Source: The People of the State of California v. George W. Hall (1854). Transcript available at http://www.cetel.org/1854_hall.html.

Document 2
PAGE LAW

On March 3, 1875, the Page Law is enacted, which defined "undesirable" migrants as anyone from Asia (Chinese, Japanese, and "Mongolian") who were "contract laborers," Asian women suspected of prostitution, and felons. It was the first restrictive federal immigration law that was named after its sponsor, Representative Horace F. Page, Republican of California. Page introduced it to "end the danger of cheap Chinese labor and immoral Chinese women." The law required the consul-general to ascertain the labor status and moral character of the immigrants. The law proscribed a maximum fine of $2,000 dollars and imprisonment for any U.S. citizen or legal *resident who transported Asian contract laborers. In addition, the law made it a felony to "knowingly and willingly" transport Asian women into the United States for the purposes of prostitution: this carried a penalty of $5,000 fine and imprisonment of up to five years. This resulted in a near-total ban on Chinese women, which impacted the formation of Chinese American families and community composition.*

FORTY-THIRD CONGRESS. SESSION II. CH.141. MARCH 3, 1975 CHAPTER 141.

An act supplementary to the acts in relation to immigration

[Only the pertinent sections are included.—Ed.]

Be it enacted by the Senate and House of Representatives of the United States of America in Congress-assembled,

That in determining whether the immigration of any subject of China, Japan, or any Oriental country, to the United States, is free and voluntary, as provided by section two thousand one hundred and sixty two of the Revised Code, title "Immigration," it shall be the duty of the consul-general or consul of the United States residing at the port from which it is proposed to convey such subjects, in any vessels enrolled or licensed in the United States, or any port within the same, before delivering to the masters of any such vessels the permit or certificate provided for in such section, in ascertain for a term of service within the United States, for lewd and immoral purposes; and if there be such contract or agreement, the said consul-general or consul shall not deliver the required permit or certificate. . . .

SEC.3. That the importation into the United States of women for the purposes of prostitution is hereby forbidden; and all contracts and agreements in relation thereto, made in advance or in pursuance of illegal importation and purposes, are hereby declared void; and whoever shall knowingly and willfully hold, or attempt to hold, any woman to such purposes, in pursuance of such illegal importation and contract or agreement, shall be deemed guilty of a felony, and, on conviction thereof, shall be imprisoned not exceeding five years and pay a fine not exceeding five thousand dollars. . . .

SEC.5. That it shall be unlawful for aliens of the following classes to immigrate into the United States, namely, persons who are undergoing sentence for conviction in their own country of felonious crimes other than political or growing out of or the result of such political offenses, and women "imported for the purposes of prostitution." Every vessel arriving in the United States may be inspected under the direction of the collector of the port at which it arrives, if he shall have reason to believe that such obnoxious persons are on board; and the officer making such inspection shall certify the result thereof to the master or other person in charge of such vessel, designating in such certificate are person or persons, if any there be, ascertained by him to be of either of the classes whose importation is hereby forbidden. . . .

Source: Page Act of 1875 (Sect. 141, 18 Stat. 477, 1873–March 1875).

Document 3
"APPEAL FROM CALIFORNIA. THE CHINESE INVASION. WORKINGMEN'S ADDRESS."

In October 1877 Denis Kearney organized anti-Chinese meetings in San Francisco, and established the Workingmen's Party of California charging Chinese workers willingly work for lower wages, poorer conditions, and longer hours, which displaced white workers. The slogan "The Chinese Must Go" was being widely repeated and popular. Anti-Chinese anxiety characterized politics in the American West, particularly labor politics, in the late 19th century. Labor leaders like Denis Kearney and H. L. Knight of California's Workingmen's Party often resorted to popular racist discourses to defend the exclusion of Chinese immigrants. In this 1878 address, Kearney and Knight described the Chinese as a race of "cheap working slaves" who undercut American living standards and thus should be banished from America's shores to protect white laborers. Anti-Chinese sentiments grew and eventually resulted in passage of the Chinese Exclusion Act of 1882 that banned skilled and unskilled Chinese laborers.

Our moneyed men have ruled us for the past thirty years. Under the flag of the slaveholder they hoped to destroy our liberty. Failing in that, they have rallied under the banner of the millionaire, the banker and the land monopolist, the railroad king and the false politician, to effect their purpose.

We have permitted them to become immensely rich against all sound republican policy, and they have turned upon us to sting us to death. They have seized upon the government by bribery and corruption. They have made speculation and public robbery a science. The have loaded the nation, the state, the county, and the city with debt. They have stolen the public lands. They have grasped all to themselves, and by their unprincipled greed brought a crisis of unparalleled distress on forty millions of people, who have natural resources to feed, clothe and shelter the whole human race.

Such misgovernment, such mismanagement, may challenge the whole world for intense stupidity, and would put to shame the darkest tyranny of the barberous past.

We, here in California, feel it as well as you. We feel that the day and hour has come for the Workingmen of America to depose capital and put Labor in the Presidential chair, in the Senate and Congress, in the State House, and on the Judicial Bench. We are with you in this work. Workingmen must form a party of their own, take charge of the government, dispose gilded fraud, and put honest toil in power.

In our golden state all these evils have been intensified. Land monopoly has seized upon all the best soil in this fair land. A few men own from ten thousand to two hundred thousand acres each. The poor Laborer can find no resting place, save on the barren mountain, or in the trackless desert. Money monopoly has reached its grandest proportions. Here, in San Francisco, the palace of the millionaire looms up above the hovel of the starving poor with as wide a contrast as anywhere on earth.

To add to our misery and despair, a bloated aristocracy has sent to China—the greatest and oldest despotism in the world—for a cheap working slave. It rakes the slums of Asia to find the meanest slave on earth—the Chinese coolie—and imports him here to meet the free American in the Labor market, and still further widen the breach between the rich and the poor, still further to degrade white Labor.

These cheap slaves fill every place. Their dress is scant and cheap. Their food is rice from China. They hedge twenty in a room, ten by ten. They are wipped curs, abject in docility, mean, contemptible and obedient in all things. They have no wives, children or dependents.

They are imported by companies, controlled as serfs, worked like slaves, and at last go back to China with all their earnings. They are in every place, they seem to have no sex. Boys work, girls work; it is all alike to them.

The father of a family is met by them at every turn. Would he get work for himself? Ah! A stout Chinaman does it cheaper. Will he get a place for his oldest boy? He can not. His girl? Why, the Chinaman is in her place too! Every door is closed. He can only go to crime or suicide, his wife and daughter to prostitution, and his boys to hoodlumism and the penitentiary.

Do not believe those who call us savages, rioters, incendiaries, and outlaws. We seek our ends calmly, rationally, at the ballot box. So far good order has marked all our proceedings. But, we know how false, how inhuman, our adversaries are. We know that if gold, if fraud, if force can defeat us, they will all be used. And we have resolved that they shall not defeat us. We shall arm. We shall meet fraud and falsehood with defiance, and force with force, if need be.

We are men, and propose to live like men in this free land, without the contamination of slave labor, or die like men, if need be, in asserting the rights of our race, our country, and our families.

California must be all American or all Chinese. We are resolved that it shall be American, and are prepared to make it so. May we not rely upon your sympathy and assistance?

With great respect for the Workingman's Party of California.

Dennis Kearney, President
H.L Knight, Secretary

Source: Dennis Kearney, President, and H. L. Knight, Secretary, "Appeal from California. The Chinese Invasion. Workingmen's Address," *Indianapolis Times,* February 28, 1878.

Document 4
HO AH KOW V. NUNAN (1879)

Ho Ah Kow v. Nunan (1879) is an early example of civil rights litigation among Chinese Americans. Ho Ah Kow was a Chinese laborer living in San Francisco. At the time, there was a San Francisco municipal ordinance called the "Cubic Air Law" that forbid sleeping in a room with less than 500 cubic feet of air space per person. This ordinance was justified on a basis of public health, namely, as a way to prevent overcrowding and unsanitary living conditions. It was an ordinance that targeted the Chinese residents because they often lived in cramped quarters in the segregated Chinatown community. If the Chinese were arrested for violating the ordinance they were given two options: pay a fine or go to jail. As a form of resistance, the Chinese selected to go to jail instead of pay the fine. In 1876, the San Francisco Board of Supervisors responded with the "Queue Ordinance" (also referred to as the "Pigtail Ordinance"). This ordinance allowed the prison wardens to cut and shave the hair of all prisoners to one inch of hair. This ordinance clearly targeted the Chinese men who wore their hair long and in a braid known as a "queue," and cutting it was shameful and disgraceful. Ho Ah Kow protested the discriminatory treatment and sued Sheriff Matthew Nunan for damages. U.S. Supreme Court Justice Stephen J. Field ruled that the Queue Ordinance violated the Equal Protection Clause of the Fourteenth Amendment and was applicable to the Chinese as persons. Ho Ah Kow was awarded $10,000 for his damages and the law was overturned. Ho Ah Kow was an early fighter for civil rights in San Francisco, and the Queue Ordinance is a concrete example of the racist laws that were used against Chinese immigrants.

Circuit Court, D. California. July 7, 1879.
12FED.CAS.—17

HO AH KOW V. NUNAN.
[Only the pertinent sections are included.—Ed.]

1. The board of supervisors of the city and county of San Francisco, the body in which the legislative power of the city and county is vested, is limited in its authority by the act which consolidated the government of the city and county,

generally known as the consolidation act. It can do nothing unless warrant be found for it there, or in a subsequent statute of the state. . . .

4. Accordingly, where an ordinance of the city and county of San Francisco, passed on the fourteenth of June, 1876, declared that every male person imprisoned in the county jail, under the judgment of any court having jurisdiction in criminal cases in the city and county, should immediately upon his arrival at the jail have the hair of his head "cut or clipped to an uniform length of one inch from the scalp thereof," and made it the duty of the sheriff to have this provision enforced, it was held, that the ordinance was invalid, being in excess of the authority of the board of supervisors, whether the measure be considered as an additional punishment to that imposed by the court upon conviction under a state law, or as a sanitary regulation, and constituted no justification to the sheriff acting under it.

5. The ordinance being directed against the Chinese only, and imposing upon them a degrading and cruel punishment, is also subject to the further objection, that it is hostile and discriminating legislation against a class forbidden by that clause of the fourteenth amendment to the constitution, which declares that no state "shall deny to any person within its jurisdiction the equal protection of the laws." This inhibition upon the state applies to all the instrumentalities and agencies employed in the administration of its government; to its executive, legislative and judicial departments, and to the subordinate legislative bodies of its counties and cities.

6. The equality of protection thus assured to every one whilst within the United States implies not only that the courts of the country shall be open to him on the same terms as to all others for the security of his person or property, the prevention or redress of wrongs and the enforcement of contracts, but that no charges or burdens shall be laid upon him which are not equally borne by others, and that in the administration of criminal justice he shall suffer for his offenses no greater or different punishment.

7. The legislation of congress carrying out the provisions of the fourteenth amendment in accordance with these views cited. . . .

This was an action to recover damages from the defendant [Matthew Nunan] for alleged maltreatment of the plaintiff. The facts of the case are sufficiently stated in the opinion of the court, with the exception of the law of April 4, 1870. The act of the legislature of that date, entitled "An act to establish a quarantine for the bay and harbor of San Francisco and sanitary laws for the city and county of San Francisco," in its second section creates a board of health for the city and county of San Francisco, consisting of the mayor of the city and county and four physicians residing there, to be appointed by the governor; and in its ninth section provides that the said board of health "shall have general supervision of all matters appertaining to the sanitary condition of said city and county, including the city and county hospital, the county jail, almshouse, industrial school, and all public health institutions provided by the city and county of San Francisco; and full powers are hereby given to said board to adopt such orders and regulations and appoint or discharge such medical attendants and employees as to them seems best to promote the public welfare and not in contravention of any law." St. 189–70, 717, § 9. By the thirty-fifth section "all acts or parts of acts in conflict with this act, or any of its provisions," are repealed. To the action two defenses were set up by the defendant; the second being a justification of his conduct under an ordinance of the city and county of San Francisco, which is mentioned in the opinion. To the plea setting up this justification the plaintiff demurred, and the case was submitted upon written arguments.

Source: Ho Ah Kow v. Nunan, 12 F. Cas. 252 (C.C.D. Cal. 1879).

Document 5
CHINESE EXCLUSION ACT (MAY 6, 1882)

In the spring of 1882, the Chinese Exclusion Act was passed by Congress and signed by President Chester A. Arthur. Section 14 of the Act declares, "hereafter no State court of the United States shall admit Chinese to citizenship; and all laws in conflict with this act are hereby repealed." Section 15 states, "That the words 'Chinese laborers,' wherever used in this act, shall be construed to mean both skilled and unskilled laborers and Chinese employed in mining." By 1888, the act was extended to include all Chinese, not just laborers. It was renewed by the Geary Act of 1892, and extended indefinitely in 1902. The Chinese Exclusion Act was the first U.S. law ever passed to prevent immigration and naturalization on the basis of race, which later was extended and expanded to include other Asian immigrants, such as the Japanese, Korean, and Indian. The flow of immigration (encouraged by the Burlingame Treaty) was stopped by the Chinese Exclusion Act. The exclusionist policies led to an immediate and sharp decline in the Chinese population: from 105,465 in 1880 to 89,863 in 1900 to 61,639 in 1920. The Chinese population declined until the Act was repealed in 1943 by the Magnuson Act.

AN ACT TO EXECUTE CERTAIN TREATY STIPULATIONS RELATING TO CHINESE

Whereas, in the opinion of the Government of the United States the coming of Chinese laborers to this country endangers the good order of certain localities within the territory thereof: Therefore,

Be it enacted by the Senate and House of Representatives of the United States of America in Congress assembled, That from and after the expiration of ninety days next after the passage of this act, and until the expiration of ten years next after the passage of this act, the coming of Chinese laborers to the United States be, and the same is hereby, suspended; and during such suspension it shall not be lawful for any Chinese laborer to come, or having so come after the expiration of said ninety days, to remain within the United States.

SEC. 2. That the master of any vessel who shall knowingly bring within the United States on such vessel, and land or permit to be landed, any Chinese laborer, from any foreign port or place, shall be deemed guilty of a misdemeanor, and on conviction thereof shall be punished by a fine of not more than $500 for each and every such Chinese laborer so brought, and may be also imprisoned for a term not exceeding one year.

SEC. 3. That the two foregoing sections shall not apply to Chinese laborers who were in the United States on the 17th day of November, 1880, or who shall have come into the same before the expiration of ninety days next after the passage of this act. . . .

SEC. 4. That for the purpose of properly identifying Chinese laborers who were in the United States on the 17th day of November, 1880, or who shall have come into the same before the expiration of ninety days next after the passage of this act, and in order to furnish them with the proper evidence of their right to go from and come to the United States of their free will and accord, as provided by the treaty between the United States and China dated November 17, 1880, the collector of customs of the district from which any such Chinese laborer shall depart from the United States shall, in person or by deputy, go on board each vessel having on board any such Chinese laborer and cleared or about to sail from his district for a foreign port, and on such vessel make a list of all such Chinese laborers, which shall be entered in registry-books to be kept for that purpose, in which shall be stated the name, age, occupation, last place of residence, physical marks or peculiarities, and all facts necessary for the identification of each of such Chinese laborers, which books shall be safely kept in the custom-house; . . .

SEC. 7. That any person who shall knowingly and falsely alter or substitute any name for the name written in such certificate or forge any such certificate, or knowingly utter any forged or fraudulent certificate, or falsely personate any person named in any such certificate, shall be deemed guilty of a misdemeanor; and upon conviction thereof shall be fined in a sum not exceeding $1,000, and imprisoned in a penitentiary for a term of not more than five years.

SEC. 8. That the master of any vessel arriving in the United States from any foreign port or place shall, at the same time he delivers a manifest of the cargo, and if there be no cargo, then at the time of making a report, of the entry of the vessel pursuant to law, in addition to the other matter required to be reported, and before landing, or permitting to land, any Chinese passengers, deliver and report to the collector of customs of the district in which such vessels shall have arrived a separate list of all Chinese passengers taken on board his vessel at any foreign port or place. . . .

SEC. 9. That before any Chinese passengers are landed from any such vessel, the collector, or his deputy, shall proceed to examine such passengers, comparing the certificates with the list and with the passengers; and no passenger shall be allowed to land in the United States from such vessel in violation of law. . . .

SEC. 11. That any person who shall knowingly bring into or cause to be brought into the United States by land, or who shall knowingly aid or abet the same, or aid or abet the landing in the United States from any vessel of any Chinese person not lawfully entitled to enter the United states, shall be deemed guilty of a misdemeanor, and shall, on conviction thereof, be fined in a sum not exceeding $1,000, and imprisoned for a term not exceeding one year.

SEC. 12. That no Chinese person shall be permitted to enter the United States by land without producing to the proper officer of customs the certificate in this act required of Chinese persons seeking to land from a vessel. . . .

SEC. 13. That this act shall not apply to diplomatic and other officers of the Chinese Government traveling upon the business of that government, whose credentials shall be taken as equivalent to the certificate in this act mentioned, and shall exempt them and their body and household servants from the provisions of this act as to other Chinese persons.

SEC. 14. That hereafter no State court or court of the United States shall admit Chinese to citizenship; and all laws in conflict with this act are hereby repealed.

SEC. 15. That the words "Chinese laborers," wherever used in this act, shall be construed to mean both skilled and unskilled laborers and Chinese employed in mining.

Approved, May 6, 1882.

Source: An act to execute certain treaty stipulations relating to the Chinese, May 6, 1882; Enrolled Acts and Resolutions of Congress, 1789–1996; General Records of the United States Government; Record Group 11; National Archives.

Document 6
EXCERPT FROM "THE CHINESE MUST STAY" BY YAN PHOU LEE

Chinese exclusion lasted from 1882 to 1943. Many Chinese Americans took to the pen to express their frustration with the discriminatory law. Some did so anonymously while in detention at Angel Island craving poems and prose into the wooden walls of the barracks. Others, including Chinese diplomats, merchants, and students educated at American universities wrote essays, articles, and opinion pieces to challenge the law and anti-Chinese sentiments in popular magazines and journals. Moreover, some gave speeches to middle- and upper-class Anglo-Americans to debunk negative stereotypes and forester empathy and understanding as they evoked equitable treatment. Lee Yan Phou (1861– ca. 1938) was a Chinese student brought to the United States by the Chinese Educational Mission in Hartford, Connecticut. Lee graduated from Yale College (now University) and converted to Christianity. In "The Chinese Must Stay" Lee enjoins Americans to live up to their founding principles of equality and refutes scapegoating arguments used to legitimate their exclusion. In 1887 Lee published his memoir, When I Was a Boy in China, *which countered negative portrayals of the Chinese in popular American culture in the late 19th century.*

No Nation can afford to let go its high ideals. The founders of the American Republic asserted the principle that all men are created equal, and made this fair land a refuge for the whole world. Its manifest destiny, therefore, is to be the teacher and leader of nations in liberty. Its supremacy should be maintained by good faith and righteous dealing, and not by the display of selfishness and greed. . . .

How far this Republic has departed from its high ideal and reversed its traditionary policy may be seen in the laws passed against the Chinese.

Chinese immigrants never claimed to be any better than farmers, traders, and artisans. If, on the one hand, they are not princes and nobles, on the other hand, they are not coolies and slaves. They all came voluntarily, as their consular papers certified, and their purpose in leaving their home and friends was to get honest work. They were told that they could obtain higher wages in America than elsewhere, and that Americans were friendly to the Chinese and invited them to come. In this they were confirmed by certain provisions of the treaties made between China and the United States, by which rights and privileges were mutually guaranteed to the citizens of either country residing in the other. No one can deny that the United States made all the advances, and that China came forth from her seclusion because she trusted in American honor and good faith.

So long as the Chinese served their purposes and did not come into collision with the hoodlum element afterwards imported to California, the people of that State had nothing to complain of regarding them. Why should they, when, at one time, half the revenue of the State was raised out of the Chinese miners? But the time came when wages fell with the cost of living. The loafers became strong enough to have their votes sought after. Their wants were attended to. Their complaints became the motive power of political activity. So many took up the cry against the Chinese that it was declared that no party could succeed on the Pacific coast which did not adopt the hoodlums' cause as its own. . . .

It has been urged:

I. That the influx of Chinese is a standing menace to Republican institutions upon the Pacific coast and the existence there of Christian civilization.

That is what I call a severe reflection on Republican institutions and Christian civilization. Republican institutions have withstood the strain of 13,000,000 of the lower classes of Europe, among whom may be found Anarchists, Socialists, Communists, Nihilists, political assassins, and cut-throats; but they cannot endure the assaults of a few hundred thousands of the most peaceable and most easily-governed people in the world! . . .

IV. That the Chinese have displaced white laborers by low wages and cheap living, and that their presence discourages and retards white immigration to the Pacific States.

This charge displays so little regard for truth and the principles of political economy that it seems like folly to attempt an answer. But please to remember that it was by the application of Chinese "cheap labor" to the building of railroads, the reclamation of swamp-lands, to mining, fruit-culture, and manufacturing, that an immense vista of employment was opened up for Caucasians, and that millions now are enabled to live in comfort and luxury where formerly adventurers and desperadoes disputed with wild beasts and wilder men for the possession of the land. Even when the Chinaman's work is menial (and he does it because he must live, and is too honest to steal and too proud to go the almshouse), he is employed because of the scarcity of such laborers. . . . You may as well run down machinery as to sneer at Chinese cheap labor. Machines live on nothing at all; they have displaced millions of laborers; why not do away with machines? . . .

V. That the Chinese do not desire to become citizens of this country.

Why should they? Where is the inducement? [*Yan Phou Lee recited the laws discriminating against Chinese to argue they have not been encouraged to become citizens.*] . . . Are you sure that the Chinese have no desire for the franchise? Some years ago, a number of those living in California, thinking that the reason why they were persecuted was because it was believed they cared nothing for American citizenship, made application for papers of naturalization. Their persecutors were alarmed and applied to Congress for assistance, and the California Constitution was amended so as to exclude them. . . .

Source: North American Review, 148 (April 1889): 476–83.

Document 7

UNITED STATES v. WONG KIM ARK (1898)

Wong Kim Ark was an American citizen by birth. U.S. citizenship law is grounded on two legal traditions: jus soli *"right of the soil" and* jus sanguinis *"right of the blood." Under* jus soli, *a child is granted automatic citizenship if born on the soil* of the United States of America, without regard to the political status of the child's parents. Under jus sanguinis, a child's citizenship status is linked to the status of the parent. The citizenship laws in the United States have followed both principles since the Naturalization Act of 1790. Wong Kim Ark was born in San Francisco to immigrant Chinese parents in 1873. In 1895, he visited China, and upon reaching the port of San Francisco, he was not allowed reentry on the grounds that he was not a citizen. Moreover, federal Chinese exclusion acts prohibited him from entering as an immigrant. Thomas Riordan, a lawyer for the Chinese Consulate in San Francisco and the Chinese Six Companies, filed a writ of habeas corpus on behalf of Wong Kim Ark in federal district court. Citing Wong Kim Ark's birth in the United States and relying on the authority of In re Look Tin Sing, 21 F. 905 (1884), the court ordered him discharged from custody. The decision was immediately appealed to the U.S. Supreme Court.

The U.S. Supreme Court appeal hinged upon the interpretation of the first clause of the Fourteenth Amendment, which states, ". . . all persons born or naturalized in the United States, and subject to the jurisdiction thereof, are citizens of the United States." The government argued that Wong Kim Ark was not a citizen because his Chinese parentage made him subject to the emperor of China. In a 6-2 decision (Justice McKenna did not participate), Justice Gray wrote the majority opinion that a child born to two Chinese nationals legally present on American soil was an American citizen. The case was a landmark legal victory for Asian Americans during a period of intense anti-Asian sentiment.

SYLLABUS

A child born in the United States, of parents of Chinese descent, who, at the time of his birth, are subjects of the Emperor of China, but have a permanent domicile and residence in the United States, and are there carrying on business, and are not employed in any diplomatic or official capacity under the Emperor of China, becomes at the time of his birth a citizen of the United States, by virtue of the first clause of the Fourteenth Amendment of the Constitution,

All person born or naturalized in the United States, and subject to the jurisdiction thereof, are citizens of the United States and of the State wherein they reside.

This was a writ of habeas corpus issued October 2, 1895, by the District Court of the United States for the Northern District of California to the collector of customs at the port of San Francisco, in behalf of Wong Kim Ark, who alleged that he was a citizen of the United States, of more than twenty-one years of age, and was born at San Francisco in 1873 of parents of Chinese descent and subjects of the Emperor of China, but domiciled residents at San Francisco, and that, on his return to the United States on the steamship Coptic in August, 1895, from a temporary visit to China, he applied to said collector of customs for permission to land, and was by the collector refused such permission, and was restrained of his liberty by the collector, and by the general manager of the steamship company acting under his direction, in violation of the Constitution and laws of the United States, not by virtue of any judicial order or proceeding, but solely upon the pretense that he was not a citizen of the United States.

At the hearing, the District Attorney of the United States was permitted to intervene in behalf of the United States in opposition to the writ, and stated the grounds of his intervention in writing as follows:

. . . Because the said Wong Kim Ark, although born in the city and county of San Francisco, State of California, United States of America, is not, under the laws of the State of California and of the United States, a citizen thereof, the mother and father of the said Wong Kim Ark being Chinese persons and subjects of the Emperor of China, and the said Wong Kim Ark being also a Chinese person and a subject of the Emperor of China.

Because the said Wong Kim Ark has been at all times, by reason of his race, language, color and dress, a Chinese person, and now is, and for some time last past has been, a laborer by occupation.

That the said Wong Kim Ark is not entitled to land in the United States, or to be or remain therein, because he does not belong to any of the privileged classes enumerated in any of the acts of Congress, known as the Chinese Exclusion Acts, which would exempt him from the class or classes which are especially excluded from the United States by the provisions of the said acts.

Wherefore the said United States Attorney asks that a judgment and order of this honorable court be made and entered in accordance with the allegations herein contained, and that the said Wong Kim Ark be detained on board of said vessel until released as provided by law, or otherwise to be returned to the country from whence he came, and that such further order be made as to the court may seem proper and legal in the premises.

The case was submitted to the decision of the court upon the following facts agreed by the parties:

That the said Wong Kim Ark was born in the year 1873, at No. 751 Sacramento Street, in the city and county of San Francisco, State of California, United States of America, and that his mother and father were persons of Chinese descent and subjects of the Emperor of China, and that said Wong Kim Ark was and is a laborer.

That, at the time of his said birth, his mother and father were domiciled residents of the United States, and had established and enjoyed a permanent domicile and residence therein at said city and county of San Francisco, State aforesaid.

That said mother and father of said Wong Kim Ark continued to reside and remain in the United States until the year 1890, when they departed for China.

That during all the time of their said residence in the United States as domiciled residents therein, the said mother and father of said Wong Kim Ark were engaged in the prosecution of business, and were never engaged in any diplomatic or official capacity under the Emperor of China.

That ever since the birth of said Wong Kim Ark, at the time and place hereinbefore stated and stipulated, he has had but one residence, to-wit, a residence in said State of California, in the United States of America, and that he has never changed or lost said residence or gained or acquired another residence, and there resided claiming to be a citizen of the United States.

That, in the year 1890 the said Wong Kim Ark departed for China upon a temporary visit and with the intention of returning to the United States, and did return thereto on July 26, 1890, on the steamship *Gaelic,* and was permitted to enter the United States by the collector of customs upon the sole ground that he was a native-born citizen of the United States.

That after his said return, the said Wong Kim Ark remained in the United States, claiming to be a citizen thereof, until the year 1894, when he again departed for China upon a temporary visit, and with the intention of returning to the United States, and did return thereto in the month of August, 1895, and applied to the collector of customs to be permitted to land, and that such application was denied upon the sole ground that said Wong in Ark was not a citizen of the United States.

That said Wong Kim Ark has not, either by himself or his parents acting for him, ever renounced his allegiance to the United States, and that he has never done or committed any act or thing to exclude him therefrom.

The court ordered Wong Kim Ark to be discharged, upon the ground that he was a citizen of the United States. 1 Fed. Rep. 382. The United States appealed to this court, and the appellee was admitted to bail pending the appeal.

Source: United States v. Wong Kim Ark, 169 U.S. 649 (1898).

Document 8
WEBB-HANEY ACT (ALIEN LAND LAW), CALIFORNIA, 1913

Living in America was difficult. Attempts to settle and create families was not easy, especially with the passage of alien land laws that made it illegal for immigrants ineligible to become naturalized citizens from buying and owning real estate. In 1913 California passed its first alien land law (the Webb-Haney Act). This law also stipulated that aliens ineligible for citizenship may not lease land for agriculture for terms longer than three years. January 19, 1920, the 1913 California Alien Land Law was amended to close a loophole that permitted Asian immigrants to own or lease land under the names of their native-born children. Soon after, on February 26, 1921, Arizona passed an Alien Land Law; on March 8, 1921, Washington State legislature passed an Alien Land Law; in April 1921 Texas passed an Alien Land Law; in 1922 New Mexico passed an Alien Land Law; in 1923 Idaho, Montana, and Oregon passed Alien Land Laws. On November 12, 1923, the U.S. Supreme Court in Terrace v. Thompson *upheld the constitutionality of Washington's Alien Land Law; on November 12, 1923, the U.S. Supreme Court in* Porterfield v. Webb *upheld the constitutionality of California's Alien Land Law. On November 4, 1924, Nevada passed an Alien Land Law; and in 1925 Kansas passed an Alien Land Law. On April 17, 1952, the California Supreme Court found California's Alien Land Law of 1913 unconstitutional.*

§ 1. All aliens eligible to citizenship under the laws of the United States may acquire, possess, enjoy, use, cultivate, occupy, transfer, transmit and inherit real property, or any interest therein, in this state, and have in whole or in part the beneficial use thereof, in the same manner and to the same extent as citizens of the United States, except as otherwise provided by the laws of this state.

§ 2. All aliens other than those mentioned in section one of this act may acquire, possess, enjoy, use, cultivate, occupy and transfer real property, or any interest therein, in this state, and have in whole or in part the beneficial use thereof, in the manner and to the extent, and for the purposes prescribed by any treaty now existing between the government of the United States and the nation or country of which such alien is a citizen or subject, and not otherwise. . . .

§ 7. Any real property hereafter acquired in fee in violation of the provisions of this act by any alien mentioned in Section 2 of this act, . . . shall *escheat* as of the date of such acquiring, to, and become and remain the property of the state of California. . . .

Proposition 1: Permits acquisition and transfer of real property by aliens eligible to citizenship, to same extent as citizens except as otherwise provided by law; permits other aliens, and companies, associations and corporations in which they hold majority interest, to acquire and transfer real property only as prescribed by treaty, but prohibiting appointment thereof as guardians of estates of minors consisting wholly or partially of real property or shares in such corporations; provides for escheats in certain cases; requires reports of property holdings to facilitate enforcement of act; prescribes penalties and repeals conflicting acts.

Source: Webb-Haney Act, also known as the Alien Land Law of 1913. Cited in *Sei Fujii v. State of California*, 38 Cal. 2d 718 (1952).

Document 9

GOVERNOR GARY LOCKE'S INAUGURAL ADDRESS, 1997

Gary Faye Locke was born on January 21, 1950, in Seattle, Washington. Locke is a third-generation Chinese American whose paternal lineage is from Taishan, China. Locke is the second oldest of five siblings. His father, James Locke served as a staff sergeant in the U.S. Fifth Armored Division during World War II, and his mother, Julie Locke is from Hong Kong. Locke's paternal grandfather left China in the 1890s and emigrated to the United States and worked as a "house-boy" in Olympia, Washington in exchange for English-language lessons. Locke's political career began in 1982 when he was elected to the state of Washington's South Seattle district in the Washington House of Representatives. Locke became the first Chinese American governor in U.S. history when he won the general election for governor of Washington in 1996. Locke won reelection in 2000 and did not seek a third term. He was the 21st governor of Washington. Locke was chosen by the Democrat Party to give his party's response to President George W. Bush's 2003 State of the Union Address. Locke received racist slurs and threats to him and his family after his rebuttal, which influenced his decision to not seek a third term.

Mr. President, Mr. Speaker, Madam Chief Justice, distinguished justices of the Supreme Court, statewide elected officials, members of the Washington State Legislature, other elected officials, members of the Consular Corps, fellow citizens, and friends of Washington state across America and around the world.

I am humbled by the honor of serving as your governor. And I am deeply grateful to all those who have made our American tradition of freedom and democracy possible.

I also want to express my gratitude to members of my family, and to introduce them to you. First I'd like you to meet my father, Jimmy Locke, who fought in World War II and participated in the Normandy invasion. I'd like you to meet my mother, Julie, who raised five children, learned English along with me when I started kindergarten, and who returned to school at Seattle Community College when she was nearly 60. . . . And finally, it is my greatest pleasure to introduce Washington's new First Lady, Mona Lee Locke. This truly is a wonderful day for the Locke family.

One of my ancestors—a distant cousin, actually—was a merchant who immigrated to Olympia in 1874 and became a leader of the Chinese-American community just a few blocks from this state capitol. He acted as a bridge between the Chinese and white communities, and became friends with the other downtown merchants, and with the sheriff, William Billings.

In 1886, an anti-immigrant, anti-Chinese mob threatened to burn down the Chinese settlement here. But what happened next is a story that every Washington resident ought to know: Sheriff Billings deputized scores of Olympia's merchants and civic leaders. And those citizen deputies stood between the angry mob and the Chinese neighborhood at Fifth and Water streets. Faced by the sheriff and the leading citizens of Olympia, the mob gradually dispersed. Not a single shot was fired, nor a single Chinese house burned.

For the Locke family, that incident helped establish a deep faith in the essential goodness of mainstream American values:

- The values that reject extremism and division, and embrace fairness and moral progress;
- The value of working together as a community; and
- The values of hard work, hope, enterprise and opportunity.

Just a few years after that Olympia show of courage, my grandfather came to America to work as a "house boy" for the Yeager family, who lived in a house that's still standing, less than a mile from here.

His purpose was to get an education, and so the Yeager family agreed to teach him English in return for his work. Like everyone else in our family, my grandfather studied and worked hard, and he eventually became the head chef at Virginia Mason Hospital in Seattle. . . .

Our family history is more the norm than the exception. . . . There are millions of families like mine, and millions of people like me—people whose ancestors dreamed the American Dream and worked hard to make it come true. And today, on Martin Luther King's birthday, we are taking another step toward that dream.

In the 108 years since Washington became a state, we have gone from riding horses to flying in jets; from sending telegrams to sending e-mail; and from woodstoves to microwave ovens. Can anyone even guess what the next hundred years will bring? . . .

To keep the American Dream alive in a high-tech and unpredictable future, we have to raise our sights, and our standards. . . .

The principles that will guide me in this quest for higher standards—and the principles that will guide my response to legislative proposals—are clear and simple.

- My first principle is that education is the great equalizer that makes hope and opportunity possible. That's why I am passionately committed to developing a world-class system of education.

In the last century, the drafters of our Constitution made the education of children the "paramount duty" of the state. But learning is not just for kids anymore. For the next century, the paramount duty of this state will be to create an education system for lifelong learning—a system that every person regardless of age can plug into for basic skills, professional advancement or personal enrichment.

- My second principle is to promote civility, mutual respect and unity, and to oppose measures that divide, disrespect, or diminish our humanity. I want our state to build on the mainstream values of equal protection and equal opportunity, and to reject hate, violence and bigotry. And I want our state to be known as a place where elected officials lead by example.

- My third principle is to judge every public policy by whether it helps or hurts Washington's working families. Everyone who works hard and lives responsibly ought to be rewarded with economic security, the opportunity to learn and to advance in their chosen field of work, and the peace of mind that comes from knowing that the essential services their families need—like health care insurance and child care—will be affordable and accessible. And every senior citizen who has spent a lifetime contributing to the freedom and prosperity we enjoy deserves dignity and security.

- My fourth principle is to protect our environment, so that future generations enjoy the same natural beauty and abundance we cherish today. . . .

. . . As most of you already know, Mona and I are expecting our first child in March. So in very rapid succession, I will be blessed with two titles that carry immense responsibility and immense honor: Governor and Dad.

As the advent of fatherhood gets closer, I am more and more conscious that everything I do as governor—and everything we do together—we do for our children.

Our child will be a child of the 21st Century. He or she will come of age in a world that we can scarcely imagine. But it is his or her world that we must now work together to create. For our children and yours, I want to foster a new century of personal responsibility, of community, and of hope and optimism.

Please help me carry on the Locke family tradition of focusing on those three crucial values: get a good education, work hard, and take care of each other.

With your hand in partnership, and with an abiding faith in the essential goodness of the people of our great state, I want to devote the next four years to making the American Dream come true for children whose faces we have yet to see.

Thank you.

Source: Governor Gary Locke, official webpage, http://www.digitalarchives .wa.gov/GovernorLocke/speeches/speeches.asp.

Document 10

CONGRESSWOMAN JUDY CHU AND H. RES. 683

Congresswoman Judy Chu authored H. Res. 683 to express the regret of the House of Representatives for passing the Chinese Exclusion Act in 1882. The Chinese Exclusion Act prevented Chinese migrants from coming to the United States and prohibited them from becoming naturalized American citizens and, by extension, voting. The Chinese Exclusion Act lasted for 60 years until 1943, impacting the Chinese American community for generations. This was the first and only federal law in U.S. history that excluded a single group of people from immigration on no basis other than their race.

Sponsor: Rep. Chu, Judy [D-CA-32] (Introduced 06/08/2012)

H.Res.683—Expressing the regret of the House of Representatives for the passage of laws that adversely affected the Chinese in the United States, including the Chinese Exclusion Act.

In the House of Representatives, U. S.,

June 18, 2012.

Whereas many Chinese came to the United States in the 19th and 20th centuries, as did people from other countries, in search of the opportunity to create a better life;

Whereas the United States ratified the Burlingame Treaty on October 19, 1868, which permitted the free movement of the Chinese people to, from, and within the United States and made China a ``most favored nation'';

Whereas in 1878, the House of Representatives passed a resolution requesting that President Rutherford B. Hayes renegotiate the Burlingame Treaty so Congress could limit Chinese immigration to the United States;

Whereas, on February 22, 1879, the House of Representatives passed the Fifteen Passenger Bill, which only permitted 15 Chinese passengers on any ship coming to the United States;

Whereas, on March 1, 1879, President Hayes vetoed the Fifteen Passenger Bill as being incompatible with the Burlingame Treaty;

Whereas, on May 9, 1881, the United States ratified the Angell Treaty, which allowed the United States to suspend, but not prohibit, immigration of Chinese laborers, declared that ``Chinese laborers who are now in the United States shall be allowed to go and come of their own free will,'' and reaffirmed that Chinese persons possessed ``all the rights, privileges, immunities, and exemptions which are accorded to the citizens and subjects of the most favored nation'';

Whereas the House of Representatives passed legislation that adversely affected Chinese persons in the United States and limited their civil rights, Including. . . .

Whereas Chinese-Americans continue to play a significant role in the success of the United States; and

Whereas the United States was founded on the principle that all persons are created equal: Now, therefore, be it Resolved,

SECTION 1. ACKNOWLEDGEMENT.

That the House of Representatives regrets the passage of legislation that adversely affected people of Chinese origin in the United States because of their ethnicity.

Source: H. Res. 683 (2011–2012). Available at: https://www.congress.gov/bill/112th-congress/house-resolution/683/text.

Bibliography

Barde, Robert E. 2008. *Immigration at the Golden Gate: Passenger, Ships, Exclusion, and Angel Island.* Westport, CT: Praeger.

Brooks, Charlotte. 2009. *Foreign Friends: Asian Americans, Housing, and the Transformation of Urban California.* Chicago, IL: University of Chicago Press.

Brooks, Charlotte. 2015. *Between Mao and McCarthy: Chinese American Politics in the Cold War Years.* Chicago, IL: University of Chicago Press.

Cassel, Susie Lan, ed. 2002. *The Chinese in America: A History from Gold Mountain to the New Millennium.* Walnut Creek, CA: AltaMira Press.

Chan, Anthony B. 1983. *Gold Mountain.* Vancouver, BC: New Star Books.

Chan, Jachinson. 2001. *Chinese American Masculinities: From Fu Manchu to Bruce Lee.* New York: Taylor & Francis.

Chan, Sucheng. 1986. *This Bitter-Sweet Soil: The Chinese in California Agriculture.* Berkeley: University of California Press.

Chan, Sucheng, ed. 1991. *Entry Denied: Exclusion and the Chinese Community in America, 1882–1943.* Philadelphia, PA: Temple University Press.

Chang, Iris. 2003. *The Chinese in America: A Narrative History.* New York: Penguin Books.

Chee, Maria W. L. 2005. *Taiwanese American Transnational Families: Women and Kin Work.* London: Routledge.

Chen, Carolyn. 2009. *Getting Saved in America: Taiwanese Immigration and Religious Experience.* Princeton, NJ: Princeton University Press.

Chen, Jack. 1980. *The Chinese of America.* San Francisco, CA: Harper & Row.

Chen, Shehong. 2002. *Being Chinese, Becoming Chinese Americans.* Champaign: University of Illinois Press.

Chen, Yong. 2014. *Chop Suey, USA: The Story of Chinese Food in America.* New York: Columbia University Press.

Chennault, Anna. 1962. *A Thousand Springs: the Biography of a Marriage.* New York: Paul S. Eriksson.

Chew, Ron, and Cassie Chin. 2003. *Reflections of Seattle's Chinese Americans: The First Hundred Years.* Seattle, WA: Wing Luke Museum.

Chin, Frank, ed. 1974. *Aiiieeeee! An Anthology of Asian-American Writers.* Washington, DC: Howard University Press.

Chinn, Thomas W., Him Mark Lai, and Philip P. Choy, eds. 1969. *A History of the Chinese in America, A Syllabus.* San Francisco, CA: Chinese Historical Society of America.

Choy, Philip. 2007. *Canton Footprints: Sacramento's Chinese Legacy*. Sacramento, CA: Chinese American Council of Sacramento.

Chu, Daniel. 1967. *Passage to the Golden Gate: A History of the Chinese in America to 1910*. Garden City, NY: Doubleday.

Chun, Gloria Heyung. 1999. *Of Orphans and Warriors: Inventing Chinese American Culture and Identity*. New Brunswick, NJ: Rutgers University Press.

Chung, Sue Fawn. 2011. *In Pursuit of Gold: Chinese American Miners and Merchants in the American West*. Champaign: University of Illinois Press.

Chung, Sue Fawn, and Priscilla Wegars, eds. 2005. *Chinese American Death Rituals: Respecting the Ancestors*. New York: AltaMira Press.

Clark, Hugh. 1975. *Portland's Chinese: The Early Years*. Portland, OR: Center for Urban Education.

Coe, Andrew. 2009. *Chop Suey: A Cultural History of Chinese Food in the United States*. London, UK: Oxford University Press.

Dong, Arthur. 2014. *Forbidden City, USA: Chinese American Nightclubs, 1936–1970*. Los Angeles, CA: DeepFocus Productions.

Echenberg, Myron. 2007. *Plague Ports: The Global Urban Impact of Bubonic Plague, 1894–1901*. New York: New York University Press.

Friday, Chris. 1994. *Organizing Asian American Labor: The Pacific Coast Canned-Salmon Industry, 1870–1942*. Philadelphia, PA: Temple University Press.

Gyory, Andrew. 1998. *Closing the Gate: Race, Politics, and the Chinese Exclusion Act*. Chapel Hill: University of North Carolina Press.

Hing, Bill O. 1993. *Making and Remaking Asian American Through Immigration Policy 1850–1990*. Stanford, CA: Stanford University Press.

Huang, Eddie. 2013. *Fresh Off the Boat: A Memoir*. New York: Spiegel & Grau.

Jung, Moon-Ho. 2006. *Coolies and Cane: Race, Labor, and Sugar in the Age of Emancipation*. Baltimore, MD: Johns Hopkins University Press.

Kwong, Peter. 1996. *The New Chinatown*. New York: Hill and Wang.

Kwong, Peter, and Dusanka Miscevic. 2007. *Chinese America: The Untold Story of America's Oldest New Community*. New York: The New Press.

Lai, David Chuenyan, and Pamela Madoff. 1997. *Building and Rebuilding Harmony: The Gateway to Victoria's Chinatown*. Victoria, BC: University of Victoria.

Lai, Him Mark. 1980. *Island: Poetry and History of Chinese Immigrants on Angel Island*. San Francisco, CA: Hoc Doi.

Lai, Him Mark. 2004. *Becoming Chinese Americans: A History of Communities and Institutions*. Walnut Creek, CA: AltaMira Press.

Laurie, Clayton D. 1990. "'The Chinese Must Go!': The United States Army and the Anti-Chinese Riots in Washington Territory, 1885–1886." *Pacific Northwest Quarterly* 81: 22–29.

Laurie, Clayton D. 1990. "Civil Disorder and the Military in Rock Springs, Wyoming: The Army's Role in the 1885 Chinese Massacre." *Montana* 40 (3): 44–59.

Lee, Erika. 2003. *At America's Gates: Chinese Immigration During the Exclusion Era, 1882–1943*. Chapel Hill: University of North Carolina Press.

Lee, Erika, and Judy Yung. 2010. *Angel Island: Immigrant Gateway to America*. Oxford, UK: Oxford University Press.

Lee, Jonathan H. X. 2015. *History of Asian Americans: Exploring Diverse Roots*. Santa Barbara, CA: ABC-CLIO.

Lee, Jonathan H. X., and Kathleen Nadeau. 2011. *Encyclopedia of Asian American Folklore and Folklife*. 3 vols. Santa Barbara, CA: ABC-CLIO.

Lee, Murray. 2011. *In Search of Gold Mountain: A History of the Chinese in San Diego, California*. Virginia Beach, VA: Donning Company Publishers.

Loewenstein, Louis K. 1984. *Streets of San Francisco: The Origins of Street and Place Names*. Illustrated by Penny deMoss. San Francisco, CA: Lexikos.

López, Kathleen. 2013. *Chinese Cubans: A Transnational History*. Chapel Hill: University of North Carolina Press.

López-Calvo, Ignacio. 2009. *Imaging the Chinese in Cuban Literature and Culture*. Gainesville: University Press of Florida.

Louie, Vivian S. 2004. *Compelled to Excel: Immigration, Education, and Opportunity Among Chinese Americans*. Stanford, CA: Stanford University Press.

Lum, Arlene, ed. 1988. *Sailing for the Sun: The Chinese in Hawaii 1789–1989*. Honolulu: University of Hawai'i Center for Chinese Studies.

Lydon, Sandy. 1985. *Chinese Gold: The Chinese in the Monterey Bay Region*. Capitola, CA: Capitola Book Co.

Marchetti, Gina. 2012. *The Chinese Diaspora on American Screens: Race, Sex, and Cinema*. Philadelphia, PA: Temple University Press.

Mayer, Ruth. 2013. *Serial Fu Manchu: The Chinese Supervillain and the Spread of Yellow Peril Ideology*. Philadelphia, PA: Temple University Press.

McCunn, Ruthanne Lum. 1988. *Chinese American Portraits: Personal Histories, 1828–1988*. San Francisco, CA: Chronicle Books.

McCunn, Ruthanne Lum. 2014. *Chinese Yankee*. San Francisco, CA: Design Enterprises.

Metzger, Sean. 2014. *Chinese Looks: Fashion, Performance, Race*. Bloomington: Indiana University Press.

Morton, James. 1973. *In the Sea of Sterile Mountains: The Chinese in British Columbia*. Vancouver, BC: J. J. Douglas.

Moy, Victoria. 2014. *Fighting for the Dream: Voices of Chinese American Veterans from World War II to Afghanistan*. Los Angeles: Chinese Historical Society of Southern California.

Nash, Robert. 1973. "The Chinese Shrimp Fishery in California." PhD diss., University of California, Los Angeles.

Ng, Franklin. 1998. *The Taiwanese Americans*. Westport, CT: Greenwood Press.

Nokes, R. Gregory. 2009. *Massacred for Gold: The Chinese in Hells Canyon*. Corvallis: Oregon State University Press.

Pan, Erica Y. Z. 1995. *The Impact of the 1906 Earthquake on San Francisco's Chinatown*. San Francisco: Peter Lang.

Pfaelzer, Jean. 2009. *Driven Out: The Forgotten War Against Chinese Americans*. Berkeley: University of California Press.

Scott, Janet Lee. 2007. *For Gods, Ghosts, and Ancestors: The Chinese Tradition of Paper Offerings*. Seattle: University of Washington Press.

Seward, George F. 1881. *Chinese Immigration in its Social and Economic Aspects*. New York: Charles Scribner's Sons.

Tchen, John Kuo Wei. 2014. *Chinese American: Exclusion/Inclusion*. New York: New-York Historical Society.

Tong, Benson. 2000. *The Chinese Americans*. Westport, CT: Greenwood Press.

Wegars, Priscilla. 1993. *Hidden Heritage: Historical Archaeology of the Overseas Chinese*. Amityville, NY: Baywood.

Wegars, Priscilla. 2003. *Polly Bemis: A Chinese American Pioneer*. Cambridge, ID: Backeddy Books.

Wei, William. 1995. "The Anti-Chinese Movement in Colorado: Interethnic Competition and Conflict on the Eve of Exclusion." *Chinese America: History & Perspectives* 9: 179–97.

Weinstein, Robert A. 1978. "North from Panama, West to the Orient: The Pacific Mail Steamship Company." *California History* 57: 46–57.

Wong, K. Scott. 2005. *Americans First: Chinese Americans and the Second World War*. Philadelphia, PA: Temple University Press.

Wong, Marie Rose. 2004. *Sweet Cakes, Long Journey: The Chinatowns of Portland, Oregon*. Seattle: University of Washington Press.

Woo, Wesley. 1991. "Chinese Protestants in the San Francisco Bay Area." In *Entry Denied: Exclusion and the Chinese Community in America, 1882–1943*, edited by Sucheng Chen, 213–45. Philadelphia, PA: Temple University Press.

Wunder, John R. 1983. "The Chinese and the Courts in the Pacific Northwest: Justice Denied." *Pacific Historical Review* 52: 191–211.

Wunder, John R. 1986. "Chinese in Trouble: Criminal Law and Race on the Trans-Mississippi Frontier." *Western Historical Quarterly* 17: 25–41.

Xu, Guoqi. 2014. *Chinese and Americans: A Shared History*. Cambridge, MA: Harvard University Press.

Yang, Fenggang. 1999. *Chinese Christians in America: Conversion, Assimilation, and Adhesive Identities*. University Park: Penn State University Press.

Yeh, Chiou-ling. 2008. *Making an American Festival: Chinese New Year in San Francisco's Chinatown*. Berkeley: University of California Press.

Yep, Kathleen. 2009. *Outside the Paint: When Basketball Ruled at the Chinese Playground*. Philadelphia, PA: Temple University Press.

Yun, Lisa. 2009. *The Coolie Speaks: Chinese Indentured Laborers and African Slaves in Cuba*. Philadelphia, PA: Temple University Press.

Yung, Judy. 1995. *Unbound Feet: A Social History of Chinese Women in San Francisco*. Berkeley: University of California Press.

Zesch, Scott. 2012. *The Chinatown War: Chinese Los Angeles and the Massacre of 1871*. New York: Oxford University Press.

Zhu, Liping. 2000. *A Chinaman's Chance: The Chinese on the Rocky Mountain Mining Frontier*. Denver: University of Colorado Press.

Zhu, Liping, and Rose Estep Fosna. 2004. *Ethnic Oasis: The Chinese in the Black Hills*. Pierre: South Dakota State Historical Society.

Zinzius, Birgit. 2005. *Chinese America: Stereotype and Reality: History, Present, and Future of the Chinese Americans*. New York: Peter Lang.

List of Contributors

Ryan J. T. Adams, PhD
Western Michigan University
Kalamazoo, Michigan

Linda Bentz, BA
Ventura County Chinese American
Historical Society
Ventura, California

Bennet Bronson, PhD
Chinese in Northwest America
Research Committee
Bainbridge Island, Washington

John Cappucci, PhD
University of Windsor
Windsor, Ontario, Canada

Benji Chang, PhD
Columbia University
New York, New York

Sheau-yueh J. Chao, MLS, MS
Bernard M. Baruch College
New York, New York

Ching-In Chen, MFA, PhD
University of Wisconsin Milwaukee

May May Chiang, MA
Independent scholar and
Ethnomusicologist
Phoenix, Arizona

Yvette M. Chin, MPhil
Independent scholar, writer, editor
Boston, Massachusetts

Patricia P. Chu, PhD
George Washington University
Washington, DC

James Chuck, PhD
First Chinese Baptist Church
San Francisco, California

Sue Fawn Chung, PhD
University of Nevada, Las Vegas

Linda Sun Crowder, PhD
California State University,
Fullerton

Lan Dong, PhD
University of Illinois, Springfield

Lorraine Dong, PhD
San Francisco State University

Joel S. Franks, PhD
San Jose State University
San Jose, California

Yan He, PhD
Dr. Shao You-Bao Overseas Chinese
Documentation and Research Center
Ohio University

Ryan W. Higgins, PhD candidate
Johns Hopkins University
Baltimore, Maryland

Chuimei Ho, PhD
Chinese in Northwest America
Research Committee
Bainbridge Island, Washington

Kevin Hogg, MA
Mount Baker Secondary School
Cranbrook, British Columbia, Canada

Adam R. Hornbuckle, MA
Independent historian and
freelance writer
Spring Hill, Tennessee

Frank Jacob, PhD
Würzburg University, Germany

Russell Jeung, PhD
San Francisco State University

Wendell G. Johnson, MLS, PhD
Northern Illinois University
DeKalb, Illinois

Douglas R. Jordan, BA
Independent Scholar

Andrew Kelly, PhD
University of Western Sydney
Australia

William P. Kladky, PhD
American Institutes for Research
and College of Notre Dame of
Maryland

Zachary S. Kopin, PhD
American University
Washington, D.C.

Ashok Kumar, doctoral student
St John's College
Oxford University

Tammy Ho Lai-Ming, MPhil
Hong Kong Baptist University

Alejandro Lee, PhD, MLIS
Central Washington University
Ellensburg, Washington

Heather R. Lee, PhD
Massachusetts Institute of Technology
Cambridge, Massachusetts

Genevieve Leung, PhD
University of San Francisco

Amy Lively, MA
Grand Canyon University
Phoenix, Arizona

Haiming Liu, PhD
California State Polytechnic University
Pomona, California

Lisa Rose Mar, PhD
University of Maryland, College Park

Ruthanne Lum McCunn, BA
Author
San Francisco, California

Sean Morton, PhD candidate
Brock University
St. Catharines, Ontario, Canada

Edy Parsons, PhD
Mount Mercy University
Cedar Rapids, Iowa

Mary Thi Pham, MA
San Francisco State University

Matthew Quest, PhD
Georgia State University
Atlanta, Georgia

Nancy Yunhwa Rao, PhD
Rutgers, the State University of
New Jersey

David Alan Rego, MA
Independent scholar, writer, editor
Boston, Massachusetts

Scott Nicholas Romaniuk,
doctoral student
University of Trento
Italy

Wei Shao, PhD
Freelance writer, poet, and translator
Dallas, Texas

Elijah Siegler, PhD
College of Charleston
Charleston, South Carolina

Esther Spencer, doctoral student
Florida State University
Tallahassee, Florida

Alice Tam, MA
San Francisco State University

Angela Tea, MA
University of California,
Los Angeles

Kathleen A. Tobin, PhD
Purdue University Calumet
Hammond, Indiana

Don E. Walicek, PhD
University of Puerto Rico, Río Piedras

Elizabeth Evans Weber, PhD
candidate
University of California, Los Angeles

Priscilla Wegars, PhD
University of Idaho
Moscow, Idaho

James A. Wren, PhD, DPhil, DSc
San Jose State University

Emily S. Wu, PhD
Dominican University of California
San Rafael, California

Ben Wynne, PhD
University of North Georgia
Gainesville, Georgia

Carlise Womack Wynne, PhD
University of North Georgia
Gainesville, Georgia

Edmond Yee, PhD
Pacific Lutheran Theological Seminary
Graduate Theological Union
Berkeley, CA

Xuefeng Zhang, PhD
Westmont College
Santa Barbara, California

Macy Zheng, MLS
East Asian Studies Librarian
McGill University
Montréal, Quebec, Canada

About the Editor

Jonathan H. X. Lee, PhD, is an associate professor of Asian American studies who specializes in Southeast Asian and Sino-Southeast Asian American studies at San Francisco State University. He received his doctorate in religious studies from the University of California at Santa Barbara in 2009. He is the founder and program co-chair of the Asian American Religious Studies section for the American Academy of Religion, Western Region (AAR/WR) conference. His work has been published in *Peace Review: A Journal of Social Justice; Nidan: International Journal for the Study of Hinduism; Chinese America: History & Perspectives—The Journal of the Chinese Historical Society of America; Empty Vessel: The Journal of the Daoist Arts; Spotlight on Teaching/American Academy of Religion; Asia Pacific Perspectives; Pacific World: Journal of the Institute of Buddhist Studies; JATI: Journal of Southeast Asian Studies; Amerasia Journal*; and other journals and anthologies, both nationally and internationally. His published works include ABC-CLIO's *Encyclopedia of Asian American Folklore and Folklife* (2011); *Encyclopedia of Asian American Religious Cultures* (2015); and *History of Asian Americans: Exploring Diverse Roots* (2015). In addition, he is author of *Cambodian American Experiences: Histories, Communities, Cultures, and Identities* (2010, reprint 2015); *Asian American Identities and Practices: Folkloric Expressions in Everyday Life* (2014); *The Age of Asian Migration: Continuity, Diversity, and Susceptibility,* volume 1 (2014); and *Southeast Asian Diaspora in the United States: Memories and Visions, Yesterday, Today, and Tomorrow* (2015). He has published extensively on Chinese, Cambodian, Vietnamese, Chinese-Southeast Asian, and Asian American histories, folklore, cultures, and religions. Currently, Lee serves as editor-in-chief of *Chinese America: History & Perspectives*, a peer-review journal published by the Chinese Historical Society of America.

Index

Note: Page numbers in **bold type** indicate main encyclopedia entries; page numbers followed by a *p* in *italics* indicate photographs.